I0580964

The First Step

The girl was obviously practising a solo. She spun round in a series of dazzling pirouettes and then seemed to fly across the room, landing with a lightness that suggested an ethereal spirit rather than a flesh and blood girl.

Moth realised that she had been watching an artist...

Also available in Lions

Dancer in the Wings *Jean Richardson*
One Foot on the Ground *Jean Richardson*

Homecoming *Cynthia Voigt*
Anastasia Krupnik *Lois Lowry*
The Exiles *Hilary MacKay*
Elidor *Alan Garner*
Apple Bough *Noel Streatfeild*
White Boots *Noel Streatfeild*
Isaac Campion *Janni Howker*
A Small Person Far Away *Judith Kerr*
The True Confessions of Charlote Doyle *Avi*
Little House on Rocky Ridge *Roger Lea MacBride*

The First Step

Jean Richardson

Illustrated by
Julia Pearson

Lions
An Imprint of HarperCollins*Publishers*

First published in Great Britain by Knight Books in 1979
First published by Lions in 1994
3 5 7 9 10 8 6 4 2

Lions is an imprint of HarperCollins Children's Books,
a division of HarperCollins Publishers Ltd,
77-85 Fulham Palace Road,
Hammersmith, London W6 8JB

Revised edition text copyright © Jean Richardson 1994
Illustrations copyright © Julia Pearson 1994

ISBN 0 00 674666 7

The author asserts the moral right to be
identified as the author of the work.

Printed and bound in Great Britain
by HarperCollins Manufacturing Ltd, Glasgow

Conditions of Sale
This book is sold subject to the condition
that it shall not, by way of trade or otherwise,
be lent, re-sold, hired out or otherwise circulated
without the publisher's prior consent in any form of
binding or cover other than that in which it is
published and without a similar condition
including this condition being imposed

1

No Money

It was failing her audition that began it all. The audition was for a place at White Lodge – the lower school of the Royal Ballet – and, as Moth Graham soon realised, she was only one of several hundred children who wanted to become dancers.

Moth had been dancing ever since she could remember. Her brother liked to tease her about the photograph of her aged six taking part in a Christmas show and wearing what Toby unkindly called her 'soppy swan face'. Moth hadn't known anything about *Swan Lake* or indeed any other ballet at the time. It was just that her feet wanted to dance, and while other children found it hard to remember steps, Moth picked them up at once and instinctively matched them to the music.

The Grahams lived in a small town, so Moth didn't have much opportunity to see ballets. Touring companies sometimes did a week at the nearest big town, but going to the ballet, let alone taking part in one, wasn't something the rest of the family ever thought of doing.

Moth didn't know why she herself was so drawn to it. Certainly she hadn't inherited her love of dancing from her parents, both of whom had their feet very firmly on the ground. She'd gone to dancing classes in the first place because her mother thought it would teach her to 'walk nicely'. She was proud that Moth had done well in her grade exams and taken part in one or two local festivals, but she'd never expected Moth to take dancing seriously.

And Moth hadn't, until the day when a ballerina who was the guest of honour at one of the school's shows had complimented her on her dancing. She'd also spoken to Moth's teacher, Mrs Shaw, who then spoke to Moth's surprised parents. As a result, it was decided that Moth should audition for a place at White Lodge.

The fact that she didn't get one should have settled the matter, but the audition gave Moth ideas. Only when it seemed that the chance of proper training was not being offered to her, did Moth realise that the one thing she really wanted in life was to learn to dance. And to dance so well that one day she would become a member of the Royal Ballet Company.

Her parents were amazed at the sudden change in her. Until then, she had been a rather quiet, unambitious child with no plans for the future. Now, overnight, she talked of nothing but going to a full-time dancing school. It was a ridiculous idea, but she was so insistent that at last they agreed to talk it over with Mrs Shaw. She wasn't very encouraging.

'It's impossible to say at eleven,' she told them. 'At the moment, Moth has good proportions and a nice line, but she could easily grow into the wrong shape for a dancer. She might become too tall or too plump, which happens to a lot of girls. Her feet might not be strong enough to take the strain of *pointe* work. Or she might simply change her mind. I know you're set on dancing now,' she said, turning to Moth, 'but by the time you're fifteen, you may decide you'd like to go to university or do something else.'

Moth didn't say anything. It was a waste of time to argue. Grown-ups were all the same. They always saw the difficulties and drawbacks and tried to put you off. They said things like, 'This is a new idea. You didn't want to do this last week. You'll soon forget about it.' But Moth knew she wouldn't, not this time. Deep down she'd always wanted to be a dancer, though she hadn't realised it until the audition had provided a glimpse of the kind of place that would make it possible. Now if they would only let her have the chance, she would work as never before, even at the things she hated.

It was also a question of money. If Moth had got a place at White Lodge, she would have received a grant that paid for her fees. But there were few grants for other schools, at least until you were older.

'And it's not just a matter of the fees,' her mother pointed out, when Moth started up the argument yet again while her mother was getting supper.

'There's no suitable dancing school near here, and it would cost a fortune to send you to a boarding school. I'm sorry, darling, but we can't afford it. We've got Toby and Lyn to think of, too.'

'But they don't want to be dancers,' said Moth. 'Toby wants to be a footballer, and that doesn't cost money. Footballers earn loads of money.'

'Perhaps,' said her mother, dodging past Moth to get a couple of pizzas out of the freezer. 'But one day they may get expensive ambitions too, and it wouldn't be fair if we'd spent all our money on you.'

She put the pizzas in the oven, set the timer, and began washing some salad.

'You can go on having lessons with Mrs Shaw.' She was shouting now, to be heard above the splashing water. 'Then you can try again for the Royal School when you're sixteen. If you get in, there'll be no trouble getting a grant.'

Moth couldn't imagine ever being sixteen. Her mother had turned off the tap now, but Moth felt too angry to speak quietly.

'Mrs Shaw isn't good enough to teach me,' she said furiously. 'No one from her school ever

becomes a real dancer. It's just a game. She doesn't even like ballet that much. She'd rather I did tap and modern dancing like everyone else, so I could be in some horrid pantomime. I hate you and daddy. You can do the things you want because you're grown-up, but I can't afford to wait, not even until I'm sixteen. If I'm going to be a proper dancer I've got to start now, before my bones get set. And you won't let me.'

She rushed upstairs, slammed her bedroom door so hard that the house shook, and burst into tears.

Her mother went on calmly getting supper. Toby, attracted by the prospect of a family row, and by the delicious smell of freshly-baked pizza, wandered into the kitchen and was told to lay the table. Sensing this was no moment to protest, he did as he was told for once.

Moth heard the call for supper, but she didn't feel hungry. Toby could have her share. He was such a pig he could easily eat a whole pizza.

She looked at herself in the mirror and began to practise *pliés*. Her feet were in the second position, and she checked that they formed a straight line, though she was too young for her hips and whole leg to turn out. She looked at her reflection mournfully. Mrs Shaw wasn't a very strict teacher. By the time Moth was sixteen, she'd probably have the kind of bad habits it was too late to correct.

She sat down on the bed and tried to think what she could do. She could leave home. But where could she go? She could stop eating so that she got thinner and thinner, and then they'd be sorry. But she wasn't sure she could keep it up. She was already wishing she hadn't turned her back on the pizza. It had looked like her favourite: spicy ham, tomatoes, mushrooms, melted cheese . . .

'It's so unfair,' she said to her bear Humpidge, who was sitting on her pillow watching her with his usual concern. 'I bet if Toby said he wanted to be a doctor, or Lyn turned out to be a mathematical genius, they'd do everything they could to help them. Why is dancing so different?'

'But it's not as though we'd be investing in a worthwhile career,' said Moth's father, as he and her mother talked it over a few days later. 'Of course I want Moth to be happy, and I hate to see her going round looking like a wet week, but this dancing lark is so uncertain. There's no safe job at the end of all this training. Dancers have to be brilliant and lucky to get into the Royal Ballet, and even then, if they hurt themselves, they can be off work for weeks and perhaps never dance again. Sounds like a recipe for heartache to me.'

'Job security isn't everything,' said Mrs Graham, 'especially when you're Moth's age. She isn't worried about her future, but she'll make herself ill if she goes on like this. She's a pain to live with: moody, snapping at everyone, shutting herself up in her bedroom. If we could afford it, I'd be for giving her a chance. She's more likely to do well at school if she's happy, and as long as she passes her GCSEs she can change course once she's over this dancing craze. At least it will have taught her to move gracefully.'

'Possibly,' said Mr Graham, looking for a newspaper so that he could check when the Cup match was on, 'but as we can't afford it, it's no use Moth going on like this. She'll come to terms with it in a few weeks, I expect.'

He switched on the TV and was soon miles away at the match, alternately groaning and cheering at the antics of his favourite team.

But Mrs Graham found she couldn't dismiss the matter so easily. She was worried by the change in Moth and more sympathetic to the cause. When she was Moth's age she'd wanted to be a skater, and although it now seemed ridiculous – when had she last gone skating! – she remembered how passionately she had minded being denied her chance. If only there was some way she could earn some money.

She'd trained as a teacher – not of skating – and had planned to go back to teaching once the children were old enough to manage without her. Lyn was at school now, so perhaps it was time to see if she could still manage a class. She wrote to her local authority and found that they were short of teachers and would be delighted to welcome her back.

'It'll only be part-time at first,' she explained,

when the family looked alarmed at the idea of any changes in their routine. 'You'll have to be a little more independent, that's all. Keep your rooms a little tidier, for example,' she added for the benefit of Toby and Lyn.

At the same time, without telling Moth or her husband, she found out how much it would cost to send Moth to a full-time dance school. The fees for boarding schools were a shock: far more than she'd expected, and more than she would probably earn from teaching. The one school that sounded affordable was miles away in London and didn't take boarders, which left the problem of where Moth would live in term-time.

'If only we knew someone who lived nearby,' Mrs Graham said, explaining the problem to her husband. 'I suppose we could advertise or ask the school, but Moth's rather young to live with strangers, and they'd need to be paid. I seem to have raised Moth's hopes for nothing. She's going to be even more disappointed, and she was so thrilled when she saw the prospectus.'

'There is someone,' Mr Graham said reluctantly, after he had read the details of the school and consulted a road map of London, 'though I'm not sure she'd be willing, or suitable. However, since you both seem to have made up your minds, we could ask her. But if she says no, that's final.'

Moth virtually held her breath until her father, who insisted on writing a letter rather than phoning – 'she must have time to think about it'

– received an answer. She felt she didn't care whom she lived with as long as she could dance.

Though when it was all settled, it did seem slightly alarming to be leaving home to live with someone Moth hardly knew.

2

Doubts

'You must remember,' Moth's father said, as the car sped along the motorway towards London, 'that your great-aunt is an elderly lady. I'm sure she'll do her best for you, but you'll have to make allowances.'

Moth was silent. She was still dazed at the way in which her life had suddenly been turned upside down. She could hardly believe that she was leaving home to live with someone she didn't know in a strange place in order to go to a new school. It was enough to silence anyone, especially someone who'd never been away from home before, except to spend a few days with her best friend. Now she didn't have a best friend any more.

'Penny for your thoughts,' said her father.

Moth sighed. She didn't know what to say. How could she even begin to explain that after wanting something so badly, getting it had not turned out to be quite the thrill she'd imagined.

There was so much to sort out and arrange. And supposing she wasn't really any good at dancing? Supposing she discovered that her body had become earthbound and her feet wouldn't obey her? Would they all feel – her parents, who were spending such a lot of money, Great-Aunt Marion, whose offer of a home in term-time had finally made the dream come true, Mrs Shaw, the new school – that she had let them down.

Her father was surprisingly understanding.

'You can always come back if you don't like it, you know. But as we've got this far, I think you should give it a try. We don't want you to grow up into one of those people who feel they've never been given a chance. If you don't like dancing after all, or if it doesn't like you, at least you'll have got it out of your system and you'll be free to find something else you do like.

'Now cheer up and stop looking as though it's the end of the world. We're nearly there, and I need someone who's wide awake to do a bit of map reading and tell me which way to go.'

Great-Aunt Marion lived in the top half of an Edwardian house that had been built in the days when families had lots of children. Land had been cheaper then, so large houses like this could afford to have large gardens.

Great-Aunt Marion had been born in the house and had lived there all her life. Her four brothers had left home to get married or work overseas, and when her elder sister died and she found herself alone, she had sensibly decided to convert the house into two flats.

Although it meant climbing a lot of stairs, she had chosen to live in the top flat. This allowed her to keep her old bedroom with its treasured view of the garden, which every spring without fail was a foaming sea of pink and white blossom.

As a small boy David Graham had been her favourite nephew, but she hadn't seen much of him or his family since the Grahams had moved to the Midlands. Neither she nor Moth knew quite what to expect of each other.

When she opened the door, Marion Graham saw a thin, rather anxious-looking child with a pale face, tawny eyes and long straight hair.

Moth saw a tall, elegant, elderly woman, with a severe expression and white hair swept back from her face and pinned up in a very neat French pleat. She stood up very straight, her eyes were very alert, and she had an air of authority, as though she was used to giving orders and being obeyed. Moth's heart sank. She'd expected someone more frail, not someone who looked as though she might be a retired headmistress.

As Moth's father had to drive back almost at once, Great-Aunt Marion suggested they have tea straight away. Moth wasn't hungry. She didn't feel at ease with the lace tablecloth and delicate flowered china and thought wistfully of the sturdy mugs they used at home. There they had tea round the kitchen table, and Toby fought her for the bun with the most currants or the right to scrape out the last of the jam. It was impossible to imagine behaving like that at Great-Aunt Marion's table, and everything looked so dainty and fragile that Moth was afraid she might spill her tea or drop jam on the spotless cloth.

'At least the grub's good,' her father said, trying to make her smile as he helped himself to another scone. 'You'll probably get so used to all this stylish living that we'll seem a very uncouth lot when you come home.'

'I wish I was home now,' said Moth, overcome by the feeling that she had made a terrible mistake. She was about to ask her father if she could change her mind and come back with him, when her great-aunt returned from the kitchen with a splendid fruit cake. Moth felt too shy to say anything in front of her.

After tea they trooped up a flight of steep narrow stairs to inspect Moth's room. It was tucked up under the roof, which in parts sloped down to the floor, but there was so much space that Moth saw at once that she'd be able to practise here. The furnishings were old and well worn, but it was a different kind of worn from the room that Moth shared with Lyn. There was a patchwork quilt on the bed, which had a tall brass railing at its head and foot, a wardrobe with a long mirror, and a matching chest of drawers with an old-fashioned swing mirror on it.

Even more unusual than the brass bed was a quaint little desk that Moth fell in love with at once. The top was open to show a flap lined with faded green leather and two rows of intriguing little pigeon-holes. Two ornate gilt candlesticks, complete with candles, showed that it dated from the days before gas or electric lighting.

Moth longed to know if the desk had any secret drawers, but she didn't like to ask her great-aunt in case she thought it a silly question. She had always wanted a desk like this, and the thought of it comforted her and somehow made the moment when she had to say goodbye to her father a little easier.

'Keep your pecker up,' he said, as he unlocked the car. 'You'll find your great-aunt's quite human underneath that starchy exterior. I expect you'll soon be so busy that you won't have time to miss us.'

'I will miss you, I will,' Moth protested, throwing her arms around her father. 'I wish I'd never wanted to dance. I wish I was still having lessons with Mrs Shaw and going to school with Jenny.'

Her father rumpled the top of her hair. He wasn't sure what to say. Moth had upset the whole family and now she wanted to change her mind. She'd been so insistent, so sure, that he didn't understand what had happened. Perhaps she felt homesick.

'It's a big break, I know, but everyone has to

leave home and find themselves sooner or later. I didn't go away to school, but I sometimes envied boys who did.' He knew he would have hated to have left home, but this was no moment to admit it to Moth. 'Eleven is young to strike out on your own, but not if you've found something you really want to do. Think of it as a great adventure, with you as the heroine who has to battle away all by herself. At the worst you need only survive until Christmas, then you can tell us all about your ordeal and come back home if you want to. And talking of Christmas reminds me: here's a little good-luck present to open when I've gone.'

Moth took the small packet, gave her father a last hug and kiss, and watched him ease the car away from the kerb and drive off. When the car had turned the corner, the street seemed very empty and there was no warmth in the evening sun. Moth had never felt so alone.

She walked slowly back to the house, stopped, and sat down on one of the steps up to the front door. She had taken the first step into a world that she wouldn't be able to share with her parents, and it was frightening. She wanted to wait a few minutes until the threat of tears had worn off. She looked down and saw she was clutching the packet her father had given her. She unwrapped it.

Inside was a box padded with cotton wool to protect the little silver figure of a dancer attached to a silver chain. A card read: 'To bring our dancer luck, with lots of love from Mummy and Daddy.'

Moth slipped the chain over her head and tucked the dancer inside her shirt. She didn't want anyone, least of all her great-aunt, to see her secret link with her parents. Then she went round the side of the house to the door for the top flat and went in. She could feel the outline of the dancer pressing against her, just below her heart, as she ran up the stairs to face her great-aunt.

3

A New World

The days before term started marked off Moth's old life from her new one. She had brought a few familiar things with her: Humpidge, who seemed to approve of her attic bedroom, a photograph of the family sitting on the beach and looking as she liked to remember them, and her collection of Degas postcards.

She'd been collecting these for several years, and it had become a family custom to send Moth ballet cards, often of paintings by Degas, at Christmas and on her birthday. The young girls the famous French artist had drawn and painted were long dead, but they seemed very real to Moth. He had captured them off stage and on, tying their shoes, rehearsing, taking a bow, and had portrayed the hardship and addictive attraction of the dancer's life. Although Degas had worked about a hundred years ago, there was a timeless quality about the world of his dancers.

Moth would like to have stuck up the cards in

her bedroom – there were acres of empty walls – but she was still too in awe of her great-aunt to ask if she would mind. She found it impossible to work out what she could or could not do, because her great-aunt's lifestyle was so unfamiliar.

For one thing, it was so quiet and orderly. There was no shouting, no rushing around, no family squabbles and, to Moth's dismay, no television. Great-Aunt Marion disapproved of television and said so in a way that made it plain she wasn't prepared to argue. Her days had a regular pattern: she liked to read the morning paper rather than talk at breakfast; after that, she usually went shopping and changed her library books; in the afternoon she went for a walk or had a friend to tea; and after supper she would either play Patience or read.

Moth realised that although her great-aunt wanted her to feel at home, she wasn't prepared to change her life to suit someone much younger. Moth was expected to make her own bed, tidy her room, lay the table and help with the washing-up. And then what? Great-Aunt Marion's answer seemed to be: reading.

Meals were dignified occasions and felt more like eating in a hotel. Great-Aunt Marion didn't seem to have heard of crisps, fishfingers, burgers, pizzas, chips, jacket potatoes or ice cream. She prepared dishes with sauces and strange vegetables. Moth discovered that she liked avocados, wasn't sure about artichoke soup and hated aubergines.

One thing her great-aunt surprisingly did know was where to buy ballet shoes and the dark blue leotards that were the only uniform the Fortune School insisted on.

The shop had been making ballet shoes for years, and the walls were lined with signed photographs of all the famous dancers who'd been customers. Moth, much impressed, hoped they'd want a photograph of her one day.

Then, to her surprise, her great-aunt took her round the corner to a little bookshop that seemed to stock every book on dance and ballet that had ever been written. There were so many that they spilled over on to the floor and jostled for space on tables stacked with magazines and trays of photographs.

'I thought you might like one or two pictures for your room, to inspire you,' her great-aunt said, as though she had read Moth's thoughts.

There were dozens of photographs to sort through, but her great-aunt waited patiently until Moth decided on a spectacular picture of the Russian dancer Mukhamedov striding through the air, and one of Darcey Bussell, a graduate of the Royal Ballet Schools who was only twenty when she was promoted to the rank of Principal Dancer. She'd had a dream career so far and was young enough for Moth to identify with her, unlike the dancers her great-aunt admired, legendary prima ballerinas like Margot Fonteyn and Natalia Makarova.

'One day I'm going to see Darcey Bussell dance,' Moth promised herself, 'but just looking at her makes me feel that's how I'd like to be.'

As well as making sure that she had everything on the school list, Moth also found out exactly where the school was. She dreaded having to turn up in the custody of her great-aunt, and as the school was only a short walk away, she begged to be allowed to go on her own.

'Not on your first day,' said her great-aunt firmly. 'Everyone will have a parent or adult with them, and your mother would expect me to take her place.'

Moth thought wistfully of her mother, whom she knew would have dropped her outside and driven off with an unembarrassing wave. Being escorted by a white-haired old lady, however well-meaning, would be very different.

Unlike Moth's previous schools, the Fortune School of Dancing had once been a private house, though a very grand one. It had been built for a fashionable Victorian artist, who'd given bohemian parties in the elegant drawing room, filled the maze of bedrooms with a horde of children and friends, lazed in a hammock under the apple tree in the large, untidy garden, and painted portraits of beautiful women in the barn-like studio.

The studio had been turned into a theatre, the drawing room still had a grand piano but was

now lined with mirrors and practice barres, the library was still a library, though the books were no longer bound in leather, the study was occupied by the school's headmistress, Miss Lambert, and the bedrooms were now classrooms. Most of the garden was used as a playground, but there were flowering shrubs, some apple and cherry trees, and corners still carpeted with grass thick with clover.

Even in its heyday the house could never have known such noise and bustle as on the first day of term. It spilled out on to the pavement, where to her relief Moth saw a sprinkling of parents. She was glad that at least her great-aunt wasn't holding on to her, unlike one determined-looking woman who was holding fast to a small boy who seemed anxious to escape. Moth looked away, though she felt sympathetic. She guessed they might be in the same class, though the boy wasn't as tall as she was.

Several men festooned with cameras and recording equipment were waiting in the road, and when a limousine turned the corner and purred to a halt they went into action. The driver got out and ran to open the rear door. Moth expected to see someone famous, but to her surprise the only person to get out was a girl of about her own age. She was obviously used to being photographed, because she paused and smiled and waved to the press before going up the path. The chauffeur followed, carrying several bulging holdalls. Moth wondered what on

earth was in them: certainly not just a leotard
and a pair of ballet shoes.

'I'd better go in now,' she said, moving away
before her great-aunt had time to do anything
embarrassing, like kissing her. 'See you at four
o'clock,' and she was halfway up the path before
Great-Aunt Marion could say anything.

The noise inside was deafening. Girls chat-
tered and squealed as they pushed their way to a
large noticeboard covered with lists of names.
All of them seemed to be weighed down with
schoolbags, music cases and holdalls stuffed with
books and clothes. Some had already changed
into practice dress, on top of which they had
piled sweaters, sweatshirts and thick woollen
legwarmers. Somewhere in the background a
piano was pounding out the routine accompaniment to a class.

Suddenly a girl appeared at the top of the
stairs and began ringing an old-fashioned hand-
bell. The chattering rose in a crescendo and then
faded away down the corridors. Soon the hall
was empty, apart from a handful of apprehensive
girls, the reluctant small boy, and a skinny boy
with a fizz of curly hair. Like Moth, they were
the newcomers.

Moth hardly said a word the rest of the day. She
felt confused by the amount of information
she had to absorb and the number of things
she needed to remember. There were lockers,
classrooms and desks to sort out. There were

instructions on how to get ready for a class, where to change, how to put your hair up, the right way shoes must be darned and ribbons sewn on. There was the timetable to copy down, a timetable that was disappointingly full of English, French, history, maths, biology and geography, as well as more promising subjects like choreography, notation and mime. Dancing was only allotted an hour a day, with extra classes on Saturdays.

As well as the two boys, there were six other girls in Moth's form. One of them was the girl in the limousine, who told everyone that her name was Selsey James. When no one seemed impressed, she explained that she was a film star and therefore someone very special.

'I'm just here for a term,' she said, 'to get some background for my next picture, in which I'm playing a young ballerina. My agent knows the headmistress and she just begged him to let me come here. She can probably do with the publicity.'

Moth was relieved to see that the rest of the class were just ordinary and, like her, too shy to talk about themselves. She found herself a desk in between a tall thin girl who said her name was Jane, and Ruth, who looked too round and plump for a dancer but had a nice smile. The two boys, reluctant Tom and curly-haired Drew, were in the row behind.

Moth was glad when it was time to go home because she didn't feel she could sensibly take in any more. But the day had one more surprise in store – and it wasn't a pleasant one.

The new girls had been told that they had to make their own skirts for character dancing and that Mrs George, who looked after the wardrobe, would explain the kind of material they needed to buy. The wardrobe was right at the top of the house, in what had once been the attics, but Moth couldn't find the right staircase. She was wandering along the top landing, wishing there was someone she could ask, when she heard music coming from one of the rooms. The door was half-open, so she was tempted to look inside.

As with all the practice rooms, the walls were lined with mirrors and at first it looked as though there were several people dancing, though in fact there was only one. The music came from a cassette-recorder, and the sole dancer was a slight girl with arms and legs so fragile that Moth felt with alarm that they could easily snap. She had dark hair cut into a fringe and enormous eyes, but her face was striking rather than pretty and seemed too grown-up for the rest of her. But it was her dancing rather than her expression that stopped Moth from saying anything.

The girl was practising an obviously difficult solo. She spun round in a series of dazzling *pirouettes* and then flew across the room, landing with a lightness that suggested an ethereal spirit rather than a flesh and blood girl. Her arms had an instinctive grace and Moth, who was always being told to relax her fingers, noticed that her hands made a beautiful shape. Her final attitude had such control that she seemed to freeze into stillness.

Until she saw Moth.

'What do you want?' she said angrily. 'How dare you come snooping round here. This room is private and no one is allowed in, so get out.'

She stormed towards the door, eyes blazing. She was not much taller than Moth although she was obviously older, but her anger was the more terrifying because it was so unexpected. She was not just cross because she had been disturbed while practising. Moth realised that she had been watching an artist, and that talent of this order wasn't kind or considerate. It was unreasonable, determined and ruthless, and it was dangerous to get in its way.

She fled down to the cloakroom and seized her things. She wanted to run home to the things and people she understood; but then she remembered. Home was hundreds of miles away and waiting outside was not her mother, longing to hear all about her first day, but the distant figure of Great-Aunt Marion.

4

Caught Out

It took a fortnight for Moth to convince her great-aunt that she knew the way to school, that she would look both ways before crossing the main road, that she wouldn't speak to strangers and would *never* accept lifts.

She knew that her great-aunt meant well when she fussed, but Moth felt that she understood the risks and could be trusted not to do anything silly. If she was old enough to leave home, she reasoned, then she was surely old enough to take herself to school.

Getting used to the ways of the Fortune School and making new friends was more of a challenge. She liked plump, cheerful Ruth best, and the feeling seemed to be mutual, as they tended to choose each other as partners.

At their first class Miss Pearson, a teacher with a brisk, no-nonsense manner, asked everyone to say why they wanted to dance and what kind of dancing they'd done so far.

Moth was pleased to discover that no one had higher grades than she had, though Jane had danced a small part in a real ballet.

Selsey, who expected by right to be the star of any class, was disappointed to find that dancing was considered more important than acting. Although she looked the part of a baby ballerina in her leotard, and like to stand round as though she was posing for a photograph, she didn't know much more than the five positions and was soon in trouble.

'I don't care if you never dance another step after this term,' Miss Pearson said, trying yet again to persuade Selsey's knees to turn out, 'but while you're in my class, you'll at least make an effort to do *pliés* properly.'

Selsey made a face behind Miss Pearson's back, but no one laughed because class was a serious business. They all knew they'd have to practise the routine for the rest of their dancing lives, because all dancers, even the greatest, need the daily discipline of a class to keep their bodies supple and to correct any faults that may have crept in.

Moth was dismayed to find how stiff her shoulders and arms were. Miss Pearson was always finding fault with her, or so it seemed. She was no longer a star pupil, as she was used to being, and much of the time she felt rather like Alice in Wonderland when the Red Queen told her, 'It takes all the running *you* can do, to stay in the same place. If you want to get somewhere else, you must run at least twice as fast as that!' She could see in the mirrors that lined the studio that Ruth had far more control, and she despaired of ever looking as elegant as Jane.

Selsey never missed a chance to make it clear what she thought of dancing.

'I wouldn't dream of being a dancer,' she said, when it was her turn to tell the class about her background. 'Dancers don't earn big money, like actresses, and they aren't famous in the same way. When I go shopping lots of people recognise me because they've seen my films, but who's interested in dancers? Also, they have to retire when they're still quite young, but I'm going to go on and on acting until I'm very old. There are lots of famous old actresses, but who's ever heard of an old dancer?'

'What about Margot Fonteyn?' said Tom, who despite being so small could jump higher than anyone else in the class and somersault with the ease of an acrobat. 'I've seen her on video, and she went on dancing for years and was very famous.'

'Have you got the video of *Ondine*?' said Jane. 'My mother saw her dance that when she was younger than me. That's why she wanted me to be a dancer.'

Jane's parents seemed to have bought her every ballet video there was and were always taking her to Covent Garden. Only the week before, she'd seen Mukhamedov dancing with Darcey Bussell.

Hearing the others talk about who they'd seen upset Moth. She'd seen very few ballets, except on television, and couldn't trade any top names. She wasn't even sure where Covent Garden was, though if she was to keep up with the others, she'd obviously have to go there as soon as possible. She wondered if her great-aunt would take her.

The current programme for Covent Garden – or, as Jane called it, The Garden – was pinned up on the noticeboard in the hall, and Moth saw that ballets were not put on every night but spaced out between operas. The leading male dancer seemed to be the Russian Irek Mukhamedov, whom she had heard of, but she didn't recognise any of the other names.

In the ballet history class they were learning about famous choreographers, and Mrs Fraser had started with Marius Petipa, who created some of the most famous ballets in the world for the Imperial Russian Ballet. Nearly everyone in the class had seen *The Sleeping Beauty* or *Swan Lake*, and Jane had seen the less well-known *La Bayadère*.

'I saw Sylvie Guillem and Mukhamedov,' she boasted, 'and Kumakawa as the Idol. He only had one dance, but he was fabulous.'

'How about you, Moth?' said Mrs Fraser. 'Have you seen any Petipa ballets?'

Afterwards, Moth couldn't think why she'd done it, but before she could think of the consequences, she heard herself saying, 'Yes, I've

seen *Bayadère* too. I saw Mukhamedov and
Darcey Bussell.'

'Did you?' said Mrs Fraser. 'That must have
been quite a performance. Well, in that case,
perhaps you'd like to do a special project on *La
Bayadère*. Find out all you can about it, and
then give a little talk about what you've discovered and what you thought of the ballet.
Now, who'd like to do *Swan Lake*?'

She went on to list some books that told the
story of Petipa's ballets and gave details of the
famous dancers who had appeared in them, but
Moth didn't hear a word. How could she have
made such a stupid boast, especially when Jane
had actually seen the ballet and would be bound
to realise that Moth hadn't. And how could she
talk about Darcey Bussell, when the nearest
she'd come to seeing her was in a photograph on
her bedroom wall. There was only one way out.
Somehow, and as soon as possible, she had to
see *La Bayadère* – and a performance in which
Bussell was dancing.

She was so quiet and withdrawn that evening
and ate so little that her great-aunt was
concerned.

'I hope you're not sickening for something,'
she said. 'Perhaps you'd better go to bed early
with an asprin and some hot milk.'

Moth was so preoccupied that she forgot to
say that she hated hot milk. She was thinking
about how she could get to the vital perform-

ance, and the only way seemed to be to ask her great-aunt to come with her. She had an idea that tickets for Covent Garden were rather expensive, but perhaps she could offer to pay, and it might help to say that the school wanted her to go.

'I need to go to Covent Garden,' she said, in a nervous tone that would at once have made her mother suspicious. 'I have to do a project on *La Bayadère*, so I want to see it. Daddy gave me some money for emergencies and extra expenses, and I could pay for the tickets out of that. It's on a Friday, at 7.30 – and I'd like you to come as my guest.'

Her great-aunt looked as though she'd been given an unexpected present. 'What a lovely idea,' she said. 'I can't remember the last time I went to the ballet. If you tell me the date I'll ring up for tickets first thing in the morning, and it must certainly be my treat.'

Moth ought to have slept well now that her problem seemed to be solved, but she had an anxious dream in which she was supposed to be going to the theatre only to find that it kept disappearing. It was always just round the corner or at the top of the next street, but whenever she got there it had vanished.

She reminded her great-aunt about the tickets at breakfast, and as soon as she got home from school she dashed upstairs and asked before anything else, 'Are we going?'

'I'm afraid not,' said her great-aunt. 'You seem

to have chosen a very popular programme. The only seats they had left were stalls at £50, and I didn't think we ought to pay that much. I'm sorry you're disappointed,' she added, for Moth looked ready to burst into tears, 'but perhaps there's something else you'd like to see. I believe *La Fille Mal Gardèe* is lovely, or perhaps we could go to *The Nutcracker* at Christmas?'

Moth wanted to explain that it had to be *Bayadere* because she was supposed to have seen it, but she wasn't sure that her great-aunt would understand why she'd told a lie. She suspected that lying would be something of which she strongly disapproved.

Moth went up to her room and sat down on the bed. She couldn't bear to look at the photograph of Darcey Bussell, and considered taking it down. Even if she read up about Petipa and the story of *Bayadère*, she was sure the others would guess that she hadn't really seen it. Jane would be sure to interrupt with some question Moth couldn't answer, and what would everyone think of her? That she was a worse show-off than Selsey, who at least told the truth, even if she exaggerated it.

Not surprisingly perhaps she'd been worse than ever in class today. She hadn't even put up her hair properly, and it had come tumbling down, earning her a sharp remark about being unprofessional from Miss Pearson. Could it be that she wasn't destined to be a dancer after all? That she would never be able to compete with girls like the fiery, temperamental Marina – the girl in the attic whom she'd since discovered was the school's star pupil – or self-assured Jane? Maybe ballet was a lofty, superior world to which you either belonged – or you didn't.

5

Floral Street

By now Moth knew her way round the school and had no further trouble finding the wardrobe room. She was expected to make her character skirt with the expert help of Mrs George, who began by giving them all a little talk about how important it was for dancers to be able to sew.

'And it's not just a question of sewing ribbons on your shoes and darning the toes to stop them wearing out so fast. You don't know what you may be asked to do once you join a company, and you won't be much use to them if you can't take your turn at the sewing machine.'

'I bet you don't have to use a sewing machine at Covent Garden,' said Jane, who was finding it hard enough to fold her skirt material the right way. 'My mother says they have proper wardrobe staff who look after all the costumes and mend and iron them.'

'And what makes you think you'll be dancing at Covent Garden?' said Mrs George, who was

showing Moth how to pin on the pattern. 'Only
a very few dancers ever get into the Royal Ballet
companies. Most of you, if you're lucky, will
probably end up in small companies struggling
to make both ends meet, and you'll have to do
worse things than a little sewing. But before any
of you become stars, and when you've finished
your skirts, I'd like some help with the
Christmas show. We're very proud of the fact
that we never hire any costumes here. Everything's made by hand, and we're famous for our
beautiful displays.'

The walls of the wardrobe were lined with
photographs confirming this, and as Moth
looked up at the rows of past angels, snowflakes,
fairies and flowers she saw miles of sewing
ahead.

She had been to the noticeboard several times
to check the Covent Garden programme in the
hope that she might have made a mistake or the
management decided to cancel one of the operas
and put on another performance of *Bayadère* –
by special request. The last time her eye was
caught by the words 'Booking on the day',
which read:

65 Rear Amphitheatre seats are sold from
10 a.m. on the day of performance to personal
callers. Tickets are limited to one per person.

Moth did think of telling her great-aunt about
this, but she doubted whether an elderly lady,
however active, would be willing to get up early
on a cold November morning to stand in a

queue for a couple of hours. And if she said no
to the idea of Moth standing in a queue, it would
be an act of deliberate defiance to go against her
wishes. Whereas if she didn't know . . . But even
if Moth were to get a ticket, she doubted
whether her great-aunt would let her go out at
night by herself.

She was concentrating so hard on trying to
think of a way round her problem that several
lessons completely passed her by, but it was
impossible to be miles away in class, especially
when they were doing exercises to the irresistible
piano accompaniment of Russell Watson. A
young man with unruly red hair that flopped
over his eyes when he was feeling depressed,
Russell scraped a living as an accompanist while
writing a symphony in his evenings. He had a
natural feeling for dance, and when he was
feeling cheerful could invent just the right tune
for any set of steps.

Gradually Moth worked out a plan that had
two stages. First, she had to see if she could get
a ticket, which would involve leaving home no
later than 8 o'clock, or even earlier. She decided
to tell her great-aunt that she had to go to school
extra early for a meeting about the Christmas
show. Then when she arrived at school late, she
would have to say she hadn't felt well – and pray
that no one had rung her great-aunt to ask where
she was.

As a normally truthful person, Moth was
worried about having to tell lies, but she told

herself that it was something she must make herself do if she wanted to become a dancer. She did want to be honest, but it wasn't her fault that this was the only way she could get a ticket for *Bayadère*.

She was also concerned about how to get to Covent Garden. She was still overawed by the vastness of London, by the warren of back streets she'd glimpsed behind Oxford Street and Regent Street, which were the only places she felt she could recognise. She'd found out that there was a station called Covent Garden, but was it really near the opera house or some kind of joke like Piccadilly Circus, which all Londoners knew wasn't the kind of circus that had acrobats and performing animals.

When it came to the Friday morning, she woke up far too early. It was dark outside, but a streetlight dappled the sloping ceiling so that she could just see Darcey Bussell flying through the air. It gave her courage as she wondered whether she was brave enough to cope with the unknown city. At home she knew all the streets and shops, which seemed to become smaller and closer together as she grew older, but she couldn't piece London together at all. At that moment, she thought, if she'd been a bird, she wouldn't have known which way to fly to make sure of landing on Covent Garden.

But the reality wasn't so difficult. Her great-aunt didn't ask any awkward last-minute questions, and Moth ran to the station, hardly aware of a grey chilliness that made the crowded warmth of the Underground almost welcome.

The trains arrived so tightly packed that at first Moth was afraid to try and squeeze in. She remembered how they'd all laughed when her father told them that in Japan, so he'd heard, they employed people to cram as many passengers as possible into the carriages. They certainly weren't needed on this platform, where no one could have found room for another arm or leg, let alone a whole person.

Jammed up against a fat woman with an equally fat briefcase, a spiky umbrella and something bulky with wheels, Moth tried desperately to see past her whenever the doors opened. Baker Street . . . Oxford Circus . . . Piccadilly. She was ejected on to the platform like a pea bursting from a pod and swept along passageways and down another escalator. At Covent Garden, as she waited impatiently for a lift, she was almost tempted to race up the stairs.

It was now 8.45. Which way was the opera house?

A newspaper-seller, sensing her desperation, asked: 'Lost something, miss?'

'I'm looking for Covent Garden,' said Moth.

'Well, you've come to the right place,' he said, 'unless you want the old market. That went a long time ago.'

'No, I want the opera house, where they do ballets.'

'Dancer, are you?' said the man. 'Well, just

you dance round the corner, cross the road and go along Floral Street. You can't miss it.'

And she didn't, though she was surprised that Floral Street was such an ordinary little street. Ordinary, that is, on one side. On the other, a handsome cream building with doorways labelled 'Amphitheatre' and 'Stage Door' soared up. Opposite was a kind of shop with the sign 'Box Office' and an alarmingly long queue. It stretched almost to the corner of Floral Street, and by the time Moth had reached the end she had almost given up hope of getting a ticket.

The last person in the queue was a young man in an overcoat so large that it seemed to be wearing him. The collar was turned up to protect his ears and the back of his neck, but a crescent of dark wavy hair was just visible above it. He wore glasses and was intent on reading a book.

'Please,' Moth said, hoping this wouldn't count as speaking to strangers, 'is this the queue for tonight?'

'Hope so,' the young man replied. 'I wouldn't want to stand around in this weather if it wasn't.'

'It's a very long queue. Do you think it's worth waiting for a ticket?'

'Yep,' he said confidently. 'They're limited to one each, and if you count, you'll see that there aren't sixty-five people yet.'

Moth tried to check, but it was difficult to count the huddle of anoraks tucked into doorways or perched on stools. Some people were sheltering from the cold in cars and cafés, taking turns to relieve their partners or bring them a mug of hot coffee. She decided it was worth taking a chance.

By the time they'd reached the box office, Moth had learned quite a lot about how the queue system worked and also about the young man, whose name was Robert. She was sure her great-aunt wouldn't have approved of her talking to him, but there were plenty of other people around and he seemed quite harmless.

He told her that as he couldn't afford any other seats – 'They're not priced for students' – he always queued on the day and had always got a ticket. He liked ballet and loved opera, and he reckoned he'd seen all the most famous dancers and singers.

'You meet some odd people in the queue,' he said. 'In the summer, when the tourist hordes are here, it's like the United Nations. People are very friendly, perhaps because they feel we've got something in common.'

Moth was tempted to tell Robert how she came to be in the queue, but just then it started to move, and she was too nervous to talk as the straggling line began to fold up like a concertina.

When at last it was her turn at the window, there was no need to speak. The man pushed the ticket across to her as though he were a machine. To him it was a chore he did every day, but for Moth the ticket was something special. She tucked the precious little piece of cardboard into the pocket with a zip, fled, and arrived at school on wings. The hardest thing was pretending that she had not felt well, when she suspected that everyone could see that she felt absolutely marvellous.

6

The Back Row

Getting away from her great-aunt was more of a problem. Usually after they'd had supper and Moth had helped with the washing-up, she did her homework while her great-aunt read or listened to the radio. Moth liked to work in her room, her books spread out on the green leather desk with the gilt candlesticks. She would like to have had tall candles flickering in them, but her great-aunt was terrified of fire and had firmly forbidden it. Moth had found a bunch of old seals in a drawer, and she imagined one of the desk's previous owners melting wax at the candles to seal his, or maybe her, letters. One of the seals said 'Forget me not' underneath a little flower, and Moth longed to seal a letter with this.

The day before, sitting there holding the seal as though it were a lucky charm, she had decided that the best plan was to leave a note for her great-aunt. She had thought of saying that someone at school had given her a ticket, but this would only lead to embarrassing questions about who she was going with and, more important still, who would see her home. It seemed best to leave a simple message:

Have gone to Covent Garden to see *La Bayadère*. Please don't worry. I'll come straight home.

She would have to miss supper to get there in time, and she realised that her great-aunt would find out that she had gone when she called up to Moth to come and lay the table. She might well think of ringing up the school, or Moth's parents, or even the police, so the best place to leave the note seemed to be on top of the telephone. That way her great-aunt wouldn't be able to call anyone without first seeing the note.

Great-Aunt Marion was busy in the kitchen when Moth tiptoed down the stairs. There was a delicious smell from the oven and its appetising warmth made the chill darkness outside even less inviting. Streetlights cast puddles of light on the pavement, but in between were the distorted shadows of walls, bushes, hedges and trees. There was no one about. As Moth ran along, she could hear her steps echoing and tried to hush them. She felt safe near houses, but at one point she had to brave being boxed in by a line of parked cars and a sinister wall that she reminded herself only concealed a disused tennis court. It was beginning to rain, and the harsh orange lights of the main road were blurred with mist.

But when she reached Floral Street it was bright and crowded: there were people trying to sell tickets at the last moment, people waiting for friends, people fumbling in bags and wallets for tickets and change for programmes before stampeding up the stone stairs with an energy that put life back into frozen hands and feet. Up and up. Moth felt she would never get there as each bend curved round into yet more stairs.

Then suddenly, breathless, she found herself among bars and foyers, attendants with programmes, and on the threshold of the theatre itself, tumbling down in a blaze of lights past tiers of gilded boxes to an enormous stage curtained in red velvet with a flourish of golden royal monograms. Far below she could see the stands of the orchestra with tiny figures tuning up, and as she made her way to P15 in the last row of all, Moth felt that she might easily lose her balance and roll down into the distant stalls.

She found Robert still engrossed in a book. He had shed his overcoat but was now dwarfed by an enormous pair of binoculars that looked more suitable for sighting enemy submarines than dancers.

'I'll let you have a look,' he said generously, 'so that you can actually see Mukhamedov's face. I expect you want to drool over him. You get a marvellous view of the pattern of a ballet from up here. All the best people, the ones who really love ballet and don't just come because their firm pays for the tickets or because it's the

OK thing to do, sit up here.'

Moth wondered where Jane and her parents usually sat. Were they the best sort of people, in the sense that Robert meant?

Robert told her that she must have a programme as a souvenir. They cost nearly as much as a book, but after a few minutes of looking longingly at Robert's, Moth knew that she had to have one. She needed to know all about this ballet, starting with the story.

The bayadère of the title, she discovered, was a temple dancer called Nikiya who was in love with a noble Indian warrior called Solor. They had sworn eternal love, but as a reward for his valour, Solor was given the hand of the Rajah's beautiful daughter Gamzatti. She overheard the High Brahmin, a priest of the temple who was also in love with Nikiya, telling the Rajah about Solor's love for Nikiya and decided to have her killed. Moth tried to get the names sorted out in her mind before reading on.

The High Brahmin brought Nikiya to dance at the betrothal of Gamzatti and Solor, where she was bitten by a snake hidden in a basket of flowers and died. Solor was haunted by a vision of Nikiya in the Kingdom of the Shades, and before he could marry Gamzatti the gods, angered by the killing of Nikiya, destroyed the temple, killing everyone in it. The spirits of Nikiya and Solor were now free to unite in eternal love.

'It's the usual cheerful story,' Robert said.

'Don't worry if you can't take it all in at first. What matters is the dancing. You can check up on the details in the interval.'

Moth persevered with the details but had to give up when the lights dimmed. There was applause for the conductor, and leaning forward until she could just see him, Moth was aware of a tense expectancy all around her. The magic was about to begin.

They were tiny figures, far below, except when Moth summoned them to her through Robert's binoculars. She could only guess at the difficulty of steps that were made to look effortless. Nikiya was danced by a Russian ballerina who provided a touching, fragile contrast to the long-legged Bussell as Gamzatti. Mukhamedov as Solor looked suitably noble. When he flew through the air Moth willed him to do still more soaring *jetés* because they were so exciting.

In the first interval Robert took her on a grand tour of the foyers and staircases while telling her about all the productions and dancers he'd seen. 'Wait till the Shades come on,' he said. 'It's one of the most magical entrances for a corps de ballet ever devised. I must have seen it at least half a dozen times, and every time it's as mysterious and beautiful as ever. But seeing it for the first time is something special.'

Moth liked the way Robert took it for granted that she cared as much about ballet as he did. She felt flattered that he talked to her as though they were the same age.

In the second act, Solor conjured up a vision of the dead Nikiya in the Kingdom of the Shades. The shades came on one at a time, moving along a ramp that sloped gently down to the stage. They appeared in profile and advanced slowly, tilting forward into an arabesque at each step. When the first dancers reached the stage they formed a line while continuing to repeat the same arabesque. As each dancer began to move down the slope, she was replaced at the top by another, and yet another. Every time a new dancer stepped forward, Moth felt she must surely be the last. Yet there was still more, until the line of dancers extended into four rows that filled the stage. Moth was aware of a strange sensation that she guessed must be her hair standing on end. Robert was right: the procession of shades had a mysterious, compelling beauty.

Once assembled, the corps echoed the movements of Nikiya as Solor tried in vain to recapture his lost love. He tried to bind her to him with a long scarf, but their parting was inevitable.

In the second interval Moth began to worry about how she was going to get home and the sort of reception she would get from her great-aunt. She was so subdued that Robert noticed and asked whether she was enjoying herself.

'It's wonderful,' Moth said, 'and quite different from on the TV. It's so much more exciting seeing the real people and knowing there's

nothing automatic about them. They could make
a mistake, or fall over. It's sounds silly, but the
risks of dancing are thrilling. Or perhaps,' she
added tremulously, feeling that she just had to
tell someone, 'I just feel that because I took a
risk in coming here.'

'Why is coming to the ballet a risk?' Robert
asked.

'Because . . . because I ran away to come. My
great-aunt didn't know I was coming. She'd
never have let me come by myself, and she's
going to be so angry.'

'But it was worth it, wasn't it?' Robert said.
'Don't spoil the rest of the evening by worrying
about what'll happen later. She'll probably be so
glad to see you safe home, that she won't be too
upset.'

Moth tried to follow his advice. Certainly the
nimble Tetsuya Kumakawa, making all too brief
an appearance as the Bronze Idol who sat outside
the temple, banished all other thoughts. He
darted about the stage like quicksilver, and Moth
saw at once why he was Tom's hero.

The destruction of the temple was most
impressive, and the spirits of the lovers were
united to provide a happy ending.

Moth was glad that Robert insisted on staying
until the very last curtain. They both clapped
and stamped and Robert shouted '*Brava!*' whenever the ballerinas appeared. Moth had never
seen so many curtain calls: Asylmuratova, Bussell, Mukhamedov, Kumakawa, the corps de

ballet. Sometimes together, sometimes slipping out from behind the curtain on their own to a great roar from their fans, who were in no hurry to go home. Someone in a box kept hurling flowers on to the stage, and Mukhamedov gallantly retrieved them and presented them to Bussell and Asylmuratova, who had both already carried off an armful of bouquets.

Then suddenly it was all over and Moth and Robert raced down the stairs and burst out into a wet night full of jostling umbrellas and gleaming limousines swallowing up couples in evening dress. Moth felt lost.

'Which way do you go?' said Robert, who had retrieved his vast overcoat from under his seat and was turning up the collar against the rain. 'Bus or tube?'

'Tube,' said Moth, trying to get her bearings. But before they could set off for the Underground, Moth's arm was seized and her heart did a great leap as she recognised her great-aunt. She looked round for Robert, wanting at least to say goodbye, but she was hustled towards a waiting taxi and bundled in with no chance to turn round.

As the taxi set off down a side road on the kind of traffic-dodging route only taxi drivers know, she found herself trapped on the back seat with a very angry great-aunt.

7

Preparations

Nothing was said during the journey home, perhaps because Great-Aunt Marion didn't wish to scold Moth within the hearing of the taxi driver.

Moth found the silence more frightening than the angriest words would have been. Travelling by taxi was a new experience, but it was impossible to enjoy it sitting next to someone who was presumably saving her words until they were alone. Moth wondered whether to say she was sorry that her great-aunt had been put to so much trouble, but she was nervous of saying anything. She was also, she realised, surprisingly hungry.

Her great-aunt had anticipated this, because a hot drink and sandwiches came before the lecture, which was about responsibility.

'Your parents trusted me to take care of you, and they trusted you to behave properly and not be deceitful. Supposing anything had happened to you. A child of your age' – Moth felt indignant at being called a child – 'isn't old enough to be wandering around London at night by herself. Why couldn't you have waited until we could go to the ballet together, instead of sneaking off in this underhand way?'

'I – I had to see this particular performance,' stammered Moth, who suddenly felt very tired, too tired to go into details about the project.

'I'm sure the school didn't expect you to go and see it by yourself,' said her great-aunt. 'No school would. I've a good mind to complain to your headmistress.'

'They didn't . . . It wasn't . . .' Moth couldn't stop herself yawning. The evening seemed to be turning into a nightmare.

'You'd better go to bed. You look worn out,' her great-aunt said in a kinder tone. 'We'll say no more about this, but if you ever go off again without telling me, I shall tell your parents that I can't accept the responsibility of looking after you. Do you understand?'

Moth nodded. She had just enough strength to go upstairs and get undressed, but even the prospect of being sent home in disgrace couldn't keep her awake. She fell asleep as soon as her head touched the pillow.

Her great-aunt didn't refer to the matter again, and Moth was glad that she wasn't a person who sulked or bore a grudge. There was enough to cope with at school, what with end of term exams, the project on *La Bayadère*, for which

Moth had little enthusiasm, and the preparations for the Christmas show.

Although the main show took place at the end of the summer term, when all sorts of agents and talent-spotters were invited, the parents liked and expected an entertainment at Christmas. Mrs Fraser firmly refused to stage yet another Nativity play.

'I insist on a rest from kings and shepherds and hordes of wretched angels,' she said at a staff meeting. 'And I'm sure Mrs George must be fed up with reviving those everlasting wings, which looked very tatty last year.'

It was agreed, however, that there ought to be some kind of religious theme, so it was decided to recite and mime *The Ballad of St Christopher*, the story of a huge giant who wanted to serve the mightiest king in the world. He was so strong that he was given the task of ferrying travellers across a dangerous river. He didn't realise that the little boy who wanted to cross the river one stormy night was in fact the Christ child, and for carrying him across the river the giant was given the name 'Christopher', the Christ bearer.

One of the seniors was tall enough to play the giant, and much to his fury Tom, as the smallest boy in the school, was chosen as the Christ child. He minded very much about his lack of inches and hated the idea of a part that emphasised this, but apart from scowling and looking gloomy there was nothing he could do about it.

Selsey saw the Christmas show as an obvious chance for her to shine. She hated not being continually in the limelight and announced that she wanted to do a dance number on her own. Her class was the despair of Miss Pearson, who was always complaining that she still couldn't do a *plié* properly. She was also hopeless at keeping in time with the rest of the class, but instead of being ashamed, Selsey always managed to imply that everyone else was in the wrong.

'Of course they won't let you do a solo,' said Jane. 'You're about the worst dancer in the class and you haven't passed any exams.'

'Who cares about silly little exams.' Selsey enjoyed winding up Jane. 'I'm a star and everyone wants to see me. I'm the only person here who's been in films and you're lucky I'm here.'

And so it seemed. Because when the programme was pinned up on the noticeboard, Selsey was down for a solo tap dance.

Like everyone else Moth was puzzled. It was a ballet school and the only other soloist was Marina, the star pupil Moth had disturbed on her first day, but she was glad not to be in Selsey's shoes. Moth still felt nervous about dancing in front of an audience, and her part as one of the berries in the Christmas garland ballet was enough for her.

Each class made up part of a garland of holly and mistletoe, with dancers in red, green, and tinsel costumes and Marina a lone figure in white. 'The effect,' promised Miss Pearson, 'will be stunning, if you can only get it right.'

Each year learnt their steps separately, and then during the last week, when exams were over, the whole school was given over to preparing for the show. Moth was also in the choir and sang carols until her head rang with glorias and ding-dong merrily on highs. Miss Ellison drilled the choir mercilessly while Russell Watson thundered away on the piano, but even he began to flag as his fingers had to plod through yet another chorus of 'Here we come a-wassailing'.

When she wasn't either dancing or singing, Moth was kept busy sewing buttons and velcro on the stack of clothes being run up by Mrs George and her helpers. The seniors cut out and machined the costumes under her direction while Moth and the other juniors, who were not considered reliable enough with the sewing machines, had to do all the fiddly things that needed to be done by hand.

'We never hire anything. We make everything ourselves', was Mrs George's motto, and whenever she said this, which was all too often, Jane would whisper, 'More's the pity'. She hated sewing even more than Moth did, and was so careless that she attached the velcro the wrong way round.

'What a stupid little girl you are,' said Mrs George unsympathetically. 'You'd better do some unpicking instead.' She dumped on Jane an old costume that reeked of mothballs because it had been in a trunk for so long, and told her to unpick the red lining which was needed for one of the holly berries.

Although the first year's dance was very short and simple, Moth loved rehearsals. They took place in the studio-theatre, and were the nearest she'd yet come to appearing on a real stage. As each year was taking part in the ballet, she had a chance to watch the older dancers at work and see how the various strands of the garland fitted together.

The atmosphere was an intoxicating blend of hard work and excitement. Music went on all the time, either provided by Russell Watson, who had written special Christmas music with clever echoes of carols, or by a tape recorder which did duty for him when he was needed elsewhere.

Dancers cast off sweaters and legwarmers, did a few *pliés* or stretched in careless arabesques, put on *pointe* shoes, tried out steps off and on stage, asked for their music again, and yet again. Miss Pearson sat in the third row and kept leaping up on to the stage to reposition a dancer or show them just what she had in mind. Each dance was designed to emphasise the level of a particular class, and they all came together in the finale to compose the garland. Moth found her greatest problem was not doing the right steps but arriving in the right place on the crowded little stage at the right moment.

'Do let's have some smiles,' implored Miss Pearson, as a grimly serious troupe of holly berries scattered across the stage. 'You all look as though you were attending an execution. And I said smile, not leer,' she added, as the berries made a ferocious effort to look happy.

As a reward for submitting to the part of the Christ child, Tom had been given some solo steps that exploited his gift for jumps and somersaults. He shot round the stage like a firework, becoming a real menace after he'd heard one of the seniors say, 'That little kid's rather good'.

The only people who seemed immune to the magic of rehearsals were Selsey and Marina. Surprisingly, they had much in common. Both hated waiting for their turn and expected to have the stage to themselves. Both preferred to practise in secret. Both were cut off from the others in their class: Selsey because everyone was fed up with her showing off, and Marina because she was so intense.

Moth was looking forward to her father coming to the show because she wanted him to see how much she'd already improved, and why dancing was so important to her. She felt sure that when he saw someone as good as Marina, he would realise that ballet deserved to be taken seriously as a proper career.

The day before the show, he telephoned to say that he wouldn't be able to get away in time. 'I'm sorry, love, but I've got an important meeting with a chap from head office and I can't leave early.'

'But you promised,' wailed Moth. 'Daddy, you promised you'd come and see me dance.'

'And I will one day. You know I'd much rather be watching you than stuck in the office, but it can't be helped. I'm afraid it means the others won't be able to come either, as I need the car, but we'll all be thinking of you.'

Moth put down the phone and sighed. Why were offices so much more important than people, at least to her father? Her great-aunt was coming to the show, so at least there would be someone who belonged to her, but her father and her family were special and no one could take their place.

8

The Christmas Show

The show took place on the evening of the last day of term. School finished at midday, and that morning classrooms were either empty or taken over by small groups trying to sort out last-minute changes to a step or a sequence. They were furious at being interrupted.

'Can't you find somewhere else,' said a senior crossly when Moth and Ruth came to collect some books from their desks. 'Come back later. We must get this dance worked out and the stage is tied up all morning.'

They crept away. They were supposed to ask Mrs George if she needed a hand with any last-minute sewing, but both of them felt they couldn't face any more velcro. There was a final choir practice after break, but until then they decided to be childish and play hide and seek, which seemed to suit the party mood of the day.

'We can't use the whole building,' Ruth said sensibly. 'It would take too long and you might never find me. Let's stick to the rooms on this side of the hall.'

Apart from Miss Lambert's study, which neither of them would have dared to hide in, this meant the library, various classrooms, an odd little waiting room which was sometimes used as a sick room, the art room, the old kitchen, and some dusty rooms at the very top of the house where no one ever went.

Ruth hid first, and after a ten-minute search that seemed more like an hour, Moth was ready to call the whole thing off. The rooms right at the top, which seemed such obvious hiding-places, turned out to be full of a jumble of old stage equipment and faded flats from earlier shows that flaked paint if you so much as breathed on them. Moth felt sure they housed spiders too, and she couldn't imagine Ruth would take the risk of their crawling on her as she crouched among the musty relics.

She drew a blank in the library and found the art room occupied by a couple of scene painters putting the finishing touches to the props for St Christopher. They had no time for children playing games. She was about to pass the little waiting room that led to Miss Lambert's study when it struck her that although it didn't offer much scope for hiding-places, Ruth might think it daring to be so near the lion's den and count on Moth not being bold enough to look round.

The door was shut, and Moth had to nerve herself to turn the handle and go in. The room seemed to be empty, and the door leading to the study was ajar. Moth tiptoed across to look behind the settee, the only obvious hiding-place, and then froze at the sound of ugly sobbing. It came from the study and was interrupted by the calm voice of Miss Lambert, who was obviously trying to quell the tears.

'I understand how you feel, my dear, but is anything going to be solved by your withdrawing from the Christmas show? You asked me to let you show everyone what you can do, and I agreed because I appreciate that this term has not been easy for you. After being thrust into the limelight, you've had to take a back seat and have discovered you can't do some things as well as the others. I know you've been criticised, and you've resented it, but this isn't a school for budding film stars but for dancers, who are being trained for careers that will mean a lot of hard work and perhaps not very much glamour.'

'Nobody likes me,' said a voice Moth hardly recognised because it was so unlike the confident way in which Selsey usually spoke. 'But they all knew that I was a star. Now everyone'll think I'm not when they hear that the film has been cancelled. It's in all the papers,' she added with a sob.

'I doubt if anyone here has had much time to read the papers today,' said Miss Lambert gently. 'I suspect they're all much too busy. And as you're not coming back next term, you won't have to face them then. But it's too late to change the programme for tonight. The audience will be expecting to see you. I'm sure you'll get another part before long, so why not leave us on a brave note. Go ahead with your dance and prove that you believe in the old stage tradition that the show must go on whatever has happened to those taking part.'

Moth had not been able to stop herself listening. She knew it was wrong to eavesdrop on other people's conversations, especially when she had no right to be there, but a scary excitement, a longing to know what happened next, had rooted her to the spot. But now the spell was broken and she slipped quickly out of the room, not quite closing the door after her in case the slightest sound should alert Miss Lambert.

She still hadn't found Ruth, but she didn't want to go on with the game. She'd never liked silly Selsey and thought it was ridiculous for her to be playing a ballerina when she couldn't do the most simple exercises properly, but she also saw what a blow it must have been when the film fell through. And she was surprised to find that she felt sorry for Selsey.

Suddenly she remembered the choir practice and scampered across the hall to the music room, where a harassed Russell Watson was trying to cope with the exacting demands of Miss Ellison, who was determined to get her crescendos absolutely perfect. Moth was just in time to take her place next to Ruth, and there was no chance to breathe a word until afterwards.

'Wherever did you get to?' said Ruth, when they had finally carolled the last *'Gloria in excelsis'* to Miss Ellison's satisfaction and were making their way to the cloakroom. 'I waited ages for you and then Jane came in and asked me to a secret meeting.'

'What was the secret?'

'It's about Selsey. Everyone's fed up with her showing off and going on about being famous, so Jane suggested we should do something to spoil her precious dance. We thought we might put something in her tap shoes to give her a little surprise.'

'But she'll notice that when she puts them on, and it won't stop her dancing,' Moth pointed out, surprised by how protective towards Selsey she felt. 'I think the whole idea is silly, anyway. Let her show off if she wants to.'

Moth sounded so disapproving that Ruth felt she was being scolded. 'All right,' she said, 'don't join in. I thought you'd enjoy the joke instead of being so snotty about it.'

And she walked off, leaving Moth with a problem. She didn't like Selsey, and she didn't want to quarrel with Ruth, but it was a joke that could turn out to be very hurtful. So should she warn Selsey?

Moth worried all the afternoon about what to do. She thought of asking her great-aunt's advice but guessed what it would be: that Moth should tell Selsey about the plan and risk getting the others into trouble. She knew that she couldn't do this, but she decided that she would find out where Selsey was changing and then stay nearby to stop anyone meddling with her things.

Her form were to change in their classroom and then file over to the studio just before the performance began. Selsey was not there and as the minutes wore on Moth began to think that perhaps she'd decided not to dance after all. But at twenty-five past seven Selsey appeared. She had changed at home and looked like a miniature Fred Astaire, with a top hat, white tie and tails. Instead of trousers she was wearing black fishnet stockings, and her glitzy glamour was in striking contrast to the demure charm of the holly berries in their scarlet tutus with matching headbands and pale tights. Ruth and Jane giggled, but Selsey took no notice of them and looked scornfully at Moth as she changed places so that she was next to Selsey. From the looks of the others Moth guessed that they had some plan for getting Selsey's shoes away from her.

Each group remained in their seats until just before their piece was due. There wasn't much room off-stage and it was necessary to move very quietly. Selsey's tap shoes would have made this impossible, so she was carrying them and intended to put them on in the wings.

When it was coming up to her turn, Selsey bent down to pick up her shoes but couldn't seem to find them in the dark. There were murmurs of 'shush' as she scrabbled about on the floor, and at first Moth thought that hiding them was the plan, but then they were passed up from the end of the row. Selsey seized them and Moth sensed that no one was disappointed. Everything, it seemed, was going according to plan. But what could they have done to the shoes in the dark? And then suddenly she guessed the answer. None of them had any pockets in which to carry anything, but there was one very simple place in which to carry something: in one's mouth.

Moth got up and pushed her way along the row muttering, 'Sorry, must go to the loo.' There were several in the corridor leading back-stage and she rushed down it looking for Selsey. She was not in sight, but she had parked her unmistakable tap shoes on a chair in the wings, perhaps while she too went to the loo.

Moth picked them up and looked at the soles: they were covered with blobs of chewing gum. She managed to drag most of it off, but suddenly Selsey was beside her. She snatched the shoes away and said accusingly, 'What are you doing to my shoes?'

There was no time to reply, for at that moment the boy who was stage managing came up to check that Selsey was ready and hissed, 'Shut up. You're on in a minute.'

Moth sped back to her seat and was in time to see Selsey come on. Some of the parents had seen her on the screen, and the whole audience was curious to see such a pint-sized personality at first-hand.

Selsey sensed their interest and exploited it. Her song and dance act was an imitation of something far beyond her years. She was aping an adult glamour, pretending to be one of the great stars of Hollywood, and she would have been laughable but for her personality. She believed in herself. She believed that she was fun to watch, and the brashness that made her so unbearable off-stage helped her to sparkle in front of the footlights.

It wasn't the kind of dancing Moth liked at all, but she knew it had taken courage to go on. The audience saw only the person on stage and that was what mattered; they responded to Selsey's verve and vitality, which were far more important than her attempt at dancing.

There were more carols, and St Christopher, with a radiant Tom perched on the giant's shoulders, and then came the garland finale.

Moth was too dazzled to see into the darkness beyond the footlights, but she felt herself the focus of dozens of eyes. It was quite different from dancing for an audition. On stage it was as though she had stepped into another atmosphere, was breathing pure oxygen. She wanted it to last for ever. She wanted to transfix the audience so that they couldn't go home, so that she could stay in that small square of light where all her movements had a purpose and where she was conscious not only of the need to shape her steps to the music but of being part of the design that moved around her.

Each class added to the garland: red and white berries, light and dark green leaves, gold and silver tinsel, and finally Marina, a simple figure in white. Crowded in the wings as she waited to come on for the final grouping, Moth watched Marina's solo and knew why she wanted to be a dancer. The steps were so matched to the music that they seemed to unfold it, and Marina danced with a confidence that lifted dancing above mere steps. She made it look so easy that when it was Moth's turn to run on and take her place in the bouquet forming around the centre of spinning whiteness, she felt that the whole secret of dancing was there in front of her, if she could only reach out and catch it.

The applause was tremendous. There were flowers for Marina and Miss Lambert, who made a speech thanking everyone for all their hard work. Then dancers flowed over into the audience, looking for parents and friends, while a distraught Mrs George made frantic appeals for everyone to get changed first and not to fling their costumes down anywhere.

Moth recognised Great-Aunt Marion's white hair and edged towards her, anxious to avoid any confrontation with Selsey. She saw to her amazement that her great-aunt was not on her own but talking to a familiar figure, and she flew into the arms of her mother while Toby and Lynette capered round her.

'I saw you, I saw you,' chanted Lynette, her eyes shining with pride.

'We only decided to come at the last minute,' said her mother, laughing at Moth's surprise, 'and as we weren't sure whether the car would make it in time, I told Marion to keep it a secret. She's very good at keeping secrets, as you'll find out.'

'Why, is there another one?' said Moth, hoping this meant that her father would suddenly appear.

'Yes,' said her mother, 'there's a really big secret, but this isn't the place to tell you. Go and get changed and then we can go back to Marion's and she can tell you all about it.'

9

The Awful Secret

Moth thought about the secret all the time she was changing. What could it be? She tried to work out what she would like best in the world and decided that it would be for her father to get a job in London, so that they could all live together again. Perhaps this was it. Or perhaps they had won top prize on the premium bonds.

A favourite family game, often played on long journeys, was to plan what they would do if their number ever came up, the sort of house they would move to, how they would have a pony and a boat. Mrs Graham also wanted a holiday in a really luxurious hotel where she would be waited on hand and foot and not have to plan meals and do all the shopping and cooking and washing. The family felt quite guilty when she spoke like this, but then she would laugh and tell them not to be silly. She enjoyed looking after them and she loved cooking. It was doing it all the time that got her down, because it didn't leave her much time to be a person in her own right.

Moth was secretly alarmed at the thought that her mother wanted to be someone different; she loved her just the way she was. But as she struggled out of her tutu and took off her ballet shoes she decided that the secret couldn't be anything as drastic as that. Her mother's expression had been teasing rather than transformed.

She bumped into Ruth as she made her way into the hall; their quarrel of that morning seemed forgotten.

'Have a super Christmas,' said Ruth. 'Perhaps you'd like to come over in the holidays and see my things.'

'I'd love to if I'm back in time,' said Moth, overjoyed by the way in which the future was suddenly opening up and promising to be more fun.

She squashed into the back of the car with Toby and Lyn.

Toby had been very impressed by Tom's antics. He and Drew had done a tumbling dance of whirling leaps and somersaults and Toby envied their lightning speed. He wanted to know if they played football.

'I expect so,' said Moth, 'though we don't do it at school. I know Tom has a skateboard and he's even better at it than you are.'

'You haven't seen me for ages,' protested Toby indignantly. 'I can crouch right down now with one leg out and no hands.'

'So can Tom.'

'Bet he can't. Bet you wouldn't know a christie if you saw one.' Toby began to press Moth
against the side of the door, reinforcing his
argument with his familiar strong-arm tactics.
Moth prepared to fight back.

'Stop it, you two,' said her mother. 'You've
no idea how tiresome children can be,' she said
to Great-Aunt Marion. 'These two are always
squabbling and competing, and it nearly always
ends in blows.'

Great-Aunt Marion smiled. 'I seem to remember that my brothers were much the same. They
always wanted to be bigger and stronger and
better at everything than me. I spent hours one
summer jumping to and fro over the washing
line because I did so want to be best at
something.'

'And were you?' asked Moth, trying to imagine her great-aunt sailing over the high jump.

'Yes, but it didn't last long. They soon had
even longer legs and I could only beat the
younger ones.'

When they arrived back at the flat they found
that Great-Aunt Marion had prepared what she
called 'a high supper'. Even Toby was impressed
by the food, and the gracious setting didn't
inhibit him from tucking in.

There were rolls of ham speared with gher-
kins, sausage rolls hot from the oven, several
kinds of savoury biscuits, two flavours of crisps

(to which Moth had introduced her great-aunt), bowls of nuts and dainty sandwiches of smoked salmon decorated with a twist of lemon.

'What's that funny pink stuff?' said Toby suspiciously, and then had to be restrained from making a pig of himself when he discovered that he liked the salty tang of the salmon.

Lynette sat contentedly munching a sausage roll and blowing bubbles through her straw while Moth suddenly realised how hungry all the excitement had made her.

'What's the great secret?' she said, demolishing two sausage rolls and then scooping up a handful of crisps.

'Well, I think your great-aunt should tell you,' said her mother. 'It's really her secret.'

Great-Aunt Marion took a sip of sherry and the amber liquid caught the light and sparkled like a jewel. 'It was my idea,' she began, 'and perhaps I should have talked it over with you first, but I didn't want you to be disappointed if it didn't work out. You see, it's worried me that you've had to be so much on your own. I'm not much company for someone of your age, so I thought you might be much happier if you had someone of your own age living here.'

Moth wondered whether she ought to apologise for not having seemed happier.

'As you know, two of my brothers went out to live in Australia, and when I wrote to Jack about Moth he told me that his granddaughter Libby was very keen on dancing too and having lessons. Libby's mother was killed in a car crash a few years ago, and ever since she's been living with her grandparents. I gather from Jack that they find her rather a handful at times, and as she hasn't any brothers or sisters I think she's missing a lot. Her father is an airline pilot, so he would be able to come to London and see her sometimes, and he agrees that it would be lovely for her to join a real family, especially as you're both so keen on dancing.'

Great-Aunt Marion paused to take another sip of her drink; she was obviously very proud of her secret. 'Libby will be arriving here after Christmas, and I've arranged for her to go to school with you next term. You'll be able to look after her and show her the ropes, and I'm sure you'll have lots of fun sharing a room and being able to talk about your dancing.'

There was silence. Everyone was waiting for Moth to say something.

'Well, Moth,' said her mother at last, when the silence had become embarrassing, 'don't you think it's a good idea?'

'No, I don't.' Moth didn't stop to think what she was saying. 'It's a rotten idea. I don't want some horrid Australian round my neck. You might have asked me first.'

'Moth,' said her mother, 'stop this at once. How dare you talk to your great-aunt like that.'

'How dare she make plans behind my back,' shouted Moth. 'I never asked for some awful cousin to come poking her nose in here. I don't

want her and I won't help her. She can find her
own way to school, just like I did. I hate her.
And I hate all of you.'

Moth rushed out of the room and ran up the
stairs to her bedroom. She slammed the door
and used all her strength to turn the big old-
fashioned key. Then she flung herself down on
the bed and gave way to choking sobs.

After a while she turned over on her back and
looked round the room. In the last couple of
months she'd become very attached to it. The
drawers of the green leather desk were full of
her possessions, her ballet postcards were
arranged on one wall, the little white bookcase
was gradually filling up with her library of
paperbacks, and high up on the sloping wall
Mukhamedov and Bussell looked down in shad-
owy splendour.

It was the only room Moth had ever had all to
herself, and although she missed the family, the
room had somehow consoled her and become a
symbol of growing up, of the independent life
she was slowly learning to make for herself.
Now this pride of possession was to be shattered. The room would have to be shared – and
with a complete stranger. The future, which had
begun to look so much more promising after a
term of trial, was now uncertain and upset, and
the joy of seeing the family had been changed
into the misery of a row.

Moth hoped that her mother would come
upstairs and rattle the door. She longed to let

her in and explain why she had been so angry. But no one came. From below came sounds of clearing away, then noises in the kitchen, footsteps in the hall, and silence. Presumably Mrs Graham and the children had been stowed away on camp beds and settees.

Moth was too exhausted to cry any more or to get undressed. She lay there listening for her mother and willing her to come upstairs, until eventually she fell asleep.

10

Home Again

Moth was very subdued on the journey home. She sat in the back of the car with Lyn and hardly spoke. Nothing more had been said about Libby at breakfast, and her great-aunt had said a cool goodbye that sounded more as though she was disappointed than angry.

They stopped for lunch at an ice-cream parlour that also sold giant hot dogs. Toby managed to eat two, smothered in ketchup and relish, and then spent ages weighing up the merits of thirty-two different flavours of ice cream. He narrowed the choice down to toffee, coconut, blueberry or New York butter pecan, and finally decided on the latter because he wanted to try pecan nuts. Moth just pointed to the nearest one, a garish green with chips of almond in it, and couldn't remember afterwards what the taste was.

She had so looked forward to going home, but as the car drove under the arch of the old town wall and past the historic Market Cross, now stranded in a sea of parked cars, she felt no pleasure at the sight of familiar shops and streets. Her temper had worn her out. She felt faded by crying and as though she had become a pale person without the strength to feel anything any more.

Not surprisingly, she had one of her headaches, and by the time they arrived home it was so bad that she had to lie down. It was strange being in such a small bedroom again. Her half looked unnaturally tidy, with her books put away and her dolls stacked in a forlorn row. She put her bear on her pillow – she'd refused to hand him over to Lyn – and she was glad of his silent sympathy. Humpidge was always on her side.

It was too dark to see much of the garden, though the lights from downstairs spilled over onto the lawn. The familiar swishing of the wind – so much fiercer than the wind in London – sounded like the sea, and when she touched them with her cheek, the window panes stung like ice. Moth loved the contrast between the wildness outside and the safe security of indoors.

She left the curtains open and went back to her bed. Rain began to tap at the window, and as she lay in the dark listening to the wind, the pain in her head slowly eased. She heard the front door bang and knew that her father had come home. She hoped he would come up to her, but he went into the living room and she pictured him sitting in front of the fire. The smell of fried sausages drifted upstairs.

At first Moth felt she was too ill to eat, but as the smell became stronger and more tempting, and she remembered the crispness of her mother's chips, she had second thoughts. She hadn't eaten much all day and suddenly she felt hungry.

As she stood outside the kitchen door, she wondered for a moment if she still belonged. Then she went in to light and warmth. Toby was supposed to be laying the table, there was a hiss of frying from the cooker, where her mother was just about to serve up, Lyn was grizzling with impatience, and her father was sitting at the table orchestrating the confusion.

'We're all in our places with bright smiling faces,' he chanted, swinging Lyn up from the floor and planting her firmly on a chair. 'Hello,' he said to Moth. 'You decided to join us?'

Moth nodded and sat down in her old place. Toby had given her a huge fork and a small knife and he hadn't forgotten her mug. Everything was gloriously the same, except for some new drawings by Lyn which included a spidery 'My Daddy'. When her mother set down a dish of fat sausages (two and a half each and four for her father) Moth knew she was home.

After they had all helped with the washing up, Mrs Graham put Lyn to bed and Toby shut himself in his room to work on a Christmas secret. Moth and her father sat in front of the fire.

The Grahams still had a proper coal fire,

though Mrs Graham sometimes complained, half-heartedly, about the amount of work it made. Moth loved the uneven patterns of the firelight and the occasional live coals that flared and spluttered with untapped energy. She saw that her mother had remembered to buy some chestnuts as a winter treat, and her father took up a handful and began to slit the shells with his penknife.

'Sorry I missed seeing you as a holly berry,' he said. 'Even Toby was impressed. Promise I'll come next time, even if it means missing the most important conference of the year.'

He picked up the shovel, arranged the chestnuts on it, and then balanced it carefully between two slabs of coal. The orange ashes flared up, scorching the underneath of the shovel.

'I gather there were a few fireworks afterwards, though. And that instead of being pleased that your cousin is coming to join you, you staged one of your tantrums and were very rude to your great-aunt.'

Moth was silent. The cracks in the chestnut shells widened and she could see the white kernels beginning to turn pale yellow.

'It's too late to put her off, you know,' said her father. 'And it's going to be much worse for her. She's already had to cope with losing her mother, and now she's being sent halfway round the world to a country where everything will be strange and new. I expect you've made some friends at school, but she'll be the new girl who

83

comes in in the middle of everything. Even if your dancing is much the same all over the world, she's bound to do some things differently. You know now what it's like to be homesick, so what do you think it'll be like for her?'

Moth tried to imagine. She pictured someone with a pushy personality and a brash Australian accent. Someone who would share her room and see all her things. Someone who would be there for every meal, and perhaps get on better with her great-aunt. Someone who would want to sit next to her at school and walk home with her every day, just when she was making friends with Ruth. And, said a voice inside her head, perhaps she'll be someone who can dance better than you, who'll get all the attention and sympathy because she hasn't a mother and is far from home, who'll . . . But Moth made the voice stop. It was also telling her that she was mean, whereas her father was asking her to be generous.

I can't help it, I can't help it, she thought. I bet he wouldn't like it if someone new turned up at his office and he had to share everything with them.

The chestnuts were now splintering and turning black. Her father put the shovel in the hearth to cool and looked for an old *Radio Times* to put the shells on. He didn't press Moth for an answer.

'Give it time,' he said. 'Wait and see what

she's like. You may be in for a pleasant surprise.'

He put his arm round Moth and she snuggled against him as they watched the fiery turrets in the fireplace topple and disintegrate. Moth felt better.

A few minutes later Toby switched on the light and said indignantly, 'Hey, you've been roasting chestnuts. That's not fair. I want some.'

He bounced across the room and Moth sat up and began to do battle for the deliciously charred nuts that were now cool enough to eat.

11

Opposites

Christmas went in a flash, though beforehand it seemed as though it would never come. More and more cards arrived. There were whispered conferences about presents. Mrs Graham ticked her way through endless shopping lists. There was the usual argument about whether to have a real Christmas tree or a plastic one, and the usual frantic search for last year's decorations. Then in a glorious rush of opening stockings and presents and eating too much it was all over.

Great-Aunt Marion gave Moth a record of Prokofiev's music for *Romeo and Juliet* and a promise to take Moth to see the ballet the next time it was on in London. 'And this time we'll get the tickets in good time,' she wrote on her card.

Moth was still at the stage of being a little wary of music she didn't know. Once she had a tune to hold on to, or felt that she could dance to the music, it was all right, but she tended to get lost or even bored without some guidelines. But the bold dramatic music was as exciting as Tchaikovsky (her favourite composer), and when she heard the lovers' theme she added Juliet to the roles she intended to dance one day.

She was surprised to find how much she was looking forward to going back to school. She felt that she wanted to get on with life instead of just marking time at home. Her former best friend came to tea, but there wasn't much to talk about. Jenny still went to the same dancing classes, and she seemed to accept that Moth wasn't interested in them any more.

Increasingly Moth felt that she was suffering from what her granny called 'the hump'. This was the way you felt when you had nothing to do, it was pouring with rain, and you didn't want to read, paint, listen to music, or finish a jigsaw.

'I shall be glad when you've gone back,' said Mrs Graham, when Moth had made Lyn cry yet again by being too bossy. Toby was no help either. He'd been given a huge box of old stamps, many of them still stuck on scraps of envelope, and he spent hours in the bathroom soaking them off and leaving the washbasin full of soggy paper.

Moth had managed to forget about Libby, but as she and her father drove back to London the thought of her cousin loomed up and spoilt the pleasure of having her father all to herself. He told her about Great-Aunt Marion's younger brothers, whom he had known when he was a small boy.

'They were both in the navy during the war,' he said, 'and I can remember being terribly impressed when they were home on leave. And I was rather frightened of Cousin Rex, Libby's father. He was older than me and used to play the most awful practical jokes. He once got me into the cupboard under the stairs by pretending that he'd invented some marvellous new light. Then he shut the door and left me there in the dark.'

'Were you frightened?'

'Terrified. I howled so loudly that someone soon came and let me out – and Rex was in disgrace afterwards.'

Moth wondered if Libby would take after her father. I shan't let her frighten me, she thought.

To their surprise, Libby had already arrived. She had flown in with her father, who'd breezed across London, scooped up Great-Aunt Marion and taken her out for a meal.

'Rex is so full of life,' she told them. 'He insisted on taking us to one of those restaurants where you help yourself by carving off huge joints of meat. I told him I had a small appetite, but he carved me a great plate of roast lamb, then some roast pork, and after we'd eaten enough meat for a family for a week, he went back again and got himself a great plate of roast beef. He must cost a fortune to feed,' she said with a laugh, turning to Libby.

'Sure, Dad likes his food,' agreed Libby with a grin. She had grey eyes, short wavy hair and a suntan that was miles away from an English winter. Unlike Moth, she didn't seem at all shy and was brimming over with the excitement of the past few days.

'I've seen Big Ben and the Houses of Parliament, and Buckingham Palace and Nelson's Column, and had a ride on the Underground, and seen the soldiers who wear those big black fur hats, and . . .'

Her great-aunt and Moth's father both laughed.

'I can see she's been keeping you busy,' David Graham said.

'Yes, but I've enjoyed it. If you've lived in London all your life, like me, you take these things for granted. You know they're there and you tell yourself that you'll have a look at them one of these days, but it takes someone like Libby to make you realise how exciting London is. Do you know, after all these years, I'd never seen the Changing of the Guard. Until yesterday.'

'I know what you mean. And I'm delighted that Libby's so keen. I hope you'll now have two enthusiasts on your hands, though I hope you won't find them too exhausting.'

'Well, I don't think my legs are up to walking miles, but I have promised Libby the Tower of London and a trip down the river when the weather's better. And I've been thinking about some of the things you and Rex and Patrick liked doing when you were young. Do you remember being taken to Pollock's and all buying toy theatres?'

'What's Pollock's, Daddy?' asked Moth. She'd been feeling out of the conversation and guilty about not having shown more interest in London. She remembered that her great-aunt had offered to take her sightseeing, but she hadn't shared Libby's enthusiasm.

'Pollock's,' said her father, 'was a very old shop that sold toy theatres that you could make yourself. They were all based on real theatres that had existed years ago, and you got not only a cardboard model of the theatre but the text of some bloodthirsty play and all the scenery and characters to go with it. I remember I spent hours cutting them out, and Patrick was very keen on the Penny Plain ones that you had to colour yourself.'

'Did they really cost a penny in those days?' said Moth disbelievingly.

'Well, they did originally, when they were first printed, but not by the time I bought them. The first ones were sold for a penny plain and twopence coloured, and this expression became famous. I'm surprised that Pollock's is still going. Are you sure?'

'Yes,' said Great-Aunt Marion. 'As soon as I remembered the name, I looked them up in the phone book and rang up. They're in Scala Street now, just off Goodge Street, but they still sell toy theatres and they've got a toy museum. So I thought we might add that to our list of sights.'

'When can we go?' said Libby impatiently. 'Is it open tomorrow?'

'You're certainly going to have your hands full with this one,' said David Graham, exchanging amused smiles with Great-Aunt Marion. 'I only wish I could help out, but it's time I was getting back. Libby must come and stay with us in the holidays. She'll put my lot to shame. I don't think they know much about where we live, though it does have quite a history.'

Moth couldn't be bothered to protest. Libby was obviously going to be flavour of the month. She went downstairs with her father to say a private goodbye. It was raining, and the light outside splotched on the liquid pavement.

'She's just as I feared she'd be,' she said quietly. 'She doesn't seem at all homesick and she's awfully pushy.'

Her father pulled her hair playfully. 'I like her, and I think she'll be good for you,' he said. 'You could do with a little more push yourself.'

Moth hugged him reproachfully and then shivered as she watched the car turn the corner. And it was not on account of the chill damp. Perhaps he was right. She was still uncertain about so many things, above all about herself and her ability, but the last thing she felt she needed was a confident cousin who didn't look as though she had a nerve in her.

Then she remembered the shared room. She had meant to sort out her treasures and put the more private ones away. What had Libby done to them? She rushed upstairs and flung open the bedroom door. The room was in darkness apart from the reflections on the ceiling. There was no sign of Libby or of a second bed.

She could hear voices in the kitchen as she went down to join them. Her great-aunt had started the washing-up and Libby was helping. She was telling her great-aunt about a fabulous beach picnic her friends had arranged as a good-bye party.

'Where am I going to sleep?' said Moth abruptly, breaking into Libby's account of sun-bathing on Christmas Day.

'In your room, as usual,' said her great-aunt, groping with her rubber gloves for the last spoon.

'What about Libby?'

'She's got her own room,' said Great-Aunt Marion, smiling at Moth as though they shared a private joke. 'I decided that you were quite right about the room. It isn't really big enough for two. So I cleared out the other attic, and although Libby has to share her room with a few old trunks and odds and ends, she doesn't seem to mind.'

Moth was surprised to find that she was both relieved and disappointed. She had made up her mind to put up with her cousin, to swallow her down like some nasty medicine. Now it seemed there was no need. She could keep her room all to herself. No one wanted her to be a martyr.

As she went back upstairs to start unpacking, she thought how unsettling it was that nothing ever turned out to be quite as one expected.

12

'Twopence Coloured'

Libby longed for it to snow because it never did at home, except in the mountains, but the weather refused to oblige and just went on sulkily raining. The damp tweaked at Great-Aunt Marion's arthritis, and made her put off any more sightseeing until there was only one day left before term began.

'Please,' begged Libby, 'please can we go to Pollock's tomorrow? If we don't go then, we shall have to go on a Saturday when there'll be lots more people. And you said it isn't a place for crowds.'

The next day was as damp and grey as ever, but Great-Aunt Marion gave in. Pollock's turned out to be on the corner of a row of faded houses quaintly squashed together. On one side someone had painted a mock shop window and, on the brickwork above, the figure of Harlequin pointed in the direction of another false window. Moth noticed that even the real windows were crooked, and slanted as though they had been drawn by a child.

Libby had run ahead of them and was pressing her nose against the shop window. The chill mist outside made the small bright room look comforting and cosy. It was a jumble of drawers, trays and boxes spilling over with puppets, models, cutouts, and an assortment of doll's house miniatures, from tiny glasses, mugs and plates to minute jars of jam and elaborate cakes.

The entrance to the toy museum was through a door inside the shop. The assistant explained that it was two small houses joined together and that you went up the stairs of one house and down the stairs of the other. Moth felt as though they had suddenly stepped into a giant doll's house and been reduced to miniatures themselves. The narrow stairs, painted in bright colours, twisted sharply, and the rooms leading off them were small and had sloping ceilings, uneven floors and black lead fireplaces. On every side, on the walls and in cabinets, were displayed the leftovers of childhood, the toys and games of children who were probably now as old as Great-Aunt Marion.

Although Moth and Libby felt that they were too old for dolls and doll's houses, they looked at them to please their great-aunt, who wasn't too old to enjoy them. The French dolls had kept their beautiful pale complexions and had soft curling hair, shining eyes and delicately painted eyebrows. Their clothes were trimmed

with lace and had rows of tiny buttons that must
have taken ages to undo. They looked rather
vain, and Moth noticed that one of them had her
own brush and comb, and a proper garden-party
hat trimmed with faded blue ribbon.

What she liked best was the room with the
bears. There were two that were more than
eighty years old, and they looked their age.
Moth felt sorry for one sitting in a chair who
was described as the oldest known teddy bear.
He had only one ear and seemed to be stuffed
with straw. There was also a doll and a bear
called Freda and William, who had apparently
never been parted. The sight of so many aged
bears made Moth feel that she must be a little
kinder to Humpidge when she went home. It
was sad to be neglected just because someone
had grown too old for you.

Libby wanted to know how old the houses
were. She'd always lived in a modern house in a
modern city, and she was very impressed by the
age of everything in London. 'How many
hundred years?' she asked Great-Aunt Marion,
who said she thought the houses had probably
been built at the end of the eighteenth century.

They saw the toy theatres that Uncle Patrick
had loved, and just as their fathers had done,
they clamoured to buy one. They found the
books with the cardboard models in the shop,
and Moth couldn't decide whether she wanted
the Victoria Theatre with *Cinderella*, or the
Regency Theatre with *The Sleeping Beauty*. Her

great-aunt suggested that Moth and Libby should each have a different one, but they wavered over who was to have what.

They were busy comparing the scenery when Moth was startled by an amused voice that said, 'I think you're more of a Cinderella myself. I should have that one.'

It was Robert, looking like a character in a melodrama with his vast greatcoat and a long striped scarf wound round and round his neck.

Just then Great-Aunt Marion came out of the other room, saying that she had found enough presents to last her for the rest of her birthdays and Christmases. Moth introduced Robert to her great-aunt and Libby. She had told her great-aunt how kind he'd been at Covent Garden, and was relieved that she didn't regard him as a dangerous stranger, won over perhaps by his good manners.

'It's a pleasure to meet you,' he said gallantly, 'but I'm afraid I can't stay because Morris is sitting on a yellow line. I just called in to pick up a new play. But I'd be happy to give you all a lift home, especially as it's such a foul day.'

So they bought one Victoria and one Regency theatre and hurried off to rescue Robert's car. It was dark now, and as they waited while Robert folded down the front seat and threw his junk into a corner of the back seat, Moth looked back at the toyshop and thought how easy it was to believe that you could step inside and back into the past.

Robert was asked to tea, and he proved a great help in getting the theatres assembled. Libby wanted to start on hers as soon as they got home and pestered her great-aunt for scissors and sharp knives and glue before she had time to put the kettle on.

'Surely it'll wait a few minutes,' she protested, as Libby overturned her sewing box in search of another pair of scissors. Moth had bagged the first pair and was already cutting out the stage of her theatre under Robert's direction.

'I'm hopeless at doing things myself,' he said, stretching out on the floor and propping himself up on one of the best flowered cushions, 'but very good at telling other people what to do.'

Moth bent the edges of the stage under, tucked the corners round and glued them together. Then she began cutting out the proscenium arch. This went round the front of the stage and bore a splendid coat of arms with lots of ornamental twirls. The gilt boxes on either side of the stage were hung with swags of red velvet, and in one of them a man with a monocle was quizzing the stage. The people in the boxes reminded Moth of her visit to Covent Garden, though none of the people there had worn such grand clothes. It was tricky cutting round the row of footlights and along the fringe of the looped-up curtain, and Moth was glad when her great-aunt brought in tea.

She had made a stack of toast, and there were two kinds of jam and Marmite for Moth, who much preferred savoury toast.

Robert was obviously a jam man, and just as he was about to bite into a slice laden with fruit, Libby asked him what he did and why he'd been buying a play at Pollock's.

Moth had been too shy to ask. She guessed that he didn't work in an office because he didn't dress or talk like her father.

Robert finished his toast and helped himself to another piece before replying. 'I'm a student,' he said.

'A student of what?'

'Well, life, really. But officially I'm supposed to spend my days in the Reading Room of the British Library, sending for piles of books, making lots of notes, and eventually, I suppose, writing a book myself.'

'What'll the book be about?' said Libby.

'The theatre. In the nineteenth century. In fact about the very kind of theatres you're busy making. Which is why I know about Pollock's. I used to go there when I was a schoolboy, and it was playing about with model theatres that started my interest in theatre history.'

'Do you get paid for playing with toy theatres?' said Libby, who was shamelessly inquisitive.

Robert laughed. 'Yes and no. I've got a grant to write my thesis, and so far I've managed to persuade the authorities that I'm working very hard. But I expect they'll find me out some day, and then I'll have to work like everyone else.'

'I expect you work very hard,' said Great-Aunt Marion. She didn't really approve of modern students, but she liked Robert and was determined to think well of him.

After tea they got down to the theatres in earnest. Robert and Great-Aunt Marion read the instructions aloud and held corners in place. Moth and Libby wielded the scissors, and were sometimes in such a hurry that they chopped off odd corners and even vital parts. But by supper time there were two resplendent theatres with stout columns at the four corners and sturdy wings with slits to take the scenery.

'My fingers won't cut any more,' said Libby, throwing the torturing scissors down. 'We'll have to do the characters tomorrow.'

'Wouldn't it be lovely to dance on a stage like this?' said Moth, putting her theatre on the sideboard and kneeling down to look into the stage. 'It would make a beautiful setting for a ballet.'

'Diaghilev had the same idea,' said Robert, and added proudly, 'and I bet not many people could tell you that.'

'What did he do?'

'Went to Mr Pollock's shop, which in those days was in the East End, and fell in love with the old engravings of the pantomime characters. Then when he wanted to commission a new ballet, which he was always doing, he suddenly remembered the old prints and decided that he would build a ballet round them.'

'Can we go and see it?' said Libby.

'Heavens, no. It was staged a long time ago and everyone's forgotten about it by now, though you sometimes come across photographs of it. But Moth's right about the theatre. It would be a lovely setting for a ballet, so perhaps you should try and make one up.'

Libby looked doubtful, but Moth thought it was a good idea. She took her theatre up to bed with her and stood it on her chest of drawers. When she was in bed, she switched off her bedside lamp and got out the torch she kept under her pillow. She'd always had one there since the days when she was very small and afraid of the dark. Now she switched it on and directed the beam on to the empty stage, moving it round as though it were a spotlight. The theatre looked more alive by torchlight, and the stage was so inviting that Moth longed to step on to it.

'That's the sort of theatre I shall dance in one day,' she said to herself. And then she fell asleep.

13

Tom's Challenge

To Moth's surprise and secret dismay, Libby soon proved to be the most promising dancer in their class. She was well proportioned, had been well taught and had a nice relaxed style, and Miss Pearson was delighted with her.

As she'd done Cecchetti examinations in Australia, she fitted into the class without any trouble and like the rest of them was soon hard at work on Grade 4.

This involved various exercises such as *pliés* and *battements* at the barre, and then *port de bras* and more *battements* in the centre. In the adage, the slow movements section, there were *grands ronds de jambe en l'air* with an arabesque, and Moth tried to model herself on her poster of Darcey Bussell, who didn't look as though she ever wobbled.

Libby was very good at pirouettes and at the different jumps, the *changements*, *echappés*, *temps levés* and *jetés*. In the final part of the examination, they had to do a sequence made up by the examiner, and then a dance of their own. The dance had to be no longer than a minute, but Moth felt sure that it would be one of the longest minutes of her life. The examination ended, like all classes, with a bow or a curtsey, which was considered a polite way of thanking the teacher or examiner.

There was always a break after class while they changed out of their tights and leotards. The school was too small to have a uniform, but Miss Lambert made it very plain that she didn't approve of sloppy clothes and even Drew, who carried round his possessions in a curious ex-army haversack, managed to conform as far as wearing grey flannels.

Break was the first chance to swap news, because Miss Pearson made everyone work so hard that there was no time for talking in class. Moth and Ruth's favourite private place was in the shelter of an old wall in one corner of the playground. It was near the few trees left, which had been carefully preserved in neat squares cut out of the asphalt. Moth had feared that Libby would expect to join them, but she much preferred the company of Tom, who shared her restless energy. He, in turn, liked her enough to tell her about his great problem.

His way to and from school lay past the local comprehensive school, a vast untidy complex of buildings that took up the whole of one street. Some of the boys who went there had found out that Tom went to the Fortune School of Dancing, and they let him know just what they thought of it.

'Mind you don't get a ladder in yer tights.'

'Made yer fortune yet?'

''oo's afraid of football?'

Sometimes they came along in a group, boys who were all taller than Tom although about the same age, and walked close behind him, so close that they trod on his heels. He tried to take no notice, but then they would start to jostle him, until his fear of being attacked got the better of him and his walk became a run and he would hare off up the road while the boys laughed and called insults after him.

He was afraid to tell his mother. He knew that she would insist on coming down to the boys' school and making a fuss, and then they would have something else to jeer at. Dancing might not be sissy, and require far more strength and muscle than most of the boys who made fun of Tom possessed, but how could he make them see that? Their heroes were footballers, and although Tom had heard of a football team that had tried ballet exercises and found them exhausting, this wasn't the sort of thing he could explain in the street.

He began to think of his day as having two danger zones, two periods that had to be lived through somehow. He worked out that it didn't take more than a couple of minutes to walk past the school, and he told himself that a couple of minutes wasn't very long. There were ways of getting through the danger zone. Sometimes when he turned the corner, someone else came along: an elderly lady on her way back from the shops, a mother with a toddler in a pushchair. Tom would tag along just behind them and use them as a kind of shield. He knew that the boys wouldn't attack him when anyone was about. Their bullying was strictly private.

Libby was the only person Tom felt he could confide in. She shared his indignation and felt that they must fight back.

'I bet they're not good at anything,' she said. 'I bet none of them could jump as high as you or turn cartwheels as fast as you can.'

Tom was flattered and comforted by her admiration. But it wasn't much practical use.

'Lots of grown-ups feel like they do,' he said. 'My grandfather's always making awful jokes about me turning into a little swan. *Swan Lake* is the only ballet he's ever heard of, and he thinks it's terrible that I should be doing girls' stuff.'

But, ironically, it was Tom's grandfather who provided Libby with a way in which she felt Tom could show his tormenters that dancing was for real boys. For Tom's eleventh birthday, his grandfather gave him a complete skateboard outfit: board, crash helmet and knee pads. The present was meant as a challenge: a challenge to Tom's mother, whom he thought was to blame for all this ballet nonsense, and a challenge to

Tom to show that he really was a normal boy.

Mrs Blundell-Smith was predictably furious. She didn't realise that Tom already owned a rather battered skateboard and she saw the present as a dangerous threat. 'Tom could have a very nasty accident and ruin his chances of dancing for ever. It's a most unsuitable present for a child in his position, and I insist that you take it back.'

Tom's grandfather was a wily old man. He loved his grandson and wanted to be proud of him, but he saw nothing to be proud of in a boy who wanted to dress up in fancy clothes and jig round a stage. It wasn't his idea of being manly, and he was sure it was all the fault of Tom's mother. He winked at Tom, packed the present up, and as soon as Mrs Blundell-Smith was out of the room told Tom that he could keep it if he was prepared to hide it away.

'But where?' Tom asked Libby. 'My mother would find it wherever I put it. She's always dusting and poking about in my room.'

'Why not give it to me,' suggested Libby. 'My bedroom's already got lots of things stored in it. I could easily hide your gear behind one of the trunks, and then we could share it.'

Tom brought his present to school in instalments, and Libby managed to take them home without even Moth finding out. Moth and Ruth liked to dawdle on the way home, whereas from now on Libby and Tom raced back. Libby would tell her great-aunt that she was going out to play with Tom, smuggle the skateboard downstairs, and off they would scoot in search of a suitable slope.

If Great-Aunt Marion was at all surprised, she wasn't over-curious. She was pleased that Moth and Libby had their own friends, and as long as they weren't too late for tea, she enjoyed having a little more quiet time on her own.

Libby and Tom had a marvellous time experimenting with the skateboard. Both had a natural sense of balance and they were fearless. Their ballet training had taught them to relax, and although they kept falling off, they were soon inventing all kinds of variations, mostly thought up by Libby.

The competition was her idea too. It came to her when Tom arrived very late for class one day and couldn't put a foot right. He told her afterwards that he'd been set on by a couple of boys who'd snatched his holdall, emptied it out, and made fun of his practice clothes.

'They pretended to dance round in them and then threw the rest of my things all over the place,' he said, almost crying with anger. 'It took me ages to find everything, and I knew Miss Pearson would be furious if anything was missing.'

'Never mind,' said Libby consolingly. 'They only do it because it makes them feel stronger than you. But they're not, not really. I bet they can't skateboard half as well as you.'

And then she had her idea.

'Why don't you challenge them to a skate-board competition? You could show them once and for all that dancers aren't cowards or sissies.'

14

Out of Control

It proved surprisingly easy to provoke the boys to a contest the next time they came across Tom on his way home and started their familiar jostling.

'D'you like fairy stories?' asked one of them, a skinny boy with a T-shirt featuring a monster-like gorilla. 'Read fairy stories, do you?'

The others laughed as though the Beast had made a brilliant joke. One of them bumped into Tom and trod heavily on his foot.

'Sorry,' he said with mock politeness. 'Hope I haven't hurt yer twinkletoes.'

'That's a good name for 'im,' said one of the others. 'Little Fairy Twinkletoes.' And they all began to chant 'Fairy Twinkletoes, Fairy Twinkletoes'.

Tom felt sick. In desperation he looked down the road, hoping that some woman would come along so that he could walk close behind her. He was sure that the boys wouldn't actually attack

110

him in the presence of an adult. But the only movement in the street came from the shadows of the newly fledged trees basking in the spring sunlight.

One of the boys had a skateboard and was shunting along on it. Tom remembered Libby's challenge and wished she was there to support him.

'Bet you can't do a handstand on that,' he said. He had meant to say it in an offhand assured way, but his voice sounded shrill and unsteady.

'Hark at Twinkletoes,' jeered the Beast. 'Fancies himself on wheels. Does Mummy let you play with nasty dangerous wheels?'

Tom flushed at the mention of his mother. 'If you think you're so good,' he said, 'prove it. Let's have a contest to see who's really afraid.'

The boys started chanting 'Twinkletoes on wheels, the garden gnome on wheels', but the Beast was considering.

'Right,' he said, 'yer on. Know the ramp outside David Morgan House? We'll see you there on Thursday after school. You can show us how well you can dance, little fairy.'

And with that the gang lost interest in Tom and ran off down the street, jumping up here and there to strip the branches of their young leaves.

Tom told Libby what had happened the next day and was comforted by her enthusiasm. 'We'll show them,' she said.

Both she and Tom were determined to master a christie by Thursday. This involved crouching down on the board with one leg sticking out in front and both arms stretched out to balance. Libby fell off several times and grazed her hand and knees. She had a stoical disregard for injuries, even when they brought tears to her eyes, but Great-Aunt Marion was far more upset.

'What *have* you been doing?' she said, when Libby arrived home with grubby handkerchiefs round both her knees. 'These cuts must be bathed at once and properly disinfected.' And she made Libby sit still while she bathed her knees and hand with hot water and then applied antiseptic cream. 'You can get an infection very easily,' she said, swabbing out the pieces of grit.

'You can get lockjaw,' said Moth cheerfully. 'Perhaps you'd better keep your mouth open all the time so that it doesn't get stuck.'

'Don't be silly,' said her great-aunt crossly. 'There's no need to worry as long as you disinfect cuts properly and make sure there aren't any splinters in them.'

Great-Aunt Marion had done a First Aid course during the war, and Moth could imagine her being marvellous in a crisis because she was so cool and unfussy. But she was less calm and unruffled when Libby developed a sore throat and a streaming nose.

'Back to bed with you, my child,' she said firmly, after Libby had picked at her breakfast and mopped her way through half a box of tissues.

'I must go to school,' protested Libby, struggling to find the energy to defy a cold and her great-aunt.

'Nonsense. Moth can explain, and I'm sure they won't want you spreading your germs all round the school.'

Libby gave in only after a promise that she could go tomorrow *if* she was better, but when Moth came home in the afternoon she found Libby much worse and obviously in need of several days in bed. Her face was flushed, she had a temperature, and her chest wheezed like a concertina.

Moth assured her that she wasn't missing much, but as soon as Great-Aunt Marion had gone downstairs, Libby told her about Tom and the contest.

'If he doesn't turn up, the others will think it's because he's afraid, and then they'll tease him even more. And it'll be all my fault because it was my idea in the first place.'

Her hoarse voice sounded painfully urgent and Moth could tell from her flushed cheeks and bright eyes that she was really ill.

'You'll have to take the board in tomorrow,' Libby said. 'I've hidden it under that big bush in the front garden.'

Moth was appalled. She hated her brother's skateboard and the whole beastly pastime, and she remembered that they had all been warned in their first term of the injuries that skateboards and roller skates could cause.

'If you don't,' croaked Libby, 'I shall get up and take it myself, when Gam isn't looking.'

Moth knew she meant it.

'All right,' she said miserably, 'I'll take it.'

David Morgan House was a block of flats called after one of the local councillors. It was part of an estate that had been designed with some thought for the people who had to live there, and the various blocks were linked by square patches of grass and oblong flower beds cut out of the surrounding concrete. The gardens were at different levels and were joined together by steps and ramps that were ideal for boarding.

There was also a dismal sunken basin that had started out as a pond but had been drained when all the fish disappeared and several toddlers fell in. It had gradually filled up with rubbish and dead leaves until one of the boys on the estate had seen a film about boarding and realised its potential. Cleaned out, it wasn't quite up to a Hollywood swimming pool, but the sloping sides had their moments.

There was a raw March wind blowing on Thursday and Moth dug her chin well down into her scarf which was wound several times round her neck. She would like to have disappeared right inside it, so that she was invisible, because she so wished that she hadn't felt obliged to turn up with Tom. But he had obviously been relying on Libby for moral as well as practical support.

The Beast was wearing a leather jacket decorated with metal studs, and torn jeans. The jacket zip was broken and another lurid disaster, this time featuring a car chase, was stencilled across his T-shirt. A Walkman clamped to his ears emitted an incessant tinny beat.

Moth felt afraid of him and his friends. There was a casual violence about them, about the way in which they moved in a pack, kicking at anything that got in their way and viciously grabbing any trees and bushes that crossed their path. One of them had found an old can and kept hurling it against a wall. The jangling crash seemed to amuse him, but suddenly he tired of the game and leapt on the can, using his full weight to crush it as he might have crushed an enemy.

'Brought our girlfriend, 'ave we?' said one of them, eyeing Moth.

'Well, she's not 'is mother,' said another. And they all laughed as though they had only one laugh between them.

'Right, let's go.' The Beast shot forward on his board and flipped down on to the next level of the gardens. Tom shunted along behind him and Moth followed them, trying to pretend that she just happened to be passing. When they got to the empty basin, the Beast began to ride up the curve of the sides, flicking the board round in a turn as he reached the top.

115

Tom studied the Beast's technique. He and Libby had not found anywhere like this to practise, but he was used to copying an exercise and his agility and sense of balance, sharpened for a very different purpose, stood him in good stead. He rattled down one side and shot up the other, matching the Beast's speed and daring.

The Beast was unimpressed. He jumped out of the basin and zigzagged through the gardens, dodging round the cutouts of spring green grass and the beds spiked with roses. Tom pursued him, angling his body so that his board rolled and bucked obediently. Finally they came to a longer slope where a ramp wound down to the street. The Beast crouched down until he was lying across the board and his body seemed to graze the paving as it spun past.

'Let's see yer handstand,' he called up as he clattered to a standstill in the middle of his gang.

Tom gripped the ends of his board, launched it with two or three steps and then kicked his legs up and locked his elbows. His body was poised vertically over the board and the watching boys were impressed.

'Magic,' said one admiringly.

The board gathered speed and at that moment a large mongrel came bounding up the ramp.

'Tom, look out,' shouted Moth, but her warning was too late. Tom swerved to avoid the dog but had no time to cartwheel upright. The board bounced off the side wall of the ramp and Tom thudded down on to the pavement.

The First Step

The boys scattered at the scent of trouble, leaving Moth and the dog alone with Tom. He was obviously hurt, but Moth couldn't tell how badly because Tom didn't say. He just lay there on the ground without moving.

15

Taking the Blame

Although it was only a couple of minutes before Tom opened his eyes, it seemed like eternity to Moth. In the meantime, the dog licked him, decided he wasn't something to eat, looked hopefully at Moth, and then ambled away.

Moth knelt down and tried to see where Tom was hurt. There wasn't any blood so far as she could see, but she was frightened by his stillness. Supposing he was dead? People did die from a knock on the head. How would she know? Just then Tom made a noise, a whimper of pain that increased as he tried to turn his head.

Moth wondered whether to help him sit up. She had an idea that you weren't supposed to move people after an accident, in case it made them worse. And weren't you supposed to keep them warm? Perhaps she should put her raincoat round him.

She looked desperately round the gardens to see if anyone had noticed them. The Beast and his gang had vanished – they didn't want to be mixed up in any trouble – and the windows of the flats towering above her looked down on Moth like so many blank faces that just didn't want to know.

Tom sat up and didn't seem sure where he was. When he tried to stand up, his eyes filled with fear and tears.

'My foot hurts,' he sobbed. 'It feels all funny and as though it won't hold me. How am I going to get home?'

Moth saw that he was trying hard not to cry, but the pain and uncertainty about what had happened to his foot were too much for him. She knew that when she was ill, the one person she wanted was her mother, and she guessed that Tom might feel the same.

'Perhaps I should phone your mother?' she said. 'Then she could come and take you home.'

Tom didn't answer. His head ached, his foot throbbed, and he couldn't cope with the voices calling him a coward and his mother fussing and worrying about his career. He just wanted someone to come along and take care of everything, and he left the decision to Moth.

Summoning Mrs Blundell-Smith seemed to be the best idea, but telephoning her wasn't that easy. There was a phone box outside David Morgan House, but even if it worked, which was doubtful, it only took cards, and Moth didn't have the money to buy one. When she asked a passer-by if there was anywhere else with a phone, the woman looked at her suspiciously and muttered something about some shops just round the corner. Moth couldn't think straight as she found herself faced with a greengrocer, a launderette, and an Indian restaurant. Then she saw that the last shop was a sweet-shop-cum-paper-shop-cum-post-office. Surely they would help.

She rushed in, looked around wildly for a phone, and burst into tears.

The woman behind the counter had just reached the most exciting moment in a romantic thriller, and she was not pleased at being disturbed. 'What's the matter?' she said crossly.

'It's Tom. He's hurt his ankle and he can't walk. I must get in touch with his mother and the phone outside only takes cards. Could I use yours?'

'Well,' said the woman, 'I'm not supposed to let the public use the phone, but seeing as it's an emergency, I s'pose it's all right. But make it quick.'

She lifted up a flap in the counter and led Moth into the back of the shop. It was dark and small and stacked with bundles of newspapers and magazines and a pile of cardboard boxes that seemed to be full of bars of chocolate. The mere sight of them made Moth feel faintly sick.

She was remembering the rather overbearing woman who had brought Tom to school that first day, and she didn't look forward to having to tell Mrs Blundell-Smith that her darling had been injured.

Nothing was easy. It took Moth ages to find the number – did one look under Blundell or Smith? – and then she wasn't very good at explaining where they were. In the end, Mrs Blundell-Smith said imperiously 'Some estate called David Morgan' and left it to the taxi driver.

By the time she arrived, Moth had propped Tom up against a wall and covered him with her raincoat. His legs stuck out awkwardly and he looked like a small child's attempt at fashioning a guy. He kept touching the swelling on the back of his head to see if it was getting bigger, and his face was smudged with dirt and tears.

'My poor little treasure,' said Mrs Blundell-Smith, scooping Tom up and smothering him in an embrace. 'Whatever's happened to my poor boy?'

Moth was glad that no one else was about to hear these endearments, but Tom was too upset to care. He limped along between his mother and Moth, wincing every time his left foot touched the ground. His mother took no notice of Moth; all her attention was concentrated on Tom. She helped him tenderly into the taxi, told the driver her address, and drove off without a word of thanks to Moth. When she looked at her watch, Moth saw that the whole incident had only lasted about an hour; she wouldn't even be very late for tea.

As she hurried home, she wondered what would happen next. Mrs Blundell-Smith was sure to find out about the skateboard and make a terrific fuss, but that Moth herself might be blamed in some way was something that never occurred to her.

Tom wasn't at school next day, and as Libby's cold now threatened to descend to her chest, Great-Aunt Marion insisted on keeping her at home.

Moth had not been able to tell Libby what had happened to Tom, other than that he'd been hurt, because after tea they had to humour her great-aunt, who suggested that a game of snakes and ladders might cheer up the invalid.

As Moth slithered down a particularly evil-looking snake, she reflected that life was just like that. Things seemed to be going well and you got on and then, wham: you landed on a snake and had to go right back to the beginning.

Her real-life snake turned out to be Miss Lambert, who summoned Moth to her study next morning.

'Sit down, Jennifer,' she said, looking at Moth across her desk with an expression that made Moth apprehensive. 'I understand you're a friend of Tom Blundell-Smith.'

Moth nodded. She hated being called 'Jennifer', which she never thought of as her real name. It was a proper name, shared by lots of other people, whereas 'Moth' was special and belonged just to her.

She hadn't spoken to Miss Lambert since her first interview, and was rather in awe of her. Moth had studied the photographs of Ashton ballets in the hall and found it hard to reconcile Miss Lambert's present appearance with the slim, pretty girl who had once taken her orders from Sir Fred himself.

'I think you know that Tom Blundell-Smith had an accident last night, but perhaps you don't know that he's broken his ankle.'

Moth was shocked.

'His mother is keeping him at home for a few days, and he won't be able to dance again for at least a couple of months. Mrs Blundell-Smith is very upset, because it seems that the accident was caused by a skateboard that she had forbidden Tom to use and thought had been given away. She tells me that in fact he gave it to you, and that you encouraged him to go on using it although you'd been warned that it was dangerous.'

Moth was stunned. There must be some mistake. It was Libby not she who had encouraged Tom. She hadn't known anything about the skateboard. She tried to think of some way of explaining what had really happened without getting Libby into trouble, but Miss Lambert swept on, taking Moth's silence as an admission of guilt.

'I would like to remind you,' she said sternly, 'that unlike most schools, we are not obliged to keep any pupils here. As I told you at your interview, there are lots of reasons why pupils are sometimes asked to leave. Usually they are reasons outside their control, but they all add up to one most important reason: because the staff and I have come to the conclusion that they won't make dancers.

'One of the most important qualities a dancer needs is the ability to benefit from advice. If you ignore it and think that you know best, then you're not likely to do well at something that requires discipline above all else. Some of the rules may seem a little harsh, but I'm sure you know why you are advised not to do certain sports or take risks that might harm other pupils, don't you?'

Moth nodded. She wanted to say that it was unfair. That she didn't break rules. That it was all Libby's fault. But the words wouldn't come. She saw with dismay that Miss Lambert had no doubts about the situation.

'I've spoken to some of the staff and they're very surprised that you behaved in this silly way. But it's more than silly, because your disobedience might have resulted in the end of someone else's career. And that is something I take very seriously. If your parents were in London, I should want to discuss the matter with them, but I have decided not to involve them at this stage. Instead, I shall keep a special eye on you in the future. If you do well in the examinations and your conduct is satisfactory, then all will be well. But if you show that you're not ready to accept the school rules, then I shall have to tell your parents that you would be better off in another school.'

Moth left Miss Lambert's study with the same feeling of relief with which she usually got down from the dentist's chair. The most important thing was that it was over, and she intended to make sure that she never had to go back there again. But increasingly throughout the day she began to feel resentful towards Libby. She'd never wanted her to come in the first place, and now, thanks to her, Moth was in danger of losing the chance she valued most.

As soon as she got home, Moth ran upstairs in search of Libby. She was determined to make her promise to explain the situation to Miss Lambert, but Libby's room was empty.

Moth stood in the doorway feeling angry. Angry with her great-aunt for interfering. Angry with Miss Lambert for never doubting that Moth was to blame. Angry with Libby for preferring the company of Tom and causing so much trouble. It wasn't fair. It wasn't fair.

She felt sorry for herself and looked round the room for some way of getting back at Libby. Her eyes fell on Libby's theatre, and in a spiteful rage she knocked it off the chest of drawers and stamped on it. Her foot crashed down on the triumphant arch, the stiff curtain, the sets and actors, the footlights. The theatre crumpled under her onslaught into a heap of torn and bent cardboard.

Moth knelt down and pulled at the pieces, but all the king's horses and all the king's men couldn't have put them together again. The theatre was broken beyond repair, and the only thing to do with it was to hide the remains. Hurriedly she pushed them down the back of the chest of drawers, hoping that Libby might possibly think that the theatre had mysteriously slipped down there of its own accord.

Then she went down to tea.

She found Libby showing off as usual, telling her great-aunt about the ballets she'd seen in Sydney and the parts she was hoping to dance one day.

'When I'm older and I've finished my training,' she boasted, 'I shall go back home and become the prima ballerina of the Australian Ballet. I shall practise and practise until I'm world famous, and people will come to Australia just to see me.'

'Isn't that rather a tall order?' said Great-Aunt Marion, smiling at Moth. 'If you're so famous, you'll be asked to dance in all the great opera houses and you won't be content to stay in Australia.'

'Yes, I will,' said Libby firmly, 'because I want everyone to see how good the Australian company is. I get so fed up with everyone over here going on and on about the Royal Ballet. I bet they're not really all that good.'

It was Moth's cue to start an argument, but to her great-aunt's surprise she seemed miles away. She was wondering whether to tell the prospective prima ballerina that first she would have to own up to breaking the rules. Perhaps Miss Lambert would then threaten to send her away. She was certainly far more likely to do something else wrong before very long. But did Moth really want her to go? She wasn't sure.

So while Libby prattled on about the current stars of the Australian Ballet, Moth made a pact with herself. It wasn't so much a pact as a bargain, a case of if I do this, then that will happen. The bargain was: if I don't tell on Libby, in exchange, please let me pass all my exams. It was a deal with Fate, like holding your collar when you saw an ambulance, but it made Moth feel much better and she settled down to a large tea.

16

Sea-Break

Much of the spring term had been grey, cold and wet, the ideal weather for staying indoors and working hard, but it was much harder to concentrate in the summer term, when the sun insisted on shining.

Moth and Libby were feeling so full of energy that they enjoyed the exhausting routine of class, but it was one thing to fling oneself into *jetés* and pirouettes and quite another to concentrate on maps and sums and French verbs, especially when trees in full green looked through the windows with a very different message.

Libby never stopped complaining about being miles from the sea and having to make do with a small overcrowded swimming pool. She went on and on about how marvellous it was back home, until Moth began to picture Australia as a vast swimming pool fringed by sandy beaches creamed by surf. She didn't like swimming that much, because she so hated those first moments when the water explored her with icy fingers.

'Can't we go to the sea, just for the day?' Libby pestered Great-Aunt Marion. 'It's so near London. Back home, we think nothing of driving miles just to find an extra good beach.'

Libby was being what Moth's father, after several weeks of her persistence when she wanted her own way during the holidays, had dubbed 'irrepressible'. Lyn, who loved long words but didn't always get them right, had seized on this and kept saying that Libby was so pressable, which made Toby and Moth laugh.

'It's such a performance and so expensive,' said Great-Aunt Marion defensively. 'If we had a car, it would be different. I'm afraid you'll just have to make the most of the swimming baths.'

So Moth went on shivering down the steps and dipping in the shallow end while Libby plunged down length after length like a young dolphin.

The baths were in the same building as the library, and one day they bumped into Robert, who had tickets for libraries all over London. Libby immediately began telling him how many lengths she'd swum and how it wasn't an Olympic-sized pool, and how cramped and shut in London was.

'You sound as though you could do with a day by the sea,' said Robert sympathetically. 'I know just how you feel. The British Library is all right once you get into the Reading Room, but there are so many tourists at this time of year that it takes ages to check in, and if I have to stand around too long, I start thinking that it's much too nice a day to spend inside with a lot of books that will wait until a rainy day.'

Moth thought that he was only agreeing with Libby out of politeness. He must be old enough to have joined the ranks of grown-ups like her father who thought that it was one's duty to go to work, however tempting the day. But she was wrong about Robert.

A few days later, he rang up Great-Aunt Marion and suggested that they should all go to the sea by car on Sunday.

'I thought somewhere not too far, just in case Morris is taken short,' he explained. 'I think Southend would be a fairly safe bet.'

Libby wanted to know all about Southend.

'It's years since I've been there,' said her great-aunt, 'and I expect it's all changed, but it used to be a great favourite of Londoners, and it's got the longest pier in the world.'

'What's a pier?'

'A way of walking on the sea without getting your feet wet.'

Libby couldn't make sense of this, but Gam refused to explain and answered every question with, 'Wait and see'.

Morris seemed to have got the message that much was expected of him. Once they were through the traffic of the East End, they chugged along at what Great-Aunt Marion, who hated fast driving, thought was a very nice speed and Robert confessed was about Morris's limit.

Moth and Libby shared the back seat with a splendid hamper they had found in Great-Aunt Marion's collection of things-not-to-be-thrown-away-because-they-are-bound-to-come-in-useful-some-day. She had prepared a banquet of a picnic, with iced soup, cold chicken, boxes and boxes of unusual salads, coffee and, as a special treat, early strawberries. She'd arranged everything with such care that Moth was sure they were taking a tablecloth, too.

Libby was determined to be the first to see the sea. But as the car turned down towards the sea front and they came out on to the promenade overlooking the estuary and the further shore, there was no sudden whoop of joy.

'Where is it?' she said at last in a subdued voice. 'That's not the sea!'

Moth saw what she meant. The shore was littered with a galaxy of small boats, most of them belonging to local fishermen, but instead of bobbing about on the water, they were perched amid flatlands of grey mud. The tide was out, and so far out that it had left behind a vast foreshore, to the delight of boys in wellingtons who were furiously digging in the mud for bait.

Robert laughed, and then tried to remedy Libby's disappointment. 'I'm sorry. I should have checked the tide times and warned you.

But the tide comes in very quickly once it's turned, and we'll go out to the end of the pier and find the sea.'

The setting for the picnic was less elegant than Great-Aunt Marion would have liked, but at least Robert found them somewhere full of interest. They perched on a wall at the top of the beach like a row of hungry gulls, and while Great-Aunt Marion unpacked the hamper and fussed over the iced soup (which was a delicious concoction of tomatoes, onions, green peppers and cucumber), Robert pointed out the land-marks and swept the horizon with his binoculars.

He enjoyed ship-spotting and told them about the liners, oil tankers and cargo boats that turned off the high seas at this point and came past on their way up the estuary to the docks at Tilbury. He told Libby about cockles and Southend rock and promised her a sample, and he whetted their appetite for the narrow nautical high street at Leigh and the long streak of the pier.

Great-Aunt Marion said she didn't feel equal to tackling the pier, even if the railway was still running, so after the picnic they drove along the front and found the perfect parking place for her and Morris, where she said they could keep each other company.

The sun was shining on the pier so that Moth felt they were walking along a causeway of light. Gulls screamed overhead, and when they had got about halfway they caught up with the sea, which was curling gently back towards the land. The town dwindled behind them and they seemed to be sailing away on the deck of a great liner.

On the journey down Moth had been thinking about the exam this week and the final verdict that lay on the far side of it. Everyone seemed to have their problems. Was Jane growing too tall? Was Ruth getting too fat? Would Tom's ankle be all right? Would Marina be the first pupil to get a place in the Royal Ballet's senior school, and who would win the prize for the most promising dancer in the first form? Moth had felt herself weighed down by anxieties, but here on the pier the breeze took hold of them and carried them off as lightly as a balloon. The sea, it said, sun and summer holidays, it said, lie ahead.

As usual, Libby wanted to see everything. They had to go into the shed where the lifeboat stood poised above the slipway ready to dash down into the water. They had to go right to the end of the pier and up some stairs to a little lookout hut where they hoisted signals when it was stormy. Then downstairs to the sea itself, where passengers still boarded ships amid fearsome girders encrusted with sea moss and tiny shelled animals.

'That's what piers were really for,' said Robert knowledgeably. 'To enable people to get on and off boats when the tide was a long way out. It's a pity that nowadays going on a trip doesn't seem very exciting, and so there are hardly any real passenger-boats left.'

Libby was still very scornful of Robert's idea of the sea. The tide had turned now and the waves were hastening back, but she was used to sea on a much grander scale, to the roar of surf instead of the very English murmur of lapping water. She longed to startle Robert and Moth and so she suddenly raced back along the pier shouting, 'Bet you can't catch me.' And of course they couldn't.

Great-Aunt Marion was very glad to see them because it was very hot in Morris, and she didn't approve of people who sat in their cars as though they were still at home and never stretched their legs. Unfortunately her legs didn't stretch very far because of her arthritis, and Moth longed to walk a little faster. Robert sensed her impatience and cheered her up by quoting in a whisper:

'"Will you walk a little faster?" said the whiting to the snail. "There's a porpoise close behind us, and he's treading on my tail."'

Libby loved the fishermen's stalls with their glistening harvest of pale pink shrimps and shiny black winkles, and their dolls'-size plates of cockles, and kept clamouring to try some.

In the end Robert called for a truce in the shape of a proper seaside tea.

They sat outside a café overlooking the sea, which was striding in now, and ordered cockles, winkles, shrimps (very fiddling things to eat,

135

Robert warned), bread and butter, ice cream, tea and fizzy drinks.

Moth loved the shrimps, Libby said the cockles tasted like fishy mackintosh, and Robert admitted that he had an allergy to shellfish. It was left to Great-Aunt Marion to do the tea real justice. She said it reminded her of her school holidays, when she and her brothers spent their pocket money on plates of cockles drenched in vinegar. 'We were forbidden to eat between meals and of course this made them taste even better.'

All the boats were afloat now and the waves were nearly up to the promenade. Libby wanted to go for a swim, but Great-Aunt Marion said firmly that they hadn't time to wait for her tea

to go down. Libby sulked, and then darted off to get her feet wet looking for shells. Moth refused to part with a very smelly piece of seaweed, because she wanted to hang it up at home and see if it really would tell her when it was going to rain.

There wasn't time to go on to Leigh, but Robert promised a return visit, 'If Libby can face the possibility of more seaside without sea.'

They played I Spy and car number spotting on the way back, and it wasn't until after Robert had dropped them at the flat and rattled off in Morris that Moth remembered that they weren't on holiday yet.

Tomorrow was school – and this was the week of the Cecchetti exam.

17

No Luck

One of Miss Pearson's firmest rules was 'No jewellery'. She didn't allow even the plainest necklace or bracelet in class – 'and I don't care if you were given it by your fairy godmother at your christening' – and when Selsey had protested against removing her lucky charm bracelet, Miss Pearson had soon quelled her. 'No one, and I mean NO ONE, wears jewellery in my class,' she said, 'and if you wear that object again, I shall confiscate it.'

Moth had heeded this warning and had only worn the silver dancer her parents had given her at weekends and on her visit to Covent Garden, when she had felt in special need of good luck and protection. It seemed to have worked, and so she wanted it with her during the exam. She knew that she couldn't wear the dancer round her neck, so she decided instead to tie it in her handkerchief and tuck that in her belt.

The sensible thing would have been to put it

ready the night before, but Moth was too impulsive for that. She liked to leave everything until the last minute, and when her mother complained about this, she said that getting ready in advance made her feel much more nervous.

So it wasn't until the morning of the exam that she started looking for the dancer. She had kept it in a number of places: with her socks in the top drawer, under her pillow (when she was feeling extra worried), in one of the little drawers of the desk and, when she first discovered it, in the secret drawer that could only be opened by pressing a spring hidden under the ink well. It was only when she had searched all these places that she realised she had lost the dancer. But how, and where?

She was certain that she hadn't lost it outside the house, because she had always put it away very carefully after she'd worn it and she would have noticed then if it had been missing. And then she thought of Libby. She'd never mentioned her theatre, but she must have noticed that it had disappeared. Perhaps she'd found the crumpled remains behind her chest of drawers and this was her way of getting her own back on Moth.

Moth didn't stop to think what she was doing. She barged into Libby's room and said furiously, 'Where's my dancer? Give it back to me.'

Libby was trying to find her best pair of tights, the only ones without any ladders in them. She looked up in surprise. 'What dancer?

I don't know what you're talking about.'

'My lucky dancer. The one my parents gave me. It's on a silver chain and I wear it sometimes.'

'Oh, that. I don't know where it is. I haven't got it.'

'You must have,' said Moth, getting desperate. 'You took it because I knocked over your theatre. I'm sorry, I didn't mean to break it. Not afterwards,' she added, more truthfully.

'So it was you,' said Libby scornfully. 'I guessed it must be. Gam would have said if she'd done it, but then she doesn't creep round doing mean things.'

'Neither do I,' said Moth hotly. 'I didn't plan to do it beforehand and I've said I'm sorry. But you must have planned to take my dancer, and that's stealing.'

'I didn't take your silly dancer,' shouted Libby indignantly. 'If I'd wanted to get back at you I'd have done it openly, in a fair fight. You're the one who does things behind people's backs.'

'I'm not, I'm not,' screamed Moth, and because there seemed to be no other way of getting the truth out of Libby, she rushed across the room and began to shake her. Caught off-balance, Libby fell on the bed pulling Moth down with her, and they struggled together like a pair of enraged kittens.

'What on earth's going on?' They had not heard Great-Aunt Marion coming upstairs.

Moth and Libby let go of each other and stood up. They both looked dishevelled and angry.

'Moth's lost that dancer necklace of hers,' said Libby, 'and she thinks I've got it.'

'Have you?'

'Of course not.'

'Right. Then pick up these things from all over the floor and get ready for school, or you'll be late. Moth, go to your room.'

Moth went, and sat on her unmade bed looking tearfully at the havoc caused by her search. She had flung things everywhere and all the drawers hung out in abandon. When she'd finished despatching Libby, her great-aunt came in and shut the door.

'First of all,' she said firmly, 'you're going to tidy this room, and then you're going to tell me what all this is about.'

Moth obeyed, but she wasn't sure how best to explain the situation. She didn't want to tell her great-aunt that she'd stamped on Libby's theatre in an earlier rage, but it was the main reason why she suspected Libby now.

'It's to do with luck,' she said lamely. 'I wanted to take my dancer to the exam with me because I thought she would bring me luck. I've got to pass the exam because if I don't Miss Lambert will make me leave. I haven't changed my mind about dancing, I love it more than ever . . . and I don't want to let Mummy down when she's working to give me a chance . . . Libby's all right, but I don't want her to be here next year without me . . .' Moth's explanation became more and more disjointed and brimming with tears.

Her great-aunt looked surprisingly sympathetic. She hadn't had time yet to put on her sensible daytime expression, and she was still in a flowered dressing gown with her hair tied back in a simple plait.

'But why on earth should you fail?' she said. 'You're keen, you've worked hard, and you must be good at dancing or you wouldn't have got this far. Exams are for seeing how well you've done, not for making you feel a failure. If you do your best, you shouldn't need a lucky dancer or a lucky anything else to get you through.

'You know I used to be considered a very good judge of character when I was in the navy' – Moth managed a smile at the thought of her great-aunt in uniform – 'and I know you're going to do well. You've got it written all over you. The only trouble is that you waste so much energy on worrying about things that don't matter, instead of forging ahead. If you really believed in yourself, you wouldn't need any lucky charms.

'But you won't pass any exams if you don't get off to school, so you'd better get moving.'

Moth scrambled her things together. As she shot downstairs, her great-aunt came out into the hall and said, 'Moth, I've just remembered. I found your dancer the other day when I was hoovering your room. It must have slipped down the side of your bed and somehow made its way underneath. I put it in a safe place, meaning to tell you, but it quite slipped my memory. Anyway, you don't need it now. You'll only be worrying about losing it if you take it to school. Don't forget, you need confidence, not luck.'

Moth wasn't entirely convinced, but there was no time to argue. She would have to tell Libby, and apologise, and she was so late that she had to run all the way to school. But luck or not, even at top speed she was careful not to step on any lines.

18

Honours Even

The summer show was a much grander and more serious affair than the Christmas end-of-term show. Staged primarily for the senior students, it was designed as a showcase to attract agents, scouts, and anyone who might possibly offer the leavers a job.

Some of them had already decided to become teachers, two were going to university, a boy called Inigo, who spent his time planning impossible stage sets and experimenting with lighting, was going to art school, a girl who had formed a modern dance group had won a scholarship to a dance institute in America, two girls had been taken on by a minor German company, and Marina, it was rumoured, was going to the Royal Ballet senior school.

For all of them the summer show was a glorious chance to show off before they became small fish in much larger pools. For Miss Lambert and the rest of the staff, the show was equally important as a chance to impress parents, old pupils, friends, critics, education authorities, and those very special people who didn't look important but could turn out to be millionaires or sponsors looking for causes to support.

Although the whole production was mounted on a shoestring, the aim was elegance and sophistication. Mrs George might be combing warehouses for seconds and remnants, the cloak-room basins overflowing with exotic dyes, and the sewing machines chattering late into the night, but come the day the show would be perfect and seem effortless.

Moth's form were to start the evening with a light-hearted little ballet that made fun of the routine of class. Moth suspected that Miss Pearson had been inspired by memories of poor Selsey, who had found it so difficult to keep in step and always seemed to be on the wrong foot. Libby and Tom, whose ankle was now out of plaster and back to normal, were chosen to play the two children who couldn't put a foot right.

Moth might have been jealous of Libby's star part had she not been noticed by the intense Marina, who needed a junior in her ballet. The part was very small, but Moth was thrilled. To be honest, most of the time she sat in a corner watching, and Marina treated her like a slave and made her run errands and mind her shoes, legwarmers and sweaters, but Moth didn't mind. She would have done anything for Marina, and she resented it when Libby called her Marina's little lamb and taunted her with 'And everywhere Marina went, the lamb was sure to go.'

But then Libby wasn't one for hero-worship or modelling herself on others. She had a restless, energetic personality, and she danced as spontaneously as she ran and jumped and turned somersaults. She sometimes made Moth feel that *she* was surrounded by people who were too practical and down to earth. Moth was attracted to dancing because it was bound up with very different feelings. Marina was the first person she'd met who seemed to share these feelings and live in a world governed by them. She wasn't trying to pass exams or looking for a safe job. She danced because she had to, and Moth saw that because, for her, dancing was another way of feeling, she had more than mere technical brilliance.

The show didn't begin until eight, but beforehand there was a party for the most important guests. Moth and Libby were pressganged into helping Mrs George, who had now changed her tune to 'We do all our own catering'. They spent ages decorating squares of toast with smoked salmon or pâté topped with wisps of lemon and shiny olives, and stuffing little pastry cases with a delicious mixture of mushrooms and chicken. Moth couldn't resist helping herself and was quite glad when Mrs George banned any more sampling with the awful warning, 'You'll be sick, probably on stage.'

The party was held in the library, but the news that the most important guest had arrived soon reached the kitchen. She was, it seemed, someone legendary who, when she was not much older than Moth, had danced in Diaghilev's wonderful company. Jane said that she'd created roles in all sorts of famous ballets and was acknowledged to have been an outstanding Giselle. What they were now learning as ballet history, she had actually seen taking shape.

Determined to set eyes on this fabulous being, Moth slipped out of the kitchen and went along to the library. She pretended that she'd come to collect any empty plates as she pushed and squeezed past people in her search for someone who looked famous. The long windows were open and the party had spilled over into the garden, which was perfumed with the scent of old roses. There was a seat by a bush massed with tiny flowers and someone was holding court there.

Perhaps because Jane had mentioned *Giselle*, Moth half-expected to see a figure in white tulle with a filmy veil. What she certainly didn't expect was a little old lady who was much much older than Great-Aunt Marion. She was enveloped in an extraordinary dress that sparkled as though it was jewelled and reached from her bird-like face down to her ankles. She was wearing soft ballet slippers, and Moth saw that her feet were very small. Her eyes were still bright, but her face was creased and criss-crossed with lines as though it had long ago been folded up and put away.

Moth stared at her, then remembered that it was rude to stare and turned away. She was bitterly disappointed. It seemed natural for someone like her great-aunt or her granny to be old, but she'd forgotten that growing old happened to everyone, even to the most beautiful dancer in the world.

The sense of time passing coloured the rest of the evening, which was so exciting that Moth kept wishing that time would stand still. She saw that every minute she was moving into the future, just as inevitably as the students who had once been juniors and were now leaving.

Inigo had hidden floods and coloured lights in the trees and was impatient for it to get dark. He had worked out the most complicated lighting for one of the ballets, and after threatening either to blow a fuse or electrocute himself, he had become very calm and controlled and was now crouching in the darkness ready to switch on his master plan.

The first-form ballet was a great success. Tom's timing was so good and he tied himself up in such clever knots that a voice in front called him 'an infant Wayne Sleep' and Mrs Blundell-Smith nearly burst with pride. Libby revealed an unexpected gift for comedy, as the child who was longing to catch up with the rest of the class. When she finally managed to start on the right foot and do the right *port de bras*, her delight was so evident that it drew a round of applause.

Then came a Spanish gipsy dance with lots of tambourines and castanets, and a hornpipe by all the boys, with Tom as a very junior sailor. The third form did a mimed poem about a beautiful princess and her jealous suitors that ended up with everyone lying dead on the stage, and then two fifth formers acted the balcony scene from *Romeo and Juliet* with such passion that Mrs Blundell-Smith made a mental note to ask Miss Lambert how far co-education was allowed to go.

Marina tried Moth's devotion by being at her most imperious. She insisted on sitting in a room by herself and expecting Moth to call her when it was her turn to dance.

This meant that Moth had to hang around backstage and missed seeing *Kaleidoscope*, the modern dance ballet which was done to weird electronic sounds and disturbing patterns of light. Inigo was determined to impress a flamboyant Italian stage designer who was sitting in the front row, and to Inigo's joy he led the applause and kept shouting out '*Bravo!*'.

Marina seemed unaware of all the excitement. When it was time for her to go on, she picked her way through the tangle of ropes and wires in the wings, ignored Miss Pearson who was frantically trying to co-ordinate everyone – and electrified the audience. Moth had only a small part in the ballet, and she was so absorbed in watching Marina that she forgot to be nervous. As her mother said afterwards when they were talking about the highlights of the show, 'Moth was quite carried away. She looked so like a real dancer that I forgot I was watching my own daughter.'

The evening ended with a speech by Miss Lambert, who came on stage looking positively glamorous. She was happy to report that the Fortune School had had one of its most successful years and said parents would be delighted to know that former students were distinguishing themselves in many different fields. The current list included several teachers, a lawyer, two artists, a stage-designer, three stage-managers and four air-hostesses. 'I like to think,' she said amid laughter, 'that our students do on occasions have their heads in the clouds.'

But of course the real aim of the school was to produce dancers, and it was encouraging that so many ex-pupils were finding places in companies, both at home and abroad. 'We haven't so far ever had anyone in the Royal Ballet, but having seen her dance this evening, I know you won't be surprised to hear that Marina Guest has won a place in the Royal Ballet's senior school.' She had to stop because of the thunderous applause, and Moth couldn't resist giving Libby a 'told you so' look.

Then Miss Lambert went on to announce the examination results and Moth held her breath.

Form One: Drew, Ruth, Jane and the others had all passed and were commended; then Tom Blundell-Smith, pass with Honours, Elizabeth Graham, pass with Honours, Jennifer Graham, pass with Honours.

Moth was so relieved that she didn't really mind when the prize for the most promising dancer in the first year was awarded to Elizabeth Graham. Libby received her prize from the handsome Italian designer, who spent some minutes talking to her and seemed much amused. When Moth asked her later why he had laughed, Libby said that she had told him that she came from Australia and that was where she had really learned to dance well.

In a way it was Libby's evening, because when they had sorted themselves out afterwards and met up with Moth's parents and Great-Aunt Marion, Libby gave a whoop of joy and threw her arms round a suntanned figure in uniform. It was her father.

Lyn had already fallen in love with him because he was prepared to carry her on his shoulders – a feat that her father prudently avoided – and Toby told Moth that Uncle Rex had promised to show him round his jet and let him sit in the captain's seat.

Moth thought that Uncle Rex was just like Libby, all drive and enthusiasm, and she suddenly felt very fond of her quieter father and slipped her hand into his, so that he shouldn't feel that all his children had deserted him.

As they came out of the studio, Inigo's lights were on and the playground had turned back into a garden. The trees had haloes and threw mysterious shadows, and the scene looked as though it was waiting for some romantic intrigue. Moth could see Miss Lambert still surrounded by people in the library, and all over the house windows kept lighting up as though some wild chase was in progress.

'What a lovely house,' said Mrs Graham, but before Moth could point out her classroom, her mother was forced to attend to Mrs Blundell-Smith, who wanted to congratulate her on having such a lovely daughter who'd been so clever to win the prize. Moth thought of the skateboard and winked at Tom. She was amused to see that his father was a retiring little man who never seemed to say a word.

When they got back to Great-Aunt Marion's flat, they found that she'd arranged one of her special feasts and thoughtfully bought plenty of Australian beer for Uncle Rex, who was famous for his thirst. They all sat up late, talking first about the school and how well Libby and Moth had done, and then about the past and the rest of the family, and life in Australia.

Lyn and Toby fell asleep, and when at last everyone else was ready for bed, there was a great sorting out of rooms. Uncle Rex said he could sleep on a clothes-line and would be quite happy on the settee, Mr and Mrs Graham had Libby's room, and all the children piled into

Moth's. There was plenty of room for lilos, camp beds and sleeping bags, and Moth felt she was missing some of the fun as the only one in a proper bed.

Although it was so late, she was too excited and happy to fall asleep straightaway. She had passed her exam so Miss Lambert couldn't complain, she would be back next year and so would Libby.

'And next year,' thought Moth, 'I'll work even harder, I'll believe in myself more, and I'll win a prize. Yes,' she decided as she thought over the evening and saw in the moonlight that her cousin was already asleep, 'next year I'll beat Libby.'

The Jinny Books
Patricia Leitch

When Jinny Manders rescues Shantih, a chestnut Arab, from a cruel circus, her dreams of owning a horse of her own seem to come true. But Shantih is wild, and almost impossible to manage. Jinny perseveres, and she and Shantih have many very exciting adventures.

For Love of a Horse	£2.99
A Devil to Ride	£2.99
The Summer Riders	£2.99
Night of the Red Horse	£2.99
Gallop to the Hills	£2.99
Horse in a Million	£2.99
The Magic Pony	£2.99
Ride Like the Wind	£2.99
Chestnut Gold	£2.99
Jump for the Moon	£2.99
Horse of Fire	£2.99
Running Wild	£2.99
Jinny 3-in-1	£4.99

(contains *For Love of a Horse*, *A Devil to Ride* and *The Summer Riders*)

Order Form

To order direct from the publishers, just make a list of the titles you want and fill in the form below:

Name ....

Address ....

....

....

Send to: Dept 6, HarperCollins Publishers Ltd, Westerhill Road, Bishopbriggs, Glasgow G64 2QT.

Please enclose a cheque or postal order to the value of the cover price, plus:

UK & BFPO: Add £1.00 for the first book, and 25p per copy for each addition book ordered.

Overseas and Eire: Add £2.95 service charge. Books will be sent by surface mail but quotes for airmail despatch will be given on request.

A 24-hour telephone ordering service is avail-able to Visa and Access card holders: 041-772 2281

COLLINS GEM

DICTIONARY OF THE
BIBLE

Rev. James L. Dow M.A.

HarperCollinsPublishers

HarperCollins Publishers
P. O. Box, Glasgow G4 0NB

General Editor: W. T. McLeod

First published 1974
Reprinted 1988
Reprinted in paperback 1992

© HarperCollins Publishers 1974
Reprint 10 9 8 7 6 5 4 3 2 1

ISBN 0 00 470124 0
All rights reserved

Printed in Great Britain by
HarperCollins Manufacturing, Glasgow

FOREWORD

When the publishers asked me some three years ago to prepare this dictionary for them, I started light-heartedly enough, but soon discovered that I had taken on quite a job, especially as it had to be done at odd times snatched from a very busy life. Soon, however, my own interest in the work grew steadily as I went back over facts and figures I had thought little about since College days. My Congregation began to get the benefit of my researches. We had to make an early decision on the pattern and purpose of the dictionary – was the idea to get as many subjects as possible into it, or was it to give as much information as possible on names, subjects and words which seemed important? In other words were we to concentrate on quantity or on quality. We decided to discriminate. There are thousands of proper names and place names in the Bible which do not contribute a great deal to the meaning, purpose and message of the Bible. Thus the Book of Ezra has long lists of returned exiles who did not do anything but return, as far as the narrative goes, to put away their foreign wives – which was rather hard on the foreign wives. There seemed to be little point in giving them a mention which would simply refer the reader back to the mention they are given in the Bible. There are the names of many people who are recorded as doing very little, and even if they did it well they did not seem to us to merit space which could be devoted to others who did a great deal, even if they did it badly. We have therefore produced a dictionary which we hope will help people to understand more about the Bible and its people: for let us remember that it is a book about people and their attitude to God. There are other books of reference which spread wider and go deeper. This dictionary tries to spread as wide as possible and to go as deep as possible within the limits of its size. Our hope is that it satisfies and stimulates. I would like to record my personal thanks to my former Greenock neighbour and present friend, The Rev. W. B. Johnston, now of Colinton, for his help and advice on several points where I was in two minds.

The Rev. James Dow was ordained in the Church of Scotland in 1932. He wrote widely on religious and other subjects and his publications include *American Wit and Wisdom* (Collins, 1967); *Late and Early* (St Andrew Press, 1970); *Graham came by Cleish* (Hutchinson, 1973) and *No Better than I should be* (Hutchinson, 1975). He also wrote radio scripts and was Scottish editor of *The British Weekly* from 1953-4. James Dow died in 1977, three years after completing the work for the first edition of *Gem Dictionary of the Bible*.

ABBREVIATIONS USED IN THIS DICTIONARY

acc.	according to	fem.	female, feminine
AD	Anno Domini	ff.	following
agst.	against	ft.	foot
Aram.	Aramaic		
Apoc.	Apocalypse	gen.	generally
assoc.	associated	Gk.	Greek
AV	Authorised		
	Version	Heb.	Hebrew
		hist.	history
BC	Before Christ	H.Q.	headquarters
bet.	between		
		ie	that is
c.	circa (about)	imp.	important
cent.	century	in.	inch
cf.	compare	inc.	including
ch.	chapter		
corr.	corresponding	lit.	literally
		LXX	Septuagint
desc.	descendant,		
	descended	m.	mile
dist.	district	marg.	margin
		ME	Middle East
E	East, eastern	mistrans.	mistranslated,
eg	for example		mistranslation
Eng.	English	mod.	modern
equiv.	equivalent	MSS	manuscripts
esp.	especially	mt.	mount, mountain

ABBREVIATIONS CONTINUED

N	North, northern	S	South, southern
nr.	near		
NT	New Testament	trad.	tradition, traditional
orig.	origin, originally	trans.	translate, translated
OT	Old Testament		
Pers.	Persian	v., vv.	verse, verses
poss.	possible, possibly	Vulg.	Vulgate
prob.	probable, probably		
		W	West, western
prop.	proper, properly		
Prot.	Protestant	yr.	year
qv	which see		
R	river		
refs.	refers, references		
Rom.	Roman, Romans		
RSV	Revised Standard Version		
RV	Revised Version		

BOOKS OF THE BIBLE

Gen.	Genesis	Nahum	Nahum
Ex.	Exodus	Hab.	Habakkuk
Lev.	Leviticus	Zeph.	Zephaniah
Num.	Numbers	Hag.	Haggai
Deut.	Deuteronomy	Zech.	Zechariah
Josh.	Joshua	Mal.	Malachi
Judg.	Judges	Matt.	Matthew
Ruth	Ruth	Mark	Mark
1 Sam.	1st Samuel	Luke	Luke
2 Sam.	2nd Samuel	John	John
1 Kings	1st Kings	Acts	Acts
2 Kings	2nd Kings	Rom.	Romans
1 Chron.	1st Chronicles	1 Cor.	1st Corinthians
2 Chron.	2nd Chronicles	2 Cor.	2nd Corinthians
Ezra	Ezra	Gal.	Galatians
Neh.	Nehemiah	Eph.	Ephesians
Esth.	Esther	Philip.	Philippians
Job	Job	Col.	Colossians
Ps.	Psalms	1 Thes.	1st Thessalonians
Prov.	Proverbs	2 Thes.	2nd Thessalonians
Eccl.	Ecclesiastes	1 Tim.	1st Timothy
S. of S.	Song of Solomon	2 Tim.	2nd Timothy
Isa.	Isaiah	Titus	Titus
Jer.	Jeremiah	Philem.	Philemon
Lam.	Lamentations	Heb.	Hebrews
Ezek.	Ezekiel	Jas.	James
Dan.	Daniel	1 Pet.	1st Peter
Hos.	Hosea	2 Pet.	2nd Peter
Joel	Joel	1 John	1st John
Amos	Amos	2 John	2nd John
Obad.	Obadiah	3 John	3rd John
Jonah	Jonah	Jude	Jude
Micah	Micah	Rev.	Revelation

DICTIONARY OF
THE BIBLE

A

Aaron [āā´-rŏn]. Elder brother of Moses; married Elisheba who bore 4 sons. Family became hereditary priests. He had great influence on Moses, playing a large part in the work for liberation (*Ex.* 4). Upheld Moses' arms during battle against Amalek (*Ex.* 17, 12). Yielded to popular demand for idol (*Ex.* 32). Held office as High Priest 40 years (*Num.* 12). Quarrelled with Moses (*Num.* 12) and was denied entry into Promised Land (*Num.* 20, 25 ff.). NT refs. (*Heb.* 5, 4 & 7; *Acts* 7, 40; *Heb.* 9, 4).

Aaron's Rod. Its miraculous blooming appears in a difficult passage (*Num.* 16-18). Thereafter it was laid up forever before the Ark. But another ref. (*Heb.* 9, 4) places it within the Ark.

Ab. 5th month of Heb. calendar. *See* TIME.

Abaddon [ă-băd´-dŏn]. Word peculiar to Wisdom Literature meaning lit. death, destruction. Then: place of death. Lowest stratum of Sheol. Then personified as Angel of the Abyss, Apollyon (*Job* 26, 6; etc.).

Abana (Abanah) [ă-băn´-ă]. Sometimes Amana. With Pharpar, the rivers of Damascus. Mod. river Nahr Barada (cold river) (*2 Kings* 5, 12).

Abarim [ă-bă-´rim]. Lit. ' parts beyond and dwellers therein.' Region E of Jordan containing Mts. Nebo, Pisgah and Hor. Israel encamped on its bluffs overlooking Jordan before the final crossing (*Num.* 33, 47-49; *Deut.* 32, 49; 34, 1; *Jer.* 22, 20).

Abba [ăb′-bă]. Child's name for ' father '; term of simple affection (*Mark* 14, 36; *Rom.* 8, 15; *Gal.* 4, 6).

Abda, Abdeel, Abdi, Abdiel, Abdon [ăb′-dă ăb′-dĕel ăb′-dī ăb′dĭĕl ăb′dŏn]. Common name meaning servant, by implication ' of God.'

Abednego [ă-bĕd′-nĕ-gō]. Name given by Babylonians to Azariah, one of 3 faithful Jews who defied Nebuchadnezzar (*Dan.* 1, 7; 3, 12-30).

Abel [ā′-bĕl]. 1. Second son of Adam and Eve (*Gen.* 4; *Matt.* 23, 35; *Luke* 11, 51; *Heb.* 11, 4). The story is prob. the account of the struggle bet. the cultivators (Cain) and the herdsmen (Abel). 2. In assoc. with many place names means ' meadow.'

Abiathar [ă-bī′-ă-thăr]. Son of Ahimelech priest of Nob (*1 Sam.* 21, 1). In the line of Eli and sharing with Zadok office during reign of David. Ahimelech mentioned with him might be his son. Though loyal to David during the Absalom revolt he threw in his lot with the rebel Adonijah. Deposed from office he brought Eli's line as High Priests to an end, fulfilling the prophecy (*1 Sam.* 2, 31-35; 22, 1 ff.; *1 Chron.* 15; *2 Sam.* 15; *1 Kings* 1-2).

Abib [ā′-bīb]. The 1st month (*Ex.* 12, 1-2; 13, 4). After the captivity, name changed to Nisan (*Neh.* 2, 1; *Esth.* 3, 7). See TIME.

Abigail [ă′-bī-gāil]. Woman who on death of her husband Nabal, married David (*1 Sam.* 25; *2 Sam.* 3, 3). Also a stepsister of David (*1 Chron.* 2, 16; *2 Sam.* 17, 25).

Abihu [ă-bī′-hū]. Second son of Aaron. Became priest; slain with brother Nadab for offering strange fire (*Lev.* 10, 1 & 2; *Num.* 3, 4; 26, 61).

Abijah (Abiah) [ă-bī′-jăh]. Most important of the name are: 1. Son and successor of Rehoboam.

Also named Abijam (*1 Kings* 14, 31; *2 Chron.* 11, 20 & 22). **2.** King of Judah (*1 Kings* 15; *2 Chron.* 13). **3.** Second son of Samuel (*1 Sam.* 8, 2).

Abilene [ăb′-ĭ-lē′nē]. Town, district and people of the Anti-Lebanon some 20 m. NW of Damascus (*Luke* 3, 1).

Ability. In AV does not have mod. meaning of mental capacity, but is either material capacity (*Lev.* 27, 8; *Ezra* 2, 69; *Acts* 11, 29) or personal capability (*Dan.* 1, 4; *Matt.* 25, 15).

Abimelech [ă-bĭm′-ĕ-lĕch]. **1.** King of Gerar who took Sarah into his harem unaware that she was Abraham's wife (*Gen.* ch. 20). **2.** King of the Philistines at Gerar at whose court Isaac tried to pass off Rebekah as his sister (*Gen.* 26). **3.** Son of Gideon; a fierce and bloody king of Shechem (*Judg.* 9). **4.** Title of Psalm 34. *See* ACHISH. **5.** Priest, son of Abiathar.

Abinadab [ă-bĭn′-ă-dăb]. Man of Kirjath Jearim who housed the Ark of the Covenant when the frightened Philistines sent it back (*1 Sam.* 7, 1 & 2; *2 Sam.* 6, 3; etc.).

Abinoam [ă-bĭn′-ō-ăm]. **1.** Father of Barak (*Judg.* 4, 6 & 12). **2.** Second son of Jesse (*1 Sam.* 16, 8). **3.** Son of Saul, killed at Gilboa (*1 Sam.* 31, 2).

Abishag [ăʹ-bĭ-shăg]. Shunamite maiden appointed to look after David in his old age (*1 Kings* 1, 1-4). (*1 Kings* 2, 13-25).

Abishai [ă-ʹbĭsh-āī]. Nephew of David; brother of Joab and Asahel (*2 Sam.* 2, 18). Was prevented by David from killing Saul in the cave (*1 Sam.* 26, 5 & 9). He remained loyal during the Absalom revolt. He conquered Edom (*1 Chron.* 18, 12 & 13) and saved David's life at Ishbibenob (*2 Sam.* 21, 16 & 17).

Abner [ăb′-nĕr]. Commander-in-chief of Saul's

army (*1 Sam.* 14, 51). He met David at the slaying of Goliath (*1 Sam.* 17, 55-58). On death of Saul he nominated Saul's son Ish-bosheth. War broke out between his and David's supporters. Abner, defeated by Joab, and let down by Ish-bosheth, came over to David. He was assassinated by Joab either as revenge for the death of Asahel or because he was afraid for his own position (*2 Sam.* 2 & 3).

Abomination. Trans. of 4 Heb. words and usually refs. to men and manners abhorrent to God; including heathen deities, idols, images and other features of heathen religions: ritually unclean animals, witchcraft, tampering with weights and measures (*Lev.* 11, 10; *Deut.* 13, 14; 27, 15; *2 Kings* 23, 13; *Prov.* 11, 1; etc.).

Abomination of desolation. The negation of everything that a spiritual religion stands for; idolatry. Daniel makes much use of the phrase (9, 27; 11, 31; 12, 11). In 168 BC Antiochus Epiphanes (qv) greatly angered the Jews by stopping the daily Temple sacrifice and by superimposing on the brazen altar another on which sacrifice was made to Jupiter Olympus (cf. *Luke* 21, 20). This is undoubtedly in Daniel's mind.

Abraham [ā'-brā-hăm]. One of the noblest types of Hebrew piety. Sometimes Abram. Son of Terah he was father of the faithful and friend of God. The name may also be tribal. He married his half sister Sarah. The whole family emigrated from Ur of the Chaldees on the death of his brother Haran, probably to better themselves or to escape political disturbances. They settled in Haran where Terah died. Abraham then set off to fulfil the original mission and reached Canaan where he settled at Shechem for 10 years. Driven by famine to Egypt he fell into easy ways and lost

the sense of vocation. Then he heard the call
again and returned to Bethel to set up the old
altars. There he prospered and moved to Mamre.
He was greatly respected among the neighbouring
tribes, and was always a man of peace. Brought
up under a polytheist religion, he attained and had
revealed to him, a concept of God and of human
events far ahead of his people and times. He saw
God in control of everything and established
firmly that basis of monotheism which made the
Jews a people apart, and thus the only race
capable of producing Jesus, and of becoming the
inspiration of Christianity. He is greatly revered
both by Jews and Mohammedans to this day.
His time in history must be bet. 2300 and 2000
BC (*Gen.* 11-25 and many refs. throughout the
Bible).

Abraham's Bosom. Lit. ' in Paradise ' which is a
' feast ' (*Luke* 16, 22), cf. John and Jesus in their
positions at the last supper (*John* 13, 23).

Absalom [ăb′-să-lŏm] (**Abishalom**). Third son of
David, handsome, vain, spoiled. Banished for
fratricide, he returned after 5 years to hear that
David had nominated Solomon to be his successor.
He raised a rebellion supported by the mass of
the people, but David's veterans remained loyal.
Absalom was beaten in battle and was escaping
when his long hair was entangled in the low
branches of a tree. Joab came on him and killed
him against David's instructions. His fond father
mourned him bitterly (*2 Sam.* 15-18).

Abyss. Lit. ' bottomless pit '; the abode of the
dead (*Rom.* 10, 7). The dwelling place of Satan
and evil spirits (*Rev.* 9, 11; 17, 8; 20, 1-3) which
existed before creation.

Acacia. See SHITTAH TREE.

Accad (Akkad) [ăc′-căd]. City and dist. in Shinar

(*Gen.* 10, 10), region bet. the Tigris and Euphrates, and including Babylon. *See* BABYLONIA.

Acceptance. Being in the favour of another, esp. of God. In OT this was often won by observing a ritual (*Ex.* 28, 38; *Ps.* 20, 3). The prophets generally questioned this. In NT the conditions of acceptance are always spiritual (*Rom.* 12, 1; *Philip.* 4, 18; *1 Pet.* 2, 5). Jesus is the perfectly accepted one (*Mark* 1, 11; *Heb.* 10, 5 ff.) and so secures man's acceptance by God (*Eph.* 1, 6; *Rom.* 14, 18; *1 Pet.* 2, 20 & 21).

Access. Introduction of the seeker to God by Jesus (*1 Pet,* 3, 18; etc.).

Achaia [ă-chāī′-ă]. Greek state, then province of Rome after the Augustan conquest, known as the Peloponnesus. Its capital was Corinth.

Achan (Achor) [ā′-chăn]. Man who defied Joshua's ban on pillage after the fall of Jericho. He was discovered and stoned (*Josh.* 7, 1-26).

Achish [ā′-cĭsh]. King of Gath who gave hospitality to David fleeing from Saul (*1 Sam.* 21 & 27 & 28 & 29).

Achmetha [ăch′-mĕ-thă]. The town of Ecbatana, capital and treasure city of Medea, where decree authorising rebuilding of the Temple was found. (*Ezra* 5, 6; 6, 2).

Achor [ā′-chŏr]. Valley S of Jericho where Achan (qv) was stoned.

Achsah (Achsa) [ăch′-săh]. Daughter of Caleb, promised to the man who would conquer Debir, and won by her uncle Othniel (*Josh.* 15, 16-19).

Acts of the Apostles. The title *Acts of the Apostles* is as old as the 2nd cent. The purpose of the book is to show how Christianity spread by the work of the Apostles and the presence of the Holy Spirit, and covers the period from the Ascension to AD 61. In it Peter is prominent at first, and then Paul. The book is addressed to Theophilus (qv) who was probably a Gentile Christian in the imperial service. Luke, the companion of Paul is accepted as the author. Attempts have been made to prove that it is a compilation, but with no success. There are no anachronisms and there is a genuine similarity of style and language to the Gospel of Luke. Its unmistakable historical accuracy is substantiated by contemporary literature and by archaeological discovery. It was written not later than AD 80. There seems, however, to be a clear division at ch. 13, 8, from which point the events appear to be described by a fellow traveller. Luke explains the manner of the rise of Christianity to be a universal religion during the 33 years after the Crucifixion, the main events being Pentecost, the appointment of the 7, the conversion of Paul, the meeting of Paul and Barnabas with the Roman Sergius Paulus in Cyprus, which fired Paul with the passion to make Christianity the religion of the empire. This was followed by the Council of Jerusalem and the vindication of Paul, the call to Macedonia, the missionary journeys and Paul's trials. *See* separate characters encountered under their own names.

Adah [ā′-dăh]. **1.** One of the 2 wives of Lamech, mother of Jubal and Jabal (*Gen.* 4, 19 ff.). **2.** One of the wives of Esau (*Gen.* 36, 2 & 4). Also called Basemath (*Gen.* 26, 34).

Adam. Lit. ' man,' *homo sapiens.*

Adamant. Very hard mineral, prob. the diamond in some refs. Used of the stony heart (*Ezek.* 3, 9; *Jer.* 17, 1; etc.).

Adar [ā′-dăr]. Town in Judah; or name for the 12th month, brought back from the Exile. *See* TIME.

Adder. Different kinds of reptiles are called adders in AV, and can be the deaf adder (*see* ASP), the horned viper, the common adder, or the puff adder. In *Prov.* 23, 32 it could be the cockatrice, the Heb. being the same as in *Isa.* 11, 8; 14, 29; 59, 5 (qv).

Adonijah [ă'-dōn-I'-jăh]. Fourth son of David. Spoiled by his father he insisted on his rights to the throne and tried to seize it in rivalry to Solomon and won over to his side Joab and Abiathar. The rising failed. Later he was sentenced to death, nominally over the affair with Abishag (qv) but this was prob. a pretext (*2 Sam.* 3, 2 ff.).

Adoption. Act of taking officially the child of another to be one's own. cf. Moses, Esther, etc. (*Ex.* 2, 10; *Esth.* 2, 7). In NT it is used figuratively to signify: **1.** The choice of the Jewish nation by Jehovah (*Rom.* 9, 4). **2.** The reception of all Christians to be children of God in a particular way (*Gal.* 4, 5; *Eph.* 1, 5). Contrasted with the spirit of adoption (permanent security) there is the spirit of bondage (the temporary relationship of slave to master) (*Rom.* 8, 14-21). **3.** The body's deliverance from sin, pain and death to a blessed and glorified state (*Rom.* 8, 23).

Adria [ād'-rĭ-ă]. Conforms more or less to the Adriatic Sea.

Adullam [ă-dŭll'-ăm]. Canaanite city as old as Jacob (*Gen.* 38, 1 ff.). Near it was the cave used by David as HQ (*1 Sam.* 22 & 23).

Adultery. 1. Sexual intercourse of a man with a woman not his wife or of a woman with a man not her husband. (Polygamy was not adultery.) It was punishable by death (*Lev.* 20, 10). **2.** All sexual impurity in thought, word and deed. The 7th commandment interpreted in the spirit of *Matt.* 5, 27 & 28. **3.** Used metaphorically as the worship of false gods or as the breaking of the covenant bet. man and God (*Jer.* 3, 8 & 9; *Ezek.* 23, 37 & 43; *Hos.* 2, 2-13).

Adummim [ă-dŭm'-mĭm]. Pass from the Jordan valley to the hills, following the shortest route from Jerusalem to Jericho. Site of the trad. inn of the Good Samaritan (*Luke* 10, 34).

Advertise. Simply inform (*Ruth* 4, 4; *Num.* 24, 14).

Advocate. Gk. *parakletos*, and found only in the writings of John. Used of the Holy Spirit in the Gospel (*John* 14, 16 & 26; 16, 7). In the Epistle (*1 John* 2, 1) trans. ' comforter ' which conceals the meaning (AV). In the sense of comfort it means one called in to one's side and upon one's side. In court of law, the counsel for the defence. ' Comfortless ' (*John* 14, 18) is literally orphaned.

Agabus (ă'-găb-ŭs]. Christian of Antioch who foretold Paul's death (*Acts* 11, 28; 21, 10 ff.).

Agag [ă'-găg]. May be hereditary title of kings of Amalek, or a name which recurs in the succession. Best known are found in (*Num.* 24, 7; *1 Sam.* 15, 9 ff.).

Again. A second time (*Philip.* 4, 16) or back (*Matt.* 11, 4) AV.

Agate. *See* JEWELS AND PRECIOUS STONES.

Age. 1. Great age was attributed to the ancients, but it is significant that longevity diminishes in the record after the time of Abraham who is supposed to have died at the age of 175. David, on the other hand, was a done old man at 70, which was reckoned the allotted span. If one lived to 80 it was 'by reason of strength.' Old age was venerated in the OT and was regarded as a sign of God's favour. **2.** Age as a rendering of the Gk. *aeon*, meaning: (a) a particular, specified period of hist. past, present or future (*1 Cor.* 10, 11). Also an unspecified but very long period of time: 'Unto the ages' (*Luke* 1, 33); equals 'forever' (*Eph.* 3, 21): (b) by allusion, the world itself, where there is a sense of its duration (*Matt.* 12, 32; 13, 40; 24, 3). It can also be the world to come (*Mark* 10, 30; *Luke* 18, 30; *Heb.* 2, 5): (c) the course of the world (*Eph.* 2, 2).

Agony. Agonia was the nervous tension and fear experienced by a contestant about to enter the arena or lists for combat (*agon*). The agony in Gethsemane is properly understood thus (*Matt.* 26, 37; *Mark* 14, 33).

Agriculture. Land is the property of God and its use is granted to man. It was divided into royal estates and the estates of the nobility, and the remainder belonged to town and village communities: common lands in which each cultivator had a share. For the tools and products of husbandry, see under the individual names. The main cereal crops were wheat, barley, millet, spelt, and the pulses. As in the primitive east to-day, rain was needed to soften the baked ground for the plough, and usually fell in late Oct. The plough was simply a share and a shaft drawn by 2 oxen or 2 asses, but not by a mixed team (*Deut.* 22, 10). Seed was broadcast by hand. Failure of the spring, or latter, rains was a serious and not uncommon trial, and the blast of the sirocco, mildew, hail and locusts were all serious and common risks (*Hag.* 2, 17). According to the lie of the land, harvest stretched from mid April to early June. Reaping was by the sickle and the corners of fields and the gleanings were left for the stranger and the needy. Threshing might be done either by flail or by the treading of the unmuzzled oxen (*Deut.* 25, 4). The threshings were tossed into the air by pitchfork (the 'fan' of the AV) when a good breeze was

blowing, which separated the light chaff or husk
from the heavy grain (*Ps.* 1, 4). The grain was
then stored in jars in the granaries, or barns
(*Matt.* 6, 26). The law was very strict on tenancy,
neighbourliness, straying cattle, fencing, breeding
from proper stock, etc.

Agrippa [ă-grip-pă]. *See* HEROD.

Agur [ā'-gŭr]. Author of *Prov.* ch 30.

Ahab [ā'-hăb]. King of Israel who succeeded his
father Omri c. 875 BC. He married Jezebel (qv),
princess of Sidon, a Baal worshipper. She was
the stronger character and converted him to the
less demanding religion (*1 Kings* 16, 30 ff.). She
tried to force the entire nation to conform. Then
appeared Elijah who foretold the doom of Ahab.
Eventually the king was slain in battle at Ramoth
Gilead. *See* ELIJAH (*1 Kings* 16, 20-22, 40;
2 Chron. 18, 1-34). There was another Ahab, a
lying prophet (*Jer.* 29, 21 ff.). *See* ISRAEL.

Ahasuerus [ă-hă'-sū-ēr'-ŭs]. Persian king, husband
of Esther (*Esth.* 1, 2 & 19; 2, 16 & 17). Better
known by his Gk. name, Xerxes. He was the
son of Darius Hystaspis, succeeding in 486 BC;
but he was not the father of Darius the Mede.
The ref. (*Dan.* 9, 1) is wrong. His invasion of the
W failed and the course of hist. was changed by
the Greek naval victory of Salamis in 480 BC.
He was assassinated in 465 and was succeeded
by Artaxerxes Longimanus. There is a poss. ref.
to him in *Ezra* (4, 6).

Ahaz [ā'-hăz]. King of Judah, son of Jotham c.
735 BC. He was an idolater. Jerusalem was being
besieged by Rezin of Syria and Pekah of Israel.
Agst. the advice of Isaiah he entered into a mutual
aid treaty with Tiglath Pileser of Assyria, buying
his help with the Temple treasures. The Assyrians
defeated the alliance and Rezin and Pekah were

killed, but Ahaz found himself virtually the vassal of Assyria, and died in 721. *See* ISRAEL.

Ahaziah [ā'-hă-zī'-ăh]. **1.** King of Israel who succeeded his father Ahab (qv). He reigned only 2 years and everything he did seemed to go wrong. He died after an accident, leaving no male heir, and the throne passed to his brother Jehoram (*1 Kings* 22, 40-51). **2.** Another is king of Judah, son of Jehoram, c. 843 BC, who succeeded at the age of 23 and reigned only 1 year. *See* ISRAEL, JUDAH.

Ahijah (Ahiah) [ă-hī'-jăh]. There are 9 of the name in the OT, the most important of them being a great grandson of Eli (*1 Sam.* 14, 18) who might be Abimelech (qv). Another was a prophet of Shiloh who foretold the division of the kingdom (*1 Kings* 11, 29 ff.; *2 Chron.* 9, 29).

Ahikam [ă-hī'-kăm]. Prince of Asher in Judah who protected Jeremiah (*2 Kings* 22, 12; *Jer.* 26, 24).

Ahimelech [ă-hĭm'-ĕ-lĕch]. **1.** Chief priest of Nob (*1 Sam.* 21 & 22). **2.** Grandson of above (*2 Sam.* 8, 17; *1 Chron.* 18, 16). **3.** A Hittite follower of David (*1 Sam.* 26, 6).

Ahinoam [ă-hĭn'-ō-ăm]. Saul's wife (*1 Sam.* 14, 50). Or one of David's wives, mother of his first son, Amnon (*1 Sam.* 25, 43).

Ahithophel [ă-hĭth'-ō-phĕl]. Counsellor of David. His advice was always astute and unerring, but he was not trustworthy morally (*2 Sam.* 15-17).

Aho. For names beginning Aho-, see OHO.

Ai [ā'-ī]. In AV Hai. A town E of Bethel, scene of Achan's sin (*Gen.* 12, 8; *Josh.* 6 & 7). Or a city of the Ammonites (*Jer.* 49, 3). A fem. form used in *Neh.* 11, 31 is Aijah; another in *Isa.* 10, 28 is Aiath.

Ai Jeleth Hash Sha Har [āī'-jĕlĕth hăsh shā'-hăr].

Lit. ' the hind of the dawn.' Prob. a tune for *Ps.* 22. *See* PSALMS.

Ain ['ă-ĭn]. 16th letter of Heb. alphabet.

Akeldama [ă-kĕl'-dă-mä]. The Potter's Field. Bought as a burial place for strangers, it was called the Field of Blood (*Matt.* 27, 7 & 8).

Alabaster. *See* JEWELS AND PRECIOUS STONES.

Alamoth [ă'-lă-mŏth]. Musical term, prob. referring to soprano voices. *See* PSALMS.

Albeit. Lit. although it may be so. (*Ezek.* 13, 7; *Philem.* 19.)

Aleph [ă'-lĕph]. 1st letter of Heb. alphabet, its sound might be described as like smooth breathing through half open lips.

Alexander. 1. The Great. King of Macedonia 336 BC. He conquered Damascus, Sidon and Tyre and threatened Jerusalem, which was saved by the boldness of the High Priest Jaddua. Thereafter he granted the Jews many privileges, and was the first to bring the Jews into contact with Greece. He founded Alexandria and penetrated to India. In Babylon in 323 BC he died at the age of 33. 2. Son of Simon of Cyrene, brother of Rufus (*Mark* 15, 21). 3. Member of the priestly court at Jerusalem when Peter and John were tried (*Acts* 4, 6). 4. Man involved in Ephesus riots, poss. identical to 5 and 6 (*Acts* 19, 33). 5. Man excommunicated by Paul (*1 Tim.* 1, 19 & 20). 6. The coppersmith (*2 Tim.* 4, 14 & 15).

Alexandria. Founded by Alexander the Great in 332 BC on N coast of Egypt at the mouths of the Nile, it became one of the greatest seaports of the ancient world. A mole connected it with the island of Pharos and the lighthouse. Under both the Ptolemies and the Romans it flourished abundantly, its university and museum and library becoming the centre of the world's intellectual

life. The population was mixed, and some
600,000 to 700,000 strong, speaking Gk. as the
common tongue. Jews lived in the NE quarter
and enjoyed the same civil rights as all others.
In its library was made the trans. of the Heb.
scriptures into Gk., the Septuagint or LXX, the
work occupying time bet. 250 and 132 BC. This
was the work which became the Bible of the early
Church. The Alexandrian Jews had their own
synagogue in Jerusalem and were assoc. with the
persecution and execution of Stephen (*Acts* 2, 10;
6, 9). Christianity early penetrated to Alexandria
and produced at least one notable man in Apollos
(*Acts* 18, 24 ff.).

Algum. *See* ALMUG.

Allelujah. *See* HALLELUJAH.

Allow. In AV generally ' to approve.' Once it is
' to admit ' (*Acts* 24, 16).

Almond. Tree and fruit. The cups and branches of
the golden candlestick were modelled on its
flowers (*Ex.* 25, 33 ff.). Aaron's rod budded
almond blossoms (*Num.* 17, 8). It is usually the
first bloom of the year, and is used as a figure for
the wakefulness of God (*Jer.* 1, 11 ff.). In another
figure it is the white hairs of the aged (*Eccl.* 12,
5).

Alms. Almsgiving. This was something freely
given to the needy (*Acts* 3, 3) out of the goodness
of the heart, but not truly including the charities
which the law demanded. (*See* POVERTY.) In the
2nd cent. BC almsgiving and righteousness became
almost synonymous. At synagogue services there
was always an offering for the poor. Jesus rebuked
ostentatious charity (*Matt.* 6, 1-4; etc.). The
early Church laid great stress upon community
responsibilities (*Acts* 4, 32 & 34) and created
the diaconate to attend to them (*Acts* 6, 1 ff.).

Almug [ăl'-mŭg]. Timber much used for fine work, imported in large quantities by Solomon. Prob. red sandalwood, burned for its aromatic smell.

Aloes. Not the bitter aloes of medicine, but another, valued for its fragrance, prob. *agallocha*, a wood containing an essential oil (*Ps.* 45, 8; *Prov.* 7, 17; etc.).

Alpha. First letter of Gk. alphabet used with the last letter, *Omega*, as symbolic of God, the first and the last (*Isa.* 44, 6; *Rev.* 21, 6).

Alphaeus [ăl-phāe'-ūs]. **1.** Husband of one of the Maries, father of James the Less and of Joses (*Matt.* 10, 3) often identified with Cleopas or Clopas but there is no certain proof (*John* 19, 25). **2.** Father of Levi (Matthew) (*Mark* 2, 14).

Altar. Any raised structure upon which incense is burned or sacrifices made to the gods. The patriarchs raised altars in their encampments (*Gen.* 8, 20; *Ex.* 17, 15; etc.). In the Tabernacle there were two altars. (1) The brazen altar of burnt offering, which stood in the outer court. It was a hollow frame of acacia wood overlaid with brass (really copper) about 7 ft. 6 ins. square and 4 ft. 6 ins. high. On the upper corners were projections called horns, and it was equipped with rings and poles for portage. Its place at the entrance signified that there was no access to God for those who did not realise that they were sinners for whose sin blood had atoned (*Ex.* 27; cf. *Ps.* 118, 27). (2) The golden altar, or altar of incense, stood in the Holy Place, in front of the Veil that hung before the Mercy Seat. It was much smaller, being only 18 ins. square and 3 ft. high. It was overlaid with gold and was portable. It was the symbol, not so much of sacrifice, as of adoration being necessary for men, and for the delight of God (*Ex.* 30, 1 ff; 28, 34-37; cf. *Heb.* 9, 4).

When Solomon built the permanent temple the
size of the altars was greatly increased and new
altars were made (*1 Kings* 8, 64; 7, 48; *2 Chron.*
4, 1 & 19). These were the nation's permanent
altars (*Deut.* 12). In the 7th cent. BC the only
altars were those in the temple at Jerusalem.
Twice the law regarding the Holy Place had to
be waived: once when the Ark, the residence of
God, was in Philistine hands and when it was
lying at Kirjath Jearim, God was absent (*1 Sam.*
6, 20-7, 4; *Ps.* 78, 59-64). Then Samuel exercised
his authority and sacrificed in various places
(*1 Sam.* 7, 9-17). The other main occasion was
when the 10 tribes of the north (Israel) revolted
and seceded. They could not get through to
Jerusalem, which was in Judah. They either had
to dispense with altar worship or build 'un-
official' altars (*1 Kings* 18, 30 ff.; 19, 10).

Altashheth [ăl-tăsh'-hěth]. Name found in the titles
of Psalms, meaning ' destroy it not ' and is prob.
the name of the psalm tune (*Ps.* 57 & 58 & 59 &
75).

Amalekites [ă-măl'-ě-kītes]. Descendants of Esau
by his grandson Amalek, who settled round
Kadesh Barnea (*Num.* 13, 26). They were a
constant plague to the Heb. of the Exodus, who
were routed by the Amalekites at Kadesh (*Num.*
14, 43 ff.). They were associated with the dist.
of Ephraim and borrowed the name (*Judg.* 12,
15). Saul inflicted a disastrous defeat on them,
when their king Agag was taken and slain (*1 Sam.*
15, 7; 27, 8). The final blow agst. them was
struck by David (*1 Sam.* 15 & 30). Hezekiah
finished off the remnant (*1 Chron.* 4, 43).

Amariah [ă'-măr-ī'-äh]. Very common name.
Those mentioned are mainly priests.

Amasa [ă'-mă-să]. Nephew of David who became

commander of Absalom's troops during the revolt (*2 Sam.* 17, 25-20, 12).

Amaziah [ă'-mă-zī'-ăh]. Important one was king of Judah who succeeded his father Joash after having been regent during father's illness (*2 Kings* 14, 1). He defeated the Edomites in the Valley of Salt. He reintroduced idols and set them up as his gods. In battle agst. the Israelites he was defeated and taken prisoner. After a reign of 29 yrs. he was murdered at Lachish (*2 Kings* 14, 1-20). *See* ISRAEL, JUDAH.

Amber. Fossilised resin of *pinus succinfer*, now extinct. It is native to the Baltic and is gen. yellow in colour (*Ezek.* 1, 4 & 27).

Amen [ā'-měn]. Lit. ' firm, established.' Used of Jesus (*Rev.* 3, 14). Used also as interjection: ' so be it,' or ' may it be so ' (*Deut.* 27, 15-26; *2 Cor.* 1, 20). To make it more emphatic it may be doubled (*Num.* 5, 22). Jesus had a unique habit of starting a sentence with it instead of ending it. AV trans. this ' starting ' Amen as ' verily.'

Amethyst. *See* JEWELS AND PRECIOUS STONES.

Amittai [ă-mĭt'-tāi]. Father of Jonah (*2 Kings* 14, 25; *Jonah* 1, 1).

Ammonites [ăm'-mŏn-ītes]. Trad. desc. from Ben-ammi, second son of Lot (*Gen.* 19, 38). They fought agst. Israel (*Judg.* 3, 13) but were defeated by Saul (*1 Sam.* 11, 1 ff.) then by Joab and Abishai (*2 Sam.* 10). Relations became more friendly during the reign of Solomon who married an Ammonite princess who bore him his successor, Rehoboam. In the time of Jehoshaphat they invaded Judah (*2 Chron.* 20, 1-30) and were inveterate enemies of the Heb. (*Jer.* 49, 1 ff; *Amos.* 1, 13 f.). They worshipped Moloch and Chemosh (*1 Kings* 11, 7 & 33; *Judg.* 11, 24).

Amnon [ăm′-nŏn]. Son of David who dishonoured his half sister Tamar and was eventually murdered by Absalom, her full brother (*2 Sam.* 13).

Amok [ăm′-ŏk]. One of the principal priests who returned from Babylon with Zerubbabel (*Neh.* 12, 7 & 20).

Amon [ā′-mŏn]. **1.** Son of Manasseh, King of Judah. Succeeded when young. He followed Manasseh's evil ways and was murdered after reigning 2 yrs., being followed by his son Josiah (*2 Kings* 21, 19 ff.). **2.** A governor of Samaria (*1 Kings* 22, 10 & 26). **3.** A local god of Thebes, afterwards worshipped as Amon-Re. There are others of little importance mentioned.

Amorites [ā′-mŏr-ītes]. Their original territory ran from Palestine to Mesopotamia, and their most important king was Hammurabi (qv) the great lawgiver of about 2050 BC. They were in Canaan before the Heb. came (*Gen.* 10, 16; *Ex.* 3, 8). After the conquest a strong remnant remained (*Judg.* 1, 35; 3, 5). Ultimately they became bond servants of Solomon (*1 Kings* 9, 20; *2 Chron.* 8, 7).

Amos [ā′-mŏs]. Prophet from Tekoah in Judah, 6 m. from Bethlehem. He was a herdsman and dresser of sycamore trees (sycomore AV). There is evidence that he was widely travelled, prob. as a drover. Although a Judean his work was done in Israel, with his first prophetic appearance at Bethel where he condemned idol worship, and when accused of being a professional prophet indignantly denied it. When he appeared on the scene at the time of Uzziah of Judah and Jeroboam II of Israel (775-750 BC) Israel had been at the mercy of Syria for the last cent., but now Syria was beginning to feel the pressure of Assyria. Amos saw that this relief was only a lull, and that Assyria would be more dangerous than ever Syria

had been (5, 27; 6, 7-14; 7, 17). His theme is
that religion which is divorced from morality is
no religion at all. Before him the theory was that
Jehovah had absolute power over his own people
within stated geographical limits (*I Kings* 20, 23).
The people accepted the idea of other gods with
similar limitations. But Amos affirms God as
universal, all righteous, and holding everything
in his hands. He taught, however, that God had
a special relationship to Israel, which was not
necessarily permanent. The Israelites thought
that it was permanent so long as they observed
the set ritual. Amos said that the contract could
be broken by God at any time. His insight into
the moral character of God made it plain to him
that God could not tolerate Israel, but must
punish. He is the first of the great literary prophets, who believed in a sovereign God. His
speech is forthright and forceful, simple, but
reaching the grandeur simplicity can attain. The
book falls into three parts: (1) Introduction (chs. 1
and 2). (2) Three sermons (chs. 3-6) with a series
of five visions (7, 1 to 9, 7). (3) The Promise (9, 8
to the end). The first 2 sections are a denunciation of the way of life of king and people and
priests. His vision of the summer fruit, by the
way, is a pun (8, 1-3). *Kayis* is summer fruit, and
kes (pronounced similarly) is ' the end.' This
is the judgment of outraged God upon outraged
man. But the Promise gives hope. All the hardships are the means of cleansing, sifting, winnowing the good from the bad. It will all come again,
the glory has not departed forever. The book of
Amos is full of things that have the ring of eternal
truth, and which are as apt for to-day as they
were for his day. Social justice is the unalterable
foundation of orderly society and of permanent

peace and of human happiness. Privilege bears
inescapable duties, and failure to perform these
duties spells disaster. Once knowledge of the
right has been revealed it is sin not to live by it.
Worship is meaningless if the will is not surren-
dered. Amos is not to be identified with the
ancestor of our Lord (*Luke* 3, 25). *See* PROPHET,
ISRAEL.

Amphipolis [ăm-phī'-pŏl-ĭs]. City of Thrace of
great commercial importance, founded by Athens
in 5th cent. BC, 33 m. SW of Philippi. Paul
passed through it (*Acts* 17, 1).

Amram [ăm'-răm]. Father of Moses and Aaron (*Ex.*
6, 18-20).

Amraphel [ăm'-ră-phĕl]. King of Shinar. Has been
identified with Hammurabi (*Gen.* 14, 1 & 9).

Amulet. Anything worn as protection agst. sorcery
or the occult. May be ornamental (*Isa.* 3, 20 RV;
Gen. 35, 4).

Amusements. *See* GAMES.

Anak [ā'-āk]. Race name of the Anakim, below.
Means the long necked people (*Josh.* 14, 15;
Num. 13, 22).

Anakim [ăn'-ă-kĭm]. A hill people of great stature.
Goliath was prob. one of them. They were cut
off in the hills at the invasion of Canaan, and
Caleb chose their last refuge as part of his allot-
ment (*Josh.* 14, 12; 15, 13-19). The last of them
settled around Gaza, Gath and Ashdod (*Josh.*
11, 22).

Anammelech [ăn-ăm'-mĕl-ĕch]. Babylonian god of
the sky (*2 Kings* 17, 31).

Ananias [ă-năn-ī'-ăs]. 1. Disciple at Jerusalem,
husband of Sapphira (*Acts* 5, 1 ff.). He pretended
that his contribution to the common good was
the whole price of the land he had sold, when it
was not. When rebuked, he died of a stroke.

2. A Christian of Damascus who received the blinded Paul (*Acts* 9, 10-18). 3. High priest appointed by Herod, King of Chalcis in AD 48. He was counsel for the prosecution at the trial of Paul before Felix (*Acts* 23, 2; 24, 1). He was murdered as a Quisling c. AD 67.

Anathema [ă-nă'-thē-mă]. Gk. rendering of the word *cherem*, meaning ' put under a ban, un-redeemable '; as Achan was with his plunder (*Josh.* 6, 17). The sense is of something set aside for sacrifice which is bound to be destroyed and cannot be taken back. That is the sense in which Paul uses it (*1 Cor.* 16, 22 AV). RV prefers, ' accursed.'

Anathema Maranatha [măr'-ă-năth'-a]. The word *maranatha* is not complementary to *Anathema* (above). It is in fact difficult to regard this as a phrase at all. *Anathema* is Gk., while *maranatha* is Aram. It is not a double imprecation as AV wrongly has (*1 Cor.* 16, 22). *Maranatha* must be taken separately meaning ' Our Lord (*marana*) come! (tha).' It is the prayer for the second coming of Christ which will destroy evil (*Rev.* 22, 20).

Anathoth [ăn'-ă-thŏth]. Personal name and name of city of Benjamin allocated to the priests (*Josh.* 21, 18; *1 Chron.* 6, 60). It was the birthplace and nearly the death place of Jeremiah (*Jer.* 1, 1; 11, 21).

Andrew. Fisherman of Bethsaida, who lived in Capernaum. He was a disciple of the Baptist, who pointed out Jesus to him and called Jesus the Lamb of God. Andrew approached Jesus and became convinced that Jesus was Messiah. He is very important as having been the first to whom Jesus ' stated His case,' and his trust must have sustained Jesus in His decision about method

reached during the Temptation. Andrew brought
Peter to Jesus (*John* 1, 35-44). He became disciple
and apostle (*Acts* 1, 13). Apart from descriptive
refs. he appears in the Gospels usually in connection with questions to Jesus (*Mark* 13, 3 & 4).
He brought the inquiring Greeks to Jesus
(*John* 12, 22). He is the one who finds the
lad with the loaves and fishes (*John* 6, 8). Trad.
says he was murdered at Patrae in Achaea on the
St. Andrew's Cross, saying that he was unworthy
to be crucified on one of the same shape as the
Lord's.

Andronicus [ăn'-drŏ-nī'-cŭs]. Jewish Christian
imprisoned with Paul (*Rom.* 16, 7).

Angel. Lit. ' a messenger.' **1.** A celestial, spiritual
being with a nature superior to human nature,
but infinitely lower than God's nature (*Heb.* 1,
4; *Matt.* 22, 30). Poetically, ' the Sons of
God ' (*Job* 5, 1 RV; *Ps.* 89, 5 RV). Later there
appear gradations of degree or rank: archangels
(*I Thes.* 4, 16; *Jude* 9). There are angels fallen
and unfallen; there are differences of power and
station (*Rom.* 8, 38; *Eph.* 1, 21; 3, 10; *Col.* 1,
16; 2, 15). Cherubim and seraphim are angels
of sorts. Visitations were attributed to angels
(*Ps.* 104, 4 RV; *2 Sam.* 24, 16; *Zech.* 1, 7-17).
They appear as protectors (*2 Kings* 6, 17; *Ps.*
34, 7; *Isa.* 63, 9). On occasion they may appear
in human form as to Abraham, Hagar, Lot,
Moses, etc. Angels announce the birth of Jesus
and His Resurrection; they help Peter and Paul.
Some of the more important are named: Gabriel
and Michael (qv). In the Apocrypha appear
Raphael and Uriel. In Jesus' teaching on angels
they are not at work in the world of men, nor are
they God's spokesmen to men. The book of
Acts seems to hark back to the OT idea of angels,

but Paul is in line with Jesus. The phrase ' Angel
of the Lord ' is not a gen. term, but a specific
and particular one, meaning the direct visitation
of a human being by God. It is divine communication. 2. Angels of the churches. The phrase is
very obscure. They may be human beings (eg,
the bishops of the churches), or they may be
celestial beings, or even the personification of the
churches themselves, One ref. (*Matt.* 18, 10) is
' guardian angels,' not the souls of the children.

Anise. Vegetable like parsley (*pimpinella anisum*)
and allied to caraway, producing an aromatic
culinary seasoning. AV Marg and RV have ' dill '
which is the more common *anethum graveolens*
(*Matt.* 23, 23).

Anklechain. Chain bet. anklets (qv) forcing the
woman to take short steps, and making a tinkling
sound as she walked. (*Num.* 31, 50; *Isa.* 3, 20).

Anklets. To the ankles what bangles are to the
wrists. Called tinkling ornaments in AV (*Isa.*
3, 18).

Anna [ăn'-nă]. Hannah, an aged woman seer who
proclaimed Jesus in infancy to be the Messiah
(*Luke* 2, 36-38).

Annas [ăn'-năs]. High Priest at Jerusalem before
Caiaphas, his son-in-law, in AD 26 (*Luke* 3, 2).
At the time of the arrest and trial of Jesus he had
ceased to act officially, but was still the power
behind the throne. He acted, too, at the arrest
of Peter and John (*Acts* 4, 6).

Annunciation. Intimation by the archangel Gabriel
to Mary that she would bear Jesus (*Luke* 1,
26-38). *See* MAGNIFICAT.

Anoint. To apply oil to a person or thing, especially
to the head. Among Jews ordinary anointing was
simply part of the normal toilet, and to refrain
from it was a sign of mourning (*2 Sam.* 12, 20;

Dan. 10, 3; *Matt.* 6, 17). It was the courteous and hospitable gesture to a guest (*Luke* 7, 46). Priests, prophets and kings were anointed officially and ceremonially (*I Kings* 19, 16). The titles Christ and Messiah mean the anointed one. The altar, the Tabernacle, and the furnishings were anointed (*Ex.* 29, 36; 30, 26; 40, 9-11). There were also medicinal and surgical anointing (*Isa.* 1, 6; *Luke* 10, 34; *Rev.* 3, 18). The recipe for the oil is given (*Ex.* 30, 22-25; 37, 29).

Anon. At once.

Antichrist. Lit. ' agst. or in place of Christ.' Used only by John in NT (*1 John* 2, 18-22; 4, 3; *2 John* 7). The antichrist was supposed to appear immediately before the second coming of Christ, not necessarily as an individual—there might be many. Their purpose would be to descry and deny Christ as the Incarnate Son of God, and to oppose all the moral obligations of the Christian who believed in the Incarnation and the Resurrection, and who accepted the implications of this in his own way of life. When John was writing, this kind of opposition was already present in the Church, and appeared as agnosticism and cynicism, as well as in a watery compromise with philosophy. When Jesus spoke of false Christs (*Matt.* 24, 23 & 24; *Mark* 13, 21 & 22), He did not mean antichrists in the Johannine sense, but simply ' pretenders.' Antichrist is the devil incarnate as Christ is God Incarnate.

Antioch [ăn′-tĭ-ŏch]. 1. Great city of Syria founded in 300 BC by Seleucus Nicator (qv) and named by him after his father Antiochus (qv). It stood about 15 m. up the Orontes river, which was navigable to the sea. Under Rom. rule it was still capital of Syria in 64 BC. After the martyrdom of Stephen many Jerusalem Christians fled to

Antioch and preached mainly to Jews already settled there. Barnabas was sent from Jerusalem to confirm the work and to establish it among the Gks. He sent for Paul. The disciples were first called Christians here (*Acts* 11, 19-26). It became the centre of a great missionary effort (*Acts* 14, 6). Paul's 2nd missionary journey began and ended at Antioch (*Acts* 15, 33 & 36; 18, 22). It was the scene of controversy bet. Peter and Paul over the place of Judaism in Christianity (*Gal.* 2, 11). **2.** Town in Asia Minor, of the same origin as above. It was in Phrygia and was known as Pisidian Antioch to distinguish it from the other. It had a synagogue (*Acts* 13, 14) and was visited by Paul and Barnabas (*Acts* 13, 14-52; 14, 19-21; *2 Tim.* 3, 11).

Antiochus [ăn-tĭ'-ŏ-chŭs]. **1.** Great king of Syria, 6th of the Seleucidan dynasty, and father of Epiphanes (below). His dates are 223-187 BC. He invaded Europe but was defeated at Thermopylae and at Magnesia in 190 BC. **2.** Epiphanes. The 8th of the dynasty who reigned from 175-163. For 15 years he was held in Rome as hostage for his father's good conduct. Epiphanes was a strong king who offended the Jews by robbing the temple of its treasures, and by setting up a statue of Jupiter (*see* ABOMINATION). He pulled down the walls of Jerusalem, forbade circumcision, forced priests to sacrifice swine, and destroyed sacred writings. He was responsible for the revolt of the Maccabees. **3.** Eupator. He reigned as a minor and was murdered. **4.** Antiochus, another minor who met the same fate. **5.** Antiochus, who besieged and took Jerusalem (AD 138-128).

Antipas [ăn'-tĭ-păs]. Contraction of Antipater. **1.** Christian martyred at Pergamos (*Rev.* 2, 12

& 13). **2.** Son of Herod the Great. *See* HEROD 2.

Antipater [ăn-tĭp-ā-tĕr]. Father of Herod the Great.

Antipatris [ăn-tĭp′-ā-trĭs]. Town founded by Herod the Great bet. Jerusalem and Caesaraea. Paul was in prison here on the first night of his journey as a prisoner (*Acts* 23, 31).

Antonia [ăn-tōn′-I-ā], **Tower of.** It overlooked the Temple area and figures largely in the Rom. siege of Jerusalem. Paul was in custody here and addressed the mob from the stairs (*Acts* 21, 30 ff.).

Appelles [ă-pĕll′-ĕs]. Christian of Rome greeted by name by Paul (*Rom.* 16, 10).

Apocalypse [ă-pŏc′-ā-lўpse]. Lit. Gk. ' unveiling.' The Jews under the persecutions and during the time of the domination of the great empires sought to recapture the prophetic hope of Zion, the Jewish Utopia, which would come not by evolution but by divine intervention in human affairs. The lit. produced includes *Daniel* and many of the Apochryphal books written bet. 170 BC, and AD 100. It includes also, of course, the Book of *Revelation* (qv) with which the name Apocalypse has become identified.

Apocrypha [ă-pŏ′-crŷ-phā]. Lit. ' the secret, or hidden things.' The name was orig. used of writings whose content could be revealed only to initiates, but it is now used to describe ancient writings included in the early Latin and Gk. versions of Scripture which were not admitted as canonical by the Jews. The Apocrypha are in Gk., and the Palestinian Jews admitted into the canon only books which were originally in Heb. Jesus and the apostles do not allude to them although the books were written between 250 BC and the early Christian cents. The early Church allowed them to be read, but did not admit them into the canon; that is, they could be read in private, but not at public worship. The books are *1* and *2 Esdras, Tobit, Judith*, the *Rest of Esther*, the *Wisdom of Solomon, Ecclesiasticus, Baruch*, with the *Epistle of Jeremy*, the *Song of the Three Holy Children*, the *History of Susannah, Bel and the Dragon*, the *Prayer of Manasses, 1, 2, 3, 4 Maccabees*. The Roman Catholic Church retains certain of these books which were approved by the Council of Trent in 1546. They were orig. in the King James edition but are seldom nowadays printed with the AV. But they are important in that they bridge the gap of nearly 400 years bet. the writing of the Old and New Testaments.

Apollos [ă-pŏl′-lŏs]. An Alexandrine Jew, a disciple of John the Baptist. He neither met nor saw Jesus, but believed passionately. When he met Aquila and Priscilla (qv) he was taken further in the faith and was introduced to the brethren in Achaia. He was a brilliant thinker and great controversialist, who delighted in confuting the Jews who lived in the Gk. cities by demonstrating to them that Jesus was indeed the Messiah of prophecy (*Acts* 18, 24 & 28). Paul had a very high regard for him (*1 Cor*. 16, 12; *Titus* 3, 13). *See* HEBREWS (EPISTLE).

Apollyon [ă-pŏll′-yŏn]. Lit. ' a destroyer.' *See* ABADDON (*Rev*. 9, 11).

Apostle. Lit. ' like an angel, a messenger '; ' the deliverer of a message '; ' an ambassador '; ' a delegate '; ' one commissioned.' There are two types: 1. Men selected by Jesus as eye witnesses of events in His life, as hearers of His word, and as witnesses of His Resurrection. To qualify they must be able to give first hand testimony (*Matt*. 10, 2-42; *Acts* 1, 2 ff.; *1 Cor*. 9, 1). The first of them seems to have been Andrew,

then Peter (Simon), James, John, Philip, Nathanael (Bartholomew), Matthew (Levi), Thomas,
James, son of Alphaeus, Judas, the brother of
James, Judas Iscariot, and Simon the Zealot,
who was not a Canaanite but a Cananaean, which
is the Aramaic for Zealot. They were looked down
upon by the Jewish authorities, but they were
intelligent men, and even, some of them, men
of education. Yet they did not quite comprehend
Jesus, thinking to the end that His kingdom was
of this world, and that they would be elevated
to high places in it (*Matt.* 20, 20-28). They completely failed him at Gethsemane and Calvary
(*Matt.* 26). The apostles were also called disciples,
or pupils (*Matt.* 11, 1). (*See* under their individual
names). After the death of Judas Iscariot their
number was maintained at 12 by the election of
Matthias (*Acts* 1, 15-26). The transformation
of the apostles was at Pentecost (qv) (*Acts* 2).
In the fellowship, Peter, James and John were
most prominent (*Acts* 3-5; 9, 32-12, 18). Paul's
claim to apostleship was that he fulfilled the
conditions because of the adventure of the Damascus road. He had known Christ living, he had
seen Christ risen (*1 Cor.* 9, 1). **2.** Applied to more
prominent converts like Barnabas (*Acts* 13, 3;
14; 4 & 14). It was a name even applied to Jesus
(*Heb.* 3, 1).

Apothecary. Word is found in 8 refs. and should be
' perfumer ' (AV).

Appii Forum [ăp′-pĭ-ĭ Fŏ′-rŭm]. Town on the
Appian Way some 40 m. from Rome (*Acts* 28,
15).

Apple. There are 6 refs. (3 in *S. of S.* and 2 in
Prov. with *Joel* 1, 12). The description of the
fruit is not quite of apples as the W world knows
them. They may be the quince or the apricot.

Apple of the eye. The pupil of the eye (*Deut.* 32, 10; *Ps.* 17, 8; *Zech.* 2, 8).

Aquila [ă´-quil-ă]. Jew born in Pontus who lived with his wife Priscilla in Rome. He was banished with the rest of the Jews by Claudius in AD 52 and went to Corinth where he worked as a tentmaker. There they encountered Paul who was also a tentmaker, and Paul lodged with them (*Acts* 18, 1-3). Later they settled in Ephesus (*1 Cor.* 16, 19). He travelled part of the way with Paul on a journey to Syria (*Acts* 18, 18 ff.). Aquila had a house church in Ephesus (*1 Cor.* 16, 19) and had great influence upon Apollos (qv), leading him into the secret place of the Most High (*Acts* 18, 26). Later they seem to have returned to Rome (*Rom.* 16, 3) and then to have left it again (*2 Tim.* 4, 19).

Arabah [ăr´-ă-băh]. Lit. ' desert.' The great depression, part of the great Rift Valley in which lie the Sea of Galilee, the Jordan and the Dead Sea. AV sometimes trans. it as ' plain ' or ' wilderness.' (*Ezek.* 47, 8; *Amos.* 6, 14).

Arabia [ă-rā´-bĭ-ă]. The largest peninsula on earth, bounded E by the Persian Gulf and Gulf of Oman, S by the Indian Ocean, W by the Red Sea. It is about 1,800 m. long by 600 broad and is largely desert. Ptolemy, geographer of Alexandria, divided it into Arabia Felix (happy, fertile) and Arabia Deserta. It is regarded as the cradle of the Semitic peoples, and its civilisation is very ancient, Arab tribes were constantly in touch with the Hebs. from the earliest times (*Gen.* 37, 28-36; *Judg.* 6-8). Solomon traded with Arabia (*2 Chron.* 9, 14). Arabs were present on the day of Pentecost (*Acts* 2, 11). Both Christianity and Judaism were in Arabia when Mohammed founded Islam in AD 632.

Aram [ā'-răm]. A person, a people and a region (*Gen.* 10, 22 & 23; *1 Chron.* 1, 17). It is a plain inhabited by the Arameans, which stretched from the Lebanon mts. to the Euphrates river, and from the Taurus mts. to Damascus. The maternal ancestry of Jacob's children is Aramean (*Deut.* 26, 5). The regions of Aram were: (1) *Aram-na-ha-ra-im*, Aram of the rivers (Euphrates and Kabur) where Padan Aram was prob. situated (*Gen.* 24, 10; 28, 5). This is ‘Aram beyond the river’ (*2 Sam.* 10, 16); (2) Aram Damascus (*2 Sam.* 8, 5; *1 Kings* 15, 18). Its inhabitants waged constant war on the borders agst. Israel; (3) Aram Zobah, W of the Euphrates, a powerful kingdom in the time of Saul, David, and Solomon (*1 Sam.* 14, 47; *2 Sam.* 8, 3; 10, 6). Damascus was one of the its chief cities; (4) Aram Maacah; E of Jordan in the Mt. Hermon area (*Josh.* 12, 5). Their language was Aramaic, a N Semitic dialect sometimes wrongly called Chaldean (*Dan.* 2, 4). Aramaic is a very ancient language, inscriptions having been found dating to 800 BC. Examples are to be found in parts of *Ezra* (4, 8-6, 18; 7, 12-26). Parts of *Daniel* are in Aramaic (2, 46-7, 28). Occasional words and phrases crop up elsewhere in OT and NT. The Aram. used by Laban (*Gen.* 31, 47) was a kind of Lingua Franca of the ancient world. It was in international use for commerce and diplomacy (*2 Kings* 18, 26 RV), and began to replace Heb. (*Neh.* 13, 23 ff.). In time it became the vernacular language while Heb. remained the classical language.

Ararat [ăr-ă-răt]. Mountainous country N of Assyria, and itself a kingdom (*Jer.* 51, 27) equiv. to mod. Armenia (*2 Kings* 19, 37). In the Noah story the ark rested here (*Gen.* 8, 4). The name Ararat has been given to a single mt. about half-

way bet. the Black and the Caspian seas. It is
about 17,000 ft. high. *See* FLOOD.

Araunah [ă-rāun'-ăh]. Jebusite whose threshing
floor on Mt. Moriah was bought by David as the
site for an altar (*2 Sam.* 24, 18-25; *1 Chron.* 21,
15-28). It became the site of Solomon's temple
(*2 Chron.* 3, 1). Called Ornan in *Chronicles*.

Archelaus [ăr'-chĕ-lā'-ŭs]. Son of Herod the Great
by Malthace, a Samaritan woman. Elder brother
of Antipas (qv), he was educated at Rome with
him and their half brothers, Herod and Philip.
The father left the greater part of the kingdom to
him in 4 BC, with tetrarchies for Antipas and
Philip, and cities for his own sister, Salome. The
Jewish kingdom was a protected state under the
Romans, and Archelaus decided to go to Rome for
official sanction before mounting the throne.
Before he could depart, riots broke out at Passover
and he had to assume the kingship to suppress
them, which he did at the cost of 3,000 Jewish
lives. A deputation of Jews went to Rome to
petition Augustus agst. the succession. Herod
seized the chance to ask for the throne himself.
Augustus gave the kingdom to Archelaus, but
with reduced status as ethnarch (ruler of the
people). Soon after this Joseph and Mary returned from Egypt with Jesus and settled in
Galilee which was outside Archelaus' jurisdiction
(*Matt.* 2, 22). He was deposed and banished
c. AD 6.

Archippus [ăr-chĭp'-pŭs]. Christian at Colossae
(*Col.* 4, 17; *Phil.* 2).

Arcturus [ărc'-tū'-rŭs]. Lit. " Keeper of the Bear";
the bright star behind the tail of the Great Bear
(*Job* 9, 9; 38, 32).

Areopagite [ăr'-ĕ-ŏp'-ă-gūte]. A member of the
court of Areopagus below. (*Acts* 17, 34).

Areopagus [ăr-ĕ-ŏp′-ā-gŭs]. **1.** Low hill W of the Acropolis in Athens, consecrated to Areis God of War, corresponding to Roman Mars, ie, The Mars Hill. **2.** The supreme court of Athens before which Paul appeared. It is not likely that he was on trial on a charge, but rather that he received an invitation to speak before these interested intellectuals (*Acts* 17, 16 ff.).

Ariel [ā′-rĭ-ĕl]. Should not have been transliterated from the Heb., but trans. ' altar ' or ' hearth ' as in RV (*Isa.* 29, 1 & 2 & 7; *Ezek.* 43, 15-16). Also a personal name (*Ezra* 8, 16).

Arimathea [ă′-rĭm-ă-thē′-ă]. The town of the councillor, Joseph, who received Pilate's permission to remove the body of Jesus from the cross (*Matt.* 27, 57-70; *Mark* 15, 43; *Luke* 23, 51-53; *John* 19, 38).

Aristarchus [ă′-rĭs-tăr′-chŭs]. Macedonian of Thessalonica who was with Paul at Ephesus (*Acts* 19, 29).

Aristobulus [ă′-rĭs-tŏ-būl′-us]. Son and grandson of Herod the Great. The latter lived in Rome and those addressed (*Rom.* 16, 10) are people of his household, prob. slaves.

Ark. Noah's was built of gopher wood (prob. cypress) and was 450 ft. long, 75 ft. beam, and 45 ft. deep, daubed with bitumen. It had 4 decks with ports round the upper decks and a large cabin on the upper deck (*Gen.* 6, 14 to 8, 19). Moses' ark was a basket platted of papyrus reeds and coated with bitumen (*Ex.* 2, 2-6). The Ark of the Covenant or Testimony was a chest some 3 ft. 9 in. long, 27 in. broad and deep. It was made of acacia wood and overlaid with gold. Rings were fitted and staves for carrying it. It was covered with a golden lid called the Mercy Seat which bore the figures of 2 cherubim (qv),

who faced one another, their wings overarching
the Mercy Seat. God dwelt bet. the cherubim and
spoke from there (*Ex.* 25, 10 ff.; 30, 6; *Num.* 7,
89; *1 Sam.* 4, 4). There is no mention of the Ark
in the hist. books after it had been deposited in
Solomon's temple (*1 Kings* 8, 1 ff.). Poss. it was
carried away by Shishak along with the treasures
of the House of the Lord in 930 BC, but it may
still have been there in Jeremiah's time (3, 16 ff.),
and then looted by Nebuchadnezzar in 587 BC.
To begin with the Ark was regarded almost as a
fetish, but the attitude changed with the passing
years till it became simply the receptacle for the
testimony on the tables of stone (*Ex.* 31, 18). It
was placed in the Holy of Holies and was the
most venerated object in the worship of the Jews.

Armageddon. Acc. to (*Rev.* 16, 16) this is the world's
last battlefield; the kings of the earth and the
Beast agst. God. Actually it is the Mt. of Megiddo
around which several bloody battles had been
fought (*Judg.* 5, 19; *2 Kings* 9, 27; 23, 29; *Zech.*
12, 11).

Armlet. (*Ex.* 35, 22 RV; *Num.* 31, 50 RV; cf.
2 Sam. 1, 10.) A kind of metal bracelet worn round
the upper arm, frequently by royalty.

Armour. Complete armour is described (*Eph.* 6,
11): (1) Shield, buckler, target. Of 2 sizes.
Large carried by heavy spearmen and lancers
(*1 Chron.* 12, 8 & 24 & 34; *2 Chron.* 14, 8).
Smaller carried by archers (*1 Chron.* 5, 18;
2 Chron. 14, 8). Could be round or oblong or
square, usually of wood overlaid with leather,
or of thicknesses of leather alone, oiled (*Ezek.*
39, 9; *Isa.* 21, 5). Might be wood covered with
brass or all brass (*1 Kings* 14, 27). Special shields
could be of gold (*1 Kings* 10, 17; *2 Chron.* 9, 16).
The warrior might have his own shield bearer

(*1 Sam.* 17, 7). (2) Helmets were of leather, iron, or brass (*1 Sam.* 17, 5; *2 Chron.* 26, 14). (3) Breastplates or coats of mail made of leather, or quilted cloth, or of brass or iron (*1 Sam.* 17, 5; *Rev.* 9, 9). (4) Greaves or shin guards of metal or leather (*1 Sam.* 17, 6). (5) Sometimes laced boots coming almost to knee, and heavily studded with nails (*Isa.* 9, 5 RV marg).

Army. For a major campaign the orig. Israelite army consisted of all fit males over 20 yrs. and under 50, made up as spearmen, slingers and archers, all on foot (*Num.* 1; *2 Sam.* 24, 9). The Levites were not conscripted but there was no rule agst. them fighting (*Num.* 1, 48-50). For minor skirmishes each tribe mobilised the number of men needed (*Num.* 31, 4; *Judg.* 20, 10; *Josh.* 7, 3). After the settlement, in the event of war, the army was summoned by proclamation (*Judg.* 6, 34-35; 19, 29; *1 Sam.* 11, 17). The political and military unit was the Thousand, usually of related clansmen under their own Chief. Because of differences in the size of these tribal units the Thousand was often only that in name, and consisted of fewer men (*Ex.* 12, 37; *Num.* 1, 2 & 3 & 16 & 46). These were sub-divided into companies of 100, half companies of 50 and platoons of 10 (*Ex.* 18, 25; *Num.* 31, 14 & 48). The officers of the Thousands met together under the commander-in-chief, in the Council of War. Saul, however, formed a small standing army with many mercenaries in it (though payment seems to have been no more than a share of the loot) about 3,000 strong (*1 Sam.* 13, 2; 14, 52; 30, 24). David's standing army was nearer 24,000 strong in 12 divisions (*1 Chron.* 27). Solomon introduced cavalry and chariots, posting them at strategic points in the kingdom (*2 Chron.* 17, 13-19; 25,

5 & 6; 26, 11-15). *See* FORTIFICATION AND SIEGE, LEGION, WAR.

Arpad (Arphad) [ăr′-păd]. Important city prob. nr. Aleppo (*2 Kings* 18, 34; 19, 13; *Isa.* 10, 9).

Arrowsnake. (*Isa.* 34, 15 RV.) *See* OWL, SERPENT.

Artaxerxes [ăr′-tă-xĕr′-xĕs]. Third son of Xerxes who succeeded to the throne of Persia 465 BC. He is called Longimanus, maybe for the length of his hands, but more likely from the extent of his power. He allowed Ezra to lead the Jews back from Babylon to Jerusalem (*Ezra* 7, 1 & 11 & 12 & 21) in 458 BC, and Nehemiah to rebuild the city in 445 BC (*Neh.* 2, 1). He appointed Nehemiah governor of Jerusalem in 433 (*Neh.* 13, 6). Artaxerxes died in 424. *See* ISRAEL, JUDAH.

Artemas [ärt′-ĕ-măs]. Trusted companion of the ageing Paul (*Titus* 3, 12).

Artemis [ärt′-ĕ-mĭs]. (*Acts* 19, 24 RV marg.). *See* DIANA.

Artillery. Simply weapons; an antique word with nothing to do with the mod. meaning (*I Sam.* 20, 40 AV).

Arts and crafts. The Jew had a very high regard for manual labour and thought it right that all men should have a craft and skill. They may be classified as: (1) workers in wood (*1 Chron.* 22, 15) more commonly carpenter, who in Scotland would be described as a ' wright.' This was the trade of Joseph and Jesus (*Matt.* 13, 55). They used axe (*Deut.* 19, 5); hammer (*Jer.* 10, 4); the adze or hatchet (*Jer.* 10, 3; *Ps.* 74, 6 RV); saw (*Isa.* 10, 15); drill worked with bow and string; measuring line (*Isa.* 44, 13); stylus or metal scriber (ibid.); planes (more prob. broad chisels) and compasses. (2) Metal workers. The metals

used are found in (*Num*. 31, 22). Brass (qv) is
bronze or copper. Iron begins to be used about
1000 BC (Time of Saul). There is the coppersmith
(*2 Tim*. 4, 14); and the blacksmith (*2 Kings* 24,
14). They used hammer and anvil, tongs and
bellows (*Isa*. 41, 7; 44, 12; *Jer*. 6, 29). (3) Stone
workers. Masons (*2 Sam*. 5, 11). They hewed
from the quarry (*1 Kings* 5, 17 RV; 6, 7 RV).
Stonesquarers (*1 Kings* 5, 18 AV) are more
correctly Gebalites (as RV), imported highly
skilled labour. They worked from plans (*Ex*. 25,
9) or models, using the measuring reed (*Ezek*.
40, 3); the plumbline (*Amos* 7, 7); the mell
(*Jer*. 23, 29); and the pick (*1 Kings* 6, 7) trans.
' axe ' AV. (4) Workers in clay. Brickmaking
was not regarded as a craft, nor was plastering
with clay (*Lev*. 14, 42). The real craftsman was
the potter (qv). (5) Leather workers. The tanner
was important (*Acts* 9, 43) but since he worked
with skins of unclean animals it was not a trade
highly thought of. As a strong-smelling trade it had
to be done outside the city (*Acts* 10, 32). *See* BOTTLE.
(6) Clothing trades. There was the weaver (*Ex*.
35, 35) (*see* SPINNING AND WEAVING), the em-
broiderer, the fuller, and the dyer. The fuller was
both a worker in raw material and a kind of
laundryman (*Isa*. 7, 3; *Mal*. 3, 2; *Mark* 9, 3).
The ' soap ' of the *Mal*. ref. may be fuller's earth.
(7) ' Toilet ' workers: the barber (*Ezek*. 5, 1);
and the perfumer, trans. AV ' Apothecary.' *See*
HAIR, PERFUMES. (8) Food workers. The cooks
killed, dressed and prepared the food, but were
employed only by the well-to-do. Ref. (*1 Cor*. 10,
25) trans. AV ' shambles ' was not the slaughter
house alone, but the meat market. There was a
Jerusalem street of the bakers (*Jer*. 37, 21). People
ground their own corn, but there were also public

grain mills. The great millstone (*Matt.* 18, 6) was certainly not the domestic quern. *See* MILL. (9) Agricultural workers are dealt with in the articles AGRICULTURE, SHEEP, VINE, etc. (10) Miscellaneous workers. Paul, Aquila and Priscilla were tent-makers (*Acts* 18, 3). *See* TENT. Many refs. are to fishermen. Others will be found under SCRIBES, MEDICINE; etc. The various crafts seem to have kept together in their own quarter of the town (as still obtains in the east); and to have formed themselves into guilds (*Neh.* 3, 8 & 31; *Ezra* 2, 42; *Acts* 19, 25). *See* WAGES.

Asa [ā′-să]. Most important is king of Judah, son of Abijam, and grandson of Rehoboam. On the distaff side he was grandson of Absalom (2 *Chron.* 14, 1). His reign began peacefully, and he cleaned up pagan practices in religion (*1 Kings* 15, 9-13; *2 Chron.* 14, 1-5; ch. 15-16). At first he could not eradicate them but later succeeded in restoring Jehovah worship. Too weak to resist the inroads of Baasah of Israel he hired the support of Ben Hadad of Damascus by giving him the Temple treasures. He died after a reign of 41 yrs. *See* ISRAEL, JUDAH.

Ascension. (*Mark* 16, 19; *Luke* 24, 50 f.; *Acts* 1, 1-12). Forty days after the Resurrection Jesus disappeared from the sight of his disciples at the Mount of Olives. It was necessary that His Resur-rection body should be seen to pass away to establish the reality and the permanence of His spiritual presence of which they became aware at Pentecost. The Jesus of the Gospels becomes the Universal Christ of the Acts and the Epistles and of the Christian history.

Ascents. Called 'degrees' in AV. Appears in RV titles of 15 Psalms (120-134): and is called 'Songs of ascents.' The songs were prob. sung by pilgrims coming up to Jerusalem (*1 Sam.* 1, 3; *Ps.* 42, 4; 122, 4; *Isa.* 30, 29).

Ash. Tree. In RV and LXX it is fir or pine (*Isa.* 44, 14). *See* FIR.

Ashdod [ăsh′-dŏd]. (*Josh.* 13, 3; *1 Sam.* 5, 1 ff.) A Philistine city, centre of Dagon worship, to which the Ark was carried after its capture, and the centre of much fierce fighting for many yrs. (*2 Chron.* 26. 6; *Isa.* 20, 1).

Asher [ăsh′-ĕr]. Proper name (*Gen.* 30, 12; 13; 35, 26; 49, 20; *Deut.* 33, 24). Particularly the tribe Asher which stemmed from Jacob (*Josh.* 19, 24-31). May also be town E of Shechem (*Josh.* 17, 7).

Asherah [ă-shēr′-äh]. Heb. rendering of Canaanite goddess Ashirtu. Has 2 pl. forms: *Asherim* (masc.) and *Asherah* (fem.). Frequently and wrongly trans. ‘ grove ’ in AV. Nearest approach to a grove was the single pole, or stripped tree trunk, poss. phallic in significance which stood at Canaanite places of worship (*Ex.* 34, 13 and RV marg; *Judg.* 6, 25 & 28 RV). Where it is not definitely the name of the goddess as in *Judg.* 3, 7 RV; *1 Kings* 18, 19 RV; *2 Kings* 21, 7 RV, it means a symbol of fertility. It was priests of Asherah who were slain after Elijah's challenge on Carmel (*1 Kings* 16, 33 RV). Josiah destroyed the symbol (*2 Kings* 23, 6 RV).

Ashkelon (Askelon) [ăsh′-kĕ-lŏn]. One of 5 main Philistine cities (*Josh.* 13, 3). It stood 12 m. N of Gaza (*Jer.* 47, 5 & 7). Centre of worship of Derceto, the fish goddess.

Ashtaroth [ăsh′-tă-rŏth]. Pl. form of Ashtoreth (qv) is general name for the goddesses of the Canaan-ites. It is also a city, the ancient Bashan, centre of the worship of Astarte (*Deut.* 1, 4; *Josh.* 9, 10).

Ashtoreth [ăsh′-tŏ-rĕth]. The Phoenician and

Canaanite parallel to Astarte; identified with Venus or Aphrodite, goddess of love. Rites included sexual orgies. Appears also as goddess of war (*I Sam.* 31, 10). Worshipped in Sidon (*I Kings* 11, 5 & 33; *2 Kings* 23, 13).

Asia. In NT is always the Roman province of Asia which comprised Syria, Mysia, Lydia, Phrygia and Caria (*Acts* 6, 9; 27, 2; *I Pet.* 1, 1; *Rev.* 1, 4 & 11). With Africa it was the richest and most important province in the Empire. Sometimes a distinction is made bet. Asia and Phrygia (*Acts* 2, 9 & 10; 16, 6). The names of the smaller territories making up the province were still used (*Acts* 16, 7 RV; *Rev.* 1, 4 & 11). The capital was Ephesus, where Paul preached. It was the seat of government by a proconsul. There were 7 churches in Asia (*Acts* 19, 10 & 22 & 26 & 27; 20, 4 & 16; *I Cor.* 16, 19).

Askelon [ăs'-kĕ-lŏn]. *See* ASHKELON.

Asp. Several Heb. and Gk. words are so trans. Sometimes trans. ' adder' (qv). The snake is prob. *naja haje*, of the same species as the cobra.

Asphalt. *See* BITUMEN.

Ass. 1. The wild ass, prob. *asinus onager* (*Job* 39, 5-8; 39, 5; *Dan.* 5, 21). **2.** Wild ass of Syria, *asinus hemppuis* (*Job* 24, 5; etc.). **3.** The domestic ass, *equus asinus* (*Gen.* 12, 16; 22, 3; *Deut.* 22, 10; etc.). People of importance favoured white asses (*Judg.* 51, 10; *Matt.* 21, 5). This latter was Jesus' interpretation of the prophecy (*Zech.* 9, 9).

Assassins. Dagger men dedicated to fight agst. Rome in the time of Felix, though some were less patriots than brigands (*Acts* 21, 38 RV). *See* ZEALOTS.

Assembly. *See* CONGREGATION.

Asshur [ăssh'-ŭr]. *See* ASSYRIA.

Assurance. The grounds for confidence and the

state of being confident. Paul uses it (*Acts* 17, 31) of the risen Jesus as the warrant for belief; the proof. But generally it means the inward experience induced by the outward proof. It occurs only once in OT (*Isa.* 32, 17 AV) but this is better trans. as in RSV ' Effect of (or result of) righteousness.' Assurance in the usual NT sense is the all-pervading and completely satisfying certainty of the love and power of God in Christ.

Assyria [ăs-sy̆r'-ĭ-ă]. Country and people E of R. Tigris bet. lat. 35 and 37 N. It takes its name from the ancient capital Ashur, or Assur. Later the name was extended to the whole kingdom and empire. C. 1950-1850 BC. it was under Babylonian rule but broke free to a chequered career under pressure from Hittites, Egyptians, and Hurrians. Shalmaneser 1 was one of their great kings (1280-1260). After him the Assyrian power began to decline as the Babylonian power began to increase again. With the accession of Ashur Dan in 1175 came another revival, culminating in wide conquests under Tiglath Pileser, c. 1115-1102. He secured control of the main E to W trade routes. Another decline set in c. 1100-900, which gave the Heb. under David and Solomon a chance to expand. By 900 BC the Assyrians were on the march again, however, under Tukulti-ninurta I (890-885); and Ashur-nasiripal (885-860). Next in line to the throne was Shalmaneser III who was the first Assyrian king to have direct dealings with the Israelites. There followed another decline and another revival under Tiglath-Pileser III, c. 745-728, and the Second Assyrian Empire began. He was followed in turn by Shalmaneser V, 728-722; Sargon 722-705; Sennacherib 705-681; Esar-haddon 681-669; Ashur-banipal 669-626. The Babylonians and Medes attacked and de-

stroyed Nineveh in 612, and the nation ceased
to exist after the battle of Carchemish in 605.
See ISRAEL, JUDAH.

Astrologers. Heb. lit. ' Dividers of the heavens.'
Their purpose was purely prediction which never
achieved anything, but they were the pioneers of
astronomy proper as a science. They are mentioned as ' stargazers ' (*Isa.* 47, 13). *See* MAGIC.

Athaliah [ăth´-ă-lī´-ăh]. Proper name. Principally
the wife of Jehoram of Judah and daughter of
Ahab and Jezebel (*2 Kings* 8, 18 & 26; *2 Chron.*
21, 6; 22, 2). Powerful, cruel, vindictive, she
seized the throne and reigned 6 yrs., the only Queen
of Judah. Finally murdered (*2 Kings* 11, 1-16;
2 Chron. 22, 10).

Athens. Named after goddess Athene, it was the
capital of Attica, one of the Gk. states. It grew
up around the Acropolis and became the centre
of culture, literature and the arts of the ancient
world. Its port was Piraeus. Draco and Solon
were 2 of its great early legislators. The Athenians secured the W agst. the threat from the
Persians at the Battle of Marathon, 490 BC.
Later it fell to Xerxes, but the naval battle of
Salamis meant the end of the Persian danger.
Before leaving, the Persian general, Mardonius,
burned the city in 479. Its influence continued,
however, and Athens under Pericles 459-431, was
a great imperial city state.

Atonement, Day of. On the 10th day of the 7th
month a solemn and general act of worship was
performed by the High Priest to reconcile the
nation to Jehovah (*Lev.* 16, 23-26, 32). It was the
only fast compelled by law (*Acts* 27, 9). The High
Priest, without his vestments, sacrificed a bullock
as Sin Offering for the priests, He then filled a
censer from the altar and carried it into the Holy

of Holies (the only time in the year when he entered there). He burned incense, and sprinkled the bullock blood on the Mercy Seat and floor on behalf of the priesthood. Two goats had been provided; he cast lots, killed one as a Sin Offering for the nation and sprinkled its blood in the Holy of Holies, and repeated the ceremony on behalf of the sanctuary itself and the furnishings. He placed his hands on the head of the other goat, confessed the sins of the people and sent it into the wilderness. This was the scapegoat (*see* AZAZEL).

Aven [ă'-věn]. Name applied by prophets to certain towns in condemnation of their idolatry. It means ' an emptiness; a nothingness.' Applied by Ezekiel (30, 17) to an Egyptian city of Heliopolis, by Hosea (10, 8) to a city of Bethel, and by Amos (1, 5) to a valley in Damascus.

Avenger of blood. One who fulfils upon a murderer the law of a life for a life (*Gen.* 9, 5 & 6; *Num.* 35, 31 RV). AV uses ' Revenger of blood.' Semitic law allowed the offended person to be his own judge, jury, and executioner. The nearest relative of one murdered was expected to avenge the death. Even accidental homicide justified revenge, and this usually resulted in the start or continuation of a blood feud between families. Mosaic law introduced cities of refuge (qv) to which the guilty person could flee. He was not, however, granted unconditional sanctuary. All that happened was that he got a trial. If murder was proved he was executed, if murder was not proved he went free. But of course if he left the city he was still liable to the avenger of blood (*Num.* 35, 18 & 21 & 24 & 27; *2 Sam.* 14, 11). The only limit to the stay of the ' innocent ' person in the city of refuge was until the death of the High Priest. After that he could go home, and if the avenger killed him, he made himself a murderer.

Away with. (*Isa.* 1, 13 AV). Tolerate, put up with.

Ayin (Ain) [ă-yīn]. 16th letter of Heb. alphabet. Orig. ' shape of eye.' Equiv. to Gk. *omicron* and Eng. *O*. Also place name (*Num.* 34, 11; etc.).

Azariah [ă-zăr-ĭ′-ăh]. Proper name appearing frequently. Ref. in *2 Chron.* 22, 6 prob. error for Ahaziah in verse following. Ref. *2 Kings* 15, 1 and *2 Chron.* 26, 1 is to King of Judah known also as Uzziah (qv). It was the orig. name of Abednego (qv) (*Dan.* 1, 7).

Azazel [ăz′-ă-zĕl]. Only ref. is *Lev.* 16, 8 & 10 & 26 RV. There are many interpretations. Prob. one of these 3 is correct. **1.** The evil spirit of the wilderness to whom the scapegoat bears back the sins of the people for which the evil spirit is responsible. **2.** Simply ' removal ' or ' dismissal,' ' that which escapes.' **3.** The Devil. (Unlikely). *See* ATONEMENT, DAY OF.

B

Baal [Bā′-ăl]. Orig. the Baalim were supernatural beings, each inhabiting his own tract of ground, and being responsible for its fertility. Gradually these very localised godlings were amalgamated into the single divinity, Baal. There were altars to Baal in Canaan in the time of the Judges (*Judg.* 2, 13; 6, 28-32). But the real advent of Baal worship to the nation was when Ahab married Jezebel, a princess of Tyre and a confirmed Baal worshipper. So great was the move over to Baal that Jehovah worship virtually ceased, although Elijah fought stoutly agst. it (qv) and ultimately saw the death of both Ahab and Jezebel (*I Kings* 16, 31 & 32; 18, 17-40). It persisted, however, and recovered from the damage Elijah had done it, until driven out of Israel by Jehu (*2 Kings* 10, 18-28). In Judah, however, Jezebel's daughter Athaliah usurped the throne and re-introduced Baal worship (*2 Chron.* 17, 3; 21, 6; 22, 2). After her death the temple of Baal in Jerusalem was pulled down (*2 Kings* 11, 18). From time to time there were revivals of Baalism (*Hos.* 2, 8; *2 Chron.* 28, 2; *2 Kings* 21, 3). Josiah suppressed it during his reforms (*2 Kings* 23, 4 & 5). Baal was the sun god, Ashtoreth the moon goddess, and their worship included sexual orgies, with homosexuality (*I Kings* 14, 24) and even child sacrifice (*Jer.* 19, 5). *See* BAALI, ISHI, ASHERAH.

Baali [Bā'-ălī]. Heb. word for ' husband ' used by Hosea when describing Jehovah and Israel as husband and wife (*Hos.* 2, 16). But the inroads of Baalism led to the identification of Baal the god, and Baali, the spiritual husband. Hence Hosea's command from God to cease using the title. *See* ISHI.

Baalpeor [bā-ăl-pē'-ŏr]. A Moabite god, prob. Chemosh to whose worship many Israelites were attracted (*Num.* 25, 1-9; *Ps.* 106, 28; *Hos.* 9, 10). *See* PEOR.

Baalzebub [bā-ăl-zē'-bŭb]. The particular Baal of Ekron (qv) (*2 Kings* 1, 2 & 6 & 16). *See* BEELZEBUB.

Baanah [bā'-ănăh]. A Benjamite, leader of a band of desperadoes who, looking for favour with David, waylaid and killed Saul's son Ishbosheth and brought his head to David. He executed them (*2 Sam.* 4).

Baasha [bā-ă-shā]. A usurper king of Israel (*I Kings* 15, 27; etc.).

Babbler. (*Acts* 17, 18 AV.) Lit. ' one who picks

up a precarious living.' Hastings suggests
' carpet-bagger ' as equivalent.

Babel [bā'-běl]. Nimrod's capital city, standing on
the plain of Shinar (*Gen.* 10, 10). Prob. Babylon,
as it is called in all other refs. (except *Gen.* 11, 9).
OT does not use the common phrase, ' Tower of
Babel ' a name which prob. was given to the
ziggurat at Babylon (qv). The ziggurat was a
temple built at the summit of a lofty building
constructed in tiers, like the towers children build
up with blocks, or cubes diminishing in size.
Access from one tier to another was by a ramp
(*Gen.* 11). They used sun-fired brick and bitumen,
which are both available in plenty. *See* TONGUE.

Babylon [băb'-ў-lŏn]. Proper name of Babel above,
the capital of the Babylonian empire. (*See* BABY-
LONIA below). It grew great under Hammurabi
(qv) and was at its peak in the 6th cent. BC under
Nebuchadnezzar (qv). (cf. *Dan.* 4, 30). Its hanging
gardens were one of the wonders of the ancient
world, and were really an artificial hill in a flat
land. A high wall encircled the city (*Jer.* 51, 58)
and a moat. Flowing through the city was the
R. Euphrates (qv). Scripture is filled with prophecies agst. this loathed place (*Isa.* 13; 14, 1-23;
21, 1-10; 46, 1 & 2; 47, 1-3. *Jer.* 50 & 51). The
prophecies have all been fulfilled. The Babylon
of *Rev.* (17, 3 & 5 & 6 & 9) is really Rome.

Babylonia [băb'-ўlŏn'-iă]. The regions of which
Babylon was capital are known also as Shinar
(*Gen.* 10, 10). Sometimes they are called the
Land of the Chaldeans (*Jer.* 24, 5; etc.). It was
not a large area, prob. not more than 8,000 sq. m.
of the Tigris and Euphrates basin. The orig.
inhabitants were Sumerians, living in a number of
city states; Babylon, Borsippa, Kish and a few
more in the Akkad territory, and Nippur, Lagash,

Ur and Eridu in the Sumer territory. Around
2600 BC the Sumerians were pushed out by the
Semites, and gradually an empire grew. It decayed later and was replaced by another Sumerian
empire whose capital was Ur. It endured till c.
2025 BC. The Elamites then took over and made
Babylon the capital, which named the nation also.
The great king was the 6th of the Elamite dynasty,
Hammurabi (qv) of 1792-1750 BC. There was a
short period of Assyrian domination c. 1260, then
a restoration of Babylonian kings 1225-1039 BC.
The Assyrians were back in 729, and in 689
Sennacherib burned Babylon city. This was not
the end, for the Chaldeans rose again and destroyed
the Assyrians, including Assyria and Babylonia
in their Empire. The new Babylon was built by
one of the their greatest kings, Nebuchadnezzar,
who captured, sacked, and destroyed Jerusalem
twice (597 and 586). The city and the country fell
to the Persians in 539, however, and was theirs
until Alexander the Great took it from them.
From then it had varying fortunes till the Moslem
Arabs conquered it in AD 641. *See* BELSHAZZAR,
NEBUCHADNEZZAR, CYRUS, DANIEL.

Babylonish garment. Lit. ' Mantle of Shinar ' a
costly, elaborate, embroidered cloak (*Josh.* 7, 21).

Baca [bā´-că]. Lit. ' a balsam tree,' and the name
of a valley in Palestine (*Ps.* 84, 6). It may simply
be the Valley of the balsam trees, or it may be
the Valley of Weeping (Heb. *bakah*) or the Valley
of little water (Arab. *bakaa;* to have little water).

Badger. The Heb. *tahash* is variously trans. but
it certainly is not the badger of the N (*meles vulgaris*),
which is not referred to at all in Scripture. *See*
ROCK BADGER, SEAL.

Bagpipe. (*Dan.* 3, 5 & 7 & 10 & 15.) AV and RV
trans. ' dulcimer,' which is wrong. The word is

Aram. *sumponya*, Gk. *symphonia*, a unison of sounds. The bagpipe is an ancient instrument, played in Egypt and Arabia.

Baking. *See* BREAD.

Balaam [bā′-lăam]. A soothsayer (qv) living in Pethor on the banks of the Euphrates (*Josh.* 13, 22; *Num.* 22, 5). Balak of Moab was at war with Israel, and sent to Balaam asking him to curse the enemy army before battle. Instead of engaging to do as the king asked he said that he could do no more than was revealed to him. On the way to Balak, the donkey on which Balaam is riding refuses to move. He interprets this as a warning that he may land himself in trouble if he goes his own way. He actually blessed the army he was supposed to curse, and at the same time foretold doom for Moab and Edom. But Balaam suggested that there might be a way to bring the wrath of God upon Israel without going contrary to the revelation and cursing them. If the Israelites could be persuaded to turn to Baal worship, they would bring the curse upon themselves. They found this fairly easy till Moses and Eleazar took control. During the fighting that followed, Balaam was killed (*Num.* 22 & 23 & 24; Refs. in *Deut.* 23, 4 & 5; *Josh.* 24, 9 & 10; *Neh.* 13, 2; *Micah* 6, 5; *Jude* 11; *Rev.* 2, 14).

Balak (Balac) [bā′-lăk]. Moabite king. *See* BALAAM above.

Bald locust. Heb. *solam.* An edible locust or grasshopper (*Lev.* 11, 22).

Balm of Gilead. A yellowish aromatic gum extracted from *Balsamodendron Gileadense*, and *B. opobalsamum*. It is valued for its fragrance and medicinal properties as an ointment. It is more likely, however, to be a mastic extracted from *Pistacia lentiscus*, the plant which produces the pistachio nut, and which does grow abundantly in Gilead. (*Gen.* 37, 25; *Jer.* 8, 22; 46, 11; *Ezek.* 27, 17.)

Balsam tree. Large genus of herbs included in the order *Geraniaceae* in RV marg. This is a rendering for Baca (the valley) in RV marg. (*Ps.* 84,6). AV marg. has mulberry trees. *See* BALM, MULBERRY, BACA.

Band. That which binds, a bond. Also a ribbon, sash, or girdle (*Ex.* 39, 23 RV; etc.). Also a company or troop of soldiers (*Gen.* 32, 7; *1 Kings* 11, 24; etc.). In NT it is the cohort of the Roman army, ie between 500 and 1,000 men (*Matt.* 27, 27; *Mark* 15, 16; *Acts* 21, 31).

Bank, Bankers. Money lending was a considerable business all through Biblical times, and banking practice was not unlike mod. banking practice. People made deposits with their bankers, which bore interest, and the bankers granted loans also bearing interest (*Luke* 19, 23; *Matt.* 25, 27). These loans were on mortgage or security (*Neh.* 5, 3 & 4). *See* MONEY.

Banner. An ensign: a standard, carried by soldiers. (*Num.* 2, 2.) Some refs., however, are not to flags (*Num.* 21, 8 f.) but to poles, or even masts (*Isa.* 5, 26; 11, 10; *Jer.* 4, 21; etc.). The word trans. standard bearer (*Isa.* 10, 18 AV) should be 'a sick man.'

Banquet. The meaning is slightly different from the mod. meaning. It was more a gathering for drinking than for eating and drinking (*S. of Sol.* 2, 4 is 'the house of wine'). 'Carousing' is a good trans. of *1 Pet.* 4, 3.

Baptism. It is very doubtful if any OT refs. are to baptism as even remotely understood by the mod. Church (*Ex.* 29, 4; 30, 20; 40, 31; *Lev.* 15; *Lev.* 16, 26 & 28; etc.). These cannot have meant more than ceremonial laving, or washing to remove impurity. At best they were a symbol of consecration, but not of dedication. It is not till the NT that the word in its full meaning is found (*Matt.* 3, 1; *Mark* 8, 28; etc.). Some argue that there was a ceremony of admission into Judaism which involved baptism, but scarcely in the Christian sense. John's was a baptism of repentance, but there is no indication that it was the necessary prelude to membership of a fellowship. John himself regarded it as incomplete (*Mark* 1, 8). It is very unlikely that Jesus Himself baptised anybody (*John* 4, 2). The disciples baptised, but there is nothing about baptism in Jesus' instructions to the 70 whom He sent out. The reason apparently is that baptism was to be ' of the spirit ' (*John* 7, 39) and that would be after the death and the rising, and the coming of the Holy Spirit at Pentecost. In the Apostolic Church it was certainly the normal, and prob. the essential means of admission to the fellowship (*1 Cor.* 12, 13; *Gal.* 3, 27). ' Repent and be baptised in the name of the Lord Jesus Christ ' was Peter's advice to those moved in their hearts after the first sermon of the Church (*Acts* 2, 37 & 38). Paul did baptise, but seldom (*1 Cor.* 1, 14-17). The 3 involved in baptism were (and are) the baptised person, the receiving Church (not the administrator) and the Lord of the Church. No instructions are given in Scripture as to the form and order of the Sacrament of Baptism. Several Christian denominations are divided on the practice of infant baptism. The latest valuable contribution to the subject comes from reports made by a Special Commission set up by the General Assembly of the Church of Scotland

Bar. Prefixed to proper names esp. in NT and meaning ' son of.' It is Aram.

Barabbas [bărăb'-băs]. A criminal imprisoned while Jesus was being tried. Poss. he was connected with some of the political rioting, assassination and the like prevalent at the time (*Matt.* 27, 16-26).

Barak [bā'-răk]. Commander of the Napthali and Zebulun forces when they routed Sisera. He was inspired by Deborah (*Judg.* 4; 5, 1 & 12). There is a ref. in NT (*Heb.* 11, 32).

Barbarian. Orig. one who did not speak Gk. (*Rom.* 1, 14). No offence was offered or taken by the use of the word. Later, however, it was used superciliously and snobbishly of ' people who did not belong '; who were ' non-U ' (*Col.* 3, 11) or of one who spoke an uncouth language (*1 Cor.* 14, 11).

Barjesus. *See* ELYMAS.

Barjonah [băr'-jō-năh]. The surname of the Apostle Peter, prob. meaning the son of John (*Matt.* 16, 17; *John* 1, 42; etc.).

Barley. *See* AGRICULTURE, BREAD.

Barnabas [băr'-năbăs]. The surname given by the apostles to Joseph, a Levite of Cyprus who became a Christian and gave his all to the Christian community (*Acts* 4, 36 & 37). He was sent to Antioch (*Acts* 11, 19-24) and, impressed by the opportunity offered there, travelled to Tarsus and prevailed upon Paul to return to Antioch with him (*Acts* 11, 27-30). The 2, accompanied by Mark John (qv), were on another mission when they were taken for manifestations of the gods Jupiter and Mercury by the people of Lystra (*Acts* 13, 3; 14, 28). They attended the Council of Jerusalem together (*Acts* 15, 1 & 2 & 12) and were sent round the churches to convey the findings of the Council. They quarrelled, Paul and Barnabas, over John Mark who was related to Barnabas. Paul and Barnabas went separately on their remaining missionary tours (*Acts* 15, 36 & 41) but they remained friends, who agreed to differ on the one point of John Mark, and with a warm regard and deep respect for one another (*1 Cor.* 9, 6; *Gal.* 2, 1 & 9 & 13; *Col.* 4, 10; *2 Tim.* 4, 11).

Barrel. This would be of earthenware, not of wood (*1 Kings* 17, 12 & 14 & 16; 18, 33). Elsewhere the word is trans. pitcher.

Barrenness. *See* CHILD.

Barsabbas [bärsăb'-bäs]. The surname of a man named Joseph who was one of 2 nominated to make up the number of the apostles to 12 after the death of Judas. He was not elected (*Acts* 1, 23). Also the surname of one, Judas, who was sent to Antioch with Paul and Barnabas (*Acts* 15, 22).

Bartholomew [bärthŏ'-lŏmēw]. One of the 12 disciples, of Jesus prob. the same man as Nathaniel, who was introduced to Jesus by Philip (*Matt.* 10, 3; *Mark* 3, 18; *Luke* 6, 14; *Acts* 1, 13; etc.).

Bartimaeus [bär'-tīmāe'-ŭs]. A blind man of Jericho, healed by Jesus (*Mark* 10, 46).

Baruch [bär'-ŭch]. **1.** A scribe and faithful friend of Jeremiah, who wrote down the book to Jeremiah's dictation (*Jer.* 36, 1-8). Both were carried off as prisoners to Egypt after the siege and fall of Jerusalem (43, 1-7).

Barzillai [bärzĭll'-āi]. Three of the name are noted. Most important is a wealthy man of Gilead who was of great help to David and his army during the Absalom rebellion. David was royally grateful to him (*2 |Sam.* 17, 27-29; 19, 31-39; *1 Kings* 2, 7).

Basemath, (Basmath), (Bashemath) [băs'-ĕmăth, băs'-măth, băsh'-ĕmăth]. The name of 2 of Esau's wives, one of whom was known also as Adah

(*Gen.* 26, 34; 36, 2 & 3 & 4 & 13 & 17). *See* ADAH. Also a daughter of Solomon (*1 Kings* 4, 15).

Bashan [bā´-shăn]. A territory E of Galilee whose main cities were Golan (*Deut.* 4, 43), Edrei and Ashtaroth (*Deut.* 1, 4), Salecah (*Deut.* 3, 10). It contained the region of the Argob (*Deut.* 3, 4 & 5; *1 Kings* 4, 13). The inhabitants in Abraham's day were celebrated for their great size and strength, and were known as the Rephaim (*Gen.* 14, 5). Their last king was Og (*Num.* 21, 33 & 35; *Deut.* 3, 1-7).

Basket. Many Heb. and Gk. words are so trans., signifying baskets of all shapes, sizes and materials varying from the conical fruit basket (*Jer.* 24, 1) to one of the size of a hamper (*Acts* 9, 25).

Basin (Bason). Words used to trans. Heb. and Gk. for bowls and dishes of various kinds, as well as for the basin understood domestically to-day. There are 3 main kinds. **1.** A small vessel trans. ' cup ' (*Isa.* 22, 24) and ' goblet ' (*S. of S.* 7, 2) RSV retains ' bowl ' for the latter. **2.** A shallow vessel used in the kitchen (*2 Sam.* 17, 28) and in the temple (*Ex.* 12, 22; *Jer.* 52, 19) RV has ' cups,' and RSV ' bowls.' **3.** A large bowl used mainly in the service at the great altar (*Num.* 4, 14; 7, 13; etc.). Ref. *Amos* 6, 6, ' drink wine in bowls ' might be the mod. slang, ' by the pailful.'

Bat. In the list of the unclean (*Lev.* 11, 13 & 19; *Deut.* 14, 11 & 12 & 18) the bat is classed as a bird, which, of course, it is not.

Bath. *See* WEIGHTS AND MEASURES.

Bathing. The word frequently means washing without entering the water, which is not the mod. meaning. There were also ceremonial bathings, prob. springing from the very necessity for bathing regularly (*Lev.* 14, 8; 15, 5; 17, 15;

Num. 19, 7 & 8). Travellers and guests were always offered the facility (*Gen.* 18, 4; etc.; *John* 13, 10). To resume bathing after a death was the sign that the mourning was ended (*Ruth* 3, 3; *2 Sam.* 12, 20; *Matt.* 6, 17). The priests had to bathe before conducting service (*Ex.* 30, 19-21; *Lev.* 8, 6; 16, 4 & 24). There were public baths at Tiberias, Gadara and Callirrhoe in Roman times.

Bathsheba [băth-shē′-bă]. Daughter of Eliam and wife of Uriah, a Hittite mercenary in David's army. After his intrigue with her, when he ordered Joab to put Uriah in the forefront of the battle so that he would be killed, David married her. Their 1st child died in infancy; the 2nd was Solomon (*2 Sam.* 11, 3 & 4; 12, 24; *1 Kings* 1, 11-53).

Bay tree. The trans. of the Heb. in the AV is not good here (*Ps.* 37, 35). Better the RV 'a green tree in its native soil'.

Bdellium [bdĕll′-ĭūm]. Could be a fragrant gum, or could be a rock crystal (*Num.* 11, 7; *Gen.* 2, 12).

Beans. See AGRICULTURE, FOOD.

Bear. The *ursus syriacus*, which is an omnivorous animal but normally vegetarian in its habits. It is yellowish brown in colour and its fur is both handsome and useful. The bear of (*Dan.* 7, 5) is prob. symbolic of the land of Media. See ARCTURUS.

Beard. The beard was the symbol of manhood, virility and wisdom, and the Jews took great pride in them. To neglect the beard was a sign that something was badly ado (*1 Sam.* 21, 13; *2 Sam.* 19, 24). To damage it wilfully was a sign of mourning (*Ezra* 9, 3; *Isa.* 15, 2; *Jer.* 41, 5). The king of the Ammonites perpetrated an unforgiveable insult and indignity on David's emissaries

when he shaved off half their beards (*2 Sam.*
10, 4 & 5). The Egyptians normally were not a
bearded people (*Gen.* 41, 14). The Jews were
forbidden to round off the hair on their temples
or to ' mar the edges of their beards ' (*Lev.* 19,
27; *Jer.* 9, 26 RV; 25, 23 RV) the reason for
this being that certain other races did.

Beast. 1. Any mammal not man, bird, or creeping
thing (*Gen.* 1, 29 & 30). The beasts were divided
into those in the wild state, and those which had
been domesticated (*Lev.* 26, 22; *Isa.* 13, 21 & 22;
34, 14; *Mark* 1, 13). 2. All or any of the inferior
creatures (*Ps.* 147, 9; *Eccl.* 3, 19; *Acts* 28, 5).
These were divided into the ceremonially clean
and the unclean. 3. Metaphorically the four great
empires which had made the nation's life miserable
down through hist. (*Dan.* 7). These beasts are
combined and conjoined (*Rev.* 13, 1-10; 17, 3-18)
Rome taking the place of Babylon.

Beatitudes. The word is not scriptural, its earliest
appearance being in the Vulg. (*Rom.* 4, 6). The
word means blessedness, and is universally
associated with Jesus sayings (*Matt.* 5, 3-12;
Luke 6, 20-23). This form of pronouncement is
met with in the OT (*Ps.* 32, 1). The 2 collections
of beatitudes in *Matt.* and *Luke* are generally
reckoned to have been taken from some earlier
work. There are points of similarity and points
of difference. Beatitudes 3, 5, 6 and 7 in *Matt.*
do not appear in *Luke*, and where *Luke's* are in
the second person, *Matt.'s* are in the first person
except in No. 8 (*Matt.* 5, 11 & 12).

Beautiful Gate. *See* TEMPLE.

Bed. A mattress or simply the ground with the outer
garment used as mattress or quilt (*Gen.* 28, 11; *Ex.*
22, 27 unless the sense implies clearly ' bedstead '
(*2 Kings* 1, 4 & 6; 4, 10; etc.). *See* HOUSE.

Bee. Mainly the wild bee, but bees were kept in earthenware hives (*Ex.* 3, 8; *Ps.* 81, 16; *1 Sam.* 14, 25; *Ezek.* 27, 17; *Matt.* 3, 4). *See* HONEY.

Beelzebub [bĕ-ĕl′-zĕ-bŭb]. The prince of the demons (qv) (*Matt.* 10, 25; 12, 24; *Mark* 3, 22; *Luke* 11, 15 & 18 & 19). He was by Jesus identified with Satan (*Matt.* 12, 26; *Mark* 3, 23; *Luke* 11, 18). Baalzebub (qv) was the god of Ekron, but should prob. be Baalzebul, 'Lord of the dwelling place.'

Beer [bē′-ĕr]. Found in many place names meaning a well.

Beer-sheba [bē′-ĕr-shē′-bă]. A place where Abraham and Abimelech of Gerar concluded a non-aggression pact, after a series of squabbles about the well. Sheba may mean an oath, or No. 7 (*Gen.* 21, 22-32; etc.). A town rose at the place (*Josh.* 15, 28) and has been immortalised in the trad. description of the bounds of the nation: 'from Dan to Beer-sheba' (*Judg.* 20, 1; etc.).

Beetle. *See* CRICKET, LOCUST.

Behemoth [bĕ′-hĕ-mŏth]. The creature described (*Job* 40, 15-24) is very prob. the hippopotamus, which is now extinct in Egypt but which was not so in scriptural times.

Bel. Sun god of Babylon whose proper name was Marduk or Merodach in Heb. (*Isa.* 46, 1; *Jer.* 50, 2; 51, 44).

Belial [bĕl′-ĭăl]. Lit. 'worthlessness; ungodliness' (*Ps.* 18, 4 RV). The sons of Belial are evil scoundrels (*Deut.* 13, 13; etc.) and evil scoundrels are sons of Belial.

Bell. Part of the adornment of the High Priest's robes (*Ex.* 28, 33 & 35). They were also used on animal harness (*Zech.* 14, 20) but these may rather

have been small metal discs which clinked together.

Bellows. The Egyptian form consisted of 2
leather bags with tubes leading from them. The
bags were squeezed flat by the feet and the
operator recharged the bags by pulling them out
again by means of leather thongs.

Belshazzar [bĕl-shă′-zzăr]. He was the first son of
Nabonidas and was co-regent with him. His
father was the last king of the Neo-Babylonian
empire. He himself was never king but carried
on effective government in his father's old age,
553-539 BC. He had commanded troops in
Akkad for 11 yrs., and was prob. commander-in-
chief when Babylon fell to Cyrus. *See* BABYLONIA,
CYRUS, DANIEL.

Benaiah [bĕn-aī′-ăh]. There are a dozen or so of
the name but the 2 most notable were among
David's mighty men (*2 Sam.* 23, 30). Of the 2
the son of Jehoiada was the more distinguished
and had several feats of great gallantry to his
credit (*2 Sam.* 23, 20 & 21; *1 Chron.* 11, 22 & 23;
2 Sam. 8, 18). He rose to be commander-in-chief
of David's army (*1 Kings* 1, 38; 2, 25 & 29—34
& 46).

Benefactor. This is a title of honour and should
be spelled with a capital (*Luke* 22, 25).

Ben Hadad [bĕn hă′-dăd]. Two kings of Damascus
bore this name. One was engaged by Asa of
Judah to oppose Baasha of Israel. He invaded
Israel and so relieved the blockade of Judah
(*1 Kings* 15, 18-21; *2 Chron.* 16, 1-6). The other
twice besieged Samaria and was defeated by Ahab
(*1 Kings* 20, 1-34). Ahab and Ben Hadad preserved the peace for 3 yrs. (*1 Kings* 22, 1). The
Syrians and the Israelites were in a state of almost
constant warfare at this time, relieved only when

they had to combine to resist Assyrian aggression. (*1 Kings* 22, 2—*2 Kings* 6, 23; *2 Kings* 6, 24—7, 20). There was a 3rd Ben Hadad, a son of Hazael, the usurper of the throne of Damascus and murderer of the Ben Hadad named above. He succeeded his father, but that was his only success. Refs. to the palaces of Ben Hadad are to the buildings of Damascus (*Jer.* 49, 27; *Amos* 1, 4).

Benjamin. The man and the tribe. The man was the youngest of Jacob's sons, and Rachel died giving him birth (*Gen.* 35, 16-20). He was greatly loved by his father (*Gen.* 43, 1-17 & 29-34; 44, 1-34). He became the founder of one of the 12 tribes (*Gen.* 46, 21; *Num.* 26, 38-41; *1 Chron.* 7, 6-12; 8). The tribe gave its name to the territory allocated to it after the invasion and occupation of Canaan (*Josh.* 18, 1-20). Among its chief towns were Jerusalem, Jericho, Bethel, Gibeon, Gibeath and Mizpeh (*Josh.* 18, 21-28). The tribe gave Israel its first king, Saul (*2 Sam.* 2, 9-15) and was naturally intensely loyal to Saul (*2 Sam.* 16, 5; 20, 1-22). But when the 10 tribes separated under Jeroboam, the Benjamites remained loyal to Judah (*1 Kings* 12, 31; *Ezra* 4, 1). The name ' Saul ' was popular with Benjamites of whom Paul was one (*Philip.* 3, 5).

Benjamin gate. A gate of the Temple.

Benoni [běn'-ō'-nī]. Rachel's name for Benjamin (*Gen.* 35, 18).

Bernice [běr-nī'-cê]. The oldest daughter of Herod Agrippa I. She married her uncle Herod, king of Calchis, causing a scandal because of this unnatural alliance. When he died she caused another scandal by her unnatural attachment to her brother Agrippa. Ultimately she married Polemo, the king of Cilicia, but deserted him after a little while and came back to Agrippa. She was in court when Paul was on trial (*Acts* 25, 23 —26, 30).

Beryl. *See* JEWELS AND PRECIOUS STONES.

Besom. A broom made by binding stiff twigs to a pole—like a witch's broomstick (*Isa.* 14, 23 AV.

Beth. 2nd letter of the Heb. alphabet. Gk. *Beta* Eng. *B.* Used as a numeral it means 2.

Bethany [bĕth'-ănў]. There are 2 towns of the name. (*Beth* signifies ' house of '). The first is a small town on the Mt. of Olives (*Mark* 11, 1; *Luke* 19, 29) between Jerusalem and Jericho. This was the town of Martha, Mary and Lazarus at whose home Jesus often stayed (*Matt.* 21, 17; etc.; *John* 11, 1). Here stayed also Simon the leper (*Matt.* 26, 6-13). The Ascension took place near this Bethany (*Luke* 24, 50 & 51.) The other Bethany was a place E of the Jordan (*John* 1, 28 RV).

Bethel [bĕth'-ĕl]. Lit. ' The House of God.' This was a Palestine town W of Ai and S of Shiloh where Abraham encamped on his 1st journey (*Gen.* 12, 8; 13, 3; *Judg.* 21, 19). The Canaanites knew it as Luz. The name Bethel was given to it by Jacob after his vision (*Gen.* 28, 18-19; etc.). After the conquest of Canaan it was assigned to Benjamin, and during the loss of the Ark of the Covenant it was created the site of a temporary altar (*1 Sam.* 7, 16; 10, 3). It became the centre of idolatry during the reign of Jeroboam (*1 Kings* 13, 1-32; *2 Kings* 10, 29). The prophets often had occasion to denounce it and what was assoc. with it (*Jer.* 48, 13; *Hos.* 10, 15; *Amos* 3, 14; 4, 4). Amos called it Bethaven, the house of nothingness (5, 5 & 6). Josiah destroyed the altars during his reforms (*1 Kings* 13, 1-3; *2 Kings* 23, 4 & 15-20).

There was another town of the same name in Simeon (*1 Sam.* 30, 27).

Bethesda, (Bethsaida) [běth-ěs′-dă, běth-sā′-ĭdă]. RSV has Bethzatha. It was a pool nr. the Sheep Gate of Jerusalem, whose waters were supposed to possess healing properties (*John* 5, 2 & 3; RV and RSV omit v. 4). There is an intermittent spring called the Virgin's Fount which connects with the Pool of Siloam, and had trad. healing virtues. Some commentators identify Bethesda with it, for the sake of v. 4 (the angel troubling the water). But the Virgin's Fount is SE of the temple and Bethesda (Bethzatha) must be in the section of the city N of the temple. According to *Neh.* (ch. 3) the Sheep Gate was N of the temple.

Bethhoron [běth-hō′-rŏn]. These were 2 towns on the border between Ephraim and Benjamin (*Josh.* 16, 3 & 5; 18, 13; *1 Chron.* 7, 24). They lay in a narrow pass bet. Jerusalem and the plain, and controlled access to it. Solomon fortified them (*2 Chron.* 8, 5; *1 Kings* 9, 17). They were the scene of a good deal of fighting from time to time (*Josh.* 10, 10 ff.; *1 Sam.* 13, 18).

Bethlehem [běth′lĕ-hěm]. There were 2: one a town in Zebulun of which little is heard (*Josh.* 19, 15; *Judg.* 12, 8-11). The other is one of the best loved names in Scripture. It lay in the hill country of Judah and was orig. known as Ephrath, Beth-ephrath or Bethlehem Judah to distinguish it from the other town of the same name (*Gen.* 35, 19; *Judg.* 17, 7; *Micah* 5, 2). Rachel died giving birth to Benjamin and was buried near here (*Gen.* 35, 16 & 19; 48, 7). A branch of stout Caleb's family settled here (*1 Chron.* 2, 51 & 54). And here dwelt Boaz and Ruth (*Ruth* 4, 21 & 22). The prophets foretold that the Messiah would be born in Bethlehem (*Micah* 5, 2; *Matt.* 2, 5; *Luke* 2, 1-20).

Bethpeor [bĕth-pē´-ŏr]. A town and military camp nr. Pisgah (*Num.* 21, 20; 23, 28). Moses was buried here (*Deut.* 34, 6).

Bethphage [bĕth´-phãge]. A village not far from Bethany and standing close to the road from Jerusalem to Jericho (*Mark* 11, 1; *Luke* 19, 29).

Bethsaida [bĕth-sā´-ĭdã]. A town on the sea of Galilee nr. the mouth of the Jordan. Many incidents in the life of Jesus centre around this place (*Luke* 9, 10; *John* 6, 1; *Mark* 6, 45 & 53). Bethsaida was the native town of Peter, Andrew and Philip (*John* 1, 44; 12, 21).

Betrothing. *See* MARRIAGE.

Beulah [beū´-lãh]. Lit. ' married ' (*Isa.* 62, 4). As applied to Israel it is the blissful land when God's favour was restored.

Bewitch. *See* MAGIC.

Bewray. The meaning in the AV is not quite ' betray,' but rather ' reveal ' (*Isa.* 16, 3; with ' betrayeth,' *Prov.* 27, 16; 29, 24; *Matt.* 26, 73).

Bezalel [bĕz´-ālĕl], (Bezaleel AV). Principal architect of the temple, (*Ex.* 31, 1-11; 35, 30-35).

Bible. The name is not in Scripture at all, and is derived from the Phoenician city of Byblos the principal exporter of papyrus (cf. Damask, Hessian, Calico, etc.). The word was drawn into the Gk. language as *biblos*, and into Latin, the pl. form being *biblia*, books. It is a neuter pl. which was regarded as a fem. singular, and became ' the Book.' The OT refers to ' The Books, the Heb. being trans. *bibloi* in LXX (*Dan.* 9, 2), but the NT word is ' the Scriptures ' (*Matt.* 21, 42; 22, 29; *Luke* 24, 32; *Acts* 18, 24; etc.). Sometimes they are called the Holy Scriptures (*Rom.* 1, 2; etc.) and sometimes ' the sacred writings '

(*2 Tim.* 3, 15 RV). All these refs. are, of course to the books of the OT as we now know it. It is wise to remember that the Biblia which gave the name, 'The Book' is prop. 'The Books' for that is what the Bible is, a collection of books, a library of books, now accepted as a unity, divinely guided. The OT was orig. written in Heb. with a few passages in Aram. The NT was written in Gk. There were no chapters and verses. Prob. Stephen Langton, Archbishop of Canterbury (died 1228) was responsible for the chapter divisions, while the Jewish Masoretes divided the OT Heb. text into verses. NT verses were introduced by Robert Stephens when he published Gk. and Lat. versions in 1557. The Genevan edition of the Bible was the first to be divided into chs. and vv. RV and RSV prefer the paragraph to the verse. *See* CANON, PENTATEUCH, VERSIONS, APOCRYPHA, ETC.

Bildad [bĭl'-dăd]. A friend of Job (qv) (*Job* 2, 11).

Birds. The Heb. included ' all things that fly,' ie, bats and winged insects. A score of these are named as birds ceremonially unclean when, of course, they are not birds at all (*Lev.* 11, 13-19; *Deut.* 14, 11-20). The only birds used for sacrifice were turtle doves and young pigeons (*Lev.* 1, 4). Doves and chickens were domesticated (*Isa.* 60, 8; *Matt.* 23, 37; etc.). Wild birds were hunted (*Amos* 3, 5; etc.). Jeremiah takes note of their migratory habits (8, 7). *See* under bird names.

Birthday. Royal birthdays are the only ones mentioned as being festivals of any kind (*Gen.* 40, 20; *Matt.* 14, 6).

Birthright. This was the privilege and prerogative of the first son born in the household, no matter which of a number of wives produced him. He inherited the headship of the household or clan and a double portion of property left by his father (*Deut.* 21, 17; cf. *2 Kings* 2, 9). This birthright could be passed on only by the one who had received it (*Gen.* 25, 31; *Heb.* 12, 16) although it could be forfeited (*1 Chron.* 5, 1). If a man died childless the heir was the firstborn of his widow, fathered by the nearest kinsman of the dead man (*Deut.* 25, 5-10).

Birthstool. In AV merely stool (*Ex.* 1, 16). A special chair upon which a woman might sit or crouch during parturition.

Bishop. The episcopus, from Gk. *Episcopos*, an overseer, religious or political (*Num.* 4, 16; 31, 14). The first occurrence of the word in the NT is in the exhortation of Paul to the elders (presbyters) of Ephesus (*Acts* 20, 17 & 28). He makes no distinction bet. elders, presbyters and bishops (*Titus* 1, 5-7) but regards them as holding office equal and identical. This opinion is strengthened by the fact that he does draw a distinction bet. bishop and deacon (*Philip.* 1, 1; *1 Tim.* 3, 1-13). The bishop in the Apostolic Church was the shepherd taking charge of the flock of God (*Acts* 20, 28; *1 Pet.* 5, 2; *1 Thess.* 5, 14; *Heb.* 13, 17; *1 Tim.* 3, 1-7; *Titus* 1, 7-9). There was a considerable number of them, even in a single congregation (*Philip.* 1, 1; *1 Tim.* 4, 14). They held meetings to discuss Church affairs (*Acts* 15, 6 & 22; 16, 4; 21, 18). The name is given figuratively to Jesus (*1 Pet.* 2, 25). It was not until the 2nd cent. that differences and distinctions began to appear bet. elders, presbyters, and bishops, a move inspired largely by the Epistles of Ignatius, who died in c. AD 115. The RC Council of Trent in the 16th cent. ordained that bishops are the successors of the apostles, and are to govern the Church. They are superior to presbyters and elders. This assumes, with practically no good reason, that the apostles did in fact govern the Church of their day, exercised a gen. oversight, and ordained deputies in local congregations. Anglicans justify episcopacy on the grounds of the peculiar position of James, the fact that there were some called Angels of the Churches; and on the functions of Timothy and Titus (*1 Tim.* 1, 3 ff.; *2 Cor.* 12, 18). But the fact of the matter is that Timothy was ordained in the first place by presbyters (*1 Tim.* 4, 14). There is nothing in the NT to demonstrate that the apostles nominated, ordained, or set apart in any way their immediate heirs and successors. *See* ELDER, PRESBYTERS, CHURCH.

Bithynia [bǐ-thӯ-nǐ-ǎl. A region on the Black Sea in NW Asia Minor. Paul and Silas tried unsuccessfully to enter it (*Acts* 16, 7).

Bitter herbs. These were salads eaten at Passovertime (*Ex.* 12, 8; *Num.* 9, 11). Something considerably more bitter than these is referred to in (*Lam.* 3, 15).

Bitter water. (*Num.* 5, 18). *See* JEALOUSY.

Bittern. The activities assoc. with the bittern AV (*Isa.* 14, 23; 34, 11; *Zeph.* 2, 14) certainly are not characteristic of the bittern, which is a wading bird. RV trans. the Heb. 'porcupine'. LXX and Vulg. prefer ' hedgehog.' RSV uses both.

Bitumen This is, in the Bible, asphalt, still known as Jew's Pitch. It is found in a liquid and semi-solid state nr the Dead Sea and in other parts of the ME. The Gk. and Rom. called the Dead Sea, ' Lake Asphaltitis.' Asphalt is meant when the AV uses ' slime ' (*Gen.* 11, 3; 14, 10).

Blain. An inflammatory swelling, bleb, blister, boil, which was the 6th plague of Egypt. It occurs in the mod. compound ' chilblain ' (*Ex.* 9, 8-11). *See* MEDICINE.

Blasphemy. Language or actions defaming God and derogating from His honour (*Ps.* 74, 10-18; *Isa.* 52, 5; *Rev.* 16, 9 & 11 & 21). It was punishable by death (*Lev.* 24, 16) and was the accusation brought agst. Stephen (*Acts* 6, 11) and agst. Jesus (*Matt.* 12, 22-32; etc.). Paul was accused of blasphemy agst. the local god (*Acts* 19, 37).

Blasting. *See* MILDEW.

Blemish. *See* MEDICINE.

Bless. The action of God bestowing favour and favours (*Gen.* 1, 22; 2, 3; 9, 1-7). Or the giving of thanks and adoration by man to God (*Ps.* 103, 1; *Matt.* 26, 26). Or asking God to bestow His favour on a person other than one's self (*Gen.* 27, 4 & 27-29; *1 Chron.* 16, 2; *Ps.* 129, 8). At its lowest level it is merely a kindly or benevolent greeting from one to another (*1 Sam.* 25, 5 & 6 & 14; *2 Kings* 4, 29).

Blessedness. The word does not appear at all in the OT, and in the NT (AV) it is used wrongly (*Rom.* 4, 6 & 9; *Gal.* 4, 15) which should be respectively : ' David pronounces a blessing upon . . .'; and ' What has happened to that fine spirit of yours ? '

Blessing. Favour and benefit granted by God (*Gen.* 39, 5; *Deut.* 28, 8; *Prov.* 10, 22). Or the act of asking this in favour of another (*Gen.* 27, 12). Or a gift given in goodwill (*Gen.* 33, 11; *Josh.* 15, 19; *2 Kings* 5, 15).

Blindness. This was and is a common condition in the ME, due in the main to ophthalmia and congenital syphilitic diseases. There was little for the blind to do but beg unless he had money or friends to support him (*Matt.* 9, 27; 12, 22; 20, 30; etc.). It could, of course, come in old age by the processes of time (*Gen.* 27, 1; *1 Sam.* 4, 15; etc.). Prisoners of war were sometimes blinded (*1 Sam.* 11, 2; *2 Kings* 25, 7). Temporary blindness is noted (*2 Kings* 6, 18-22; *Acts* 9, 9; etc.). The Mosaic law commanded kindness towards the blind (*Lev.* 19, 14; *Deut.* 27, 18). See MEDICINE.

Blood. In the OT it was believed that the life of a person was in his blood, or even that it was his life; where the soul lived (*Lev.* 17, 11 & 14; *Deut.* 12, 23; *Ps.* 104, 29 & 30). It was not Abel's blood that cried from the ground; it was his life (*Gen.* 4, 10). This identification of the life with the blood was the reason why taking the blood of the lower animals was forbidden although their flesh could be eaten (*Gen.* 9, 3 & 4; *Acts* 15, 20 & 29). The blood (the life) of animals was used in the Sin offering (*Lev.* 17, 10-14), Blood (life) was the price of atonement (*Heb.* 9, 22). The blood of animals slain for food or sport was always buried (*Deut.* 12, 15-16). There are, of course, many refs. to the blood of Jesus, always signifying his work of atonement. See AVENGER OF BLOOD.

Blood, Issue of. See MEDICINE.

Bloody flux. See MEDICINE.

Bloody sweat. See SWEAT, MEDICINE.

Boanerges [bō-ăn-ĕr′-gēs]. The sons of thunder, or wrath. A nickname given by Jesus to the brothers James and John (*Mark* 3, 17).

Boar. The word is applied to the wild variety of pig, esp. to the male (*Ps.* 80, 13). The same word is trans. ' swine,' when applied to domesticated pigs. See SWINE.

Boat. See SHIPS AND BOATS.

Boaz (Booz) [bō′-ăz]. **1.** A man of means who lived in Bethlehem. Related to Ruth's late husband, he married her to offer her the security which the

law encouraged, when a nearer kinsman than he
refused to carry out the Heb. custom of protecting
the widow of a close relative in this way. Their
son's son was Jesse, father of David, and from
their line came Jesus (*Ruth* chs. 2-4; *Matt.* 1, 5).
2. The pillar on the left, or N side of the porch of
Solomon's temple (*1 Kings* 7, 15-22).

Boil. With blains (qv), boils were the 6th plague
of Egypt (*Ex.* 9, 8-11). They could be one of the
symptoms of leprosy (*Lev.* 13, 18-20). Job was
plagued by them (*Job* 2, 7). Hezekiah's disease
(*2 Kings* 20, 7) may have been pyaemia, for which
a poultice of figs would be a perfectly proper
treatment. *See* MEDICINE.

Bolster. The word is used only in the AV (*1 Sam.*
19, 13 & 16; 26, 7 & 11 & 12 & 16). It should
simply be trans. ' at the head.'

Bondage, Bondmaid, Bondman. In translating the
Heb. word gen. used, the context has to be
watched, for its meaning is wide (cf. *2 Sam.* 9, 2
where the meaning is simply ' servant,' with v. 10,
where it is obviously ' bondman ' and with v. 11
where it appears to be no more than the polite
greeting still used in correspondence ' your
humble servant '). The Heb. is the same for all
3. It was possible to be a servant without
being a slave, who, of course, is one in bondage.
This distinction has to be kept in mind, and in
this article only this last class will be dealt with.
From the beginning bondsmen and women were
regarded as possessions, property. In the Ten
Commandments they are lumped with the cattle
(*Ex.* 20, 17). The bondman had no rights at all;
he could be flogged to the point of death (*Ex.* 21,
21). The maidservant was in the same position
and was almost certainly not only work-slave,
but concubine (*Ex.* 21, 7 ff.). If a maidservant

was criminally assaulted, the compensation was paid to her owner, not to her. She might be the slave of the wife, prob. having formed part of the dowry (*Gen.* 29, 24 & 29; etc.). Most slaves were, of course, captives of war, though some might be bought from slave traders. Joseph was sold by his brothers to slave traders (*Gen.* 37, 28). Poverty or debt might compel the freeborn to sell themselves as slaves (*Ex.* 21, 2; *Amos* 2, 6; 8, 6; etc.). According to *Neh.* (7, 66 ff.) the Jews after the Exile numbered 42,360 with 7,337 slaves, a proportion of about 1 slave to 6 freemen. The Ten Commandments granted slaves at least 1 rest day a week and they took part with the rest of the household in religious feasts (*Deut.* 12, 12 & 18; 16, 11 & 14). Before being allowed to take the Passover, however, the slave had to be circumcised (*Ex.* 12, 44). Kidnapping, or shanghai-ing into slavery was forbidden and punishable by death (*Ex.* 21, 16). On the whole, however, slaves appear to have been pretty well treated (they were valuable property, after all). The trusted slave was a man of very considerable importance and influence in the household (*Gen.* 15, 1-4; *Judg.* 19, 3 ff.; *1 Sam.* 9, 5 ff.; etc.). There was nothing to prevent one born to the master by a slave girl from inheriting even the birthright (*Gen.* 16, 1 ff.; 21, 13; etc.). There was provision for the release of Heb. slaves, but not of foreign-born slaves, after 6 yrs. of bondage (*Ex.* 21, 1-6). The slave could, however, contract to remain in bondage. If he did this willingly the lobe of his ear was pierced and he remained a slave for life. This law operated for men but not for women. *Deut.* altered this harsh law as it affected women and made provision for their release (15, 12-18). There is a further reading of

the law in *Lev.* (25, 39-55). This indicates a gradual
mellowing of the attitude of the Heb. to slaves,
but it is not until we reach *Job* (31, 13-15) that
we find a real change in the attitude to slavery,
and some questioning of the moral justification
for it. Jesus said nothing in criticism of the practice of slavery, but in apostolic times decision
was forced upon the Church, since many slaves
had become Christian (*Rom.* 16, 10; *1 Cor.* 1,
11; etc.), and Paul summed up all the conflicting
ideas when he said that in Christ there is neither
bond nor free (*1 Cor.* 12, 13). When he persuades
Onesimus the runaway slave to return to his
master Philemon, he does not even suggest to
Philemon that he should release Onesimus. In
short, to the early Church, one's position in
society did not matter. This may have been
partly due to their expectation of the imminent
end of the age, and the second coming of Christ,
but there must also have been the conviction that
the important thing is not one's standing in the
eyes of society, but one's standing in the eyes of
God. *See* PHILEMON.

Bonnet. The word does not appear in the RSV.
The AV (*Isa.* 3, 20) is a fem. headdress (the word
used by RSV). RV has a ' sash ' Ref. is to the
headdresses of priests in (*Ex.* 28, 40; 29, 9; 39,
28; *Lev.* 8, 13; *Ezek.* 44, 18). In the last ref.
listed, RSV trans. ' turbans ' (ornamental headdresses). *See* DRESS.

Book. The first writing was on tablets of soft clay
which were then baked. Later, papyrus and
parchment were used, and were kept rolled round
rollers—*volumen*, hence volumes (*Ps.* 40, 7; *Jer.*
36, 2; *Ezek.* 2, 9). The Heb. prob. began to write
when they were in Egypt (*Ex.* 17, 14). The books
of the Bible and Apocrypha are by no means the

whole literature of the Heb. and there are numerous refs. to books which have now disappeared. (cf. *Num.* 21, 14; *Josh.* 10, 13; *1 Chron.* 27, 24; 29, 29; *2 Chron.* 9, 29; 12, 15; 13, 22; 20, 34; 24, 27; 26, 22; 32, 32; 33, 18 & 19; etc.). *See* PAPYRUS, BIBLE.

Book of Life. The Jews believed in a record which would determine the final judgment. There would also be a list of those fated to enjoy the blessings of the Messianic age. From this derived the notion of a Book of Life, and a Book of Death. The Apocalyptic writers made Michael the Recording Angel.

Boot. *See* DRESS.

Booth. This was a kind of substantial bivouac made of interlacing branches, used by growers when they were keeping an eye on their crops, notably vegetables and vines (*Gen.* 33, 17; *Job* 27, 18; *Isa.* 1, 8 RV). Sometimes the word is trans. 'cottage, hut, tent, pavilion.' During the Feast of Tabernacles (qv) the Jews had to live in booths for a week, partly to celebrate the vintage, and partly to remind themselves that they were orig. a nomadic people led by God (*Lev.* 23, 39-43; *Neh.* 8, 14).

Booty. Plunder of war, masculine, feminine or neuter (*Gen.* 14, 11 & 12 & 16). During the actual invasion of Canaan the Israelites were forbidden to take any booty, but in other wars were allowed to help themselves, after the enemy males had been killed (*Num.* 33, 52; *Deut.* 20, 14-16). Sometimes a fixed proportion of the spoil had to be handed over (*Num.* 31, 26-47; *Josh.* 6, 19; etc.). David made a law of fair shares (*1 Sam.* 30, 23-25). *See* WAR.

Border of garment. These are the fringes which the Israelites were ordered to have on their robes

(*Num.* 15, 37 ff.). RV and RSV have 'tassels.'
The command is slightly different in *Deut.* (22,
12) which seems to mean more of a twisted cord
stitched to the corners of the plaid-like upper
garment, with blue thread (*Num.* 15, 38 RV,
RSV). This is the ' hem ' of Jesus garment (*Matt.*
9, 20; 14, 36) and the ' border ' (*Mark* 6, 56;
Luke 8, 44). The exact reason for the command is
obscure, but it was undoubtedly a distinguishing
mark.

Borrow. Simply 'to ask as a favour,' as in RV
(*Ex.* 3, 22; 11, 2; 12, 35). There might sometimes
be an understanding, or merely the obligation to
return it, whatever it was (*2 Kings* 6, 5) and
sometimes there was none (*Judg.* 5, 25; 8, 24).
The reciprocal act or response was to lend (*Ex.*
12, 36 AV), ie, to grant such a favour as had
been asked (RV). *See* DEBT.

Botch. Mod. verb means to ' make a mess of '
something. But here (*Deut.* 28, 27 & 35) it is a
noun meaning a boil. *See* MEDICINE.

Bottle. These were made of leather or of earthenware, not of glass. Trans. sometimes as wineskins (*Job* 32, 19; *Matt.* 9, 17; etc.). *See* CUP-
BEARER.

Bottomless pit. *See* ABYSS.

Bow. A weapon of war and of the hunt. It was
carried both by officers and men of the infantry
and the cavalry alike, and by charioteers. The
arrows were made of cane or polished wood (*Lam.*
3, 13; *Isa.* 49, 2; *Ezek.* 39, 9) and the heads were
of iron, copper, or stone according to the period.
Sometimes the tip was poisoned (*Job.* 6, 4).

Bowels. In Scripture these were regarded as the
seat of the emotions as the heart is nowadays,
for no better reason.

Bowl. *See* BASIN.

Box 79 **Bra**

Box. 1. Any small container with a lid, made of wood, leather, metal or stone (*Matt.* 26, 7 AV). **2.** The box wood, *buxus longifolia* (*Isa.* 60, 13).

Bozrah [bŏz'-răh]. **1.** A city of Edom (*Gen.* 36, 33; etc.) noted for its sheep (*Micah* 2, 12). The prophets foretold its doom (*Amos* 1, 12; *Jer.* 49, 13 & 22). **2.** A city of Moab (*Jer.* 48, 24).

Bracelet. An ornament worn on the wrist, forearm or upper arm, and by men and women alike (*Gen.* 24, 22; *Ezek.* 16, 11). The vessels for the Tabernacle were made from them donated (*Num.* 31, 50). Some refs. trans. as ' cords or chains or brooches ' (RV).

Bramble. Although the same word is trans. ' thorns ' (*Ps.* 58, 9) AV has ' bramble ' (*Judg.* 9, 14 & 15) as have RV and RSV who also have ' bramble ' in (*Luke* 6, 44) but in (*S. of S.* 2, 2) RV has ' thorns ' and RSV ' brambles.'

Brasier. See COAL.

Brass. In all refs. brass should be copper or an alloy other than the alloy copper and tin or zinc. Copper was mined and smelted in the land and at the time (*Deut.* 8, 9; *Job* 28, 2) but brass as it is known to-day is not so ancient. RV marg. and RSV prop. have copper or bronze. It was used for making utensils (*Ex.* 38, 3; *Lev.* 6, 28; etc.), armour (*2 Sam.* 21, 16) and many other items (*Ex.* 38, 8; *2 Kings* 25, 13-17; *Isa.* 45, 2; *Matt.* 10, 9; *1 Cor.* 13, 1; *Rev.* 9, 20). Where the metal has been shaped by casting it is certainly bronze (*1 Kings* 7, 41-46; *2 Chron.* 4, 1-7). See BRONZE.

Bravery. Simply ' showy splendour ' (*Isa.* 3, 18 AV).

Brazen Sea. See MOLTEN SEA.

Brazen serpent. Actually a bronze serpent which was the symbol raised by Moses in the wilderness when the people were plagued by snakes; it

restored their faith and will to live, for many of
them were prob. dying of fright rather than of
venom (*Num.* 21, 8 & 9). The bronze serpent
was preserved but began to be regarded with
superstitious awe and then as an idol. It was,
as a result, destroyed by Hezekiah (*2 Kings* 18, 4).

Breach. An outburst of anger (*2 Sam.* 6, 8; *1
Chron.* 13, 11; *Job* 16, 14 AV).

Bread. This was not baked in loaves as we understand them, but rather as flat cakes of various
thicknesses. The material was wheat or barley,
ground each day in a handmill. Gen. the flour
was unfermented (cf. American sourdough) but
when leavened bread was wanted, a piece of
rather old dough was put in the mixture, and
some fermentation was produced (*Gen.* 19, 3;
1 Sam. 28, 24; etc.). The oven was a small,
usually portable affair (*Lev.* 2, 4). Scones (American biscuits) were cooked in pans (*Lev.* 2, 5).
Sometimes the dough was simply laid on hot
stones (*1 Kings* 19, 6). Usually the housewife
did her own baking, but in the towns there were
professional bakers (*Jer.* 37, 21). There is a list
of the various kinds of bread (*Lev.* 2). The word
as used in (*Luke* 11, 3) means merely ' food.'

Breakfast. *See* MEALS, FOOD.

Breastplate. Part of the regalia of the High Priest
(*Ex.* 28, 15-30). *See* HIGH PRIEST. It was also
part of a soldier's armour (qv). It is used figuratively (*Isa.* 59, 17; *Eph.* 6, 14). for righteousness and (*1 Thess.* 5, 8) for faith and love.

Brethren of the Lord. They were James, Joses (or
Joseph), Simon and Judas (*Matt.* 13, 55 RV;
Mark 6, 3). They were not enamoured of Jesus'
conduct and could not credit His claim (*John* 7,
4 & 5). But after the Resurrection they came into
the company of the apostles (*Acts* 1, 14; *1 Cor.*

9, 5; *Gal.* 1, 19). James became one of the prominent and influential leaders of the early Church (*Acts* 12, 17; 15, 13; *Gal.* 2, 9) and wrote the *Epistle of James.* Their exact relationship to Jesus cannot be more than a matter of speculation. Some reckon that they were children of Joseph by a former marriage but that is untenable (*Matt.* 1, 25; *Luke* 2, 7). It is also suggested that they might be cousins. But all these notions are obviously due to reluctance to admit that Joseph and Mary lived a normal married life. There is still the wish to preserve the sense of the perpetual virginity of Our Lord's Mother. The brethren are always assoc. with Mary in the Gospels, and it seems perfectly clear that they were the children of Mary and Joseph, born after Jesus (*Matt.* 1, 25; *Luke* 2, 7).

Bribery. *See* CRIME AND PUNISHMENT.

Brick. Might be sun-dried or kiln-dried and baked (*Ex.* 5, 7; *2 Sam.* 12, 31; *Nahum* 3, 14). In the last ref. the RV marg. and RSV have 'brickmould' prop. There are differences elsewhere (*Jer.* 43, 9) where AV has 'hide them in the clay in the brick kiln,' RV has 'in the brickwork' and RSV has 'in the mortar,' which is prob. right.

Brier. In Heb. there are 6 different words thus trans. and 1 Gk. LXX trans. (*Isa.* 55, 13) as 'fleabane,' and Vulg. has 'nettle.' Where AV has 'briers' (*Heb.* 6, 8) RV and RSV have 'thistles.' The Gk. is *tribolos*, trans. thistle in AV (*Matt.* 7, 16). In other refs. brier and thorn appear to be more or less interchangeable.

Brigandine. A brigand in the Eng. of the AV was not a highwayman but a light infantryman. The brigandine is his coat of mail, usually light overlapping metal discs on leather (*Jer.* 46, 4; 51, 3).

Brimstone. In most refs. is sulphur; volcanic deposits (*Gen.* 19, 24; *Deut.* 29, 23).

Bronze. A brown-coloured alloy of copper and tin sometimes with some zinc or lead. Up till the middle of the 18th cent. AD it was classed as brass. ' Brass ' in the Bible is usually bronze, and always bronze when it is something cast. The Bronze Age in its 3 periods covered roughly 3200 BC to 1300 BC, and was followed by the Iron Age. The patriarchs lived in the Bronze Age.

Brook. Gen. a wadi or watercourse which flows after rain but is dry at other times. *See* RIVER.

Broom. The word is rendered ' juniper ' in the AV, but is more prop. broom, *retana retem.* The root is still burned to make charcoal (*Ps.* 120, 4).

Brother. A male of the same parentage as oneself, or at least by the same father (*Gen.* 28, 2) or of the same mother (*Judg.* 8, 19). It is sometimes used a little more loosely of a man of the same direct ancestry (*Gen.* 14, 16) and even merely of one of the same nation or people (*Deut.* 23, 7; *Neh.* 5, 7; *Jer.* 34, 9). Again it may be used of an ally (*Amos* 1, 9) or of one of the same faith (*1Cor.* 6, 6). Familiarly used of one greatly beloved (*2 Sam.* 1, 26). Finally, one of the brotherhood of man (*Gen.* 9, 5; *Matt.* 5, 22; 18, 35). *See* FAMILY.

Brotherly love. The love that a brother *ought* to have for another.

Bruit. Rumour or report (*Nahum* 3, 19 AV).

Buckler. *See* ARMOUR.

Builder. *See* ARTS AND CRAFTS.

Bul. The 8th month of the Calendar. *See* TIME.

Bull. Male of the species *bos taurus. See* OX. But should be ' antelope,' not wild ox, wild bull (*Deut.* 14, 5; *Isa.* 51, 20 AV).

Bullock. These were used as draught animals (*Judg.* 6, 26; *Jer.* 31, 18 AV). The 2nd ref. is trans. 'untrained calf' in RSV which fits the context better. But, of course, it was being trained as a draught animal. Bullocks could be sacrificed (*Ex.* 29, 1).

Bulrush. RSV retains AV bulrush (*Ex.* 2, 3) but changes it to papyrus (*Isa.* 18, 2). It seems likely that the papyrus is meant in both instances (qv).

Burden. Word used lit. and metaphorically for a heavy load (*Ex.* 23, 5; *Num.* 11, 11 ff.). It is used also of a prophecy foretelling heavy judgments (*Isa.* 14, 28; 15, 1; *Ezek.* 12, 10; *Hos.* 8, 10; *Nahum* 1, 1). Ref. (*Gal.* 6, 5) is a military allusion: 'every man to carry his own kit.'

Burglary. See CRIME AND PUNISHMENT.

Burial. As in all E lands burial followed death within 24 hours (*Gen.* 23, 3 & 4). Cremation was sometimes, but seldom, employed (*1 Sam.* 31, 11-13; *2 Sam.* 21, 12-14). There was an extravagant display of grief at the burial, professional mourners sometimes being employed to increase the wailing (*Mark* 5, 38; *Jer.* 9, 17). The body of the dead was washed, and either rolled in a sheet or swathed in bandages (*Matt.* 27, 59; *John* 11, 44). Spices and perfumes might be bound in (*John* 12 , 7; 19, 39). The body was carried on a bier to the place of interment which was gen. in a sepulchre hollowed in the rock and not often in a grave in the ground (*Gen.* 25, 9 & 10; *2 Sam.* 3, 31; *Matt.* 27, 60; *Luke* 7, 14). See MOURNING, TOMB.

Burning. See CRIME AND PUNISHMENT.

Burning bush. Seen by Moses (*Ex.* 3, 2 & 3; *Deut.* 33, 16; *Mark* 12, 26). Prob. one of the many flowering thorns of the acacia variety. The miracle was not that it seemed to burn, but that it was not consumed.

Bushel. *See* WEIGHTS AND MEASURES.

Butler. *See* CUPBEARER.

Butter. As understood in Biblical times it was more curds than butter as we know it. Curdled milk, not churned from cream (*Gen.* 18, 8; *Deut.* 32, 14; *Prov.* 30, 33; *Isa.* 7, 15-22). RSV prefers ' curds,' using ' butter ' only once where the sense seems to call for it (*Ps.* 55, 21). *See* FOOD.

By and by. Not ' in a little while ' but ' instantly.'

Byway. *See* ROADS.

C

Cab. *See* WEIGHTS AND MEASURES.

Caesar. Orig. the family name of the Julian house, which became the official title of the Rom. Emperors, after it had been adopted by Octavius, nephew of Julius in AD 44. He became Augustus Caesar. He was succeeded by Tiberius, Caligula, Claudius and Nero who were all of the Julian house. The name was accepted as the official title and was retained by the next 6 emperors although they were not ' Julians ': Galba, Otho, Vitellius, Vespasian, Titus and Domitian. The emperors referred to in NT are: (1) Augustus (*Luke* 2, 1) who became sole ruler when the triumvirate of himself, Lepidus and Antony broke up in 31 BC. He was not unfriendly to the Jews and respected their worship and institutions. Augustus died at the age of 67 in AD 14. (2) Tiberius (*Matt.* 22, 17; *Mark* 12, 14; *Luke* 3, 1; 20, 22; *John* 19, 12) was born in 42 BC and was both stepson and son-in-law of Augustus. Pilate served under him, and Herod Antipas built Tiberias on Galilee in

his honour. He died in AD 37 and was succeeded
by the mad Caligula who reigned till AD 41.
(3) Claudius, nephew of Tiberius followed. He
banished all Jews from Rome (*Acts* 18, 2) and
died in AD 54. (4) He was succeeded by Nero
(*Acts* 25, 12 & 21; 26, 32; *Philip.* 4, 22) who was
the adopted son of Claudius. Power went completely to his head. The great fire of AD 64 which
destroyed a 5th of the city was blamed on the
Christians, though it is just poss. that Nero was
responsible for it. Christians were hunted down
and martyred by the score, including, according
to trad. Peter and Paul. (5) Titus, son of Vespasian a Rom. general who became emperor.
Succeeding to the command of the army of Judea
he conducted the siege of Jerusalem in AD 70.
Becoming emperor in 79, he died within 2 yrs.
There were, of course, other Caesars but these
are the Caesars of Scripture.

Caesar's household. Christians engaged in the imperial service (*Philip.* 4, 22; *Rom.* 16).

Caesarea [căes′-ă-rē′-ă]. A city built on the coast
by Herod the Great in 25-13 BC. It is some 60
m. from Jerusalem and was a great and prosperous
port. It was named in honour of Augustus Caesar
and was the Rom. capital of Palestine. Philip
brought the Gospel to the city (*Acts* 9, 30) and it
is mentioned again (*Acts* 10, 1 & 24). Herod
Agrippa died here (*Acts* 12, 19 & 23). There was
a Christian church (*Acts* 18, 22; 21, 8 & 16).
Paul was taken to the city as a prisoner under
heavy escort (*Acts* 23, 23 & 33) and was tried
before Festus and Agrippa (*Acts* 25, 1-4 and 6-
13).

Caesarea Philippi [phĭl′-ĭ-ppī]. A city nr. Mt. Hermon at the spring where the Jordan rises. Herod
built a magnificent temple here. It was the scene

of Peter's great confession of Jesus (*Matt.* 16, 13; *Mark* 8, 27).

Caiaphas (caī'-ă-phäs]. He was appointed High Priest c. AD 18 by Valerius Gratus the Rom. procurator who preceded Pilate. His father-in-law was the High Priest Annas (*Luke* 3, 2). An astute politician, he negotiated the death of Jesus (*John* 11, 49-53; 18, 14). After the arrest Jesus was taken to Annas, who sent him to Caiaphas (*John* 18, 24) who sent him to Pilate (18,28]. He worked Pilate into a difficult position, and secured his objective. He was also involved in the trial of Peter and John (*Acts* 4, 6) and was deposed by Vitellius in AD 36.

Cain. Elder brother of Abel, and elder son of Adam and Eve. He prob. represents the tiller of the soil as the natural enemy of the herdsman. He killed Abel, but founded a race from which the pioneers of many arts sprang (*Gen.* 4, 1-25).

Cake. *See* BREAD.

Calamus (căl'-ă-mŭs]. A sweet smelling plant (*S. of S.* 4, 14) from which a perfume was extracted for scenting anointing oils (*Ex.* 30, 23). It is prob. the *acorus calamus.*

Caleb [cā'-lĕb]. There are 2 of the name. **1.** A son of Hezron (*1 Chron.* 2, 18 & 42). **2.** Son of Jephunneh (*Josh.* 15, 17) of the tribe of Judah. He was one of the 12 spies sent into Canaan. A man of great courage, he was Joshua's right-hand man all through the campaigns (*Num.* chs. 13-14; *Josh.* 14, 6-14). At the allocation of land he was spokesman for Judah, but chose for his own plot the hill land still unconquered (*Josh.* 14, 14; 15, 13 & 14 & 15-19).

Calendar. *See* TIME.

Calf. A young bull or cow, *bos taurus,* and used in sacrifice or as food. The young bull symbolised virility and sexual power and was a common idol of the ancient world (*Ex.* 32, 4).

Calvary. A low eminence outside Jerusalem where Jesus was crucified (*John* 19, 17 & 20 & 41; *Heb.* 13, 11-13). The name is the Latin *calvaria*, trans. of the Heb. *golgotha*, via the Gk. *kranion*—a skull. There are many ' explanations ' of why it was called Skull Hill.

Calves of the lips. (*Hos.* 14, 2 AV). May simply be the offering or sacrifice of our lips. But a very slight change in the Heb. makes ' calves ' into ' fruit ' (RSV).

Camel. The one-humped camel, or dromedary. There is the draught animal (*2 Kings* 8, 9) and the racing camel (*Isa.* 66, 20 RV, RSV). Camels were ceremonially unclean (*Lev.* 11, 4). Cloth was woven from the longer hair (*Matt.* 3, 4).

Camp. *See* WILDERNESS, WAR.

Camphire. Henna (*S. of S.* 1, 14; 4, 13 AV). This is a small shrub which grows abundantly in the Engedi dist. When powdered and mixed with water the plant supplied a red or orange dye.

Cana [că′-nä]. Cana of Galilee. A village in the Nazareth area where Jesus performed his first miracle at the wedding feast (*John* 2, 1). Nathanael was a native of Cana (*John* 21, 2).

Canaan [că′-năan] (**Chaanan**). The grandson of Noah, son of Ham (*Gen.* 9, 18 & 22; 10, 6) and the land to which he gave his name—Palestine (qv).

Canaanite. The orig. inhabitants of Canaan. In NT the word is used (*Matt.* 10, 4; *Mark* 3, 18) in quite a different sense, in connection with the disciple Simon. The word should be Cananaean, which has nothing to do with the land of Canaan. The Cananaeans were members of a revolutionary party dedicated to overthrow Rom. rule. Founded by Judas of Gamala, they are known elsewhere (*Luke* 6, 15; *Acts* 1, 13) as the Zelotes, or Zealots.

Candace [căn-dă-cē]. The queen whose vizier was converted to Christianity after hearing Philip preach (*Acts* 8, 26-39).

Candle. Not the wax candle. *See* LAMP.

Candlestick. Prob. a lamp stand. The 7 branched candlestick was an upright with 6 curved branches which raised the 7 lamps to the same level (*Ex.* 25, 31-40; 40, 24; *Lev.* 24, 2-4). These lamps (qv) had wicks floating in olive oil and burned continually. The stand and the lamps were of beaten gold ornamented with the almond blossom design. Solomon added 10 more lamp stands (*1 Kings* 7, 49) but they were all taken away to Babylon at the Exile (*Jer.* 52, 19).

Cankerworm. Prob. the caterpillar or locust in its larva stage (*Jer.* 51, 27; *Joel* 1, 4; 2, 25; etc.).

Canon. Lit. 'a measuring rod, a standard, a model' (*2 Cor.* 10, 13-16; *Gal.* 6, 16); deriving from that, the genuine as agst. the false. Applied to Scripture it is the difference between one set of books and another, the canonical and the non-canonical. The main division is, of course, bet. OT and NT, a distinction which did not occur until the Christian literature was in existence and known. 'Testament' is the Gk. *Diatheke* (dī-ă-thē′-kē) which trans. the Heb. *Berith*, or Covenant. Considering the OT first, there were 3 stages in the formation of the canon. The Holy Scripture in the age of *Ezra* and *Nehemiah*, consisted of the Pentateuch, the first 5 Books of our OT. Later, but before 200 BC, the prophets were admitted to the canon of Holy Scripture: these included the early prophets, *Joshua, Judges, 1 Samuel* and *2 Samuel, 1 Kings* and *2 Kings.*

The late prophets are the 3 major: *Isaiah, Jeremiah* and *Ezekiel*, and the 12 minor: *Hosea, Joel, Amos, Obadiah, Jonah, Micah, Nahum, Habakkuk, Zephaniah, Haggai, Zechariah* and *Malachi*. Other Books were gradually incorporated by 132 BC, but it was not until the Synod of Palestinian Jews, held at Jamnia, nr. Joppa, in AD 90, that the present OT was declared canonical and official sanction was given to 'The Writings': *Psalms, Proverbs, Job, Song of Solomon, Ruth, Lamentations, Ecclesiastes, Esther, Daniel, Ezra, Nehemiah, 1st and 2nd Chronicles*. The Jewish canon is therefore in 3 parts: The Law, the Prophets, and the Writings, while the Eng. Bible canon is in 4 parts (OT): the Pentateuch (or Law), the Historical (*Josh.-Esth.*) the Poetical (*Job-S. of S.*, including the Wisdom Literature) and the Prophets. Books cannot be written unless people can write, and the start of Heb. literature cannot be before 1400 BC or later than 900. There is no space to go into the arguments for this claim. In the early days of the Heb. people, they were not 'the people of the Book.' The will of God was conveyed through the voices of selected people (*Deut.* 18, 18; 19, 17; 21, 5; 24, 8). But round c. 800 BC, it began to be seen that there was value in the written word, the permanent record (*Isa.* 30, 8); which means that there must have been a considerable literature in existence, though it was not yet regarded as absolutely authoritative. Samaria fell in 722 BC, and the 10 tribes of the N Kingdom cease to have any influence upon Jewish thought. The custodians of the Heb. heritage are now Judah and the Levites. Josiah reigned over Judah c. 621, and it is during his reign that the literature begins to be collected into something that can be called canonical. The in-

spiration of this was the discovery in the Temple of a
Book approximating to the OT book *Deuteronomy*
which became the basis of the renewed Covenant
bet. Jehovah and His people. There came, however, the Exile, and then the return to Jerusalem
of the remnant of Judah and Levi. During the
Exile it was impossible to practise the trad. religion
which had centred upon the Temple. What held
the people together was no longer the Temple, but
the literature which they had taken with them. *Ezra*
and *Nehemiah* who had been greatly involved in
the later captivity and in the return, were therefore
well aware of the value of the literature and
gathered together what is now the Pentateuch,
and gave it official sanction (*Neh.* chs. 8-10). Just
when the prophetic books were incorporated in
the canon is not known, but, *Mal.*, *Jonah* and
Zech. were not written earlier than 430 BC, or
thereabouts. The apocryphal Book of *Ecclesiasticus* is known to have been written c. 200 BC,
and the present prophetic canon was an established
fact by then (cf. *Ecclesiasticus* chs. 44-50). The
Writings (Gk. *Hagiographa*) were incorporated
later, and there was some hesitancy over *Esther,
S. of S. and Eccl.*, though the others were accepted
readily enough. The final decision was made at
the Synod of Jamnia in AD 90, and our present
OT is their decision. Many Books were excluded,
which now form part of the Apocrypha, but it is
very likely that the growth of Christian literature
inspired these Jews to ' close the door ' once and
for all upon the canon. The NT recognises the
OT, of course, and speaks of the 3 divisions (not
4) (*Luke* 24, 44). And the 2 refs. (*Matt.* 23, 35;
Luke 11, 51) seem to indicate that they recognised
Genesis as the earliest Book and *Chronicles* as the
last). The NT, however, does not quote from

Esth., *S. of S.* or *Eccl.*, implying that there was some doubt about them being canonical. The oldest MS of the OT is more recent by 400 yrs. than the oldest MS of the NT. The date is AD 916. The formation of the NT canon was simpler, in that the hist. range was so much less, and authorship was less in doubt. It was reckoned that any writings which had apostolic sanction should be read in churches. The first writings which would be read, would be, or course, epistles directed to named churches, or circular letters. Exactly when the Gospels were set down (or the writings on the life and teaching of Jesus which preceded the Gospels) is not known. But they were in existence by the beginning of the 2nd cent. AD, and were being read. From the writings of the early fathers, Clement, Tertullian and Irenaeus it is clear that the idea of a new canon was being discussed bet. 180 and 200, and it appears that at that time only 7 books of the present NT were in any doubt: *Heb.*, *James*, *2 Pet.*, *2* and *3 John*, *Jude* and *Rev*. One or two of the apocryphal books were as nr. inclusion in the canon as these were. In 327 Athanasius suggested as the NT canon, the 27 books which now constitute the NT. The synod of Hippo Regius (393) and the 2 synods of Carthage (397 and 419) ratified this conclusion. This was universally accepted until the RC Council of Trent (1546) uttered an anathema on anyone who did not accept as canonical all the books included in the Vulg. The Vulg. contains all the pre-Christian books classed by the Prot. churches as apocryphal.

Canticles. *See* SONG OF SOLOMON.

Caper berry. RV trans. of (*Eccl.* 12, 5) where AV and RSV have 'desire.' LXX supports RV. It is poss. that the caper-berry was used as a stimulant or aphrodisiac.

Capernaum [că-pĕr′-nă-ŭm]. After being rejected by his own people at Nazareth, Jesus centred much of His work on this town on the NW shore of Galilee (*Matt.* 4, 13-16; 9, 1). It was a Rom. military post and a tax centre (*Matt.* 8, 5-13; *Mark* 2, 1). The town was the scene of several of Jesus' miracles (*Matt.* 8, 5-13; *Luke* 7, 1-10; *Matt.* 8, 14-17; *Mark* 1, 21-28; 2, 1-13; *John* 4, 46-54; *Matt.* 8, 16-17; *Mark* 1, 32-34; *Luke* 4, 23 & 40 & 41). After the feeding of the 5,000 Jesus preached here (*John* 6, 24-71), Matt. was called to discipleship at Capernaum (*Matt.* 9, 9-13; etc.).

Caph [căph]. The 11th letter of the Heb. alphabet. Gk. *kappa*. Eng. *K*.

Capital. Chapiter AV and RV (*1 Kings* 7, 16 & 19 & 20; etc.). The top of a column or pillar.

Cappadocia [căp′-pă-dō′-ciă]. Territory in E Asia Minor which became a Rom. province in AD 17. There was a colony of Jews in the town (*Acts* 2, 9; *1 Pet.* 1, 1).

Captain. The title is used rather loosely in scripture, and the status of men so described can only be determined by the context (*Gen.* 21, 22; *1 Sam.* 8, 12; *2 Sam.* 10, 16; *1 Kings* 16, 9; etc.). In NT it means an officer of about the rank of military tribune, ie, superior to a centurion, but inferior to the commander of the legion. Ref. ' captain of the temple ' (*Acts* 4, 1; 5, 24 & 26) means simply a priest in charge of the temple police.

Captivity. *See* ISRAEL, JUDAH.

Caravan. *See* TRADE AND COMMERCE.

Carbuncle. *See* JEWELS AND PRECIOUS STONES.

Carchemish [căr′-chĕmĭsh] (**Charchemish**). One of

the 2 capitals of the Hittites where Chaldea defeated Egypt, 605 BC (*2 Chron.* 35, 20).

Careful. Lit. ' full of care, over-anxious.'

Careless. Lit. ' without a care in the world.'

Carmel [căr′-mĕl]. A long ridge of hills, 1700 ft. high at the SE end and some 15 m. long, running out to the sea at Haifa. The scene of Elijah's overthrow of the priests of Baal seems to have been at the S end, looking down to the plain of Esdraelon (*1 Kings* 18, 17-46).

Carpenter. *See* ARTS AND CRAFTS.

Carpus [căr′-pŭs]. A man of Troas with whom Paul left his cloak (*2 Tim.* 4, 13).

Carriage. Only in AV and meaning baggage—that which is carried (*Isa.* 10, 28; *Acts* 21, 15; etc.).

Cart. Usually a 2 wheeled wooden vehicle drawn by oxen or bullocks. It could be covered or un-covered (*1 Sam.* 6, 7; *2 Sam.* 6, 3-6; etc.).

Casement. Better trans. lattice (*Prov.* 7, 6 AV).

Cassia. The bark from the cassia tree is very like cinnamon (qv) (*Ex.* 30, 24; *Ezek.* 27, 19).

Castanets. *See* MUSICAL INSTRUMENTS.

Castle. AV. A citadel, stronghold or palace except (*Gen.* 25, 16; *Num.* 31, 10; *1 Chron.* 6, 54) where it clearly means a nomadic camp.

Castor and Pollux. These were twin divinities of Greece and Rome, known as the *Dioskouroi*, the protectors of mariners (*Acts* 28, 11).

Caterpillar. *See* LOCUST.

Cattle. Lit. ' wealth, possessions,' which for an agricultural community is obviously the domes-ticated farm animals.

Caul. A net cap or cowl: a hair net (*Isa.* 3, 18). Medically, an investing membrane, the *epiploon* or *omentum* (the fatty membrane wrapping the liver) (*Ex.* 29, 13; *Lev.* 3, 4 & 10 & 15). Or the *pericardium* (the membrane surrounding the heart) (*Hos.* 13, 8).

Causey. (*Prov.* 15, 19 AV margin). A raised pavement or footpath; causeway.

Cave. The most notable are Makkedah (*Josh.* 10, 16-27) and Adullam (*1 Sam.* 22, 1; *2 Sam.* 23, 13).

Cedar. The characteristic tree of the Lebanon (*1 Kings* 5, 6). Its timber was valuable (*2 Sam.* 5, 11; *1 Kings* 6, 9 & 10 & 18; *Ezek.* 27, 5).

Cenchreae [cĕn-chrē′-āē]. (**Cenchrea** AV). The S harbour of Corinth (*Acts* 18, 18). There was a Christian church (*Rom.* 16. 1).

Censer. Container for burning incense (*Num.* 16, 6 & 7 & 39; etc.). *See* FIREPAN, INCENSE.

Census. The Heb. system was counting heads of families, then septs, then tribes (*Num.* 1, 18; *Ex.* 18, 25). Three military registrations are recorded (*Num.* 1; 26, 1-51; *2 Sam.* 24, 1-9). There was a count of the repatriated Jews after the Exile (*Ezra* 2). And, of course, the census ordered by Augustus which brought Joseph and Mary to Bethlehem (*Luke* 2, 1). *See* QUIRINIUS, THOUSAND.

Centurion. Company commander in Rom. legion, ranking with the mod. sergeant. Two are named; Cornelius (*Acts* 10) and Julius (*Acts* 27, 1 & 3 & 43). There are 2 unnamed (*Matt.* 8, 5-13; *Matt.* 27, 54).

Cephas [cē′-phās]. Aram. *kepha*, meaning rock or stone. The name given by Jesus to Peter (cf. Gk. *petros*, a rock or stone). *See* PETER.

Chaff. *See* AGRICULTURE.

Chalcedony. *See* JEWELS AND PRECIOUS STONES.

Chaldea [chăl-dē′-ă]. *See* BABYLONIA.

Chaldean. Inhabitant of Chaldea but in *Dan.* (1, 4; 2, 2 & 4) it means a sorceress.

Chaldees. Same as Chaldeans, but this form of the

word has been attached to the city of Ur (of the Chaldees) (*Gen.* 11, 31; *Neh.* 9, 7).

Chalk stones. Ref. indicating that Israelites burned and slaked lime (*Isa.* 27, 9).

Chamberlain. The major domo of a palace, like Blastus (*Acts* 12, 20) or the palace treasurer like Erastus (*Rom.* 16, 23). In OT the word usually means eunuch (qv).

Chambers of the South. *See* STARS.

Chameleon [chăm-ē'-lĭon]. It may simply be any of the smaller lizards (*Lev.* 11, 30).

Chamois. Not the true chamois which is not indigenous to Palestine. It is more likely the mountain sheep *ovis tragelaphus* (*Deut.* 14, 5).

Champaign. AV. Simply open country (*Deut.* 11, 30). *See* ARABAH.

Changes of raiment. Mod. slang ' glad rags ' not just a change of clothing. (*Gen.* 45, 22; *Judg.* 14, 12 f.)

Chapiter. *See* CAPITAL.

Chapman. A travelling merchant; a packman (2 *Chron.* 9, 14) trans. merchantmen (*1 Kings* 10, 15).

Charger. 1. A large, usually decorative, dish or platter used for serving (*Matt.* 14, 8; *Num.* 7, 13; etc.). Trans. plate or platter is RSV. 2. (*Nahum* 2, 3 RSV). The horse of the cavalryman. The phrase is quite wrong in AV which trans. ' the fir trees be terribly shaken.' RSV has ' the chargers prance.'

Chariot. A 2 wheeled vehicle used in war, for state processions, and for private, peaceful use. It was drawn by 2, 3 and sometimes 4 horses. The charioteer stood, and might be accompanied by a driver, to leave him free for combat. There is a description (*1 Kings* 7, 33). War chariots might be of metal or overlaid with bronze, and with sword blades protruding from the hubs. A 4 wheeled vehicle is ref. (*Rev.* 18, 13).

Charity. From Lat. *caritas*, used in the Vulg. to trans. Gk. *agape*: found in NT for OT 'Loving Kindness' of God for men, which inspires the same bet. humans. Not abstract love but the spirit of brotherly love.

Chebar [chē'-băr]. River and canal of Chaldea. Here *Ezek.* in Exile saw some of his visions (*Ezek.* 1, 1 & 3; 3, 15 & 23; 10, 15 & 20).

Checker work. Better as 'net work pattern' on the pillars of the temple (*1 Kings* 7, 17).

Chedor-Laomer [chē'-dŏr-lă-ō'-mĕr]. King of Elam in the time of Abraham (*Gen.* 14).

Cheese. Really pressed curds (*Job* 10, 10; etc.). *See* MILK, FOOD.

Chemosh [chĕm'-osh]. The Moabite god (*Num.* 21, 29; *Jer.* 48, 46). Josiah destroyed the place where Chemosh worship was practised (*2 Kings* 23, 13).

Cherethites [chĕr-ĕ-thī'-tes]. People of the S portion of the Philistine country (*1 Sam.* 30, 14). Sometimes called Carites. They formed the core of David's standing army.

Cherith [chē'-rĭth]. The brook or *wadi* beside which Elijah stayed awhile. In Gilead, E of Jordan (*1 Kings* 17, 3 & 5).

Cherub, Cherubim. They are not the representation or even the sublimation of any creatures found in nature. They appear to be more the personification of the storm cloud (*Ps.* 18, 10). Babylonian influence on the idea of the cherubim is clear, for they tally in *Ezek.*'s description (*Ezek.* 1; 10, 2) with the massive figures unearthed by archaeology in Babylonia, with human head, bull's body, and eagle's wings. They were the guardians of sacred things, and were a symbol not a reality. Cherub is also the name of a place in Babylonia (*Ezra* 2, 59; *Neh.* 7, 61).

Chestnut tree. The plane tree.

Cheth [chĕth]. (*Heth, Hheth* in RV.) The 8th letter of the Heb. alphabet: Eng. *H*, though the Heb. is not guttural.

Chidon [chĭ'-dŏn]. The place where Uzzah (qv) was struck dead when he touched the Ark of the Covenant (*1 Chron.* 13, 9).

Child, Children. Possession of children was a great cause of delight and satisfaction; to be childless was to be sorrowful. Children were signs of God's favour and were His gifts (*Gen.* 4, 1). Barrenness was a disgrace and a misery, showing as it did that God's favour was absent (*Gen.* 16, 4; *Luke* 1, 25; etc.). The size of the family and esp. the number of sons was the guarantee of security and prosperity. Children were completely dominated by their parents (*Judg.* 11, 39; etc.) and at one time could even be sacrificed (*Lev.* 18, 21; 20, 2 & 3; *2 Kings* 23, 10; *Jer.* 32, 35). The Law commanded children to be obedient and respectful (*Lev.* 19, 3; *Deut.* 27, 16). *Prov.* gives a great deal of space to the duty of parents and children (*Prov.* 3, 12; 13, 24; 15, 5; 22, 6; 29, 15; etc.). It must not be thought, however, that it was a harsh over-disciplined relationship. Many instances appear of deep genuine affection (*Gen.* 37, 35; 43, 14; *2 Sam.* 12, 16; *2 Kings* 4, 18 ff.; *Ps.* 131, 2; *Matt.* 18, 3; 11, 25). See FAMILY.

Children (sons) of God. The phrase sometimes refers specifically to angels (*Gen.* 6, 1-4; *Job* 1, 6; 2, 1; etc.) or to the Judges (*Ps.* 29, 1 RV Marg.; 82, 6). Otherwise it is simply the relation of humans to God or of the nation to God (*Ex.* 4, 22; *Deut.* 1, 31; 8, 5; 14, 1 f.; *Hos.* 1, 9).

They can lose this kinship (*Deut.* 32, 5). The NT changes the whole conception and makes it intensely personal, for the title of God is not now Jehovah, but Father. All men are truly the sons of God when they have come to the Father through His unique son, Jesus Christ (*John* 14, 6). Then there is a re-birth, a spiritual sonship (*John* 1, 13; 3, 3 & 8). This idea was carried on by Paul (*Gal.* 3, 26; *Philip.* 2, 15; etc.). *See* ADOPTION. The height and perfection of it is (*Rev.* 21, 7).

Chios [chī'-ŏs]. Island in the Gk. Archepelago (*Acts* 20, 15).

Chislev [chĭs'-lĕv]. The 9th month. *See* TIME.

Chiun [chī'-ŭn]. The planet Saturn (*Amos* 5, 26).

Chloe [chlō'-ē]. A Christian woman of Corinth (*1 Cor.* 1, 11).

Choir. *See* MUSIC.

Choler. Bitter anger (*Dan.* 8, 7; 11, 11 AV).

Chorazin [chŏr-ăz'-ĭn]. A town nr. Capernaum which featured largely in Jesus' ministry (*Matt.* 11, 21; *Luke* 10, 13).

Chosen People. The term was applied by the Israelites to themselves. They believed themselves to be the people of the Covenant, and their hist. and the hist. of the Apostolic Church cannot begin to be understood unless this persistent idea is kept in mind. Only the Messiah could restore what had been interrupted by the Exile. Any reforms or reconstructions which took place were inspired by a return to the orig. Covenant (*see* DEUTERONOMY). The Passover was the link with the bondage in Egypt, when God had renewed the Covenant with Abraham. Tragically the conviction of the Covenant produced spiritual pride instead of humility. They failed to see that God's method was not national election, but individual selection, and that the Divine purpose was to build a pyramid of which the Jewish race was the base, and Jesus the apex (*Deut.* 4, 37; 14, 2; *Isa.* 41, 8 & 9; *Acts* 13, 17; *John* 4, 22; etc.).

Christ. The Heb. and Aram. title Messiah as trans. in LXX. Orig. the anointed king, then the royal son of David (*Ps.* 2, 2; *Dan.* 9, 25). ' The Christ ' is Jesus as the fulfilment of the Messianic hope (*Matt.* 16, 16 & 20; etc.). The word became so assoc. with our Lord's name that it became part of it: Jesus Christ (*John* 1, 17; *Acts* 11, 17; *Rom.* 1, 1 & 3; etc.).

Christian. The word was first used at Antioch c. AD 43, and not necessarily as a term of respect (cf. Puritans, Wesleyans, Papists,.) (*Acts* 11, 26) and is used only 3 times (*Acts* 26, 28; *1 Pet.* 4, 16).

Chronicles, Books of. With *Ezra, Neh., S. of S., Dan.* and *Esth.*, the *Chron.* was among the last of the OT books to be written: some time bet. 250 BC and 125 BC. It is quite poss. that *Chron.*, *Ezra* and *Neh.* were written by the same man, prob. a Levite, or by the same team. Some have credited *Ezra* with the authorship (cf. *2 Chron.* 36, 22 & 23 with *Ezra* 1, 1 & 2). Whoever he was, there is nothing obscure about his purpose; to show the unique connection bet. God and Israel as demonstrated by hist. His hist. runs parallel to the hist. of *Sam.* and *Kings*, but is sometimes given a twist towards ecclesiasticism. The David of *Chron.* is not he of *Sam.* The author is more interested in the Temple than in the palace: in religion more than in politics: in Judah more than in Israel. Occasionally his estimates are wild: like David's army of one and a half million men (*1 Chron.* 21, 5) and the contribution of a million pounds in gold to the temple construction (*1 Chron.* 22, 14). The book begins with genealogical tables down to (9, 44) then the hist. of the kings of Israel, David receiving much attention, as does Solomon, the temple builder himself (*1 Chron.* 29, 25—2 *Chron.* 9). From that point the hist. turns to Judah alone and its kings from Rehoboam to Zedekiah. The Heb. title is ' Words of Days '; the LXX title, ' The Omissions.' The present title dates from 4th cent. AD.

Church. Gk. *Kyriakon doma:* The Lord's house. But the word trans. church in the NT is *ecclesia,* lit. a gathering together of citizens summoned for a civic responsibility (*Acts* 19, 32 & 41). This sense was transferred to the gathering of the faithful summoned by its Head, Jesus Christ (*Matt.* 16, 18; 18, 17; *Acts* 2, 47 AV). But there are 3 senses of the word in the NT: (1) The local, summoned, worshipping fellowship; (2) The combination of all, everywhere, who met and worshipped thus; (3) All who have gathered and worshipped thus, and who are now dead, plus all who are doing it and are alive, plus all who ever will do and who are not yet born (*1 Cor.* 1, 2; 12, 12 & 13 & 27 & 28; *Col.* 1, 24; *1 Pet.* 2, 9 & 10). They had to come together to listen to the apostles (the only true witnesses); to break bread (the command of Jesus at the Last Supper); to obtain the stimulus to faith of the society of others (again at Jesus' command); and to worship together (man is a worshipping creature). In giving a sense of order and regularity, the natural people to look to were the apostles, but they did not greatly concern themselves, living in daily expectation of Jesus' second coming. But the church grew too big for that. It was necessary to regularise things and to announce that this was a church in its own right. The Council of Jerusalem did this officially in AD 50. The rule of the apostles was not, however, either aristo-

cratic or autocratic (*Acts* 5, 2; 15, 2 & 4 & 6 &
22 & 23; etc.). But it became increasingly plain
that some kind of order was needed. Elders,
bishops, deacons, were created (qv). They dealt
with matters of day to day organisation as they
occurred, and they discussed them round the
table. The local church, meeting for worship,
would follow by and large the Jewish convention
of synagogue worship: scripture, prayer, preaching and praise, with, of course, baptism when
called for, and the breaking of bread always.
There would also be the offering.

Churches, Robbers of. (*Acts* 19, 37). Prop.
sacrilegious persons.

Cilicia [cĭl-ĭ´-cĭa]. Territory in SE Asia, chief town
being Tarsus, birthplace of Paul. One of the
earliest places visited by evangelists (*Acts* 15, 23)
and by Paul (*Acts* 15, 41).

Cinnamon. An aromatic bark, yielding an oil
burned for its fragrance (*S. of S.* 4, 14; etc.).

Circumcision. A rite practised by Jews even to-day,
but not of Israelite origin. It may have begun as
an act of hygiene, but is trad. religious, or tribal.
It was the initiation performed at any age after
the 8th day (*Gen.* 17, 10-27; etc.). The uncir-
cised were those beyond the pale. The ' Circumcision' was the Jewish church and nation (*Gal.*
2, 8). Paul wrote of circumcision of the heart,
signifying complete rejection (*Col.* 2, 11). Insistence on the rite as an essential for entry into the
Christian church was the cause of an early and
serious dispute (*Acts* 11, 2; etc.).

Cistern. A built reservoir to preserve water; normally not very large (*Deut.* 6, 11 RSV; *Jer.* 2, 13).

Cities of the Plain. *See* PLAIN, CITIES OF.

City. The number of houses is immaterial but there
is usually an enclosing wall (*Gen.* 4, 17; 18, 26;

etc.). A distinction is drawn (*Deut.* 3, 5). Hilltops were preferred, but they lacked water. Lower lands were good, but vulnerable (*Josh.* 2, 5 & 15).

City of David. *See* DAVID, CITY OF.

City of Refuge. *See* AVENGER OF BLOOD. A device introduced by Moses to end the blood feuds caused by the law of an eye for an eye. He named 3 cities E of Jordan; Bezer in Reuben, Ramoth Gilead in Gath and Golan in Bashan (*Deut.* 4, 41-43) and 3 more W of Jordan; Kedesh in Naphtali, Shechem in Ephraim, and Kiriath arba, or Hebron, in Judah (*Josh.* 20, 7).

Claudia. A Christian woman (*2 Tim.* 4, 21).

Claudius Lysias [lўs'-ĭ-ăs]. Commander of 1,000 men and prob. military tribune of the Rom. garrison of Jerusalem. (*Acts* 22, 26ff.; 23, 26).

Clean. *See* PURIFICATION.

Clement. A Christian at Philippi, assoc. with Paul (*Philip.* 4, 3).

Cleopas [clē'-ō-păs]. One of the 2 men on the Emmaeus Road (*Luke* 24, 18) but not he of (*John* 19, 25) who was known also as Clopas.

Cloak. *See* DRESS.

Clopas. *See* ALPHAEUS, CLEOPAS (above).

Closet. Lit. ' a room within a room.'

Cloud, Pillar of. Cloud in the form of a pillar which seemed to roll before marching Israel. At night it glowed (*Ex.* 13, 21 & 22). It concealed God when he spoke to the people (*Num.* 12, 5).

Clout. Word still common in Scotland, where a dishcloth is a clout (pronounced cloot). Orig. did not have the meaning of a rag (*Jer.* 38, 11-12). Also the verb meaning to patch (*Josh.* 9, 5).

Coal. In Scripture this is charcoal (*Ps.* 120, 4) which was burned in a brazier (*Jer.* 36, 22 ff.). In 2 places it should simply be a hot stone (*1 Kings* 19, 6; *Isa.* 6, 6).

Coast. The border bet. 2 places, or the immediate neighbourhood of a place.

Coat. *See* DRESS.

Coat of Mail. *See* ARMOUR.

Cock. *Gallus domesticus.* Cockcrow is the 3rd watch of the night (*Matt.* 26, 34 & 74 & 75; *Mark* 13, 35).

Cockatrice. Lat. *cocatrix:* the crocodile. Trad. a fabulous monster based on cocatrix, with baleful breath and baneful glance (AV only. *Isa.* 11, 8; 59, 5; *Jer.* 8, 17).

Cockle. An ill-smelling plant (*Job* 31, 40). ' Foul weeds ' is better.

Coffin. Heb. did not use coffins. Ref. (*Gen.* 50, 26, burial of Joseph) is the Egyptian mummy case *sarcophagus.*

Coins. *See* MONEY.

College. In connection with Huldah (qv) (*2 Kings* 22, 14; *2 Chron.* 34, 22) it means the 2nd quarter or ward of the city.

Colony. Not used in the mod. sense. It was an organised group of Rom. citizens (of any nationality orig.) settled anywhere in the empire and recognised by the Senate as a community. Rom. soldiers often settled down where they were serving (*Acts* 16, 12).

Colossae [cŏl-lŏs'-săe]. A city of SW Phrygia in Asia Minor, important at one time but superseded by Laodicaea and Hierapolis (*Col.* 2, 1; 4, 13).

Colossians, Epistle of Paul the Apostle to the. With *Eph.*, *Philem.* and *Philip.*, the letter was written from prison in Rome, and was carried to Colossae by Tychicus. Paul had not visited the church there, but reports of heresies and deviations had come to his ears. The main heresy seems to have been a departure from the view that the full and final revelation of God to man was Jesus. Paul's theme, therefore, is the supremacy of Christ. The 'new thought' of Colossae was a mixture of Judaism and oriental ideas, about the essentially evil nature of matter. The flesh was to be mortified, the spirit sublimated, and God could be reached by contact with angelic beings. Paul takes them sharply to task. He writes an introduction (1, 1-8), follows with a section on sound doctrine (1, 9—3, 4), then an exhortation to mend their ways (3, 5—4, 6), and closes with salutations (4, 7-18). He tells them that the heart, not the body, needs discipline and purifying: that Christ is absolutely and eternally pre-eminent: that they must not separate the religious life from the social life of the community.

Colt. Although it is always applied to the young of the horse outside Scripture, it never means this in Scripture.

Coming, Second. *See* PAROUSIA.

Common. Ceremonially unclean (*Acts* 10, 14 ff.).

Communication. Conversation, talk, having dealings with another (*Col.* 3, 8).

Communion. Gk. *koinonia* is trans. communion in AV (*1 Cor.* 10, 16; *2 Cor.* 6, 14 'concord'; 13, 14), but is not so trans. in RSV which has 'participation,' 'fellowship,' 'accord.' AV renders the word as fellowship 12 times, the RV has 'fellowship' 15 times, and once 'contribution' (*Rom* 15, 26) and once 'distribution' (*2 Cor.* 9, 13). *Koinonia*, however, means a common sharing in something (or in anything). 'Partners' (*Luke* 5, 10) is *koinonos*. It is first used (*Acts* 2, 42) in all 3 vv. as fellowship, and omitting the definite article, but it is 'the fellowship' of all things in common, the community of goods. This *koinonia* ('communism' in its true sense) was replaced by the *diakonia*, which was the distribution of goods to the needy, but Paul continued to regard sharing as an essential part of the fellowship of the church. But gradually *koinonia* came to mean the shares distributed rather than the spirit of fellowship which inspired the distribution (*Rom.* 15, 26; *2 Cor.* 9, 13). The essence of communion, in Paul's view, was the common sharing of Jesus by all Christians. He was the ' great possession ' held in common (*1 Cor.* 1, 9). This fact is set forth in the central rite of the faith (*1 Cor.* 10, 16). There was also common participation in the Holy Spirit (*2 Cor.* 13, 14). The apostles gave the right hand of fellowship (Gk. *koinonia*) to Paul and Barnabas (*Gal.* 2, 9) and by doing so recognised that these 2 had been given the same grace, and included in the same service—the apostles to those of the circumcision and the 2 for the ' heathen.' The same sense of *koinonia* is in (*Heb.* 13, 16). Paul uses the word again in a more sublime sense when he speaks of drinking the cup that Christ drank, and so sharing His sufferings, death, and resurrection (*Philip.* 3, 10). John uses the word (*1 John* 1, 3 & 6 & 7) as communion, and again as fellowship with the Father and with the Son (*John* 15, 4). *See* LORD'S SUPPER.

Concision. Mutilators of the flesh. The word is applied contemptuously by Paul to the physical circumcision that had no spiritual meaning (*Philip.* 3, 2).

Concubine. Under the system of polygamy, she was a secondary wife often from the slaves or captives. She could be put away without divorce (*Gen.* 21, 10-14) but she had certain legal rights (*Ex.* 21, 7-11; *Deut.* 21, 10-14). *See* MARRIAGE.

Concupiscence. To use the adjective ' evil ' with it (*Col.* 3, 5) is tautology. It is always evil and is usually applied to sexual lust.

Coney. *See* ROCK BADGER.

Confection. Really ' perfume ' (*Ex.* 30, 35). The
confectionary is the perfumer (*1 Sam.* 8, 13 AV).

Confession. May be either a statement of faith, or an
admission of guilt or sin. **1. Confession of faith.**
In this sense the word is used only once in OT
(*1 Kings* 8, 33-35), but profession of faith occurs
frequently. In NT the word is used in connection
with Jesus; first merely the acknowledgment that
He was Messiah (*John* 1, 41), then it was taken
further by Peter (*Matt.* 16, 16). The orig. confession in the apostolic church was simply ' Jesus
is Lord ' (*1 Cor.* 12, 3), but as heresies began to
appear it was necessary to make the confession
more definitive (*1 John* 4, 2 & 3 & 15; *2 John* 7).
Jesus expected public confession of faith from
His followers (*Matt.* 10, 32 ff.; cf. *Rom.* 10, 8-10).
2. Confession of sin. This was of prime importance
in OT. The form and order for confession by
individual, community, or nation is laid down
(*Lev.* 5, 1 ff.; 16, 21; 26, 40). Confession runs
al' through the Penitential Psalms, and the prophets (*Ezra* 10, 1; *Neh.* 1, 6 & 7; *Dan.* 9, 4 ff.
& 20). It was necessary for forgiveness (*Ps.* 32,
5; *Prov.* 28, 13). It is not commanded so often
in NT, but is still a condition of pardon (*Matt.*
3, 6; *Jas.* 5, 16). It is in the Lord's Prayer and
is implied in the parable of the Prodigal (*Luke*
15, 18). Jesus commands offenders to confess
to those whom they have offended (*Matt.* 5, 23
& 24; *Luke* 17, 4).

Confirmation. Occurs twice in AV and is retained
in RSV (*Philip.* 1, 7; *Heb.* 6, 16). The Gk. verb
occurs often, however (*Acts* 14, 22; 15, 32 & 41).
There is no sign of any formal ritual. In mod.
confirmation the practice of laying on hands may
be traced to (*Acts* 8, 15 & 17). But this itself may

have sprung from the OT (*Gen.* 48, 14). *See* LAYING ON OF HANDS.

Congregation. The assembly. **1.** The people of Israel (*Ex.* 12, 3 & 19 & 47; etc.). **2.** The church-nation: the gathering or assemblage for worship (*1 Kings* 8, 14 & 65; *Num.* 10, 7; etc.). **3.** The community of those called by God to salvation ('solemn assembly' does not mean 'reverent,' but formal, regular, stated, appointed). 'Mt. of the congregation,' 'mt. of the assembly' (RSV) is the Babylonian Olympus, the seat of the gods (*Isa.* 14, 13). *See* TABERNACLE, CHURCH, SYNA-GOGUE.

Conscience. Lit. 'joint knowledge,' esp. bet. a standard and an inclination. There must be choice, allied to a feeling that only one course of action is right.

Consecration. Dedicatory act of a person or thing to God (*Ex.* 29, 9; *Lev.* 8, 33; *1 Chron.* 29, 5). Also setting apart from a common use and pur-pose to a sacred and holy use (*Josh.* 6, 19; *2 Chron.* 31, 6).

Convenient. Often means befitting (*Rom.* 1, 28; etc.)

Conversation. Has nothing to do with talking except in so far as talk is part of one's conduct and way of life. It means 'a way of life' (*Ps.* 37, 14; *Eph.* 4, 22; etc.).

Convocation. This occurred when the people laid aside their daily work and met for worship. This they did every Sabbath (*Lev.* 23, 1-4); on the 1st and 7th days of the Feast of Unleavened Bread (*Ex.* 12, 16); Pentecost (*Lev.* 23, 15-21); the 1st and 7th days of the 7th month, the latter being the Day of Atonement (*Lev.* 23, 24-28); and the 1st and 8th days of the Feast of the Tabernacles (*Lev.* 23, 34-36).

Copper. *See* BRASS.

Cor. *See* WEIGHTS AND MEASURES.

Corban [cŏr'-băn]. The important ref. is in NT (*Matt.* 27, 6; *Mark* 7, 11). Something intended for God was corban (*Lev.* 1 2 & 3; 2, 1; etc.). Families neglecting the care of their aged might say that their money was corban (' dedicated,' ' spoken for '). This could not, by law, be used for any other purpose.

Coriander. A seed used in seasoning (*Ex.* 16, 31).

Corinth. A Gk. city which became a great seaport and suffered from the mod. disease of prosperity. Paul came to it c AD 52, and stayed 18 months with Aquila and Priscilla (qv). He was arrested and discharged. When he left, the work was carried on by Apollos (qv) (*Acts* 18, 1-18; 24-28). He sent 4 letters to the church here.

Corinthians, Epistles of Paul the Apostle to the. Ref. (*1 Cor.* 1, 9) shows that Paul had already sent one letter now lost. The 2nd letter which is *1 Cor.* was written in Ephesus in the year Paul finished his work there (AD 55). The Corinthians had asked his advice about certain matters, and he took the chance to remind them of some other matters, to him more important. It is well attested as the genuine work of Paul. After the greetings he deals with rumours that have reached him of things he does not care for (1, 12; 6, 20). Then he goes on to answer categorically the questions they have asked in their letter to him. He deals with divisions and factions, and holds high above all factions the supreme Christ without whom none of them is anything. Then he appeals for order: there must be rules, there must be discipline. People must conform to something larger than themselves. Where there is no precedent, he is prepared to give advice (chs. 5 & 6 & 7). They

should not give the impression or the appearance
of evil. They must also guard agst. sensationalism
and must keep the sacraments simple, leaving
room for the Holy Spirit (11, 2-24). They must
believe firmly in the life after death (ch. 15). This
letter did not accomplish all that Paul expected,
though it did achieve as much as any letter could
have done. Some were asking who this man Paul
was and by what authority he laid down the
law like this (ch. 4). This was the reaction to the
lost letter, and maybe to a visit Paul paid himself. Another letter seems to have followed (2
Cor. 2, 4; 7, 8) and some scholars consider part
of it to be in the scripture (chs. 10-13). Things
seemed to get better after this and a more cheerful
note is struck in the 4th letter (2 *Cor.* chs. 1-9).
Timothy carried a least 1 of the letters, and Titus
another (2 *Cor.* 2, 13; etc.).

Cormorant. The sea bird. Ceremonially unclean
(*Lev.* 11, 17). The word appears wrongly in AV
(*Isa.* 34, 11; *Zeph.* 2, 14) where the Heb. is clearly
' pelican.'

Cornelius [cŏr-nē′-lĭ-ŭs]. Centurion stationed at
Caesarea, who with his family was baptised by
Peter, giving a lead to other non-Jews (*Acts* 10).

Corner stone. The stone so cut that it forms part
of end wall and part of side wall of a building,
binding them together. The chief corner stone is
the one at the foundation of the house; the head
of the corner is the one at the top of the wall (cf.
Rom. 9, 33; *Matt.* 21, 42).

Cornet. E. Used to trans. 3 Heb. words. **1.** The
trumpet (qv) (*Lev.* 25, 9; *Ps.* 98, 6; etc.). **2.**
Should be castanets (2 *Sam.* 6, 5). **3.** The
horn, orig. animal horn, later of metal (*Dan.* 3,
5 & 7 & 10 & 15). *See* MUSIC (INSTRUMENTS).

Corruption, Mount of. A hill nr. Jerusalem where

Solomon built altars where his heathen wives might worship (*2 Kings* 23, 13).

Cos [cŏs], **(Coos)** [cō´-ŏs]. Island in the Gk. archepelago bet. Rhodes and Miletus.

Cotton. Prob. Indian cotton (*Esth.* 1, 6; *Isa.* 19, 9) trans. ' hangings ' and ' networks ' in AV.

Coulter. Better ' ploughshare.' The Heb. plough had no coulter (*1 Sam.* 13, 20 f.).

Council. A governing body which prob. came into being during the Exile, when normal processes of government were suspended. It came back with the returning Jews and became a recognised part of the civic order (*Ezra* 7, 25 & 26; 10, 14). It was the *gerousia*, or senate, exercising considerable authority. Later, BC 57-55, the Romans divided Judea into 5 dist. and set over each a *synedrion* (mod. synod, sanhedrin). The *gerousia* continued to function, too, but there was such overlapping of authority that the provincial sanhedrins were done away with, and complete authority given to the Sanhedrin of Jerusalem (qv).

Counsellor. Prob. princes of Media and Persia acting as advisers to Artaxerxes on local politics (*Ezra* 7, 14; *Esth.* 1, 13-14).

Countervail. To make up for; compensate for (*Esth.* 7, 4 AV).

Court. Space enclosed by buildings grouped with a central square. It was unroofed, and, if of a private house, might contain a well (*2 Sam.* 17, 18) or a garden (*Esth.* 4, 11). Because of the division and subdivision of the Temple there were several courts (*Ps.* 65, 4; 84, 2).

Cousin. Not strictly the child of uncle or aunt, but in gen., a fairly close kin (*Luke* 1, 58).

Covenant. An agreement bet. individuals or peoples, and more particularly bet. individuals or peoples,

and God, involving the formality of a binding
oath and some ritual of witness (*Gen.* 21, 27 &
32; *1 Sam.* 18, 3; 23, 18; *1 Kings* 20, 34; etc.).
Noah's covenant (*Gen.* 6, 18); Abraham's (*Gen.*
15, 8); Israel's (*Ex.* 19, 5); Phineas' (*Num.* 25,
12 & 13); David's (*Ps.* 89, 20). Then came the
the New Covenant (*Jer.* 31, 31-34; *Heb.* 8, 8 & 11,
and, of course, *Matt.* 28, 19 & 20). Of this, Jesus
Christ is the intermediary bet. the 2 parties. The
OT and NT are the hist. of the initiation and
operation of the Old and New Covenants. In
the old, bet. God and man, there were conditions
on both sides (cf. Jacob, *Gen.* 28, 20 ff.). It was,
in fact, a bargain. The 10 Commandments were
the tables of the Covenant. The box in which
they were kept was the Ark of the Covenant.
The words (*Ex.* chs. 20, 22-23, 33) were the Book of
the Covenant, though this was later extended to
include *Deuteronomy* (*Deut.* 31, 9 & 26).

Cow. The farm animal: it figured in the covenant
ritual bet. Abraham and God (*Gen.* 15, 9); in
the ceremony for professing innocence of murder
(*Deut.* 21, 1-9); as a peace offering (*Lev.* 3, 1);
as a sin offering (*Num.* 19, 2-9); and even,
though rarely, as a burnt offering (*1 Sam.* 6, 14).

Craft. In the sense of handicraft it is dropped in
RV and RSV except once (*Rev.* 18, 22). *See*
ARTS AND CRAFTS.

Crane. Prop. the swallow (*Isa.* 38, 14).

Creation. In Scripture this is always an act of God.
It is used specifically of the creation of the world
and all that is in, on, and around it. The Heb.
insisted upon God at the beginning, thus creating
the distinctive characteristic of their recorded
hist. It is completely theistic. In *Gen.* there are
2 accounts of creation: (1) Belongs to the Priestly
code (*Gen.* 1, 1—2, 4); (2) Belongs to the earlier

Jahvistic code (*Gen.* 2, 4-25). It begins with a
short ref. to the orig. chaos, in which God forms
a garden for man whom he has moulded out of
the dust. The garden he can enjoy except for the
fruit of the tree of good and evil. God then creates
the animals, and, finally, woman. The Priestly
account is longer and more detailed. There is
the primeval chaos, and then, day by day the
emerging order. These writers were not trying to
be scientific; they were religious men affirming,
'In the beginning, God.' If one forgets this
essential purpose in their minds, it is easy to confuse one's own mind by trying to co-relate *Gen.*
and geology. Such speculation is trivial. Science
can no more tell us in scientific terms the last
word about God, than religion can in religious
terms tell us the last thing about relativity. The
truth about God is eternal, and it was the truth
that these writers were seeking; not the truth
about whether the hen or the egg came first. They
affirm that there is a personal God who is in
control and who has always been in control of a
created world, which, like all created things, must
have sprung out of design, will, thought, and
activity. *See* PENTATEUCH.

Creditor. *See* DEBTS.

Creeping thing. Prob. 'swarming.' There is no
distinction bet. creatures which creep on legs, like
caterpillars or lizards, and those which crawl,
like snakes (*Lev.* 11, 41; *Ps.* 104, 25; etc.).

Crescens [crĕs'-cens]. Companion of Paul in his
last imprisonment. Sent to Galatia (*2 Tim.* 4, 10).

Crete. Mediterranean island off SE coast of Greece.
It was prob. the first European land to reach a
high standard of artistic civilisation. There were
important and thriving colonies of Jews (*Acts* 2,
11). Titus was the most influential member of

the Church there, going to Crete to counter a
tendency to Judaise the faith (*Titus* 1, 5 & 14).
The Cretans of that day had rather an unsavoury
reputation (*Titus* 1, 12).

Crib. *See* MANGER.

Cricket. Heb. word includes the locusts and grass-
hoppers. They were ' clean ' because they did
not creep, but leap (*Lev.* 11, 22). AV trans.
' beetle ' but this must be wrong, since the beetle
creeps and is thus unclean.

Crime and punishment. Crime in Scripture usually
means not the act, but the charge. Actual crimes,
civil and religious, were catalogued with appropriate penalties in several codes (*Ex.* 20, 2-23, ch.
33; *Deut.* chs. 12-28; *Lev.* chs. 17-26). The last
code is the Priestly code gathered together. The
crimes listed are; worship of heathen deities and of
heavenly bodies with idolatry, blasphemy, black
magic; and were all punishable by death by
stoning. For working on the Sabbath, failing to
observe special days, sacrilege; the penalty was
to be cut off from the people, ie excommunicated. Adultery; death for both. Seduction;
with parental consent, the man must marry the
girl. Rape; if victim was betrothed, death.
Incest; death for both. Prostitution; death.
Physical cruelty to parents; death. Bribery, per-
jury, slander; heavy penalties, including fines
Theft and burglary, interfering with boundaries,
false weights and measures, trespass, arson; full
restitution. Assault; the assaulted to return in
kind (*jus talionis*). Kidnapping; death. Murder;
death at the hands of the next of kin (*see* AVENGER
OF BLOOD and CITY OF REFUGE). Restitution could
be up to 5 times the value for animals stolen
and slaughtered. Compensation was a money
payment. Imprisonment was rare. The stocks

were known (*Jer.* 20, 2 f.). Beating and scourging were practised. Indecent assault could be punished by mutilation. Stoning was the usual means of execution, and was the penalty for 18 crimes. Hanging was not a means of execution and is mentioned only of suicide, among the Jews. Crucifixion and beheading were mainly Rom. methods. A whole community might be destroyed for a crime (*Deut.* 13, 15-17).

Crisping pins. Prob. satchels. RSV has handbags. (*Isa.* 3, 22 AV).

Crispus [crĭs'-pŭs]. One of the few converts baptised by Paul, and ruler of the Jewish synagogue at Corinth (*Acts* 18, 8; *1 Cor.* 1, 14).

Crocodile. See LEVIATHAN, LIZARD.

Cross. A NT word, although crucifixion (qv) was common in the ancient world. Jesus uses the word as a symbol of sacrifice (*Matt.* 10, 38; 16, 24). It was a wooden gibbet, heavy, but not beyond a man's strength to carry on his shoulder, or drag (*Matt.* 27, 32; etc.). The victim might be fastened to it before it was raised, or after. Before it became the glory of the Christian faith it was reckoned the most shameful and loathsome of objects (*John* 19, 31; *1 Cor.* 1, 23; *Heb.* 12, 2). There were 3 main forms of cross in use in Rom. times: the *crux commissa*, shaped like the letter T; the *crux immissa* or *ordinaria*, in which the upright projected beyond the junction with the cross member; and the *crux decussata*, the St. Andrew's cross, with the 2 beams forming an X. Prob. Jesus was crucified on the *crux immissa* which would allow the superscription to be nailed above his head.

Crown. Symbol of authority of one kind or another, worn on the head. The king's crown was normally a circlet of gold with or without precious

stones (*Ps.* 21, 3; *2 Sam.* 12, 30; *Zech.* 9, 16).
They might be worn by idols (*2 Sam.* 12, 30).
This one weighed a talent, which was somewhat
heavier than a man could wear. Persian kings
wore an ornamental hat with a blue and white
circlet called the diadem. Assyrian kings wore
a kind of fez with a circlet of gold and jewels.
The High Priest wore a headdress like the mod.
episcopal mitre with a plate of gold on the front,
inscribed ' Holy to Jehovah.' The Romans who
had an ancient prejudice agst. crowns granted
them as symbols of victory to successful generals.
These could be of laurel or of gold modelled on
the leaves (*2 Tim.* 2, 5; 4, 8). The word is also
used to describe the ornamentation round the
temple furnishings (*Ex.* 25, 11 & 24 & 25; etc..)

Crucifixion. A very ancient method of execution
known to Assyrians, Persians, Gks. and others
(*Ezra* 6, 11). It was adopted by the Romans,
but was reserved only for those guilty of the most
heinous crimes, or for slaves. Death usually came
as a result of heat, thirst, exposure and exhaus-
tion. Death might be hastened by physical assault
(*John* 19, 31 & 33).

Cruse. Small vessel for holding liquids or for
carrying them (*1 Kings* 17, 12; *1 Sam.* 26, 11).
Sometimes a diff. Heb. word is used, better trans.
' bottle ' (*1 Kings* 14, 3) or ' bowl ' (*2 Kings* 2, 20).

Cubit. *See* WEIGHTS AND MEASURES.

Cuckoo (cuckow). *See* SEAMEW.

Cucumber. Rather smaller than the W vegetable.
Booths were built to shade them in the season
(*Isa.* 1, 8.)

Cummin. Cultivated for its seeds, used as a condiment (*Isa.* 28, 25 & 27). They were common and
cheap, and Jesus used the tithes on them to make
the Pharisees look ridiculous (*Matt.* 23, 23).

Cunning. As a noun, means skill or knowledge.

Cup. The vessel or its contents, used figuratively for pleasant or unpleasant experiences (*Ps.* 23, 5; *Isa.* 51, 17; *Matt.* 26, 39).

Cupbearer. Important and trusted official in an age when poison was a political device (*Gen.* 40, 9-14; *Neh.* 1, 11; 2, 1 & 2 'butler').

Cush [cūsh]. The son of Ham, and his clan who settled in S Arabia and N African coast (*Gen.* 10, 6-8; *1 Chron.* 1, 8-10). They gave their name to a territory (*2 Kings* 19, 9; etc.).

Custom. This was not the hated tribute raised by the publicans under the 'farming out' system. It was a tax on goods, not a poll tax, which in Galilee and Peraea went to Herod, and in Judea to the procurator (*Matt.* 17, 25; *Rom.* 13, 7).

Cut off from the people. *See* CRIME AND PUNISHMENT, EXCOMMUNICATED.

Cymbal. *See* MUSIC.

Cypress. Often trans. 'box' (*Isa.* 41, 19; 60, 13). One ref. (*Isa.* 44, 14) prob. the holm trees.

Cyprus. Third largest of the Mediterranean islands, it lies to the E, 60 m. W of Syria. Famous for copper ore in early times, the woods were felled for charcoal for smelting, and the land became arid in the interior through erosion. Strong Jewish communities flourished there in apostolic times (*Acts* 4, 36; 11, 19 & 20). Barnabas and Paul visited it (*Acts* 13, 4) and Barnabas and Mark (*Acts* 15, 39). *See* KITTIM.

Cyrene [cȳ-rē'-nē]. Ancient city of N Africa; mod. Tripoli. It lay bet. Alexandria and Carthage on the hills 9 m. from the coast. It was famed for its medical school, and had a large Jewish pop. One, Simon, carried Jesus' cross (*Matt.* 27, 32). Cyrenians in Jerusalem formed a synagogue

(*Acts* 6, 9) and there were conversions among them, notably Lucius (*Acts* 11, 20; 13, 1).

Cyrus. King of Persia 600-529 BC and real founder of the Persian empire; regarded by Isaiah as the created instrument of God to end the Exile by defeating the Babylonians. He was son of Cambyses, son of Cyrus, son of Teispes, son of Achaemenes, kings of Elam, the territory bet. Persia and Babylonia. He united Media and Persia and transferred the capital from Ecbatana to Susa. He was a humane conqueror and allowed the exiled Jews to return home and rebuild. He fell in battle in 529. This is Cyrus the elder. The Cyrus of Xenophon's Anabasis is Cyrus the younger, who is not mentioned in scripture (*Isa.* 44, 28; 45, 1-14; *Dan.* 6, 28; *Ezra* 1; 5, 13 & 14; 6, 3).

D

Dagon [dā'-gŏn]. The Philistine national god. He had temples in Canaan (*Judg.* 16, 23; *1 Sam.* 5, 1-7; *1 Chron.* 10, 10). Trad. Dagon was the father of Baal. The upper parts of the idol were human, the lower part was the body of a fish.

Daleth [dā'-lĕth]. 4th letter of the Heb. alphabet; Gk. *delta*; Eng. *D*. In early Heb. MSS the letters D (daleth) and R (resh) were very similar, and copyists' errors have caused some confusion (cf. *Gen.* 10, 4 and *1 Chron.* 1, 7).

Dalmatia [dălmă'-tiä]. Territory on the E coast of the Adriatic. In the Rom. empire it formed part of Illyricum (*Rom.* 15, 19). Titus went to Dalmatia (*2 Tim.* 4, 10).

Damascus [dămăs'-cŭs]. The capital of Syria and

the oldest of surviving cities (*Gen.* 14, 15), it was
the centre of the 3 main trade routes of the ancient
world. It stands by the rivers Abana and Pharpar
(qv) (*2 Kings* 5, 12). David captured it (*2 Sam.*
8, 5 & 6). Under the rule of Rezin, an ambitious
and able king, it developed into a powerful kingdom which was a constant thorn in Israel's flesh
(*1 Kings* 11, 23 & 24; etc.). Ahab had a treaty
with Damascus (*1 Kings* 20, 34) and was in alliance with the Damascenes agst. the Assyrians.
Pekah of Israel and Rezin of Damascus combined
agst. the combination of Ahaz of Judah and
Tiglath Pileser of Assyria, who took Damascus
(*2 Kings* 16, 5 & 9; *Isa.* 7, 1-8, ch. 17; *Amos* 1, 3-5).
Damascus rose again (*Ezek.* 27, 18). After being
occupied in turn by Assyrians, Chaldeans, Persians,
and Macedonians, it was taken by the Romans in
64 BC, and Syria became a province. There was
a strong Jewish community with a synagogue in
which there was an early appearance of followers
of Jesus, enough at least to inspire Saul of Tarsus
to deal with the situation (*Acts* 9). On the way he
had the vision, and in the town he received kindly
treatment from those he was travelling to arrest.
At a later period he had to escape hastily from
Damascus when the Jews were threatening his
life (*Acts* 9, 24 & 25).

Damnation. All words stemming from 'damn'
ref. to being condemned to everlasting punishment, but in the AV they usually mean no more
than condemnation in general. 'Judgment' is a better
trans. in many refs. (*John* 5, 29).

Dan. Son of Jacob and founder of the clan bearing
his name (*Gen.* 30, 5 & 6; 49, 16 & 17; *Deut.* 33,
22). Also the territory which they occupied (*Num.*
1, 12 & 38 & 39; *Josh.* 19, 40-48). The town of
Laish, renamed Dan, is assoc. with Beer-sheba

in defining the N and S limits of the occupation (*Judg.* 20, 1; *1 Chron.* 21, 2). Samson was a Danite (*Judg.* 13, 2 & 24).

Dance. Dancing was gen. restricted to fem. on ceremonial occasions (*Judg.* 11, 34; *1 Sam.* 18, 6 & 7; etc.). Children danced, but prob. not formally (*Job* 21, 11; *Matt.* 11, 16 & 17). Salome danced before men, prob. a form of ballet or pantomime, and not of a high moral tone at that (*Matt.* 14, 6). It was part of heathen ritual, and poss. frenzied (*Ex.* 32, 19; *1 Kings* 18, 26). Some of the religious festivals of the Heb. included ceremonial dancing (*Ex.* 15, 20; *Judg.* 21, 21 & 23). And David danced before the Ark of the Covenant when it was brought home (*2 Sam.* 6, 14-23).

Daniel. There are several men of the name: **1.** A son of David (*1 Chron.* 3, 1) called also Chileab (*2 Sam.* 3, 3). **2.** A priest (*Ezra* 8, 2; *Neh.* 10, 6). **3.** But the important Daniel is the Jewish prophet in Babylon. His ancestry was noble (*Dan.* 1, 3-7). He was one of Nebuchadnezzar's captives (*Dan.* 1, 1; *Jer.* 25, 1). Specially trained for high office of state, he held an important government post till the capture of the city by Cyrus in 538 BC. All the time he insisted upon obeying the Mosaic law scrupulously (*Dan.* 1, 8) and created bitter and powerful enemies (*Dan.* 6, 3-23). He saw and foretold the end of the captivity, and looked forward to the final struggle bet. God and the kingdoms of the world for supremacy. NT refs. are (*Matt.* 24, 15; *Mark* 13, 14; *Heb.* 11, 33).

Daniel, Book of. In the Heb. canon the book is placed with the Hagiographa headed by the *Psalms*, and not with the prophets, prob. because prophecy was not Daniel's main occupation and true vocation. He does not introduce his state-

ments with the trad. prophetic foreword; 'Thus
saith the Lord.' The Book is apocalyptic
literature, like the book of *Revelation*, and it was
written not long before the Christian era. It is
certainly not contemporaneous with the situation
which it purports to describe, or with the hist.
which it relates. Its purpose is to show that as the
older kingdoms of the world could not endure agst.
the might of God, neither would the oppressive
rule of Antiochus and the Romans endure. Two
languages are used by the author or authors: Heb.
and Aram. of a style identical to the language current in Palestine in the couple of cent. before
Christ. Scholars are fairly unanimous that the date
of the book is c. 168 BC, and that its purpose was
to give courage and confidence to the persecuted
Jews. Jesus knew the book well and valued it
highly (*Matt.* 24, 15). *See* APOCALYPSE.

Danjaan [dan'-ja'-an]. Ref. *2 Sam.* 24, 6 places it
bet. Gilead and Sidon. Text may be corrupt and
these may be 2 places. Reading may be 'And they
came to Dan and Ijon' (*1 Kings* 15, 20).

Daric [dă'-rĭc]. *See* MONEY.

Darius [dă'-rĭus]. Three of the name are mentioned
in scripture: **1.** Darius the Mede, son of Ahasuerus (qv) who reigned over Babylon after its
capture by Cyrus (*Dan.* 5, 31; 6, 1 & 27; 9, 1).
Prob. he was acting only as regent for Cyrus
who was still busy on his work of conquest. He
is not the man who qualified for the title, 'Darius
the king.' **2.** The king of Persia 521-486 BC, and
son of Hystaspis. He is important for his connection with the Jews still in Babylon when it
was taken, and with his interest in their return
to their own land. Cyrus had given permission
to the repatriated Jews to rebuild the Temple.

Complaints came from neighbouring tribes who resented the return of the Jews, that there was no authority for this. After representations had been made by the Jews Darius ordered a search to be made for the missing charter, which was found at Achmetha (qv) Ecbatana (*Ezra* 6, 1-12). He attempted the invasion of the W, but his armies were defeated by the Gks. at Marathon in 490. **3.** The last of the Achaemenian kings of Persia, 336-330 BC. He crossed swords to his cost with Alexander the Great in 333 and 331, and was murdered by his own underlings. Poss. he is the Darius the Persian of *Neh.* 12, 22.

Darling. Lit. 'an only son,' but used by the Psalmist to describe his life, dear to himself (*Ps.* 22, 20; 35, 17 AV).

Date. *Phoenix dactylifera.* Trans. 'honey' in *2 Chron.* 31, 5.

Dathan [dā'-thăn]. A rebel agst. Moses' rule (*Num.* 16, 1-35; etc.).

Daughter. 1. The true fem. child (*Gen.* 30, 13; *Matt.* 9, 22; etc.). **2.** A fem. indigenous to a country or city (*Gen.* 24, 3; *Judg.* 21, 21; etc.). **3.** A fem. worshipper (*Isa.* 43, 6; *Mal.* 2, 11; etc.). **4.** The total citizenry of country or city (*Ps.* 9, 14; 137, 8; *Lam.* 4, 21; *Zech.* 2, 10).

David. The 2nd king of Israel. He was the youngest of the 8 sons of Jesse, of the tribe of Judah, settled in or nr. Bethlehem. Chosen as Saul's successor by Sam. (*1 Sam.* 16) he came into court circles and was appointed armour bearer to the king. He greatly distinguished himself by his courage and confidence agst. Goliath (*1 Sam.* 17). Saul grew jealous of David's popularity and David had to take to the hills for his life, where he became the leader of an outlaw band. Though given the chance to kill Saul, he refused to take it

(*1 Sam.* chs. 24 & 25 & 26). When Saul and his son Jonathan died in battle agst. the Philistines at Gilboa, David succeeded to the throne. His nomination was opposed by the 10 tribes of the N, known particularly as Israel, but they ultimately accepted him. In deference to their feelings, however, he moved his capital from Hebron to Jerusalem which was then an independent city not connected with any of the 12 tribes (*2 Sam.* 5). During his reign he was in a state of constant war with Philistines, Edomites, Moabites, Syrians and Ammonites, and was vexed in his declining years with a rebellion in favour of and inspired by his son Absalom (qv). Like all great men he could be guilty of the meanest of sins, and his affair with Bathsheba was something he suffered for sorely all his life. Nathan brought home to him the meanness of the crime agst. Uriah (*2 Sam.* 11, 1-27). His life's ambition was to build a temple, but the sense of his own guilt deterred him, and he died, an unhappy and frustrated man at the age of 71, naming Solomon, the 2nd son of Bathsheba (the 1st had died in infancy) to be his successor. As poet and singer he soared to the heights and sounded the depths of human experience, the necessary experience of the great poet. About 70 of the psalms are undoubtedly his, but he set a pattern of poetry which others followed to the enrichment of experience and praise.

David, City of. The title is sometimes used of Jerusalem, the stronghold of the Jebusites which David took and made his capital, thus satisfying both Israel and Judah, and sometimes of Bethlehem, his ancestral home, and poss. his birthplace (*Luke* 2, 4).

Day. The Heb. reckoned the day to stretch from

evening to evening (*Ex.* 12, 18; *Lev.* 23, 32). This convention was prob. due to dating from the phases of the moon. Before the captivity in Babylon, the days of the week were numbered, not named, except for the Sabbath (qv). The day itself was divided not into hours but into recognisable periods: sunrise, the heat of the day, the cool of the day, etc. During their stay in Babylon they adopted the Chaldean convention and divided the day into marked time periods, the 6th hour being mid-day (*John* 4, 6). The 9th hour was the time of prayer (*Acts* 3, 1). The word 'day' is used also to define an occasion, as the Day of Trouble (*Ps.* 20, 1); Day of Wrath (*Job* 20, 28); Day of the Lord (*Isa.* 2, 12). In NT it is used of the Second Coming of Christ (*1 Cor.* 5, 5; *2 Pet.* 3, 10; etc.).

Day of the Lord. The day of God's victory over the powers of evil, which were identified with Israel's enemies. It was not merely a prophetic phrase (*Amos* 5, 18) for Amos gave it a new meaning which included judgment upon Israel itself (*Amos* 5, 18-20; etc.). Later prophets used it to describe the day of doom and judgment—*dies irae, dies illa* (cf. *Ezek.* 30, 3; *Obad.* 15-17; *Isa.* 2, 12-21; *Joel* 2, 1 ff.). It is the day when God 'takes over' the world.

Day's journey. A completely indefinite indication of distance which depended entirely upon circumstances, unlike the Sabbath Day's journey (qv) which was definite.

Daysman. An arbiter, an umpire (*Job* 9, 33 AV).

Dayspring. Simply the dawn. The 'Dayspring from on high' is a poetical phrase for the Messiah from heaven (*Luke* 1, 78).

Daystar. *See* LUCIFER.

Deacon. Lit. servant; messenger (*Matt.* 20, 26).

Later, an official of a Christian congregation
(*1 Tim.* 3, 8; *Acts* 6, 1-6; *Philip.* 1, 1). Their
particular responsibility was matters of finance
and benevolence.

Deaconess. Certain women in the early church did
hold an office akin to that of deacon (*Rom.* 16,
1; *1 Tim.* 3, 11).

Dead Sea. The Salt Sea of (*Gen.* 14, 3; *Num.* 34,
12; etc.) known also as the Sea of the Arabah
or Plain (qv) (*Joel* 2, 20; etc.). It is part of the
Great Rift Valley which extends from the African
lakes to the Caspian and includes the Red Sea
and the Jordan gorge. The Jordan flows into it,
and it is about 50 m. long by 10 broad. There is
no outlet, with the result that the chlorides of
sodium, calcium and magnesium carried into it
by the Jordan and a few smaller streams are
highly concentrated by evaporation. The Dead
Sea is 4 times more salt than the oceans, and there
is almost no organic life in it (*Ezek.* 47, 6-12).

Deafness. *See* MEDICINE.

Deal. A share, a part (*Ex.* 29, 40 AV) cf. mod. 'a
great deal.'

Dearth. Shortage of food. *See* FAMINE.

Death. The earliest beliefs in death as a state of
being, and of the dead as being in some state of
existence vary considerably. To the Heb.
Sheol was the abode of the dead from which
spirits could be recalled to the world by necromancy. But the real belief was that the dead
were in a state of unconsciousness and silence
(*Ps.* 88, 12; 94, 17; 115, 17; etc.). The dead
have no communication with Jehovah, but since
it is absence from consciousness it is also absence
from worry, fear, suffering and wretchedness,
and as such can be desirable (*Job* 3, 17 ff.). A
new idea comes with the prophets who had

tremendous respect for the worth of human personality, and reckoned that something so worthwhile deserved something better than Sheol and its condition (*Jer.* 31; *Ezek.* 18). People who saw the hand of God in everything saw that death must have a divine as well as a human significance, a religious as well as a physical meaning (*Deut.* 30, 15; *Prov.* 15, 10; 14, 32). An entirely new conception of death and its meaning comes with Jesus. Note that He adds no information about the place of death, and none to information about the fact of death. He does not regard death as the enemy, or as being in itself evil. When He raises the dead it is not because He believes life to be better than death, but because he is moved by compassion for the bereaved. In John's Gospel it is obvious that the thing to be afraid of is not physical death, but spiritual death. Only the presence of sin makes death to be feared.

Deborah [dĕ´-bŏrăh]. **1.** The nurse of Rebekah, wife of Jacob (*Gen.* 24, 59). **2.** A prophetess, wife of Lappidoth. She was one of the Judges, and inspired Barak to fight and defeat Sisera (*Judg.* 4, 4-14; 5).

Debt. There is considerable legislation on the subject mainly for the protection of the debtor, the reason being that credit was not a business convention or practice, but simply the answer to the despair of the poor. Debt was always regarded as a misfortune (*Deut.* 28, 12 & 44). All 3 codes of the Law forbid usury (*Ex.* 22, 25; *Deut.* 23, 19; *Lev.* 25. 36-37) the reason being that this was taking advantage of the misfortunes of another. The nature of pledges was strictly controlled and provision was made for remission of indebtedness in the Year of Release which occurred every 7th year. This proviso appears only in one place (*Deut.* 15) and not in the other codes except in the case of persons enslaved for a pledge. There are many OT refs. which show that the laws agst. usury were continually flouted (*2 Kings* 4, 1-7; *Isa.* 50, 1; *Matt.* 18, 23; etc.). There must have been a considerable traffic in credit (*Ps.* 15, 5; *Prov.* 19, 7; 28, 8; *Isa.* 24, 2; *Jer.* 15, 10; *Matt.* 25, 27; *Luke* 16, 5; 19, 23).

Decalogue. See TEN COMMANDMENTS.

Decapolis [dĕ-căp'-ŏ-lĭs]. Territory at the mouth of the Jordan on the plain of Esdraelon, which was occupied by Gk. settlers after the campaigns of Alexander the Great. There were 10 cities (hence the name): Damascus, Dion, Gadara, Gerasa, Hippos, Kanatha, Pella, Philadelphia, Raphana and Scythopolis. Jesus visited Decapolis (*Matt.* 4, 25; *Mark* 5, 20; 7, 31).

Dedan [dē'-dăn]. These were people of Canaanite stock (*Gen.* 10, 7) who settled on the trade routes and were considerable merchants (*Ezek.* 27, 15 & 20; 38, 13; etc.).

Dedication, Feast of. After the Maccabean revolt agst. Antiochus Epiphanes (qv) the temple which he had desecrated was restored and purified. The day was remembered each yr. and became an annual festival, sometimes known as the Feast of Lights. It lasted 8 days, beginning on 25 Chislev (Dec.) (*John* 10, 22).

Deer. Prob. the roebuck (*Deut.* 14, 5; *1 Kings* 4, 23 AV only).

Defenced. AV only. Simply, provided with a fence.

Degrees. See ASCENTS.

Delilah [dĕ-lī'-läh]. A Philistine woman of Sorek who wiled Samson from his Nazirite vows (*Judg.* 16, 4-22).

Deluge. *See* FLOOD.

Demas [dē'-mas]. Assoc. with Paul (*Col.* 4, 14; *Philem.* 24). He later abandoned the cause (*2 Tim.* 4, 10).

Demetrius [dē-mē'-trĭ-ŭs]. King of Syria; called Soter, 162-150 BC, and his son and successor, called Nicator, 148-129. Father was a nephew of Antiochus Epiphanes (qv) who usurped the kingdom on his uncle's death. He was attacked, defeated and killed by Alexander Balas in 150 BC. The son in alliance with Egypt defeated Balas, and ascended the throne of Syria in 145. Balas' son, Antiochus claimed the throne and civil war ensued. Nicator, during an expedition into Persia, was taken and imprisoned for 10 yrs. On his release he regained the throne in 129 but was defeated in battle by another claimant, fled to Tyre and was assassinated. Two more of the name are mentioned in NT. He of *Acts* 19, 24-41 was a silversmith of Ephesus who made and sold models of the temple of Diana (qv). He stirred up a riot agst. the Christians who were threatening his livelihood. The other (*3 John* 12) was a highly respected member of the church.

Demon. Gk. *daimon*: an inferior dignitary. Sometimes a spirit watching over an individual's fortunes. The Scripture use of the word always implies evil. An evil genius, as Mephistopheles was to Faust (*Deut.* 32, 17; *Ps.* 106, 37; *Luke* 4, 33; 8, 29; 10, 17-20). *See* DEMONIAC.

Demoniac. One in the thrall of a demon: a ' possessed person ' (*Matt.* 4, 24). Many ailments, diseases and esp. functional disorders were attributed to such possession (*Mark* 9, 17-29; etc.). Epilepsy particularly was thus accounted for (*Mark* 1, 23 & 24). It was believed that the demons had some kind of spiritual reality, prob.

created by the person himself (*Matt.* 8, 31 ff.).

Derbe [děr´-bě]. A city of Asia Minor visited by Paul (*Acts* 14, 6 & 20; 16, 1; 20, 4).

Desert. *See* WILDERNESS.

Deuteronomy, Book of [dēū-těr-ŏ´-nŏmy]. Lit. ' The law repeated.' Scholars are far from agreed about authorship and date, but it is clear enough that the author is not Moses. It is a compilation, edited and arranged after the Exile, and is surely the Book of the Law discovered in the temple in the reign of Josiah (qv). The reforms carried out by Josiah were precisely those advocated in *Deut.*: nationalisation of religion and its centralisation at Jerusalem. What the authors have done is to put into the mouth of Moses a rehearsal of the Law in the form of a series of speeches delivered to Israel before entering the Promised Land. This literary device is common in the OT. But the situation to which *Deut.* speaks is more obviously post-Exile Judah than pre-Canaan Israel. The 1st sermon (1, 6—4, 40). The 2nd sermon (5—26). The 3rd sermon (26 & 27). These contain a restatement of the Mosaic law, written now to give it permanence. Then follows the Song of Moses (31) and the Book concludes with his valedictory and death. *Deut.* is a glorious book, the most quoted of all OT books in the NT. Jesus was steeped in its teaching, to which He went for the great commandment (*Deut.* 6, 4 f.; *Mark* 12, 29). In the Temptation He fortified himself by recalling it (*Deut.* 6, 13 & 16; 8, 3; *Matt.* 4, 4 & 7 & 10).

Devil. There is a distinction bet. the devil and demons and where AV uses ' devils ' it usually means ' demons ' (qv). Demons are evil spirits subject to the devil who is prob. Satan, Lord of the fallen spirits (*Rev.* 12, 9; *Matt.* 4, 8-11; etc.).

Satan fell through pride (*1 Tim.* 3, 6) and the sin he brought to Eden was self-sufficiency. Satan is constantly at work in the world, tireless in his efforts to uproot good and sow evil. He is not only the enemy of God, he is the enemy of man. He wins when he persuades humans that his ways are in their best interests. Scripture teaches that the Devil is the personification of evil, and the type and example of the confirmed, determined, deliberate evil doer who delights in it.

Dew. Used figuratively as the silent invisible refreshment of the soul (*Ps.* 110, 3; *Prov.* 19, 12; etc.).

Diadem. Prob. not a star or decoration but simply a headdress of the turban kind, esp. the royal or High Priestly headdress (*Job.* 29, 14; *Isa.* 62, 3; *Ezek.* 21, 26; etc.).

Dial. A sun dial (*2 Kings* 20, 11; *Isa.* 38, 8). These were in use in ancient Babylon to record time by the movement of the sun, but the ref. here to 'steps' seems to point to something different, like reading time by watching the progress of some shadow (of an obelisk or the like) upon a flight of steps.

Diamond. *See* JEWELS AND PRECIOUS STONES.

Diana [dī-ă′-nă]. The Rom. moon goddess, Gk. Artemis. But this is not the goddess of the Temple of Diana at Ephesus. She was the Asiatic Artemis, a different proposition altogether (*Acts* 19, 24 & 35). The western Artemis (Diana) was goddess of chastity, the Asiatic was goddess of fertility.

Didrachma [dī′-drăch′-mă]. *See* MONEY.

Diet. Prob. a ration, allowance (*Jer.* 52, 34 AV).

Didymus [dĭd′-ymŭs]. *See* THOMAS.

Dill. *See* ANISE.

Dinah [dī'-năh]. Daughter of Jacob and Leah (*Gen.* 30, 21) she was the cause of trouble bet. the sons of Jacob (except Joseph) and the Hivites (*Gen.* 34, 1-30; 49, 5-7).

Dinner. *See* FOOD, MEALS.

Dionysius [dī-ŏ-nў'-sĭŭs]. A member of the Areopagus (qv) converted after Paul's preaching (*Acts* 17, 34).

Diotrephes [dī-ŏt'-rĭ-phēs]. An unworthy member of the Church (*3 John* 9, 10).

Disallow. Disown (*1 Pet.* 2, 4 & 7 AV). Disapprove (*Num.* 30, 5 & 8 & 11 AV).

Disciple. Lit. ' pupil.' Commonly the follower of any religious teacher, esp. the 12 followers of Jesus.

Discover. Uncover (*Ps.* 29, 9 AV). Disclose (*Prov.* 25, 9 AV). Catch sight of (*Acts* 21, 3; 27, 39 AV).

Diseases. In Scripture these were regarded as being closely connected with sin, or at least traceable to some breach of the Law. Since physical and moral law were closely identified, this is no wonder. Disease was therefore a visitation, and often a punishment from God. Job argued vigorously agst. this idea (chs. 3-42). Jesus was not persuaded of the sin element in gen., though He did recognise the poss. of there being a direct connection bet. a particular disease and a particular way of life (*John* 9, 1-3; *Matt.* 9, 2). *See* MEDICINE, for specific diseases.

Dispersion. *Diaspora.* In the Mosaic Law, one of the penalties forecast for breach of the Law was the break up of the nation (*Lev.* 26, 14 & 33; *Deut.* 4, 27; 28, 64-68). This happened over a period of yrs. beginning with the captivities of Israel and Judah from which many Jews chose not to return. Then for many reasons, commercial, political and religious, thousands of Jews moved into the thriving cities of the empire of Alexander the Great, and later, of the Romans. They took Judaism with them and established synagogues in every city of importance in the known world. Gentiles were frequently converted to the Jewish faith, and it was these colonies of Jews and proselytes who formed the core of the early Christian church, and gave it a chance to move into all the world (*Acts* 2, 5-11; *1 Pet.* 1, 1; etc.). *See* ISRAEL, JUDAH.

Distaff. *See* SPINNING AND WEAVING.

Divination. Simply fortune telling, soothsaying. Sometimes the diviner went into a form of trance, real or pretended, or claimed to have mystic awareness of coming events (*Acts* 16, 16). More often they read natural processes and phenomena as signs and portents: the flight of birds, the appearance of the organs of slaughtered animals and birds, esp. the liver, the examination of water and of objects dropped into it, casting lots, star-gazing, and even spiritualism (*Gen.* 44, 5; *Num.* 22, 6; *1 Sam.* 28, 8; *Isa.* 47, 13; *Ezek.* 21, 21; etc.). *See* MAGIC.

Diviner. One who practised divination (*Deut.* 18, 9-12; *Isa.* 19, 3; etc.). Some were professionals (*Num.* 22, 7 & 17 & 18; *Acts* 16, 16). To consult diviners was forbidden by Mosaic Law but nevertheless practised (*Lev.* 19, 31; 20, 6; *1 Sam.* 28, 8; *Micah* 3, 6 & 7 & 11; etc.).

Divorce. For the man this was fairly easy under Mosaic Law. If dissatisfied with his wife on grounds of some indecency (widely interpreted) he could give her a bill of divorcement and put her away. Both were free to remarry (*Deut.* 24, 1-4; *Jer.* 3, 8). Jesus had strong views on divorce, stating that the only permissible grounds were fornication including adultery. If the wife were put away for any other reason, no matter what the Mosaic Law said, the man or woman would commit adultery if they married again, according to Jesus (*Matt.* 5, 31-32; 19, 3 & 9; *Mark* 10, 6-12). Paul subscribed to this view (*1 Cor.* 10-17). *See* MARRIAGE.

Doctors. Simply, the teachers, the rabbis (*Luke* 2, 46 AV; *Luke* 5, 17 AV; *Acts* 5, 34 AV). *See* EDUCATION.

Doctrine. Several Heb. and Gk. words so trans.: **1.** What is received; instruction '*Deut.* 32, 2; *Job* 11, 4; *Prov.* 4, 2; *Isa.* 29, 24). **2.** *logos:* the word, the reason rather than doctrine itself. **3.** *didache:* teaching. **4.** *didaskalia:* the content of the teaching, in a sense, doctrine. In the Pastoral epistles *didaskalia* is common but it is used only in a disparaging way, as something not worth teaching, outside these epistles (*Matt.* 15, 9; *Mark* 7, 7; *Eph.* 4, 14; *Colos.* 2, 22; except *Rom.* 12, 7; 15, 4). The word used of Jesus' teaching is always *didache.* These were truths, not just ideas or notions. The Christian doctrines were, of course, not drawn up until much later.

Doe. In *Prov.* (5, 19) prob. the wild goat.

Doeg [dō'-ĕg]. A bloodthirsty Edomite, herdsman to Saul (*1 Sam.* 21, 7) responsible for the massacre at Nob (*1 Sam.* 22, 7-23).

Dog. Mostly the pariah dog of the E (*Ex.* 22, 31; *1 Kings* 14, 11; etc.). They are and were filthy untamed brutes covered with fleas and sores. Shepherds trained dogs (*Job* 30, 1). They were known in houses (*Mark* 7, 28). They were unclean by law, and when the name was applied to a human, it was the grossest of insults (*1 Sam.* 17 43; *2 Kings* 8, 13; *Matt.* 7, 6; etc.).

Doleful creatures. RSV has 'howling creatures' (*Isa.* 13, 21), prob. jackals.

Door, Doorkeeper, Doorpost. *See* HOUSE, PRIESTS and LEVITES.

Dorcas [dôr′-căs]. Or Tabitha, a Christian woman of Joppa whose name has become synonymous with acts of charity towards the poor (*Acts* 9, 36-43).

Dove. Any of the *columbidae*, doves or pigeons: the wood pigeon, rock dove, ash humped dove. It is the type of harmlessness and helplessness (*Ps.* 74, 19; *Matt.* 10, 16). They were used for sacrifice (*Lev.* 5, 7; 12, 6; etc.).

Dove's dung. Eaten during the siege of Samaria, appears to be just what it implies (*2 Kings* 6, 25).

Dream. Even in the mod. world there is a pseudo-science of dream interpretation. In Scripture there is a sense of something more than a heavy supper causing dreams, and since God is the prime cause of everything, dreams must be a form of communication bet. God and man, conveying messages of encouragement or warning (*Judg.* 7, 13; *Matt.* 27, 19). Mosaic law, whilst accepting the divine orig. of dreams was not always ready to accept the dreamer's word that his dream had been as he revealed it (*Deut.* 13, 1-5). *See* VISION.

Dress. Orig. materials were animal skins (*Gen.* 3, 21) then came wool and flax (*Prov.* 31, 13). Linen (qv) would be imported from Egypt. Garments were woven, too, of goat and camel hair. Silk is mentioned (*Rev.* 18, 12) but the silk of (*Prov.* 31, 22; *Ezek.* 16, 10 AV) is prob. linen of high quality. The basic garment for men was the loin-cloth, worn much as it is worn in the ME today. AV refers to it as the girdle, but this is misleading and involves trans. 2 Heb. words by the same Eng. word. The girdle prob. was worn on top

of the clothes, but the other is a waistcloth or
loin-cloth worn next the skin as in RSV (*Job* 12,
18; *Isa*. 5, 27; 11, 5; *Jer*. 13, 1 ff.). The aprons
(*Acts* 19, 12) were short kilts worn mainly by
manual workers. When worn by priests they
were called ephods (*I Sam*. 2, 18). But the
Priestly Code insisted on priests wearing 'linen
breeches,' a kind of drawers, for the sake of
propriety (*Ezek*. 44, 18). Breeches of the more
mod. sort may have been worn (*Dan*. 3, 21 AV).
Hosen is the pl. of hose, but the meaning of the
orig. Aram. is obscure, and could be turban or
tunic. The common undergarment was the tunic,
usually rendered 'coat' in AV. Fitting fairly
close at neck and waist it reached to the ankles
and could be with or without sleeves. Joseph's
celebrated coat of many colours is really a long
garment with sleeves (*Gen*. 37, 3). The tunic could
be a sewn garment, or woven in one piece (*John*
19, 23). *See* SPINNING AND WEAVING. The true
girdle could be simply a rope (*Isa*. 3, 24) or something more elaborate (*Rev*. 1, 13). Usually it
was a long piece of cloth folded narrow and
wrapped tightly round the waist like a cummer-
bund, for support and protection. In it the sword
or the inkhorn might be thrust (*2 Sam*. 20, 8;
Ezek. 9, 3 & 11; *Matt*. 10, 9). Money was kept
in the folds. To 'gird up the loins' was to hitch
up the tunic by pulling it through the girdle till
it was knee length. The upper garment was the
cloak, which served also as a blanket. Note the
humanity of the Law which would not allow the
cloak, given as a pledge, to be retained after
sunset (*Ex*. 22, 26 ff.). It was variously called
garment, cloak, clothes, raiment. Jesus' bidding
to 'give the cloak also' (*Matt*. 5, 40) is really
to give what cannot be demanded by law. The

cloak was draped over the left shoulder and carried round the right arm, like the toga. The hanging corners were the skirts. People of high rank might wear an elaboration of the cloak, called by another word, and trans. 'robe' (*1 Sam.* 2, 19; *Ex.* 28, 31 ff.). The prophets seem to have favoured another variation of goat or camel hair (*Gen.* 25, 25; *Zech.* 13, 4; *Matt.* 3, 4; etc.). There was also a light linen upper garment trans. 'sheet,' having tassels (see FRINGES) on the corners (*Prov.* 31, 24; *Eccl.* 9, 8; *Matt.* 27, 59). The cloak placed on Jesus by the soldiers was the military cloak (*Matt.* 27, 28 & 31). Paul's was a travelling cape (*2 Tim.* 4, 13). Elaborate headdress was not common, a square of cloth held in place by a circlet of rope or twisted camel hair sufficing normally (*1 Kings* 20, 31 f.). Men of the upper class might wear a turban, their ladies, a hood. The hats (*Dan.* 3, 21) are either the conical Babylonian hats, or not hats at all but mantles. The napkin (*John* 11, 44) is the kerchief or head covering. Vail, or veil, might be like the garment still worn by Moslem women in purdah, or just the end of the cloak held across the face. In the home they went barefoot; outside they wore sandals or shoes. The sandal was a leather sole held in position by thongs or straps: the shoe latchets (*Gen.* 14, 23; *Mark* 1, 7). The ref. (*Isa.* 9, 5 RV marg.) may be a military boot. 'Changes of raiment' were not spare clothes, but festal garments (mod. slang 'glad rags.')

Drink. Normally water, milk or wine. See MEALS, WINE AND STRONG DRINK.

Drink offering. See OFFERING.

Dromedary. See CAMEL.

Drunkenness. See WINE AND STRONG DRINK.

Drusilla [drū-sĭl′-lă]. Daughter of Herod Agrippa I, born c. AD 38. She married Azizus, king of Emesa, who adopted the Jewish faith, but she left him for Felix (qv) becoming his 3rd wife while still in her teens. She was with him when Paul defended her faith (*Acts* 24, 24 & 25).

Dukes. Word found only in AV (*Gen.* 36, 15-21; etc.) and means simply, 'leaders' or 'chiefs.'

Dulcimer. Prob. the bagpipe (qv) (*Dan.* 3, 5 & 10 & 15). See MUSIC (INSTRUMENTS.)

Dumbness. *See* MEDICINE.

Dung. Was used as fertiliser and as fuel (*Ezek* 4, 12 & 15). The Law gives directions for personal and social hygiene (*Deut.* 23, 10-14). The word was often used to express contempt or disgust (*2 Kings* 9, 37; *Jer.* 9, 22) or worthlessness (*Philip.* 3, 8).

Dung gate. A gate of Jerusalem.

Dwarf. May simply be one emaciated by disease (*Lev.* 21, 20).

E

Eagle. 3 Heb. words are so trans. but prob. none is the true eagle: more likely to be vultures.

Ear. To give ear is to pay attention (*Isa.* 6, 10; *Matt.* 11, 15; *Rev.* 2, 7). The uncircumcised ear (*Jer.* 6, 10) is the unperceptive. The open ear (*Ps.* 40, 6) speaks of understanding. Slaves' ears were pierced (*Ex.* 21, 6; *Deut.* 15, 16 ff.). The priest's ear was consecrated (*Ex.* 29, 20; etc.).

Earing. 17th cent. word for ploughing (*Gen.* 45, 6 AV) (cf. *Deut.* 21, 4).

Earnest. Money in part payment to bind a bargain or secure an option. Fig. a pledge or promise of something to come (*2 Cor.* 1, 22; 5, 5; *Eph.* 1, 13 & 14).

Ear-ring. Worn more often by women but not confined to them (*Ex.* 32, 2; *Ezek.* 16, 12). Sometimes it was an amulet (*Isa.* 3, 20). Word may mean a nose stud or nose ring (*Gen.* 24, 22 & 30).

Earth. Place of man's habitation as distinct from heaven. Also the land as distinct from the sea. Also the productive soil, and, by metonymy, the inhabitants of the world (*Heb.* 2, 5).

Earthquake. There are several descriptions of earthquakes slight and severe (*Ps.* 18, 7; *Isa.* 6, 4; *Jer.* 4, 24; *Amos* 1, 1; *Zech.* 14, 4 & 5; *Matt.* 27, 45 & 51-54; 28, 2; *Acts* 16, 26). The walls of Jericho were prob. brought down by earthquake.

East. Lit. 'the front.' Heb. faced E when determining direction, as we face N. It was the direction of the sunrise. The first rays of the sun at the spring and autumn equinoxes shone through the E gate of the temple into the Holy of Holies. Used in phrases, eg, Children of the E, the E country, it means the territories and peoples on the Moab and Arabian borders (*Gen.* 25, 1-7; 29, 1 & 4; *Ezek.* 25, 4 & 10).

East (eastern) Sea. The Dead Sea (qv).

East wind. The drought-bringing desert wind (*Gen.* 41, 23 & 27; *Ezek.* 17, 7-10; 19, 10-12; *Hos.* 13, 15).

Easter. Not a scriptural term. Found only in (*Acts* 12, 4 AV) where it should be passover.

Ebedmelech [ĕ′-bĕd-mē′-lĕch]. Ethiopian eunuch who pulled Jeremiah up from the dungeon and prob. saved his life thereby. It may not be a proper name, but simply 'servant of the king' (*Jer.* 38, 7-13).

Ebenezer [ĕ-bĕn-ē′-zĕr]. Lit. Stone of Help, set up by Samuel nr. Mizpah to commemorate a battle (*1 Sam.* 7, 10 ; & 12).

Ecbatana [ĕc-bă′-tănă]. *See* ACHMETHA.

Ecclesiastes [ĕc-clēs′-ĭ-ăs′-tēs]. Has been called the Sphinx of Heb. lit. and there was some hesitation before it was admitted into the Heb. canon. It is never ref. to in NT. Although the authorship is ascribed to Solomon, mod. scholars place the date much later. The title means ' one who discourses in an assembly ' and has passed by way of LXX and Vulg. into ' The Preacher.' The date cannot be later than 200 BC, the date of the apocryphal book *Ecclesiasticus*, which presupposes its existence. It consists of a series of musings upon life in gen. and the search for absolute good; the conclusion being that it cannot be found under the sun. Man's chief end and duty is to fear God and obey Him. The much quoted ch. (12, 1-7) is a description of the physical break up of a man in old age.

Eden. Lit. ' delight; unalloyed pleasure.' The first abode of Adam and Eve; earthly paradise (*Gen.* 2, 8-25). It seems likely that it lay somewhere around the head of the Persian Gulf, an area which satisfies most of the rather vague geographical details given in Scripture. It is ref. to by several of the prophets (*Isa.* 51, 3; *Ezek.* 28, 13; 31, 9 & 16-18; 36, 35; *Joel* 2, 3). A Mesopotamian region of the same name is mentioned, but this is prob. Beth-Eden, and is not the garden (*2 Kings* 19, 12; *Isa.* 37, 12; *Ezek.* 27, 23 & 24).

Edom (Idumea) [ē′-dŏm, ĭ-dūm-ē′-ä]. It is a name of Esau, and, through him, of a race of people, the Edomites, and their land, known orig. as Seir. This was a hilly country of red sandstone, and was less fertile than Canaan. Important towns were Bozrah, Teman and Sela (later Petra). The Gks. knew Edom as Idumaea. The wilderness of Edom (*2 Kings* 3, 8 & 20) is the Arabah. Edomites were recognised by the Israelites as being of the same stock (*Deut*. 23, 7 & 8) but there was little love lost bet. them (*Num*. 20, 14-21) and there was even active hostility (*I Sam*. 14, 47; *Ezek*. 35, 5 & 6; etc.). The Herods were of Edomite stock.

Education. This was markedly religious among the Heb.; the fear of the Lord was the beginning of wisdom (*Prov*. 1, 7). The script used in early records and correspondence was Babylonian cuneiform, at the time of the settlement of Canaan and it is unlikely that very many were able to read or write it; but as the Heb. language took shape and the script developed, education advanced. There were no schools as we understand them to-day; the word in its mod. sense occurs only once (*Acts* 19 9), as does schoolmaster (*Gal*. 3, 24 & 25). Schools of prophets were like schools of philosophy, or schools of thought. Children were taught at home (*Deut*. 6, 20-25; etc.), and the emphasis was on the traditions and faith of the nation. After the Exile, the Book of the Law became the text book of education (*Neh*. 8, 1 ff.). The synagogues were created, which were places for teaching rather than for worship, and a kind of communal instruction in classes began to operate. Note the recurrence of ' teach ' and ' teacher ' (cf. *Matt*. 4, 23; *Mark* 1, 21). As Wellhausen has said: ' the Bible became the spelling book, the community a school.' The orig. teachers were the scribes (qv) (*Ezra* 7, 6). Under Gk. influence more secular schools began to appear c. 250 BC (cf. *Eccl*. 12, 12). Bet. 160 BC and AD 70 elementary schools were established in towns and villages, children enrolling at 6 yrs. The teachers were the doctors of the law (*Luke* 5, 17). Reading was taught from the Scriptures. The scholars sat on the floor round the master (*Acts* 22, 3) learning by rote, reading, writing and arithmetic. Girls did not attend these schools but were taught at home. Bright boys could go on to college.

Egg. *See* FOOD.

Eglon [ĕg´-lŏn]. King of Moab who occupied Jericho (*Judg.* 3, 12-30). Also a town taken over by Judah (*Josh.* 15, 39).

Egypt. The Egypt of scripture is the Nile basin from the Mediterranean to the 1st cataract, with a few scattered oases. Upper Egypt was the valley of the Nile and Lower Egypt was the delta. The whole made some 13,000 sq. m. of most fertile soil, and was a strip 550 m. long and as broad as the overflow of the river and irrigation ditches could reach. Around it was uncompromising desert. Under various dynasties the Egyptians pushed their territory further up the river as far as the 4th cataract. Orig. known as Cushites (*Gen.* 10, 6) there were so many invasions and infiltrations that the stock became very mixed. They had a written hist. extending over 5,000 yrs. The main scriptural interest is, of course, in Egypt's connections with the Heb. people. Abraham had been there for a while, but it was not till the time of Joseph during the Middle Empire of 2150-1580, and which included the Hyksos dynasty (1730-1580) that there was a real Heb. settlement in Egypt (*Gen.* 45, 9-11; 46, 8-25; 47, 4 & 29 & 30; 48, 21). They settled in Goshen and remained there for the best part of 400 yrs. until the Exodus (*Ex.* 8, 22; etc.). The Hyksos (shepherd) kings of Egypt were of Semitic stock, like the Heb., and had conquered Egypt. The oppressions began when the Hyksos were driven out by Rameses II. Merenptah was poss. the Pharaoh of the Exodus in the 13th cent. BC, but there is no certainty. *See* NILE, EXODUS, JOSEPH, MOSES, etc.

Egyptian, the. One of the assassins for whom Paul was mistaken by Lysias (*Acts* 21, 38).

Ehud [ē´-hŭd]. One of the judges, who slew Eglon of Moab. (*Judg.* 3, 12-20).

Ekron [ĕk´rŏn]. One of the 5 great Philistine cities, centre of much fighting for centuries.

Elam [ē´-lăm]. Country on he E of the lower Tigris whose capital was Shushan, or Susa, the heart of a great empire (*Gen.* 14, 1 f.). This would be around 2300 BC, but it faded after Hammurabi (qv) had freed Babylon from the Elamites (*Gen.* 14). With the threat of the rise of Assyria, Elam and Babylonia came together again to resist the danger in the 8th and 7th cents. Susa fell in c. 645 BC. Later the country and its capital came under the domination of Persia (*Isa.* 21, 2 ff.; *Jer.* 49, 34 ff.). The Elamites tried to interfere with the rebuilding of the Temple (*Ezra* 4, 9). In AD 1901-1902 the famous Code of Hammurabi was found at Susa.

Eldad [ĕl´-dăd]. One of Moses' 70 elders who, with Medad, was absent when the Holy Spirit came down upon ᴠhe others, assembled with Moses (*Num.* 11, 26-29).

Elder. In OT was firstly the hereditary head of a household, the oldest son succeeding the deceased father. It was an office which depended on respect rather than on statutory authority. In Moses' day, elders were chosen by himself, and he established government by aristocracy After the settlement the system continued in the towns and villages. They now had legal sanction and authority; they administered the Law. During the Exile they held the nation together and later prob. formed the nucleus of the Sanhedrin(qv) There

are many refs., a few representative ones being
(*Ex.* 3, 16 & 18; 24, 1; *Num.* 22, 4; *Deut.* 16,
18; *1 Sam.* 4, 3; 8, 4; *Ezra* 10, 8; *Jer.* 29, 1;
Amos 2, 3). In NT the elder became an official
of the early Christian church. Elder, Bishop,
and Presbyter were prob. interchangeable terms
(*Acts* 20, 17 & 28; *Titus* 1, 5 & 7). They may
not have meant exactly the same, however. It
was not till the 2nd cent. that 2 orders emerged:
elder or presbyter on the one hand, and bishop
on the other. Paul left new elders behind him
as he travelled (*Acts* 14, 23) but they were working
everywhere (*Jas.* 5, 14; *1 Pet.* 5, 1). Bishops and
elders worked together in the same local churches
(*Acts* 11, 30; 20, 17 & 28; *1 Tim.* 3, 4 & 5; 5,
17; *Titus* 1, 9; *Jas.* 5, 14; *1 Pet.* 5, 1-4). They
appear also in the Apocalypse. *See* BISHOP.

Eleazar [ĕl'-ĕa'-zăr]. There are several of the name,
the most notable being the following: **1.** 3rd son
of Aaron, consecrated priest and head of the
Levites. He succeeded his father as High Priest.
He played an important part in the settlement
and was in turn succeeded in office by his son
Phineas (*Ex.* 6, 23; 28, 1; *Num.* 3, 2 & 32; 20,
25-28; *Josh.* 14, 1; 17, 4; 19, 51; 21, 1). **2.**
Son of Abinadab, made keeper of the Ark (*1
Sam.* 7, 1).

Elect, Election. The choice of one or a few out of
many. In this context it is always election of
man or men by God. It is characterised by a
call. Of all mankind, Abraham is elected (*Gen.*
12, 2). Isaac, not Ishmael; Jacob, not Esau. Israel from all nations (*Isa.* ch. 41-49). The reason
is God's good purpose for the world, and the
whole process culminates in Jesus. Scripture
insists that God does not merely choose from
the available material but deliberately creates

his elect at the time of need (*Isa.* 45, 5; *Jer.* 1, 5; *Gal.* 1, 15). In NT the idea changes. The OT conception started with the choice of Israel and then concentrated gradually on an individual. NT starts with the individual. These elect individuals come together to form the church. In OT, the nation and then the individual were elected to fulfil God's eternal purpose. In NT they are elected to salvation for their own sakes. This does not cancel such statements as the elect being the light of the world (*Matt.* 5, 13-16), or that they are to be workers together with God (*I Cor.* 3, 9) or that they are to be living epistles (*2 Cor.* 3, 2 & 3). Paul believed that the prime purpose of election was to select those who would tell it out among the heathen (*Acts* 9, 15).

Elect lady. The address of the *2 Epistle of John.* Some think this is an individual woman of Ephesus and her family; others regard it as the personification of a church. Prob. the obvious answer is right and it is a woman whose name is now lost.

Elephant. The hippopotamus (*Job* 40, 15 AV).

Elhanan [ĕl-hăn′-ăn]. The son of Jair, who slew Lahmi, the brother of Goliath (*1 Chron.* 20, 5). He is also credited with the death of Goliath (*2 Sam.* 21, 19). This is due to corrupt text.

Eli [ē′-lī]. The very weak judge and High Priest who preceded Samuel. The more we read about him the more clear becomes the need for Sam. Scripture says he died of a broken neck (4, 1-18) but he really died of a broken heart.

Eli, Eli, Lama Sabachthani [ē′-lī, ē′-lī, lă′-mă-să′-băch-thă′-nī]. The words of Jesus from the cross (*Matt.* 27, 46; cf. *Ps.* 22, 1). The word is also given as *eloi* (*Mark* 15, 34). The Aram. in which the words were spoken would be *elahi*. *Eli* is Heb. and *eloi* is an Eng. transliteration from Gk. The meaning is the same: My God, my God, why hast Thou forsaken me?

Eliab [ĕ-lī'-ăb]. Common male name. Most prominent is David's eldest brother (*1 Sam.* 16, 6 & 7; 17, 13).

Elias [ĕlī'-ăs]. *See* ELIJAH.

Elihu [ĕlī'-hū]. Several of the name; the best known being one of Job's ' comforters.'

Elijah [ĕlī'-jăh]. Elias is the Gk. form of the name. He appears in the reign of Ahab (876-854 BC) and disappears during the reign of Ahaziah (854-853). A man of Gilead (*1 Kings* 17, 1), he presented a pretty grim picture when he stepped on to the stage (*2 Kings* 1, 8). His name means ' Jehovah is God ' and that was the substance of his preaching and activity. Ahab (qv) had married the Phoenician Jezebel (qv) and had fallen into the congenial worship of Baal (*1 Kings* 16, 32). Jehovah's champion was Elijah, who begins with a grim warning of impending drought (17, 3). The drought does come and Elijah suffers with the rest from the famine, though he shared the ravens' food and was treated kindly by a poor widow of Zarephath (*1 Kings* 17, 9 ff). *See* RAVEN. Choosing the moment when the people were desperate, he challenged the priests of Baal, using Obadiah the king's chief steward as his intermediary. He encounters the king and treats him brusquely. He heaps scorn upon the priests. He calls them all to Carmel, and prays to God for a sign. Lightning strikes the sacrifice that the priests had been unable to kindle. The people cry, ' Jehovah, He is God.' Elijah calls for the blood of the priests and they are massacred at Kishon (18, 1-40).

Elijah affirms his loyalty to Ahab as the Lord's anointed (18, 41-46) but Jezebel's hatred is implacable. Elijah is scared, and runs for his life, completely dispirited. Courage returns at Horeb (19, 1-8) and he hears the still, small voice. (Heb. lit. 'a sound of gentle stillness.') He sees that Ahab and Jezebel must be driven off the throne. Hazael is to be anointed king of Syria to be the scourge of idolatrous Israel. Jehu is to succeed to the throne of Israel, and Elisha is to be set apart to continue the work he himself has begun. He realises that he is not alone, as he had feared, but that God never leaves Himself without witnesses. The kings are anointed, though not by Elijah himself, and he remains for a while in the desert nr. Damascus. He next appears when Jezebel fabricates a charge agst. Naboth, in order to secure his vineyard for Ahab (ch. 21). He challenges Ahab, denounces him, and foretells his gory end. At last he disappears from Elisha's sight in a ' chariot of fire.' Elijah is a tremendous character who gave to Heb. prophecy its direction and function. In later yrs. no one was more revered than Elijah, and the people believed that he would come again (*Mal.* 4, 5 & 6). Many reckoned John the Baptist to be the re-incarnation of Elijah (*Matt.* 11, 10 ff.). He was to be the herald of the Messiah. Other Elijah's of little moment appear (*1 Chron.* 8, 27; *Ezra* 10, 21).

Elim [ē'-lĭm]. An oasis, the 3rd halt of marching Israel after crossing the Red Sea (*Ex.* 15, 27; *Num.* 33, 9).

Elimelech [ĕlĭm'-ĕlĕch]. Husband of Naomi and father-in-law of Ruth (*Ruth.* 2, 1 & 3).

Eliphaz [ĕ'-lĭ-phăz]. **1.** Son of Esau (*Gen.* 36, 4). **2.** One of Job's ' comforters.'

Elisabeth. Wife of the priest Zacharias (qv) and

mother of John the Baptist. She was a kins-woman to Mary (*Luke* 1, 5-45).

Elisha [ĕ-lī'-shă]. Son of a comfortable farmer of Abel-mehola in the Jordan valley. He was ploughing when Elijah chose him by casting his mantle over him. He responded and followed the prophet (*I Kings* 19, 16 & 19; *2 Kings* 3, 11). He became leader of the Sons of the Prophets (*see* PROPHECY) and his work appears to have stretched over some 50 yrs. (855-798) during the reigns of Jehoram, Jehu, Jehoahaz, and Joash of Israel (*2 Kings* 3, 1 ff.). In disposition he was different from Elijah, more diplomatic and tactful in his dealings with people and problems. He preferred society to solitude, and the town to the desert. Many miracles are credited to Elisha (*see* MIRACLES). He anointed Jehu king, on the instruction of Elijah, and so spelled the doom of Ahab's house. His influence in Israel and Syria was enormous, and he was given credit for tri-umphs and disasters alike. *See* ISRAEL.

Elishah [ĕ-lī'-shăh]. Race of people, 'sons' of Javan (*Gen.* 10, 4) who were manufacturers of the Tyrian dye, a purple much in demand, which was extracted from shellfish.

Elkanah [ĕl-kă'-năh]. There are several of the name, the most prominent being the husband of Hannah and father of Samuel (*I Sam.* 1, 1; 2, 11 & 20).

Elm. *Pistacia terebinthus*, the turpentine tree (*Hos.* 4, 13 AV) trans. ' oak ' (*Gen.* 35, 4; *Judg.* 6, 11 & 19).

Eloi. *See* ELI, ELI.

Elon [ē'-lŏn]. A judge. (*Judg.* 12, 11 & 13).

Elymas [ĕl'-ў-măs]. A charlatan calling himself Bar-Jesus encountered by Paul in the Cyprus town of Paphos. He tried to dissuade the Rom.

deputy Sergius Paulus from listening to Paul.
His discomfiture by the apostle confirmed the
Roman's judgment (*Acts* 13, 6-12).

Embalm, embalming. Only the bodies of Jacob and
Joseph were dealt with in this conventional
Egyptian way (*Gen.* 50, 2 f. & 26).

Embroidery. Needlework. Lat. *acu pingere:* ' to
paint with a needle.' Both ' embroidery ' and
' needlework ' are used to trans. single Heb. word
(*Judg.* 5, 30; *Ps.* 45, 14). The 1st of these (AV)
should be ' a piece or two of embroidery.' The
same word is trans. ' embroidered work ' (*Ezek.*
16, 10; etc.). A different word is used in other
places and trans. ' embroider,' which might be
better ' weave ' (*Ex.* 28, 39). RV and RSV have
' chequer work ' for AV embroidery (*Ex.* 28, 4).
The threads and the process are described (*Ex.*
39. 3). See SPINNING AND WEAVING.

Emerald. See JEWELS AND PRECIOUS STONES.

Emerods. Haemorrhoids (*Deut.* 28, 27; etc.). See
MEDICINE.

Emim [ē'-mĭm]. People of great height, inhabiting
part of Moab (*Deut.* 2, 10 f.).

Emmanuel. See IMMANUEL.

Emmaus [ĕm-māē'-ŭs]. **Emmaus** AV. Village 60
furlongs from Jerusalem (*Luke* 24, 13).

Encampment by the Sea. Camp site used by marching Israel after they left Elim (qv). Prob. on
shore of Gulf of Suez (*Num.* 33, 10).

Enchantment. See MAGIC AND SORCERY.

Endor [ĕn'-dŏr]. Town 6 m. SE of Nazareth (*Josh.*
17, 11). Here king Saul consulted with a 'medium'
or witch before the battle of Gilboa (*1 Sam.* 28).
It was also the scene of the rout and annihilation
of Sisera and Jabin (*Ps.* 83, 10).

Engedi [ĕn-gē'-dī]. On the W shore of the Dead Sea
formerly called Hazazon-Tamar (*Gen.* 14, 7; 2

Chron. 20, 2). David hid here for a while (*1 Sam.*
23, 29; 24, 1). Jehoshaphat fought the Moabites
and Ammonites in and around Engedi (*2 Chron.*
20, 2).

Engines. *See* FORTIFICATION AND SIEGE (*2 Chron.*
26, 15; *Ezek.* 26, 9 AV).

Enoch [ē'-nŏch]. 7th in line from Adam (*Gen.* 5,
18-24; *Jude* 14). He became a legendary figure
in Apocalyptic literature, as preacher, teacher
and prophet. AV suggests no more than that
he was a man of great and noble character (5,
24).

Enos [ē'-nos] **(Enosh).** Son of Seth (*Gen.* 4, 26; 5,
6-11; etc.).

Enrogel [ĕn-rō'-gĕl]. A well outside Jerusalem
identified with both the Virgin's Well (qv) and
Job's Well (qv). It was in the Kidron Valley.
During the Absalom rebellion David's spies were
posted here (*2 Sam.* 17, 17).

Ensample. AV. Simply example.

Envy. Gen. regarded as the direct antithesis of
Christian love. All through Scripture the outcome of envy is shown as something evil, bringing
disaster (cf. Cain and Abel; Jacob and Esau;
Rachel and Leah; Joseph and his brothers;
Saul and David; the Prodigal son and the elder
brother).

Epaenetus [ĕp-āē'-nĕtŭs]. One of the 1st Asian
converts, greatly beloved by Paul (*Rom.* 16, 5).

Epaphras [ē-pă'-phrăs]. A native or resident of
Colossae, he established a church there (*Colos.*
1, 7; 4, 12). It is poss. that he brought the faith
to Laodicea and Hierapolis (4, 13). When Paul
was 1st imprisoned in Rome Epaphras brought
him news of the church at Colossae and may have
asked for guidance in dealing with the heresies
which were vexing that church. Paul then wrote

the letter to the Colossians and Epaphras took it back with him.

Epaphroditus [ĕpăph'-rō-dī'-tŭs]. He, too, was in Rome during Paul's 1st imprisonment (*Philip*. 2, 25-30; 4, 18), having come from Philippi with supplies and money to ease Paul's condition. He became involved in the work at Rome and laboured so hard that he had a breakdown. This was a great grief to Paul and to Epaphroditus' friends at home, and Paul persuaded him to return to Philippi in all probability bearing with him the epistle to the Philippians.

Ephah [ĕ'-phăh]. *See* WEIGHTS AND MEASURES.

Ephes Dammim [ĕ'-phĕs-dăm'-mĭm]. Encampment of the Philistines when David slew Goliath (*1 Sam*. 17, 1). Also called Pas-dammim (*1 Chron*. 11, 13).

Ephesians, Epistle of Paul the Apostle to the. First of the epistles of the captivity, written in Rome bet. AD 61 and 63. Although addressed to the saints at Ephesus, 2 of the best texts (Sinaiticus and Vaticanus) omit this greeting, indicating that it may have been for gen. distribution and circulation. Further evidence that this may be so is the fact that there are no particular and personal greetings to friends at Ephesus, and no discussion of matters appropriate only to the church at Ephesus. Marcian (AD 140) actually calls it the Epistle to the Laodiceans. Paul had spent a long time in Ephesus and it is rather remarkable, if the letter was meant for them alone, that he does not refer to his stay. Many commentators reckon that the address was left blank for Tychicus, who was delivering several copies of it, to fill in as he delivered each. If so, and it is a circular letter, it is prob. the one referred to (*Col*. 4, 16). There is much internal evidence that it was written at the same time as *Colossians* but whereas the emphasis of *Col.* is on the pre-eminence of Christ, the emphasis in *Eph.* is on the Church catholic, or universal, as the fulfil-ment of the eternal purpose of God. It is the body and Christ is the head. The accent is always upon unity, and that is not to be wondered at, for the churches of Asia were multi-racial to a high degree. In prison Paul must have been thinking deeply of the success of the apostolic work and of the certainty now of the establish-ment of the church of his dreams. He saw also the degrees of separateness, esp. bet. W and E. It is worth noting that this letter to the E was written when he was in the W and that the letter to the W (Romans) was written while he was in the E (at Corinth).

Ephesus [ĕph'-ĕsŭs]. An ancient city of Asia stand-ing at the mouth of the R. Cayster, bet. Miletus and Smyrna. Its foundation was Gk. c. 1000 BC, but it was successively in the domain of Lydia, Persia, Macedonia (Alexander) and Rome, when it became the seat of government for the Rom. prov. of Asia (qv). The temple to Diana (qv) was one of the 7 wonders of the ancient world. There were settlements of Jews in Ephesus long before the Christian era, and they had their synagogue (*Acts* 18, 19; 19, 17). Paul's 1st visit was on his 2nd missionary journey with Aquila and Priscilla (*Acts* 18, 18-21). His next stay lasted more than 2 yrs., and to support himself he worked at his trade of tentmaker. After the riot, stirred up by Demetrius the silversmith (qv), who was incensed at the threat to his trade in models of the temple and statue, he left the city and Timothy took over (*1 Tim.* 1, 3). That was his last visit, though he did meet the elders of the

Ephesian church in conference at Miletus (*Acts* 20, 16 & 17). He wrote the letter (qv) from Rome.

Ephod [ē′-phŏd]. A linen ' waistcoat ' worn by by priests, but notably by the High Priest (qv).

Ephphatha [ĕph′-phā-thă]. Aram. lit. ' be opened ' (*Mark* 7, 34).

Ephraim [ĕph′-rā-ĭm]. Grandson of Jacob and 2nd son of Joseph by Asenath. His elder brother was Manasseh (*Gen.* 41, 50 ff.). They were, of course, born in Egypt, but Jacob adopted them into the clan, and in spite of protests by Joseph, conferred the birthright upon Ephraim not Manasseh (*Gen.* 48, 14 ff.). Ephraim (now used as a tribal name) became the most powerful of the 12 and received the choicest land at the settlement of Canaan. Joshua himself was an Ephraimite, which may explain it. The 1st king of Israel (the N kingdom after the separation from Judah) was an Ephraimite, Jeroboam. Eli and Sam. were 2 more notable tribesmen, and the most important cities of the N kingdom, Shechem, Tirzah and Samaria were in Ephraim's territory. The tribe dominated the hist. of independent Israel until the fall of Samaria.

Ephraim Gate. A gate of Jerusalem.

Epicureans [ē′-pĭcū-rē′-ăns]. A school of philosophy founded by Epicurus 341-270 BC. He was born in Samos, though his parents were Athenians orig. and to Athens he returned when about 36 yrs. old to found a school of philosophy in his garden. He divided philosophy into 3 parts: Canonics (logic, the theory of knowledge), Physics and Ethics. Judgment by the experience of the senses was the only warrant of opinion (ie, a thing is not hot unless it feels hot). His theory of physics was atomic. All bodies are formed by the combination of infinite numbers

of atoms in infinite space. There is a soul, but
it is a substance, composed, too, of atoms. There
are gods, composed of the finest quality atoms
only with no adulteration; but the gods are
quite detached from the world of men and not
at all interested in it. At death the atoms of the
body go back into their orig. state and the atoms
of the soul are dispersed, never to assemble again.
The image of an object passes through the air to
the eye of the beholder. In ethics he counts
pleasure to be the highest good, and the only
happiness. There are degrees of pleasure, none
of them bad, but rest, freedom from pain and
discomfort—tranquillity, is best. The mod. word
Epicureanism has come to mean self-indulgence,
esp. in food and drink. True Epicureanism was
a far nobler idea than that. Paul encountered
some of them in Athens along with the Stoics
(qv) (*Acts* 17, 15-34).

Epilepsy, Epileptic. *See* DISEASES, MEDICINE.

Erastus [ē-răs'-tŭs]. Name occurs three times,
but quite poss. it is only 1 man. He sends greetings to the Rom. church (*Rom.* 16, 23) and is described as treasurer (AV Chamberlain) of Corinth.
He is sent by Paul from Ephesus to Macedonia
(*Acts* 19, 22) and later he is found again at Corinth
(*2 Tim.* 4, 20).

Erech [ē'-rĕch]. An ancient city founded by Nimrod
(*Gen.* 10, 10).

Esaias [ĕs-aī'-ăs]. NT spelling of Isaiah (qv).

Esarhaddon [ĕ'-sär-hăd'-dŏn]. Son, but not heir
of Sennacherib of Assyria (qv). His 2 older
brothers, incensed at the father's partiality to him,
killed Sennacherib 681 BC (*2 Kings* 19, 36 & 37).
Civil war broke out, and winning it, Esarhaddon
ascended the throne. He was a great king and
soldier, conquering in turn Sidon, Judah, Edom,

Moab, Ammon, Gaza, Ashkelon, Ekron and Ashdod. He ruled both Assyria and Babylonia (*Isa.* 37, 37-38; *Ezra* 4, 2).

Esau [ē'-saū]. Sometimes known as Edom. The name means shaggy, and ruddy. He is the ancestor of the Edomites (*Gen.* 36, 9 & 43; *Jer.* 49, 8 ff.) and was the son of Isaac, twin brother of Jacob. He and his brother had nothing else in common (*Gen.* 25, 22; *Hos.* 12, 3). The incident of the sale of the birthright (qv) is well known (*Gen.* 25, 29 ff.). He was a man who lived in and for the moment and held nothing sacred. He married outside the clan, two Hittite women (*Gen.* 26, 34 & 35) then married one of his own people (28, 8 & 9). He was cheated out of his birthright; apparently changed his mind about its value when inheriting it seemed closer (27, 41) and he determined to kill Jacob. His brother avoided him, however, for 20 yrs. until they were reconciled (33, 4). He then settled down at Seir (35, 29; etc.).

Eschew. Used only in AV (*Job* 1, 1 & 8; 2, 3; *1 Pet.* 3 11). It means simply 'to turn away from.'

Esdraelon [ĕs'-drä-ē'-lŏn]. Gk. corruption of Jezreel (qv). The valley of Jezreel or the great plain to the N of the Carmel range was the cockpit of Palestine. Deborah and Barak fought Sisera here (*Judg.* 4). Saul fought the Philistines (*1 (Sam.* ch. 28-31). Josiah was slain in battle (*2 Kings* 23, 30).

Esdras [ĕs'-dräs]. *See* APOCRYPHA.

Eshcol [ĕsh'-cŏl]. **1.** An Amorite ally of Abraham (*Gen.* 14, 23 & 24) living nr. Hebron (*Gen.* 13, 18). **2.** A valley nr. Hebron, poss. named after above (*Num.* 13, 23 & 24; *Deut.* 1, 24).

Eshtaol [ĕsh'-tă-ŏl]. City of Judah (*Josh.* 15, 33)

allotted to Dan (*Josh.* 19, 40-41). Samson was
buried nearby (*Judg.* 16, 31).

Essenes [ĕss'-ēnes]. An odd monastic order which
rose in Judea about the time of the Maccabean
wars, and which persisted till the 3rd cent. AD.
Its origins are obscure but it may have sprung
from an intense desire to recapture the purity
and piety of the pre-temple times of Moses. They
held the Gk. idea of the immortality of the soul,
though not of the resurrection of the body. They
prayed facing the sun (as the Parsees), not facing
Jerusalem and the temple. They believed in
absolute predestination. They led a most austere
life, keeping strictly to the letter of the Mosaic
law. Finding it difficult to pursue their ways in
society, they withdrew into communities where
everything was held in common, and where they
supported the community by their daily labour.
They suffered grievously at the hands of the Romans, mainly for their refusal to co-operate. Unfortunately, if inevitably, they were fairly guilty
of spiritual pride, and later became tainted with
the Gnostic idea of the essential evil of matter.
The Herods favoured them. but orthodox Jews
hated them.

Estate. In AV usually means the same as the alternative word 'state' or 'condition' (*Col.* 4, 7).
There is another meaning, however, (*Acts* 22, 5)
more like, say, 'The Three Estates,' ie, people
of a particular sort in council assembled.

Esther [ĕs'-thĕr]. Heroine of the book of the same
name. This is a Pers. form of the Heb. proper
name, Hadassah. She was daughter of Abihail,
but, left an orphan, was reared by her cousin
Mordecai in Shushan. Her singular beauty
attracted the king, and she was taken into the
palace, succeeding Vashti as queen when she was

put away. Xerxes did not know that she was a
Jewess. Haman, a favourite at court, hated
Mordecai, and envied his growing influence. He
persuaded Xerxes to authorise a massacre of the
Jews. Mordecai inspired Esther to risk her life
by revealing her nationality to the king. Impressed by her courage he rescinded the order
and Haman was hanged. Mordecai was raised
to a position of honour and the Jews were allowed
to avenge themselves on the guilty Persians. Two
decrees were issued by Esther and Mordecai:
that there should be an annual feast of rejoicing
on the 14th and 15th days of the month of Adar;
and that there should be an annual day of mourning to recall the orig. decree. For historicity,
see article below.

Esther, Book of. There were many objections to
the inclusion of Esther in the canon of the OT,
both by Jewish and by Christian authorities.
Finally the Jewish authorities admitted it among
the Hagiographa. The name of God is never
mentioned in *Esther*. Athanasius regarded it as
uncanonical (AD 373). And so did others of the
Fathers. Luther would have none of it. The date
of authorship is undoubtedly late: certainly not
earlier than 300 BC. On the face of it, this is the
hist. of the orig. of the Jewish feast of the Purim,
but not many scholars will agree that the account
is genuine. It could be Babylonian, the struggle
being bet. the Babylonian and the Elamite gods,
with the victory going to the Babylonian. Esther
is the Babylonian goddess Ishtar, whose cousin
was Marduk (Mordecai). Haman is Humban,
god of the Elamites, whose capital was, of course,
Shushan, or Susa. Haman's wife, Zeresh, is the
goddess Kirisha. Vashti also was an Elamite
goddess. But this does not explain Purim, unless

it was orig. a Babylonian feast of celebration of victory over Elam. There is, however, nothing to support it.

Ethanim [ĕ'-thăn-ĭm]. The 7th month of the Heb. calendar; 3 great celebrations fell in the month: the Feast of Trumpets; the Day of Atonement; and the Feast of Tabernacles. *See* TIME.

Ethiopia [ē'-thĭ-ō'-pĭä]. The Lat. name for a territory known to the Heb. as Cush. It is the land N of the 1st cataract of the Nile (Nubia). A fairly barren land, and thinly populated: the mod. Sudan. At first a province of Egypt, it attained independence as Egypt declined, with Napata as its capital. Ethiopian kings are first heard of c. 730 BC. The territory came into the Pers. domain, but was independent after that till invaded by the Romans in 24 BC. They destroyed the capital in retaliation for an attack upon Egypt. There are several refs. (cf. *Ps.* 68, 31; *Acts* 8, 26-42).

Ethiopian Eunuch. Shortly after the martyrdom of Stephen, Philip met this man on the road. He was an important minister of Candace, queen of Ethiopia. Luke may have heard of the incident from Philip himself. This was an important day for the mission to the world (*Acts* 8, 26-40).

Ethiopian woman. Moses' connection with a coloured woman (Cushite) was a scandal to Miriam and Aaron. Some think the woman was Zipporah, as there is no record of her death. But it is likely that she was simply a negro slave girl (*Num.* 12, 1).

Eubulus [ēū-bū'-lŭs]. Prominent member of the Christian community at Rome. The name is Gk. (*2 Tim.* 4, 21).

Eunice [ēū-nī'-cĕ]. Mother of Timothy (*Acts* 16, 1; *2 Tim.* 1, 5).

Eunuch. There is some doubt as to whether or not all described as eunuchs were, in fact, emascu-

lated, Arguments for and agst. are about even.
There is the married ' eunuch ' (*Gen.* 39, 1) rendered ' officer.' But hist. records examples of eunuchs
marrying. There is no certainty.

Euodia [eu-ō'-diă]. The AV form, Euodias, is
wrong. It is the fem. form of Euodias, and clearly
a woman is intended. Paul rebuked her for
bickering and quarrelling with Syntyche at
Philippi, where poss. both were deaconesses
(*Philip.* 4, 2).

Eupator [ēu-pă'-tŏr]. *See* ANTIOCHUS.

Euphrates [ēu-phră'-tĕs]. The W river of
Mesopotamia, the other being the Tigris, which
it joins before entering the Persian Gulf. The
plain bet. the 2 rivers was the cradle of W civilisation. After joining the Tigris it becomes the
Shatt el Arab. The Heb. kingdom at the peak
of its expansion reached the river (*Gen.* 15, 18;
1 Kings 4, 21 & 24). It separated the E empire
of Assyria-Babylonia from the W empire of
Egypt, and was the E limit of the Rom. empire.
Babylon was the greatest city on its banks.

Euraquilo [ēu-ră'-quilŏ]. (*Acts* 27, 14) mod. *Gregale*,
the violent NE wind which blows across the Mediterranean in early spring.

Eutychus [ēu'-tȳchŭs]. The earliest recorded
listener who fell asleep during the discourse
(*Acts* 20, 9 & 10).

Evangelist. Lit. ' one who proclaims good tidings '
(*Acts* 21, 8; *Eph.* 4, 11; *2 Tim.* 4, 5). Philip is
called the Evangelist and he is first seen actually
preaching in Samaria, in the desert and in the
coast cities (*Acts* 8, 4 & 5 & 12 & 25 & 35 & 40).
An evangelist is, therefore, orig. a Christian
missionary on tour in foreign parts—' foreign '
being ' heathen.' The gift of being able to evan-
gelise is ref. to as being a special and valuable

gift, comparable to prophecy, teaching and preaching (*Eph.* 4, 11). But this does not mean that the early church recognised separate orders. In the 3rd ref. (*2 Tim.* 4, 5) evangelism is obviously a function, not an office. Timothy is bidden to be an evangelist as well as being many other things, including a settled pastor.

Eve. Wife of Adam; the first woman; mother o all living (*Gen.* 3, 20). It is prob. a generic name for life itself. In *Gen.* she is the personification of motherhood. In the NT her deception by the serpent is noted (*2 Cor.* 11, 3; *1 Tim.* 2, 13-15).

Evening. *See* TIME.

Evidently. Clearly, openly (*Acts* 10, 3 AV).

Evil. Sometimes in AV has the antique sense of ' ill ' ie unwell (*Jer.* 24, 3; *Matt.* 7, 18). But in the OT at first, all ills are evil, or at least connected with evil. God is responsible for the ills that flesh is heir to, and they are a judgment upon the evil in man (*Isa.* 45, 7; *Lam.* 3, 38; *Ezek.* 14, 9; *Amos.* 3, 6). God presents man with moral decisions which involve moral temptations (*2 Sam.* 24, 1; etc.). Sometimes these temptations are personified (*1 Sam.* 16, 14; *Judg.* 9, 23; etc.). Later there is the complete personification of evil and the identification of evil with Satan, the adversary (*Zech.* 3, 1; etc.). This dissociation of God from evil (making Satan responsible for it) stresses the growing sense of the essential holiness of God (*Deut.* 32, 4; *Hab.* 1, 13). In the NT God is never regarded as being responsible for evil (moral evil) (*Jas.* 1, 13). It is the work of the Evil One (*Matt.* 6, 13; *John* 3, 27; *Rev.* 12, 9). In the great day the Evil One will be overcome and bound with chains (*Rev.* 20, 2 & 10). Pain and suffering (the ills or evils of the OT) may come from God for a purpose that is good. In other words, ills are not necessarily evils any more (*Rom.* 8, 28; *1 Thes.* 3, 3; *Rev.* 3, 19). The Bible does not explain the orig. of evil.

Evil Merodach [mĕ-rō'-dăch]. Son and successor of Nebuchadnezzar (qv). He reigned lawlessly for 2 yrs. (562-560 BC) then was assassinated.

Evil Spirit. *See* DEMON.

Excellent, Excellency. That which excels. The meaning is much stronger than the mod. meaning. Pre-eminent, pre-eminence (as in RSV).

Exchanger. *See* MONEY CHANGER.

Exile. *See* ISRAEL.

Exodus. The migration of the Heb. from Egypt. The route is hard to trace, and the time spent is hard to determine. They did not take the direct route to Palestine, but frequently doubled back on their tracks. *See* ISRAEL, MOSES.

Exodus, Book of. The scope of the book is from the death of Joseph to the end of the second yr. out of Eygpt. After listing the sons of Israel it describes the treatment of the Jews at the hands of the Egyptians. There follows the call of Moses, the appointment of Aaron, the plagues, the institution of the Passover. It is indicated that the reason for the choice of the Red Sea route was to show the pre-eminence of Jehovah over the gods of Egypt. Some of the halting places are listed, and they reach Sinai where Moses received the Law. He is instructed about the building of the Tabernacle and the Ark and the Tabernacle are made. In these latter and priestly parts of the book, the intention is to stress the fact that Israel depends entirely upon Jehovah, and to give an account of the origin of the religious practices and ecclesiastical institutions. The Jahvist portions of the book give a fuller account of the life of the Heb. in Egypt, of the plagues and of the escapes. The destruction of the pursuing Egyptians is described in detail; but there is considerable clashing bet. Jahvist and Priestly writers. In one, the Heb. are cattle owners in Goshen; in the other they live among the Egyptians and have no cattle (1, 6 & 8 & 12, cf. with 1, 15 & 20 & 21, and cf. 12, 29 & 34 with 11, 1-3; 12, 35 ff.). The same confusion occurs in the account of the actual departure (cf. 14, 21 & 24 & 25 & 27 & 28-30 with 14, 15 & 16 & 19 & 20 & 29). These differences continue (chs. 19-33). But in and through it all there runs the fact of the Decalogue and the spirit of it, a work that was continued by *Deut. See* AARON, EGYPT, ISRAEL, MOSES, PASSOVER, PENTATEUCH, SINAI, TABERNACLE.

Exorcism. The expulsion of an evil spirit by performing a conventional rite which included the invocation of a holy name. In early Christian times there were professional exorcists (*Acts* 19, 13 & 19) and other amateurs, reputed to have the gift, did practise it (*Matt.* 12, 27; *Luke* 11, 19). When our Lord cast out evil spirits there was no incantation. He commanded on His own authority (*Matt.* 8, 16; *Mark* 1, 25; 9, 25). He gave His disciples power to exorcise (*Matt.* 10, 1 & 8; etc.). The apostles remembered His authority and used His name (*Acts* 16, 18; 19, 13-16).

Experience. Really, 'learned by experiment' (*Gen.* 30, 27 AV). Or 'by divination' (RSV).

Experiment. Proof (*2 Cor.* 9, 13 AV). The word is used in the assaying of metals. 'Under the test' (RSV).

Ezekiel [ĕz-ē′-kĭĕl]. He was son of Buzi, a priest in the line of Zadok, reared in and around the temple and familiar with Jeremiah and his teaching. Ezekiel was carried into captivity in Babylon

along with King Jehoiachin in 597 BC (*2 Kings*
24, 8 ff.). At that time he would be a man of
around 30 yrs. The exiles settled together on the
banks of the Chebar for at least 22 yrs. (*Ezek.* 1,
2; 29, 17) and there he had a vision and a revelation calling him to the task of prophecy. He was
not at first well received (3, 7) and never had the
success with the people that he had hoped for.
But nothing deters the man with the true call,
and not even the death of his dear wife made
him swerve from his purpose (24, 15-18). Unlike
the other major prophets he exercised a priestly,
or at least a pastoral office as well (4, 14). His
later life is completely unknown, but for many
cent. Jews made pilgrimage to a grave nr. Baghdad, reputed to be his.

Ezekiel, Book of. Its place in the historic succession
of books should be immediately after Jeremiah.
The text of the book is very corrupt, but it is
quite clearly a year by year account of a man's
words and works, set down by himself. Its style
lacks the punch and bite of, say, *Amos*, and the literary grace of *Isaiah* and *Jeremiah*. Fact and fancy
are mixed together: plain statement and involved
imagery. But he knows what he is trying to do,
and he does it most successfully. He tends to be
prolix and repetitive; certain words and phrases
occur time and time again. But other authors
have done the same. When he comes to the
prophetic role of condemning the sins of the
people the authentic thunder is there, and he has
the real ring of conviction. The prophecies fall
into two distinct sections—those delivered before
the siege of Jerusalem (24, 1 & 2) and those delivered after the siege and the fall of Jerusalem,
at which, of course, he was not present. He was
already in exile. The account of how the news

of the fall of Jerusalem reached him is described
(33, 21). Chs. 1-24 are the denunciation of the
sins of the people and warnings of the impending
and inevitable doom. Came the siege and the
fall of the city, which was the vindication of his
prophecy. Then from chs. 25-48 he speaks of the
hope of the future. His dating of the warnings
and the events which followed is most accurate.
(*See* the beginning of chs. 1, 8, 20, 24, 26, 29,
31, 32, 40 & 29, 17; 30, 20; 32, 17; 33, 21).
He makes no excuse for Israel's conduct from
the Exodus, and sees no good in anything that
the nation has done to date. He allows that those
in exile with him are not quite such a bad lot as
those still in Jerusalem, but points out that that
is a fact which signifies very little (14, 22 ff.).
Every wrong thing that they could possibly do,
they have done. They are in such straits that it
almost looks as if God Himself can do nothing
for them. But that is not true; God will restore
them in His time and quite without their help.
The people must not delude themselves that their
present troubles are the result of the working of
the law about the sins of their fathers being visited
on the children. Very far from it. Their own
sins have done it; their own ways are wrong, and
they had better mend them. God is longing to
help them but He cannot, for their sin (18, 23 &
31; 33, 11). The last 8 chs. describe the change
that will take place when they go home. The
organisation of the nation will be theocratic, not
political. There will be a new temple, described
in great detail. A new priesthood will operate
—those of the line of Zadok (which, of course,
was his own line) and they alone. There will be
no High Priest, and the king's authority will be
no more than nominal. The king will have an

income, and will provide the sacrifices for the temple, but will exercise no real rule. God will speak to the priests and the priests will tell the people what God's will is. What, in fact, Ezekiel was doing, was laying the foundations of the Judaism which ultimately crucified Jesus.

Ezion Geber [ĕz'-iŏn gĕ'-bĕr]. A port of the Red Sea (*Deut.* 2, 8; *1 Kings* 9, 26; etc.). The Israelites encamped nr. here (*Num.* 33, 35). It had smelting works for copper, due to the natural funnelling which the topography gave to the prevailing winds, creating a ' natural ' forced draught.

Ezra [ĕz'-rä]. The man was a Jewish scribe living in exile in Babylon under Artaxerxes Longimanus (qv). He was prob. descended from the High Priest, Seraiah. When Babylon fell to Nebuchadnezzar c. 605 BC, he was allowed to return to Jerusalem, where he discovered that the descendants of those who had not been captured had intermarried with surrounding tribes. He tried to restore the old exclusive order. His position was strengthened by the arrival of Nehemiah 13 yrs. later, and bet. them they managed to recreate some of the former order, rule and worship. His main interest was the Law, for he was a scribe rather than a prophet, and the real Jews were in captivity still in Babylon, not free in their native land. When he left Babylon for Jerusalem he set up a gen. divorce court to get rid of the ' heathen ' wives, regardless of the hardships imposed on the hapless women and children. Carrying on the work of Ezekiel (qv) he established Judaism, bringing the Law back with all the impact it had previously possessed and so giving the Jews a fresh start as a people apart.

Ezra, Book of. It joins on with *Neh.* as a single work, and since *Neh.* is a continuation of *Chron.*,

the 3 are really 1. The book divides into 2 at
the end of ch. 6. The first part is the account of
the events at the Persian court which led to the
return to Jerusalem of 40,000 Jews under Zerubbabel 538-537 BC, and of the start of the work
of restoring the Temple; the suspension of the
work because of the hostility of neighbouring
tribes, and the resumption of the work after
representations had been made to Artaxerxes.
Haggai and Zechariah were the inspiration of
this. The work was completed in 515. This is
all historical, and Ezra himself played no part
in it. Not till 60 yrs. later did the events in which
he was personally concerned occur. This account
begins with ch. 7 which tells of how he left Babylon in 458. The rest is the record of his dealing
with the intermarriage of the remnant Jews. It
is partly autobiographical, (7, 11-28) but the
rest of the book has been edited or re-written by
the Chronicler, prob. from an Aram. account of
c. 450, of the building of the city walls and the
temple. Commentators are persuaded that the
following passages are by the Chronicler, not by
Ezra (1; 3, 2-4; 7; 4, 24; 6, 16-17; 11; 8, 35
& 36). *See* NEHEMIAH, BABYLON, EXILE, etc.

F

Fable. A short story devised to convey some useful
lesson or moral. In the OT there are two, neither of
them conveying a message from God. **1.** Jotham's
fable points out the stupidity of the men of
Shechem (*Judg.* 9, 8). **2.** The fable of Jehoash is
to rebuke Amaziah (*2 Kings* 14, 9). In the NT
the word occurs 5 times AV. In RV and RSV
the word is trans. ' myth,' quite a different mean-

ing from the OT fable. It now is a fiction calculated to deceive (*1 Tim.* 1, 4; 4, 7; *2 Tim.* 4, 4; *Titus* 1, 14; *2 Pet.* 1, 16).

Fair Havens. Harbour on the S coast of Crete nr. Lasea. Paul's ship sheltered here on the voyage to Rome (*Acts* 27, 8).

Faith. Word occurs only twice in AV OT (*Deut.* 32, 20; *Hab.* 2, 4). The 2nd is really faithfulness, fidelity. In RSV it occurs 18 times with the following re-translation from AV (*Lev.* 5, 15; 6, 2; *Num.* 5, 6; *Deut.* 32, 51; *Josh.* 7, 1; 22, 22; *Ezra* 10, 2). Where AV has 'trespass' or 'transgression,' RSV has 'breach of faith.' Then (*Judg.* 9, 15 & 16 & 19) where AV has 'dealing truly,' RSV has 'acting in good faith.' Another group (*Job* 39, 12; *Ps.* 78, 22; 106, 24; 116, 24) AV 'belief' becomes RSV 'faith' and 'disbelief' becomes 'having no faith.' Another difference (*Ps.* 146, 6; *Isa.* 26, 2) is where 'keeping the truth' (AV) becomes 'keeping faith' (RSV). Further slight modifications are (*Hab.* 2, 4) where 'the just shall live by faith' becomes 'the righteous shall live by faith.' And (*Deut.* 32, 20) where 'faith' becomes 'faithfulness.' One of the key passages to the meaning of faith in the OT is (*Gen.* 15, 6). Abraham believed Jehovah, and He counted ('reckoned' RSV) it to him for righteousness. That is, taking a promise at its face value. Paul brought this to its logical and sublime conclusion (*Rom.* 4, 9 & 22; *Gal.* 3, 6) justification by faith. But in the OT the human side is more the nation than the individual. The OT faith is backward looking to Egypt and the Exodus, while the NT faith is forward looking to the Kingdom. Where the OT is saying 'believe that it will happen yet,' the NT is saying, 'believe that it has happened.' This idea developed in the NT into (1) Trust in the pledge of a person, Jesus Christ; and (2) belief in the evidences—the witness. Ultimately this becomes 'The Faith,' something very different from, simply, 'faith' (*Acts* 6, 7; 24, 24; *Rom.* 1, 5; etc.).

Faithless. In AV, 'untrustworthy.'

Falcon. Prob. a bird of prey not a vulture. They were unclean.

Fall. The story of the fall of man is told (*Gen.* 3) and is the tragedy of the inexpert use of human freewill. Orig. sin is not 'sex'; it is pride; the sense of self sufficiency; knowing all the answers. The story is an attempt to explain why a perfect creation should produce such ills as the pains of childbearing, the blood, toil, sweat and tears of human existence. The explanation is that man reckoned he knew better than God how creation should be used. Man makes up his own mind about what is right and wrong instead of taking instruction. Right and wrong are not relative but absolute values. Man forgets that the distinction bet. right and wrong is not a thing of man's choice, but of God's decree. The redemptive work of Christ was to restore this sense of the eternal worth of truth and goodness: that they are fixed and immutable.

Fallow deer. Prop. the hart (*Deut.* 14, 5) or gazelle (*1 Kings* 4, 23).

Familiar spirit. Spirit of a dead person called by a medium, to speak either through the medium or apart (*Deut.* 18, 11; *Lev.* 20, 27; *Isa.* 29, 4). The medium was the possessor, or lord, of the spirit (*1 Sam.* 28, 7).

Familiars. Intimate friends (*Jer.* 20, 10).

Family, Families. The family was 'the house' (*Gen.* 7, 1), that is everyone who lived beneath the goodman's roof, including servants and slaves.

For reasons of security, and because the family wealth is in lands and cattle, people tended to keep together in the one place. The family might even be the nation. Abraham was always regarded as the father of the people. *See* MARRIAGE, BIRTHRIGHT, CHILD, BONDAGE.

Famine. This was due usually to failure of the rains (*Lev.* 26, 19; *Amos* 4, 6 & 7). Man-made famine occurred during sieges of cities (*2 Kings* 6, 25; etc.). To avoid the risk of famine, not only had there to be rain but it had to come at the right time. The early rain fell in Oct.-Nov. and the latter rain in Mar.-Apr. Since God sent the rain, a drought must be a sign of His displeasure (*1 Kings* 17, 1; *Ezek.* 5). Famine could also occur because of the destruction of the standing crops by hail, locusts or flood (*Ex.* 9, 31; 10, 15; etc.). A natural result of famine was disease (*1 Kings* 8, 37; *Jer.* 21, 9; etc.). Notable famines are the one which drove Abraham into Egypt (*Gen.* 12, 10) and that one which drove Jacob to Egypt (*Gen.* 26, 1). Famine struck Egypt, too, owing to the failure of the rains in the Abyssinian mts. (*Gen.* ch. 41 ff.) dealt with by Joseph (qv).

Fan. The winnowing fork of 5 or 6 prongs used to toss the grain after it had been threshed to allow the wind to blow away the chaff, or husk (*Isa.* 30, 24; *Jer.* 15, 7). *See* AGRICULTURE.

Farthing. *See* MONEY.

Fast, Fasting. There are 2 kinds: fasting by necessity and fasting by choice. Latter is the commoner usage. In AV OT the phrase ' to afflict the soul ' is often used for fasting (*Lev.* 16, 29-31; etc.). RSV has ' afflict yourselves.' Fasting begins in the OT after the captivity in Babylon. The fasts might be individual and voluntary as was David's

when the first child of Bathsheba was dying; or
national and ordained, as the Day of Atonement
(qv) (*Neh.* 7, 73; 9, 38). After the return from
Babylon there appear to have been 4 statutory
fasts (*Zech.* 7, 3 & 5; 8, 19). One in the 10th month
recollecting the start of the siege of Jerusalem
(*2 Kings* 25, 1). One in the 4th month recollecting
the fall of Jerusalem (*2 Kings* 25, 3 & 4). One in the
5th month recalling the destruction of the temple
(*2 Kings* 25, 8 & 9); and one in the 9th month recalling the murder of Gedaliah and the remaining
Jews (*2 Kings* 25, 25). *See* PURIM. The Pharisees
fasted on Thursdays and Mondays (*Luke* 18, 12).
The Baptist's disciples fasted but Jesus' did not
(*Matt.* 9, 14 & 15). The mod. Jewish calendar
prescribes 22 fasts in addition to the Day of
Atonement, the 4 of *Zech.* (8, 19), and the fast
of Esther. Jesus Himself fasted in the desert, but
He did not advocate fasting as a practice, at least
for its own sake (*Matt.* 6, 16 & 18; etc.). The
Apostolic Church held fasts before certain solemn
occasions (*Acts* 13, 2; 14, 23). Paul made a practice of it (*2 Cor.* 6, 5; 11, 27). This may have been
the result of his Pharasaic origin.

Fat. The fat of sacrificial animals belonged to the
Lord (*Lev.* 3, 16; 7, 23 & 25). Prob. because the
offering would not have burned without it. The
fat of animals slaughtered for food could be
eaten (*Deut.* 12, 15 & 16 & 21-24). *See* FOOD,
SACRIFICE. In AV (*Joel* 2, 24; *Isa.* 63, 2) it is a
wine vat.

Father. Several meanings are noted. **1.** The immediate male parent or grandfather, or even a more
distant relative (*Gen.* 42, 13; 28, 13; 17, 4).
2. The pioneer of some craft or occupation (*Gen.*
4, 20); or the mayor or provost of a town (*1
Chron.* 2, 51). **3.** A courtesy title for one who had

acted like a benevolent father (*Gen.* 45, 8), or simply an old and revered teacher (*1 Sam.* 10, 12). **4.** God Himself (*Mal.* 2, 10; *Matt.* 11, 26; *Rom.* 8, 15). *See* FAMILY, GOD.

Fathom. Gk. *orguia*, the measurement from fingertip to fingertip of the outstretched arms, which is normally the same as a person's height. English fathom is 6 ft.,

Favour. In AV means goodwill. When used as 'well-favoured,' 'ill-favoured,' it describes not temperament but appearance. It can mean mercy (*Josh.* 11, 20).

Fear (Fear of the Lord). In the OT it means to be aware of the power, the holiness, the presence of a power beyond oneself; ie, it is the opposite of self sufficiency which is orig. sin. In the NT to fear means rather to appreciate, value, and honour. There is, of course, another fear which is not fear of the Lord. Those who fear the Lord fear none other, as a matter of course. It is the presence of sin which creates the fear that is not the fear of the Lord, but only in those who know that sin bears a punishment, and who have deliberately, and in the face of this knowledge, chosen the way of sin.

Fearfulness. As used in the AV is not the mod. sense of the word, where it might describe, say, the operations of total war. In Scripture it is introvert rather than extrovert; something felt rather than something expressed or done; a feeling of fear, not the cause of fear. In some RSV refs. it is 'full of fear' or of foreboding. This is the meaning.

Feast(s). This can simply be a sumptuous meal 'with all the trimmings' (*Dan.* 5, 1), but it is particularly used, esp. in OT, to denote sacred festivals. To begin with, the feasts were indeed

celebrations when the Heb. figuratively, and prob.
lit., ' let their hair down.' They were ' occasions.'
But later, some of the occasions became serious
or even grim. Nevertheless the name persisted.
See ATONEMENT, DAY OF. In the beginning, however, they were jollifications and junketings (*Judg.*
21, 21) tending at times to get out of hand (*1
Sam.* 1. 13; *Amos.* 2, 7). These were local affairs,
but there were national occasions better described
as festivals. The Rom. church still distinguishes
bet. festivals and fiestas (*Ex.* 23, 14 & 17; 34,
23; *Deut.* 16, 16). In determining these festivals
the number 7 was regarded as being peculiarly
sacred; that numeral and its multiples figure
very largely in Jewish religious practice. (1) *The
Sabbath.* There are three theories. (a) It was the
day when Creation was completed (*Ex.* 20, 11;
31, 17). (b) It was the day when they won away
from Egypt (*Deut.* 5, 14 & 15). (c) It was good
for people and animals to have a rest (*Deut.* 23,
12). Therefore work of any kind was prohibited
(*Num.* 15, 32-36). Very little was heard of this
practice till after the Exile. *See* SABBATH. (2) The
New Moon. This was a special day in the month
(*Num.* 10, 10; 28, 11-15). No business was done
and no work (*Amos* 8, 5). (3) Feast of the trumpets
took place on the 7th new moon of the yr., Tishri,
Oct. *See* TRUMPETS. (4) The Sabbatical year (qv).
The 7th yr. when even the land had to rest. (5)
The Year of Jubilee. The 7 times 7th yr. Slaves
were released, debts forgiven. mortgaged land
returned to the owner. *See* SABBATICAL YEAR. In
addition there were the national festivals. For
further information *see* under separate titles:
Passover or Feast of Unleavened Bread; Pentecost or end of the corn harvest; Tabernacles or
end of the fruit and wine harvest; Purim; Dedi-

cation. The Lord's Supper is a feast of the Christian church.

Felix Antonius [fē'-lĭx ăn-tō'-nĭŭs] (*Acts* 23, 24 ff.) was procurator of Judea c. AD 52. He may have been a freedman. Felix was cruel, vindictive and oppressive as the record of Josephus indicates. During his term of office there was a good deal of political and religious agitation leading to riots which he put down with the utmost severity. Paul was involved in one such (*Acts* 21, 38) and was sent to Caesarea to be tried before Felix who undoubtedly was hoping for a bribe from Paul or from Paul's friends. Paul defended himself with great vigour before Felix and the procurator's wife, Drusilla, but sentence was deferred and he was still in prison when Festus succeeded Felix.

Fellow. AV use of the word does not involve the patronising or even disparaging meaning of the mod. word, cf. Tyndale (*Gen.* 39, 2) ' and the Lord was with Joseph and he was a luckie fellowe.' In many refs. it simply has the meaning of ' companion.'

Fellowship. *See* COMMUNION.

Fenced city. *See* FORTIFICATION AND SIEGE.

Ferret. Prob. the gecko (*Lev.* 11, 30). *See* LIZARD.

Festus. Porcius. He was successor to Felix as procurator of Judea. He ' inherited ' Paul in prison and had to deal with the case which Felix had suspended. This he did justly, refusing to surrender Paul to the Jews untried.

Fever. Trans. of Heb. *kaddahath*, lit. ' burning,' and of Gk. *pyretos*, lit. ' fire.' *See* MEDICINE.

Field. Eng. usage defines an enclosure of some kind, but this meaning is not in Scripture. It has nothing to do with enclosure or dimension (*Gen.* 37, 7 & 14-16; *Matt.* 6, 28; etc.). The boundaries bet. one man's holding and another's were marked by stones (*Deut.* 19, 14).

Fiery serpent. *See* SERPENT, SERAPHIM.

Fig. *Ficus carica* or common fig, providing an important part of the staple diet of Palestine (*Jer.* 5, 17; *Hab.* 3, 17). The barren fig tree is a self sown one; all male fig trees are erratic croppers. They are deciduous and put on their first foliage and the fig bud simultaneously; but since the male and female flowers are separate, insects are necessary for pollination; a variety of small wasp performs this function normally. The green fig (*S. of S.* 2, 13) is the immature green fig, wind fallen. The ripened fruit might be eaten fresh from the tree or dried and pressed into cakes (*1 Sam.* 25, 18; etc.). It could be used medicinally, too (*2 Kings* 20, 7; *Isa.* 38, 21).

Fine, Fines, Fined. *See* CRIME AND PUNISHMENT.

Fir, fir tree. Prob. the cypress (qv), a conifer whose excellent wood was much used in building.

Fire, fire pan. For ordinary domestic use of fire for cooking, heat, etc., *see* HOUSE. But fire was needed also for the sacrifice of burnt offerings (*Gen.* 8, 20; etc.). The sacrificial fire of the tabernacle was not allowed to go out (*Lev.* 6, 9-13). Fire worship was a common heathen practice (*2 Kings* 16, 3; 21, 6; etc.). The fire pan was of bronze, silver or gold (*Ex.* 27, 3; *1 Kings* 7, 50). These were not unlike domestic frying pans. Sometimes trans. 'censer' when used in conjunction with incense (*Lev.* 10, 1; 16, 12; etc.). The 'snuff dishes' (RSV 'snuffers' *Ex.* 25, 38; *Num.* 4, 9) are the same containers used for removing the burnt wick of the lamps. They were not snuffers in the mod. sense, for there were no candles in the mod. sense.

Firkin. *See* WEIGHTS AND MEASURES.

Firmament. The heavens; the sky (*Gen.* 1, 8).
Compared with a tent (*Ps.* 104, 2; *Isa.* 40, 22).
Upon it were placed the stars, and it divided the
upper and the lower waters (*Gen.* 1, 6). Through
apertures in it the rain fell (*Gen.* 7, 11). *See*
CREATION.

Firstborn, Firstling. A very ancient practice was
the dedication of the firstborn to God (*Ex.* 13,
11-16; etc.). The firstborn may even have been
sacrificed (*2 Kings* 3, 27; *Micah* 6, 7). To the
firstborn came the birthright (qv). The son took
over the headship of the clan with a double portion of the inheritance (*Deut.* 21, 17). If a man
died childless, the firstborn of his widow by his
next of kin was the heir (*Deut.* 21, 15-17). The
most grievous blow suffered by Egypt before the
Exodus was the death of the first born (*Ex.* 11,
4-8; 12, 29 ff.). The word is used of Jesus (*Rom.*
8, 29; etc.). *See* OFFERINGS.

First-fruits. A later form of offering since there would
be no fruits until the land was settled and cultivated. It means that the first of a crop to ripen
was given to God. But it became largely symbol-
ical as the sheaf at the Feast of Unleavened Bread
and the 2 loaves at the Feast of Weeks (*Lev.* 23,
10 & 17). It is used figuratively in the epistles
(*Rom.* 8, 23; *1 Cor.* 15, 20 & 23; *Rev.* 14, 4; etc.).
See OFFERINGS.

Fish, Fishing. All the Palestine waters except the
Dead Sea are teeming with fish. Members of the
carp family are most common. The catfish could
not be eaten because it has no scales (*Deut.* 14, 9).
The fishpools (*S. of S.* 7, 4 AV) should be ' pools
in Heshbon.' But there is a false ref. to ponds
for fish (*Isa.* 19, 10 AV). RSV trans. this as
' those who work for hire.' This is right.

Fitch. Black cummin, or *nigella sativa*, used as a condiment (*Ezek.* 4, 9).

Flag. Prob. not the iris, but any weedy plant growing in fresh or salt water margins (*Gen.* 41, 2; *Ex.* 2, 3 & 5; *Job* 8, 11).

Flagon. Container for liquids. In refs. (*Ex.* 25, 29; 37, 16) where AV has 'covers' and RV has 'cups' the Heb. is the same as (*Num.* 4, 7) which is prob. flagon. There are 4 mistranslations in AV (*2 Sam.* 6, 19; *1 Chron.* 16, 3; *Hos.* 3, 1; *S. of S.* 2, 5). The Heb. word is not flagon, or any other kind of utensil, but a pressed cake of dates, figs, raisins, meal or the like, as in RV and RSV.

Flax. May have been harvested at one time in the wild state, but it was cultivated (*linum usitatissimum*); the plant from whose fibres linen is made (*Josh.* 2, 6; *Hos.* 2, 9; etc.). The leaves were cooked or steamed (*Ex.* 9, 31) to separate the fibres, and were dried on the flat roofs of the houses (*Josh.* 2, 6). A further soaking followed, and the leaves were then combed out (*Isa.* 19, 9 RV, RSV). From the seeds comes linseed oil. *See* SPINNING AND WEAVING.

Flea. *Pulex irritans.* It irritated then, as now, and spread disease, though the disease was not then assoc. with the flea. They are, of course, parasitic on animals and on man (*1 Sam.* 24, 14; 26, 20).

Flesh. There are 6 main uses of the word. **1.** The material of the body (*Gen.* 41, 2; etc.). **2.** The quality of the body (*Ex.* 4, 7). **3.** Kinship of one to another by birth or marriage (*Gen.* 2, 24; etc.). **4.** Man as an ephemeral creature as contrasted with eternal God (*Isa.* 31, 3; etc.). **5.** The physical self as contrasted with the spiritual self (*Ps.* 63, 1; *Matt.* 26, 41; etc.). **6.** The element prone to sin in the human being (*Rom.* 7, 14; etc.) which has its own 'works,' products, characteristics (*Gal.* 5, 19-21).

Flesh hook. A 3 pronged fork used in temple sacrifice (*Ex.* 27, 3; *1 Sam.* 2, 13; etc.).

Fleshy, Fleshly. The two have quite different meanings in AV where 'fleshly' means carnal (RSV has sensuous), while 'fleshy' means simply human as opposed to inanimate (*2 Cor.* 3, 3). 'The fleshy tables of the heart,' in contrast to tables of stone.

Flesh pot. The large pot we would call a soup pot or a stock pot (*Ex.* 16, 3; *2 Kings* 4, 38; *Jer.* 1, 13; etc.).

Flint. Geologically a form of silica, which is very hard. Sparks can be struck from it with steel. It shows a sharp edge when chipped, and was one of the lethal weapons of the Stone Age (*Ex.* 4, 25; *Deut.* 32, 13). Figuratively it was used to describe hardness of heart, or firmness and determination of purpose (*Isa.* 50, 7; *Ezek.* 3, 9).

Flood. The scriptural account of the flood, with the ark and Noah is well known. Very similar accounts of a flood occur in the literature of the other peoples of the ancient ME world and give clear proof that at a point in hist. there was an inundation upon a considerable scale. The *Gen.* account characteristically gives a religious explanation. The world has grown wicked—too wicked to redeem. God decides to destroy it and build again from the remnant of Noah and his family, with the living creatures rescued in the ark. In *Gen.* however, there are 2 narratives, 1 Jehovistic and 1 priestly. *See* PENTATEUCH. The priestly is as usual, more elaborate, and there are differences of detail. Both bear close resemblance to the Babylonian account.

Floor. This can be either the floor or the ceiling (which is, of course, the floor of the room upstairs)

(*1 Kings* 7, 7). It might be made of packed earth (*Num.* 5, 17) or of wood (*1 Kings* 6, 15). It might be the floor of the sea (*Amos* 9, 3). There is also the threshing floor (*2 Kings* 6, 27; AV ' barn-floor '. *Hos.* 9, 1. AV and RV ' cornfloor '). *See* AGRICULTURE.

Flour. Made by pounding, rubbing, or grinding wheat or barley. There were 3 qualities (*Lev.* 2, 14 & 16; *Gen.* 18, 6; *1 Kings* 4, 22): coarse, medium and fine. *See* BREAD, FOOD.

Flowers. Various words are so trans. some of them meaning fruit blossom (*Ex.* 25, 33; *Isa.* 18, 5, ' buds '). Palestine abounds in flowers for a very short season in March and April. Because of this they become the symbol of impermanence (*Job* 14, 2; *Ps.* 103, 15). The lilies of the field (*Matt.* 6, 28) are prob. all the flowers: anemone, iris, gladiolus, etc. The roses of the OT are prob. not true roses, but the crocus, narcissus and poly-anthus. A flower is meant by the ' rolling thing ' and ' the wheel ' (*Isa.* 17, 13; *Ps.* 83, 13). This is a kind of tumbleweed, the Rose of Jericho.

Flute. *See* MUSIC (INSTRUMENTS).

Flux. *See* MEDICINE.

Fly. Baalzebub, worshipped in Ekron, was lord of the flies (*2 Kings* 1, 2) which are a constant plague. They were one of the plagues of Egypt. Cholera, enteric fever, etc. carried by the flies might well have been the plague. Flies prob. included mosquitoes, the fem. *anopheles* being the carrier of malaria.

Folk. Word still common in Scotland meaning ' people ' (AV *Mark* 6, 5; *John* 5, 3; *Acts* 5, 16). But in OT it means more than this, the nation (cf. folk song, folk dances, etc.). Metrical version of *Ps.* 100 is wrong with ' flock ' it should be ' folk.'

Food. The Heb. ate little meat, prob. because it was almost imposs. to keep it fresh. For this reason they were not allowed to hang meat; it had to be eaten as soon as the animal was killed. Corn (AV) or grain (RSV) was the staple food-stuff and consisted in the main of wheat, barley, millet and spelt (grain of poor quality). The last 2 were eaten only when there was nothing else. The grain might be rubbed bet. the hands and eaten raw (*Deut.* 23, 25; *Matt.* 12, 1) but this was not eating seriously. The whole ear, un-husked, might be roasted on a hot plate (parched grain) (*Ruth* 2, 14) but it was usually ground or pounded into flour and baked. The poorer folk ate barley bread (*Judg.* 7, 13). *See* BREAD, FLOUR. Ref. to dough (*Num.* 15, 20; *Neh.* 10, 37; *Ezek.* 44, 30) is either coarse meal or porridge (brose in Scotland). The pulses were another imp. item of diet, lentils and beans being the most common. There were also the salad vegetables (*Ex.* 12, 8; *Num.* 11, 5; *Prov.* 15, 17; *Matt.* 13, 31). Olives were eaten raw or pickled, or were rendered into oil. Figs were eaten green, or dried and pressed (*1 Sam.* 25, 18). Grapes were eaten from the vine, or dried as raisins (*Num.* 6, 3). These appear to have been pressed into bulk, too (*1 Sam.* 25, 18; etc.). AV ref. (*Hos.* 3, 1) ' flagons of wine ' (made of ' grapes ') is wrong, and should be ' cakes of raisins ' (as RSV). It is poss. that this is some kind of fermented sweetmeat, but the meaning is quite obscure. Most of the grape harvest went to the making of wine (qv). *See* HONEY. Dates are mentioned, but a better trans. is ' honey ' (*2 Chron.* 31, 5). Yet dates must have been known then as they are now. The palm is mentioned (*Joel* 1, 12) and since the ref. is to fruits it must be the date palm. *See* ALMOND,

APPLES, NUTS, POMEGRANATES. The ' husks ' (*Luke*
15, 16) are the pods of the carob tree. As far
as meat is concerned, limits were imposed by the
' clean-unclean ' legislation (*Lev.* 11, 23; *Deut.*
14, 4-20). The main flesh diet (such as it was)
was goat, as it still is in the ME. It was the poor
man's meat, which the elder brother compared
to the fatted calf (*Luke* 15, 29). Eating sheep was
discouraged, prob. because the fleece was more
valuable than the flesh, and any mutton tender
enough to eat didn't have a fleece worth killing
it for. A sheep was better alive than dead. The
flesh of cattle was permissible, if not very appetising. Veal was the daintiest, but poss. the calves
were eaten because the cow's milk was needed
for human consumption. Animals were specially
fed for the table—the stalled ox (*Prov.* 15, 17).
Milk was obtained from cows, goats, ewes and
camels (*Gen.* 32, 15; *Deut.* 32, 14; *Prov.* 27, 27).
See MILK. Seven kinds of game are mentioned (*Deut.*
14, 5) any of which may have been the venison
which Esau brought for his father's delight (*Gen.*
25, 28). Pigs were taboo for the Heb. then as
now for Jews and Mohammedans and most
Hindus. As far as fish were concerned they were
allowed to eat any that had scales and fins (*Deut.*
14, 9 f.). Fish was a favourite food, and fishing
a prosperous industry (*Deut.* 33, 19; *Neh.* 3, 3;
13, 16). Fishes were salted and dried, and the
fishes of Jesus' miracle were certainly of this kind.
Raw fish would have gone bad in the time and
the heat. The list of fowl is explicit (*Lev.* 11,
13-19; *Deut.* 14, 11—18). Birds bred for the
table were pigeons (*Isa.* 60, 8), poultry (*Matt.* 23,
37), fatted fowl (geese ?) (*1 Kings* 4, 23), wild birds
that might be shot or snared and eaten were
partridge and quail (qv), sparrows (*Matt.* 10, 29).

The eggs of the farmyard fowl were valued (*Deut.* 22, 6; *Isa.* 10, 14; *Luke* 11, 12). The famous ' is there any taste in the white of an egg ' (*Job* 6, 6) is a doubtful trans. but it is so good a phrase that it deserves to be correct. There were also edible insects (*Lev.* 11, 22 ff.). Dishes in hot countries usually require a good deal of seasoning to produce the sweat which is nature's way of cooling off. Salt is also an essential because of the loss of body salt through sweating. *See* SALT. The condiments are: coriander (*Ex.* 16, 31), black cummin (*Isa.* 28, 25), mustard (*Matt.* 13, 31), capers (*Eccl.* 12, 5 RV). *See* MINT, ANISE, CUMMIN, RUE. All meat had to be kosher—the blood had to be drained off. *See* BLOOD. There were also restrictions on the eating of fat. *See* CAUL (*Lev.* 3, 3 ff.; 7, 22 ff.). ' Braxy ' meat— from an animal that had died—was forbidden, prob. because any animal dead any time at all would give food poisoning (*Deut.* 14, 21; etc.). The confusion bet. animals killed for eating and those killed for sacrifice appears several times (*Dan.* 1, 8; *Acts* 15, 20 & 29; *I Cor.* 8, 1-10; 10, 19 & 28). In earlier days a man's own flocks and herds supplied all his needs, and, of course, meat and milk had to be the staple diet before the settlement. But as they settled, professional suppliers came into being (*Neh.* 3, 1 & 3; 13, 15 f.; *John* 4, 8; *I Cor.* 10, 25; ' meat market ' RSV; ' shambles ' or ' slaughter-house ' AV). There were also foodshops (*Matt.* 25, 9).

Fool. There are many Heb. words for fool, but of course there are many ways of being foolish. One is the man who can't keep his mouth shut (*Prov.* 18, 7; *Eccl.* 5, 1 ff.). Another is the man who does silly things (*2 Sam.* 13, 13; *Isa.* 44, 25). Then there is the man who won't take advice (*Prov.* 1,

7; 5, 23; 12, 15 & 16; 24, 7 & 9; 27, 3). There is
also the use of the word as a euphemism. Scots
will say of a confirmed drunkard: ' He's a wee bit
foolish ' (*Deut.* 22, 21; 32, 6; *Josh.* 7, 15; *Ps.*
14, 1; 74, 18; *Jer.* 29, 23). In the NT it can mean
' not quite all there ' (*Luke* 24, 25), or silly (*Eph.*
5, 18), or ' just plain daft '; ' 1oco ' (*Luke* 12,
20), or ' about fifteen shillings in the pound '
(*Rom.* 1, 21).

Foot. If a man's head is his greatest glory, his
feet are the opposite. To sit at the feet of anyone
or to fall at the feet was a gesture of great significance, saluting the least honourable part, and
so humbling oneself (*Luke* 7, 38; 10, 39; *Acts*
22, 3). The symbol of victory was to place the
foot (the lowest) on the neck (the highest) (*Josh.*
10, 24). To ' water with the feet ' (*Deut.* 11, 10)
must ref. either to some kind of splash feed for
irrigation, or to opening or blocking a gap in the
low earth ridge round a plot of land. A hot and
dusty land naturally dirtied the feet of walkers
and several practices stem from that fact (*Ex.* 3,
5; *Deut.* 25, 9; *Josh.* 5, 15; *Ruth* 4, 8). Ref.
(*Jer.* 2, 25) 'withhold thy foot from being unshod'
(AV), or ' keep your feet from going unshod'
(RSV) is prob. ' don't wear the soles off your
shoes running around.' Hospitality demanded
facilities for the guest to wash his feet (*Gen.* 18,
4; *Luke* 7, 44). For the host to attend to this
personally was a very high compliment to his
guest.

Footman. **1.** A soldier of the infantry (*1 Sam.* 4,
10; 15, 4). **2.** An aide-de-camp of the king; lit.
' a runner.' These acted both as despatch carriers
and as bodyguard (*1 Sam.* 8, 11; *2 Sam.* 15, 1).
Sometimes even as executioners (*1 Sam.* 22, 17).
In (*Jer.* 12, 5) ref. is to competitive running.

Forbearance. *See* LONG-SUFFERING.

Foreigner. In AV a stranger—one not a Jew (*Deut.* 29, 22; etc.). Captives ceased to be foreigners when they were enslaved (*Gen.* 17, 12). Word is used also of proselytes to Judaism (*Gen.* 34, 14-17). Foreigners could not eat the Passover (*Ex.* 12, 43) or enter the sanctuary (*Num.* 1, 51) or become king (*Deut.* 17, 15). Inter-marriage was deplored (*Ex.* 34, 12 & 16). Business could be done with foreigners (*Deut.* 14, 21; 15, 3; 23, 20). Orthodox Jews of NT times would not assoc. with foreigners (Gentiles) at all (*Acts* 11, 3; *Gal.* 2, 12). But Gentiles could be admitted to Judaism; they then ceased to be foreigners (*Gen.* 17, 27; *Matt.* 23, 15). *See* STRANGER.

Forerunner. Lit. ' one who goes or runs ahead of another '; military scout; diplomatic herald or courier. The precise word is not applied to John the Baptist, but the meaning is there (*Matt.* 11, 10; etc.). It is very important as used in (*Heb.* 6, 20). AV has ' whither the forerunner is for us entered (heaven, as the High Priest entered the Holy of Holies), even Jesus.' RSV has ' Where Jesus has gone as a forerunner on our behalf.' The AV meaning is not quite correct for it identifies Jesus with the High Priest who was never a forerunner. No one could possibly follow him (*Heb.* 9, 7).

Forgiveness. Heb. conception of God was as one all-powerful, which meant that He could forgive if He so chose, any sin agst. Himself (*Deut.* 9, 19; *Neh.* 9, 17; *Jer.* 36, 3). But the transgressor himself had to admit penitence (*Ps.* 86, 5) and show that he was going to mend his ways (*Josh.* 24, 19; *Jer.* 5, 1 & 7). Once this had been done there was no hesitation on God's part (*1 Kings* 8, 36 & 50; *Ps.* 103, 3). The Heb., however, did

not reckon that injury to another person could
be blotted out merely by securing God's pardon.
There had to be restitution and a demonstration
of atonement (*Lev.* 6, 2-7). Ignorance was no
excuse (*Lev.* 4, 13; *Num.* 15, 22-26). Paul appreciated the sense and worth of the Levitical law
in this regard (*Gal.* 3, 24). The prophets, even
when they were denouncing the sins of the people,
did not tell them that there was no hope of forgiveness. It was still God's nature to forgive, but
first the people had to repent and atone (*Ezek.*
33, 11; *Hos.* 14, 1). To Jesus the author of forgiveness was always God, and when He spoke of
His own power to forgive sins He always saw
Himself as God's representative and spokesman
(*Mark* 2, 10; etc.). The apostolic writings carry
this idea further, and in them Jesus becomes the
mediator (*Eph.* 4, 32; *1 Pet.* 5, 10). But the OT
insistence remains implicit in the NT (cf. *Ps.* 32,
5 with *1 John* 1, 9). The sin of the Pharisees was
that they would not make the gesture to God because they did not think it necessary (*John* 9,
40 ff.). At the heart of Jesus' teaching was the
insistence that the human who would not forgive
the human could never be forgiven by God. There
was, too, a limit to God's power to forgive the
sin agst. the Holy Spirit (*Matt.* 12, 32). It is a
sin of speaking blasphemy. Mark calls it the
eternal sin. This sinner never has forgiveness (3,
29). Jesus said this after His clash with the Pharisees and He is referring to a condition of soul
apparent in the Pharisees by their words, actions
and attitude. In life their souls were dead; they
were completely impervious to the influence of
the Holy Spirit. Such a soul cannot possibly
find its way back to the beginning and start again.
It is, in fact, dead. God cannot forgive such a

soul for such a soul is unable to receive and appreciate forgiveness. It has gone too far ever to
return. The word 'forgive' occurs only once in
the Gospel according to John (RV). But this is a
most imp. ref. (*John* 20, 23). This is the account of
the occasion when Jesus granted to the apostles the
power of absolution, and that power can only
follow upon the granting of the gift of the Holy
Spirit. The Church becomes the body of Christ
and as such is able to make judgment of things
spiritual and to pronounce a verdict (*1 Cor.* 2,
12 & 15). Not only does the Church proclaim
the fact of divine forgiveness, but the Church by
her spiritual authority can indicate that the forgiveness has been granted (*Acts* 2, 38).

Fornication. *See* CRIME AND PUNISHMENT.

Fortification and siege. The way of life was so
perilous in ancient days that it was practically
suicide to live the completely rural life, just as it
was in the Scottish-English border country, or in
the pioneering days of Canada and the American
west. There had to be strong points, towers,
'castles' or walled cities into which the people
of the surrounding countryside could disappear
when enemies appeared in any force. The cities
were not big, but they were surrounded by a defensible wall. AV has 'fenced cities' (*Deut.* 9,
1; etc.). The walls might be of mud brick or of
random rubble or of dressed stone, but usually
had stone nr. the base to guard agst. deterioration
from damp, and to offer better resistance to
battering rams. The walls might be anything up
to 30 ft. thick. At strategic points there were
towers (*2 Chron.* 26, 15) from which an enemy
might be enfiladed. Along the top of the wall,
which would be around 30 ft. high, were the
battlements and embrasures (*Zeph.* 1, 16; 3, 6).

Sometimes there would be an inner and an outer wall—the rampart (*1 Kings* 21, 23) or bulwark (*Isa.* 26, 1). Within would be the keep trans. variously ' palace ' (AV), ' castle ' (RV), ' citadel ' (RSV) (*1 Kings* 16, 18). In other places it is called the stronghold. Apart from the fortified cities there were fortified strong points at key positions (*1 Kings* 9, 15; *2 Kings* 17, 9; etc.). The gates, being the most vulnerable part of the defences. received special attention (*2 Chron.* 26, 9). The gateway was a deep, narrow opening, flanked by towers and usually with more than one gate across it (*2 Sam.* 18, 24). The passage was L-shaped. The ' gates of brass ' were of bronze (qv) (*Ps.* 107, 16; *Isa.* 45, 2). This was prob. plates of bronze bolted on to thick wood. The enemy might burn the gates (*Judg.* 9, 49 & 52) or scale the walls (*1 Chron.* 11, 6) or win by stratagem (*Judg.* 9, 42 ff.) or by blockade (*2 Sam.* 12, 26). They might build an earth ramp up to the height of the walls (*2 Sam.* 20, 15). They might use battering rams (*Isa.* 22, 5; *Ezek.* 4, 2; 21, 22; 26, 9). The artillery (*1 Sam.* 20, 40) was not, of course the artillery of to-day but merely bows and arrows and slings. The Assyrians had catapults (*2 Chron.* 26, 15). A prolonged siege was a grim business indeed (*2 Kings* 6, 25 ff.).

Fortunatus [fŏr'-tūnā'-tŭs]. A Corinthian of the household of Stephanas who with Stephanas and Achaicus came to see Paul at Ephesus (*1 Cor.* 16, 17).

Fountain. A spring, as distinct from a well, and of prime importance in time of drought (*Judg.* 1, 15).

Fowl. Any kind of bird.

Fowler. A catcher of birds or game by snares, which could be running nooses, pegged down (*Amos* 3, 5), or nets (*Prov.* 1, 17). There was also the gin or trap (*Amos* 3, 5). The word is used figuratively for the enticer of the innocent (*Ps* 91, 3; 124, 7; *Hos.* 9, 8).

Fox. In some refs. undoubtedly the jackal (*Judg.* 15, 4; etc.). Where many foxes are talked about they must be jackals which are gregarious while foxes are not (*Ps.* 63, 10).

Frankincense. White fragrant tree gum, part of the blend of the anointing oil (*Ex.* 30, 34). It was used in sacrifice, but not for the sin offering or the jealousy offering (*Lev.* 5, 11; *Num.* 5, 15). It was imported from Arabia (*Isa.* 60, 6).

Fray. Verb. Simply, ' scare ' (*Zech.* 1, 21 AV).

Freely. Sometimes has the meaning, ' gratuitously,' cf. mod. slang ' for free ' (*Num.* 11, 5; *Matt.* 10, 8).

Friend of the King. Simply privy councillor (*Gen.* 26, 26).

Fringes. *See* BORDER OF GARMENT.

Frontlets. *See* PHYLACTERY.

Froward. Lit. ' the opp. to toward' as in to and fro. A froward person is one who persists in going fro when he should be coming to. It does not mean ' forward' but ' perverse ' RSV trans. (*Prov.* 2, 14; *Isa.* 57, 17; *1 Pet.* 2, 18).

Fruit. *See* FOOD.

Fuel. Wood or charcoal (*see* COAL) and animal dung (*Ezek.* 4, 12-15).

Fuller. *See* ARTS AND CRAFTS.

Furnace. 1. A smelting furnace (*Deut.* 4, 20). *See* IRON. **2.** A crucible for refining precious metals (*Prov.* 17, 3). *See* ARTS AND CRAFTS, SMITH. **3.** A baker's oven (*Neh.* 3, 11). *See* BREAD.

Furniture. In AV often used for ' furnishings ' (*Ex.* 31, 7 & 8; *Num.* 3, 8 RV). The camel's furniture (*Gen.* 31, 34) is the palanquin.

G

Gabbatha [gă'-bă-thă]. A raised pavement of tesselated work—prob. a square in Herod's palace (*John* 19, 13).

Gabriel [gāb'-rĭ-ĕl]. *See* ANGEL.

Gad. A man, a tribe, a dist. The man was son of Jacob by Zilpah, Leah's handmaid. His tribe was highly commended by Moses (*Deut.* 33, 20) at, of course, a much later date. They were respected warriors (*1 Chron.* 12, 8 & 14). In the two census counts they numbered about 40,000 (*Num.* 1, 24 & 25; 26, 15-18). Moses settled them E of Jordan (*Num.* 32, 20-32). They supported David agst. Saul. With all Israel they were taken captive by Tiglath Pileser of Assyria in 734 BC, and are not heard of again.

Gadara [găd'-ă-ră]. A town some 6 m. SE of Galilee in Decapolis (qv). Famous for its hot medicinal springs. The inhabitants were the Gadarenes (*Mark* 5, 1).

Gaius [gāi'-ŭs]. Name mentioned 4 times. **1.** A man who entertained Paul at Corinth and was converted (*Rom.* 16, 23; *1 Cor.* 1, 14). He may have been the same as **2.** Gaius of Derbe (*Acts* 20, 4). He accompanied Paul to Asia. **3.** Gaius of Macedonia, a fellow traveller of Paul who was involved in the riot at Ephesus (*Acts* 19, 29). He may just possibly be **4**, a man addressed by John (*3 John* 1.)

Galatia [găl-ā'-tĭ-ă]. Territory in Asia Minor, partly in Phrygia and partly in Cappadocia. The inhabitants were Gauls (Galatae). A Gaulish expedition had reached the territory c. 278-279 BC, as part of a larger migration which overran E Europe till they were defeated by Attalus of

Pergamos (241-197). He forced the remnant of the Gauls to contain themselves within the dist. which became Galatia. It later became a province under Augustus. Refs. to Galatia are apt to be confusing as it is sometimes not clear whether the orig. territory is meant or the province. There is even a theory that the Galatia to which Crescens went (*2 Tim.* 4, 10) was Gaul (France). But it seems reasonably clear that the Galatians to whom the Epistle of the name was addressed lived in the Phrygian part of Galatia which included the towns of Derbe, Lystra, Iconium and Pisidian Antioch: towns which Paul visited.

Galatians, Epistle of Paul the Apostle to the. There seems little doubt that the churches addressed were all founded at the same time (4, 13-15). The date of writing is most uncertain, but was certainly after Paul had visited Jerusalem twice (ch. 2). It seems obvious that he had visited Galatia twice before he wrote the letter. The epistle to the Romans and that to the Galatians have distinct points of similarity. Some think this means that Paul had reached a certain stage of theological development and wrote the two letters at the same time while his mind was on the one track. It can be argued, however, that the similarities are due to the fact that he wrote both letters more or less on the same subject. Prob. the best clue is the absence of refs. to Barnabas, which seems to point to a date after their quarrel. Poss. the letter was written while he was on tour some time bet. the 2nd and 3rd missionary journeys. The inspiration of the letter is the attack being made on Paul by a person or persons unknown, who were preaching the need for circumcision to the Galatians, telling them that Paul had ' let the side down ' by preaching the freeness of the new faith and its indepen-

dence from Judaism. They were saying that Paul
in his heart still believed that circumcision was
necessary, but was playing the hypocrite to win
converts the easy way, and to be popular. Paul
therefore begins by proving his apostleship, which
was being challenged. (Chs. 1 & 2.) He tells of
his conversion, of his dealings with the apostles,
of his visits to Jerusalem, of his relationship to
Peter. He then goes on to insist that the Gospel
is not rooted in Judaism (3, 1—5, 12). The Law
has now been superseded. There follows an im-
passioned plea to ' hold fast by freedom ' (5, 13—
6, 10). It closes with a reiteration of his objections
to the ' circumcision school of thought.' There
is a mistranslation in the AV (6, 11). The words
are not ' see what a large letter I have written
unto you with my own hand.' It is plainly not
a large letter at all, but a short one. The correct
trans. is ' see with what large letters I am writing
to you with my own hand.' There is something
very human in this, as there is in the phrase (6,
17) ' let no man henceforth trouble me.' Which
savours of, ' I can't be bothered with these
characters.' The date is anywhere bet. AD 48 and
AD 57, and the place of writing could be Antioch.

Galbanum [găl'-bă-nŭm]. A kind of sweet scented
resin; an ingredient of the incense (*Ex.* 30, 34)

Galilaean (Galilean). Native or inhabitant of the
dist. round Lake Galilee.

Galilee [găl'-ĭ-lēē]. Little is heard of this N province
in OT times. It was orig. in Naphtali, Asher
and Zebulun and the pop. seems to have been
mainly non-Jewish (Galilee of the Gentiles) (*Isa.*
9, 1; *Matt.* 4, 15). The dist. was badly hit by the
Assyrian wars, and after the captivity it was
handed over to the Assyrians, though the pop.
remained mixed. The orthodox Jews had little

respect for the Galileans, and Jesus' attachment to
Galilee did him no good in Jewish eyes. Herod
the Great ruled Galilee in 47 BC, and his son
Antipas ruled in 4 BC. Jesus it was who has
made Galilee known, for almost His entire life
was spent in and around that area. Round the
Lake is a well-watered and fertile plain, and there
were settlements of Greeks of fair social standing,
as well as of Romans with their military posts.
But the sneer still was: 'Can any good thing come
out of Nazareth (in Galilee)?' (*John* 1, 46). Their
Aram. may or may not have been uncouth, but
it was certainly recognisable (*Matt.* 26, 73).

Galilee, Sea of. The sea is really part of the R.
Jordan which spreads at that point in a pear-
shaped depression, the narrow end being S. It
is about 13 m. long and 8 m. broad, and lies deep
among high hills, down whose gorges sudden
squalls can swirl. Tiberias (qv) was the largest
town on its shores. Other cities on the lake were
Bethsaida, Capernaum, Chorazin and Magdala.
The fishing was and is excellent, 22 species having
been classified *See* SEA.

Gall. Both animal and vegetable. **1.** The liver bile
(*Job* 16, 13; 20, 25). It was used metaphorically
for venom, malignancy (*Acts* 8, 23). **2.** Poisonous,
bitter herb (*Deut.* 29, 18). Sometimes trans. hemlock (*Hos.* 10, 4) or poison (*Job.* 20, 16). The
wine mingled with gall (*Matt.* 27, 34) was prob.
myrrh (qv) (*Mark* 15, 23) which the Romans
gave to lessen suffering.

Gallery (*S. of S.* 7, 5) mistranslation of ' long hair,'
' tresses.' Another Heb. word so trans. occurs
(*Ezek.* 41, 15 & 16; 42, 3 & 5) and seems to
mean a long room or corridor, or even verandah.

Galley. *See* SHIPS AND BOATS.

Gallio [găll´-ĭ-ō]. Proconsul of Achaia when Paul

was in Corinth, and Claudius was emperor (*Acts* 18, 12-17). He refused to judge Paul on what was a purely religious issue which the Jews themselves were competent to deal with.

Gallows. Occurs in Esther (AV) but is prob. a sharpened stake or pole on which criminals were impaled.

Gamaliel [găm-ā'-lĭ-ĕl]. **1.** Head of Manasseh in the wilderness (*Num.* 1, 10). **2.** Highly respected Pharisee and authority on the Law. He was tolerant and liberal in his outlook, free from Pharisaism in the bad sense. He taught Paul (*Acts* 22, 3). His advice when his fellows were agitated about the new teaching was that if it was man-made it would fail; if it was God-made, there was nothing they could do about it (*Acts* 5, 34-40).

Games. The Jews were not much given to playing games. Their dances were either devotional or, when the subject of their devotions was not Jehovah, dances started as devotional, degenerating into an orgy. They were not by nature (though they occasionally were by choice) socially inclined (*Ps.* 150, 4; *Jer.* 31, 4; etc.). Isaiah condemned secular song (5, 12). They had nothing at all comparable to the athletic contests of the Greeks; although there might be some hint of competitive prowess (*1 Sam.* 17, 10; *2 Sam.* 2, 13-16). Children played at children's games then as now, and there was prob. very little difference (*Zech.* 8, 5; *Matt.* 11, 16-17; *Luke* 7, 31 ff.). Paul, of course, and other Jews with a Greek background could not be ignorant of athletics even if they were not themselves particularly athletic (*Rom.* 9, 16; *1 Cor.* 9, 24-27; *Gal.* 2, 2; 5, 7; *Philip.* 2, 16; *2 Tim.* 4, 7; etc.). There is one prob. allusion to boxing (*Eph.* 4, 27). The AV trans. is 'neither

give place to the devil.' RSV has: ' give no
opportunity to the devil.' But the meaning really
is: ' when you're fighting the devil keep your
guard up.' The prize, ' palms ' (*Rev.* 7, 9) could
be the trad. award to the winning athlete.

Garden. Word used for all cultivated ground under
vegetables, fruit or flowers. Eden was a garden,
and so was Gethsemane and the place of the
sepulchre.

Garden House (*2 Kings* 9, 27). The Eng. trans. of
a place called Bethhaggan.

Garland. A wreath of flowers for bedecking a
sacrificial animal (*Acts* 14, 13).

Garlic. *Allium satirum.* The bulbous plant of the
onion family (*Num.* 11, 5).

Garment. *See* DRESS.

Garner. Simply to gather what is to be stored in a
granary; and sometimes the granary itself.

Garnish. Simply to ornament anything.

Garrison. A military post and the men who man
it. *See* FORTIFICATION AND SIEGE.

Gate. *See* FORTIFICATION AND SIEGE.

Gath. One of the great Philistine cities—Penta-
polis. It was the last ' hide-out ' of the giant
Anakim (qv) who were too tall to hide from Caleb.
(*Josh.* 11, 22). Goliath was one of them. David
captured Gath (*1 Chron.* 18, 1). It was held
alternately by Israelites and Philistines till Uzziah
broke its walls to ruins (*2 Chron.* 26, 6). No
more is heard of it, though Amos hints (6, 2)
that something pretty dreadful had happened to
it.

Gauls. *See* GALATIA.

Gaza [gā'-ză]. Like Gath it was one of the 5 great
Philistine cities (*Gen.* 10, 19; *Josh.* 11, 22). Samson had adventures here (*Judg.* 16, 1-3 & 21-
30).

Gazelle. AV has roe and roebuck; but they are gazelles: *gazella dorcas*. It is hunted (*Prov.* 6, 5; *Isa.* 13, 14) and was ceremonially clean (*Deut.* 12, 22). It was a favourite name for girls (Ghazaleh) and has the same meaning as Dorcas (qv) and Tabitha.

Geba [gĕ'-bă]. City of Benjamin assigned to the Levites (*Josh.* 21, 17).

Gebal [gĕ'-băl]. City N of Sidon, called Byblos by the Gks. Also an area S of the Dead Sea.

Gecko. *See* LIZARD.

Gehazi [gĕ-hā'-zī]. He was Elisha's servant and confidant, and prob. Elisha thought Gehazi was to him what he himself had been to Elijah. How wrong he was. But like most of his kind Gehazi was found out. His is a sordid and sorry story (*2 Kings* 4, 17-37; 5, 20 ff.).

Gehennah [gĕ-hĕn'-nă]. The name of a valley W of Jerusalem. It was assoc. with the horrid rites of Moloch and Tammuz (*2 Kings* 23, 15; *Jer.* 7, 31; 32, 35). During his reforms Josiah defiled the place (*2 Kings* 23, 6 & 10). It became a public rubbish dump. The names 'hell' and 'Gehennah' became interchangeable. *See* HELL.

Gemariah [gĕm-ă-rī'-ăh]. **1.** Son of Shaphan the Scribe who tried to prevent Jehoiakim (qv) from burning Jeremiah's scroll (*Jer.* 36, 10 ff.). **2.** Son of Hilkiah (qv) who carried a letter from Jeremiah to the Jews in Babylon (*Jer.* 29, 3).

General. The word has lost meaning since the AV was written. Here it means 'universal' as 'generally' means 'universally.'

Generation. 1. The act of begetting child, and the child who is begotten (*Gen.* 2, 4; 5, 1). **2.** A period of time quite undefined in duration (*Ps.* 10, 6 RV; 102, 24; *Isa.* 51, 8). **3.** All people living at a particular time (*Gen.* 6, 9). **4.** A particular type of people (*Prov.* 30, 11-14). **5.** Offspring (*Matt.* 3, 7). **6.** A race of people (*1 Pet.* 2, 9).

Genesis, Book of. Name of the 1st book of the Bible derived from LXX (*see* VERSIONS) and meaning *genesis kosmoi*—the origin of the world. Even better is ' Book of the beginnings.' There are 3 clear divisions: (1) Creation of the world and God's prime part in it. (1, 1-2, 3). (2) Hist. before Abraham and God's part in that (2, 4-11, 26). (3) The story of the Covenant from the time of Abraham (11, 27-50, 26). The book is certainly not the work of one hand. This was seen as early as 1753 when scholars noted God was ref. to by two distinct names: Jahweh and Elohim (trans. respectively Jehovah and The Lord). It was plain that passages containing the one name differed radically, characteristically and consistently in style, language, expression and emphasis from passages containing the other name. The mod. position briefly is that there are three main sources in the book, called for convenience J writings, E writings and P (priestly) writings. It seems that at some point the J and E writings were combined to become JE, and that parts of the narrative were subsequently rewritten by some priestly author whose main interest was the orig. and hist. of sacred and ecclesiastical institutions. Whatever may be thought of *Gen.* as a hist. record, its opening affirmation: ' in the beginning God ' is still unassailable. It is interesting to note in passing that the stages of Creation in *Gen.* are geologically correct in their order. *See* PENTA-TEUCH, FALL, FLOOD, etc.

Gennesaret. *See* SEA.

Gennesareth [gĕn-nĕ′-săr-ĕt(h)]. Dist. on W shore of Galilee.

Gentiles. All peoples other than Jews. They were,

however, within the Promise (*Isa.* 2, 2-4). When Peter had social and friendly dealings with Cornelius (*Acts* 10, 28; 11, 3), Christian Jews were outraged. Paul was bitterly attacked for claiming that he had a mission to the Gentiles (*Acts* 22, 21 & 22). There were far more Gentiles than Jews in the early Church, and the decision not to make them subscribe to the Law of Moses was fundamental to the spread of the Gospel (*Acts* 15, 1-29).

Gentle, Gentleness (*1 Thes.* 2, 7). This is the gentleness of a nurse with a young child. There is another gentleness with a certain amount of firmness for the child's own good (*2 Tim.* 2, 24). The word is also used meaning consideration, fairness, understanding, as opposed to the single-minded judgment of the Law (*Titus* 3, 2; *Jas.* 3, 17; *1 Pet.* 2, 18).

Gera [gē´-rä]. *See* WEIGHTS AND MEASURES.

Gerar [gē´-rär]. City nr. Gaza (*Gen.* 10, 19).

Gerizim [gĕr-ī´-zĭm]. Mt. the Samaritan equivalent of the Jewish Zion. It is the scene of Jotham's parable (*Judg.* 9, 7).

Gershom [gĕr´-shŏm]. 1. Son of Moses (*Ex.* 2, 22). 2. Son of Levi (*1 Chron.* 6, 16). 3. Desc. of Phineas (*Ezra* 8, 2).

Geshur [gē´-shŭr]. Aramaean kingdom bet. Hermon and Bashan (*2 Sam.* 13, 37). Absalom fled here after the murder of Amnon.

Gethsemane [gĕth-sē´-măn-ē]. Lit. ' oil press.' A garden, most prob. of olives, E of Jerusalem across the Kidron brook. The scene of Jesus' agony. There are two trad. sites, but no certainty.

Gezer [gē´-zēr], (**Gazara, Gazera**). An ancient Canaanite town (*Josh.* 10, 33). It was given by one of the Pharaohs to Solomon as his daughter's dowry (*1 Kings* 9, 16).

Ghost. Simply a spirit, cf. Holy Ghost.

Giant. A race of demi-gods, the Nephilim, comparable to the Titans of classical mythology (*Gen.* 6, 4). Other race names are given to peoples of remarkable stature who were aboriginal in Palestine before the conquest: Raphaim (*Deut.* 2, 11); Emim (*Deut.* 2, 10); Zamzummin (*Deut.* 2, 20); Zuzim (*Gen.* 14, 5); Anakim (*Josh.* 15, 13); Og of Bashan's bed (or, better, sarcophagus) was 13 ft. 6 in. long by 6 ft. broad. Goliath of Gath was 9 ft. 9 in. tall.

Gibeah [gĭb´-ĕ´-äh]. **1.** Village of Judah (*Josh.* 15, 57). **2.** Town of Benjamin nr. Ramah (*Judg.* 19, 13). Saul lived here (*1 Sam.* 10, 26). **3.** Town or hill in Ephraim where Eleazar was buried (*Josh.* 24, 33).

Gibeon [gĭb´-ē-ŏn]. Principal city of the Hivites (qv) inc. the Amorites (*Josh.* 11, 19; *2 Sam.* 21, 2). They were in treaty with Joshua, but deceived him (*Josh.* 9). Later the treaty was ratified (*Josh.* 10, 1-11). Saul, however, went back on it (*2 Sam.* 21, 1-9). Scene of the victory by David over the Philistines (*1 Chron.* 14, 16). Before the Temple was built the Tabernacle and brazen altar stood here (*1 Kings* 3, 4-15). The Gibeonites were taken into captivity with the Jews and were released with them (*Neh.* 7, 25).

Gideon [gĭd´-ē-ŏn]. Son of Joash of Ophra in Manasseh, he was called to liberate the people from the Midianites (*Judg.* 6). He offended the people by destroying the altar to Baal, but his father asked that Baal should be allowed to avenge himself—if he could. When there was no ' divine ' vengeance, Gideon earned the name of Jerubbaal (let Baal contend). He mobilised 4 tribes, reduced his numbers to 300, and defeated Midian in a night attack (*Judg.* 7). He refused a call to the throne and returned to private life (*Judg.* 8, 22 & 23). *See* JUDGES.

Gier eagle [gī′-er]. The Egyptian vulture—Pharaoh's Chicken (*Lev.* 11, 18; *Deut.* 14, 17). *See* OSSIFRAGE.

Gifts, Giving. Very often the gift was something expecting a *quid pro quo*. It can even be a bribe (*Prov.* 18, 16). Otherwise gifts may be in the nature of tribute (*2 Sam.* 8, 2 & 6); rewards (*Dan.* 2, 48); coming-of-age presents (*Gen.* 25, 6); or dowry (*Judg.* 1, 15). They could be the payment by the groom to the bride's father (*Gen.* 34, 12), or simply marriage presents (*Ps.* 45, 12). Gifts were required also for religious purposes (*Matt.* 5, 23 & 24; *Acts* 11, 29; *Philip.* 4, 16). In its religious use in NT, the gifts of God are the graces and virtues (*John* 14, 16; 16, 7; *Acts* 5, 31; *Rom.* 12, 6; *Gal.* 5, 22).

Gihon [gī′-hŏn]. A spring nr. Jerusalem; scene of Solomon's coronation (*1 Kings* 1, 33).

Gilboa [gĭl-bō′-ă]. Range of hills not higher than 1,700 ft., forming the watershed bet. the Kishon basin and the Jordan valley. They run for about 8 m. circling E of the plain of Esdraelon. Here Saul was defeated and slain by the Philistines (*1 Sam.* 28, 4; 31, 1; *2 Sam.* 1, 17 ff.).

Gilead [gĭl′-ē-ăd]. There are 3 persons of the name (*Josh.* 17, 1; *Judg.* 11, 1; *1 Chron.* 5, 14). But the chief Gilead is the mountainous country E of Jordan (*Deut.* 3, 16; etc.). Gad occupied the S part, and Manasseh had the N. Laban and Jacob met there for the last time (*Gen.* 31, 21). The dist. was celebrated for its balm (qv) (*Jer.* 8, 22). The name is given also to a mt. which may be Gilboah (*Judg.* 7, 3), and to a city (*Hos.* 6, 8).

Gilgal [gĭl′-găl]. **1.** First settlement of Israel after crossing the Jordan, and HQ for the conquest (*Josh.* 4, 19-24). Later a town was built (*Josh.* 15, 7). Saul forfeited his right to form a dynasty when he made a sacrifice here when his army was mobilised to fight the Philistines (*1 Sam.* 13, 4-15; 15, 20-23). It was a holy place which later became a centre of idolatry (*Hos.* 4, 15; *Amos* 4, 4). **2.** Village in Bethel connected with Elijah and Elisha (*2 Kings* 2, 1-4). **3.** Town on plain of Sharon (*Josh.* 12, 23).

Gimel [gĭm′-ĕl]. 3rd letter of Heb. alphabet—as Eng. *G*. *See* ALPHABET.

Gin. Snare:—a noose of rope or leather laid on ground or suspended over animal's run (*Job.* 18, 9; *Amos* 3, 5).

Girding the loins, Girdle. *See* DRESS.

Gittith [gĭt′-tĭth]. Musical term (*Ps.* 81; *Ps.* 84 titles). Derived from a musical instrument popular in Gath, or a tune of Gath; prob. a marching tune to which the *Ps.* was to be sung (*2 Sam.* 15, 18).

Glass. 1. A mirror (*Ex.* 38, 8; *1 Cor.* 13, 12). *See* MIRROR. **2.** Trans. of Heb. ' crystal ' (*Job* 28, 17). But very prob. simply glass as we know it to-day, which is far older than the Exodus.

Gleaning. For the sake of the poor, the farmer was not allowed to rake his field after reaping, nor to gather fallen fruit, nor to come back for grapes that were not ripe at the official grape harvest. These were the perquisite of the needy (*Lev.* 19, 9; *Judg.* 8, 2; *Ruth* 2, 2).

Glede. The kite (*Deut.* 14, 13).

Glory. In OT: (1) The honour due to God or to man. (2) The qualities which call for such honour, esp. the qualities of God. ' The wise shall inherit glory ' (*Prov.* 3, 35). It is used even of things, eg Lebanon (*Isa.* 35, 2). Used of one's own soul

(*Ps.* 16, 9). As a verb it is the shewing forth of God's qualities (*Isa.* 6, 3). It can be the Divine presence itself (*Ezek.* 1, 28). In NT it is the trans. of the Gk. *doxa* (except in *1 Pet.* 2, 20, where it means renown). *Doxa* is the reputation, the honour, of God. As applied to things it may mean splendour (*Rom.* 2, 7-10). Used as a verb it means to boast, to exult in (*1 Cor.* 1, 29). The moral and physical meanings appear together in (*Matt.* 16, 27; *Rev.* 21, 23).

Gnat. (*Matt.* 23, 24). Small fever-bearing, irritating blood-sucking insect. In this passage ' strain at ' is a mistrans. for ' strain out.' The fly falls into the glass and the drinker carefully strains it out. Then he swallows the camel without batting an eyelid.

Goad. A means of jogging cattle along, still used by E bullock cart drivers (*Eccl.* 12, 11; *Acts* 9, 5).

Goat. One of the highly valued domestic animals. The Eng. word trans. a wide variety of Heb. and Gk. words, but is perfectly adequate as the shades of meaning do not matter. Normally they were herded with the sheep but were separated for milking. They preferred the rougher grazing and were apt to be destructive of trees, crops, etc., which the sheep did not fancy. Hence the differentiation bet. sheep and goats. Goat hair was woven into fabrics. The skin made a bag for carrying water or wine. It was a sacrificial animal.

Goat, wild. This is a species of ibex with horns 3 ft. long, found mainly in Engedi (*Deut.* 14, 5; *Job* 39, 1; *Ps.* 104, 18).

God. Scripture teaches that God is not fully understood until He reveals Himself fully, and is fully accepted at His face value. Scripture is the hist. of God revealing Himself and of the various

responses of human beings to that progressive
revelation. It culminates in the revelation to
Jesus, and Jesus' response to it. The Eng. word
'God' is simply 'the object of worship.' The
Gk. word means 'spirit,' and the Heb. word
means 'The Power.' To the Christian, God is
the Almighty Spirit Who must be worshipped. The
only warrant for calling God 'He,' is that in
early Scriptural times women did not matter.
There is no reason why God should not be called
'She.' The writers of the books of the Bible
have been like artists trying to paint a picture.
The portrait changes with the passing years. The
Genesis portrait is not Isaiah's portrait. Till at
last in Jesus comes the portrait that remains
because it cannot be improved. Every attempt
to improve it results merely in one of the earlier
portraits emerging. When the Christian thinks
of God he thinks of his own mental and spiritual
portrait of Jesus and asks for nothing more because
he knows there is none better. All races have and
have had ideas of the Almighty spirit. Christianity
is the only religion which is satisfied with the
portrait it has. The names of God as they appear
in Holy Scripture are: Elohim, used of all gods,
for the early writers acknowledged the existence
of other gods (*1 Sam.* 28, 13). El, the Strong One,
the Ruler—a name often attached to a place or
to some attribute of the god (*Gen.* 31, 13; *Ex.* 20,
5). El Shaddai, God Almighty (*Ex.* 6, 3; *Num.* 24,
4). El Eligon, the Most High (*Gen.* 14, 18; *Ps.* 82,
6). Adonai, a word of relationship as of master
to servant, or of wife to husband. Jehovah,
Yahweh, Jahweh: He Who was, is, and will be
always (*Ex.* 3, 14). In other words, the orig. and
essential quality of life, the only true life, existence,
the One without Whom there can be no existence

at all, the only One who has existence that is self
derived (cf. *John* 5, 26). The name Jahweh was
so sacred that it was never spoken. Adonai was
used in its place when Scripture was being read.
In Heb. script, the vowels of Adonai were added
to the consonants of Jahweh, and so the name
Jehovah was created. Jah is Jahweh, and is used
in Heb. poetry and in forms such as Hallelujah.
Yahweh Tsebaoth is often rendered in Eng. as
Lord of Hosts (*Isa.* 1, 9; etc.). The God assoc.
with the army (which was a host of people). From
that came God with the hosts of heaven, and all
the forces of nature. There is no space to trace
the development of the idea of God from patriarchal to Messianic times, but it is interesting to
note that the anthropomorphism which could see
God walking in the garden in the cool of the day
(*Gen.* 3, 8) sees God again as Jesus hanging on the
Cross in the heat of the day.

Gog. 1. A Reubenite (*1 Chron.* 5, 4). **2.** Prince of
Resh, Mesech and Tubal (*Ezek.* 38, 39). Taken
as a type of the heathen agst. God. **3.** A mysterious person who was to appear before the end of
the present world (*Rev.* 20, 8-15). The last
struggle agst. God by heathendom was to be led
by Gog and Magog.

Gold. The precious metal which was found at
Havilah (*Gen.* 2, 11); at Sheba (*1 Kings* 10,
2); and at Ophir (*1 Kings* 22, 48). It was used
more or less as it is to-day. It serves as a
symbol of worth and value (*Lam.* 4, 2; *Rev.* 3,
18).

Golgotha [gŏl'-gŏth-ă]. *See* CALVARY.

Goliath [gŏ-li'-ăth]. Either there are two of the name
or there is some confusion. There was a Goliath
of Gath slain by David (*1 Sam.* 17, 4-10, 41-51
He was one of the Anakim (*Num.* 13, 33). But there

is another killed by Elhanan (*2 Sam*. 21, 19). *See* ELHANAN.

Gomer [gō'-mĕr]. **1.** Wife of Hosea (qv) (*Hos*. 1, 3). **2.** Race of people desc. from Japheth—the Gimmera or Cimmerians (*Gen*. 10, 2).

Gomorrah [gŏ-mŏr'-rah]. *See* PLAIN, CITIES OF.

Goodman. Means husband (*Prov*. 7, 19).

Gopher wood. Timber from which the Ark (Noah's) was made (*Gen*. 6, 14). Prob. cypress.

Goshen [gō'-shĕn]. **1.** Egyptian dist. on Nile delta (*Gen*. 46, 34). The Heb. were allowed to settle there after the reunion of Joseph with his father and brothers (46, 28). **2.** Region SE of Judah (*Josh*. 10, 41). **3.** Town in Judah (*Josh*. 15, 51).

Gospel. Both the good tidings and the books which contain the hist. of Him who brought them. In NT the word means always the message and not the Book. Not till post-apostolic times was the word applied to the books. The 4 Gospels have always been credited to Matthew, Mark, Luke and John and were from the beginning accepted as authoritative. The first three as they are in our Bible were called the Synoptics, because by and large they tell the same story in the same way. And although they differ in details, they all differ in more than detail from *John*, which concentrates largely on the divinity of Jesus and His claim to Sonship; while the others are more concerned with objective narrative. The only incident prior to the Crucifixion which appears in all the Gospels is the feeding of the 5,000. The Synoptics concentrate upon Jesus' teaching about God's will and human behaviour. *John* concentrates upon Jesus' teaching about Himself. But each is necessary to the others. The Synoptics become clear only because we read them along with *John*. The Synoptics themselves are pointed in different

directions. Matthew writes from the Jewish
point of view, claiming Jesus as Messiah. In
support of his contention he quotes a great deal
of OT texts. Mark concentrates on Jesus' power
to save, using the miracles as proof. Luke, the
friend and companion of Paul, shows Jesus the
tender Saviour, loving the poor, the outcast, and
the sinner. John shows Jesus as God Incarnate;
the portrait and the pattern of the Father. None
of them pretends to be or was ever intended to
be, the complete life story of the Lord. Mark
prob. heard much from Peter, and may have
known Jesus personally, though only when Mark
was a lad. He may well be the only one who had
any first-hand knowledge. Luke's knowledge was
obtained from listening to eye-witnesses, who
were not few (*Luke* 1, 1-4). They may not have
begun by writing. They may have started by
preaching; and when they finally came to writing,
they wrote about those aspects of Jesus' ministry
that they had been preaching about, the parts
that appealed to themselves as being significant.
John, having read what the rest had written must
have decided to fill in the gaps, and to build the
foundation for it all. It seems certain, however,
that there was some written account, however
sketchy, before the first Gospel was put on paper.
Most of Mark is in Luke and Matthew. When
it comes to the order of incidents, Mark is
never alone. Either Matthew has the same order and
Luke has not, or Luke has the same order and
Matthew has not. Mark is never in a minority of
one. Matthew and Luke were assuredly dependent
on Mark, but both of them seem to have had access
to some writings earlier than Mark's, which were
not available to Mark. The most complete story
of the life of the Lord is made by putting the

Gospels together. All of them were written well within the first Christian cent.

Gourd. (*Jonah* 4, 6-10). Prob. the castor oil plant, *Palma Christi*, or Christ's palm, though it is not a palm. It grows to 8 or 10 ft. very rapidly.

Governor. Several Heb. words are trans. ' governor,' and usually the meaning is fairly plain. Joseph was prob. Prime Minister under Pharaoh (*Gen.* 42, 6) (cf. *1 Kings* 18, 3). Persian governors of Judea were satraps (AV) (*Esth.* 3, 12); (*Ezra* 5, 3). The proper title of the Rom. governor in the NT is procurator (AV) (*Luke* 3, 1; *Acts* 23, 26). It was a special office reserved for territories fairly recently conquered and not yet organised on Rom. lines. In another place (*2 Cor.* 11, 32) 'ethnarch' is better, that is the ruler of a people who still retain their own way of life. Other refs. might be better rendered as ' steward ' (*Gal.* 4, 2); ' steersman ' or ' pilot ' (*Jas.* 3, 4); ' master of ceremonies ' is better than ' governor ' of the feast (*John* 2, 8).

Grapes. *See* WINE AND STRONG DRINK.

Grasshopper. Probably the locust (qv).

Grave. The Jews did not normally bury in holes dug in the ground but more usually in natural or artificial caves (*Matt.* 27, 60).

Graven image. *See* IDOL.

Greaves. *See* ARMOUR.

Grecians. Sometimes used of the people of Greece (*Joel* 3, 6). Also used of Jews who spoke Gk. in preference to Aram. (*Acts* 6, 1; etc.).

Greece. The Gks. called themselves Hellenes and their land Hellas. The Graeci were an ancient tribe whose name was adopted by the W world in preference to the other. The land is a peninsula on the SE corner of Europe. The written records of Greece date back to the 1st Olympiad, 776 BC. Orig.

there were 4 tribes: the Aeolians, the Acheans, the Dorians and the Ionians. The Athenians were desc. from the Dorians and the Spartans from the Ionians. Up till around 500 BC the states were independent but with a common language and culture. The states were allied politically and were known to the Jews who called their land Yavan—Ionia (*Gen.* 10, 4). Greece found herself in the struggle agst. the Persian power that had swept through the E and was threatening Europe. Cyrus took the Gk. cities of Asia Minor in 546 BC; Darius crossed the Hellespont and captured Macedonia in 510. But the Persians were routed by the Gks. at Marathon in 490 and in the sea battle off Salamis in 480, followed by defeats at Plataea and Mycale in 479. For once the Gk. nation was one and Athens emerged as the leading city state. Civil war broke out later bet. factions headed by Athens and Sparta and the Peloponnesian war dragged on disastrously from 431 till 404. Athens fell and Sparta became supreme. In 338 Philip of Macedonia, father of Alexander the Great, brought the whole of Greece within his empire. Alexander moving E as far as India, took Judea in his stride and for the first time Gk. influence was really felt in the land. One very important service rendered by this people was to provide the whole civilised world with a common language, and this greatly accelerated the spread of Christianity. By 146 Greece had fallen to the Roms. and became a province under the name of Achaea. The contribution of Greece to philosophy and the arts has been, of course, of incalculable value.

Greek. 1. A native of Greece (*Acts* 16, 1) or one of the Gk. race not living in Greece. The title is sometimes used simply for Gentile as contrasted with Jew (*Rom.* 1, 14; etc.). The Gks. who wished to see Jesus (*John* 12, 20) were simply foreigners, who may or may not have been Gks. **2.** The name is used also of the language which is very full, complete, expressive, and precise. The OT was trans. into Gk. before Jesus was born. *See* VERSIONS.

Greyhound. Dogs not unlike greyhounds or staghounds are depicted on Assyrian monuments; but the word is prob. a mistrans. of another word, meaning a warhorse (*Prov.* 30, 31). There is another similar word meaning a starling.

Grinder. In (*Eccl.* 12, 3) means the women grinding corn. *See* MILL. In *Job* (29, 17) it means the molar teeth.

Grove. This is a mistrans. for the *asherah* (qv) or poles set up for pagan worship. The exception is *Gen.* 21, 33 where the meaning is tamarisk tree (qv).

Grudge (*Ps.* 59, 15; *Jas.* 5, 9) has an old sense of grumbling. Later the word came to mean the feeling which produces grumbles.

Guard, bodyguard. The military necessity is obvious, and the guard had to be trustworthy: men like Potiphar (*Gen.* 37, 36), and Benaiah (*2 Sam.* 23, 22) who commanded David's bodyguard who were all foreign mercenaries. Some bodyguards had to kill the royal food and presumably taste it.

Guilt offering. *See* OFFERINGS.

H

Habakkuk [hă-bă′-kkŭk]. A prophet of Judah in pre-exilic times c. 608-598 BC, and contemporary with Jeremiah. The kings reigning during his

period were Jehoahaz and Jehoiakim. The threatened Chaldean invasion mentioned at the beginning of the book is that of (*2 Kings* chs. 24 & 25).
The style of the book is dialogue bet. the prophet
and God. Judah has fallen away from God and
there can be no complaint if God's justice uses
the Chaldeans to punish them. From that point
he moves to a new and noble idea; the unjust
will die, but the just will live (2, 4). This will be
true of the Jews and Chaldeans alike. In the
last chapter he reaches a great and moving
thought which is used 3 times in the NT (*Rom.*
1, 17; *Gal.* 3, 2 & 11; *Heb.* 10, 38). Ch. 3 is a
psalm which could be sung during public worship.

Habergeon. A coat of mail (*2 Chron.* 26, 14). *See*
ARMOUR. There is a wrong ref. (*Job* 41, 26).
This should be 'a pointed shaft.'

Hachilah [hă-chī′-lăh]. Hill SE of Hebron (*1 Sam.*
26, 1-3) where David hid and Saul camped.

Hadad [hā′-dăd]. **1.** God of the Arameans, found
in prop. names, eg Ben Hadad. **2.** King of
Edom whose capital was Pai (*1 Chron.* 1, 50).
3. King of Edom whose capital was Avith (*1
Chron.* 14, 6). **4.** Edomite prince who as a child
escaped the Joab massacres and was taken to
Egypt where later he married a princess. He
returned to Edom and became the enemy of
Solomon (*1 Kings* 11, 14-22).

Hadadezer [hăd′-ă-dē-zĕr]. Sometimes Hadarezer.
King of Zoba in Syria and mortal enemy of
David (*2 Sam.* 8, 3-13; 10, 16-19). *See* BEN HADAD.

Hadassah [hă-dăs′-săh]. Jewish name of Esther
(qv).

Hades. *See* HELL.

Haft. Handle (*Judg.* 3, 22).

Hagar [hā′-găr]. Egyptian bondwoman or slave to
Sarah, wife of Abraham. Sarah was barren, and

according to a prevailing custom sanctioned union bet. Abraham and Hagar, who began to put on airs, and ran into trouble, and disappeared. However she had a vision of the race that would spring from the child she would bear and returned (*Gen.* 16, 1-16). She gave birth to Ishmael, but later Sarah gave birth to Isaac. Mutual jealousies, understandable enough, led to Hagar's banishment with her son. After much suffering she got through the desert to Paran and eventually returned to Egypt (*Gen.* 21, 1-21). The Arabs trace their desc. from Abraham through Hagar. Paul uses the story as an illustration (*Gal.* 4, 21-31). *See* ISHMAEL.

Haggai [hăg′-gā-ī]. A Jewish prophet, post-exilic, of the Medo-Persian period, with a date c. 520 BC. More or less contemporaneous with Zechariah and Malachi. Prob. born in Babylon during the captivity he would return, on their release under Cyrus, with Zerubbabel. His task was to persuade and encourage the people to finish building the Temple. His four sermons are quite distinct and cover a period of only a few months (1, 2-11; 2, 1-9; 2, 10-19; 2, 20-23). The message might be summed up as ' whatsoever your hand finds to do, do it with all your might.' He first points out that their troubles have come on them because they rebuilt their own houses before God's. He encourages them by telling them how the new Temple will outshine the old. The blessing will come and God will rule through his servant Zerubbabel.

Hai [hā′-ī]. *See* AI.

Hail. One of the most devastating of natural disasters to the E farmer. The hailstones are often of considerable size and flatten crops, beat leaves and fruit from trees, and even kill the birds that keep the ground clean. Usually a hailstorm is short and limited to a clearly defined area (*Ex.* 9, 26; *Josh.* 10, 11).

Hair. Many usages, traditions and superstitions were assoc. with the hair of the head. Egyptian men shaved the face and head but often wore wigs. Assyrians wore their hair long, and Jews wore theirs fairly long, though in NT times men wore the hair cut much shorter. The edge of the hair—at the corners of the temples—was not to be cut, as this was a heathen ceremonial connected with male puberty. Heb. women were gen. black haired, wearing long braided or unbraided tresses often with ornaments. Both men and women used oil on the hair (*Matt.* 6, 17). There must be no shaving of the head (*Lev.* 21, 5). If a Heb. took as his wife a fem. captive her head was shaved in purification and initiation. The Nazirite under vow did not cut his hair at all. When his vow was accomplished he could cut it, but if he failed in his vow his head was shaved (*Num.* 6, 18). *See* BEARD.

Hall. 1. The court of the High Priest's palace (*Luke* 22, 55). **2.** The Governor's official residence and the judgment court or praetorium (qv) (*Matt.* 27, 27).

Hallel [hăl′-ĕl]. Lit, ' praise.' A name given to certain Psalms in which ' Hallelujah ' keeps recurring. There is the Egyptian Hallel (*Ps.* 113-118) and the Great Hallel (*Ps.* 120-136). These were sung at the great festivals.

Hallelujah. ' Praise ye the Lord ' normally occurs at the beginning or end or both of the Psalm, The exception is (135, 3). Prob. it should only be a heading indicating that certain Psalms are particularly suitable for synagogue praise. When taken into NT trans. ' Praise ye the Lord.'

Hallow. To make holy or to regard as holy. The latter is the meaning in the Lord's Prayer—its only mention in the NT.

Halt. To limp or stumble, cf. stringhalt, a form of lameness in horses. ' How long halt ye bet. two opinions' does not mean to stand motionless bet. them, but to stumble bet. them (*1 Kings* 18, 21).

Ham. Second son of Noah (*Gen.* 5, 32; 6, 10). He incurred a curse by unfilial conduct though it was more Noah's fault than his (*Gen.* 9, 22-27). Trad. forefather of S Arabians, Ethiopians, Egyptians, and Canaanites. Also called Canaan. The name is used poetically for Egypt (*Ps.* 78, 51; etc.).

Haman [hā′-măn]. Son of Hammedatha (*Esth.* 3, 1). Also called the Agagite. The story of his hatred for Mordecai, his attempt at a massacre of the Jews, and his discomfiture by Esther and eventual death is told in the book of *Esther* (qv).

Hamath [hā′-măth]. Hemath (*Amos* 6, 14). A city on the Orontes N of Hermon, 120 miles N of Damascus, founded by the Hittites. Solomon conquered it (*2 Chron.* 8, 3 & 4). It was later taken by the Assyrians (*2 Kings* 18, 34).

Hammeah, Tower of [hăm′-mē-ăh]. Part of the walls of Jerusalem bet. the Sheep gate and the Fish gate, with the tower Hananel (RV) beside it.

Hammer. Handtool used more or less as it is to-day. Used fig. as any crushing force (*Jer.* 50, 23). Another Heb. word is used for the mallet for driving pegs, which would be wooden (*Judg.* 4, 21).

Hammiphkad (Miphkad) [hăm-mǐph′-kăd]. Gate, prob. of the Temple.

Hammurabi [hăm′-mū-rä′-bǐ]. King of Babylon c. 1728-1686 BC. He was a good king, chiefly famed for his reform of the laws, and for collecting the written statutes. Mosaic law is not, of course, a mere re-write of the laws of Hammurabi.

Hamor [hā'-môr]. Prince of Shechem whose son violated Dinah. (*Gen.* 34). Also spelled Emmor.

Hamutal [hă-mū'-tăl]. Mother of Jehoahaz and Zedekiah (*2 Kings* 23, 31).

Hananel [hăn'-ă-nĕl] (Hananeel). Tower on walls of Jerusalem.

Hand. W people face N when describing directions. The left hand is W and the right hand E. But E peoples face E when describing directions, so that ' on the right hand ' is S and on the left is N. In prayer the two hands were raised (*Ex.* 17, 11; etc.), one hand was raised for a vow (*Gen.* 14, 22). When making a vow to a person the hand might be placed under the thigh (*Gen.* 24, 2). *See* OATH. To lay the hands on the head conveyed a blessing (*Gen.* 48, 14). This was the origin of ordination. *See* LAYING ON OF HANDS. Sin could be transferred thus (*Lev.* 16, 21). To wash the hands was to deny responsibility (*Deut.* 21, 6; *Matt.* 27, 24). Clapping hands was a sign of anger (*Num.* 24, 10). A contract could be sealed by shaking hands (*Prov.* 6, 1). Left handedness was an asset in war (*Judg.* 3, 15 & 21). God's power rested in His hand (*Deut.* 2, 15; *John* 10, 28 & 29).

Handbreadth. *See* WEIGHTS AND MEASURES.

Handkerchief. Contradiction in terms; a kerchief is for the head. Better as ' napkin.'

Handstave. (*Ezek.* 39, 9) a club or throwing stick.

Hanging. *See* CRIME AND PUNISHMENT.

Hangings. Curtains (*Ex.* 26, 36; 35, 17). ' Screens ' as in RV is better.

Hannah [hăn'-năh]. Wife of Elkanah and mother of Samuel. She was one of two wives and prob. had not borne a child. She vowed that if she did she would dedicate him to God. This she does. Her song of triumph, natural enough under the circumstances, is echoed in Mary's Magnificat (*1 Sam.* 2, 1-10; *Luke* 1, 46-55).

Hanun [hă´-nŭn]. King of the Ammonites (*2 Sam.* ch. 10).

Hap, haply. A ' hap ' is what happens, a happening. There is always the element of chance. Orig. haply was purely ' by chance ', but it has now come to mean ' by good chance.'

Haran [hā´-răn]. **1.** Brother of Abraham, father of Lot (*Gen.* 11, 29). **2.** A Levite (*1 Chron.* 23, 9). **3.** Mesopotamian city of great commercial importance, where Terah died (*Gen.* 11, 31; 12, 4 & 5). **4.** Son of Caleb (*1 Chron.* 2, 46).

Hararite [hăr´-ă-rīte]. Descriptive name applied to several of David's heroes. Prob. means ' the highlander ' (*2 Sam.* 23, 11 & 33).

Hard. Sometimes means ' nearly ' cf. ' hard by ' (*Judg.* 9, 52; *Ps.* 63, 8). It can mean ' harshly ' (*Gen.* 16, 6), or ' with difficulty ' (*Ex.* 13, 15; *Matt.* 19, 23). ' Hardness ' can be ' hardship ' (*2 Tim.* 2, 3).

Hare. An unclean animal since it chews the cud and does not part the hoof (*Lev.* 11, 6). Actually the hare does not chew the cud; it is a rodent. There are 4 varieties known in Palestine.

Harlot. Member of the oldest profession in the world. It might be carried on simply as an easy way of making a living, or it might receive official sanction from religions which made reproductivity part of their great good . As in India to-day at the Holi festival there were seasons of sexual orgy in many ancient religions, when the temple precincts were an inglorious brothel (*Prov.* 6, 24; *Amos* 2, 7; *Hos.* 4, 13). This idea of unnatural

and wicked abasement of sex, and the revolt
agst. marriage vows was used by prophets to
point the evil of apostasy. The tendency to
identify religious fervour and sexual excitement
was present even in NT times (*Acts* 15, 20; *Rom.*
1, 24; *1 Cor.* 6, 9).

Harmageddon [här'-mă-gĕd'-dŏn]. *See* ARMAGED-
DON, MEGIDDO.

Harness. Armour (qv).

Harod [hā'-rŏd]. A spring, assoc. with Gideon
(*Judg.* 7, 1).

Harp. *See* MUSICAL INSTRUMENTS.

Harrow. Agricultural implement for breaking clods
after ploughing, and for covering seed. It consisted of iron or wooden teeth mounted on a frame.
One ref. (*2 Sam.* 12, 31) is certainly not this implement but has something to do with forced
labour using picks.

Harsith [här'-sĭth]. One of the gates of Jerusalem,
called (AV) the East of Sun Gate, and (RV) the
Gate of the Potsherds (*Jer.* 19, 2).

Hart. Male deer over 5 yrs. old. *See* DEER.

Harvest. *See* AGRICULTURE.

Hashum [hă'-shŭm]. Personal and family name
often encountered in *Ezra* and *Nehemiah.*

Hasenaah [hăs'-ĕn-ă'-ăh]. Personal and place name
prominent at the rebuilding of Jerusalem (*Neh.*
3, 3; etc.).

Hat. *See* DRESS. One ref. (*Dan.* 3, 21) should be
' mantle.'

Hattin [hăt'-tĭn]. Hill bet. Tiberias and Nazareth.
There is a trad. that it is the scene of the Sermon
on the Mount

Haunt. In Scripture it has no ghostly or unworthy
sense. One's haunt is the place one frequents for
legitimate reasons. The word has become debased
(*1 Sam.* 30, 31; 23, 22).

Hauran [hă'-ū-răn]. Fertile dist. SE of Hermon, bordering on Gilead (*Ezek.* 47, 16; etc.).

Havilah [hăv'-ĭ-lăh]. **1.** Son of Cush (*Gen.* 10, 7). **2.** Son of Joktan (*I Chron.* 1, 9). It is really a place and tribal name for the Cushite dist. where Joktan settled (*Gen.* 2, 11 & 12).

Havoth Jair [hăv'-vŏth jā'-ĭr]. Unwalled towns (lit. ' tent villages ') in Bashan (*Deut.* 3, 4).

Hawk. There are many varieties of this predatory bird in Palestine. It was ceremonially unclean (*Lev* 11, 16)

Hay. Sometimes trans. grass; sometimes herbage in gen. It is not always, in AV, sun-dried grass.

Hazael [hăz'-ă-ĕl]. A Syrian. Elijah was ordered by God to anoint him king of Syria (*I Kings* 19, 15) c. 840 BC. Ben Hadad, however, was king. He later sent Hazael to Elisha to ask advice about recovery from illness. Elisha told Hazael that the king would not recover and that he would succeed him. Hazael told Ben Hadad that he would recover, and next day murdered him and usurped the throne (*2 Kings* 8, 7-15). He was persuaded not to sack Jerusalem by being bought off with the Temple treasures (*2 Kings* 12, 17 & 18). The ' House of Hazael ' is the city of Damascus (*Amos* 1, 4).

Hazel. Prob. the almond (qv) (*Gen.* 30, 37).

Hazeroth [hă-zēr'-ŏth]. One of Israel's camping grounds, where Miriam and Aaron complained about Moses' leadership (*Num.* 12).

Hazor [hă-zŏr]. **1.** Capital of Canaan at the invasion, taken and burned by Joshua (*Josh.* 11, 1-13). The king was Jabin, though there was another Jabin in the time of Deborah. Its inhabitants were later taken into captivity by the Assyrians (*2 Kings* 15, 29). **2.** Town in S Judah (*Josh.* 15,

23). **3.** Village of Benjamin (*Neh.* 11, 33). **4.** Desert region of Palestine (*Jer.* 49, 28-33).

He [hay]. Fifth letter of the Heb. alphabet, pronounced as Eng. *H*.

Head. The heart was the seat of intellect; the head was the seat of life; (*Matt.* 5, 36) swearing by the head. The word was also used, of course, for the chief or ruler of a household or community. To ' lift up the head ' is to be successful (*Ps.* 27, 6). Dust and ashes on the head, or covering the head, was a sign of mourning (*2 Sam.* 1, 2; 15, 30). To uncover the head and let the hair hang any way was also a mourning sign (*Lev.* 10, 6). To lay the hands on the head was part of the sacrificial rite, and also of blessing and ordination (qv) (*Lev.* 16, 21; *Gen.* 48, 14 ff; *Acts* 6, 6). *See* HAIR.

Headband. Prob. a sash (*Isa.* 3, 20). *See* DRESS.

Headstone. Should be ' head ' (or most important) stone, not a tombstone. *See* CORNERSTONE.

Head tire. Lit. ' head attire ' (*Ezek.* 24, 17 RV). AV has ' tire of the head.' ' Round tires ' are metal ornaments trans. ' crescents ' in RV. *See* ORNAMENT, DRESS.

Heady. Headstrong (*2 Tim.* 3, 4).

Health. 1. Healing (*Prov.* 12, 18; 13, 17; *Jer.* 8, 15). **2.** Soundness of heart and soul (*Ps.* 42, 11; 43, 5; 67, 2). **3.** Gen. well-being, not merely physical, ' heartiness ' (*Acts* 27, 34; *3 John* 2).

Heart. Generally speaking the word is not used much in the physical sense; the physical function of the heart was not understood. Yet Jacob's heart was weak in his old age, as was Eli's (*Gen.* 45, 26; *1 Sam.* 4, 13 ff.). But in the main the word is used in the spiritual and psychological sense; that which is dearest and most important to anyone; the inspiration of an action good or bad (*Gen.* 6, 6; 8, 21). This is what the Psalmist

means when he asks for a clean heart (51, 10).
The same is true of the prophet Ezekiel's prayer
(36, 26). The heart is also the centre and source
of the emotions and passions (*Deut.* 19, 6; *1
Kings* 8, 38). The Hebs. believed the head to be
the centre of life and the heart the centre of intel-
ligence and memory (*Ex.* 14, 5; *1 Kings* 4, 29; *Job*
34, 10; *Prov.* 14, 10; *Isa.* 10, 7). The heart also
holds the conscience (*Job* 27, 6). In NT and early
Christian thought these ideas persist (*Matt.* 5, 8;
13, 19; *Luke* 8, 15; *Rom.* 8, 27). St. John often
uses ' heart ' when he means conscience.

Hearth. *See* HOUSE.

Heath. (*Jer.* 17, 6). Could be tamarisk (qv) or
juniper. *See* BROOM.

Heathen. Strictly a person who does not worship
the God of the Bible, but many refs. are interchangeable with ' nation of people ' as RV and
RSV have it correctly

Heaven, the heavens. Hebs. believed that the
cosmos was in three layers; Earth being flat, and
bet. the Pit of the Dead and the Heaven of God
and the angels. Later an idea developed that the
proper route for the deceased righteous should
be up and not down. The heavens had to have
some support (*2 Sam.* 22, 8). There was more than
one heaven (cf. ' The Seventh Heaven '). Aravoth,
the highest of all was the abode of God. The third
heaven may have been the dwelling place of the
redeemed (*2 Cor.* 12, 2). This is, of course, OT
thinking. The NT does not pretend to be so
precise except in the *Revelation*.

Heave offering. To heave, was simply to select and
elevate from the mass and dedicate to God (*Lev.*
22, 12 RV; *Num.* 5, 9; etc.). The priests would take
to their own use those parts of offerings which
did not require to be burned (*Num.* 18, 8-11).

In other words the heave offering was the selected part of the whole which was the perquisite of the priests and of their families.

Heaviness. That which bears one down: grief.

Hebrew. Lit. 'a desc. of Eber: a wanderer. Scripture says they came orig. from the other side of the Euphrates (*Gen.* 12, 5; 14, 13). The name Habiri is frequently found in cuneiform inscriptions dating from 2600 BC to 1700 BC. They were invading Palestine c. the later 1300's. The Israelites could have been the Habiri, though it is not an ethnic name. The word ' Hebrews ' was applied, however, strictly to the Israelites, but by NT times it was applied only to Jews who spoke Heb. (*Philip.* 3, 5). The language is one of a related group called Semitic. The written language consisted of consonants only (22 of them) and the vowel signs were the invention of Heb. scholars in the 6th cent. AD (the Massoretes). Apart from *Daniel, Ezra* and one or two odd passages which were in Aram., the entire OT was written in Heb Gradual'y Aram. supplanted it as a spoken language, though it remained the classic language esp. of religion. In most NT refs. ' Hebrew ' means Aram.

Hebrews, Epistle to the. Although claimed in the AV as Pauline, this letter almost certainly is not. Clearly it is addressed not to Christian Jews in gen. but to some particular group of them, and it is unlikely, from internal evidence, that the group was in Jerusalem (2, 3). Some believe that it was sent to Christian Jews in Alexandria, yet later Alexandrines attributed it to Paul. The style and the argument are entirely diff. from Paul's. The only geographical clue in the letter is: ' they of Italy salute you ' (13, 24). It could therefore have been written in Rome and sent to someone else, or it could have been written anywhere where there was an Italian settlement and sent back to Rome. But it is obviously written for Jews and the Roman church was essentially Gentile. It could have been sent to a Jewish house-church in Rome (*Rom.* 16) or even to a Jewish Christian synagogue there (*Heb.* 10, 25). The strong argument that it was sent to Jewish readers is the warning agst. apostasy, not to paganism, but to Judaism. The writer is telling them that anything found good in Judaism is found better in Christianity. He constantly refs. back to the OT which would have been of little interest to Gentiles. The early Church fathers omitted this letter from the canon of Scripture, showing clearly that they did not believe that Paul had written it. Tertullian attributed it to Barnabas. The Alexandrines attributed it to Paul. Origen thought that the ideas were Pauline but that the style was not. The E Church accepted Paul as author, and the 'rad. was gradually accepted by the W Church, although Augustine and Jerome were not at all sure of it. If it had been sent to Jerusalem it is just poss. that Barnabas was the author. If the destination were Rome it cannot have been his. Luther suggested that the author was Apollos, who fills the bill in almos' every respect. Others fa our Priscilla and Aquila, or at east Aquila. They started Apollos on the right road, after all (*Rom.* 16, 3-5). There is little evidence about date, but what there is would seem to indicate a date bet. the death of Paul and the start of the persecution under Nero. The substance of the letter is as follows. **1.** An exposition of the superiority of Christianity over Judaism and all other faiths simply because there is no one superior to Jesus Christ (chs. 1-4).

2. The place of Jesus as High Priest and Mediator (chs. 5-7). **3.** The fact that His ministry as High Priest is now performed from heaven (chs. 8-10, 18). **4.** Exhortations to live the Christian life through all trials and tribulations (10, 19 ; 12, 29). **5.** Further exhortations on specific items of life, belief and conduct. It should be noted that no other epistle refs. to Jesus as priest.

Hebron [hē'-brŏn]. This is used as a personal name (*Ex.* 6, 18), but the imp. Hebron is the town in Judah (*Josh.* 15, 54). It was there when Abraham came (*Gen.* 13, 18), and there Sarah died and was buried (*Gen.* 23, 2 & 19). Joshua's spies had a look at it (*Num.* 13, 22). The king of Hebron and his three allies were defeated by Joshua (*Josh.* 10,1-27), and the town was destroyed. Later it was re-settled, but Caleb reduced it again (*Josh.* 14, 13-15 ; *Judg.* 1, 10). It became one of the Cities of Refuge (qv) and for a while David used it as his capital (*1 Chron.* 11,1-3 ; *2 Sam.* 2, 1-3, 11). The place was a fertile plot some 20 m. SE of Jerusalem, and the centre of the Absalom revolt (*2 Sam.* 15, 7).

Hedge. A ' boma ' or thorn hedge built for defence. In some refs. prob. a stone wall (*Ps.* 89, 40). In NT any kind of partition (*Mark* 12, 1 ; etc.).

Heifer. A cow which has not calved. For religious uses, *see* PURIFICATION.

Heir. The principle of inheritance was early acknowledged (*Gen.* 15, 3). Property, which was mainly animals, went to the sons of the wife or wives, but not to the sons of concubines (*Gen.* 21, 10). Daughters could inherit (*Job* 42, 15). The law stated that the oldest son received a double portion (*Deut.* 21, 17). If there were no sons, daughters would inherit but must not marry outside the clan (*Num.* 27, 1-8 ; 36). If there was no issue, the man's brother inherited (*Num.* 27,

9-11). The word is also used metaphorically of man's relationship to God (*Rom.* 8, 16-17; *Heb.* 9, 15).

Heli [hē'-lī]. Father of Joseph of Nazareth (*Luke* 3, 23).

Hell. In AV the trans. of Heb. *Sheol* and Gk. *Hades*. RV and RSV use the transliteration, 'the place of the dead.' The nature of Sheol was never clearly defined, one writer thinking one thing, and another, another. It was the lowest of the three shelves of the cosmos and was under the earth, which was flat (*Num.* 16, 30). The dead did nothing. They were shades living in a shadow (*2 Sam.* 22, 6). Nothing ever happened there, though it was just possible to get back to earth from it (*1 Sam.* 28, 8-19). It was not out of God's province and interest (*Job* 26, 6; *Ps.* 139, 8). From this there developed the idea of a distinction bet. those who had pleased God and those who had not, and eventually there was the idea of a complete separation; hell being the place of punishment and heaven the place of reward (*Job* 19, 25-27; *Ps.* 16, 8-11). But the full idea of eternal bliss and of eternal punishment came with the teaching of Jesus and the NT writers (*Luke* 23, 43; *2 Cor.* 5, 6-10). Thus hell became the place of misery by contrast, and the Gk. becomes in places Gehennah which was the valley of Hinnom where human sacrifices had once been made to Moloch. The assoc. of fire and filth made the name of hell synonymous with sin, and eternal, burning punishment. *See* HEAVEN, PARADISE, GEHENNAH, MOLOCH.

Hellenist. A non-Gk. who spoke Gk. as his language, and who by implication lived after the Gk. mode (*Acts* 6, 1; 9, 29). AV has Grecians.

Helmet. *See* ARMOUR.

Helps. It means in one ref. AV 'emergency measures' (*Acts* 27, 17); the frappings for keeping together a storm-battered ship whose seams are opening. It is included by Paul in the list of services rendered to the church (*1 Cor.* 12, 28), 'helps and governments.' These two Gk. words are not used elsewhere in the NT, but 'helps' means people who are helpful esp. to the poor and needy. 'Governments' means people qualified by nature and by training to exercise control and give guidance. The steersman of a ship was called the governor; cf. the Victorian title for one's father, the governor.

Helve. Handle of an axe (*Deut.* 19, 5).

Hem. *See* BORDER OF GARMENT.

Hemlock. *See* GALL, WORMWOOD.

Hen. Usually the fem. in the bird world. But the name does occur as a person in the AV (*Zech.* 6, 14). It is prob. a mistrans. for 'kindness' as in RV and RSV.

Henna. AV trans. 'camphire,' a fragrant plant with yellow flowers (*S. of S.* 1, 14). The leaves and twigs were pounded into powder and used as colouring for the nails, soles of the feet, and sometimes the hair and beard.

Herald. One who proclaims the king's commands (*Dan.* 3, 4). Used in RV margin of Paul (*1 Tim.* 2, 7; *2 Tim.* 1, 11) and Noah (*2 Pet.* 2, 5).

Herb. A green thing, herbage or grass, vegetables of sorts.

Hereafter. May mean 'from this time on' (*Matt.* 26, 64; *Mark* 11, 14; *Luke* 22, 69), or simply, 'some time in the future' (*John* 13, 7).

Heresy. The Gk. word does not have the mod. sense of a doctrinal departure from the faith, when used in the NT. It means rather a faction or party or sect (*Acts* 5, 17; etc.). The word 'sect' is usually used, though Paul uses 'way' (of thinking) (*Acts* 24, 14). Later it took on the meaning of schism or split (*1 Cor.* 11, 18 & 19). But when Peter uses the word, he means something closer to the mod. meaning (*2 Pet.* 2, 1); false teaching.

Hermas [hĕr'-măs]. Christian at Rome (*Rom.* 16, 14). Common name among slaves.

Hermes [hĕr'-mēs]. Dif. man, but same explanation as above.

Hermogenes [hĕr-mŏ'-gĭn-ēs]. An Asian Christian who with others abandoned Paul (*2 Tim.* 1, 15).

Hermon [hĕr'-mŏn]. Mt. at S end of the anti-Lebanon range over 9,000 ft. high. There is always snow in the gullies. It was the limit of the conquest of Canaan (*Josh.* 11, 3).

Hermonites. Prop. 'the Hermons,' for the mt. has 3 peaks (*Ps.* 42, 6 AV).

Herod. Founder of the ruling house was Antipater, an Idumaean, not a Jew by birth. As Governor of Idumaea he stood well with the Romans who did not themselves want to assume full control of Palestine after the conquest by Pompey. They made him Governor of Judea and he died in 33 BC. His 5 children were Phasael, Herod, Joseph, Pheroras and Salome. His son Herod was both ambitious and able. He married Mariamne, daughter of Simeon the High Priest, a wise political move, apart from its romance. It brought him into the ancient Hasmonaean house, the Maccabees. He served the Romans well and they backed him strongly. He could have been a great man and a great king in the best sense. He realised that there was no place for Judea as a political entity in a world dominated by Roman rule and Greek thinking, but he kept the Jews a nation; something which his Jewish enemies did not always realise or appreciate. By his 10 wives he had 6 sons and 3 daughters. The Jews had foolishly petitioned to be brought directly under Rom. rule, but the Romans refused, and carried out the terms of Herod the Great's will. One son, Archelaus, was given Judea and Idumaea; another, Antipas, had Galilee and Perea. The 3rd, Philip, had Batanaea, Trachonitis and Auranitis. This division was made in AD 4. The Jews made things so difficult for Archelaus that the Romans had to take over the province from him, which was what the Jews had wanted; Archelaus went into exile. There followed uprisings by the Zealots. Herod Antipas of Galilee was a wilier man altogether. He ruled till AD 39, but bitterly offended the Jews by marrying his brother Philip's widow, who was his own niece Herodias, mother by her 1st marriage, of Salome. Jealous of his nephew Herod Agrippa, Antipas approached the Emperor Caligula, asking for wider power. The Romans became suspicious of his ambitions and looked into his affairs. They did not like what they saw, and banished him. Herod Philip was not a bad type, and ruled in peace and obscurity on the outposts of empire (*Luke* 3, 1). He is not the father but the half-brother of the Philip who was Herodias' 1st husband (*Matt.* 14, 3). Herod Agrippa was the son of Aristobulus and brother of Herodias who married 2 of her uncles. Agrippa was raised at the Rom. court where he was kept as hostage for his father's good conduct. He had the doubtful honour of being a close friend of Caligula, and of Claudius, who succeeded Caligula, and who sent him back to Judaea to rule. That was in AD 39. Gen. he was well thought of, but he tried to ride 2 horses, Rome and Jewry, and came to a horrible end (*Acts* 12, 20 ff.). His son was also Herod Agrippa who also was brought up in Rome, and Claudius appointed him to the small kingdom of Chalchis to which were later added some of the territories over which his uncles had ruled. It was when he was on a visit to the Rom. procurator Festus that he was invited to ' sit in ' on the trial of Paul. His sisters were the notorious Berenice and Drusilla. After the fall of Jerusalem he retired to Rome where he died in AD 100.

Herodians [hĕr-ō′-dĭ-ăns]. Not a sect or party but more prob. a number of influential Jews who supported the Herods, and so, indirectly, Rome; though poss. they dreamed of an ultimately independent kingdom (*Matt.* 22, 16).

Herodias [hĕr-ō′-dĭ-ăs]. Daughter of Aristobulus and half-sister of the 1st Herod Agrippa. She married her uncle Philip (not Philip the tetrarch) (*Matt.* 14, 3). His half-brother, her half-uncle had a passion for her, divorced his wife, and married Herodias while Philip was still alive, though separated from her. Reproved by John the Baptist, she worked for his death and contrived it through her daughter Salome (*Matt.* 14, 3-22). She went into exile with Herod. *See* HEROD.

Herodion. Christian of Rome (*Rom.* 16, 11).

Heron. Wading bird, prob. the ibis, though true herons are found in Palestine (*Lev.* 11, 19; *Deut.* 14, 18).

Heshbon [hĕsh′-bŏn]. City on boundary bet. Reuben and Gad (*Josh.* 13, 26).

Hexateuch [hĕx′-ă-tēuch]. Gk. word meaning 6 volumes. A name invented for the 5 books of the Pentateuch (qv) with the book of *Josh.* added. Scholars felt that the ' closed shop ' of the first 5 books ascribed to Moses was wrong, and that

style and content made the natural group the 6
instead of the 5.

Hezekiah (Ezekias) [hĕz'-ĕ-kī'-ah]. Prince of Judah
and son of Ahaz, c. 728 BC (*2 Kings* 18, 2).
He cleansed the corrupt religion of the nation
and restored the temple (*2 Chron.* ch. 29,). He was
a good general and statesman and restored his
people's fortunes, even if he was under constant
assault from the Assyrians, who had reduced
Samaria and enslaved the 10 tribes in 722 BC
(*2 Kings* 18, 9). The hist. of the Assyrian invasions in 3 waves is recorded (*2 Kings* 18; *Isa.*
chs. 36-37). Under threat from Assyria, Hezekiah
was tempted to ally with Babylonia (*2 Kings* 20,
12). He was warned agst. this by Isaiah (*Isa.* 39).
The alliances were disastrous. Later Sargon of
Assyria and his son Sennacherib invaded the land
and demanded tribute which Hezekiah paid, but
when a direct attack was mounted agst. Jerusalem
Isaiah urged him to resist and Sennacherib's army
was decimated by plague (*2 Kings* 19, 35). Hezekiah died c. 693 BC, and was succeeded by Manasseh. There are others of the name, but of minor
importance. *See* ASSYRIA, ISRAEL, JUDAH.

Hiddekel [hĭd'-dĕ-kĕl]. The Tigris river (*Gen.* 2, 14).

Hiel [hī'-ĕl]. Man of Bethel who fortified Jericho
and who seems to have sacrificed his sons in the
process (*1 Kings* 16, 34; *Josh.* 6, 26).

Hierapolis [hī'-ĕr-ăp'-ō-lis]. Mentioned only once
(*Colos.* 4, 13). A city in Asia Minor nr. Colossae.

Higgaion [hĭg-gă'-iŏn]. Lit. 'a deep sound.' A
musical term (*Ps.* 9, 16; etc.).

High Places. These are comparable to Stonehenge
and to Druid circles in Britain. Mts., springs,
rocks, even trees, could have sacred assoc., and
would become places of pilgrimage and of worship (*Gen.* 12, 6 ff.; *Ex.* 3, 1; *Ps.* 121, 1). Most

of the high places of the OT were there before the invasion, and many of them were taken over, and their origin attributed to the patriarchs (*I Sam.* 21, 1; *I Kings* 3, 4; *Amos* 7, 13). The pattern is a level platform with an altar and standing stones. Evidence there is in plenty of sacrifices; there is blood, including human blood. But these evidences are from before the Heb. invasion. At first the worship was natural and simple, but as religion became corrupt, the High Places became assoc. with practices far from spiritual and became the object of bitter denunciation by the prophets. Hezekiah and Josiah destroyed the High Places (*2 Kings* 23, 5 ff.). But they were revived time and time again until the Exile which finished them altogether.

High Priest. The man who spoke for the nation to God, and who reported God's will to the nation. The 1st to be appointed was Aaron, though the later formalities of the office had not then been determined (*Ex.* chs. 27 & 28). Later Aaron's sons were in a way set apart, and the office became hereditary, unless there were factors making this impossible (*Lev.* 21, 16-23). The High Priest had complete authority in the sanctuary and had to perform the rites and ceremonials on days set apart. When the Sanhedrin was engaged on matters theological he presided over it. He wore the breastplate, which was a square of linen ornamented with gold and 12 precious stones in 4 rows of 3. *See* JEWELS AND PRECIOUS STONES. The breastplate was really a wallet containing the stones Urim and Thummim (qv). He wore also the Ephod which hung down front and back and was clasped on the shoulders, the clasps being of onyx stones with the names of the 12 tribes inscribed on them. Round the waist he wore a girdle. Below the Ephod was a robe of blue, without sleeves and ornamented with golden pomegranates and bells. On his head he wore a kind of turban with a triple crown and a plate inscribed, ' Holiness to Jehovah ' (*Ex.* ch. 28). He laid aside these garments when he entered the Holy of Holies on the Day of Atonement. For ' consecration ' see (*Ex.* ch. 29). Herod and the Romans discouraged life tenure of the office. Notable High Priests (to be consulted under their names) are: Aaron, Eleazar, Phinehas, Ahijah, Ahimelech, Abiathar, Zadok (back to the orig. line which ended with Phinehas). Zadok replaced Abiathar after the revolt agst. David, but Zadok was a direct desc. of Aaron. Others are Azariah, Johanan, Azariah II (in the reign of Uzziah 750 BC), Amariah, Ahitub, Zadok II, Shallum, Hilkiah (during reign of Josiah c. 621 BC) and Jehozadok, who was High Priest at the time of the exile. His son Jeshua came back with Zerubbabel (*Ezra* 2, 2). Jonathan was High Priest during the reign of Artaxerxes. Then came Simon the Just; Eleazar (c. 260 BC). During Maccabean times the High Priests were mainly of royal blood; John Hyrcanus, Aristobulus being names which recur. When Herod the Great appeared the custom of life tenure of the office disappeared, and appointments were made either by the tetrarch or by the Roman governor. Thus Annas was appointed by Quirinius, governor of Syria c. AD 6. He retired and was followed by 3 who held office for only a couple of yrs. bet. them. Caiaphas was son-in-law to Annas and was appointed by Valerius Gratus procurator of Judea in AD 18 and held office for 18 yrs. Annas, however, remained the power behind the office.

Hilkiah [hĭl-kī'-äh]. There are several of the name,

the most important being: **1.** The father of Jeremiah (*Jer.* 1, 1). **2.** High Priest in Josiah's reign, who found the book of the Law (*2 Kings* 22, 4). **3.** Priest who returned from exile (*Neh.* 12, 7).

Hill. There is no distinction bet. hills and mts. RV and RSV sometimes trans. hills as mts.

Hin [hĭn]. *See* WEIGHTS AND MEASURES.

Hind. Fem. deer.

Hinge. The only hinge that was known was the pin and socket type (*Prov.* 26, 14).

Hinnom Valley. Nr. one of the gates of Jerusalem (*Neh.* 2, 13). Part of the boundary bet. Judah and Benjamin (*Josh.* 15, 8). *See* GEHENNAH.

Hippopotamus. *See* BEHEMOTH (*Job* 40, 15).

Hiram [hī'-răm]. **1.** King of Tyre. An early example of international co-operation is his friendly trading with David (*2 Sam.* 5, 11). This continued with Solomon to whom Hiram supplied materials for the temple. There is confusion in one deal bet. them (cf. *1 Kings* 9, 10-14 with *2 Chron.* 2, 11 ff.). **2.** This was also the name of a skilled craftsman who worked on the Temple (*1 Kings* 7, 13; *2 Chron.* 4, 11).

Hire, Hireling. Because of Jesus' comparison of the man who does a job for money and the man who does it for love (*John* 10, 12 & 13), the word has gained a bad meaning which it does not really possess.

Hittites. Apart from refs. in the Bible the Hittites had completely disappeared from hist. till AD 1900 when it was substantiated that they had been a great people in the ancient world. Their empire at one time had stretched from the Euphrates to the Aegean.

Hivites [hĭv'-ītes]. A tribe occupying part of Canaan at the invasion (*Ex.* 3, 8).

Hobab [hō′-băb]. Acc. to the Heb. Masoretic text, he was the father-in-law of Moses (*Judg.* 4, 11 AV). But elsewhere it is clearly stated that Moses' father-in-law was Jethro or Reuel (*Ex.* 3, 1; etc.). Hobab is named son of Reuel (*Num.* 10, 29; AV Raguel) and is almost certainly brother-in-law of Moses.

Hoham [hō′-hăm]. King of Hebron defeated by Joshua. [*Josh.* 10, 3).

Holiness. 1. Of God. Essential attribute of God, and what the worshipper thinks of God will establish his idea of the meaning of holiness. Worshippers of a God of fertility might regard chastity as unholy. The servant of God would call himself a holy man as he felt that he was doing what God wanted him to do. But that might be exceedingly unholy by Christian standards, and this not infrequently is so in countries into which Christianity has recently penetrated, like India and Africa. Israel at a stage much earlier than that of other nations reached an idea of God which gave them an idea of the meaning of holiness much loftier than that held by their neighbours (*Lev.* chs. 17-26). But unless this was revealed by God, then it was due to naturally good men wishing God's holiness to be the sublimation of their own conscious goodness, and so attributing to God in a perfect form the values which they themselves appreciated and cherished. Of course in the chs. of *Lev.* quoted, the moral qualities and the ceremonial demands are mixed up, but the real thing is there when we come to the prophets. The accent changes. They found so much of the ceremonial empty and abhorrent to themselves that they could not believe it to be pleasing and acceptable to God. With them it was ethical and moral values that made the amalgam of holiness. God's holiness then becomes the complete absence of evil and imperfection; a holiness which is majestic in its superhuman grandeur (*Isa.* 57, 15). **2.** Holiness of persons and objects. Everything and everybody connected with God and His worship was holy for his and its own sake and in his or its own right. The prophets (themselves accounted holy for the same reason) fought agst. this, but it was Jesus and the apostolic writers who brought things and people into perspective. The word 'Holy' is there used seldom of God, but often of His Spirit. *See* HOLY SPIRIT. 'Holy' is used of Jesus 10 times, when He is called the Holy One of God. But in the NT Christians are very often called Holy Ones. There are in fact, 3 Gk. words used: (1) *Hagiotes:* the quality of holiness; (2) *Hagiosyne:* the state of holiness; (3) *Hagiosmos:* the evidence of holiness.

Holm tree. *See* CYPRESS.

Holy of Holies. *See* TABERNACLE, TEMPLE.

Holy One of Israel. Favourite title of God with Isaiah, whose attitude stems from the form of his own call and its effect upon him (*Isa.* 6).

Holy Ghost. *See* HOLY SPIRIT.

Holy Spirit. The third person of the Christian Trinity in theology. The word 'ghost' has so changed and narrowed in meaning that it is better not now to be used, esp. since its assoc. with the unreal and the inactive is so completely remote from the true meaning of the Holy Spirit; which is holiness (God) in action in the real world. Although the combination of words, Holy Spirit, is used only 3 times in the OT (*Ps.* 51, 11; *Isa.* 63, 10 & 11), the idea was there of God in action in the realm of human affairs and emotions, and the word 'spirit' is used frequently. Both in Heb. and in Gk., the word means breath, or wind. It is a force invisible but palpable. It is the energy of creation, the activating force of the cosmos; it is God's agent in the making of the world and man; it is the source of prophecy; it is the life force of the world. With the realisation that God is not physical person but spiritual being, the separation of the world of the Spirit from the work of God ceased to apply. The work of the Holy spirit was simply to function in application of the God nature. In the NT there are fewer refs. simply to the Spirit, and more to the Holy Spirit, the accent being upon the work of God on the moral and ethical, rather than on the physical plane. But some confusion is caused by refs. to the spirit of the Risen Christ, which seems to have been reckoned to approximate to the Holy Spirit (*2 Cor.* 3, 17). St. John understood the Holy Spirit as the Spirit of Truth by which men would be led to the truth itself (*John* 16, 13). In other words, to him it was the Spirit of God that would lead men to God. The spirit came with power at Pentecost, and continued in the early Church. It was the spirit that made the Apostles 'able.' The word inspiration retains the sense of breathing.

Homer. *See* WEIGHTS AND MEASURES.

Honey. The only method of sweetening anything was to use honey; there was no sugar. Honey was greatly valued as food, and is prob. the finest of all foods. There is no evidence that the Hebs. kept bees (qv). Gifts of honey were made with the first-fruits, but it could not be incorporated in cooked dishes for it caused fermentation (*Lev.* 2, 11).

Hoods. (*Isa.* 3, 23.) Prop. turbans, as in RV and RSV. *See* DRESS.

Hook. There are several kinds mentioned. Curtain hooks (*Ex.* 26, 32). Flesh hooks, for lifting hot meat from the pot (*Ex.* 27, 3). Ref. (*Ezek.* 40, 43) is more prob. a slab or shelf. Thorn-shaped hooks used for fishing (*Amos* 4, 2). To keep a caught fish fresh it was sometimes necessary in hot weather to fasten it by hook and line to a pole in the water (*Job* 41, 2). Wild animals might be led by a hook through the lip, like the ring in a bull's nose (*Ezek.* 19, 4 RV; where AV has ' chains '). Prisoners were sometimes led in that way too (*2 Chron.* 33, 11 RSV).

Hoopoe. Common bird of the E which AV calls lapwing (*Lev.* 11, 19; etc.).

Hophni [hŏph′-nī]. Like Phinehas, a son of Eli. Both the sons were slain when, agst. the law, they took the Ark into battle agst. the Philistines (*1 Sam.* 2, 22 ff.).

Hor [hŏr]. Mt. on border of Edom (*Num.* 33, 37).

Horam [hō′-răm]. King of Gezer, slain by Joshua (*Josh.* 10, 33).

Horeb [hō′-reb]. Same mt. as Sinai (qv).

Hormah [hŏr′-măh]. Orig. Zephath nr. Ziklag. The Israelites insisted on advancing in spite of warnings and were defeated here (*Num.* 14, 45).

Horn. Animal horns were made into trumpets (*Josh.* 6, 13), or flasks (*1 Sam.* 16, 1). When God exalts the horn of a man it is a sign of favour and power (*Ps.* 89, 24). But when a man exalts his own horn it is a sign of arrogance (*Ps.* 75, 4 & 5), cf. mod. ' to blow your own trumpet.' The horns of the altar were projections to which sacrifices were bound (*Ps.* 118, 27). To cling to these was to be ' in sanctuary ' (*1 Kings* 2, 28).

Horned snake. *See* SERPENT.

Hornet. Insect like a wasp, only bigger. There are 3 refs. (*Ex.* 23, 28; *Deut.* 7, 20; *Josh.* 24, 12) and all refer to hornets as instruments to drive out the Canaanites. One of the insignia of Egypt was a hornet-like insect, and this may be the meaning.

Horonite [hŏ'-rŏn-īte]. Sanballat was so called (*Neh.* 2, 10).

Horse. First appearance of the domesticated horse was among the nomads E of the Caspian. The Hittites brought the horse W and they were being used in war in 2000. BC. Chariots were in use c. 1800 BC. The topography of Palestine did not lend itself to wheeled transport. Horses were known in Egypt (*Gen.* 47, 17; *Ex.* 14, 9). Sisera's army had cavalry (*Judg.* 4, 15). Israel's army trad. did not favour cavalry (*Deut.* 17, 16). Solomon imported horses and chariots, prob. for their prestige value, and they were later used in war (*1 Kings* 10, 28; 22, 4).

Horsegate. A gate of Jerusalem.

Horse-leech. This is not a kind of veterinary surgeon, but a variety of the ordinary leech which clings to a human or animal and sucks blood until it is full, when it falls off (*Prov.* 30, 15). There is also some idea of the vampire in the use of the word. *Aluka* is a leech; *anluka* is a goblin; and *aluk* is a ghoul.

Hosanna [hō-săn'-nă]. Occurs in the Gospels only in connection with Jesus' entry into Jerusalem (*Matt.* 21, 9; etc.). It is an imperative, meaning ' save now! ' The cry was trad. raised at the Feast of the Tabernacles (*Ps.* 118, 25). The Heb. word was transliterated into Gk. and became an accepted expression of praise and joy.

Hosea [hō-sē'-ă]. He was an Israelite who could see the doom impending for his country. He blamed the king and the aristocracy for the ills of the nation (5, 1). ' On you is the sentence.'

Kings, he reckoned, ought to be selected by God, not by man. Hosea looked forward to the eventual reunion bet. Judah and Israel. Most of Hosea's prophecy falls into the time of anarchy following the death of Jeroboam II in 743 BC. There followed 6 kings in 20 yrs. Hosea believed that the split bet. Israel and Judah was a disaster. He believed also that the only kings who ruled by divine right had been the line of David. Israel, as distinct from Judah, had 9 different dynasties in 200 yrs. The only hope for Israel, then, was re-union with the old line, and with Judah. This was the only way to stable government and devotion to God. Hosea forecast the fall of Samaria and the destruction of Israel. Reunion was not effected; the kings flirted in turn with Assyria and Egypt (5, 13; 7, 11; etc.). Hosea warned them time and again about this. Although he was all for reunion he was not blind to the faults and failings of Judah (4, 15). But he still preferred Judah's ways to Israel's (1, 7). Part of the book may be biographical, though some critics argue that his refs. to his unfortunate marriage are allegorical. Something gave Hosea an idea of God that was pretty unusual for his people and his time, and when a man discovers something new about God it is usually because he has dis-covered something new about himself. A very human and commonplace story is revealed if parts of the book are regarded as autobiographical (1, 1-9; 3, 1-5; 2, 2-23; 1, 10-2, 1) in that order. Through this experience he made the great discovery that if he could love the faithless, if he could not live without one of them because of his so great love, if he could forgive, and seek, and save at a price, then God must have the same feelings towards erring humans and an erring

nation. Otherwise Hosea must be a better being
than God, which was absurd. Something brought
Hosea to that discovery. Why not his marriage?
Hosea is the prophet of the love of God. He must
have been that kind of man himself.

Hosen. Pl. of hose: trunks, really, not stockings
(*Dan.* 3, 21 AV). But the orig. might not be this
at all, but coats or tunics.

Hoshea [hŏ-shē'-ă]. **1.** Joshua (qv). **2.** Prince of
Ephraim (*1 Chron.* 27, 20). **3.** A son of Elah who
usurped the throne of Israel by assassinating
Pekah (*2 Kings* 15, 30), c. 730 BC. He reigned
for about 9 yrs. He loved to play power politics
with Assyria and Egypt and paid the usual price.
He lost the kingdom to Sargon, and the nation
was never heard of again. *See* SAMARIA, SARGON,
ISRAEL. **4.** The prophet Hosea (qv). **5.** A returned
exile (*Neh.* 10, 23).

Hospitality. This was a necessity among nomadic
desert peoples, where a traveller's life might de-
pend upon the reception he got (*Gen.* 18). It was
accounted one of the prime virtues (*Judg.* 19, 15).
When Jesus sent the disciples out on their preaching He told them to rely on hospitality (*Matt.* 10,
9; *Luke* 10, 4). The disciples were furious when
Jesus was denied hospitality (*Luke* 9, 53-54). In
Jesus' vision of judgment the division is really bet.
the hospitable and the non-hospitable (*Matt.* 25,
35). All of the larger houses had guest chambers
(*Luke* 22, 11). The guest was absolutely safe even
if it were discovered that he was one who had
good cause to be thrown in prison, or even
executed. Among Arabs to-day the guest is safe
for 36 hours after his departure. Salt might be
offered to the newly-arrived guest as a sign of trust
(like the Red Indian calumet); but the word
trans. ' salt ' has a larger meaning and covers

more or less all food. Like the Scots word, ' kitchen.'

Host. In the military sense. *See* ARMY.

Hosts, Lord of. This means far more than Lord of the armies. It is the Lord of the hosts of heaven and earth; the universal Creator and commander.

Host of Heaven. Mentioned in connection with idolatrous worship of the sun, moon and stars (*Deut.* 4, 19; *2 Kings* 23, 4 & 5 & 12). On the other hand the stars are often ref. to as the hosts, or armies, of the Lord (*Gen.* 2, 1; *Ps.* 33, 6; *Isa.* 34, 4; etc.). The host of heaven can also be the angels (*1 Kings* 22, 19). There was a tendency to identify stars and angels (*Isa.* 14, 12; *Rev.* 9, 1 & 11).

Hough. The part of the leg bet. the knee and the fetlock of an animal, cf. ' hock.' The word hough is still common in Scotland for the back of the knee joint. The verb ' to hough ' means to hamstring by cutting through the tendons behind the knee. It was a favourite stroke of infantrymen when fighting cavalry (*Josh.* 11, 6 & 9).

Hour. *See* TIME.

House. Tent-dwellers eventually settle down and become house-dwellers. The Feast of the Tabernacles was the annual reminder to the Hebs. that once they had been nomadic. Building was normally of clay of which there was ample supply, and the sun dried the clay brick hard. More elaborate edifices were built with stone (*Isa.* 9, 10). These had obvious advantages over ' clay ' houses. (*Job* 4, 19; *Ezek.* 12, 6; *Matt.* 7, 24 ff.). Clay or bitumen (qv) was used bet. the wrought stones. Wood was used for roofing but not normally for walls. The ' closet ' had nothing to do with sanitation but was the larder or store-room. Rooms were built gen. around an open court (*2 Sam.* 17,

18) and these could be extended as the family grew. There were celebrations at the laying of the foundation, or corner stone '(*2 Chron.* 8, 16; *Job* 38, 6). In the very early days, under Canaanite influence, there might be human sacrifice as has been revealed by excavation. There might be an act of dedication (*Deut.* 20, 5) as there always was with public and sacred buildings (*Lev.* 8, 10; *Ezra* 6, 16). Floors were made of clay and the walls were whitewashed (*Matt.* 23, 37; *Acts* 23, 3). The inside walls might be panelled with wood (*2 Chron.* 3, 5; *1 Kings* 6, 15). These panelled walls are sometimes called 'ceiled' in the AV. Roofs were gen. flat, supported by stout beams, with a kind of sarking on top and finished off with brushwood, earth, and clay (*Luke* 5, 19). The finish was not really tiles as we understand them, but the usual kind of roof which could easily be broken away. The joists might be supported by upright posts or pillars standing on flat stones. Round the roof was a parapet (battlement AV, *Deut.* 22, 8), and was reached by a stair outside. The roof was used a good deal—the housetop. The door had a frame of 2 jambs and a lintel and the door itself was hung by pins operating in sockets ('hinges,' *Prov.* 26, 14). These were not in the jambs or doorposts, but top and bottom in the threshold and lintel. The threshold, or sill, was of stone (*Judg.* 19, 27). The doorposts were of wood or stone and to them was fixed a small metal or wooden case containing words of Scripture (*Deut.* 6, 4-9; 11, 13-20). This is still done among the Jews. The lock was most ingenious. Inside the door was a slab of wood with a hole bored in it from left to right. Resting in this hole was a wooden bolt (*Neh.* 3, 3; 'lock' in AV). In this bolt were 3 or more vertical holes. When the

bolt was shoved home into a hole in the jamb, metal pins fell down from the slab of wood in which the bolt ran, and engaged these holes. To ' unlock ' from the outside, it was necessary to insert through a hole in the door (S. of S. 5, 4) a piece of wood into the hollow part of the bolt where the pins were engaged. On this piece of wood, or key, were pins approximating to the pins which were holding the door. So the pins which had fallen into the holes in the bolt were eased back and the bolt could then be slid aside. Windows were small and high up the wall for coolness' sake. In the E everything is closed in the heat of the day, whereas in the W everything is thrown open. The hearth was in the centre of the floor or in a corner, and burned wood or dried animal dung—a very good fuel (Ezek. 4, 15). There was no chimney. One ref. (Hos. 13, 3 AV) is not ' chimney,' but ' window.' In cold weather there might be a brazier or firepan (Jer. 36, 22; Zech. 12, 6 RV). Mats were spread on the floor and on them they sat and slept. The wealthy had beds and bedrooms (2 Sam. 4, 7; 2 Kings 11, 2), with cushions (Amos 3, 12 RV). They had chairs and stools not unlike mod. ones, with footstools and hassocks. Tables were more or less as at present and of all shapes and sizes. ' Candlesticks ' are lampstands. They did not have candles. See LAMP. Mirrors were known (Job 37, 18), also ' aids to beauty ' (2 Kings 9, 30). Prob. there would be the spindle and the loom. See SPINNING AND WEAVING. The utensils used in the house were: the earthen vessels (clay pottery) (2 Sam. 17, 28); the pitcher, the barrel, the jar (Gen. 24, 15). Water was kept in the house in waterpots, which being of porous clay would keep the water cool by evaporation (John 2, 6). Similar jars held wheat, barley, olives, oil and the like, though the cruse was more assoc. with oil (*1 Kings* 17, 12-16). Water was often collected in a waterskin (*Num.* 24, 7), 'bucket' (AV). There were no bottles as we understand them; the word so trans. should be 'wineskins' (*Matt.* 9, 17). 'Millstones' are to be understood as something like querns in which grain was hand-ground into flour or meal. *See* MILL. Other utensils were woven baskets (*Deut.* 26, 2); kneading trough, or baking board (*Ex.* 12, 34); bowls (*Judg.* 6, 38); pots, pans, kettles, cauldrons, of which the flesh-pot was the largest (*1 Sam.* 2, 14; *Ex.* 16, 3). *Lev.* mentions metal utensils, baking pan and frying pan (2, 5 & 7 RV). There were knives, forks, and flesh-hooks for removing meat from the pot (*Gen.* 22, 6; *Josh.* 5, 2; *1 Sam.* 2, 13).

Huldah [hŭl'-dăh]. Wife of Shallum; a prophetess. Josiah sought her advice when the Book of the Law was found in the Temple c. 621 BC (*2 Kings* 22, 3-20).

Hunter, Hunting. As popular then as it is now, with the same kind of people. Some of the 'clean' animals could be had only by hunting them, but the blood was always poured out (*Deut.* 12, 15; 15, 22). There was also hunting to get rid of vermin (*Ex.* 23, 29). There was hunting 'for the pot' (*Gen.* 27, 3), and simply as sport.

Hur. 1. Man of Caleb's house (*1 Chron.* 2, 18). 2. King of Midian (*Num.* 31, 8). Two others of slight importance.

Husband. *See* FAMILY.

Husbandman. A tiller of the soil: a farmer or crofter.

Husks. The pod of the carob tree, sometimes called locust, or St. John's (the Baptist) bread. It is a common cattle food.

Hyacinth, Jacinth. A colour or a precious stone (*Ex.* 28, 19; *Rev.* 9, 17). See JEWELS AND PRECIOUS STONES.

Hyena. A rather loathsome animal useful as a scavenger of carrion: trans. 'speckled bird' (*Jer.* 12, 9).

Hymenaeus [hȳ'-mĕn-āe'-ŭs]. Author of an ancient heresy concerning the resurrection. He was excommunicated by Paul (*1 Tim.* 1, 20).

Hymn. A spiritual theme which could be sung. The main examples are the *Psalms* but other hymns are (*Ex.* 15, 1-19; *Deut.* 32, 1-43; *Judg.* 5; *1 Sam.* 2, 1-10; *Luke* 1, 46-55). There are also refs. to psalms, hymns and spiritual songs as if they were all different (*Eph.* 5, 19). When Jesus and the disciples sang a hymn before the Last Supper it would be the Hallel (qv). The early Church used hymns (*Acts* 16, 25; *1 Cor.* 14, 26; etc.). Parts of some of these can be recognised (*Eph.* 5, 14; *1 Tim.* 3, 16; *Rev.* 15, 3 & 4).

Hypocrite, Hypocrisy. To appear before men as one who is not the same before God. This can be deliberate deception (*Matt.* 6, 2 & 5 & 16) or the hypocrite can deceive himself (*Matt.* 23). In OT AV the word really means godless (*Job* 8, 13; *Isa.* 9, 17).

Hyssop. A plant like a small cedar used often as a sprinkler, being dipped into a liquid and then shaken (*Ex.* 12, 22; *Lev.* 14, 4). The hyssop on which the vinegar was put at the Crucifixion must either have been a pad saturated with vinegar, or it is a mistrans. Possibly the hyssop of Calvary was an extract from the plant.

I

Ibis. (*Lev.* 11, 19 RV Marg). Wading bird venerated by the Egyptians. *See* HERON.

Ibleam [ĭb'-lē-ăm]. City of Issachar. Here Ahaziah, King of Judah was killed by the followers of Jehu (*2 Kings* 9, 27).

Ibzan [ĭb'-zăn]. A lesser Judge who ruled for 7 yrs. (*Judg.* 12, 8-10). *See* JUDGE.

Ichabod [ĭ'-chă-bŏd]. Grandson of Eli. The name means ' the glory is departed ' and commemorates the loss of the Ark (*I Sam.* 4, 21).

Iconium [ĭ-cō'-nĭ-ŭm]. Ancient city on W edge of the central plateau of Asia Minor. It was the most easterly city of Phrygia, but was on the E borderline of Lycaonia (qv). It became a Rom. province in 25 BC and was named Galatia, though it did not become a Rom. colony till the time of Hadrian AD 117-138. Paul and Barnabas visited the city twice on the 1st missionary journey (*Acts* 13, 51; 14, 21) and Paul twice more (*Acts* 16, 6; 18, 23).

Idol. The manufactured image of a person or being, to be worshipped. It represents the presence of that being (*Ex.* 20, 4; etc.). Silver, gold, wood and stone were used in their manufacture. The metal ones were molten (moulded) images; and the stone or wooden ones were graven (carved) images (*Isa.* 40, 19 & 20; *Jer.* 10, 9). Some were the small household gods, the teraphim (qv) (*Gen.* 31, 19 Marg). They might be enormous (*Dan.* 3, 1). They first appear in Christian churches c. AD 300, were forbidden in 736 and sanctioned finally by the Council of Nice in 787.

Idolatry. Images of various kinds were used in patriarchal times (*Gen.* 31, 30 & 32 & 35; *Josh.*

24, 2). The Israelites were ordered to destroy the
Canaanite idols (*Ex.* 23, 24). the 2nd commandment was directed agst. them (*Ex.* 20, 4 & 5).
When the Philistines placed the ark in the temple
of Dagon the idol was shattered (*1 Sam.* 5, 3-5).
The Council of Jerusalem forbade Christians to
eat flesh of animals which had been sacrified to
idols (*Acts* 15, 29). Paul clarified the position
(*1 Cor.* 8, 4-13; 10, 18-33).

Idumea (Idumaea) [id′-ū-mē′-a]. The land of Edom
(*Isa.* 34, 5 & 6 AV; *Ezek.* 35, 15; *Mark* 3, 8).
After the fall of Jerusalem in 586 BC they
began to infiltrate but were gradually contained
and came under the rule of the Jews by 126
BC.

Illyricum [ill-ÿ′-rĭ-cŭm]. Mentioned only once
(*Rom.* 15, 19). It was a Rom. province stretching
along the Adriatic from Italy to Macedonia.
The S portion was called Dalmatia (AV), a
name which was extended to take in the whole
province. Paul had a preaching tour which included it.

Image. (*Gen.* 1, 27; 9, 6; *1 Cor.* 11, 7; *Colos.* 3,
10.) At one time it was prob. believed that God
had the same form as man, and that man was the
proof of this, being made in the image of God.
But even in later OT days and certainly in NT
days it was recognised that God is a spirit, and
that likeness to God consists in man's endowment
of rationalism, morality, appreciation of values,
and spiritual perception. It was inevitable that
this idea should be taken at the point of its highest
probability in assessing the nature of Jesus ' the
image of the invisible God' (*Colos.* 1, 15; *Heb.*
1, 3). Jesus believed this Himself (*John* 14, 9).
Hist. is a frame which in all ages has surrounded
man's attempts to portray God—to discover His

nature and to see Him clearly. All were tentative and imperfect until Jesus appeared within the frame—the perfect portrait, the speaking likeness. *See* IDOL.

Imagination. Usually has a bad sense—a contrivance, a device, a false reasoning (*Rom.* 1, 21; *2 Cor.* 10, 5; etc.).

Immanuel [ĭm-măn′-ū-ĕl] (Emmanuel). The 2nd is the Gk. form of the word, meaning ' God with us.' He was foretold by Isaiah (7, 14). Before His coming terrible events were to take place (7, 16 & 17). He would be of the line of David, which alone had divine sanction to rule; He would be of Judah, and He would be the Messiah. Matthew (1, 22 & 23) claims Jesus as the fulfilment of the prophecy, satisfying all the conditions. ' Virgin ' should be ' maiden ' as the word is trans. in (*Isa.* 7, 14). The orig. prophecy dates from c. 734 BC and though Isaiah saw the coming of ' the Son ' as inevitable he did not see it as imminent. In fact Isaiah's word to Ahaz when disaster was threatening Judah (7, 3-11 ; 13 & 14) was that Judah's continued existence was guaranteed by God until Messiah should come (*2 Sam.* 7, 11-17). The detail of the prophecy was fulfilled in the timing of Jesus' birth. The N kingdom had disappeared, and the 10 tribes were lost. Judah was still in existence, but was a vassal state and had been to one or other of the great powers since the days of Ahaz. Many believe, however, that the idea that was in Isaiah's mind was that any child born at the time of the prophecy would see the destruction of Israel and the enslavement of Judah before reaching maturity. Supporting this view is the fact that Isaiah has very little to say about Messiah in later chs. But whatever Isaiah meant, the fact is that Jesus fulfilled the conditions.

Aware of this, He deliberately chose the Messiah's way for his entry into Jerusalem (*John* 12, 14; *Zech.* 9, 9).

Immortality. There is so little ref. in the OT to life after death that it can almost be said that the Hebrews did not believe in personal immortality or in judgment, reward, and punishment after death. Reward and punishment occurred in life. But they did believe in a realm of disembodied souls under the earth, which they called Sheol (qv). One passage in Job is mistakenly thought to prove belief in the resurrection of the body (19, 26) but the proper trans. is, ' away from my body I shall see God.' Other refs. to some kind of existence are: (*Job* 14, 12; *Ps.* 49; 73, 18-25; 88, 12; 94, 17; 115, 17; *Eccl.* 9, 10). The meaning of the last verse of the beloved *23rd Psalm* is far more for this present life and world than for the next. Only in a later literature is there any suggestion of a resurrection or a liberation (*Isa.* 26, 19; *Dan.* 12, 2). A distinction must be made between immortality (belief in which is not confined to Christians) *and* the Christian concept of eternal life, in which Jesus believed as a simple fact upon which He did not elaborate. There was a non-physical resurrection, and a judgment with a reward or punishment. The NT writers complicated their thinking and confused immortality with the end of the age—the second coming, which they believed to be imminent. The *Revelation* brings together the idea of immortality and the idea of Apocalypse (the Day of Jehovah). The new age, judgment, Resurrection of the Saints, war with Satan and the gen. resurrection which might be of the good only, or of all the sleeping inhabitants of Sheol—all this happens together. There is little or nothing of the thought

of the individual soul passing unto God at the
moment of the death of the body.

Importunity. Orig. shamelessness, impudence; but
here ' persistence ' (*Luke* 11, 8).

Impotent. Lit. ' without strength ' (*John* 5, 3 & 7);
without power (*Acts* 14, 8).

Imprisonment. *See* CRIME AND PUNISHMENT.

Incarnation. Christianity being faith in a person
who is at once God and man, requires the birth
of that person to be evident as a simple and unassailable fact. The OT had firm faith in the
divine origin of men (*Gen.* 1, 26; 2, 7) and their
early concept of God was frankly anthropomor-
phic—One with human attributes (*Gen.* 3, 8).
Therefore even from earliest times the idea of
God in man, man in God, was not foreign to
their way of thought. The NT does not for a
moment hesitate over regarding Jesus as a man
born of woman. The question of virgin birth is
far too vast to be discussed here fully. The word
used by Isaiah (7, 14) is not ' virgin ' in the mod.
sense, but ' maiden.' It stems from a root meaning ' mature, nubile, of marriageable age.' The
mother of our Lord is ref. to in this way only at
the beginning of *Matt.* and *Luke*. *Luke* is usually
reliable, but in the other genealogy of Jesus recorded in *Matt.*, Jesus' descent from David is
traced back through Joseph, not Mary. Virgin
birth of Jesus is not mentioned elsewhere even
where it might have been expected (*Gal.* 4, 4;
cf. *Rom.* 1, 3). During the first 30 yrs. of Jesus'
life, no one, and certainly not His own family,
seem to have seen anything remarkable about
Him (*Matt.* 13, 55). His physical and mental
characteristics, His emotions and His mortality
were all human. But the whole NT clearly believes
that He was more than human. He believed this

Himself (though He always refers to Himself as the Son of Man) because He believed Himself to be the Messiah. *See* IMMANUEL. In discourses recorded by John He speaks of His existence before birth and after death. As far as the first Christians were concerned, the proof of the Incarnation was the Resurrection. *See* JESUS CHRIST.

Incense. Aromatic gums and spices burned for their fragrance esp. at religious services. Stacte, opobalsammum, anycha, galbanum and pure frankincense were mixed in equal quantities; salt was added. This special mixture was for religious use only (*Ex.* 30, 34-38). *See* ALTAR, TABERNACLE.

India. (*Esth.* 1, 1; 8, 9.) E boundary of the empire of Ahasuerus. The Heb. is prob. for the R. Indus. Articles of trade which must have come from India are mentioned in *Ezek.* (27, 15 & 19 & 24).

Indite. To write; but more prop. to dictate to a writer or even to inspire a writer (*Ps.* 45, 1).

Infidel. Merely an unbeliever (*2 Cor.* 6, 15; *1 Tim.* 5, 8 AV).

Ingathering, Feast of. *See* TABERNACLES, FEAST OF.

Inheritance. *See* HEIR.

Iniquity. *See* SIN.

Injurious. Means both insult and injury (*1 Tim.* 1, 13) ' insolent.'

Ink. One ref. in OT (*Jer.* 36, 18). It was not ink in the mod. sense but something much less permanent prob. made from lamp black. In NT (*2 Cor.* 3, 3; *2 John* 12; *3 John* 13) it means ' black.' *See* WRITING.

Inkhorn. A case for reed pens incorporating a container for the writing liquid; worn slung at the side or stuck in the belt (*Ezek.* 9, 2).

Inn. Most travellers were pretty sure of bed and

breakfast at private houses (*see* HOSPITALITY).
The inn of the E was a ' be it ever so humble '
place of abode, rather than a hotel in anything
like the mod. sense: a ' battered caravanserai.'
It consisted of a number of small unfurnished
rooms opening at one side on to a court where
there was a well. The traveller usually attended
to all his own needs though there might be a
manager with a shop of sorts (*Luke* 10, 34 & 35).

Inspiration. Used only twice (*Job* 32, 8 AV; *2 Tim.*
3, 16). In Job it means that man requires an
extra quality ' breathed into ' him by God to give
him a proper understanding. Paul uses it to show
why the OT writings are different from all other
writings of the time. God had breathed upon the
word. The Gk. is not merely ' inspired' but
' God inspired.' Thus the Scriptures are a means
of grace by which God reaches us by the Holy
spirit.

Instant. In AV means ' urgent ' (*Luke* 23, 23).
' Earnestly ' (*Luke* 7, 4).

Instrument. Any utensil, implement or weapon.
See MUSIC (INSTRUMENTS).

Interest. *See* USURY.

Interpretation. 1. Dreams were reckoned to have
meanings which had to be elucidated and interpreted (*Gen.* 41, 8; *Dan.* 2, 2 ff.; *Matt.* 1, 20;
2, 12). **2.** (*Gen.* 42, 23) seems to imply a professional translator of one language into another; an
interpreter in the mod. sense (*Ezra* 4, 7; *Matt.*
1, 23; 27, 46; etc.). **3.** The prophets were inter-
preters of the will of God (*Isa.* 43, 27). Note how
often they begin, ' Thus saith the Lord.'

Intreat (Entreat). May mean to beseech or plead
with, but it can mean also to treat, use or abuse,
depending on the addition of the adverb ' well '
or ' ill.' Where it means ' to beseech ' it means a

little more: to beseech successfully, to prevail upon (*Gen.* 25, 21).

Inward parts. This may be anatomical—the 'innards' (*Ex.* 29, 13; *Lev.* 3, 3). But as the heart is one of the 'innards' there comes the assoc. of certain inward parts with certain qualities: as the seat of wisdom, of truth, of the affections and so on (*Job* 38, 36; *Ps.* 51, 6; *Jer.* 31, 33). Evil lurks there too (*Ps.* 5, 9; 62, 4 AV; *Prov.* 20, 27). Jesus used the words (*Luke* 11, 39) of the ability of the hypocrite to assume an appearance of virtue.

Iron. Although the patriarchs lived in the Bronze Age, Moses lived in the Iron Age (*Num.* 35, 16; *Josh.* 6, 19 & 24; 17, 16). Armour and weapons were made of iron (*1 Sam.* 17, 7), as were nails and builders' tools (*1 Kings* 6, 7), fishing hooks (*Job* 41, 7), farming implements (*2 Sam.* 12, 31); gates and chains (*Ps.* 105, 18; 107, 10) were also made of iron, whose prob. source was around the Black Sea (*Jer.* 15, 12; *Ezek.* 27, 12). There was iron ore in the Lebanon mts. (*Deut.* 8, 9). Prob. it was the Hittites who hit upon the secret of smelting ore c. 1400 BC (*Deut.* 4, 20; *1 Kings* 8, 51). The smelting fuel was charcoal, brought to a high temperature by bellows (*Ezek.* 22, 20). The Philistines would not share the secret with the Hebs. (*1 Sam.* 13, 19). When David crushed the Philistines the secret must have been forced from them for the Hebs. thereafter became smelters of iron. *See* SMITH, EZION GEBER.

Isaac. Son of Abraham and Sarah (qv). He was born somewhere nr. Beer-sheba (*Gen.* 21, 14) in the old age of his parents, and given a name which means, 'One laughs.' Abraham had laughed at the idea of Sarah bearing a child; but Sarah had the last laugh (*Gen.* 17, 17; 18, 9-15). While Isaac was a boy Abraham decided the only way he could prop. show gratitude to God was by sacrificing what was dearest to him—Isaac (22, 8). Isaac had submitted to his father's authority, and his nature seems to have been somewhat submissive and retiring. When he was about 40 he married Rebecca, but remained without sons for 20 yrs. (*Gen.* 25, 20 & 26). Famine drove the family N from Beerlahairoi to Gerar (26, 1-6). He was thinking of going to Egypt when he was reminded of the covenant with his father and God, and the covenant was renewed to himself (26, 2-5). Following his father's bad example he passed off his wife as his sister to avoid trouble, and similarly got into more trouble (26, 6-11). From Gerar he went back to Beer-sheba, and there built an altar and made a treaty with the king Abimelech (26, 24-33). When the sons were born it was a divided house, Isaac favouring Esau, and Rebecca favouring Jacob. This culminated in the deception for the paternal blessing and inheritance. Rebecca persuaded him to send Jacob away to find a wife, but her real motive was to keep Esau and him apart (27, 46; 28, 5). Isaac died in Hebron at a ripe old age (35, 27 ff.). In the NT he is called a child of the promise and one of the faithful (*Gal.* 4, 22 & 23; *Heb.* 11, 9 & 20).

Isaiah. He is the statesman prophet whose whole life was devoted to trying to save the state. To all problems he applied certain basic principles. Judah, he believed, was chosen by God, therefore Judah must serve God. In this alone, and not in political manœuvrings lay Judah's safety. In pursuit of his convictions he did not hesitate to defy kings. By 734 BC the Assyrians had crossed the Euphrates and were advancing W. Rezin of Damascus and Pekah of Israel were organising a

federation of states to resist them. Ahaz of
Judah, on Isaiah's advice, refused to join, and the
others, frightened of a neutral Judah to their rear
tried to conquer Judah by arms (*2 Kings* 15, 37;
16, 5-9; *2 Chron.* 28, 5-18). The king was terrified
(*Isa.* 7, 2) and made an alliance with the Assyrians
which virtually made them their vassal. He
paid them tribute to keep Israel and Damascus too
busy to fight him. Isaiah was agst. the whole idea
and said so (7, 4). The prophet foretold the destruction of Israel and Damascus within a lifetime (7, 16). *See* IMMANUEL, MESSIAH. He maintained that Assyria was the real danger. Things
turned out as he had said. Assyria subjugated
Damascus and Israel and forced Judah at peril
of invasion to pay heavy annual tribute, which
kept them in constant friction with the Assyrians
and in fear of them. Ahaz was succeeded by his
son Hezekiah c. 720, and he began a series of
reforms of worship and government. Other vassal
states of Assyria urged him to stop paying the
tribute, but Isaiah was afraid of the consequences.
Hezekiah said that he would ally with Egypt, but
Isaiah reckoned this to be even worse (ch. 20). He
persuaded Hezekiah to pay up, but this annoyed
the Egyptians who did not want an Assyrian vassal
state right on their borders. Assyria dealt in no
uncertain manner with the other revolting states,
Philistia, Edom, Moab and Ashdod, but they left
Judah alone. Sometime later a man called Merodach Baladan usurped S Babylon (an Assyrian
possession) and called himself king (*2 Kings* 20,
12; *Isa.* 39). He made an approach to Hezekiah,
who was cordial; but Isaiah saw more danger than
ever in this and foretold that Judah would end
up enslaved to Babylon. Sargon of Assyria
defeated the usurper king and restored S Babylon

to his empire. Later, however, when Sennacherib had succeeded Sargon, Merodach Baladan the Chaldean came back and re-took it. One by one the states went down till Judah was alone, the Egyptian allies defeated. The Bible account and the Assyrian inscriptions agree in the details of the invasion (2 Kings 18). Sennacherib conquered the provincial cities, till only Jerusalem remained. Hezekiah tried to buy peace by offering tribute. Sennacherib accepted it, then changed his mind and demanded the surrender of the city. Not knowing what to do, Hezekiah turned again to Isaiah whom he had ignored (2 Kings 19). Isaiah advised him to hang on. Sennacherib's army was decimated by plague (2 Kings 19, 35 ff.). He returned to Assyria and was murdered by his sons. Isaiah was vindicated. He is the evangelical prophet and one of the greatest of them all. His words are the product of a considerable intellect and his literary style is tremendous in its sweep and resource.

Isaiah, Book of. The book is not a unity, but is a collection of writings and sayings of prophets before and contemporary with Isaiah. These are anonymous, but the main author's own work is not. It was written some 300 yrs. after the events of which it tells, that is towards the end of the 3rd cent. BC. Chs. 1-12 are prophecies concerning Israel and Judah: (1) The great indictment (1-5). (2) Isaiah's call and commission (6). (3). The promise for the future (7-12). Chs. 13-23 are prophecies agst. foreign nations: **1.** Babylon (13-14, 27). **2.** Philistia RV (14, 28-32). **3.** Moab (chs. 15-16). **4.** Damascus (17). **5.** Egypt (18-20). **6.** Babylon (21,1-10). **7.** Edom (21, 11-12). **8.** Arabia (21, 13-17). **9.** Jerusalem (22). **10.** Tyre (23). Chs. 24 & 25 are prophecies of deliverance and of doom. Beginning with the picture of universal judgment (24) it continues with a group of songs (25-27); then comes a collection of 'woes' (28-33). This section concludes with a comparison of the future of Judah with that of other nations (34-35). This completes the prophetic section. The historic section consists of chs. 36-39, and deals with the Assyrian and Babylonian wars and entanglements described in the preceding article. There follows the Messianic section (41-66) which tells of the relationship bet. God and Judah, God's people and the heathen, and goes on to describe the deliverer and the delivered. *See* MESSIAH.

Iscariot. *See* JUDAS.

Ishbi Benob [Ĭsh'-bī bē'-nŏb]. Philistine giant (*2 Sam.* 21, 16).

Ishbosheth [Ĭsh'-bō'-shĕth]. Fourth son of Saul, who disputed David's succession; also called Eshbaal (*2 Sam.* 2, 8-12).

Ishi [Ĭsh'-ī]. Name used by Hosea for God to replace 'Baali' a name which had heathen assoc. (2, 16).

Ishmael [Ĭsh'-mā-ĕl]. 1. Son of Abraham and Hagar (qv). His daughter married Esau (*Gen.* 28, 9). *See* ISHMAELITE, ABRAHAM. 2. Desc. of Jonathan (*1 Chron.* 8, 38). 3. Man of Judah (*2 Chron.* 19, 11). 4. Son of Jehohanan (*2 Chron.* 23, 1). 5. Scion of the royal house of Judah who assassinated Gedaliah, Nebuchadnezzar's governor of Judah, at the instigation of the King of Ammon. After massacring many people and carrying off prisoners, he was chased to Gibeon by Johanan (*2 Kings* 25, 25; *Jer.* ch. 40-41). 6. Returned exile (*Ezra* 10, 22).

Ishmaelite (-eelite). A race founded by Ishmael, son of Abraham, therefore of mixed Heb. and

Egyptian stock. *See* HAGAR, ABRAHAM. He had 12 sons who were princes (*Gen.* 17, 20). They were nomadic, and their ' beat ' was in N Arabia bet. Havilah and the Euphrates. It was to wandering Ishmaelites that Joseph was sold and taken to Egypt (*Gen.* 37, 25-28).

Ish Sechel [ïsh-sě'-chěl]. Proper name, prop. substituted by RV for AV ' man of understanding ' (*Ezra* 8, 18).

Isle, Island. The word means more than the English word does: **1.** Habitable land as contrasted with water (*Isa.* 42, 4). **2.** Island in the usual sense (*Jer.* 47, 4 AV Marg, RV). **3.** Coastland (*Isa.* 20, 6 RV). Maritime areas (*Gen.* 10, 5). **4.** Remote regions (*Isa.* 41, 5).

Israel. This was the name of Jacob (qv) and was later applied to the clan and nation desc. from him (*Gen.* 32, 22-32). To begin with ' Israelite ' was just an alternative name for Heb., but yrs. after the settlement of Canaan by the Hebs., a distinction was drawn bet. the people of the N (Israel) and the people of the S (Judah). The S was somewhat isolated by natural barriers, and the 2 most powerful tribes, Ephraim in the N and Judah in the S were ancient rivals. These facts have to be borne in mind as we discuss this people. The hist. of their origins lies buried in the book of *Genesis*. Both Arabs and Jews (the last survivors of the Israelites) regard Abraham as the orig. man of the stock. His city was Ur of the Chaldees, a city of Mesopotamia, but the whole clan, led by Terah, Abraham's father, emigrated, prob. simply on the kind of impulse that has always sent families roaming the world. They crossed Syria and the Damascus desert, and arrived at Canaan (Palestine). By this time Terah was dead and Abraham was chief of the clan.

The people of Ur were highly civilised for their day and age, and Abraham was by no means the least civilised of them (*Gen.* 14). His point of greatest remarkability, however, was his conviction that he stood in a special relationship to God, about whose nature he was more than a little vague. He felt that he was under a compulsion: that the call to the desert was neither accidental nor incidental. Like Joan of Arc, he heard voices, and the burden of the message was that from him would come a people who would be in a special relationship to God. He waited for his dreams to come true and he waited a long time. But he believed himself to be in covenant with God, and this is the important thing: that he did so believe. He passed the promise on to his son, Isaac, but he too experienced nothing that would make him believe that the promise was being fulfilled. His sons, like himself, were late in coming, and it is from Jacob that the name Israel comes. He was both prolific and prosperous; and the clan began to mean something numerically. if for no other reason. They multiplied and they prospered. Then came one of the periodic famines, when no rain meant no crops, and they went down to the world's granary, Egypt, in search of grain. They found the long lost brother, Joseph, food minister of Egypt. *See* JOSEPH. The prospect of living under the patronage of this important brother was too much for them, and the whole clan moved into Goshen, a border dist. of Egypt and gradually forgot all about the Land of Promise. From this point they were known as Beni Israel—the Children of Israel (Jacob). Their stay did them no harm in one way but plenty in others. It civilised them, but it weakened them, too. One member of the clan, however, had not forgotten, and he

was the one who might have been forgiven for
forgetting—Joseph. He made a will which had
a clause ordering that his bones should be laid
to rest in Canaan, the land of the Promise. By
this time Joseph was an old man and his contribution to the land of Egypt had been forgotten.
There was a new dynasty and they were being
threatened on all sides. They felt that the Israelites in their midst were a very present trouble in
time of help. Joseph's people were not popular;
harsh laws were passed agst. the ' foreigners ' by
Rameses II, and the Hebs. found themselves
virtually in a state of slavery or forced labour
(*Gen.* 15; 45, 25-46, 7; *Ex*, 1, 1-14). Like most
nations they were saved by an inspired individual.
See MOSES. Whatever his origin may have been
he was brought up as an Egyptian aristocrat. He
too, felt the call, the promise and the urge (*Ex.*
3). It was a considerable task that was set him,
for not only were the Egyptians a powerful
people, but Israel now had a slave mentality.
Their leaders were not impressed by Moses, but
Pharaoh was, and clamped down even more
heavily on the people, thus making a resigned
people angry, which was exactly what Moses
wanted. Pharaoh assoc. certain natural calamities,
called the Plagues, with his own treatment of
Israel, and saw in them the manifestation of
divine wrath. He decided to let them go under
Moses. For the rest of their hist., the Israelites
(later the Jews) have regarded the Exodus (qv)
as their beginning as a nation. The round figure
of 600,000 is given as their number (*Ex.* 12, 37),
but that is prob. vastly exaggerated. They gathered
in their clans and the family subdivisions, and it
was an organised expedition that went on trek
into the desert along the regular caravan trail to

Syria. When Pharaoh recovered from his 1st shock he went after them, and the people turned agst. Moses as they were to do many times during the next 40 yrs. Their route was by the Bitter Lakes, round the N of the Red Sea. The words trans. ' Red Sea ' are really the ' Sea of Reeds.' The Israelites on foot managed it, but the Egyptians in their chariots got bogged down and a change of wind and tide overwhelmed them. It was Israel's 1st sign that the Exodus was not just Moses' idea, but the will of God. For some 40 yrs. they moved about the oases of the deserts and the most reasonable explanation for this lengthy period is that Moses had decided deliberately that it would take that time to make a slave people into a free nation. There cannot be a nation without the Law and the Church; Moses established both at Sinai (qv). He described the nature of God—vastly different from their ideas of the Egyptian gods, and he gave them a code of individual behaviour without which communal life would have been impossible. He taught them at the outset that the whole nation was in covenant and alliance with God. They were a chosen people. The law of Moses is contained in: (*Ex.* 25-*Num.* 30). It begins with the broad principles of the Ten Commandments (qv) and then applies these to the details of social living. At the same time he built the foundations of religious order and practice, with the Tabernacle and the Ark of the Covenant (qv). A priesthood was organised. To do all this was Moses' function. When his work was done, he died, leaving the leadership to Joshua. The lawgiver was followed by the soldier, for the work before them now was the work of conquest (*Josh.* 1, 1-9; 6, 6 & 20). (*See* JOSHUA). The land which th.ey eventually settled was not

a wilderness, and its people were in the main
highly civilised for the day and age. It took a
long time to reduce their cities one by one, but
eventually they conquered the territory and
partitioned it among the clans, the clan chief
being commissioned to subdivide the allotted
territory among the families. They called the
country not Canaan, but Palestine (the land of the
Philistines). The division, however, did destroy
the solidarity of the nation, and since there were
many pockets of the former inhabitants still in
the land, many of the Israelites were tempted into
foreign ways, esp. in religion. There was a gen.
deterioration, and since there was no permanent
central authority there was constant danger of
assault from neighbouring peoples who were more
united than they. The great leaders were dead:
Moses, Joshua, Caleb; but a new kind of leader
was waiting to take their place: the Judges (qv).
These were heroic figures who appeared at times
of crisis, rallied the people, and defeated the
enemy. The greatest of them was Samuel, who
appeared at the time of greatest danger—the
inroads of the skilful and powerful warrior
nation, the Philistines. All seemed lost when the
Ark of the Covenant, the sacred symbol of their
alliance with God, was captured. The nation was
never in a worse state than when Samuel appeared
upon the scene. He argued them out of their evil
and idolatrous ways and renewed the Covenant
at Mizpah (*1 Sam.* 7). Then he led them out to
war and victory. In the ensuing peace he reorganised national life on the model of Moses'
law, set up courts of justice, and began a movement called the Schools of the Prophets, which
was really a challenge to the young forward-
looking men of Israel. Their watchword was

'God and the Nation.' The Judges had never been hereditary or even political rulers of the nation, and the people demanded someone with the authority and status of Samuel to be his successor, for he was growing old. He was most reluctant to answer their demand for a king fearing that they would forget that Israel was a theocracy, not a monarchy or an aristocracy. Finally he had to accede and he chose Saul of the Benjamin clan (*1 Sam.* 9). Samuel anointed him, indicating that the king ruled by the tolerance of God, and the people accepted him gladly. The king continued to live on his own farm as the Judges had done, not regarding himself as a professional ruler, but rather as commander-in-chief of the nation under threat of war. This was in itself a pretty steady and demanding job which needed a standing army, which did not exist. In turn Saul defeated the Philistines, the Ammonites and the Amalekites. He was a success and it went a bit to his head. Political matters he had left largely to Samuel who was the fitter man to attend to them, but gradually Saul began to take more and more into his own hands and to make decisions. Samuel and he quarrelled (*1 Sam.* 13, 5-14; 22, 23). The nation divided in allegiance to the old prophet and the young king (*1 Sam.* 15, 23). Samuel told Saul that because of his disobedience the king could regard himself as rejected by God, and though there never had been a suggestion that the crown would be hereditary, the thought haunted Saul and eventually destroyed him. In the meantime Samuel decided that if there had to be kings there had to be kings, and he selected David to succeed Saul. David was of the clan of Judah. This was the inspiration of the jealousies which were later to split the nation

into 2 (*1 Sam.* 16, 1-14). Samuel anointed David
but Saul was not prepared to abdicate. In the
end David had to take to the hills like the Young
Pretender. Round him gathered some 400 out-
laws and adventurers—men who loved fighting
for its own sake and who feared nothing on earth
and very little in heaven. He even offered his
sword to the Philistines agst. Saul, but he never
drew it. Saul was defeated in a great battle at
Gilboa, but David was not with the enemy. The
king died by his own hand, and with him his 3
sons. David knew that he would have to fight
for the throne and keep fighting to hold it. He
marched into Judah, his own clan's territory and
was at once acclaimed king. But Judah was only
one out of twelve. Abner, Saul's old general, had
escaped the slaughter of Gilboa and out of loyalty
for his old master he crowned Saul's only surviving
son, Ishbosheth (qv) king. David took the fight
to him, and Ishbosheth was no match for him,
having an unfortunate tendency to offend everybody who had a mind to help him. Abner, of
course, was not much different. Eventually Ishbosheth was murdered and the whole nation
accepted David—reluctantly, apart from Judah
and Levi, who accepted him gladly. Therefore
after 7½ yrs. as king of Judah alone, David became
king of the whole nation. Neighbouring nations
were eager to take advantage of the civil disturbances in Israel, and David had to fight long and
hard to keep them off. His famous ' mighty
men ' or ' heroes ' performed deeds of spectacular
valour (*2 Sam.* 23, 16). So severe was David on
the Philistines that they disappear from hist.
altogether as a force to be reckoned with. His
greatest success was the capture of the ' impregnable ' city of Jebus, the Zion of the Amorites,

which was to become Jerusalem, the 1st capital
that the nation had had. This town had never
belonged to any of the tribes, or clans; it had
never been taken from the Amorites, which was
one of Joshua's few mistakes. It was a kind of
' free city ' lying bet. Judah and Benjamin. David
built his palace there and from there he ruled.
Remembering, however, that the real king was
God, David decided that until Jerusalem became
the centre of religion, it could not be properly
the capital. Politics was not enough, and never
is. From the days of Saul the Ark of the Covenant had been lying in a barn at Kirjath Jearim.
David brought it to Jerusalem, by that act making
this the holy city where the wandering God of
Sinai now lived permanently (*1 Chron.* 15). There
was more to do than build churches, however,
though the building of a Temple was David's
dream. The tribes of Canaan federated and conducted sporadic war with David for yrs., in which
he was steadily, and then finally victorious. He
pressed them back across the Euphrates and his
spoils were rich. He made Israel a nation ' on
top of the world.' He organised a standing army,
mostly of mercenaries, but a first class, highly-
trained, fighting machine. But a standing army
needs money, esp. if the officers and men are
mercenaries whose loyalty must be bought. That
meant taxes, which are the price any nation must
pay for national pride. Israel paid the taxes.
David set up local courts all over the country to
try civil and criminal cases, with himself as the
court of last appeal. And then David was guilty
of the most dangerous crime that the king of a
warring nation can be guilty of—he grew old.
His spoiled son Absalom rebelled, and was killed.
After 33 yrs. as king, David was now a broken

man, and he left behind him an intriguing, discontented nation, with rival claimants for the throne—his son Adonijah, and his son Solomon. Solomon got the throne, and prospered because of the foundation which his father had laid. The kingdom became of real importance in the world of the ME, and Solomon regarded himself as one who could hold up his head in any company. He made treaty arrangements with Egypt and Tyre; he lived in splendour and in peace (*1 Kings* 10, 22; 4, 25). He built the Temple, the permanent home of God, but that was about all that he did. Many stories are told of him, all to his credit, but these were in the main written by the priestly chroniclers in whose eyes Solomon could do no wrong, for he had built the Temple, and so given the priests their proper place. There was in fact nothing very remarkable about Solomon, although he did manage to make Israel of some international importance. The hist. of Israel and of the men and women who are the blood and bones of that hist., is a tale of selection and rejection. The time had now come when part of the nation was to be rejected, as being of no use in the furtherance of the transcendent purpose of God, and part of the nation was to be selected—until the time came for its rejection too. After the death of Solomon, Israel and Judah separated. It will be remembered that the 10 N tribes had preferred Saul's son, Ishbosheth, to David, Samuel's nominee. The old jealousies and rivalries had remained, and when Solomon died, the 10 tribes of the N opted for Jeroboam as their king. He was an able man, but not of the house of David. Judah, which with Levi made up the balance of the nation, decided for Rehoboam, the son of Solomon. The 2 strongest clans in the

nation were Ephraim and Judah, bet. whom there
was long rivalry. Jeroboam was of Ephraim;
Rehoboam was of Judah. Now Judah was rather
isolated geographically, and the others were more
than a little resentful not only that the capital,
Jerusalem, was in Judah, but that the only proper
place for worship was in Judah, too—the Temple.
Solomon had taxed the others heavily to make
Jerusalem and the Temple what they were; the
court had congregated there, with all the inevitable hangers-on. This jealousy and resentment, combined with a certain amount of private
pride, in which natural tendencies played some
part, had inspired the people of the 10 tribes to
set up their own more easily accessible (and more
easily corrupted) holy places. These had deteriorated towards idolatry, and Rehoboam,
backed by the priests who had a vested interest
in the integrity of the Temple, would not coun-
tenance them (1 Kings 11, 1-13; 12, 3-5). The situation was, then, that in the N were three-fourths
of the territory and two-thirds of the population.
They decided to go their own way. The Levites
naturally joined up with Judah, and 2 kingdoms
emerged. But whereas Judah was solid and united
and in a strong, naturally defensible position,
Israel was not (2 Chron. 11, 13 & 14). The 10
tribes (Israel) at first made Shechem their capital,
then Tirzah, then Samaria, a new town built by
Omri (1 Kings 12, 25; 14, 17; 15, 21; 16, 23 &
24). Jeroboam of Israel was afraid that if his
people visited Jerusalem to worship, he might lose
them: so he set up shrines in Dan and Bethel.
Israel, the N kingdom had 19 kings in all, their
reigns stretching over a mere 200 yrs. There were
plottings and assassinations and no dynasty lasted
long. Seven of their kings reigned for less than 2

yrs. each, and 8 died by their own hand or were
murdered. Under Ahab, whose wife was a
Phoenician, Jezebel, the old religion was lost
altogether in spite of the work of Elijah and
Elisha. Later came Amos and Hosea to warn
the nation, but nothing could stop their headlong
rush to ruin. Israel engaged in a fatal series of
alliances with various nations agst. Assyria and
even agst. Judah, while Judah allied with the
Assyrians agst. Israel and her friends. Finally in
722 BC Sargon of Assyria defeated Pekah of
Israel; Samaria fell and the people were carried
into captivity. The Assyrians settled in the area,
intermarried with the remnants and a new nation
of sorts emerged, the Samaritans, for whom
Judah had an eternal loathing. Israel had been
faithless to the covenant. They disappear from
hist., and Judah remains to perform the purpose
of God until in time, their turn comes too. *See*
names of individual kings, prophets, ASSYRIA,
etc.

Israelite. A desc. of Jacob, therefore an heir to the
covenant. When Nathanael is described as ' an
Israelite indeed ' (*John* 1, 47), there is the sense
expressed in the 1st ch. of *John*, ' His own received
him not.' That was what made Nathaniel exceptional—he did receive the Lord. He was what an
Israelite should be.

Issachar [is′-să-chär]. The 9th son of Jacob (*Gen.*
30, 18). Jacob did not think very much of him
(*Gen.* 49, 14 & 15). As with all the sons of Jacob
he was founder of a tribe or clan, the 5 subdivisions or septs of it being founded by his sons
(*Num.* 26, 23 & 24). By the reign of David there
were 87,000 of them (*1 Chron.* 7, 5). Moses foretold a peaceful future for them (*Deut.* 33, 18).
After the settlement they were allotted territory

bounded by Zebulon, Naphtali and Manasseh, with the Jordan as their E frontier.

Issue. Prob. a venereal disease, distinct from the ' issue of blood.' *See* MEDICINE.

Italian band. *See* article below, and BAND.

Italy. Not the Italy of mod. geography until NT times. Formerly it was only the S tip of mod. Italy. An Italian cohort was stationed in Syria (*Acts* 10, 1). Many Jews settled in Italy, their main route to the land being described in *Acts* (Ch. 27).

Itch. *See* MEDICINE.

Ituraea [ĭt′-ū-rē′-ă]. Mountainous country in the NE part of anti-Lebanon, populated by descendants of Ishmael (*Gen.* 25, 15; *Luke* 3, 1).

Ivory. Imported by Solomon from Ophir (*1 Kings* 10, 22). It was used for ornament, and Solomon had an ivory throne (10, 18; 22, 39). Amos had something to say on the luxury of ivory beds (6, 4).

Iyar [ī′-yăr]. 2nd month of the year. Same as Ziv. *See* TIME.

J

Jabal [jā′-băl]. Son of Lamech and Adah. Pioneer of the nomadic life (*Gen.* 4, 20).

Jabbok [jăb′-bŏck]. Trib. of the Jordan (*Gen.* 32, 22). Now known as Nahr ez Zerka, or Blue R. It was the boundary bet. Ammonites and Amorites (*Num.* 21, 24).

Jabesh [jā′-bĕsh]. Father of Shallum who killed King Zechariah and took the throne (*2 Kings* 15, 10 & 13 & 14).

Jabesh Gilead [jā′-bĕsh gĭl′-ĕ-ăd]. Town of Gilead (*Judg.* 21). Saul rescued it when besieged by the Ammonites (*1 Sam.* 11).

Jabez [jā'-bĕz]. City of Judah settled by desc. of Caleb (*1 Chron.* 2, 55). Also a man of Judah (4, 9-10).

Jabin (jā'-bĭn). Canaanite king of Hazor in Galilee, defeated by Joshua at Merom (*Josh.* 11, 1-14).

Jachin [jā'-chĭn]. Right-hand pillar in porch of Solomon's temple. *See* BOAZ. It was made of bronze (*1 Kings* 7, 15-22).

Jacinth. *See* HYACINTH, JEWELS AND PRECIOUS STONES.

Jackal. AV trans. 2 words 'dragon' which are certainly not so. The same word is in (*Lam.* 4, 3 AV) 'sea monsters.' But closer descriptions (*Isa.* 35, 7; 43, 20; *Jer.* 49, 33) point to the common jackal, *canis aureus*, cf. fox.

Jacob. Younger son of Isaac and Rebecca (*Gen.* 25). Favourite of his mother. By fraud he became his father's heir, and earned the enmity of Esau, but was certainly the better man to continue the Covenant. He went down to Haran seeking a wife and married the 2 daughters of his uncle Laban; Leah and Rachel. All his sons except Benjamin were born there. In Haran he prospered, and on the banks of the Jabbok (qv) received the promise of God that the Covenant would continue in him and was given the name Israel. After a reconciliation with Esau he moved to Shechem, where Joseph's brothers sold him into slavery. Driven by famine to Egypt, Jacob found the missing son in a position of high authority and settled in Goshen where he spent the rest of his life in considerable comfort. *See* ISRAEL.

Jacob's Well. (*Gen.* 33, 18-20; *John* 4, 5 & 6 & 12.) It was in Sychar, 2 m. from mod. Shechem.

Jael [jā'-ĕl]. Wife of Hebar the Kenite (*Judg.* 4, 11). The Kenites lived peaceably with both Israelites and Canaanites (*Judg.* 1, 16). When Barak de-

feated Sisera of Canaan, the beaten general took
refuge with Jael. According to the laws of hospitality (qv) he should have been safe, but Jael
murdered him (4, 21). *See* DEBORAH, SISERA, etc.

Jah [yah]. Form of name Jehovah (qv) used mostly
in poetry, usually trans. ' Lord ' (*Ps.* 68, 4; 89,
8 RV).

Jahweh [yăh'-wĕh]. *See* GOD.

Jairus [jă'-ĭ-rŭs]. Ruler of the synagogue, prob. at
Capernaum (*Mark* 5, 22; etc.). He pleaded with
Jesus to heal his daughter, which Jesus did.

Jambres [jăm'-brēs]. *See* JANNES.

James. Form of the name Jacob. **1.** Son of Zebedee, elder brother of John. The father was a
fisherman in a fairly big way (*Mark* 1, 20). The
mother was Salome, prob. sister of Mary, the
mother of the Lord (*Matt.* 27, 56; *Mark* 15, 40,
16, 1; *John* 19, 25). He was therefore a cousin
of Jesus. He worked in partnership with Andrew
and Simon Peter (*Luke* 5, 10). He was called
into discipleship (*Matt.* 4, 21) and his name is
usually found in assoc. with John's, with whom
he was nicknamed Boanerges, the sons of thunder.
He was martyred by Agrippa (*Acts* 12, 2). **2.** Son
of Alphaeus, prob. the same as Clopas (*John* 19,
25 RV). Not ' James the Less,' but ' James the
Little.' Which is a very different thing. His
mother Mary was one of the women who ministered
to Jesus at the end. He had a brother Joses
(*Mark* 15, 40). Trad. makes him Matthew's
brother, whose father was also Alphaeus. **3.**
Brother of Jesus. *See* BRETHREN OF THE LORD. He
became a believer after the Resurrection (*1 Cor.*
15, 7). And was made head of the church at
Jerusalem (*Gal.* 1, 19; 2, 1-13; *Acts* 15, 4-34;
21, 18 & 19). Trad. makes him a Nazirite (qv)
and calls him ' The Just.' He was killed by the

Scribes and Pharisees, and may be author of the Epistle below.

James, General Epistle of. Authorship gen. ascribed to James the brother of Jesus, who became head of the church at Jerusalem. While there is no direct internal evidence of this, there is nothing to contradict it. Though he does call himself ' James a servant of God and of the Lord Jesus Christ ' (1, 1) this could easily be from a proper sense of humility and fitness. To ascribe the Book simply to James surely implies one who would be automatically identified without further description. That points to the Lord's brother. He is obviously well grounded in Scripture (2, 19; 1, 17; 1, 13; 5, 4; 4, 5; etc.). And the content of the Book is on the practical lines of much of Jesus' teaching. The sins he condemns are the sins which Jesus condemned: uncharitableness, pride and superficiality (2, 1-13). His condemnation of the unbridled tongue might stem from recollection of his family's discomfort when Nazareth and Galilee began to gossip about his brother, and even from their own sorrow at their early attitude to Him. The Epistle was well known in the early Church although Origen is the 1st of the Fathers to ascribe the authorship to James. Jerome is the 1st to add ' Apostle and brother of the Lord.' Because of the literary style and the absence of refs. to Jesus' early life, and the lack of comment on the great Jerusalem controversy over the need for converts to embrace Judaism 1st, some critics deny that James is the brother of the Lord. They believe the author was a Hellenist Jew. But, as we have said, the evidence is not conclusive either way, and in these circumstances it is usually better to accept trad. until it is disproved. The letter was written for Jews living together, and does not deal with the major scandals and heresies of the early Church which inspired much of Paul's letter writing. James deals rather with faulty social behaviour and unchristian attitudes of one person to another. If James the brother is the author, the date must be before AD 62 when he was martyred. It is packed full of practical commonsense with a sure grasp upon Christianity in action. ' Faith without works is dead ' (2, 17) is the keynote of it all.

Jangling. (*1 Tim.* 1, 6; 6, 20). Chatter, foolish babbling, vain discussion (AV).

Jannes and Jambres [jăn'-nĕs, jăm'-brēs]. There is a ref. in *Exodus* to 2 Egyptian sorcerers who opposed Moses, but they are not named (7, 11 & 22). Later they are given these names (*2 Tim.* 3, 8). But these are trad. names meaning ' those who oppose, disobey, or resist.' They are not personal names.

Japheth [jă'-phĕth]. Son of Noah (*Gen.* 10, 1 & 2). Before the Flood he was married, but childless (7, 7). He is the progenitor of the inhabitants of the territory stretching from the Caspian and Black Seas to the Mediterranean.

Japhlet [jă'-phlĕt], **Japhletite.** Family and tribal name. The place was on the borders of Ephraim (*Josh.* 16, 3; *1 Chron.* 7, 32).

Jar. Vessel usually of earthenware; an earthen vessel, used for drawing water, storing wine, oil, corn, etc.

Jashar [jă'-shăr], **Jasher.** The book of Jashar (*Josh.* 10, 13; *2 Sam.* 1, 18). An ancient collection of poems, songs and ballads like those sung by troubadours and minstrels. It is quoted in the 2 passages ref. to. Other passages which are prob. quotations from Jashar are (*Judg.* 5; *1 Kings* 8, 12 & 13).

Jashobeam [jăsh-ō'-bē-ăm]. Chief of David's heroes (*1 Chron.* 11, 11).

Jashub [jā'-shŭb]. Fourth son of Issachar (*Num.* 26, 24).

Jason [jā'-sŏn]. Gk. form of Joshua, or Jesus. It was common among early Christians (*Acts* 17, 6; *Rom.* 16, 21).

Jasper. Variety of quartz, red, brown, yellow and green. *See* JEWELS AND PRECIOUS STONES.

Javan [jā'-văn]. Lit. ' Ionian.' A gen. Heb. term for Gks. In genealogy Javan is son of Japheth (qv). (*Gen.* 10, 2 & 4). It is a geographical rather than a personal name (*Isa.* 66, 19; *Ezek.* 27, 13).

Javelin. *See* LANCET.

Jaziz [jā'-zĭz]. David's chief herdsman (*1 Chron.* 27, 31).

Jealousy. Trial by ordeal for a wife suspected of adultery was to drink the water of bitterness: holy water mixed with temple dust (*Num.* 5, 11-31). This was the Jealousy Ordeal. By allusion, God is the husband, the nation is the wife, and idolatry is the adultery. God is therefore the ' jealous God ' (*Ex.* 20, 5). This is not jealousy in the mod. sense, but rather a zealousness for purity (*Num.* 25, 11; *2 Cor.* 11, 2). Sometimes it is used in a bad sense (*Rom.* 13, 13 RV; *1 Cor.* 3, 2; etc.).

Jearim [jě'-ă-rĭm]. Mt. on Judah border. Prob. Mt. Chesalon (*Josh.* 15, 10).

Jebus [jĕb'-ŭs]. Old name for Jerusalem (*Josh.* 15, 63).

Jebusite. Native of Jebus, twice ' Jebusim ' AV. They were driven out during Joshua's invasion (11, 3). The citadel, however, did not fall (*2 Sam.* 5, 6 & 7). David reduced the stronghold, but some Jebusites hung on (*2 Sam.* 24, 16 & 18). Solomon finished them off (*1 Kings* 9, 20 & 21).

Jehoahaz [jĕ-hō'-ă-hăz]. **1.** Another name for
Ahaziah prince of Judah (*2 Chron.* 21, 17). **2.**
Son of Jehu who reigned 17 yrs. from c. 817 BC.
An idolator he suffered at the hands of the Syrians,
but, reforming, conquered (*2 Kings* 13). **3.** Youn-
ger son of Josiah also called Shallum, and his
wrongful successor. He reigned only 3 months (*1
Chron.* 3, 15).

Jehoiachin [jĕ-hoi'-ă-chĭn]. Son and successor of
Jehoiakim of Judah coming to the throne c. 597
BC, aged 18 (*2 Kings* 24, 8). Given age of 8 in
(*2 Chron.* 36, 9). The bad son of a bad father he
reigned just over 3 months and lost Jerusalem to
Nebuchadnezzar, spending 37 yrs. in prison in
exile. He was released but remained in exile in
the reign of Evil Merodach (*2 Kings* 25, 27).
Jeremiah worked during his reign and refers to
him as Jeconiah, or Coniah.

Jehoiadah [jĕ-hoi'-ăd-ăh]. **1.** Father of David's
hero Benaiah (*2 Sam.* 23, 22). Prob. a priest, but
not chief priest as in AV (*1 Chron.* 27, 5). **2.** Son
of Benaiah above, though maybe some scribe has
got the names the wrong way (*1 Chron.* 27, 34).
3. High Priest during the Athaliah rebellion,
whose wife hid the young prince Joash. He led
the counter revolution and placed Joash, his
nephew by marriage, on the throne, continuing
to give him good advice (*2 Kings* 11, 1 ff.). **4.**
Priest in Jeremiah's time (*Jer.* 29, 26).

Jehoiakim [jĕ-hoi'-ă-kĭm]. Son of Joash, he was
passed by when his father died (*2 Kings* 23, 30)
his younger brother Jehoahaz being preferred.
Three months later Necho of Egypt drove the
usurper off the throne and crowned Jehoiakim
(formerly Eliakim). This was c. 608 BC when he
was 25. But he was practically a vassal to Egypt,
and, turning to idolatry, destroyed much of the

good work his father had done. Jeremiah remonstrated without effect (*Jer.* 36). Nebuchadnezzar defeated Necho and Jehoiakim changed masters (*2 Kings* 24, 1). Three yrs. later he rebelled and was imprisoned and prob. murdered by the Chaldeans, and given shameful burial (*2 Chron.* 36, 6; *Jer.* 22, 19; etc.).

Jehoram [jĕ-hō'-răm] (Joram). **1.** King of Israel, son of Ahab. He succeeded his brother Ahaziah. He failed in a campaign agst. Moab. Elijah worked during his reign (*2 Kings* 3). See JEHU. **2.** King of Judah, son of Jehoshaphat, contemporaneous with Jehoram, he married the daughter of Ahab and Jezebel, Athaliah, and was completely under her and Israel's influence. Edom broke away during his reign (*2 Kings* 8, 16 ff.).

Jehoshaphat [jĕ-hŏsh'-ă-phăt]. A few minor bearers of the name are: a historian (*2 Sam.* 8, 16), a priest (*1 Chron.* 15, 24), an official of Solomon's (*1 Kings* 4, 17), and the father of Jehu of Israel (*2 Kings* 9, 2). The most important of the name is the son of Asa of Judah, who succeeded his father after being regent. He was in power for about 25 yrs. (*1 Kings* 15, 24; 22, 41 ff.). He cleaned up Judah, sending out priests to teach the law, and securing the land (*2 Chron.* 17). In alliance with Ahab, whose daughter his son had married (*see* JEHORAM 2), he tried to retake Ramoth Gilead from the Syrians where Ahab was killed. He learned his lesson, however, and gave up territorial ambitions (*2 Chron.* 19). He successfully resisted invasion by an alliance of Moab and Edom (*2 Chron.* 20). After making a bad commercial treaty with Ahaziah of Israel which he refused to renew, he allied with Jehoram (*2 Kings* 3, 4 ff.). He died c. 850 BC.

Jehoshaphat, Valley of. This has not been identified

but might have been the valley of the Kedron.
There was a prophecy that here the world would
be judged (*Joel* 3, 2).

Jehosheba [jĕ-hŏsh´-ĕ-bă]. Daughter of Jehoram
of Judah she saved the Davidic line by hiding
the infant Joash (*2 Kings* 11, 2). *See* JOASH.

Jehovah. *See* GOD.

Jehovah Jireh [jĕ-hō´-văh jī´-rĕh]. Name given by
Abraham to the place where he found the ram
which he sacrificed in place of his son. It means
' the Lord sees and provides ' (*Gen.* 22, 14).

Jehovah Nissi [nĭs´-si]. ' The Lord is my banner.'
The name given by Moses to the altar raised after
the defeat of Amalek (*Ex.* 17, 15).

Jehovah Shalom [shā´-lom]. ' God is peace ': the
name given by Gideon to the altar he raised at
Ophra (*Judg.* 6, 24).

Jehovah Shammah [shăm´-mah]. ' God is there ': the
name given to the rebuilt Jerusalem (*Ezek.* 48,
35 Marg).

Jehovah Tsidkeni [tsĭd-kĕ´-nī]. ' God is our righteousness ': the title of the prophesied king who would
reign after the captivity (*Jer.* 23, 6 Marg).

Jehu [jĕ´-hū]. There was a Benjamite of the name
(*1 Chron.* 12, 3) a prophet who reproved Jehoshaphat for dealing with Ahab, and who wrote
the hist. of the reign (*2 Chron.* 19, 2; 20, 34); and
2 minor characters (*1 Chron.* 2, 38; 4, 35). But
the important one is the son of Jehoshaphat of
Judah and grandson of Nimshi (sometimes wrongly called ' son ') (*1 Kings* 19, 16). He was a soldier
in Ahab's army, the prophet Elijah was ordered
by God to anoint him king in place of Ahab.
This was not done until after Ahab was dead and
Jehoram was on the throne. Elisha sent word to
Jehu that his mission was to destroy the house of
Ahab. Supported by the army he marched to

Jezreel where Jehoram and Ahaziah of Judah, whose mother was Jezebel, widow of Ahab, were in conference. He disposed of all 3 (*2 Kings* 9, 1-37). He then dealt with the princes of the royal house, convinced that he was fulfilling a destiny. Hosea was not so sure (*Hos.* 1, 4). He reigned for 28 yrs., founding the 4th dynasty; paid tribute to Assyria, and was killed by Hazael of Syria. Jehu confused Divine right with his own inclinations, which is not unusual (*2 Kings* 10 & 11).

Jemima(h) [jĕ-mī′-mă]. First of 3 daughters born late in life to Job (*Job* 42 14).

Jephthah [jĕph′-thăh]. In AV NT Jephthae. The son of Gilead born out of wedlock, he was thrown out by his brothers, and fled to Haran. Being something of a swashbuckler he attracted a band of homeless men who became a force in the land. He was not a brigand, however. The Ammonites had been sitting for 18 yrs. in the E of Jordan and the elders asked him if he could help them. He rallied Gilead and vowed that if God gave him victory he would sacrifice whatever came out of his house first on his return. He defeated the Ammonites and on his return home was greeted 1st by his only child—his daughter. Afterwards Israelite women mourned her 4 times a year, though this may have been a fertility rite. Had she not been a virgin and unmarried, Jephthah could not have carried out his vow. Later he repulsed an attack by Ephraim, annoyed because he had defeated Ammon without their help. He was a Judge for 6 yrs., and is named in Hebrews as one of the men of faith (*Judg.* 11, 1—12, 7).

Jeremiah [jĕr-ĕ-mī′-äh]. He lived during the reigns of Josiah, Jehoahaz, Jehoiakim, Jehoiachin and Zedekiah of Judah c. 628-583 BC. That is about 75 yrs. after Isaiah. He was not anxious to become a prophet (qv) but felt compelled by the subservience to church and state of the self-styled prophets. He began his work of warning and advice during a peaceful part of Josiah's reign. The state was corrupt and religion decadent. To some extent (though how large or small has not been established) he was concerned with the reforms of Josiah's reign (qv). His father was priest of Anathoth in Benjamin, and in his youth he had a call to the work and a warning of its dangers (1, 4-10). First to oppose him were his own friends, and this hurt him (11, 18—12, 3). But the hostility increased rather than diminished (18, 18-23). Later he dictated his prophecies which were written down by Baruch (qv) who read them in the Temple, and later to King Jehoiakim who ordered them to be burned (36, 1-26). Another edition was written. During the siege of Jerusalem his prophecies were blamed for weakening morale, and when the Chaldeans raised the siege temporarily he tried to get away to Anathoth, and was accused of desertion (37, 1-15). He was imprisoned but was released by Zedekiah (37, 16-21). The princes soon had him back in his dungeon and had left him to die, but the plea of an Ethiopian eunuch got him released (38). When the Chaldeans took the city he received favours from Nebuchadnezzar. But when Gedaliah was murdered, though he advised the Jews to stay where they were, they ran off to Egypt taking Jeremiah with them (41, 1-44, 3). The time and place of his death are unknown.

Jeremiah, Book of. This book is a work of tremendous importance as well as being the revelation of a singularly fine personality. He begins by reminding them in the reign of Josiah that they are a Chosen People, delivered by God from Egypt, led through the wilderness and brought to a country. But they had sinned, and sin, inevitably, is punished (chs. 2-6). He goes on to define their particular sins and to call them to a proper repentance (chs. 7-9). From there he proceeds to tell of the sorrow of God over His faithless, disobedient, treacherous people (chs. 10-12). During the reign of Jehoiakim he foretells the doom of the warring nations and of Judah, pouring scorn on the false prophets who are speaking easy things. He foretells the invasion of the Chaldeans and is made to suffer for his conscience pricking pessimism. The chronology is suspect here and it has been suggested that the proper order of passages is chs. 26; 46-49, 33; 25; 36, 1-8; 45; 36, 9-32; 14-15; 16; 17; 18; 19; 20; 35; 22-23, 40; and 13. The next group of prophecies is in the reign of Zedekiah, and the suggested order is chs. 24; 27; 28; 29; 49, 34—ch. 51; then chs. 21; 34; 37; 38; 39, 15-18; 32, 33; 30; 31; 39, 1-14. These consist of the foretelling of the doom of Babylon, the account of his own imprisonment, the prophecies of revival and restoration, the account of the fall of Jerusalem and the fate of Zedekiah. All that remains are the prophecies connected with the remnant of Judah and the remnant in Egypt (chs. 40-44). Ch. 52 is a historical addition. There is a very deep human and biographical appeal in the Book, showing not only an intimate picture of the man himself, but very searching glimpses of the lives and the natures of the other figures in the hist. of that sad and perilous time. His doctrine goes deep: sin and repentance, the judgment and the Messiah; the new Covenant and Redemption, the relationship of the person to a Personal God.

Jericho [jĕr′-ĭ-chō]. A town of Palestine lying over

800 ft. below Mediterranean sea level, in very
fertile sub-tropical country, 5 m. N of the Dead
Sea. It was the 1st Canaanite city taken by Joshua
(*Josh.* chs. 1-7). Jericho was completely destroyed,
but there was a village on the site in David's day
(*2 Sam.* 10, 5). It was rebuilt by Hiel (*1 Kings* 16,
34) and became the centre of a college of prophets
(*2 Kings* 2, 4). Zedekiah's last battle was fought
here agst. the Chaldeans (*2 Kings* 25, 5). A hill
nearby is thought to be the hill of the Temptation.

Jeroboam [jĕr′-ō-bō′-ăm]. **1.** The 1st king of Israel
after the split following the death of Solomon.
His father had been one of Solomon's officials (*1
Kings* 11, 26). Solomon appointed Jeroboam
overseer of building in Jerusalem, and a prophet,
Ahijah, told him that one day he would be king
over the 10 tribes. When rumour of this got
about, Jeroboam thought it wiser to decamp, and
he found his way to Egypt where he was well
enough treated by the Pharaoh. On Solomon's
death he attended the gathering at Shechem to
decide the succession, but he made it a secession,
for the 10 tribes of the N decided to become a
nation on their own with Jeroboam as king. The
tribes of Judah and Levi possessed the land where
Jerusalem stood, the sacred city, and Jeroboam
was afraid that the attraction of Jerusalem, the
centre of worship, would be too much for his new
nation. Agst. the ancient law he established 2
centres of worship in the N kingdom: Dan and
Bethel; set up golden calves and a non-Levitical
priesthood (*1 Kings* chs. 11-12). This division of
the kingdom was the cause of its weakness and
ultimate ruin, persecution, and captivity by
surrounding peoples (*2 Kings* 17, 21-23). Jeroboam
suffered a heavy defeat at the hands of Abijam
of Judah and was taken prisoner (*1 Kings* 15, 7).

Altogether he had reigned 22 yrs. from c. 931 BC.
2. Son and heir of Joash, king of Israel. He was
of the Jehu dynasty c. 785 BC, and reigned for
41 yrs. A fine soldier, he took Damascus and
restored the old frontiers of Israel. Amos (qv)
was a thorn in his flesh (*Amos* chs. 2-7). He was
succeeded by his son Zechariah (*2 Kings* 14, 29).

Jerusalem. The Holy City to Jews, Christians and
Mohammedans, it stands on the E slope of the
Judean watershed, 2,600 ft. above Mediterranean
sea level, and distant 33 m. from that sea, and
15 from the Dead Sea. Like Rome it is built on
hills, Acra, Begetha, Zion and Ophil, which are
the spurs of the mts. bet. the Kidron and Hinnom
valleys. The area has been inhabited from the
Stone Age. Orig. called Jebus, it was the stronghold of the Jebusites and remained independent
after the Joshua invasion till it was taken by
David, who made it his capital. When Solomon
built the Temple there it became the national
shrine. There were abundant springs and cisterns,
and in all the sieges the beleaguered never suffered
from thirst. The 1st siege as a Judean city was
when Rehoboam was king and Shishak of Egypt
the enemy (*1 Kings* 14, 25). He took away the
Temple treasures which were replaced by copper
vessels. In Jehoram's reign a coalition of Philistines and Arabs plundered the city (*2 Chron.* 21,
16). Joash repaired the Temple but had to buy
off Hazael of Syria to save it again. He gave him
the Temple treasures which were later looted
from Hazael by Jehoash of Israel. Later kings,
notably Jotham, devoted themselves to streng-
thening the defences (*2 Kings* 15, 35), and the city
was able to resist both Syria and Israel in the
reign of Ahaz (*2 Kings* 16, 5). Hezekiah, aware
of the threat from neighbouring peoples streng-

thened it further and built the Siloam tunnel, a
water conduit; though when the time came it was
a mysterious affliction which decimated Sennacherib's forces and saved the city (*2 Kings* 19, 35).
Manasseh built an outer wall, and Josiah restored
the Temple (*2 Kings* 22). After a series of misfortunes due to bad royal management Jerusalem
fell to Nebuchadnezzar. The city was ruined and
the people deported. After the return from the
Exile the city was rebuilt, the defences by
Nehemiah, and the Temple by Ezra. A good description of the fortifications is found in *Nehemiah*.
This work was done under the patronage of the
Persians, who had defeated the Chaldeans, but when
they in turn were defeated by Alexander at the
battle of Issus in 333 BC, the city had an uneasy
time, being won and lost again by warring neighbours. In 168 B.C. there was a revolt agst. Antiochus
Epiphanes (qv) who desecrated the Temple. The
Rom. were called in to settle the succession.
Pompey besieged Jerusalem and again desecrated
the Temple, placing Herod on the throne in 47
BC. The Herods rebuilt the city on a grand scale,
and built a new Temple. Herod died in 4 BC.
Jesus' connection with the city is well known. He
foretold its destruction as prophets had done
before him. For a while the city prospered
under Agrippa, AD 41-44, and he and his son
added new buildings. Their work was complete
by AD 64, but 2 yrs. later the city revolted agst.
Rome and was razed to the ground in the year
70.

Jeshurun [jĕsh'-ŭ-rŭn] **(Jesurun)**. Poetical name for
Israel as a moral entity (*Deut.* 32, 15; *Isa.* 44, 2).
Jesse [jĕs'-sĕ]. Son of Obed and desc. from the Chief
of Judah in Moses' day, and from Ruth (4, 18-22).
His youngest son was David (*1 Sam.* 17, 12-14).

He lived at Bethlehem to which Samuel came in
search of a king (*1 Sam.* 16, 1-13). During the
outlaw days the other sons were with David but
Jesse and his wife were sent to safety with the
king of Moab (*1 Sam.* 22, 1-4). He was an un-
spoiled man (*Isa.* 11, 1; *Rom.* 15, 12).

Jesus. A form of the name Joshua which means
' Jehovah is salvation ' (*Acts* 7, 45; *Heb.* 4, 8 AV).
An ancestor of our Lord had this name (*Luke* 3,
29) though AV calls him Jose. There was also a
Jewish Christian of the name (*Col.* 4, 11).

Jesus Christ. The important source of information
on the Jesus of history is the first 3 Gospels which
were never meant to be the complete biography
of Jesus. They are collections of fragments of
memories, recollections and reminiscences, with
the writers more collectors than biographers. They
write in a wonderfully objective and unemotional
manner; but from their words a very real person
of flesh and blood, heart, spirit and mind can be
built up. Their Jesus is the Jesus of the months
of his ministry. Almost nothing is said about his
boyhood, though the work and the play of His
boyhood flash out many a time in what He said
and how He said it. ' My yoke is easy ': Jesus
made yokes. The rich man's bigger barns: Jesus
built barns. The children playing in the market
place: Jesus had played in the market place with
the same kind of children. Ref. is made to the
family circle (*Mark* 6, 3; *Matt.* 13, 56) and some
have tried to make out a case that Jesus' brothers
and sisters were actually His cousins. This is
because they are reluctant to believe that Mary
and Joseph carried out a normal married life and
had children after Jesus. But the incident of His
rejection by the people of Nazareth in the refs.
above loses its whole point if this cousin theory is

accepted. To argue that Jesus cannot be Messiah because He has cousins living at Nazareth is not an argument at all. We can accept Joseph and Mary, with 5 sons and at least 2 daughters. Jesus is apprenticed to the trade of country joiner—wright, we would call it in Scotland—and takes over the business on the death of His father, keeping it going till He is about 30 yrs. old (*Luke* 3, 23). It is very likely that He did this willingly until the family was independent and established. He was familiar with all the day to day activities of the home (*Matt.* 6, 30 & 32; 7, 9 & 10; 13, 33; *Mark* 2, 21; *Luke* 11, 5-7 ; 11 & 12 & 25; 15. 8). His genius for telling parables may have sprung from years of practice telling bedtime stories to His brothers and sisters. Nazareth lies at the great crossing of the caravan routes. and He must have seen and spoken to traders from the ends of the earth. He stored it all up (*Luke* 2 47), and what He did not know, He asked. His love of nature is very apparent, but it is the love of the country-bred boy who has observed: it is not at all book learning. From His early days in a house that must have been pretty crowded He may have acquired the habit of seeking solitude. In Nazareth He would see the whole pattern of oriental living, with its vast and dreadful contrasts: the very rich and the abysmally poor, the charitable and the malicious. All the characters who crowd His parables, and provide His illustrations; who draw His approval or earn His scorn, are the folk of Nazareth and around. Much of His learning came from listening to His elders, and from asking questions, which was the teaching method of the synagogue. He had His schooling and knew His scriptures thoroughly. Of His personal appearance nothing is known, but His eyes must have

been remarkable. Time and again we are told
that ' He looked,' and the look seems to have been
enough. His voice, too, must have been greatly
attractive. People do not hang on a preacher's
words for the words alone, but very often for the
way the words are spoken. Examples there are
in plenty of a kindly humour (*Matt.* 23, 24 & 25).
Even the parable of the Good Samaritan seems to
suggest a twinkle in Jesus' eye. And beneath the
humour there often was an irony: the sense of
the ridiculousness of pomposities. Compassion
was characteristic of Him: compassion and the
passion of righteous indignation agst. pretence,
pose and injustice. He could never resist the
appeal of need. His quickness in repartee is
notable and His constant ability to turn the tables,
always with the air of a simple man seeking information, upon those who foolishly tried to catch
Him in some stupidity. His was essentially a
simple mind as truth itself is simple in essence.
Like all poets He could see significance in everything from a wedding to a funeral, a shepherd
to a sower, a festival to children playing in the
street. That is the significance of the ' pictorial '
temptation of Jesus. He must have told His
disciples about this, for He was alone at the time,
and He told the story in pictures: He saw everything as a picture, vivid and real. Above every
other quality there emanated from Him a strange
power, and there was in Him an equally strange
magnetism which brought men, women, and
children willy-nilly to Him. His decision at the
temptation before His ministry began was that
He should take the way of the teacher, resisting
the political, the social or the sensational method,
and it was as a teacher that He made His first
impact and impression. The heart of His teaching

was, 'The Kingdom of God is within you.' In solitude and in the crowded ways of life He had thought and better thought of God, separating the gold from the dross of Scripture and testing all ideas by His own experience, observation and assessment of His own nature. He became totally committed to God as He understood God, and His preaching was that only such total commitment could fulfil any man's life, release his powers and bring him peace of mind. The first man to whom He revealed His thoughts was Andrew, and Andrew (qv) was immediately convinced, going to his brother Peter and telling him that he had found the Lord (*John* 1, 37-42). Jesus made the same appeal to the rest of the 12, and His purpose in having this band was certainly that He should privately teach them more intensively so that they in turn could teach others. They were a very mixed bunch, chosen, it would appear, almost at random, and they were with Him for about 3 yrs., seeing Him in all His moods and not always understanding why He should have moods at all. Very often their lack of perception and sympathy was a sore trial to Jesus, but He rebuked them forcibly very seldom. Strangely, though undoubtedly and even inevitably, the full effect of His life and personality upon them was not evident till after the Crucifixion and the Resurrection and Pentecost, when their reaction at once became, 'remember how He used to . . .' It is no use pretending as some cynics do, that Jesus had nothing orig. to say about God, just as it is pointless to say that everything He said about God was orig. But God was more real to Jesus than God has been to any man before or since. To Him, God was in and through everybody and everything, and He was constantly surprised by the inability of good people to realise this. He could not understand why they should be unable to find God when God was so easy to find; though He knew and taught that God could best be found along the road of duty and sacrifice and pain. He called only one man a fool, and that was the self-satisfied rich man who said to his soul ' Eat, drink and be merry.' To Jesus it was clear that God had thought everything out, and had created an orderly, logical world in which everything goes right so long as His will is done, but all goes wrong if His will is not done, for the world works in God's way or not at all. But Jesus does not often speak of God as the Creator and the Supreme Power: His emphasis is rather on God's passionate interest in the individual human personality —an idea both rich and new in a world where the poor little man was only a pawn in a game he could not control. This and the love of God for all, are the great accents of His teaching. The fatherhood of God is the only warrant for the brotherhood of men: the love of God is the warrant for the gen. love which alone can make the world go round. Men must practise the presence of God till human nature becomes their second nature, and divine nature their first. This is what He means by conversion, another new element in His teaching—the ability of individual human nature to change and to be changed: the rebirth. Good living, then, is living with God. Ecclesiasticism, ritual, asceticism and all superficialities have nothing whatsoever to do with it. Holiness is a natural attribute of God and of those who love God and live with Him. It implies complete trust, with no reserve and no reservation (*Mark* 11, 2; *Matt.* 10, 20). The first access to God is by way of prayer: Jesus prayed continually

(*Mark* 1, 35; 6, 46; etc.). Essential to His own prayers was: ' If it be Thy will.' Because of that He was able to say that all faithful prayer is answered (*Luke* 11, 9). Prayer answered according to God's will is still prayer answered even if those who make the prayer cannot see the answer. Prayer is a communication and a communion bet. man and God, and it is nobody's business but God's and the individual's. It must never be careless, but earnest, determined, constant and even strenuous, with the seeker believing absolutely that there is lit. nothing that God cannot do if it is His will to do it. Although He walked so closely with God, Jesus was never in the slightest out of, or above, or indifferent to, this present world. His emotions were human emotions. When He saw Jerusalem on the last journey as He turned the bend of the road He wept (*Luke* 19, 41). When He came to the Temple His gorge rose and He laid about Him in no uncertain manner (*Luke* 19, 46). His sorrow over Jerusalem was genuine and deep (*Luke* 13, 34). He loved company except for the moments when He preferred solitude. He enjoyed food and drink and good fellowship, and He wanted other people to enjoy them too. He was the friend and advocate of the poor and the hungry (*Luke* 14, 12); of the unemployed (*Matt.* 20, 9); of the widow and the orphan (*Matt.* 23, 14). His sorrow for the rich, young ruler (*Mark* 10, 17-22) was not just because he did not realise what his money could do for other people, but because he could not realise what spending his money could do for himself. He included daily bread in the prayer which He taught His disciples but He did not stop there, for He knew that men need more than bread (*Luke* 4, 4). They needed God and they were

looking for God in the wrong places (*Matt.* 9, 36).
He wanted them to know that God was looking
for them (*Luke* 15, 5). He did not blame people
for this: He was desperately sorry for them. But
He did blame those who should have known
better and who should have been teaching better.
He would not allow anyone to despise anyone
else (*Matt.* 5, 22; *Luke* 17, 2). The purpose
before His disciples, as He told them, was to
bring these poor lost sheep into the fold of the
Kingdom: to be fishers of men. He knew the
cure for human misery: 'Come unto me' (*Matt.*
11, 28) and He knew, too, that the folk most likely
to come and find their satisfaction were those
who had nowhere else to go. 'Blessed are the
poor—ye that hunger now—ye that weep now'
(*Luke* 6, 20 & 21). They were blessed not because
of their condition, which was anything but blessed,
but because their condition raised no obstacles
bet. themselves and the kingdom: there was only
one door they could try, and it happened to be the
right one. The works of healing are dealt with in the
article on Miracles. But it must be noted that these
were never performed for any reason other than
Jesus' unfailing response to human need. It was
in fact because there was so much need that He
knew for a certainty how badly He was needed.
His attitude was simply, 'What does God think
of this? What would God do here?' Actually
He never had to ask Himself that question, for He
already knew the answer. His attitude to
women is of the first importance, for it has been
largely responsible for the vast change in women's
place in society. To-day the Hindu and Moham-
medan religions have realised that unless they
change their attitude to women they are going to
be left far behind in the challenge for the soul

and mind of humanity; just as the Communist
countries are realising that they must give more
place to the rights of persons to be personalities.
To all women, good and bad, Jesus was, in the
true sense of the word, a gentleman. The mothers
brought their children to Him: Mary and Martha
loved to have Him in their home, and it would not
be at all surprising if they loved Him as a woman
loves a man. Martha's sharp complaint may have
stemmed from something more personal than
housewifely resentment at her sister. Kindness,
to Jesus, was a basic human quality, and should
be a natural action, not an enforced duty, since,
with God as father, all folk are related. Another
quality basic to Him and so to humanity, was the
ability and readiness to forgive: and again the
reason was as sound as it is simple—you must
forgive because sooner or later you will need to
be forgiven. With all His great affection for
people, however, He was under no illusions about
them and their faults and failings (*Matt.* 13, 13;
15, 8; 23, 27; *Mark* 6, 6; 8, 21; etc.). But He
' loved them just the same ' no matter how bitterly
He hated what they stood for. Even if characters
were a bit disreputable He could still mix with
people and in a way enjoy their company, though
it did not add to His popularity with the aloof
and the self-righteous (*Luke* 7, 34; 19, 1-10).
What did He think of sin, then, if His views
differed from those of His day and age? Toleration of evil cannot have a place in any religion,
but Jesus did not condone sin by mixing with
sinners and by loving them. He was there for
their good; to make them non-sinners. Jesus as
teacher followed directly upon John the Baptist
whose theme was judgment, whose conviction
was that all men were sinners, and whose advice

was to repent and hope for the best before it was too late. Jesus admired and respected John, but He did not wholly agree with him, for there was little that was new in the teaching of John. He is the last of the prophets but he is still in their line, tradition, and convention. Jesus saw that to repent in fear of judgment is only a beginning. What matters is what happens after that. The new life must be sustained, therefore it must have an active purpose, not the negative objective of avoiding punishment. Righteousness which is for one's own sake is not righteousness at all: at least it does not ' exceed the righteousness of the Pharisees.' Jesus saw simply two ways of living, a right way and a wrong way, but to turn the feet from the wrong way to the right way was only the start of the journey. This was not a road that had no turnings. It was just as easy to go off it in the last mile as it was in the first: just as easy to wander off it as never to take it at all. The end of the road is the judgment seat of God (*Matt.* 25) where the keynote of reaction is amazement: of the good that they have been good and of the bad that they have been bad. There is nothing more blind than righteousness and there is nothing more calculating than goodness. To Jesus the good man was always on the edge of wrongdoing, and would fall into it unless he kept his goodness in constant repair (*Luke* 22, 32). Jesus believed that His purpose was to find the lost; not the deliberate sinner (though He would not turn from him) but the person who did not know where he was in this business of living; to put him on the right road and to show him how to stay there. In other words His purpose was to seek the sinner, which is easy enough, and then to save him, which is another contract

entirely. But for Jesus, sin is not a gen. term.
There are millions of people in the mid-20th cent.
who are pleased to call themselves sinners, and
who pray and praise accordingly, while in their
own heart and mind they regard themselves as
being perfectly normal. They have some idea that
they are supposed to be sinners because there was
something or other called Original Sin, and because
God wants us to call ourselves sinners. They have
not the faintest idea of what Original Sin is, but
they call themselves sinners because, somehow
or other, everybody is a sinner. Jesus would have
none of this nonsense. Sin to Jesus was real and
specific and active; it was not hereditary and it
was not fated. It was a matter either of ignorance
or of choice. The people who were headed for
hell, in Jesus' view were (1) those who were indifferent to the condition of other people (*Matt.
25, 31-46*); (2) those who had dirty minds even
if they refrained from doing dirty things (*Matt.
5, 21 & 22 & 27-29*); (3) those who regarded
religion as a performance, not as a persuasion
(*Matt. 23, 23 & 24*); (4) those who knew fine
what they ought to do but who stood things on
their head to get reasons why they shouldn't do
it (*Luke 9, 62*). The thing that is sin is the thing
that God would not do. If God is understood,
sin is understood. Over agst. all this He affirmed
that there is always a way back, no matter how
far the soul has strayed, no matter how deliberately
and for how long a man has separated himself
from God. God never closes the door. We
have seen Jesus of Nazareth, of Galilee and
of Jerusalem: what of Jesus of Calvary? Why
the Cross? Looking back on the life of the
Lord we can see the Cross as inevitable, and
we can see it as inevitable only because it is

clear that it was something deliberately chosen
by Jesus. He could have avoided it, probably
even by the simple act of staying in Galilee. But
if the Cross is not a thing of choice it is a thing
without meaning. Is it then, this choice, in line
with everything that went before, or is it a last-
minute desperate attempt made because everything that had gone before had not achieved the
results that Jesus had hoped for? To us the
purpose may seem reasonably clear, but was it
just so clear to Jesus in that fatal moment of
decision? To these questions it must be replied
that from the Gospels it is patent enough that
Jesus had the Cross, or something similar (stoning
to death?) in His mind from the outset. But
equally clearly none of the disciples had for a
moment entertained the idea of anything so
dreadful (*Mark* 10, 32). His going to Jerusalem is
as deliberate as the outcome was inevitable in
Jesus' own mind. His knowledge of humanity
about which He had neither illusions nor delusions,
told Him this. The journey to Jerusalem and the
entry were a challenge, and Jesus had no doubt
at all about the response. By the manner of it
and the staging of it He was saying to all Jewry,
' Accept Me as Messiah, or kill Me as fraud and
impostor.' He does not call Himself Messiah (qv)
but He fulfils the qualifications of the Messiah.
He raises from the dead (*see* LAZARUS); He comes
through the gates in the style foretold by prophecy (*Zech.* 9, 9). He is saying to them, ' Yes,
I am Jesus of Nazareth, but I am all the Messiah
you will ever get.' He knew they would not
accept this, and He was not going to judge them
for it. But He was going to give them a chance
to judge themselves; not just the Scribes and the
Pharisees, but also His own friends, His disciples

who were maybe too familiar with Him to see Him as anybody but Jesus of Nazareth. He had done His job; He had taken teaching as far as teaching could possibly go; there must now be the act of faith. If it did not work, then He was wrong and had always been wrong. If it did work, He was right and always had been right. This was the great gamble, and only God who knows all, need not ever gamble. Jesus was betting His life that He was right, though He did not know the odds for or against. This was something that He had to do and there was no other way. Jesus was not 'half in love with easeful death' as Keats pretended to be. He hated the idea of this kind of death as anyone must, and even more than some because of His sensitivity; but He knew that nothing is worth living for that is not worth dying for, and that nothing is worth dying for that is not worth living for. Again Jesus is trying to show what God is like, and that there is lit. nothing worthy of Himself that God will not do to win and save the poorest soul alive. Jesus may have had some thought, lingering from his early training, of the scapegoat—the expiation of sin, the supreme sacrifice—but Christian theology has probably given Jesus 'credit' for some thoughts that never entered His mind. To Him it was the gamble. As James Graham, Marquis of Montrose, put it before his own cruel death: 'He either fears his fate too much, Or his deserts are small, Who puts it not unto the touch, To gain or lose it all.' He had given His life to God: if God let Him down now it was a glorious failure. He hoped and prayed in Gethsemane that it would not be so. Jesus was not a theologian: He did not speculate about God. He was possessed by God, and therefore He knew, without argument, that what He was doing was right. But since He was human He had to fight agst. the body that masquerades as the soul; agst. the fear, the frailty and the doubt as any man would in such a great adventure. You cannot think back to Jesus and attribute to Him the theological thinking of 2,000 yrs. He was of His time and of all time: He was as far ahead of the thought of his own time as He is of the thought of our times. You cannot confuse Jesus' clear ideas with Paul's theological interpretation of them. Jesus wanted people to think about God in a new way. He said to Himself, ' If they identify Me with God, this is the way I want them to think of Me—and of God.' And how right He was. *See separate articles on* MARY, IMMORTALITY, MIRACLES, etc.

Jether [je'-ther]. 1. Descendant of Judah through Perez, Hezron, Jerahmeel, Onam and Jada (*1 Chron.* 2, 32). 2. Possible descendant of Judah (*1 Chron.* 4, 17). 3. An Asherite, possibly Ithran (cf. vv. 37 & 38 of *1 Chron.* 7). 4. Form of name of Jethro, Moses' father in law (*Ex.* 4, 18 marg.). 5. Oldest son of Gideon (*Judg.* 8, 20). 6. Father of Absalom's general Amasa (*1 Kings* 2, 5).

Jetheth [je'-theth]. One of the dukes of Edom (*Gen.* 36, 40).

Jethro [jĕth'-rō]. Priest of Midian, father-in-law of Moses (*Ex.* 3, 1). Also called Reuel (*Ex.* 2, 18). He had 7 daughters, one of whom, Zipporah, Moses married while he was hiding in Midian (*Ex.* 2, 16 & 20). After Moses' return to Egypt he sent her and their 2 sons back to Jethro for safety.

Jew. The name is derived from Judah and is prop. an inhabitant of Judah or the desc. of one who was. After the division of the kingdom the name replaced ' Israelite ' as the designation of the

Chosen People. Judah had become the guardian of the tradition, and was, of course, the source of Judaism. *See* ISRAEL, JUDAH.

Jewel. The word is now confined to precious stones, but in 17th cent. Eng. it could include gold and silver (cf. *Gen.* 24, 53). Called jewelry in RV and RSV.

Jewels and precious stones. There are 3 pretty comprehensive lists of these. **1.** The High Priest's Breastplate (*Ex.* 28, 17-20; 39, 10-13). **2.** Stones worn by the king of Tyre (*Ezek.* 28, 13). **3.** The foundations of the New Jerusalem (*Rev.* 21, 19 & 20). The jewels of the High Priest's Breastplate (AV) are sardius (ruby marg.), topaz, carbuncle, emerald, sapphire, diamond, ligure, agate, amethyst, beryl, onyx, and jasper. In the RV they are given as: sardius (ruby marg.), topaz, carbuncle (emerald marg.), emerald (carbuncle marg.), sapphire, diamond (sardonyx marg.), jacinth (amber marg.), agate, amethyst, beryl (chalcedony marg.), onyx (beryl marg.), jasper. The jewels of the breastplate were pretty big, for the breastplate itself (qv) was 9 inches across and it had only 3 jewels in each row. They were also inscribed so that they can neither have been very small nor the hardest of stones. Most of them are really semi-precious stones. The diamond was not known in these days, and they had nothing hard enough to carve it, even the corundum which AV renders ' adamant ' (*Ezek.* 3, 9; *Zech.* 7, 12). The ligure is obscure. It may be jacinth and it may be amber from Liguria. Alabaster is not always the mineral known by that name now, but seems to have described any soft stone capable of being shaped into vessels. The 3 main classes of precious stones would be silicas, the quartz family; silicates, which is the combination of silica and

metallic oxides; and the alumina and alumin-
ates.

Jewry. In OT means Judah, and in NT means
Judea.

Jezebel [jĕz'-ĕ-bĕl]. Daughter of the king of Tyre
and ex-high priestess in the temple of Baal there.
She married Ahab of Israel, and at once replaced
the worship of Jehovah by the worship of Baal.
She was a woman of great strength of bad character and completely dominated her husband,
and, after his death, her sons Ahaziah and Joram
who succeeded him, for a period of 35 yrs. Her
influence penetrated into Judah where her daughter was queen, and very much of the stamp of her
mother (*2 Kings* 8, 18). Her ruthlessness is well
illustrated in her dealings with Elijah, Naboth
and Jehu (*1 Kings* 18, 19—19, 3; 21, 1-16; *2
Kings* 9, 30-37). The name occurs in *Revelation*
(2, 20) but this is prob. an imaginary character.

Jezreel [jĕz'-rē-ĕl]. Heb. name for plain of Esdraelon (qv) (*Josh.* 17, 16). It is also a city of note on
the S of Esdraelon on the Issachar border. Israel
camped here before the disaster of Mt. Gilboa
(qv). It was Ishbosheth's capital while his kingdom lasted (*2 Sam.* 2, 9). Ahab built a palace
there (*1 Kings* 21, 1). Naboth's vineyard was
here (*1 Kings* 21). Joram visited it (*2 Kings* 8, 29).
Jezebel was killed here (*2 Kings* 9). There was
another Jezreel in Judah (*Josh.* 15, 56). It is also
a personal name (*1 Chron.* 4, 3; *Hos.* 1, 4; 2,
22 ff.).

Joab [jŏ'-ăb]. There are 3 of the name. One is a
Judahite craftsman (*1 Chron.* 4, 14). Another is a
returned exile (*Ezra* 2, 6). But the really important
one is David's nephew (*1 Chron.* 2, 16). A 1st class
soldier, he is first seen in the war with Ishbosheth
(*2 Sam.* 2, 12 ff.). In the encounter with Abner

he reveals himself as a man both courageous and ruthless (*2 Sam.* 3). Even David was more than a little afraid of him. He became commander-in-chief of David's army (*2 Sam.* 8, 16), and had many successes (10, 1-14; 11, 1). He was responsible, under David's orders, for the death of Uriah —something which prob. gave him a hold over the king (11, 6-27). During the Absalom rebellion he remained loyal to David and commanded the troops who crushed it (18, 1-2). He killed Absalom, which was what the rebel deserved, though David did not want it so (vv. 9-17). He told the king why he had done it in no uncertain terms (19, 1-8). David replaced him by Amasa, and Joab murdered his rival and took over command again (20,1-22). In David's old age Joab supported Adonijah for the succession (*1 Kings* 1, 7) but deserted him when Solomon was proclaimed king (vv. 27-49). The dying David told Solomon that he wanted Joab brought to justice for the murders of Abner and Amasa. He was killed by Benaiah as he clung to the horns of the altar (*1 Kings* 2, 5 & 6 & 28-34).

Joanna [jō-ăn'-nă]. Wife of Chuza, Herod's steward, companion of Mary Magdalene and follower of Jesus (*Luke* 8, 3; 24, 10).

Joash [jō'-ăsh]. Sometimes Jehoash. **1.** Man of Judah (*1 Chron.* 4, 22). **2.** Man of Manasseh (*Judg.* 6, 11-32). **3.** A Benjamite (*1 Chron.* 12, 3). **4.** Son of Ahab (*1 Kings* 22, 26). **5.** Son of Ahaziah of Judah. He was sole survivor of a massacre of the royal house by Athaliah, his grandmother, being hidden for 6 yrs. in the temple by his aunt Jehosheba. Jehoiada the High Priest produced him in the 7th year and placed him on the throne. Athaliah was killed (*2 Kings* 11, 13-16). This was around 836 BC and he reigned for some 40 yrs. As a minor he was under the wise tuition of Jehoiada who persuaded him to restore the old religion (2 Kings 11, 1-20; 12, 1-16). But when Jehoiada died, both king and people went back to their evil ways. Zechariah, son of Jehoiada, denounced them and Joash had him murdered (2 Chron. 24, 15-22). Nothing went right after that, however. He had to pay tribute to Syria, and he fell ill, his son Amaziah acting as regent. Finally his own servants murdered him in revenge for the death of Zechariah (2 Kings 12, 20). He did, however, preserve the line of David. **6.** Son and heir of Jehoahaz, King of Israel. He reigned 16 yrs. from c. 800 BC. Although he was not loyal absolutely to Jehovah he had great respect for Elisha, who prophesied victories for him over the Syrians (2 Kings 13, 14-25). He supplied Amaziah of Judah with an army for an expedition agst. Edom. They pillaged Judah instead. Amaziah challenged Joash to battle and Joash won (2 Chron. 25). He looted the Temple and palace and took hostages. Joash died and was succeeded by his son Jeroboam II.

Job, Book of. This is one of the great books of the OT, indeed one of the great books of all time. Its central and only theme is the problem of innocent suffering; a protest agst. the current persuasion that prosperity was a sign of God's favour for good living, and that trouble and adversity were the sign of God's judgment upon bad living. When the book was written is not known but it is prob. not an early book, but post-exilic. Nobody knows who wrote it; nobody knows who the main character was about whom stories may have gathered. He is mentioned by Ezekiel (14, 14) but that may mean something or nothing. Most of the book is a poem, beginning at v. 3 of ch. 3.

The start and the conclusion (which is quite unsatisfactory and unworthy of the rest of the book) is prose. It tells the story of a man, blameless before God and man alike, who lost everything that he had but his integrity: children, money, position, and health. Satan brings the ills on him with God's permission. God is staking His own reputation on what He knows of Job's character. God never for a moment dreams that Job will let Him down. The writer puts many words into Job's mouth, and fine words they are. But the vitally important words are the words he puts into God's mouth when He speaks to Satan and when He speaks to Job. The 3 friends of Job, his 'comforters' express the human attitude to both God and man, which means that they simply keep moving round in circles without ever getting anywhere that matters. They have a fixed argument; God is omnipotent and omniscient; He has all knowledge and all power. Suffering is God's punishment for sin somewhere. God cannot possibly deal unjustly with man. Therefore there is something wrong with Job. There is sin somewhere. Job's dilemma is: God is omnipotent and God is omniscient and God is just, but here am I, sinless so far as I understand and can see. There is either something wrong with God or there is something sadly wrong with me. Although by no means a self-righteous man, Job could not see that there was anything in his way of life which would justify such punishment. Could God be wrong, then? But how to find out, since the ways of God are unsearchable? His heart told him that God could not be unjust, but his mind was not so sure. Neither his mind nor his heart would accept the arguments of his friends. But this uneasiness of soul remained in spite of logic.

Finally he flings all his faith upon God, whatever God may be, and finds himself justified. Good people whose fate it is to suffer, always want some insight into the purpose of it. If they are really good people they are prepared to endure so long as they can see some good coming out of it to somebody or to something. It is hard to find the reason and the objective benefit in *Job*. It could not be that God wanted to know Job's reactions; God already knew Job's reactions. It could not be merely to discomfit Satan, for Satan disappears from the story. Could the purpose have been to open the only door which would bring a thoroughly good man into complete communion with God? Is it possible to reach the complete and glorious vision of God only by the path of suffering? Is this what makes a saint out of a moralist? In the end of the day, if all the misfortunes had come on Job again, he would not have asked a single question and he would not have wasted his breath arguing with his friends. This is no longer thought, but knowledge; no longer persuasion, but conviction. There is no clear indication of date and authorship, but what evidence there is seems to point to a date in or around the 4th cent. BC. Briefly the analysis of the book is: (1) Prologue in prose, discussion of Job bet. God and Satan (1, 1 to 2, 10). It includes the successive afflictions. (2) The arrival of his 'comforters' (2, 11-13). (3) The poem (3-42). Job's lamentation, his questions, the 3 rounds of argument of his 3 friends (4-14; 15-21; 22-31). (4) Arrival of Elihu, and his 4 speeches to the 3 and to Job (32-37). (5) God's conversation with Job (38-42, 6). (6) The Epilogue in prose (42, 7 to the end).

Jobab [jō′-băb]. **1.** Arabian tribe (*Gen.* 10, 29). **2.** King of Edom (*Gen.* 36, 33). **3.** King of Madon

(*Josh.* 11, 1). **4.** Two Benjamites (*1 Chron.* 8, 9 & 18).

Jochebed [jŏch′-ĕ-bĕd]. Mother of Moses, Miriam and Aaron (*Num.* 26, 59).

Joda [jō′-dă]. Ancestor of Jesus (*Luke* 3, 26). AV has Juda.

Joel [jō′-ĕl]. There are several of the name but the only one of real importance is the prophet. His name is a compound of the 2 names of God, Yah and El.

Joel, Book of. For a long time there was argument about the date of the book, some scholars assigning it to the 800's BC, and others making it postexilic. The conclusion of mod. scholarship is that the date is fairly late, in the 4th cent. BC. In these last prophets like Joel (and he is prob. the last of the canonical prophets) the true prophetic ring is missing from the voice. The post-exilic prophets are rather more priestly than prophetic in the glorious trad. Amos, Isaiah and the others of old would never, as Joel did, propose a national fast when famine came as a result of drought and a plague of locusts. They had no time for this way of propitiating God; their answer would have been to start a moral revolution. Yet the matter was in Joel. At one point he rises to true prophetic stature (2, 28 ff.) when he speaks of the day when God's spirit will be poured out on all flesh. His words were the text for the first Christian sermon (*Acts* 2, 17). The sons and the daughters will prophesy, the spirit will come even to the servants and the handmaids. This is a glimpse afar off, of the priesthood of all believers. But it was because these post-exilic prophets failed in their mission that the age of conventionalism, traditionalism and legalism came upon the land. There was not a voice left to call the people back to the essentials of the true faith. John the Baptist was still to come, and Jesus Himself; but lacking revival for so long, the people rejected them.

Johanan [jō-hā´-năn]. There are about a dozen of the name, none of any great importance. **1.** (*1 Chron.* 12, 4.) **2.** (*1 Chron.* 12, 12.) **3.** (*1 Chron.* 6, 10.) **4.** (*2 Chron.* 28, 12.) **5.** (*1 Chron.* 3, 15.) **6.** (*Jer.* 40, 8 & 9.) **7.** (*Ezra* 10, 6.) **8.** (*Neh.* 6, 18.) **2.** (*Neh.* 12, 22.)

John. The name is mainly assoc. with the apostle and with the Baptist, articles on whom appear below. Simon Peter's father was called John (*John* 1, 42) though the AV calls him Jonas. There was also a member of a high priestly family of the name (*Acts* 4, 6). For John Mark *see article on* MARK.

John (the apostle). Son of Zebedee and brother of James, his mother was Salome, a sister of Mary the mother of Jesus, which makes him Jesus' cousin. With the father they were prosperous fishermen on Galilee (*Mark* 1, 19). He was attached to John the Baptist and was prob. the man who was with Andrew when Jesus was pointed out as the Lamb of God (*John* 1, 35). Later he and his brother were called to be disciples, and must have already been thinking about Jesus for they did not hesitate (*Mark* 1, 20). He and James were nicknamed Boanerges, though one has to strain the Gospel account to find much evidence of their thunderiness. The best examples of possible quickness of temper and impetuosity are (*Mark* 3, 17; *Luke* 9, 49 ff.). Either they or their mother had some ambitions for eminence (*Mark* 10, 35 ff.). John was one of the 3 who were most intimate with Jesus, the others being James and Peter, and He sometimes asked them to be alone with Him (*Mark* 5, 37; 9, 2; 14, 33). He reclined next to Jesus at the Last Supper (*John* 13, 23). He was present at the Crucifixion and was asked by Jesus to look after Mary, which he did (*John* 18, 15; 19, 27). He outraced Peter to the sepulchre when the news was told of the empty tomb, but waited till Peter arrived before he went in (*John* 20, 1-10). After Pentecost he was involved with Peter in missionary work (*Acts* 3, 1) and with Peter was imprisoned (*Acts* 4, 1-22). John remained in Jerusalem, with one journey to Samaria (*Acts* 8, 14) and was in Jerusalem when Paul came to report on his 1st missionary journey (*Acts* 15, 6; *Gal.* 2, 9). There is a trad. that he went to Ephesus to minister there, and if he wrote the *Revelation* he was on the island of Patmos. He died at a ripe old age, the revered teacher of several of the early Fathers of the Church. Five books of the NT are ascribed to him; the Gospel, the *Revelation* and 3 letters which bear his name.

John, Epistles General of. Although attempts have been made to prove that John the disciple and apostle was not the author of the letters, there can be little doubt that he was. It is obvious that this was a man who had been with the Lord, and there is a great similarity of style language and tone bet. these and the 4th Gospel. The date is uncertain, but it must have been towards the end of John's long life, prob. about AD 90. It is believed that he wrote them from Ephesus and that they were meant to be read in local churches. Heresies were beginning in the Church even then, and there was a school of thought which argued that Jesus had never indeed been man, but had only appeared to be a man. This heresy is known as Docetism. John's 1st letter is a stern denial of this heresy. He sets forth the relationship bet. Jesus and God, and shows how it is poss. for a man to live in God and for God to live in a man. At first glance the 2nd letter appears to be personal from John to a friend, the elect lady, and to her family, and since the 3rd letter is plainly a private one, so may the 2nd letter well be. On the other hand there is considerable internal evidence that John is writing from one church to a sister church, personified as the elect lady. In this letter John calls himself ' the Elder,' and the letter is simply an old man's joy at the faithfulness of the church, and a warning to beware of false teachers. John was prob. aware of the dangers of legends and the like creeping in when he, the last of the eye-witnesses was gone. The 3rd letter is so like the 2nd in many ways that it could well have been written at the same time. It is addressed to a Christian called Gaius, who was in charge of a small congregation somewhere in Asia Minor. Gaius was a very common name. The main emphasis of the letter is to take to task one by the name of Diotrephes, who is taking more business on himself than he ought as a good presbyter.

John, Gospel According to St. Much controversy has raged round the 4th Gospel and its authorship but when all the evidence is weighed, analysed, added and subtracted, there is certainly far too little left to justify a move from the trad. belief that this is the work of John, the disciple and apostle. The reader who wishes to sift the evidence for himself will have to study the library of books that have been written on the subject, and he will have a job on his hands. He will probably finish up with the same conclusion. The internal certificate of the Johannine authorship is in the words, ' This is the disciple who witnesseth concerning these things, and he who wrote these things, and we know that his witness is true' (21, 24). This verse, and indeed the whole of this ch. is an addendum to the Gospel, which may or may not have been written by the author, but this particular verse was certainly not written by the author. It is another man's certification that the author of the Gospel knew what he was writing about, and was an eye-witness of the events which he records. This was the beloved disciple, John. The opening of the Gospel, too, leaves little doubt about the fact that the writer had seen and heard what he was writing about, and the insistence upon the ' Word made flesh ' is surely well in line with the spirit and purpose of the 1st of the letters which is so adamant agst. the Docetist heresy that Jesus was not actual man. The final court of appeal agst. such heresy must be the man who knew Jesus personally and who had lived in His company. Anyone who has read the 4 Gospels will have been struck by the fact that this 4th one is certainly ' odd man out.' Its action is confined almost entirely to Jerusalem, and much that is contained in the other 3 is left out. The 4th Gospel very nearly starts off where the others finish with recognition of Jesus as Messiah in the very first chapter (v. 41). There is no building up of experience and observation culminating in this conclusion; the thing is stated at the start. Another major difference is the emphasis on the things that Jesus said, instead of on the things that Jesus did. There are no parables in the Gospel, but there are long and carefully reported sermons and discourses. Obviously the author had decided that there was no need for another account of the things that Jesus did, and of the stories which Jesus told. What was needed was a work of clarification, explanation and purpose.

He assumes that people know what Jesus did,
and that they know there was a Jesus, but he
must convince them that Jesus was indeed the
Son of God, because only when they believe that
and act accordingly can they be sure of eternal
life. Aware of the heresy that Jesus was not indeed
man at all, he insists upon the Incarnation; this
Jesus was a man who lived and laughed and wept
and suffered, felt hunger and cold and the body's
weariness. When the Roms. stab Him He bleeds.
This is a Gospel for the logical, clear thinking,
inquiring Gk. mind in the Rom. world. He lifts
the events out of their Palestinian setting, showing
how the Jews were conspiring agst. Jesus from
the beginning and insisting that this is not a thing
for Jews first and for others afterwards, but that
Jesus' mission was to the world. Nevertheless
Jesus had done everything which the Messiah of
the Jews had been supposed to do, and if the Jews
had been unable to appreciate that, it was their
own fault. The whole purpose is in fact summed
up in the words of the Gospel itself, ' These things
are written that ye may believe that Jesus is the
Christ, the Son of God; and that, believing, ye
may have life in His name ' (20, 31).

John the Baptist. He was born when his parents
were old (*Luke* 1, 7) and his mother was kin to
Mary the mother of Jesus (*Luke* 1, 36). Both his
father Zacharias and his mother Elizabeth were
of priestly descent. Even before his birth he was
dedicated as a Nazirite (qv) (*Luke* 1, 15). He was
not, however, an Essene (qv) because he did eat
meat of sorts (*Matt.* 3, 4). He was a man of the
desert; a man in the pattern of Elijah. In the
desert the truth of God came to him, and out of
the desert he marched, the last of the prophets,
but looking like, and speaking like, the first of

them. His impact upon a people who knew of
the prophets only by legend, was tremendous.
For 6 months he blazed like a comet across the
darkness of the land, and the people flocked to
hear the truth they had never heard before; the
truth about God, which they did not know; and
the truth about themselves, which they knew even
less. His message was ' Repent, the kingdom of
God is at hand ' (*Matt.* 3, 2). Claim to descent
from Abraham would not win them into the
kingdom, nor would any amount of formal lip
service to the law. Judgment was upon them, and
there was little time left (*Luke* 3, 9). He baptised
them, but his baptism was simply the sign of
repentance, the symbol of sin washed away (*Mark*
1, 4). The ceremony of baptism was known to
the Jews and is not to be confused with formal
ritualistic washings. Gentiles converted to Judaism had to experience a form of baptism. What
John was saying to them was that they as Jews
were as much outside the kingdom as the Gentiles,
and that they would have to come into the kingdom in the same way as Gentiles came into the
Jewish faith. When Jesus came to John in Jordan, at first John would not baptise Him. The
thing was to him plainly unnecessary, for here
was one with nothing to repent of (*Matt.* 3, 13;
etc.). This recognition by John was important
to Jesus, as it confirmed His own conviction about
Himself. The true greatness of John is that, just
at the moment when he had the people eating
out of his hand, and ready to acknowledge him
as the Messiah Himself, he withdrew in humility
and pointed to his own cousin, Jesus, as the
Lamb of God (*John* 1, 29). So near did he come
to the role of Messiah that there were those who
thought that Jesus was John risen from the dead

(*Mark* 6, 14). The story of his death is well known (*Mark* 6, 14 ff.). And it is plain that not only did Herod fear him, but so did Jewry of the law and the church. They were glad to be rid of him.

John the Divine, Revelation of St. This is another book about which there has been long and often bitter scholarly controversy, and it can be understood only when it is firmly placed in the time and situation which inspired it, and when it is seen that the book was for a specific purpose. This is not, in fact, a prophecy of the end of the world. It is an assurance of the end of an age in which Christians were suffering sorely. It is the affirmation that this state of things will not go on forever. In this affirmation the book is not unique: there is a great mass of literature of this sort which is called ' Apocalyptic,' and only a very little of that literature was included in the canon of the Bible. The other great canonical apocalyptic book is *Daniel.* But where *Revelation* differs widely from *Daniel* is in this: the OT book looked back over the events of known hist. and wrote the account of these events as if they still had to happen. *Revelation* does not do that. Although there is much mention of Babylon, the people who first read this book knew perfectly well that the Power referred to was Imperial Rome in the time of Nero when the early Church was being thoroughly, systematically, and brutally murdered out of existence. The religion of Rome was emperor worship, and this, of course, the Christians of the empire would not concede. The attempt was made to wipe them off the face of the earth just as Hitler fairly recently tried to wipe the Jewish race off the face of the earth, and by very much the same methods and for more or less the same reasons. Even when this is appreciated there still remain many difficulties and incongruities within the book itself, and there are some passages which would appear to have more a pagan than a Christian origin (ch. 12). There is so much figurative language, too, much of which is obscure in its meaning, that a great deal of confusion is caused. As far as the authorship is concerned, trad. and a good deal of evidence point to John the Apostle. Other evidence would seem to make it a composite work in which John may have been concerned; but there is also much that can be argued in favour of another author altogether whose name may or may not have been John— by no means an uncommon name. If the date is in the time of Nero the author could have been John. If it is of the time of Domitian, which is quite possible, the author could not have been John. The important thing is to remember that this is not a kind of mystical and magical work from which the date of the end of the world can be calculated. It is a work of its day and age, to deal with a situation in which people were living. It includes the letters to the 7 churches, and these could well be apostolic, and by the hand of John. Persecution at that time was at its height and there was a real danger of the Church being extinguished altogether. The gravest danger was the imperial order that the only object of worship was to be the emperor. The author is writing about the contemporary situation, and the situation which he believed would very soon develop. This is not Babylon, but Rome, and God will destroy Rome for more or less the same reasons that God destroyed Babylon. There is some confusion in the refs. to those who have lost their lives at the hands of 'the Beast.' If this is a

Jewish section, these are the Jews massacred at the sack of Jerusalem in AD 70. If it is a Christian section, it refers to the thousands martyred by Nero. The book itself divides into 7 visions. (1) Christ glorified in His Church. There follow 7 exhortations to the 7 Churches of Asia (1. 9—3, 22). (2) God the omnipotent and the Lamb with the Book of Life. There are the 7 seals, and the 7 acts of God (chs. 4-7). (3) The angels and the trumpets—7 of them, and the warnings of desolation to the enemies of the Church (chs. 8-11). (4) The war of Christ and the Church agst. the 7 beasts (chs. 12-14). (5) The 7 vials of wrath, God's judgment on the world, and the triumph of the saints (chs. 15-16). (6) The fall of Babylon, the harlot city: a drama in 7 scenes (18, 1—20, 15). (7) The new Church, and the new Jerusalem (chs. 21 & 22). As with all apocalyptic literature, attempts have been made to find some cryptographic clue somewhere which will determine the date of end of the present age and the second coming of the Lord. This is a misuse of Scripture and a completely wrong idea of the meaning of inspiration. The number of the beast, 666 (13, 18) has been assoc. with all sorts of people including Nero, Napoleon, Mussolini and Hitler, with more or less success. But it is possible to prove a great deal from Scripture if one starts with a fixed idea and ignores everything which contradicts it.

Jonah (Jonas, Jona). Father of Simon Peter, prob. simply John (*Matt.* 16, 17). The notable Jonah is the prophet of Israel, son of Amittai. Before the accession of Jeroboam II he foretold the recovery of Israel's ancient borders (*2 Kings* 14, 25). This would be bet. 823-782 BC, the time of Amos and Hosea.

Jonah, Book of. Among the Minor Prophets the

Book stands 5th. Most of the prophetical Books are autobiographical, but Jonah is biographical: not told in the first person singular by Jonah. It is about Jonah. Jesus knew this book and understood its purpose, which was a very good one indeed (*Matt.* 12, 39-41; etc.). That purpose was to correct the insularity and prideful nationalism of the Jews, and to claim God's interest in and dominion over the Gentile world. Jonah is unfortunately best known for his connection (temporarily) with a whale, or 'great fish,' but this is merely incidental. Jonah, all agst. his will as a Jew, is the first foreign missionary. There are only 48 verses in it, fewer than 1400 words—a very short short-story; yet it tells all that need be told and does it beautifully and perfectly. Jonah is called to a task, he runs away from it and is brought back. He speaks the word to Nineveh and the people are spared. Jonah is annoyed and God teaches him a lesson in mercy. If this book had had the effect that it should have had upon a stiff-necked race, they might have listened to Jesus with a better heart.

Jonas [jō′-năs]. *See* JONAH.

Jonathan. Son of Saul and friend of David. A brave and able soldier (*1 Sam.* chs. 13 & 14) he would prob. have made an excellent king, but the selection of David to succeed Saul made no difference to his friendship. The people loved him (*1 Sam.* 14, 44 & 45). His father trusted him in everything and constantly sought his advice (*1 Sam.* 20, 2). He met his death in battle with his wounds in front (*2 Sam.* 1). There are over a dozen others of the name, few of whom did anything notable.

Jonath Elem Rehokim. Tune title of *Ps.* 56.

Joppa. Once Japho in AV (*Josh.* 19, 46). A very

ancient seaport town of Canaan assigned to Dan
after the conquest (*Josh.* 19, 46). It was the port
of Jerusalem though over 30 m. distant. For the
building and the rebuilding of the temple, rafts
of timber were towed from Tyre to Joppa (*2
Chron.* 2, 16; *Ezra* 3, 7 RV). Peter performed a
miracle here on Tabitha (*Acts* 9, 36). And here
he lodged with Simon the tanner (*Acts* chs. 9 &
10). Jaffa is the mod. port.

Joram [jō′-răm]. *See* JEHORAM.

Jordan. The river has its source in several springs
in the N and E of the country, these streams
joining nr. Lake Huleh and flowing into it. From
the S of the Lake, which is about 4 m. long, the
Jordan proper emerges and flows some 10½ m.
to the sea of Galilee, which itself is 12½ m. long.
From Galilee to the Dead Sea, the length of the
river as the crow flies is 65 m. The total length,
including the lakes, is 104 m. Through almost
all its course the Jordan flows below ocean level.
The highest spring is at Banias, 1000 ft. above
Mediterranean level. Lake Huleh is only 7 ft.
above sea level, and Galilee is 682 ft. below, with
the Dead Sea almost twice as much below. The
name means, ' the descender.' Bet. Galilee and
the Dead Sea, which is the stretch most referred
to in the Bible, it flows through fairly open country
of sub-tropical vegetation as far as the confluence
of the Jabbok, which was the most southerly
ford (*Gen.* 32, 10). S of that point the river flows
through a gorge and there are numerous rapids
and a swift current. The stopping of the flow of
the river which enabled Israel to cross dry shod
at a fordless point is not quite a phenomenon.
Landslides caused by erosion or by earthquake
action have made this possible on several occasions. In 1927 one rock-fall stopped the flow of

the river for almost 24 hours. There is record of
the same thing happening as long ago as AD 1267.
The collapse of the walls of Jericho may be explained by earthquake too. In March and April
the Jordan overflows its banks due to the melting
of the snows on Hermon (*Josh.* 3, 15).

Joseph. There are over a dozen men of the name
in scripture. One of the best known is the 11th
son of Jacob (*Gen.* 30, 22-24). He was rather
spoiled, being the son of his father's old age and
the first-born of his beloved Rachel. The celebrated coat of many colours to which the brothers
took exception, was really a long-sleeved garment
worn by people who were not in the habit of
working manually (*Gen.* 37, 3). Joseph seems to
have had a pretty good idea of his own importance
when he admits to day-dreaming while his brothers are toiling, and then explains the dreams
as a sign that this state of affairs is ordained and
will continue. His brothers decide to murder
him and blame it on wild animals, but persuaded
by Reuben they sell him instead to Ishmaelite
slavers (*Gen.* 37, 1-35). In Egypt he was sold to
Potiphar, the captain of Pharaoh's guard, and
ultimately became his majordomo. Potiphar's
wife made advances to the good-looking young
Heb. and when he resisted these she demonstrated
the fury of a woman scorned. She told Potiphar
that Joseph had tried to assault her and Joseph
found himself in jail. But he was always a
managing kind of chap, and the head warder put
him in charge of the other prisoners. He was
able to cheer up Pharaoh's butler by giving him
an optimistic interpretation of a dream, and when
the butler was restored to favour and discovered
that Pharaoh was being troubled by dreams, he
remembered Joseph, still languishing in jail.

Hurriedly Joseph was sent for and took full advantage of his chance by telling Pharaoh that the dreams meant 7 years of good harvest, followed by famine. He offered to manage this piece of national economy for the Egyptians, and was given his chance, which again he took (*Gen.* ch. 41). Egypt's agricultural prosperity depended, of course on the annual Nile flooding, and there were years when it failed. Joseph married an Egyptian and had two sons, Manasseh and Ephraim. The famine affected more lands than Egypt, and soon hungry people were buying and begging corn from Joseph's carefully planned granaries. His brothers came to buy corn and Joseph recognised them, getting his own back on them very neatly by accusing young Benjamin of theft, and putting them all in a state of fear and alarm. He also drew their attention to the accuracy of his boyhood dream while they were down on their knees in front of him. But afterwards he let them see that there were no hard feelings (and why should there be with the position he was now in?) He invited the whole of his father's clan to settle in Egypt, which they did. Although there must be a certain amount of romancing in the story of Joseph it is basically true. Israel did settle in Egypt and found favour, and it was necessary for them to come within the influence of this great civilisation, for they could not fulfil the purpose of God while they were a nomadic people, here to-day and gone to-morrow. This is where the Arabs and the Jews parted company, and the Arabs are still a backward people. The Heb. came to Egypt during the Hyksos dynasty, and it was when that dynasty was overthrown that there came a king who did not remember Joseph and the service he had rendered Egypt, and who did not care. That was when the enslavement of the Israelites began (*Ex.* 1, 8). Joseph had asked that his remains should be taken back to the old land, and when Israel marched they remembered this; his sarcophagus (he would be mummified in the Egyptian manner) was buried nr. Shechem (*Ex.* 13, 19; *Josh.* 24, 32). His name is used poetically for the tribes desc. from his 2 sons (*Ps.* 80, 1).

The husband of Mary was Joseph, too, of course, and of a most honourable line. *See* MARY. Not much is known about him, and in the Gospels he is usually found along with Mary. But reading bet. the lines, something of his influence can surely be seen in the kind of man that Jesus became. The mother's influence is of great importance early in the life of a boy, but Jesus was about 30 when His ministry began, and was working side by side with Joseph at the bench and in the woods for a good many years. It was Joseph who taught Him how important it was that a yoke should sit easily, and who pointed the moral of the laird who ordered new barns one day. and needed a coffin the next day. From Joseph would come much of the lore of the countryside that was so much part of Jesus and even maybe the honest philosophy and the kindly and charitable outlook that grew upon Him. After all when Jesus was looking for the perfect word to describe God, he chose the word ' Father.' Some think that Joseph was still alive when Jesus began His ministry (*Matt.* 13, 55) but this is on slender evidence; a man's father may be remembered when he is dead. He must have been dead by the Crucifixion when Jesus committed Mary to the care of John (*John* 19, 26). It seems reasonable to assume that had Jesus not had home

responsibilities He might well have begun His
ministry earlier. A man of 30 in the ME is no
longer a young man. The signs are that Joseph
had died some time before Jesus left home. The
3rd Joseph of importance is Joseph of Arimathea. He was a member of the Sanhedrin,
and a seeker (*Mark* 15, 43). With Nicodemus
he was one of the 2 members of the court who would
not consent to the death of Jesus. What changed
him from a secret to an open and avowed follower
of Jesus was the Crucifixion (*Matt.* 27, 57 ff.).

Joses [jō′-sēs]. Prop. Joseph, a brother of Jesus
(*Matt.* 13, 55). Personal name of Barnabas (*Acts*
4, 36).

Joshebbasshebeth [jŏsh′-ĕb-băs-shē′-bĕth]. (2 *Sam.*
23, 8 RV.) This is corrupt text, owing to an error
of a copyist. A proper name, ' Jashobeam the
Baalite,' has become in AV, ' he that sat in the
seat.'

Joshua [jŏsh′-ū-ă]. There are several of the name,
but the only one of importance is the efficient
soldier who succeeded Moses in command of
Israel. The name appears in several forms.
Jeshua, Jehoshua, Jehoshuah. The Gk. form of
the name is Jesus. Joshua was son of Nun, an
Ephraimite (*Num.* 13, 8). The 1st victory of
Israel under his command was at Rephidim (*Ex.*
17, 8-16). He was one of the 12 sent out to report
on Canaan, and he and Caleb, his old fellow
warrior, were the only 2 who advised invasion (*Josh.*
14, 7; *Num.* 14, 6-10). Their lives were threatened for their temerity (*Num.* 14, 10). Not long
before his death Moses officially ordained Joshua
as his successor (*Num.* 27, 18; *Deut.* 31, 14).
The nation-maker's day was over; the day of the
soldier had come. As soon as Moses had died
Joshua gave Israel 3 days to get ready for invasion.

He sent out spies, and moved camp to the banks of Jordan. In one assault after another he reduced the fortified towns on the opposite banks, securing his headquarters and lines of communication. When his main body came over, the conquest was assured, though a foolish treaty with Gibeon, and neglect to occupy Jebus (later Jerusalem) caused trouble later (*Josh.* chs. 1-3). He then set about apportioning the area so far conquered (*Josh.* chs. 14-17). He asked little for himself, like Caleb (*Josh.* 19, 50). Not long before his death he called the people to Shechem and made a strong appeal to them to remain loyal to God and to themselves (*Josh.* 24, 1-28). He died at a ripe old age (*Josh.* 24, 29 & 30).

Joshua, Book of. This is the book of Joshua's deeds, not the book by his hand. It begins where *Deuteronomy* ends, and sees Joshua finishing what Moses began and inspired. Moses' death without setting foot on the ground of the Promised Land seems tragic, but the fact of the matter was that Moses' work was now done, and if the assault and invasion were to be successful there could not be a divided command. To go when the job is done is all that matters. Moses was the man for the Exodus, but Joshua was the man to cross the river. The content of the book is very much the story of Joshua himself, told above.

Josiah [jō-sī'-ah]. The important man of this name (there was only one other, *Zech.* 6, 10) is the king of Judah who succeeded his father Amon c. 638 BC, when he was only 8 yrs. old (*2 Kings* 22, 1). When he was 18 he ordered repairs to be made to the Temple which was in a dreadful condition owing to years of neglect. In the course of the repairs a Book of Instruction was found by Hilkiah the High Priest, who passed it on to

Shaphan the king's secretary who read it to
Josiah. It repeated laws, rules, regulations, and
told of a way of life which Josiah had never heard
of: the old ways. He vowed reformation of
himself and of the nation and prosecuted it with
vigour. The book was the canonical Book of
Deuteronomy (qv), and prob. parts of the Pentateuch which had been lost or destroyed apart
from this copy in the reign of Manasseh (*2 Kings*
21, 16). All the paraphernalia of Baal worshp
was destroyed. *See* ASHERAH. The place of
human sacrifice was defiled. *See* HINNOM VALLEY
and MOLECH. Josiah then called the people
to celebrate the Passover (*2 Kings* 23, 1-24).
Some 13 yrs. of uneasy peace passed in the land,
then Josiah found himself caught bet. the Egyptian armies and Assyria which they were marching
to invade. He regarded himself more or less as
a vassal of Assyria, and gave battle at Megiddo
where he was mortally wounded. He died in
Jerusalem, mourned by all, including Jeremiah.
Although only 39 when he died he had ruled
wisely and well, and his death was the beginning
of the end for the nation.

Jot and Tittle. (*Matt.* 5, 18.) *Yod* is the smallest
letter in the Heb. alphabet, as *iota* is the smallest
in the Gk. Tyndale transliterated these as ' iott.'
The tittle is a small mark distinguishing letters
that might easily be confused, like the dot over
an ' i ' or the stroke of a ' t '. Jesus' meaning
is clear enough.

Jotham [jō'-thăm]. **1.** Youngest son of Jerubbaal
who managed to escape the massacre by Abimelech of the royal house (*Judg.* 9, 5). He warned
the people in a parable (from a safe place) of
what would happen and it did (*Judg.* 9, 8-20).
2. There is another Jotham who was king of

Judah in the time of Isaiah (*2 Kings* 15, 7). His
father was Uzziah and he reigned a while as
regent. He tried to be with the sheep of Jehovah
worship and the goats of Baal. Isaiah and Hosea
were the prophets of his reign and they had a
good deal to prophesy about (*Isa.* 1, 1; *Hos.* 1,
1). There is another obscure man of the name
(*1 Chron.* 2, 47).

Joy. In Scripture it really means complete happiness as a result of the absolute co-ordination of
feelings, emotions and spiritual perceptions.
Other words for the sense are rejoicing, mirth,
gladness, blessedness. It is a state of being which
transcends all others, and which might best be
expressed as bliss.

Jubal [jū′-băl]. Son of Lamech and Adah (*Gen.*
4, 21). He was the father of music. After all,
there had to be somebody.

Jubilee. This is 7 times 7, and 7 is the great number
(*Lev.* 25, 8). The name derives from the word
for a trumpet, and it was by a trumpet that the
year was heralded. Every 7th year was a Sabbatical year (qv) and the 7 times 7 was extra special.
Jews who had sold themselves into bondage with
fellow Jews were automatically released. Ground
that had been mortgaged was returned. Land
that had been overworked was rested. The law
did not refer to real estate, which, of course, was
not in existence at the invasion of Canaan (*Lev.*
25, 8-55; 27, 17; *Num.* 36, 4). It seems to have
been honoured more in the breach than in the
observance.

Juda [jū′-dă]. *See* JUDAH, JUDAS, JODA.

Judaea (Judea) [jūd-ē′-ă]. Sometimes Jewry. The
first ref. is to a province of Persia (*Ezra* 5, 8). It
became a Rom. province governed from Caesarea,
and was part of Syria, whose proconsul lived in

Antioch (*Luke* 3, 1). It is not to be confused with the ancient kingdom of Judah.

Judah [jū′-däh]. This is the name of a person, a people and the land they lived in. The orig. Judah was the 4th son of Jacob and Leah, who married a Canaanite (*Gen.* 35, 23; 38, 1-10). He had another marriage by which he became an ancestor of David (*Gen.* 38, 11-30; *Ruth* 4, 18-22). He preserved Joseph's life (*Gen.* 37, 26 f.). He received the birthright (qv) from Jacob (*Gen.* 49, 3-10). From him sprang the tribe of Judah, which developed from his 3 sons and 2 grandsons (*Num.* 26, 19 ff.). Prob. the greatest of the princes of Judah was Caleb (*Num.* 13, 6; 34, 19). Achan was one of their worse members (*Josh.* 7, 1 & 17 & 18). They were allocated the major part of S Palestine, and tended later to separate themselves from the other tribes. David was a man of Judah, and though the clan had supported Saul, they were all in favour of their own kith and kin being the next king. But their allegiance to David was the thin edge of the wedge which eventually split the kingdom in two. The 10 tribes went their own way when David's son, Solomon, died and Judah, with Levi, became a separate nation which endured from c. 935 BC till 586 BC, being ruled by 19 kings, all of David's line. This division is a perfect example of the process which can be traced through all the OT of selection and rejection. Israel, the N kingdom was rejected. Judah, the S kingdom was chosen, so long as they carried out the purpose of God. The 10 tribes of the N disappeared, being taken into captivity. Judah, too, was taken captive, but survived, through the work of the faithful. The Israelites became the Jews—of Judah—and from them came Jesus. They were part of the purpose of God, and when they were no longer useful to that purpose, they were scattered abroad. There are several other individuals who possessed the name, but they are of little importance (*Ezra* 3, 9; 10, 23; *Neh.* 11, 9; 12, 8 & 34).

Judas. Gk. form of the Heb. Judah (*Matt.* 1, 2) or of Juda (*Luke* 3, 30). Two of the disciples carried the name, though the Gospels are careful to distinguish bet. them (*John* 14, 22). The ' good ' one was related to James (*Luke* 6, 16; *Acts* 1, 13) and was known also as Thaddaeus. One of Jesus' brothers was called Judas (*Matt.* 13, 55). Paul lodged with a man of the name in Damascus (*Acts* 9, 11). Another was a man of note in the church at Jerusalem (*Acts* 15, 22). But the most famous, or infamous, is Judas Iscariot, round whom a world of controversy has grown. It is prob. that he was not a Galilean like the others, but came from Kerioth. Commentators have fallen over backwards to prove that he followed Jesus only for what he could get out of it, quoting the fact that he was treasurer of the band—as if they ever had anything to treasure. Yet it could be that when Jesus said in the Upper Room, ' One of you shall betray me '; Judas was the only one who felt that it was not himself. All the others replied, ' Is it I ? ' The betrayal appears to be so completely pointless. Surely they knew already where to take Jesus if they wanted to take him quietly. Could it be that Judas, always feeling himself to be odd man out in the 12, never being taken into the inner circle of things, and seeing the 11 simply accepting all that Jesus was saying about His purpose in Jerusalem, because they simply did not have a clue, decided to force the issue ? Then when the legions of heaven came to the defence of the Lord of heaven, he would stand

back and say, ' Right, friends, you were supposed
to be the ones who knew all the answers; what
do you think about it now? ' Why else should he
commit suicide, than for the sudden realisation
of how wrong he had been? The man who should
have committed suicide was surely Peter, who in
the very presence of Jesus swore that he had never
known Him. This may well be all wrong, but
Judas is not one to be condemned out of hand
and automatically. In the mercy of God it is
surely right to ask why he did it.

Jude, General Epistle of. There is no good reason
for doubting that this Jude is Judas, brother of
James, and therefore brother of Jesus. Attempts
have been made to disprove this by placing the
date of the letter in the 2nd cent. AD and suggesting that the very close resemblance bet. this
letter and the 2nd letter of *Peter* means that *Jude*
is simply a late copy of *2 Peter*, with Jude's name
used to give it authority. That seems rather unlikely: the author would have chosen a more
authoritative name than Jude's. It seems as if
he had intended to write something of greater
length and importance than this short letter (v. 3).
The resemblance bet. this letter and *2 Peter*
cannot be ignored. Compare *Jude* (v. 6 ff.) with
2 Peter (2, 4-18). There can be no doubt of the
connection. Many scholars are agreed, however,
that *2 Peter* is the copy of *Jude*, not *Jude of 2
Peter*. The circumstances which made the letter
necessary were an outbreak of heresy of a particularly dangerous and immoral type. Some who
place the letter in the 2nd cent. claim that only
the Gnosticism which broke out then could fit
the description of the heresy. But it is quite likely
that Jude, like the authors of Pastoral Epistles
and the Apocalypse was attacking the beginnings

of the heresy which eventually became Gnosticism.
He does not mince his words as he condemns the
false teachers. At the end of the letter is the well-
known ascription and doxology (*Jude* vv. 24 & 25).

Judge. The orig. judge, was, of course, Moses the
lawgiver. Before his day it was the head of the
family or clan who reached all decisions. As
time went on Moses accepted advice to share
some of his judicial responsibilities (*Ex.* 18, 13-26).
There is in the verb, ' to judge ' an accent of the
oracle. Judgment was not merely a question of
weighing evidence in the mind. There was also
the idea of interpretation of the divine will. David
appointed 6,000 Levites as judges (*1 Chron.* 23, 4),
though the king remained the supreme judge of
civil matters, and there was always a right of appeal
to him. Moses had left instructions that judges
were to be appointed in all towns and communities, with the official priests as the court of appeal
(*Deut.* 16, 18-20; 17, 2-13). The name was given
also to men of worth and inspiration who acted
boldly in some national emergency, and so earned
distinction and reverence for themselves. This
was in the days before the monarchy, when there
was no commander-in-chief and no standing
army. It was the continuing need for men of this
sort which made the people appeal to Samuel to
give them a permanent judge; in other words, a
king. And Saul was chosen because he had the
qualities which the trad. position of judge demanded. Not including Ahimelech, who was a
king of sorts (*Judg.* 9), there were 12 judges in all,
each one distinguished for a dangerous and vital
service rendered to the nation: Othniel, Ehud,
Shamgar, Deborah with Barak, Gideon, Tola
with Jair, Jephthah, Ibzan, Elon, Abdon and
Samson. Eli and Samuel were known as judges

though not of the military class. This has been
called Israel's Iron Age, and it certainly was an
age of blood, toil, sweat and tears, with the most
fiendish cruelty used by both sides in war. But
it was on the anvil of that iron age that the scattered, separated, and often hostile tribes were
hammered into a nation.

Judges, Book of. The hist. of the men named above
and the things that they did, covering the period
bet. the death of Joshua and the appointment of
Saul as king—something around 300 yrs. bet.
1400 and 1100 BC. These Judges did not follow
upon one another. Sometimes there was a considerable time bet. one and another; sometimes
2 of them were operating in different parts at the
same time. It is the story of the settlement of a
land still unsubdued and surrounded by bitter and
implacable foes whose force had to be met by
force. There is a tailpiece which tells of the
apostasy of the tribe of Benjamin and the inter-
tribal war which followed (chs. 19-21).

Judgment Hall. *See* PRAETORIUM.

Judgment Seat. Prop. a tribunal.

Julius [jū´-lĭ-ŭs]. The well-disposed centurion in
whose charge Paul was placed during the journey
as a prisoner to Rome (*Acts* 27).

Juniper. Not the coniferous tree of N clime, but
an almost leafless broom (qv).

Jupiter. Zeus was the chief of the Gk. gods and
Jupiter is his Rom. counterpart. He was worshipped all over the Rom. empire (*Acts* 14, 12).

Justice. In patriarchal times justice was administered by the head of the family, the chief of the
clan, and there was no appeal agst. it, even if
the sentence were death (*Gen.* 38, 24). If injustice
or harm were done by an outsider, the whole clan
took it upon themselves to avenge. As the clans

increased in size it became necessary to have elders who would judge bet. one and another (*Ex.* 18, 13-27; *Deut.* 21, 18-21). See JUDGES. Under the monarchy, civil judges were appointed but the king was the final court of appeal to whom all had access in civil cases (*1 Sam.* 8, 20; *2 Sam.* chs. 14 & 15; *2 Kings* 15, 5). Under the system there was frequently bribery, interest and miscarriage of justice (*Isa.* 1, 23; 5, 7 & 20 & 23; *Micah* 3, 11; 7, 3). The priests were greatly involved in dispensing justice (*Deut.* 19. 15-21). The usual ' court ' was the open space nr. the town gate. After the Exile the elders still presided over a kind of bench of magistrates, 7 in smaller communities, and up to 23 in larger towns. The superior court, to which appeals could be taken was the Sanhedrin at Jerusalem (qv). The testimony of 2 witnesses was needed to substantiate an accusation, and the witnesses had to be male, of age, and free. Under the Rom. regime the minor courts and the major courts remained, but they were not allowed to pronounce the death penalty. A Rom. citizen even if he were a Jew, as Paul was, had to be tried before a Rom. magistrate, who fixed the time of hearing and put the accused in prison till that time, however long delayed, arrived. This could be open arrest with the magistrate standing surety. In any Rom. province the governor was the final court of appeal from the magistrates' courts. But if the accused were a Rom. citizen he could appeal from the governor to the emperor. The whole process can be followed in the account of the trials of Paul (*Acts* chs. 26 & 27).

Justus [jŭs′-tŭs]. This is the surname of: **1.** Joseph Barsabbas who was not elected as the 12th apostle (*Acts* 1, 23). **2.** Titus or Titius who entertained

Paul at Corinth (*Acts* 18, 7). 3. A Jew called Jesus or Joshua who was imprisoned with Paul in Rome (*Col.* 4, 11).

K

Kab [kă-b]. Dry and liquid measure. *See* WEIGHTS AND MEASURES.

Kadesh [kā́-dĕsh]. Includes Kadesh Barnea. Town, place, and spring on the S frontier of Judah (*Num.* 20, 16; *Ps.* 29, 8; etc.). Orig. called the Fountain of Judgment (*Gen.* 14, 7). Hagar's well was nr. the place or in it, and since this was on the road to Egypt, Kadesh must have been nr. the highway (*Gen.* 16, 7-14). Abraham lived there for a time (*Gen.* 20, 1). In the 2nd year after the Exodus, Israel arrived and camped in the place (*Num.* 13, 26). From there they sent the spies into Canaan (*Gen.* 13, 26). Their subsequent reluctance to advance condemned them to years of wandering. Towards the end of the 40 yrs. they came back to Kadesh (*Num.* 33, 36). Miriam was buried there, and at Kadesh Moses smote the rock for water (*Num.* 20).

Kain [as cane]. City of Judah where the tomb of Cain was supposed to be. *See* KENITE.

Kaph [as calf]. *See* CAPH.

Kedar [kḗ-dār]. Desert tribe of nomads prob. desc. from Ishmael (*Gen.* 25, 13).

Kedemah [kĕd́-ē-mäh]. Another tribe desc. from Ishmael (*Gen.* 25,15).

Kedesh [kḗ-dĕsh]. City of S Judah (*Josh.* 15, 23). Also a Canaanite town taken by Joshua (*Josh.* 12, 22; 19, 37). Barak lived there (*Judg.* 4, 6). Called Kedesh Naphtali. A 3rd town of the name was in Issachar (*I Chron.* 6, 72).

Keilah [kē-ī́-läh]. Town of the Judean lowland

(*Josh.* 15, 44). David fought the Philistines there (*1 Sam.* 23, 1-13).

Kenan [kē'-năn]. Son of Enoch; father of Mahalalel (*Gen.* 5, 9 & 12).

Kenath [kē'-năth]. City E of Jordan taken by Nobah (*Num.* 32, 42).

Kenite [kē'-nīte]. Branch of the Amalekites—a nomadic tribe, but latterly pretty well absorbed by Judah. Moses' father-in-law, Hobab, was a Kenite (*Judg.* 1, 16). Saul invited the Kenites to separate themselves from their kinsmen when he attacked the Amalekites (*1 Sam.* 15, 6). They seem to have done so, for in David's time there was a colony of the tribe in Judah (*1 Sam.* 27, 10). Cf. the place names ' Kinah ' and ' Kain ' (*Josh.* 15, 22 & 57). The Rechabites were orig. Kenites (*Jer.* 35; *1 Chron.* 2, 55). See KENIZZITE.

Kenizzite [kē'-nĭz-zīte]. Clan desc. from Kenaz; 2 of his brood being Caleb and Othniel (*Josh.* 15, 17; *Judg.* 1, 13). They were among the orig. inhabitants of Canaan (*Gen.* 15, 19-21).

Kerchiefs. (*Ezek.* 13, 18 & 21.) A covering for the head. *See* DRESS.

Kere [kē'-rē]. A variant reading on the marg. of Heb. MSS, which the Massorete revisers reckoned to be an additional word. *See* KETHIB.

Kerioth (Kirioth) [kē'-rĭ-ōth]. Town in S of Judah. Kerioth-Hezron (*Josh.* 15, 25). Same as Hazor (qv). Also town of Moab.

Kesitah [kĕs'-ĭ-tăh]. Heb. word rendered ' piece of money ' (*Gen.* 33, 19; *Josh.* 24, 32; *Job* 42, 11 RV, RSV). AV marg. has ' lambs ' but there seems to be no justification for this. The value of the Kesitah is unknown.

Kethib [kĕ'-thĭb]. *See* KERE. The *Kethib* is the word in the Heb. MSS for which the *Kere* should be substituted.

Keturah [kĕ-tū′-răh]. After the death of Sarah, this was Abraham's wife or concubine (*Gen.* 25, 1-4; *1 Chron.* 1, 32).

Key. Not a key in the mod. sense, for it did not turn to open the lock. *See* HOUSE. It was a sign of authority (*Matt.* 16, 19; *Rev.* 1, 18). It is also used figuratively for one who has access by a given means (*Luke* 11, 52).

Kid. Young goat appreciated as food, usually boiled or stewed, but not in its mother's milk (*Ex.* 23, 19; *Judg.* 6, 19; *Luke* 15, 29). *See* GOAT. The word ' kid ' appearing in *Lev.*, *Num.*, *Ezek.* and *Gen.* 37, 31, (AV) should be rendered simply ' goat ' prefixed by ' he,' or ' she ' as the case may be.

Kidnapping. *See* CRIME AND PUNISHMENT.

Kidneys. In the physical sense the word has the same anatomical meaning as now. The portion of a sacrificial animal containing the kidneys was the best portion (*Ex.* 29, 13; etc.). ' Choice meat ' (*Deut.* 32, 14) may be the kidneys. Of humans the word (AV) is always ' reins,' and were supposed to be the seat of the innermost emotions, with as much justification as mod. refs. to the heart. In the figurative sense it would be silly to replace ' reins ' by ' kidneys,' because emotions are always being ref. to. It is better to talk in mod. figurative speech and replace ' It gladdens my reins ' with ' It gladdens my heart.' To gladden the kidneys would be absurd unless we are speaking medically.

Kidron [kĭ′-drŏn]. The brook; lit. ' the wadi ': a depression which was a river during the rainy season and dry otherwise. But the Kidron was really a 3 m. long valley to the immediate E of the Jerusalem heights. It is also called the Valley of Jehoshaphat. It was, and is, a burying ground of the Jews (*2 Kings* 23, 4; *Jer.* 31, 40).

Kin, Kinsman. Certain responsibilities fell upon
the next ' of kin.' If a man was forced by circumstances to sell property, his next of kin, if it
were at all poss. should buy it (*Jer.* 32, 8 ff.).
Property already sold should be redeemed by the
next of kin (*Lev.* 25, 25). Naomi had a ' parcel
of land ' belonging to her late husband which
had to be sold and it was the duty of Boaz to
buy it (*Ruth* 4, 5). But this verse should read,
' But thou must buy Ruth the Moabitess also,
the wife of the dead.' The land has to be kept
within the clan (*Ruth* 2, 1). Should a man be
forced to sell himself as a slave, his next of kin
should endeavour to buy him back. Thus the
Heb. word *goel* takes on a meaning of ' redeemer '
(*Isa.* 41, 14; 43, 14; etc.). It was also the business
of the next of kin to avenge murder—' the avenger
of blood.' It was the business of the whole clan
to do this, though the right was restricted (*Ex.* 21,
14; *Num.* 35, 9-34; *Deut.* 24, 16).

Kine. (*1 Sam.* 6, 14 AV & RV). *See* COW.

King. The name derives prob. from a root meaning
to advise or counsel, and the first kings would be
the ' wise men.' There are many refs. in *Genesis* to
kings who were prob. no more than the ' wise
men ' of small communities (*Gen.* 14, 2), Neither
Herod nor Agrippa was a true king, yet they are
given the title (*Matt.* 2, 1; *Acts* 25, 13). God is
called King of Israel, and Jesus, ' King of the
Kingdom ' (*Ps.* 10, 16; *Rev.* 17, 14). The story
of the coming of kings to Israel is told in the
articles on ISRAEL, SAMUEL, SAUL. On Saul's death,
with the enthronement of David, the monarchy
became established and hereditary. In civil
matters the king was the final court of appeal,
and no more (*Amos* 2, 3). Although the priest-

hood resented it, the kings did regard themselves
as head of the nation's religious orders, and themselves made sacrifices (*1 Sam.* 13, 9-11). David
and Solomon both appointed and dismissed High
Priests (*2 Sam.* 8, 17). Later, priests were left to
perform the offices but they were still regarded
as civil servants (*2 Sam.* 20, 23). It was the prophets who opposed kings, priests usually agreed
with the kings. The prophets were, in fact, the
corrective to the despotism of men who were little
worse and sometimes little better than oriental
tyrants. Taxation to maintain the monarchy began
in Solomon's time. Before that the finances
would come from plunder won in war. Solomon
had certain monopolies (*1 Kings* 10, 15), and
when necessary the kings did not hesitate to
' borrow ' from the Temple treasury. Their main
officials were the commander-in-chief, or captain
of the host (*2 Sam.* 12, 27); the captain of the
bodyguard (*2 Sam.* 8, 18); the king's remem-
brancer or recorder, otherwise Prime Minister
(*2 Sam.* 8, 16); the scribe, or Secretary of State
(*2 Kings* 18, 18); the Chancellor of the Exchequer
(*2 Sam.* 20, 24); the Chamberlain of the household (*Isa.* 36, 3); and several minor officials, who
were not over-popular with the prophets (*Amos*
7, 10-17; *Isa.* 5, 8; *Jer.* 5, 28; *Micah* 3, 11).

Kingdom of God. The idea of the Kingdom of God
springs from the conviction that God the Creator
is King of His universe. Every natural phenomenon was God's : the earth, the sea, the storm,
famine, drought, pestilence; there was nothing
that was rebellious agst. God but man and the
nature of man (*Ps.* 18, 7-15; 68, 7-18; 104). As
understood by the OT writers, God had created
man in His own image and had a particular
interest in man, and an extra special interest in

certain men and a certain nation. Although at the beginning there was the concept of God as One of limited power and limited sphere of influence, it was not long before broader minds began to see that there is no room for gods in the universe, but that there is only One (*Amos* 9, 7). What the OT emphasises above all is the policy of selection for the furtherance of the purposes of God. God chooses Israel not because He is stronger than the gods of other peoples and wants to advance the cause of His favourites. He chooses Israel because He has one special thing to do, and the doing of it necessitates a gradual narrowing down until He finishes with a single man—the Messiah, the Lord Jesus. The whole burden of the OT is selection and rejection. Abraham is chosen, and from that time the process begins. The Kingdom was implicit in the hist. of this Chosen People, but it was the prophets who pointed out so clearly that choice must always involve rejection. God is the King Omnipotent who can say ' You I want. You I do not want,' and that is the end of it. There is no court of appeal; there is simply nothing else for it. The royalty of God may be a benevolent despotism, but it is still a despotism. Nevertheless a despotism is not a tyranny: those whom God chooses are those who of their own freewill have chosen God. This idea that God's choice is not haphazard is developed in the idea of the complete and absolute justice of God's ways (*Deut.* 7, 9-12). Man can have no complaint, for God is so obviously just. When catastrophe comes it is the Day of Jehovah, but only those who are blind fools cannot see why the day has come. In OT thought there was going to come a time when the kingdoms of this world were to be ruled, in this world, on the same stan-

dard and value. They thought for a while that
David was the man to do this (*Hosea* 3, 5; *Jer.*
30, 9; *Ezek.* 34, 23; 37, 24). When David failed
to live up to expectation they began to think of
someone specially sent. This was the Messianic
hope (*Isa.* 9, 6 & 7). The same idea is found in
the *Psalms* (2 & 110). This is not God come down
to earth. This is a special person who is at once
the representative and the delegate of God. He
needs God behind him and above him to make
him what he is. In the same way God uses all
sorts of earthly rulers for what they are worth,
and so long as they are advancing His cause;
but when they have done t hat they are finished
—Nebuchadnezzar, Cyrus, Alexander, are cases
in point (*Deut.* 2, 21). The Messianic idea became
conventionalised. He would be of the seed of
David, and he would come in the fulness of time;
not to take God's place, but to act as God's
representative on earth. The Messiah's kingdom,
however, would be the Kingdom of God. In the
NT the idea changes very considerably. Around
the time that Jesus was born there were elements
among the Jews who believed that the time had
come for the advent of the Messiah in the concept
of the OT. The time was ripe, the age was propi-
tious. It seemed to them that the glory of the
Jew must come when his stock was at its lowest.
This was the darkest hour that comes before the
dawn. Some thought of the coming of the kingdom in political terms, others in spiritual terms
(*Luke* 1, 67-79; 2, 25-38). Even John the Baptist
may have been disappointed that Jesus appeared
to fall bet. stools (*Matt.* 11, 2-6). Whatever the
Jews thought about it, however, our ideas of the
Kingdom of God must spring from the teachings
of Jesus Himself. He told them that the long-

awaited kingdom was at hand, and they at once
leaped to the conclusion that He was announcing
the imminence of an old idea coming true. Whereas He was doing no such thing (*Matt.* 4, 17;
Mark 1, 15). Jesus obviously had no belief at
all in the arrival of some Jewish scion of the
House of David who would raise their horn on
high. He thought John the Baptist was a fine
fellow, but He clearly thought that John was
away off the rails (*Matt.* 11, 11). John was far
too much concerned with this world and with
outward things. Jesus changes the phraseology
—Kingdom of God, becomes Kingdom of Heaven, giving the idea that this was not a thing of
this world at all (*John* 18, 36). It is a quality of
the spirit, rather than an enjoyment of either
body or mind (*Matt.* 5, 3 & 10 & 20). It is a
citizenship enjoyed by a certain kind of person
(*Matt.* 18, 3). What Jesus meant by the Kingdom
is seen and understood perhaps best in His
parables of the Kingdom. Jesus thought in pictures; His parables are always important. If
Jesus is to be king of a kingdom, that kingdom
is the human heart. The heart that is ruled by
Jesus is the kind of heart which can create, maintain, and enjoy a certain kind of earthly kingdom
which might well be called the Kingdom of God.
He is careful to point out in His parables that
the possession of the right kind of heart is not
the prerogative of the Jews (*Matt.* 21, 28-32 &
43; 22, 1-14; *Luke* 14, 16-24). When He prays
for God's kingdom to come, in the Lord's prayer,
He sees it as the day when God's will will be
done in earth as it is in heaven. The kingdom,
then, in Jesus' mind is a spiritual state that is the
result of a rebirth from above. A man can live
in any kingdom at all on earth and still be a citi-

zen of the kingdom of God if his heart is in the
right place. Paul carried this idea into the realm
of practical politics when he pointed out, in the
controversy over clean and unclean meats, that
' the kingdom of God is not eating and drinking,
but righteousness and peace and joy in the Holy
Spirit ' (*Rom.* 14, 17). There are certain types
who cannot possibly be of the kingdom, just
because they are the types they are (*1 Cor.* 6,
9 & 10; *Gal.* 5, 21; *Eph.* 5, 5). Since the very
beginning there have always been hopes that the
Kingdom of God was at hand. Innumerable
sects and persons have staked their reputation,
such as it was, on their pronouncement that the
Kingdom would come in their lifetime; some
have even given the date, and have been able,
oddly enough, to live down their miscalculation.
This is because of the confusion bet. the Kingdom and the Parousia—the second coming of the
Lord. Jesus Himself believed that He would
come again (*Matt.* 24; *Mark* 13; *Luke* 21). All
this talk of a period of time when this will happen
or that will happen is sheer nonsense. As far as
God is concerned it has all happened, except that
we are using the past tense, and with God nothing
is past. That may appear to make everything
more complicated still; but that is a very good
argument for not trying to pin down the work
of God to specified periods of a clock governed
world. Jesus spoke of the Kingdom as new wine
in old bottles, bursting through; He also spoke
of it as the leaven in the lump, a slow and gradual
process. In human hist. it has worked in both
ways, with individuals and sometimes with
communities. But Jesus never did say that one
bursting of the bottles would bring the Kingdom
to pass, or even that one working of the leaven

in the world's sour lump of dough would sweeten all. Let us remember always that Jesus was not dealing with and not talking about society at large. His concern was with the individual mind and heart and soul. The idea, then, is not to dream fondly of the day when all the kingdoms of the world shall be the kingdom of our God and of His Christ. But to pray most earnestly for the moment when our own private souls will know Him as King and acknowledge His rule, and live accordingly.

Kings, Books of. The books of the *Kings* were orig. one and they are hist. of a sort. There was history before there were literate historians, and much of the ancient history of any people was preserved in song and story before it was given the permanence of the written word. It is common enough too that when a later historian revises or improves the work of an earlier one, the importance of the earlier work diminishes, and the work itself may disappear. There is now no 'Book of the acts of Solomon' (*1 Kings* 11, 41), no 'Book of the chronicles of the kings of Judah' (*1 Kings* 14, 29) or 'Book of the chronicles of the kings of Israel' (*1 Kings* 14, 19). These lost books themselves superseded others even earlier (*2 Chron.* 20, 34; 32, 32). But if this is not how history is made, it is how history is written; though if something is gained by the more 'modern' approach, something valuable is probably lost. Kings, then, is a compilation of all sorts of works, written and unwritten, brought together by people who were interested enough in history, but who were a great deal more interested in religion. It is almost if not entirely impossible for any historian to be absolutely and consistently objective in his narrative. This is true not only of the ancients, but of the most mod. of historians. The historian has developed a theory of hist., or an idea of the purpose of hist., and with the best will in the world, he cannot help reading the meaning of events in a way which suits his particular theory. The writers of *Kings* are in this no whit different from any other historians of any period of hist. For one thing they are very much under the influence of the Deuteronomic condemnation of altars and high places which detract from and despoil the central worship of God in the Temple: and they are therefore apt to say that any king who encouraged or condoned these altars and high places was a bad king and that any king who destroyed them was a good king. No man wants to be judged by one particular pet idea which he possessed, but by and large the kings are so judged by these writers. The writers are also greatly concerned with the development of the prophets, the great and unique glory of the Jewish people, and their reading of hist. (prob. rightly) is in tracing how good came when the prophets were listened to, and how ill followed when they were not. The events narrated in *Kings* are also narrated in *Chronicles*, but with a different emphasis and with a different purpose (which maybe strengthens the suspicion that some historians have their minds made up about the point they will prove before they have started to prove it). The first 11 chs. of *1 Kings* cover a period of 40 yrs. bet. c. 1015 and 975 BC. The account was not written then, but that is the period covered. The story of Saul and most of the story of David is contained in the books of *Samuel* (qv). The 1st ch. of *1 Kings* and to 2, 11, tells of the end of David's reign, and of his choice of Solomon as his successor. The rest of the first 11 chs. tell of the reign of Solomon. They give a pretty good picture of the man. *See* SOLOMON. He made the kingdom of considerable international importance and he built the Temple, which made him the darling of the priests who wrote the *Chronicles*. A breakdown of these chs. gives us Solomon's appointment and success in spite of opposition from Adonijah (1, 1-2, 9); his accession (2, 10-46); examples of his astuteness (he was not really wise) (chs. 3-4); the preparation, construction, consecration of the Temple and notes on Solomon's greatness (chs. 5-10); Solomon's decline and the division of the kingdom at his death (ch. 11). The details of the disruption of the kingdom are given in the article on Israel; the events are recorded in *1 Kings* 12 —*2 Kings* 18. The time covered is 254 yrs. bet. c. 975 and c. 721. Israel and Judah split over the succession, Judah and Levi remained loyal to the Davidic line, Rehoboam, and the 10 tribes of the N elected Jeroboam. For the 1st 60 yrs. or so the 2 kingdoms were hostile. Then Jehoshaphat of Judah's son married the daughter of Ahab of Israel and they formed an alliance which lasted from c. 918 to c. 839. Then they fell out again owing to difference of opinion about the most profitable alliances. This hostility lasted till c. 721. During this time the N had gradually deteriorated, and by the end of this period they had disappeared altogether in bondage to Nebuchadnezzar. They are never heard of again. The best kings of Judah (on the standard of 'Temple versus high places') were Asa, Jehoshaphat, Hezekiah, and Josiah. The worst (on the same standard) were Ahaz and Manasseh. By the same standard the N kingdom had no good kings at all, for they refused to worship at Jerusalem which was in Judah. Prophets of this period were Elijah, Elisha, Joel, Jonah (not the author of the book), Amos, Hosea, Micah and Isaiah. This was the next stage in a process of divine selection; 1st the whole nation, then the fragment—Judah. The remainder of *2 Kings* is the story of Judah alone, and it covers 135 yrs. bet. c. 721 and 586 BC. During this period the nation was given 2 chances to reform and return to the old loyalties. Twice the people refused, and they ended as Israel had done. Under Hezekiah the people were delivered from the Assyrians and a religious reformation was started. It lasted only for his lifetime. But his grandson Josiah led another reformation, which lasted just as long. Isaiah was the prophet of Hezekiah's reign, and Jeremiah of Josiah's. Other prophets were Micah, Nahum, Zephaniah and Habakkuk. The end of this period and of the Books of the *Kings* is the captivity and exile, which lasted from 586 to 516, though they had been existing by courtesy of the Babylonians since 606. The Books must have been written, or at least collated, during the exile, for they do not deal with the return from the exile.

King's garden. A plot of land just outside the walls of Jerusalem, irrigated from the Pool of Siloam (*2 Kings* 25, 4; *Jer.* 39, 4; 52, 7; *Neh.* 3, 15).

King's pool. The pool of Siloam (qv).

Kiriath Jearim [kĭr′-ĭ-ăth jē′-ă-rĭm]. City on the border bet. Judah and Benjamin (*Josh.* 15, 9). Orig. of Gideon it was occupied by Danites (*Josh.* 9, 17; *Judg.* 18, 12). It may have been a 'high place' of heathen worship. The Ark lay in the town for years after it had been returned by the Philistines (*1 Sam.* 6, 19—7, 2).

Kish [kĭsh]. **1.** Benjamite father of Jeiel (*1 Chron.*

8, 30). **2.** Benjamite, son of Abiel and father of Saul (*1 Sam.* 9, 1). Also described as son of above (*1 Chron.* 8, 33). He lived at Gibeah. **3.** A Levite in David's day (*1 Chron.* 23, 21). **4.** A Levite assoc. with the Hezekiah reforms (*2 Chron.* 29, 12). **5.** Benjamite ancestor of Mordecai (*Esth.* 2, 5).

Kishon (Kison) [kīsh′-ŏn]. Stream which drains the Plain of Esdraelon. It rises in the foothills of Mt. Tabor and enters the sea E of Haifa after a course of 23 m. Here Sisera's army perished (*Judg.* 5). And here the priests of Baal were slain at Elijah's command (*1 Kings* 18, 40).

Kiss. A mark of affection, though in the orient it is commoner bet. people of the same sex than bet. man and woman. The salutation might be on the lips or the forehead, but was more commonly on the cheek or the curve of the neck. It could also be a sign of complete submission, esp. if the feet were kissed (*Gen.* 41, 40 Marg; *Luke* 7, 38). It was the symbol of the affection of Christian for Christian (*Rom.* 16, 16; etc,). The kiss could be thrown by the hand (*Job.* 31, 27).

Kite. A scavenger bird of the E and ME. But not everywhere in Scripture is the name the true trans. of the Heb. There are 3 Heb. words: (1) *ayyah* is better 'falcon' as in RV and RSV (*Lev.* 11, 14; *Deut.* 14, 13; *Job* 28, 7 where AV has vulture); (2) *daah* is the kite, though AV has vulture (*Lev.* 11, 14). (3) *dayyah* (*Deut.* 14, 13). AV uses 17th cent. word 'glede' (OE gleda) which means a kite. RSV has buzzard. It is hard to say what is correct. They were all ceremonially unclean.

Kittim [kĭt′-tīm]. Also **Chittim** AV. Prob. the island of Cyprus inhabited by the desc. of Javan (*Gen.* 10, 4).

Kneading trough. Shallow wooden bowl in which dough was kneaded either with the hands or with the feet when the quantity was large (*Ex.* 8, 3; 12, 24; *Deut.* 28, 5 & 17 RV).

Knee, Kneel. This part of the anatomy is often referred to as the part which is most greatly affected by fear or fasting. The ref. is still used —'knees knocking'; 'weak at the knees' (*Isa.* 35, 3; *Job* 4, 4; *Ps.* 109, 24). On the knees was an accepted attitude for prayer (*I Kings* 8, 54; *Ps.* 95, 6; *Acts* 20, 36). To ' bow the knee ' was to worship (*I Kings* 19, 18). For a human to kneel was to express reverence or entreaty (*Matt.* 17, 14).

Knife. Several words are so trans. Flint knives were used for circumcision (*Josh.* 5, 2; *Ex.* 4, 25). Other knives were mostly of bronze, and were used for sacrifice, dismembering carcases, and in eating. A very sharp knife was used for shaving (*Ezek.* 5, 1). The scribe's knife, used for sharpening his stylus is very prop. called ' pen knife ' (*Jer.* 36, 23 AV, RSV). The orig. pen knife was used to sharpen quill pens.

Knop. 1. Knobs ornamenting the golden candlestick (prop. lampstand) (*Ex.* 25, 31). **2.** Egg-shaped ornaments on the panelling of Solomon's Temple (*I Kings* 6, 18; ' gourds ' RV marg. and RSV).

Kohathites. The clan founded by Kohath, son of Levi. The subdivisions were the Amramites, Izharites, Hebronites, and Uzzielites (*Num.* 3, 27). Moses and Aaron were Kohathites (*Ex.* 6, 18-20). They settled ultimately in cities of Judah and Ephraim, Dan and Manasseh (*Josh.* 21, 4 & 5). They faded out after the exile.

Koph [kōph]. 19th letter of Heb. alphabet. Also *Qoph*. Eng. letter *Q* comes nearest to its sound but it is usually represented in Eng. as *K* or hard *C*.

Korah [kō′-răh]. **1.** Son of Esau by Aholibamah (*Gen.* 36, 5). **2.** Grandson of Esau, son of Eliphaz (*Gen.* 36, 16). This may be corrupt text. **3.** Levite family who rebelled agst. Moses and Aaron (*Num.* 16).

Korahite. The descendants of the above. Samuel was one of them (*1 Chron.* 6, 28). They became singers, gatekeepers and temple bakers (*1 Chron.* 15, 17; *Ps.* 42 & 44-49; 84 & 85 & 87 & 88 titles). Also (*1 Chron.* 9, 19 & 31 & 32).

L

Laban [lā′-băn]. Abraham was his great uncle. He lived at Haran (*Gen.* 24, 10 & 29; 28, 5 & 10; etc.). Rebekah was his sister, who became Isaac's wife (ch. 24). Jacob fled to Laban after the deception of Esau (chs. 29 & 30 & 31). He deceived Jacob in the matter of his daughters and made Jacob husband of both Leah and Rachel. Finally they parted after a covenant and mutual expressions of regard. They did not meet again.

Lace. The meaning goes back to the Latin word, which means a snare. In the AV it means a cord or band (*Ex.* 28, 28 & 37; 39, 21; etc.).

Lachish [lā′-chĭsh]. Town in S Judah. The people allied with the king of Jebus agst. Gibeon, and it was taken and reduced by Joshua (*Josh.* 10, 3 & 31). Rehoboam fortified it (*2 Chron.* 11, 9). Amaziah was murdered here (*2 Kings* 14, 19). Sennacherib took the town and Hezekiah made terms with him (*2 Kings* 18, 13-17). It was resettled after the Exile (*Neh.* 11, 30). Micah denounced its inhabitants (*Micah* 1, 13).

Ladder. Usually a scaling ladder used in siege. Jacob's ladder was prob. a ziggurat, the ancient temple perched on top of a mound of terraces.

Lahmi. Brother of Goliath (*1 Chron.* 20, 5). There is confusion bet. this passage and the other (*2 Sam.* 21, 19). Either may be right.

Laish [lā'-īsh]. Old name of town of Dan (*Judg.* 18, 7; etc.).

Lamb. The young of the sheep, used greatly for food, and also for sacrifice and offering (qv). A sacrificial lamb had to be without blemish.

Lamb of God. This is the Lamb provided by God, and, of course, without blemish (*John* 1, 29). This harks back to the OT (*Isa.* 53, 7; *Acts* 8, 32). Apart from the gen. idea of sacrifice and vicarious suffering, there is also the idea of the Paschal lamb, the symbol of deliverance. In short the title represents innocence, vicarious suffering, sacrifice and redemption.

Lamech [lā'-měch]. **1.** Fifth in descent from Cain, husband of Adah and Zillah and father of Jabal and Jubal, Tubal-Cain and Naamah (*Gen.* 4, 18-24). **2.** Son of Methuselah.

Lamed(h) [lā'-měd]. Twelfth letter of the Heb. alphabet corresponding to Eng. *L.*

Lamentations, Book of. This is a dirge or series of dirges attributed to Jeremiah. It is inspired by the destruction of Jerusalem and the Temple by Nebuchadnezzar in 586 BC. Each of the chs. in the AV is a separate acrostic poem. Four of the chs. have a verse for each letter of the Heb. alphabet (22) and ch. 3 has 66 vv. In the shorter poems (except ch. 5) each verse starts with the relevant letter of the alphabet in order, and in ch. 3 there are 3 vv. to each letter. The purpose is to persuade the Jews not to despise the chastening of the Lord (*Heb.* 12, 5 & 6), and not to despair under it. The 1st poem deals with the state of Zion abject and miserable. The 2nd relates why this has come about. The 3rd reveals the purpose of God that is behind it. The 4th looks back to better days, and the fate that then fell on Zion's enemies. The 5th pleads Zion's cause before God.

Lamp. This is the word that should be used gen. where AV has candles, and sometimes when it has torches. Wax candles were unknown. The lamp was a metal vessel which contained oil (usually olive oil) in which a wick, or even a dry reed, was inserted or simply floated. The oil was drawn up by capillary attraction. Sometimes the vessel was open, as the old Scots crusie, sometimes it was shaped more like a tea-pot, with the wick protruding from the spout (*Ex.* 25, 38). ' Candlesticks ' are lampstands.

Lancet. Not the surgical instrument but a javelin (*1 Kings* 18, 28; *Jer.* 50, 42—' lance ').

Land crocodile. (*Lev.* 11, 30 RV). The chameleon or some other lizard (qv).

Landmark. (*Deut.* 19, 14.) Stones and the ploughed line bet. the stones indicating the boundary bet. one holding and another (*Prov.* 22, 28; 23, 10; *Job* 24, 2; *Hos.* 5, 10 RV).

Language. See TONGUE.

Lantern. (*John* 18, 3 only.) Prob. ' torch.'

Laodicea [lå-ŏd′-ĭ-cē′-a]. (*Rev.* 1, 11; 3, 14-22). Chief city of Phrygia, founded prob. by Antiochus and named after his wife (261-247 BC). Many Jews lived there, including Epaphras (*Col.* 4, 13), who founded its church. The chief manufactures were a woven cloth of goat's hair, and a powder used in the treatment of ophthalmia.

Lappidoth [lăp′-pĭ-dŏth] Husband of Deborah (*Judg.* 4, 4).

Lapwing. (*Lev.* 11, 19; *Deut.* 14, 18 AV) (*vanellus*

cristatus.) One of the true plovers, still found in Palestine. But the meaning of the Heb. word may be the hoopoe (*upupa epops*).

Lasciviousness. Shameless conduct of any kind (*Mark* 7, 22); wantonness (*Rom.* 13, 13).

Last Supper. *See* LORD'S SUPPER.

Latchet. The leather thong fastening the sandal to the foot (*Isa.* 5, 27; *Mark* 1, 7).

Latin. The language spoken by the Rom. The Heb. adopted very few Latin words. The inscription over the Cross was in Latin, the language of government, as well as in Aram. and Gk. (*John* 19, 20).

Lattice. Crossed laths covering a window. *See* HOUSE.

Laver. Vessel for hand washing. *See* TEMPLE.

Law. 1. The law given by Moses. This was regarded as the supreme rule of private and community living. With the law came the nation. It was the law which changed a horde of ex-slaves into a proud and patriotic people. **2.** The judgments made by Moses on personal and national matters. These judgments became part and parcel of the law, written and unwritten (*Ex.* 18, 15). They were handed down and learned, passing into the tradition and constitution of the nation. They were quoted by the elders when minor causes came before them. More difficult cases were later brought to the sanctuary where the judgments were regarded as inspired (*Ex.* 21, 6; etc.). This is the orig. meaning of Torah, which later came to mean the written law (*Hos.* 8, 12). **3.** The law of the prophets was purely a moral code. The prophets recalled the people to the moral foundation and sanction of the law (*Jer.* 7, 21 & 22). **4.** The Book of the Covenant (*Ex.* 20, 22-23, 33). This is the written code of an agricultural people, and includes legislation governing the use of animals and of land. Criminal justice is concerned only with retaliation and compensation. **5.** The law of Deuteronomy is the code for a settled and civilised people. *See* DEUTERONOMY. **6.** The laws of Holiness (*Lev.* 17-26). These are concerned in the main with religious and ceremonial duties. **7.** The Priestly Code consists of the last few chs. of *Exodus*, the whole of *Leviticus* and other scattered passages. The stress is on ritual, designed to remind the people of the existence and presence of God. The danger was, of course, that the ritual itself should become more important than that which it symbolized, and this indeed happened. By Jesus' day formalism was in command, and it was that formalism which He attacked, while claiming to be Himself the fulfilment of the true spirit of the law. The Law would remain until it had achieved its object; the teaching of Jesus was that object, for He lifted man's relationship to God on to an entirely different level. Without the grace and truth which are God's gift through Jesus it is impossible for frail and fallible man to abide by the law even as it stands. Law was now written in the heart, not on paper or on stone. It was no longer imposed but accepted. Much of the Sermon on the Mount is devoted to getting behind the facade of the Law to the substance of it. This naturally brought Him into head-on collision with the formalists and with Judaism itself, they finding their heaviest complaint in Jesus' attitude to the Sabbath and to food regulations (*Mark* 2, 23-28; etc.). **8.** Paul in his letters uses the word 'law' over 100 times in *Romans* and *Galatians* alone. This is natural, for he himself was a legalist of legalists until his conversion (*Gal.* 2, 19). Nevertheless he saw the Law as the peda-

gogue who leads men to Christ (*Gal.* 3, 24).
From his knowledge of the Gk. and Latin
world he realised that many a ' heathen ' had
a far deeper and more sincere sense of goodness
and of sin than most Jews had. This brought
him to the conclusion that goodness and right
are universal and eternal (*Rom.* 3, 9-19). The fact
of death was the proof of this (*Rom.* 8, 2). The
rule becomes the rule of universal and eternal
love which conquers death (*Rom.* 13, 8-10; *Gal.*
5, 13 ff.). This law is founded on faith (*Rom.* 3,
31). The Pharisees were committed to ethical
goodness, not to ceremonial observance. Paul
sees no good, for example, in circumcision because
it is national, not universal. It is simply an unnecessary obstacle (*1 Cor.* 7, 18 ff.; etc.). James
simply takes the Sermon on the Mount as guide
and applies it to the business of living. For him
it is the law of liberty. The letters of Peter and
John do not mention the law at all.

Lawyer. *See* SCRIBE.

Laying on of hands. A symbolic act of dedication.
Thus the Levites were set apart (*Num.* 8, 5-20).
A person making a sacrifice laid his hands on it
before giving it to the priest in token that he had
made it a substitute for himself (*Lev.* 1, 4). Jacob
transferred the Covenant from himself to his sons
by laying his hands on their heads (*Gen.* 48, 5-20).
Timothy was set apart by the Presbytery in the
same way (*1 Tim.* 4, 14). The ceremony was therefore one of dedication, and at the same time of
transference and passing on of a blessing. Mothers
asked Jesus to do it to their children (*Matt.* 19,
13-15). Jesus laid hands on the sick for their
healing (*Mark* 6, 5; etc.).

Lazarus [lă'-ză-rŭs]. **1.** The beggar in the parable
(*Luke* 16, 19-31). He is the only parable character

to whom Jesus gave a name. The name, Dives, means simply ' a rich man.' **2.** The brother of Mary and Martha of Bethany; a dear friend of Jesus (*John* 11, 2). As far as Jesus is concerned, He seems to have used the death of Lazarus to emphasise his Messiahship. The sign of the Messiah was that he should raise the dead and come into Jerusalem riding on the foal of a donkey. Jesus seems deliberately to have chosen Lazarus as His ' proof.' The Jews believed that it took 3 days for the soul to separate from the body. By the 4th day the patient was really, truly, and hopelessly dead. Jesus seems to have been determined that there should be no notion that Lazarus was simply in a trance or in a cataleptic fit. He waited for the 4th day. After the miracle Jesus left Bethany, then came back, and caused a tremendous stir (*John* 12, 1-11). There followed the triumphal entry into Jerusalem which proclaimed Jesus, claim to be the Messiah. Why Lazarus does not appear again in the Gospels is a mystery, though he may have fled because of the threat to his life (*John* 12, 10 & 11).

Lead. The main sources of the metal were the Sinai peninsula, Egypt and Tarshish (*Ezek.* 27, 12). Its weight was appreciated (*Zech.* 5, 7). The ref. in *Job* (19, 24) may be to the practice, still practised, of hammering lead into carved inscriptions.

Leaf. This may refer to the foliage of a tree, or to a half door (*1 Kings* 6, 34; etc.); or to a page of a book or the column of a scroll (*Jer.* 36, 23).

Leah [lē´-äh]. Senior daughter of Laban, whom he palmed off on Jacob (*Gen.* 29, 21 ff.). Even if Jacob favoured her less than he did Rachel, he still fathered on her 6 sons and 1 daughter—Reuben, Simeon, Levi, Judah, Issachar, Zebulun and Dinah (*Gen.* 29, 31-35; 30, 18 & 20 & 21). She died before Jacob went down to Egypt and was buried at Machpelah (*Gen.* 49, 31).

Leasing. A ' leasing ' is a lie (*Ps.* 4, 2; 5, 6 AV).

Leather. *See* ARTS AND CRAFTS.

Leaven. Dough from a baking, left to ferment, and a portion of which was mixed with a subsequent baking (*Ex.* 12, 15 & 19; 13, 7). It left rather a sour taste and is now superseded by yeast or barm. Offerings made by fire to the Lord must contain none of it, though offerings that were to be eaten by humans might (*Levi* 2, 11; 7, 13; 23, 17). During the Passover season they must not eat anything containing leaven (*Ex.* 12, 39; *1 Cor.* 5, 7 & 8).

Lebanon [lĕ′-bă-nŏn]. The name occurs more than 60 times. It was a mountain range on which the snow stayed long (*Jer.* 18, 14). It was a fertile and very lovely place (*Ps.* 72, 16; *Hos.* 14, 5 & 7). Wood for the old and the new Temples was cut on its slopes (*2 Chron.* 2, 8; *Ezra* 3, 7).

Lebbaeus [lĕb-bā′-eŭs]. Judas called Thaddaeus (qv).

Leb Kamai [lĕb′-kā′-māi]. (*Jer.* 51, 1 RV) AV translates this as ' in the midst of them which rise up agst. me.' But the word is really cabalistic, like ' Abracadabra.' Read the wrong way round in Heb. the letters spell KSDIM—the Chaldeans.

Leeks. (*Num.* 11, 5.) Here the word is so trans. though it is usually trans. ' grass.' But it is surely the leek, more or less as known to-day.

Lees. The sediment at the bottom of a wine jar. After standing awhile the wine was decanted so that the lees would be separated and thrown out. *See* WINE AND STRONG DRINK.

Legion. In the Rom. army this approximated to a

battalion, about 6,000 men, infantry with cavalry
in addition. Two centuries (the command of a
centurion) made one maniple (the command of a
tribune). Three maniples made a cohort, and 10
cohorts made a legion. But in Scripture the word
is used (as it is to-day) to denote any large number
(*Matt.* 26, 53; etc.). The word is used of a man
possessed of all sorts of unclean spirits (*Mark* 5,
9 & 15; *Luke* 8, 30).

Lemuel [Lĕm′-ū-ĕl]. Author poss. fictitious, of
Proverbs ch. 31.

Lentils. The vegetable as known to-day; one of the
vetches, known in India as dhal, which must have
been Esau's pottage (*Gen.* 25, 30). It is nourishing
without being particularly appetising.

Leopard. *Felis pardus.* One of the big cats, more
ferocious than the tiger. Symbolically it is used
of a nation, prob. the Persians (*Dan.* 7, 6).

Leprosy. 1. True leprosy (*elephantiasis graecorum*)
is the disease as it is known to-day, though there
are now remedies. **2.** Black leprosy is a tubercular
or nodular disease affecting the skin and the
mucous membranes. **3.** White leprosy attacks
principally certain nerves, producing complete
numbness in these parts. It takes normally a long
time to develop, and a long time to kill the patient.
The word as used in Scripture, however, includes
various diseases of the skin which are not to-day
classed as leprosy or anything like it (*Lev.* 14, 3).
These were dermatitic, superficial, and curable
ailments, ranging from ringworm to athlete's foot.
But the ancients, unable to distinguish bet. true
leprosy and the completely superficial skin diseases, classed all alike in the interests of safety
and public health. The leprosy of garments (*Lev.*
13, 47 ff.) is no more than mildew; and the leprosy
of houses is dry rot (*Lev.* 14, 34).

Let. May mean to permit, but may also mean to hinder (*Ex.* 5, 4; *Num.* 22, 16; *Isa.* 43, 13; *Rom.* 1, 13; *2 Thes.* 2, 7).

Levi [lē'-vī]. **1.** Third son of Jacob and Leah (*Gen.* 35, 23.) He was not blessed by his father as a result of a horrible act of vengeance (*Gen.* 34, 25-31; 49, 5-7). He had 3 sons (*Gen.* 46, 11). He died in Egypt (*Ex.* 6, 16). **2.** Other name of the apostle Matthew (*Matt.* 9, 9-13; etc.).

Leviathan. Prob. simply the crocodile of the Nile.

Levites. 1. The descendants of Levi (*Gen.* 46, 11; etc.). **2.** The clan descended from them, who were given charge of the sanctuary. When Israel worshipped the Golden Calf the Levites remained faithful to Jehovah (*Ex.* 32, 26-29; *Num.* 3, 9 ff.). They carried the Tabernacle and the furnishings on the march (*Num.* 1, 50-53; etc.). The age at which their service started is given variously as 30 yrs. (*Num.* 4, 3); 25 yrs. (*Num.* 8, 24); and 20 yrs. (*1 Chron.* 23, 24). The more important duties were performed by the older men (*Num.* 8, 24-26). They retired officially at the age of 50 (*Num.* 8, 25 & 26). They wore a uniform (*1 Chron.* 15, 27). At the settlement they were divided over various towns (*Josh.* 21, 20-40). David grouped them in 4 grades (*1 Chron.* 24-26). *See* PRIEST.

Leviticus, Book of. The title is taken from the name Levi, and it is a historical book not just a book of laws. It traces the development of the religious and ceremonial practices of the people. Aaron, naturally, is the principal character. *Exodus* tells of how the nation was brought to God, *Leviticus* tells of the means employed to keep them there, mainly by means of the offerings (qv): the Burnt, the Meal, the Peace, the Sin and the Trespass Offerings. There are, too, the feasts: the Sabbath, Passover, Pentecost, Trumpets, Atonement, Tabernacles, Sabbatical Year and Jubilee. It begins with the laws governing the offerings to God (1, 1 to 6, 7), then lays down the conventional form which the offerings must take (6, 8 to 7, 38). Chs. 8, 9 and 10 deal with the place and the functions of the priesthood. In chs. 9-15 various regulations are laid down regarding food (11); illness (11-12); leprosy. The greatest ch. is prob. 16, which describes the formalities and the meaning of the Day of Atonement. Various rules and regulations follow: daily meals (17); social behaviour (chs. 18-20); priests and worship (chs. 21-23); the law of living (24). Ch. 25 deals with the Sabbatical year and the year of Jubilee. Ch. 26 treats of the Covenant, and the last deals with vows in general.

Lewd. Simply ' wicked ' in a gen. way, and not confined to the sense of lustful (*Acts* 17, 5; etc. AV).

Libertines. Prob. Jews who had been Rom. military or political prisoners—in other words ' freedmen.' The Libertines were the enemies of Stephen (*Acts* 6, 9).

Libya(ns). Country and people on the W border of Lower Egypt. The Gks. called all Africa W of Egypt by the name, but the Rom. limited it to the part bet. Egypt and their province of Africa. They divided Libya into ' inferior ' (Marmarica), and ' superior ' (Cyrenaica).

Lice. This name may include lice, fleas, sandflies and various other objectionable insects (*Ex.* 8, 16-18; *Ps.* 105, 31).

Lieutenant. *See* SATRAP.

Lignaloes. *See* ALOES.

Ligure. *See* JEWELS AND PRECIOUS STONES.

Liking. Not ' preference,' but simply ' outward appearance ' (*Job* 39, 4).

Lily. Palestine is a land of flowers, and lilies as ref. to include such plants as the gladiolus and the iris. The lilies of the field, however, are anemones.

Lime. Building material made by burning limestone and lime-bearing sea shells and the like. From it mortar was made, and whitewash (*Isa.* 33, 12; *Amos* 2, 1). This is the 'plaister' (*Deut.* 27, 2 AV) and the whitewash of the sepulchres and walls (*Matt.* 23, 27; *Acts* 23, 3).

Line. *See* ARTS AND CRAFTS.

Linen. Cloth made from the fibres of flax. It could be fine or coarse according to the treatment of the fibres and the efficiency of the weaving. It was a most popular cloth in Egypt and that was where the Heb. prob. came first in contact with it. Fine garments and hangings were made from it, and the dead were swathed in it. Actually 9 different Gk. and Heb. words are so rendered, some of them meaning fine cloth, which might be muslin or cotton. In gen. it means a cloth not woollen. 'Linen yarn' (AV *1 Kings* 10, 28; *2 Chron.* 1, 16) should be Kue—a place where Solomon bought horses.

Lintel. *See* HOUSE.

Linus [lī'-nŭs]. Christian at Rome. By trad. the first Bishop (*2 Tim.* 4, 21).

Lion. *Felis leo*: common in Palestine in the old days. Scripture uses 6 words for the animal, the distinction being usually of age and growth. 'Lion's whelps' (*Job* 28, 8) should be 'proud beasts.' Judah is described as a lion (*Gen.* 49, 9) as Jesus is, too (*Rev.* 5, 5).

Lips, calves of. *See* CALVES OF THE LIPS.

List(ed). (*Mark* 9, 13; *John* 3, 8; etc.). Has nothing to do with listening, but means to desire, or to choose.

Lively. Simply, 'full of life.'

Liver. This organ was supposed to be the seat of life itself (*Prov.* 7, 23; *Lam.* 2, 11). See DIVINATION.

Lizard. Over 40 species of lizard have been identified in Palestine, the commonest being the gecko, the land crocodile, the sand lizard and the chameleon. They were all ceremonially unclean (*Lev.* 11, 30). Creatures called in AV, ferret, mole, snail, tortoise are prob. lizards.

Loaf. See BREAD.

Loan. See DEBT, USURY.

Lock. See HOUSE.

Locust. According to the dictionary, this is an orthopterous saltatorial insect of the family *Acrididae*, esp. *Oedipoda migratoria*. A cloud of locusts, wind driven mainly, will eat every green thing in sight (*Ex.* 10, 14 & 15). In Scripture many insect enemies of the farmer were classed as locusts (*Judg.* 6, 5; *Job* 39, 20; *Jer.* 46, 23; *Num.* 13, 33; *Nahum* 3, 17; etc.). Other scourges are called palmer worm, canker worm, caterpillar, beetle, cricket, bald locust. Locusts were ceremonially clean and could be eaten (*Lev.* 11, 21 & 22).

Lodge. A shelter built by market gardeners from which they might protect their crop when fruit was ripening (*Isa.* 1, 8).

Log. See WEIGHTS and MEASURES.

Lois [lō'-is]. Timothy's grandmother. She was a devout woman of Lystra (*Acts* 16, 1; *2 Tim.* 1, 5).

Long-suffering. Word used to describe one who is not easily ruffled, 'slow to anger'; and in NT of one who is restrained, not hasty in judgment on other people—'forbearing.' It is accounted an excellent quality (*Gal.* 5, 22).

Looking-glass. See MIRROR.

Lord. The OT has 3 names for God: (1) JHWH, rendered Jehovah, which should be more like Jahweh; (2) Adonai; (3) Elohim. The AV, and in the main the RV, try to show the difference bet. the Heb. words by a change of lettering. When printed ' Lord ' the Heb. word is generally ' adon,' master (*Ex.* 23, 17; *Ps.* 114, 7); or ' adonai,' my master (*Ex.* 4, 10; *Isa.* 40, 10); or the Gk. ' kyrios,' master (*Matt.* 1, 20). When printed LORD in the AV, it is the trans. of Jahweh. Where there is no initial capital letter the word simply means a person of exalted status (*Gen.* 45, 8; *Josh.* 13, 3; *Ezra* 8, 25; etc.).

Lord of Hosts. *See* HOSTS.

Lord's Day. The ' Lord ' here is not God, but the Lord Jesus. This is a NT expression (*Rev.* 1, 10) which describes the day when the Christian Church met for worship. It is not the ' Day of the Lord ' (*2 Pet.* 3, 10) which is rather the day of the Second Coming. It is the 1st day of the week —not the Heb. Sabbath; for Jesus rose from the dead on the 1st, not the last, day of the week. This was the day when the Apostles were invaded by the Holy Spirit (*Acts* 2, 1). It early became the day when Christians gathered for the breaking of bread (*Acts* 20, 7) and when they brought the money and goods which were to be distributed as charity (*1 Cor.* 16, 2). Jewish Christians tended to observe both the Sabbath and Sunday, and although Gentile Christians did not specially observe the Sabbath there has existed even to the present day, some confusion bet. the two (*Col.* 2, 16). The observance of the Sabbath, however, was not to be regarded as necessary for salvation (*Gal.* 4, 10). It is perfectly clear that the Lord's Day is not the Jewish Sabbath.

Lord's Prayer. The important thing to remember

about this is that Jesus did not invent it on the spur of the moment when His disciples asked Him to teach them how to pray. It has been called the Lord's Prayer because He gave it to them, but surely the real sanction for the name is that Jesus himself had brought His own personal praying into the compass of these words. These are the 2 forms (*Matt.* 6, 9-13; *Luke* 11, 1-4). The doxology at the end of the Matthew version is a later liturgical addition and is omitted by RV and RSV (' For Thine is the kingdom, etc.').

Lord's Supper. The name was invented by Paul to describe the last meal which Jesus and His disciples had together before Gethsemane and Calvary (*1 Cor.* 11, 20). His account of the events is older than the Gospel account. Within 25 yrs of the death of Jesus, Paul had made the celebration a part of Christian worship (*1 Cor.* 11, 23). He does not say that he had received any information about it from apostles who had been present at it. He states his authority as being derived directly from God. It seems certain, however, that he had been told of what happened. The orig. inspirational part may well have been that Paul was the 1st to realise its significance. It seems clear that Jesus' prime intention was to provide something which would keep the disciples from scattering until the full purpose of His dying and rising had been accomplished (*Luke* 22, 19; *1 Cor.* 11, 25 & 26). It accomplished its purpose so well that from the very beginning it was recognised as the great Christian feast by people who had no knowledge of and no interest in the Jewish passover. Because of excesses, and obvious misunderstandings of the purpose of the feast (which simply took the place of the usual domestic supper) the early Church gave a form and a formality to it, which substituted the token for the actuality, thus preserving and emphasising the inner meaning of it. The Table ceased to be the ordinary dining-room table and became the Lord's Table. The Cup was known still by the Jewish name of the Cup of Blessing (*1 Cor.* 10, 16) It was also called the Cup of the Lord (*1 Cor.* 10, 21; 11, 27).

Lot. Abraham's nephew, son of Haran. He travelled with his uncle and, like him, prospered (*Gen.* 11, 31; 12, 5). Difficulties arose bet. them and Abraham decided that they had better part company, giving Lot the choice of which way he would go. Lot chose the valley of Sodom. But the people there were a bad lot, and though Lot tried to keep separate from them he got himself involved with them, and Abraham had to help him out (*Gen.* 13, 2—14, 16; *2 Pet.* 2, 7). Destruction came upon Sodom, and Lot escaped by the skin of his teeth though his wife did not. Later in life, when drunk, he became guilty of incest. From him were descended the Moabites and Ammonites (*Gen.* 19, 30-38).

Lot's wife. The story of her turning back when Lot was escaping from Sodom, and of her being turned into a pillar of salt is well known. There are great outcrops of rock salt around the Dead Sea, and it is not at all unlikely that one of them, which looked like a woman, may have started the legend.

Lots. Casting lots, usually after prayer, was an accepted way of reaching decisions. This was how Canaan was partitioned among the tribes (*Josh.* 14, 2; 18, 6). In a dispute bet. Saul and the people, lots were cast and fell in Saul's favour (*1 Sam.* 14, 40-45). The vacant place in the apostleship was decided by lot (*Acts* 1, 15-26). After Pentecost such a method was reckoned to be an insult to the Holy Spirit. *See* URIM AND THUMMIM, MAGIC.

Love feast. Trans. of Gk. *agapē* (*2 Pet.* 2, 13), RV and RSV trans. this as 'deceivings,' but this is a different word. In *Jude* (12) AV has 'feasts of charity' and RV 'love feasts.' What happened was that in order to carry out Jesus' wishes that He should be remembered when they sat down to the evening meal, they had a kind of social gathering, at the end of which there was the ceremony of the Lord's Supper (*1 Cor.* 11, 25). Sometimes, however, there was excess of eating and drinking, and the ceremony was in danger of falling into disrepute (*1 Cor.* 11, 17-34). Scandals arose, and various Councils of the early Church suppressed the practice of the agape, though it survives in certain communions.

Lucifer [lū'-cĭ-fẽr]. (*Isa.* 14, 12.) The planet Venus, brightest of all but the sun and the moon. It appears as the morning or the evening star. Owing to a confusion of passages (*Luke* 10, 18 and *Rev.* 12, 7-10 with *Isa.* 14, 12) the name has wrongly been assoc. with Satan since the 3rd cent. AD.

Lucius [lū'-cĭ-ŭs]. Christian of Cyrene who taught in the Church at Antioch (*Acts* 13, 1; *Rom.* 16, 21).

Lucre. In Elizabethan days it did not have a bad sense of money or wealth. That is why it is prefaced by 'filthy.'

Luke. Companion and fellow traveller with Paul, called the beloved physician (*Col.* 4, 14; *Philem.* 24; *2 Tim.* 4, 11). He is not Lucius (qv). He seems to have joined Paul on the 2nd missionary journey and gone with him to Philippi, and on the 3rd journey, to Jerusalem. He stayed in Palestine during the 2 yrs. when Paul was imprisoned at Caesarea, and sailed with Paul for Rome. He was not a Jew (*Col.* 4, 14). He may have been a citizen of Antioch (*Acts* 6, 5; 11, 19-27; etc.). Very ancient tradition credits him with the authorship of the 3rd Gospel and of the Acts of the Apostles which were certainly written by the same hand (*Acts* 1 1).

Luke, Gospel According to St. Many of the most dearly loved portions of the story of our Lord come to us from the pages of this book—the Annunciation, the Visitation, the Shepherds, Jesus in the Temple, Martha and Mary, the Woman who was a sinner, the Good Samaritan, the Rich Fool, the Lost Sheep, the Prodigal Son, the Penitent Thief, the Journey to Emmaus, the Ascension and others. There is a legend that Luke was an artist and he is certainly an artist in choice of incident and in words. Humanity, charity, and wonder at the grace of God characterise the Gospel as they do the Acts of the Apostles, with which the 1st book really makes one continuous story. Plainly from the intention of his introduction, Luke had decided that a new life of Jesus was needed. He had access to many documents on the subject, but they all seemed to lack something. He had therefore given himself the task of searching out the authorities on the life of Jesus; eye-witnesses, people of good memory, and of separating fact from fiction. He does not claim to be inspired. He just felt that something more was needed and that he had the capacity to supply the need. He wanted to get everything in and he wanted to get everything in the proper order—the things which Jesus ' began both to do and teach.' He addresses the whole work, Gospel and Acts, to Theophilus whom he calls ' your Excellency.' *See* THEOPHILUS. It must be remembered that Luke was not writing for the heathen. He was able to take it for granted that much of the information which he was giving was already known to his readers. His purpose was to make sure that they got the story in the right order and without fictitious accretions. The 1st few verses are peculiar to *Luke*, then he follows the pattern of *Mark* (with whose Gospel he was acquainted) up to ch. 6, v. 19. He then leaves the Marcan line (6, 20—8, 3) with an account of the Sermon on the Mount (not the same as Matthew's), the Widow's Son, etc. He then goes back to *Mark*, but inserts material not found in *Mark* (9, 51—18, 14). From there to the end he follows *Mark* fairly closely but with several insertions, and for his account of the Passion he has obviously gone to sources which *Mark* either did not know, or ignored. He is writing for Gentiles, not for Jews. That the Gospel is very accurate is attested by the great accuracy of the *Acts of the Apostles* where allusions can be checked and verified from contemporaneous historical accounts. It is unthinkable that the earlier part of the work (the Gospel) would not receive the same care and attention as the later (*Acts*). See GOSPEL, PARABLES.

Lunatic. Not quite the same as a ' possessed ' person (*see* DEMONIAC). It is poss. that the Gk. means more an epileptic (*Matt.* 4, 24).

Lust. Strong desire of any kind, not limited to sexual urges.

Lute. *See* MUSIC.

Lycaonia [lўc′-ă-ŏ-nĭă]. Dist. of Asia Minor surrounded by Galatia, Cilicia, Cappadocia and Phrygia. Its main cities were Iconium, Derbe and Lystra (*Acts* 13, 51 to 14, 23).

Lycia [lўc′-ĭ-ă]. Rom. province in Asia Minor off

which lies the island of Rhodes (*Acts* 21, 1 & 2; 27, 5 & 6).

Lydda [lỹd'-dà]. Town 11 m. SE of Joppa (*Acts* 9, 33-38).

Lydia [lỹd'-ĭ-á]. **1.** Country on W coast of Asia Minor. Croesus was its last king, being deposed by the Persians c. 546 BC. It is called also Lud. Paul lived in its largest city, Ephesus, for a long time (*Acts* 19, 1 ff.). **2.** Woman of Thyatira who earned her living by selling dyes and dyed cloth. She was Paul's 1st convert after he answered the call to leave Asia for Europe. Paul and Silas lodged with her (*Acts* 16, 14 & 15 & 40).

Lyre. *See* MUSIC.

Lystra [lỹs'-trá]. Rom. colony in Galatia nr. Iconium. Paul visited it 4 times, and was stoned there (*Acts* 14, 6-21).

M

Maacah [mā'-á-cáh]. **1.** Son of Nahor (*Gen.* 22, 24). **2.** Wife of David and mother of Absalom (*2 Sam.* 3, 3). **3.** Father of Achish of Gath (*1 Kings* 2, 39). **4.** Wife of Rehoboam (*2 Chron.* 11, 20). The name occurs several other times. **5.** It is also a small kingdom E of Galilee (*Deut.* 3, 14).

Maareh-Geba [mā'-á-rĕh-gē'-bá]. Lit. ' Meadows of Geba ' (AV *Judg.* 20, 33). But prob. the phrase means ' from the W of Geba.'

Maaseiah [mā'-á-sē'-iáh]. Common name, none bearing it were remarkable. **1.** (*1 Chron.* 15, 18). **2.** (*2 Chron.* 23, 1). **3.** (*2 Chron.* 26, 11). **4.** (*2 Chron.* 28, 7). **5.** (*2 Chron.* 34, 8). **6.** (*Jer.* 29, 21). **7.** (*Jer.* 35, 4). **8.** (*Jer.* 21, 1).

Maccabees [măcc'-á-bēēs]. Family not mentioned in the Canon, who ruled Judea from 166 BC to

37 BC. Called also the Hasmonaeans. Mattathias raised the revolt agst. Antiochus. On his death the revolt was carried on by his sons, the most important of whom was Judas who carried on successful guerrilla warfare, captured Jerusalem and restored the Temple worship. An annual feast was held in celebration (*John* 10, 22). He was succeeded by his youngest brother Jonathan when he was killed in battle in 160 BC. Other sons of Mattathias had all fallen heroically, Eleazar in single combat with an armed elephant. Jonathan had treaty arrangements with the Rom. and the Spartans, but when he was murdered in 143 BC the last brother, Simon, took over, and succeeded in having the independence of Judea acknowledged by the Syrians. He and 2 of his sons were murdered by his son-in-law, Ptolemy, in 135 BC and he was followed by his remaining son, John Hyrcanus, a shrewd politician and gallant soldier. He brought the Edomites into Judea and died after a long reign. That was the beginning of the end, however, for his sons Aristobulus and Jannaeus were weak and wild. Dissension broke out bet. the Sadducees and the Pharisees (both qv). The last of the line were called Aristobulus and Hyrcanus, but their rule was so chaotic that the Romans intervened and nominated Antipater (qv) as governor. He established his own family in the Rom. favour and his son Herod was made king. Herod's wife was Mariamne, a princess of the Hasmonaeans. Their hist. is recorded in the apocryphal *Books of the Maccabees*.

Macedonia [mă′-sĕd-ō′-nĭă]. Country to the N of Greece in the upper corner of the Aegean Sea. Under its kings, Philip (359-336 BC) and Alexander the Great (336-323 BC) it became the

centre of a tremendous, if precarious, empire. *See*
PHILIP and ALEXANDER. It later declined and
became a Rom. province in 142 BC. There is a
ref. to the empire in the OT (*Dan.* 8, 5 & 21). In
Macedonia, Paul first preached Christianity in
Europe (*Acts* 16, 9 to 17, 14). The work was
carried on by Silas and Timothy (*Acts* 17, 14 &
15; 18, 5). Paul returned with his companions
Gaius and Aristarchus, who were Macedonians
(*Acts* 19, 21 & 22; *1 Tim.* 1, 3). The Macedonian
church provided both missionaries and money
(*Acts* 19, 22; 20, 3; *Rom.* 15, 26; *2 Cor.* 8, 1-5;
Philip 4, 15).

Machpelah [măch-pē'-lăh]. Place nr. Mamre where
Abraham bought ground as a burial place (*Gen.*
23, 9; 25, 9). Isaac, Rebekah, Leah and Jacob
as well as Abraham and Sarah were buried there
(*Gen.* 49, 29-33); 50, 12 & 13).

Madmen [mad'-men]. Town in Moab (*Jer.* 48, 2).

Madmenah [măd-měn'-äh]. Town N of Jerusalem
(*Isa.* 10, 31).

Madness. *See* DISEASES, MEDICINE.

Magadan [măg'-ă-dăn]. W shore of Galilee. Another name is Dalmanutha (*Mark* 8, 10) which may
be a scribe's error. Called Magdala, see below
(AV *Matt.* 15, 39).

Magdala [măg'-dă-lă]. Town in Magadan (above).
It was nr. Tiberias and Hammath. It should be
trans. Magadan (*Matt.* 15, 39).

Magdalene [măg'-dă-lēne]. A native of Magdala,
usually applied to one of the Maries. *See* MARY.

Magi [mā'-gī]. (The g pronounced soft, as j.) The
word in the singular, ‘ magus ’ is trans. as sor-
cerer (*Acts* 13, 8). In the plural it means the
‘ Wise Men ’ (*Matt.* 2). The Magi were a sacred
caste of the Medeans. Mainly they are identified
with astrology, the interpretation of dreams

(oneiromancy) and plain magic. (*See* STAR OF THE MAGI.)

Magic. This includes divination and sorcery, all of which were designed to obtain from supernatural, or superhuman beings, information upon the destiny of individuals and nations and causes. Naturally those who professed to these powers were reckoned to be in special accord with God. Orig. the priest was the soothsayer; he made sacrifice to the god, and from the god received information which he passed on to the people. In Egypt and Babylon there were professional soothsayers (*Gen.* 41, 8; *Ex.* 7, 11). They were even found in Israel (*Mic.* 3, 5-11). The use of Urim and Thummim (qv) had divine sanction (*Ex.* 28, 30; *Lev.* 8, 8) while divination by such as the Witch of Endor had not (*1 Sam.* 28, 7). Later, of course, as the true faith developed, necromancy of all kinds was forbidden in Israel. Although in the early days it was acknowledged that there could be interpretation of dreams and the like, early legislation made witchcraft punishable by death (*Ex.* 22, 18). When Baal worship began to grow with the advance of the Assyrian empire, witchcraft was revived in Israel (*Isa.* 2, 6; *Jer.* 10, 2) but the Josiah reformation put an end to it, including the use of teraphim. *See* IMAGES. (*2 Kings* 23, 24; *Deut.* 18, 10-12.) During the Christian era and immediately before it the occult had become popular as the Mystery Religions turned towards Egypt for their inspiration. Simon Magus and Elymas were Jews who practised magic (*Acts* 8, 9; 13, 8). The methods used generally in divination (foretelling the future) were: the casting of lots (*Prov.* 16, 33): a common form was the use of Urim and Thummim (qv) which was prob. done whenever the

phrase ' Enquire of God ' is found (*Judg.* 1, 1;
20, 27; *2 Sam.* 2, 1; 5, 19 & 23). It was also
used to discover wrong-doers (*Josh.* 7, 14; *1
Sam.* 14, 41 & 42). The scapegoat was chosen
by lot (*Lev.* 16, 8). The land was distributed by
lot (*Num.* 26, 55; etc.). Men were selected by
lot (*Judg.* 20, 9; *1 Sam.* 10, 20; *1 Chron.* 24, 5).
Apart from the use of Urim and Thummim, lots
might be cast by arrows (*Ezek.* 21, 21), or simply
by pieces of stick (*Hos.* 4, 12). Revelation could
come also by dreams (*Gen.* 40, 5; etc.). But these
could be misleading (*Deut.* 13, 1-5). The prophets experience visions (*Isa.* 1, 1; *Amos* 1, 1;
Mic. 1, 1). False prophets had false visions (*Isa.*
28, 7; etc.). The movements of animals and the
use of words could be accounted omens; these
were interpreted by augurs or enchanters (*Deut.*
18, 10). They might watch the behaviour of
water (*Gen.* 44, 5); or of the clouds (*Isa.* 2, 6);
or of the stars (*Judg.* 5, 20; *Job* 38, 33). Common
in Babylon was augury by the inspection of the in-
testines of animals, esp. the liver (*Ezek.* 21, 21).
The Jews in Jesus' day demanded signs (qv).
There were people, usually women, credited with
being possessed by supernatural spirits (*Lev.* 20,
27). The dead could be called up (*1 Sam.* 28, 11;
Isa. 8, 19). To combat these baleful influences
and persons there could be exorcism (*Acts* 19, 13;
Matt. 12, 27). Amulets and charms over which
spells had been spoken were commonly worn
(*Gen.* 35, 4; *Hos.* 2, 13; *Judg.* 8, 21 & 26). Later
many Jews used phylacteries (qv). Mandrakes
(qv) were popular as love philtres (*Gen.* 30, 14;
S. of S. 7, 13). Certain people were reckoned
capable of pronouncing curses and blessings
(*Num.* 22, 6; *Judg.* 5, 23). There was also the
forerunner of the mediaeval trial by ordeal (*Num.*

5, 12-31). There was also the practice of making an image of a person hated and torturing and destroying it, in the belief that the same harm would be inflicted on the person. (*1 Sam.* 6, 5).

Magistrate. Eng. word used to trans. several Gk. and Heb. words. It can mean judge, or ruler (*Ezra* 7, 25); or ' authority ' (*Judg.* 18, 7). In the NT it means more the recognised civil authority of the Rom. empire, poss. the praetors (*Luke* 12, 11 & 58; *Acts* 16, 20-38; *Titus* 3, 1).

Magnifical. Magnificent (*1 Chron.* 22, 5).

Magnificat. Name given to Mary's hymn of praise (*Luke* 1. 46-55). It is ascribed both to Mary and to Elizabeth but is certainly later than both. It is to all intents and purposes the first Christian hymn or the last of the Psalms.

Magog [mā´-gŏg]. People desc. from Japheth (*Gen.* 10, 2). They may have been the Scythians. Ezekiel made them typical of all heathendom in the final struggle bet. the Kingdom of God and the Kingdoms of the world (*Ezek.* 38, 2 & 15; *Rev.* 20, 8 & 9). *See* GOG.

Magor-Missabib [mā´-gŏr-mĭss´-ă-bĭb]. Name given (by way of a pun) to Pashhur, who ill-treated Jeremiah (*Jer.* 20, 3).

Magus. *See* ELYMAS, MAGIC.

Mahalath [mā´-hă-lăth]. **1.** Wife of Esau (Basemath] (*Gen.* 28, 9). **2.** Wife of Rehoboam (*2 Chron.* 11, 18). **3.** Musical term (*Ps.* 53 and 88 titles).

Mahanaim [mā´-hă-nă´-ĭin]. Place on the boundary of Gad and Manasseh where Jacob had seen the angels (*Josh.* 13, 26 & 30; *Gen.* 32, 2).

Maher-Shalal-Hash-Baz [mā´-hĕr-shăl´-ăl-hăsh´-băz]. Lit. ' spoil speeds, prey hastes.' A name written by Isaiah on a tablet a year before the birth of his 2nd son; thus showing God's intention to bring down the Assyrians on Israel's enemies Damascus and Samaria (*Isa.* 8, 1-4).

Mahlon [măh′-lŏn]. First husband of Ruth (1, 2; 4, 10).

Mahol [mă′-hŏl]. Father of 3 wise men (*1 Kings* 4, 31). The name means also an instrument of music (*Ps.* 149, 3, trans. ' dance ' AV). It may therefore be merely ' the sons of music.'

Mail. *See* ARMOUR.

Make. In AV often has meaning ' do ' (*Judg.* 18, 3), It may also mean ' pretend to be ' (*John* 19, 7; *Josh.* 8, 15; *2 Sam.* 13, 5). In *Ezekiel* (17, 17) it means ' assist.'

Makkedah [măk-kĕd′-ăh]. Canaanite city where the 5 kings, pursued by Joshua, took refuge (*Josh.* 10, 10 & 16 ff.).

Malachi [măl′-ă-kī]. The name means ' My Messenger,' and could be merely a title. The date is post exilic (c. 433-397 BC), the time of Nehemiah. After the first excitements of return and rebuilding, the people grew careless and lax (*Neh.* 13, 4-31). Malachi defines and condemns their faults (*Mal.* 1, 2 & 6 & 7; 2, 17; 3, 7 & 8 & 13). He denounces them on their religious, moral, social and material attitudes. But he looks forward to the day of revival (*Mal.* 3, 10 & 16-18).

Malachi, Book of. It is worth noting that this, the last book of the OT ends with a curse. The last book of the NT ends with abundant grace. The book divides naturally into 2 portions: (1) Prophecies on people and church; (2) Prophecies concerning the Messiah and the Kingdom of God. Warnings and visions are given (1, 1-3, 12), and are followed (chs. 7 & 8) by observations on fasts and feasts. He then turns to the restoration of Judah and Israel and goes on to forecast the coming of the Messiah and the ultimate triumph. Malachi made considerable use of what has been called the Socratic method of teaching —by question and answer. The language is simple and plain with occasional flights into poetry (1, 11; 3, 1 ff.; 3, 10 & 16; 4, 2).

Malcam [măl'-căm], **Malcham**, AV. A chief of the Benjamites (*1 Chron.* 8, 9). Also an error poss. for Moloch, who was certainly the national deity of the Ammonites (*Zeph.* 1, 5).

Malchi-Shua [măl'-chĭ'shū'-ǎ]. Son of Saul slain at Gilboa (*1 Sam.* 31, 2).

Malchus [măl'-chŭs]. Servant of the High Priest, whose ear Peter wounded at the arrest of Jesus. The incident is mentioned in all the Gospels, but only John gives the name, and only Luke mentions the healing (*Matt.* 26, 51; *Mark* 14, 47; *Luke* 22, 50; *John* 18, 10).

Malice. Used in Scripture the meaning is much wider than the mod. meaning, and embraces evil and wickedness of most sorts.

Mallows. This is an error for ' salt-wort ' as in RV (*Job* 30, 4).

Mammon. It has been suggested that this was a Phoenician deity, and it may be so; but it is also the Phoenician word for ' gain.' It does not appear in OT Heb., but seems to have been ' lifted ' into NT Gk. (*Matt.* 6, 24; *Luke* 16, 9 & 11 & 13).

Mamre [măm'-rě]. A dist. of Hebron where Abraham lived on several occasions (*Gen.* 13, 18; 14, 13; 18, 1; 23, 19; 35, 27).

Man. In Scripture the importance of man stems from the fact that he is made in the image of God. He therefore is created to have dominion over all other creatures, and is able to have communion with God Himself (*Gen.* 1-2). They believed man to have been created wholly, com-

pletely and perfectly as a sentient, conscientious,
affectionate creature. At his creation there was
no room for improvement. The whole hist. of
the OT is the account of how man has tried to
win back to that blessed orig. state. The trouble
is that the spirit of God has departed from sinful
man, and with its departure has gone right judgment, wisdom, understanding, skill, ability and
courage which are only perfectly present when
the Spirit of God is in control (*Prov.* 20, 27; etc.).
The NT takes a long step forward with the idea
of sonship (*Luke* 3, 38; *1 Cor.* 11, 7). It was
Jesus who emphasised the everlasting worth of
the individual human soul, and the integrity of
the human personality (*Matt.* 10, 30; 16, 26;
Luke 10, 20). To Him all humankind had God
as Father, but only those who acknowledged this
and who lived accordingly had the right to call
themselves His children (*Matt.* 5, 9 & 45). Paul
took this idea further with his doctrine of adoption by faith. The writer of the *Hebrews* goes
back to God's first intention and sees Jesus as the
only one in whom God's intention was completely
fulfilled (*Heb.* 2). In the Creation story the breath
of God upon the dust of the earth creates the
living human soul; that soul ceases at death when
the body goes back to the dust (*Eccl.* 12, 7). To
the Jews the soul was not a separate manifestation
of life in temporary residence in the body, de-
parting from it to exist elsewhere when the body
dies. It is simply matter animated by God. That
is why the resurrection of the body became part
of the faith. Paul called the risen body a spiritual
body (*1 Cor.* 15, 44) but there is nothing odd in
that. All bodies are spiritual, in that they are
matter into which the breath (spirit) of God has
blown.

Man of sin. (*2 Thes.* 2, 3-10.) Attempts have been made to identify this with the Rom. emperor, or with the Rom. power, or with the Jews who persecuted the early Church. But it is simplest to regard it as another name for the Antichrist (qv).

Manasseh [măn-ăss'-ĕh]. Also Manasses in NT AV. **1.** Elder son of Joseph, born in Egypt of an Egyptian mother (*Gen.* 41, 50 & 51). With his brother Ephraim he was blessed by Jacob, but in a manner which showed that Ephraim would excel (*Gen.* 48, 8-21). **2.** The tribe desc. from Manasseh above. There were 7 families, one being that of his son Machir and the remaining stemming from his grandson Gilead (*Gen.* 50, 23; *Num.* 26, 28-34). One half of the tribe asked for land E of Jordan at the settlement (*Num.* 32, 33-42). Their chosen territory included part of Gilead and all Bashan (*Deut.* 3, 13-15), a rich, fertile upland. The other half settled in central Palestine bet. Ephraim, Asher and Issachar. Gideon was of the tribe (*Judg.* 6, 15). They were good soldiers loyal to David (*1 Chron.* 12, 19 & 20 & 31). **3.** Modification of the name Moses (*Judg.* 18, 30 AV). **4.** Son of King Hezekiah and his successor c. 693 BC. He ruined his good father's reforms, restored idol worship and Baal worship. He murdered his opponents, paid tribute to Assyria, was taken to Babylon, then released and restored to his throne. There he reformed his ways and restored Jehovah worship. He died after a reign of 55 yrs. (*2 Kings* 21, 1-18).

Mandrake. (*Gen.* 30, 14-16; *S. of S.* 7, 13.) ' Love apple ' RV marg. *Mandragora officinarum.* A long-rooted plant around which some superstition had gathered. Decoctions of it were used as aphrodisiacs.

Maneh [măn'-ĕh]. *See* WEIGHTS AND MEASURES.

Manger. The Eng. word is used to trans. several
Gk. and Heb. words: a place where cattle are
fattened (*Job* 39, 9); a stall (*Prov.* 14, 4); the
crib for the food (*Isa.* 1, 3). It also means a
number of animals as one would speak of a team
of horses (*2 Chron.* 32, 28). In the nativity story
(*Luke* 2, 7), if ' inn ' really means ' guest house,'
Mary and Joseph may have occupied the part
reserved for the animals but under the same roof.

Manna. Food of Israel in the wilderness (*Ex.* 16, 15).
There is no certainty about exactly what it was.
The exclamation ' It is manna ' (*Ex.* 16, 15 AV)
is better ' man hu? What is it? ' The name, then
would be simply, ' the what's it.' It resembled
the fruit (not seed) of the coriander (*Ex.* 16, 31).
It could be ground, stewed, or baked (*Ex.* 16, 23;
Num. 11, 8). Some think it was the juice of
certain trees, dried out. Others that it was a
lichen. Another theory is that it was the secre-
tion of certain insects, and another that it was
mushrooms. Whatever it was, there was a great
deal of it. The people regarded its appearance
as miraculous.

Manoah [mă-nō′-ăh]. Danite, father of Samson
(*Judg.* 13, 1-25).

Mansion. Occurs only once (*John* 14, 2). RV marg.
had ' abiding places '; and RSV has ' rooms.'

Mantle. *See* DRESS.

Maon, Maonites [mă′-ŏn]. Place and people S of
the Dead Sea. They oppressed Israel, but were
subdued by the Simeonites and later by Uzziah.
In one passage they are called Meunim (Mehunims
AV) and in another, wrongly, Ammonites (*Judg.*
10, 12; *1 Chron.* 4, 41; *2 Chron.* 26, 8).

Mara [mă′-ră]. Lit. ' Sad in spirit '; name chosen
by Naomi for herself (*Ruth* 1, 20).

Marah [mā′-răh]. Fountain or spring of bitter

water 3 days' journey from the Red Sea towards Sinai (*Ex.* 15, 23).

Maranatha [mă'-ră-nă'-thă]. *See* ANATHEMA.

Mareshah [mă-rē'-shăh]. Important city in the lowland of Judah (*Josh.* 15, 44). Fortified by Rehoboam (*2 Chron.* 11, 8). Scene of battle bet. Asa and Zerah (*2 Chron.* 14, 9 & 10).

Mark John. Disciple of Peter and author of the Gospel which bears the name. He was born and brought up in Jerusalem where his mother, a widow, had a house which may well have been the house of the Upper Room. That house became a centre of Christianity later (*Acts* 12, 12). It seems fairly certain that Mark was the lad who followed the disciples and Jesus to Gethsemane and was wounded making his escape (*Mark* 14, 52). He was therefore a Christian Jew and one of the first 'ministers' of the Church (*Acts* 12, 25). Mark was related to Barnabas, either cousin or nephew, and Barnabas remained his loyal friend even when Paul turned away from him (*Acts* 13, 13; 15, 37-39; *Col.* 4, 10). That would be about the year AD 49, but a reconciliation had taken place before Paul wrote the Colossians some 10 or 12 yrs. later. There are found in the Gospel some traces of Pauline thought (*Mark* 1, 14; 5, 23; 7, 5; 7, 22 & 23; 10, 26). But the real connection of Mark is not with Paul and Barnabas, but with Peter. The early Fathers refer to him as the interpreter of Peter, his disciple, his long-time follower. In his Epistle Peter refs. to Mark as 'my son' (*1 Pet.* 5, 13). It appears as if Mark was, in fact, Peter's private secretary. This was at Rome. Mark may have had fluent Lat. which Peter had not. But the main work done in Rome was the writing of the Gospel, which is obviously designed for

Gentile reading. He takes little time linking Jesus to the historic past of the Jews, and he is at pains to explain Jewish allusions (*Mark* 2, 26; 7, 2; 14, 12; 15, 42). Where he uses an Aramaic word, he gives the Gk. equivalent (*Mark* 5, 41; 7, 11; 14, 36; 15, 22 & 34). Sometimes he uses the straight Latin word (*Mark* 12, 14; 15, 39 & 44 & 45; 12, 42; 7, 4). It is, in fact, highly prob. that Mark, the dearly loved of Peter, wrote the Gospel more or less to the dictation of the older man.

Mark, Gospel According to St. As indicated in the article on the author, this book was written by John Mark in Rome, while Mark was with Peter. If it be true as some believe, that Mark was obliged to write Peter's testimony because Peter was dead and could not make that testimony himself, the date of the Gospel must be shortly after AD 64. If Mark wrote the Gospel to the dictation of Peter, as others believe, the motive must have been Peter's fear of his own death leaving no eye-witness. Whatever may be true, the date must fall within the 10 yrs. AD 60-70. In the beginning, with eye-witnesses present, and with a persuasion that the end of the age was near, there was felt to be little need for a written record of the life and words of the Lord. Mark's claim to a special place is that it is the objective eye-witness account of a man who played a part of the first importance in the events recorded. Its relation to the other Gospels is dealt with in the article on the Gospels (qv). The influence of Peter is clear in the Gospel from the beginning to ch. 14, 72, with the exception of the first 14 vv. of ch. 1, and the personal interpolation (14, 51 & 52). As far as the first 13 vv. of the Gospel are concerned it must be remembered that

Peter's brother, Andrew, was the first disciple. He had been there when Jesus was only thinking out His plan and policy. But where did Mark get the material of chs. 15 and 16? There was Simon the Cyrenian, and there were the women (15, 29-40). He may also have known Bartimaeus, for Mark's account of the miracle is the only example of the story told from the point of view of the man it happened to (10, 46-52). The fact is that this Gospel is very largely autobiographical, and the man who is telling the story is Peter (1, 36; 3, 16; 8, 29 & 32, 9, 5; 10, 28; 11, 21; 14, 29 & 37 & 54; 16, 7). Mark emphasises the great failures of Peter (8, 32; 14, 54). The style is simple and straightforward. The plain narrative is reminiscent of the ' J ' documents of the OT. He is not gathering together material from many sources and collating it. This is something that could have been, and prob. was, told as one, by Peter. Maybe he did not appreciate all that Jesus had said until he absorbed some of Paul's ideas about things, but he still records them. He begins with John the Baptist (1, 1-13). He goes on, without any account of the Nativity or the early yrs., to the beginning of Jesus' ministry; the ministry of Power (1, 14—3, 12). With the good news of Jesus the Messiah (3, 12—8, 30). There is the account of the setting up of the intimate group of 12 and their gradual appreciation of Jesus' purpose and person, culminating in the great confession. There are the missionary journeys of Jesus and the 12 to Tyre, Decapolis, Bethsaida, Caesarea, Philippi, Peraea and Jericho (7, 24—10, 52). Then he moves to a detailed account of the week of the passion. The Sunday of Holy Week (10, 46—11, 11). The Monday (11, 12-19). The Tuesday (11, 20—13, 37). The Wednesday

(14, 1-11). The Thursday (14, 12-72). Jesus is arrested, and there is the incident of the young man, prob. Mark himself. This includes Peter's denial. Then follows the Friday (Good Friday) (15, 1-47). This tells of the crucifixion and the burial. Then come the events of Easter Eve and Easter (15, 47—16, 6). It is prob. that the genuine end of the Gospel was lost. Ancient authorities end the Gospel at various points: at 16, 8 ' they were afraid '; at 16, 20; and at 16, 8 with a few verses stating merely that Jesus met them again and sent them out. It does appear as if something was lost after 16, 8 and that several attempts were later made to fill the gap, none of which is genuine. The Gospel ends by the hand of Mark at that point. But it is not in character with either Mark or Peter to end on the words, ' they were afraid.' What the missing portion contained can only be subject for speculation.

Market, Marketplace. ' Market ' can be interchangeable for ' merchandise ' (*Ezek.* 27, 13 & 17). RV trans. (*Ezek.* 27, 15) as ' mart.' It becomes marketplace in NT. There must be a distinction bet. Judaea and Greece here, however. When the word is ref. to Jerusalem it is the E bazaar (*Matt.* 11, 16; *Mark* 7, 4). Where the ref. is to a Gk. town it means more the public square, or civic centre (*Acts* 16, 19; 17, 17).

Marks. 1. Mark of Cain (*Gen.* 4, 15). Many of the *Genesis* incidents are designed to show the origin of some prevailing practice. There was in fact nobody to see any mark that Cain might have. According to *Genesis* there were not enough people in the world to make it matter. There may have been, later, some form of branding of a murderer. **2.** The mark of the prophet (*I Kings* 20, 35-42). This incident of the prophet being

recognised only when he unveiled himself seems
to indicate some recognisable mark, poss. incisions
on the face. This is confirmed in *Zechariah* (13,
4-6). 3. There seems, too, to have been a custom,
later forbidden as being heathen, of making marks
with a knife upon the bodies of the dead, and even
to cut oneself after the death of an intimate (*Lev.*
19, 28; *Deut.* 14, 1). 4. In the early days marks
appear to have been cut on the forehead to denote
that one was a worshipper of Jehovah. These
were later replaced by the phylacteries (qv) (*Ex.*
13, 9 & 16; *Deut.* 6, 8). 5. Paul also uses the word
in the sense of brands or stigmata (*Gal.* 6, 17). He
is referring to the marks that suffering for the
faith have made on his body (*2 Cor.* 11, 23 ff.).

Marriage. A divinely ordered state necessary for
the continuation of the human race (*Gen.* 1, 27
& 28). It is not good for a man to be alone (*Gen.*
2, 18). In NT times it was recognised that for
duty's sake a man might refrain from marriage
(*Matt.* 19, 21; *1 Cor.* 7, 8 & 26), but to do so for
merely ascetic reasons was wrong (*1 Tim.* 4, 3).
Monogamy is the ideal (*Gen.* 2, 18-24; *Matt.* 19,
5; *1 Cor.* 6, 16). And is permanent (*Matt.* 19, 6).
Marriage is dissolved by death (*Rom.* 7, 2 & 3).
But it may be dissolved for adultery and for that
alone (*Matt.* 19, 3-9). Paul included wilful desertion as ground for divorce but it is hardly likely
that this was not accompanied by adultery (*1 Cor.*
7, 15). Polygamy was, however, practised from
early days among the Hebrews (*Gen.* 4, 19). Moses
discouraged polygamy but did not forbid it. He
established the degrees within which marriage was
forbidden and established protections for 'inferior' wives (*Lev.* 18; *Ex.* 21, 2-11; *Deut.* 21,
10-17). When a man died childless his brother
took the widow (*Deut.* 25, 5). This was recom-

mended but was not compulsory. It was the
business of the father to select a wife for his son
(*Gen.* 21, 21; 38, 6). The son might ask his father's
permission to marry a particular woman, but his
father made the arrangements (*Gen.* 34, 4 & 8).
Parents of a girl might take the initiative and seek
for a suitable husband for her (*Ex.* 2, 21; *Josh.*
15, 17; *Ruth* 3, 1 & 2). Presents were exchanged
(*Gen.* 24, 22; 29, 18 & 27; *1 Sam.* 18, 25). The
' friend of the bridegroom ' was the one who acted
as intermediary bet. the ' intendeds ' bet. the
betrothal and the marriage, when they were not
allowed to see one another (*John* 3, 29). There
was no religious ceremony, but prob. an oath of
fidelity (*Ezek.* 16, 8; *Mal.* 2, 14). Later there was
a written contract. The bride, for the ceremony,
bathed, put on white robes and such jewellery as
she possessed, covered herself with a veil and put
a wreath on her head. Of prime importance was
the bridal girdle (*Jer.* 2, 32). The groom also wore
his brightest and best, and was garlanded. In a
procession of friends and relatives he went to fetch
his bride from her home (*Judg.* 14, 11). The parents handed over the veiled bride, and gave their
blessing (*Gen.* 24, 59; *Ruth* 4, 11). She was then
led back to the groom's house for the feast (*Ps.*
45, 15). If the distance was too great the feast
was held at the bride's house (*Gen.* 29, 22). After
the feast the bride was escorted to the bedroom
by her parents, and the groom by his parents and
friends (*Judg.* 14, 11). The next day the celebrations began again and might go on for days or
even weeks (*Gen.* 29, 27; *Judg.* 14, 12). The
relationship bet. God and His people is often ref.
to in terms of marriage and betrothal (*Isa.* 62, 4;
Hos. 2, 19; *Ps.* 73, 27; *Matt.* 9, 15; *2 Cor.* 11, 2
Rev. 19, 7; *Eph.* 5, 23-32; etc.).

Mars Hill. *See* AREOPAGUS.

Mart. *See* MARKET.

Martha. Sister of Mary and Lazarus of Bethany
(*Luke* 10, 38-42; *John* 11, 1; 12, 1). The contrast
in character bet. her and her sister is classic. It
is quite poss. of course, that the rivalry bet. the
sisters stemmed from their actual physical love
for Jesus, though neither they nor He ever made
mention of it (*John* 11, 1 & 2; 21-32; *Luke* 10,
38-42). Because of certain allusions (*Luke* 10, 38;
Matt. 26, 6; *Mark* 14, 3; *John* 12, 1-3) it has been
suggested that Martha was wife or widow of
Simon the leper. But there is no real evidence.
The relation of the sisters seems, psychologically,
to have been the relationship of 2 spinsters.

Mary. Gk. form of Heb. Miriam. **1.** Mary the
mother of James and Joses was one of the women
who followed Jesus from Galilee and were
witnesses of the crucifixion (*Matt.* 27, 56). She
was almost certainly the wife of Clopas (*John* 19,
25). It is not likely that she was, in fact, the sister
of Mary the mother of the Lord, for the passage
(*John* 19, 25) is ambiguous. The punctuation
should be, as in RSV, ' standing by the cross of
Jesus were His mother, His mother's sister, Mary
the wife of Clopas, and Mary Magdalene.' In
other words, 4 women. **2.** Mary, the sister of
Martha. She sits at Jesus' feet while her sister
gets on with the housework (*Luke* 10, 38-42). She
greets Him worshipfully when He comes in answer
to the call about Lazarus (*John* 11, 28-32). She
anoints His feet at Bethany (*Matt.* 26, 7-13; *Mark*
14, 3-9; *John* 12, 1-8). For her feelings towards
Jesus *see* MARTHA, above. The anointing would
be quite in character with this. **3.** Mary Magdalene, or Mary of Magdala. The name Magdala
is not mentioned in the NT. The ref. (*Matt.* 15,

39) should be Magadan. She was healed by Jesus
and thereafter would not leave the company (*Luke*
8, 2; cf. *Matt.* 12, 45; *Mark* 5, 9; 16, 9). Her
name has been given to the reformed ' fallen
woman,' but there is no Gospel evidence that she
was ever such. She was present at the crucifixion
(*Matt.* 27, 55) and followed the funeral procession
(*Mark* 15, 47). On the 3rd day she visited the
sepulchre and found it empty (*John* 20, 1 ff.). She
had the first conversation with the risen Jesus,
though it is of the utmost significance to note that
she did not recognise Him until He spoke. There
is no evidence that she was Mary the sister of
Lazarus. 4. Mary, the mother of the Lord. There
is not much mention of Mary in the NT; only
3 direct refs. in the Gospels during Jesus' ministry
(*Mark* 3, 31-35; *John* 2, 1-11 ; 19, 25 ff.). There are
2 indirect refs. (*Mark* 6, 3; *Luke* 11, 27). There is
only one ref. outside the Gospels (*Acts* 1, 14). Much
controversy has raged round this woman and her
virginity at the time of Jesus' conception. The
only evidence for or agst. is contained in Scripture
and in experience. Matthew and Luke ref. to her
condition as a virgin, Mark and John do not.
Paul takes no account of it, nor does Peter, if
Mark's Gospel is really the reminiscences of Peter.
The 2 genealogies of Jesus (*Matt.* 1, 16; *Luke* 3,
23) are the family tree of Joseph, not of Mary.
The belief in the virgin birth of our Lord does not
appear till the end of the 1st cent. AD. *See* VIRGIN.
After the birth of Jesus she had several other
children. *See* BRETHREN OF THE LORD. Mary
performed the proper offices of a mother; reared
her children at Nazareth, and was affronted at
Jesus' public conduct as He began His ministry
(*Mark* 3, 21). Jesus during His ministry, and even
on the cross, did not call her ' mother ' (*Matt.* 12,

49; *John* 19, 26 & 27). After Jesus' death she became a member of the Church (*Acts* 1, 14).
5. Mary the mother of John Mark (*Acts* 12, 12).
6. Mary, a friend of Paul (*Rom.* 16, 6).

Maschil [măs′-chīl]. Word appearing in the titles of several Psalms. It means that it is either a teaching or a meditative Psalm.

Mason *See* ARTS AND CRAFTS.

Massah and Meribah [mĕr′-ĭb-ăh]. (*Ex.* 17, 1-7.) The scene of the miraculous gift of water to the thirsty Israelites in the wilderness. There is some confusion bet. this ref. and the other (*Num.* 20, 1-13) for the one implies that this was about a year after the Exodus and the other that it was 37 yrs. after; one places the incident near Horeb and the other at Kadesh.

Master. Has the sense of schoolmaster; teacher.

Mastic. A vegetable gum used as dentifrice, or flavouring (*Gen.* 37, 25).

Matrites. Sept of Benjamin to which Saul belonged (*1 Sam.* 10, 21).

Mattanaiah [măt′-tăn-ī′-ah]. There are several of the name, mostly Levites or returned exiles. It was the orig. name of King Zedekiah (*2 Kings* 24, 17).

Mattatha(h) [măt′-tă-thă]. Son of Nathan; grandson of David (*Luke* 3, 31).

Matthew. The apostle appears under 2 names: Matthew in the Gospel of the name, and Levi in *Mark*. He was the son of Alphaeus and was a publican (qv). His place of business was on the road from Damascus to the sea, near Capernaum, where he collected customs dues for Herod. Jesus, passing by, invited Matthew to become His disciple (*Matt.* 9, 9; *Mark* 2, 14; *Luke* 5, 27). Matthew agreed and invited the others to come to his house for a meal. Jesus' acceptance of the

invitation did not add to His popularity with the
Scribes and Pharisees. In the lists of the Twelve
(*Matt.* 10, 3; *Mark* 3, 18; *Luke* 6, 15; *Acts* 1, 13)
he appears always as Matthew, not Levi. This
seems to indicate that Matthew was a surname.
Nothing is known about his life and works in
apostolic times but the trad. is that he preached
to the Jews. If he was the author of the Gospel
of *Matthew*, this would be very much in character.

Matthew, Gospel According to St. It would be as
well, before reading this article to read the article
on the Gospels. A good deal of material which is
common to Matthew, Mark and Luke has been
brought together there so that it would not have
to be included in the individual articles. The trad.
is old that Matthew, the apostle, is the author of
this Gospel—as old as the time of Irenaeus. It is
by no means certain, however, that this is so. The
Gospel certainly does not read like the work of a
man who is able to say ' I was there: this I saw
with my own eyes, and this I heard with my own
ears.' Almost everything that could be regarded
as ' eye witness reportage ' is found also in Mark,
and the Gospel according to Mark was before
the author of the Gospel according to Matthew
as he wrote. One would have imagined that had
Matthew been the Apostle he would have managed
to remember something or other which Peter, who
is really responsible for Mark, had forgotten. But
there is nothing of this sort. But it can be argued
that if somebody else wrote this Gospel and
wanted it to have the dignity of Apostolic authorship, he would surely have chosen to attribute it
to someone more prominent than Matthew—
James for example. The usually accepted explanation is that Matthew was responsible for a collec-

tion of recollections of the words of Jesus, which
was called the Logia, and which were written
in Hebrew. Mod. scholars call this document
(which was long ago lost) ' Q.' What Q contained
can only be guessed at, the clues being words and
passages found in Mark and Matthew. From
these it is supposed that Q contained the account
of Jesus' call and temptation, and a number of
His discourses, with very sketchy narratives to
emphasise special points (*Matt.* 11, 2-6). It is very
possible that Matthew was the author of these
Logia. He was a clerical worker—the only one
of the Twelve, and if any of them was likely to
write anything down, he was the one. If the
Gospel were not written by Matthew it certainly
does contain more of Q than the other Gospels
do. In fact it is possible that it contains most of
Q, with narrative additions mostly taken from
Mark. Therefore if Matthew is the author of Q,
he is well entitled to have his name attached to the
Gospel. The actual author is more a compiler.
The date is uncertain, being placed by scholars
anywhere bet. AD 65 and 100. Some claim that
it was written in Rome, others that it was written
in Palestine or Syria. There is no certainty; but
it is the work of a Christian Jew, who may as well
now be called ' Matthew.' The Gospel was written
for Jews. If it was written before AD 70, doom
was hanging over Jerusalem. If it was written
after that date, Jerusalem had already fallen and
the Dispersion of the Jews had begun. Matthew's
purpose is to bid his people hold firm and stand
fast in the faith. The Messiah is not coming, the
Messiah has come and will come again, but not
to redeem Israel—that chance has now been lost
forever. He will come to redeem those who have
accepted Him as Saviour and Lord. Jesus is the

Messiah, the Son of David, the fulfilment of all
prophecy. The Israel of God is no longer the
nation, but the Church. The Law is not the old
Law but the new. When Mark and Luke were
writing their Gospels they saw no value in insisting
upon the Palestinian and Jewish setting of Jesus'
life, work and teaching. The great value of
Matthew is that we see and appreciate the setting,
and we realise not only the tremendous opportunity which Jesus had within that setting, but
also the appalling danger of it. Mark presents a
vivid portrait of Jesus, but it is a portrait without
a background. Matthew supplies the background;
and not only that, he gives us far more fully than
the others the essential ethical teaching of the Lord.
One eminent scholar says: ' We may criticise
Matthew in more ways than one, but of all the
Gospels it is prob. his which we could least easily
spare.' As we have said, this Book is a compilation, the 2 main sources being Q and the Gospel
of Mark. He accepts Mark as having the facts
right, Peter being responsible for that (*see* MARK,
GOSPEL OF). He follows pretty generally the order
of events as Mark tells them, but he does not copy
Mark. He adapts and he paraphrases and edits,
not always for the better. He and Mark are different types: where Mark is rugged, Matthew is
smooth; and unlike Mark, Matthew is blind
to the importance of detail for a vivid story.
Matthew is also keen to explain things so that
there shall be no misunderstanding. Thus Mark's
account of what Jesus said is prob. more accurate
verbally than Matthew's, but Matthew's, even if
it includes a lot of his own words for explanatory
purposes, is more easily understood. It is harder
to explain his use of Q, since the exact nature and
content of Q is not known. But whereas in Luke

the explicit teaching of Jesus appears in little
patches all through the Gospel, Matthew has
gathered them together and gives them single
great spaces. For example the Sermon on the
Mount as it appears in Matthew may not be one
sermon, but many, preached in many places.
Matthew's arrangement is none the worse of that,
however. This device does contain a danger,
though. Matthew should not be regarded as
correct in time and order, since by bringing many
of Jesus' sayings together and writing them as one
discourse, he may be making Jesus say early in
His ministry, something which He did not say
till late in His ministry. For time and place, better
to follow Mark's order. Apart from Mark and
Q, Matthew does have a few other minor sources,
mainly in traditions of the Jews, and of Christian
Jews. Finally it has always to be remembered in
reading *Matthew*, that this is written by a Christian
Jew for Christian Jews, and that always in the
Jewish mind there was the idea and the hope of
' The Day.' Those who read into Matthew the
idea that the ' Day ' has yet to come, should
remember who wrote the Gospel and for whom.

Matthias [mă-thī'-ăs]. To fill the place left vacant
by Judas Iscariot the apostles voted bet. Matthias
and Joseph Barsabas. Matthias was elected (*Acts*
1, 21 & 26).

Mattock. A combination agricultural tool. It is
not a hoe, and not a pick, and not an axe and not
an adze, but something of a combination of these.
In places it is called a hoe. There is one wrong ref.
(*2 Chron.* 34, 6 AV) should be ' ruins.'

Maul. A kind of bludgeon used in fighting.

Maw. (*Deut.* 18, 3 AV; *Jer.* 51, 34 RV.) Old word
for stomach or gullet.

Mazzaroth [măz'-zăr-oth]. (*Job* 38, 32.) May be a

constellation of stars in the S sky; or maybe the signs of the Zodiac.

Meadow. (*Gen.* 41, 2; *Judg.* 20, 33 AV). Not the word in its mod. sense. The 1st is ' reed grass ' (RV and RSV); and the 2nd is ' west of Geba.' This is corrupt text (RSV).

Meah [mē´-ăh]. Tower at Jerusalem near the Sheep Gate (*Neh.* 3, 1).

Meal. *See* FOOD.

Meal offering. *See* OFFERINGS.

Meals. In the E it is still not customary to eat much in the middle of the day, it is too hot. The Jews ate morning and evening (*Ex.* 16, 12; *John* 21, 4; etc.). Stricter Jews of Apostolic times did not breakfast (break fast) before the hour of morning prayer, which was 9 a.m. (*Acts* 2, 15). On the Sabbath there was no food served until after the synagogue service which was at noon. The evening meal was the most important of the day. In the old days the meal was spread on a low table and the eaters sat on mats on the ground or floor, but later the Gk. and Rom. manner of reclining on couches was introduced, making the meal a leisurely business (*Ezek.* 23, 41; *John* 21, 20). Three couches would be arranged round the table, leaving the 4th side of the square for service. The highest place was to the right of the serving space. The left hand and arm supported the body and head, and the eating was done with the right. When John at the Last Supper ' lay on Jesus' bosom' it simply means that they were facing one another as they reclined (*John* 13, 23; 21, 20). The place of honour was the highest place on the highest couch—the person who had no one at his back (*Matt.* 23, 6 RV). For purposes of hygiene the hands were always washed before eating (very necessary since the eating was done without forks) but this washing later became a ceremonial which Jesus could not abide—making a virtue out of a necessity (*Mark* 7, 1-13). After a blessing had been asked, the guests helped themselves with their fingers from a common dish, or dipped bread into a gravy or soup in a common dish (*1 Sam.* 9, 13; *Matt.* 14, 19; *Acts* 27, 35; *Ruth* 2, 14; *John* 13, 26). Grace after the meal was common (*Deut.* 8, 10). On ceremonial occasions there was a polite ritual which began by receiving the guest with a kiss, and washing the feet and hands (*Luke* 7, 44 & 45). The guests wore their best, and might be anointed and garlanded by the host (*Luke* 7, 38; *Isa.* 28, 1). Portions were served separately on plates to each guest (*1 Sam.* 1, 4). There might be an entertainment of music and dancing (*Isa.* 5, 12; *Luke* 15, 25). This ceremonial owed a great deal to Gk. influence. The common dish was a stew, usually of mutton, with vegetables and spices, and often with wheat grains (*Gen.* 27, 9). The stock might be used as broth, or soup (*Judg.* 6, 19). This stewing is variously described as boiling, seething, preparing sodden meat. Roasting was popular, too, from the primitive method of simply laying it on the hot coals, to a more elaborate method (*1 Kings* 19, 6). The Passover Lamb had to be roasted in an oven on a spit of pomegranate passing through the mouth. Eggs were cooked and eaten more or less as now (*Job* 6, 6; *Luke* 11, 12). Parched corn or parched grain was the whole ear of wheat or barley roasted or toasted on an iron plate. They also made a kind of porridge of crushed grain. Very little, if any, animal fat was used in cooking, olive oil taking its place. The oil was worked into the flour in baking, or smeared on the outside of the dough (*1 Kings* 17, 12; *Lev.* 2, 4). The sweetening was honey, as sugar was unknown (*Ezek.* 16, 13). The Ruler of the Feast was master of ceremonies, toastmaster and chairman (*John* 2, 8).

Measures. *See* WEIGHTS AND MEASURES.

Measuring line. *See* ARTS AND CRAFTS.

Meat. In Scotland the word means food of any kind, cf. meat and drink. That is the Scripture meaning also.

Meat offering. *See* OFFERINGS.

Medes, Media. An ancient people who settled in the neighbourhood of the Caspian Sea and called it Media. From there they spread S till they reached the borders of Elam in the 7th cent. BC. Their chief city was Ecbatana (qv). The Assyrians under Tiglath Pileser conquered them and they were later deported by Sargon, some of them ending up in Samaria (*2 Kings* 17, 6). As the Assyrian empire began to fail, the Medes gradually rose again and in alliance with the Chaldeans, overcame Nineveh (607 BC.) This was the end of Assyria. The Medes then began to spread, and they founded the Persian empire. But the Persians made their way independently and finally the Medes were absorbed into the Persian empire in 550 BC. The word Medes is more often used than Persians, simply because the Jews were more familiar with it.

Mediator. The idea of one who mediates bet. God and man is an ancient one, but in Christianity, the one mediator is Jesus. Abraham, for example, interceded with God on behalf of Sodom (*Gen.* 18, 23-33). Moses interceded for Israel (*Ex.* 32, 30-34). Samuel interceded for Israel (*1 Sam.* 7, 8-12). Intercession is the work of a mediator (*John* 17). In the great Covenants bet. God and Abraham, however, there was no mediator; this was a free act of God (*Gen.* 12, 1-3; chs. 15 &

17). In the NT the function of Jesus as mediator
is always connected with His sacrificial death
(*1 Tim.* 2, 5; etc.). *See* ATONEMENT.

Medicine. There was, of course, absolutely no
thought of disease being connected with organ-
isms called germs, and there was no scientific
belief in infections and contagions. At the same
time they had observed certain physical facts,
like the possibility of 2 people in the same house
catching the same ailment, and the incidence of
certain specific diseases in connection with certain
specific places, conventions of diet and behaviour
and the like. In the end they worked out a fairly
sound practical law of medicine within the limits
of the day and age. Health and virtue were in
their minds connected (*Isa.* 58, 8). Disease was
a visitation, direct or indirect, from God (*John*
9, 2; *Job* 2, 7; etc.). Healing, therefore was a
sign of God's change of heart and forgiveness
(*Ex.* 15, 26). Naturally, then, the functions of
physician and priest were very close together. The
heart, to them, had nothing to do with the circulation of the blood but was the seat of mental and
moral judgment (*Deut.* 2, 28). In the reins, or
kidneys, reposed affection and conscience (*Jer.*
11, 20; etc.), and the bowels were the source of
sympathy (*Ps.* 40, 8). The words for ill-health
are ' sick,' ' sickness,' ' disease(s) ' with ' sickness
unto death ' (*Isa.* 38, 1), ' sore sickness ' (*1 Kings*
17, 17). ' incurable disease ' (*2 Chron.* 21, 28).
' Infirmity ' and ' plague ' are also used. Those
who had contracted leprosy were excluded from
communal life, but other sicknesses were treated
at home. Little or nothing is known of treatment.
Many of the diseases referred to as consumption,
wasting disease, and the like were prob. allied with
the fevers, malaria, ague, dengue, Mediterranean

fever and the rest which have a wasting effect allied to chronic anaemia. There is little evidence of tuberculosis as it is now known, and which is more a disease of later civilisation. Plagues of epidemic proportion have always been known in the E, bubonic being the most common. Diseases connected with haemorrhage (bloody flux, etc.) are prob. dysentery. Paralysis, or palsy was common, and the cause was prob. the modern one of cerebral haemorrhage and thrombosis, though these, too, are diseases of civilisation with its attendant worries (*2 Sam.* 6, 7; *Acts* 5, 5-10). Deafness and dumbness were common, though it is now known that most dumbness is the product of deafness. Epileptic fits are clearly described (*Matt.* 17, 14; *Luke* 9, 38). Dropsy was common (*Luke* 14, 2). Some think that gout was the cause of Asa's trouble with his feet (*1 Kings* 15, 23) but it is more likely to have been gangrene. The ' spirit of infirmity ' was prob. a chronic curvature of the spine (*Luke* 13, 11). Skin diseases are and were very common throughout the E and many less serious skin diseases are prob. included in the general word ' leprosy.' Botch and blains and Job's boils would be the very serious and painful sores described from the place where the sufferer lives—Baghdad sores, Assam sores, etc. They are caused by a parasite and the flesh simply rots away. ' Spots ' and ' blemishes ' are used for skin diseases; a ' wen ' is a suppurating sore. There would be deaths from the bites of poisonous serpents and scorpions, but anyone who has lived in snake country knows that these are far fewer than is supposed. Discharges and issues in some cases at least would be the result of venereal diseases. Blindness could be congenital, or caused by ophthalmia (a fly-carried infection) or by

accident. There were, of course, many cases of
infantile mortality, and of the death of the mother
by puerperal fever or other causes. Knowledge
of common hygiene was very primitive. Ab-
normalities of menstruation were regarded as
being very serious indeed (*Lev.* 15, 19; *Matt.* 9,
20). Medicines themselves were simple enough,
and treatment was scanty. The sick would be kept
as clean as poss. (*2 Kings* 5, 10), put on a diet
(*Luke* 8, 55), bandaged and treated with ointments
(*Isa.* 1, 6), or poulticed (*Isa.* 38, 21). Balm of
Gilead was used as a soothing application (*Gen.*
37, 25); mandrakes were used to stimulate conception (*Gen.* 30, 16); there was mint, anise,
cummin, salt, nitre. The apothecaries were not
chemists as we know them, but makers and sellers
of perfume. Considerable care was taken with
diet. Herbivorous animals which chewed the cud
could be eaten, as well as true fish. Birds which
lived on animal food were forbidden, and from
all blooded beasts the blood had to be drained.
Only locusts of all invertebrates could be eaten.
There was to be no cross breeding of either
animal or vegetable (*Lev.* 19, 19; *Deut.* 22, 11).
Although many of the regulations about clean-
ness and uncleanness were ceremonial, they must
have had their roots in observation of the fact
that personal hygiene did have a real effect upon
the incidence of disease. Surgical operation was
more or less unknown except for the ceremony of
circumcision which orig. would be a tribal mark.

Mediterranean. Called simply ' the Sea ' in Scripture for it was really the only ocean which they
knew (*Num.* 13, 29; *Acts* 10, 6). Otherwise it was
called the Great Sea (*Num.* 34, 6), or the hinder
or western sea (*Deut.* 11, 24). Once it is the Sea
of the Philistines (*Ex.* 23, 31). The Jews were not

fond of the sea at all. There was to be ' no more
sea ' at the millenium (*Rev.* 21, 1).

Meekness. From very early times this was regarded
as a great virtue (*Num.* 12, 3). But since this ref.
is to Moses, it is plain that meekness was no milk
and water quality. ' Devout ' might be a better
word.

Megiddo [mĕ-gĭd'-dŏ]. An ancient and important
town of Palestine. Joshua took it, slaying its king,
and it fell into Issachar's domain (*Josh.* 12, 21).
It was given, however, to the Manassites who
failed to drive out the original inhabitants (*Josh.*
17, 11). Solomon greatly improved and fortified
the town. (*I Kings* 9, 15-19; 10, 26). It commanded the passage through the mts. bet. Sharon
and Esdraelon. Mt. of Megiddo: *see* ARMAGED-
DON.

Melchizedek [mĕl-chĭz'-ĕ-dĕk]. King of Salem and
Priest of God most High. He was a friend of
Abraham (*Gen.* 14, 18-20). Salem has been identified with various places but it is most likely to
have been Jerusalem (*Ps.* 76, 2). In the hopes of
Israel, the Messiah was to be one who combined
the offices of King and High Priest (*Ps.* 110, 4;
etc.). And the only historical personage they
could recall who did combine these functions was
Melchizedek of Salem. The writer of the letter
to the Heb. took up this idea (*Heb.* 5, 10).

Melita [mĕl'-ĭ-tă]. There were 2 islands of the name,
but the island on which Paul was wrecked is
almost certainly the mod. Malta. The trad. site
of the wreck is St. Paul's Bay on the NE coast
(*Acts* 27).

Melon. The fruit more or less as known to-day,
though in a wilder state (*Num.* 11, 5).

Mem. Thirteenth letter of the Heb. alphabet,
Eng. *M*.

Memphis [mĕm'-phĭs]. An ancient Egyptian town standing on the Nile 10 m. upstream from the beginning of the delta. It was the capital of Lower Egypt up to the time of the rise of Thebes, and lost much of its commerce and importance to the new city of Alexandria. It was known to the Hebs. as Noph or Moph (*Isa.* 19, 13; *Hos.* 9, 6). Jews settled there after the fall of Jerusalem (*Jer.* 44, 1). The pyramids and the sphinx are relics of ancient Memphis.

Menahem [mĕn'-ă-hĕm]. Son of Gadi who usurped the throne of Samaria from Shallum who had murdered King Zechariah. Menahem slew him in turn (*2 Kings* 15, 14). He became a vassal to Tiglath Pileser, and reigned from c. 744 to 735 BC.

Mene Mene Tekel Upharsin [mē'-nĕ tē'-kĕl ū-phär'-sĭn]. The words that appeared mysteriously on the wall of the banqueting hall of Belshazzar (*Dan.* 5, 25 & 26). The words themselves are the names of weights and mean lit. ' a mina, a mina, a shekel, and half minas.' Daniel's interpretation depends upon some punning, becoming ' numbered, weighed, divided.' It has been suggested that it may have been a phrase used of a bankrupt, like ' a penny in the pound.'

Meonenim, Oak of [mē-ō'-nĕn-ĭm]. Only one ref. (*Judg.* 9, 37). A place near Shechem, prob. better as ' the oak of the diviners.' AV has ' plain of Meonenim,' but this is wrong.

Mephibosheth [mĕ-phĭb'-ŏ-shĕth]. Son of Saul, executed by the Gibeonites (*2 Sam.* 21, 8 & 9). Also the son of Jonathan, only 5 yrs. old when his father fell at Gilboa. His nurse escaped with him but in an accident he was lamed (*2 Sam.* 4, 4). David called him to court and restored to him the old estates of Saul (*2 Sam.* 9, 1-13). He was deprived of his estates when David believed a report

that he had supported Absalom in the rebellion.
This was denied and David restored half, which
Mephibosheth refused (*2 Sam.* 16, 1-4; 19, 24-30).

Merab [mē'-răb]. Elder daughter of Saul (*1 Sam.*
14, 49). She was promised to David but given to
Adriel (*1 Sam.* 18, 17-19).

Meraioth [mē-rā'-ī-ŏth]. Priest of the house of Eli
(*1 Chron.* 6, 6). Also the father of Zadok (*Neh.*
11, 11).

Merari [mē-rā'-rī]. Son of Levi, and a founder of
the Levites (*Gen.* 46, 11).

Merchantman (*Gen.* 37, 28; *1 Kings* 10, 15; *Matt.*
13, 45). Means simply ' merchant.' The mod.
meaning is a ship in trade.

Mercury. The Rom. name for the Gk. god Hermes,
the herald of the gods. Paul was taken for Mercury
and Barnabas for Jupiter when they healed the
cripple at Lystra (*Acts* 14, 12).

Mercy Seat. This was the covering or lid of the
Ark of the Covenant. It was made of gold and
was 3 ft. 9 in. long and 23 in. broad. Cast with it
were the 2 cherubim, one at either end, whose
wings arched over the Mercy Seat and met in the
centre. In that space was God's glory (*Ex.* 25,
17-22). The sacrifice on the Day of Atonement
was made before the Mercy Seat (*Lev.* 16, 2 &
13-17). See TABERNACLE, TEMPLE, ARK OF THE
COVENANT.

Meribah [mĕr'-ĭ-băh]. With ' Massah ' the name
given to the place where the people rebelled agst.
Moses (*Ex.* 17). Moses brought water out of the
rock, and this is the Water of Strife (*Ps.* 106, 32;
Ezek. 47, 19 AV).

Merodach [mĕr-ō'-dach]. The city god of Babylon
who became the national god of the Babylonian
empire. Also called Marduk or Maruduk.

Merodach Baladan [băl'-ă-dăn]. King of Babylon

(*2 Kings* 20, 12). He began as leader of the Chaldeans and was a man of considerable character. After doing homage to Tiglath Pileser c. 712 BC, he seized the throne of Babylon and was recognised by Sargon of Assyria in 721. He tried to persuade Hezekiah to join a confederation agst. Assyria (*2 Kings* 20, 12-19). Sargon anticipated the plan by taking on the partners one by one. Babylon was taken in 710 and the king was captured but was later restored as a prince. He only lasted another year, however, being forced to flee into Elam by Sennacherib. *See* BABYLONIA, ASSYRIA.

Merom, Waters of [mē'-rŏm]. Scene of Joshua's victory over the N Canaan confederacy (*Josh.* 11, 5-7). The waters are one of the lakes of Jordan, prob. Lake Huleh.

Meroz [mē'-roz]. A town despised because its people gave no help in the fight agst. Sisera (*Judg.* 5, 23).

Mesha [mē'-shă]. Place on the border of the territory inhabited by Joktan and his descendants (*Gen.* 10, 30). There is also a Benjamite of the name (*1 Chron.* 8, 8 & 9); and a man of Judah (*1 Chron.* 2, 42). It is also the name of a king of Moab who paid tribute of wool to Ahab (*2 Kings* 3, 4).

Meshach [mē'-shach]. Babylonian name for Mishael one of the 3 men in the fiery furnace (*Dan.* 1, 7; 2, 49).

Meshullam [mē-shŭl'-lăm]. The name of 21 men, mostly priests or Levites, none of whom seems to have done anything of very great moment.

Mesopotamia. Aram (qv).

Messiah. Also **Messias**, the Gk. form. Lit. ' The Anointed One', the Gk. equivalent of which is The Christ. Orig. it could be applied to anyone ceremonially anointed for office—the High Priest, the king, patriarchs, even Cyrus of Persia (*Isa.* 45, 1). Cyrus had been set apart by God to destroy Babylon and end the Captivity. Later it came to mean the one desc. from David to whom the sceptre would be given (*Ps.* 2, 2; etc.). When this one seemed long in coming and the prophets told of the blessed one who would come in the fulness of time and of the line of David to deliver the people, the title Messiah came to be used for Him alone (*Micah* 5, 2-5). It came to be exchangeable with the other title, Son of David (*John* 1, 41).

Metals. The metals commonly in use were gold, silver, iron, copper, lead and tin (*Num.* 31, 22).

Mete. This is not 'to dole out' but 'to measure.' A mete-yard is a merchant's yardstick (*Lev.* 19, 35).

Methuselah [mē-thū′-sĕ-lăh]. Son of Enoch and father of Lamech, noted for his persistence in remaining alive (*Gen.* 5, 21-27).

Mica. Son of Mephibosheth (*2 Sam.* 9, 12).

Micah. He is a prophet mostly of the S Kingdom during the reigns of Jotham, Ahaz and Hezekiah; at which time Pekah and Hoshea were kings of Israel. The time would be c. 750-695 BC. This was during the period of Assyrian supremacy and before the exile. Nothing is known of the man himself, except through the glimpses of character seen in the prophecies themselves. His fellow prophet in the S Kingdom was Isaiah, while Hosea was at work in the N Kingdom. All that concerned him were moral and social issues; not politics. To him the whole nation was morally corrupt and decadent (*Mic.* 2, 2 & 8 & 9 & 11; 3, 1-3 & 5 & 11). He warned them that in their spiritual and moral state, the performance of religious ceremonies and ceremonials was a patent pretence. He singled out the judges, who could be bribed to any verdict; the priests whose concern was with lining their pockets; and a new breed of people who claimed to be prophets and who would say anything that people paid for. He tells them of the judgment that will fall upon the nation, but he looks beyond that to the promise of better things. His thinking reaches its peak in the 6th ch. (v. 8) 'He hath shewed thee, O man, what is good; and what doth the Lord require of thee, but to do justly, and to love mercy, and to walk humbly with thy God.'

Micah, Book of. The book opens with a warning of the doom to come (1, 2-16). Micah then states why this is so (2, 1-11) and goes on to show the blessing that comes after the punishment (2, 12 & 13). He then reproves those who should have been leading the people but who were leading them astray (ch. 3) and repeats the promise of blessings to come (4, 1-13). Finally he lets God speak through himself in protest agst. the evil ways of the nation and the promise is given once more. The historical background will be found in the article on Israel. Much background material will be found also in the article on Isaiah, Micah's contemporary.

Micaiah [mī-cāī'-äh]. There are several of the name, which was given also to Micah, above. This was the name of the wife of Rehoboam, mother of Abijah, but is prob. an error for Maacah (2 Chron. 11, 20; 13, 2). Another of the name was a prophet commanded by Ahab to prophesy success for his arms agst. Ramoth Gilead. He tried to do this but was plainly insincere and Ahab asked him to speak the truth (1 Kings 22, 8-28). Others are: one of Jehoshaphat's princes (2 Chron. 17, 7); a man who reported the reading of Jeremiah by Baruch (*Jer.* 36, 11-13); father of Achbor (*2 Kings* 22, 12). Returned exiles (*Neh.* 12, 35 & 41).

Mice. *See* MOUSE.

Michael. There are some dozen men of the name, but the important ref. is to the archangel. *See* ANGEL. When the idea of angels was worked into Jewish thinking there were 7 regarded as being above the others. Michael was not the least of these. Most of the refs. are in Daniel (10, 13 & 21; 12, 1). He is the ' prince which standeth for the people.' He is still so reckoned in art.

Michal [mīch'-ăl]. Younger daughter of Saul, promised to David to secure his loyalty. When Saul made an attempt on David's life she accomplished his escape (*1 Sam.* 19, 11-17). Saul then gave her to Paltiel. After succeeding to the throne, David had her brought back to him, but they did not see eye to eye. She died childless and may have been divorced (*2 Sam.* 6, 16).

Michmash [mīch'-măsh]. Town near Mt. Bethel where the Philistines encamped in war agst. Saul in which Jonathan played a heroic part (*1 Sam.* 13, 5—14, 23).

Michtam [mīch'-tăm]. Word found in the titles of Psalms 16 and 56-60. Its meaning is obscure. It may mean a Psalm in epigram form, or it may mean a Psalm written under a sense of sin, and as an atonement for sin.

Midian(ites). A son of Abraham who became a desert dweller and the people desc. from him (*Gen.* 25, 1-6). The region of the name is in the Arabian desert near the Gulf of Akabah. They were settled in the peninsula of Sinai at the time of the Exodus (*Ex.* 3, 1). They allied with the Moabites in persuading Israel to apostasy and this led to war (*Num.* 22, 4; ch. 25), with dreadful slaughter (*Num.* ch. 31).

Migdol [mĭg′-dŏl]. Lit. ' a tower,' and as common in place names as ' caster ' (camp) is in England. One ref. to it in several passages was a town in the extreme N of Egypt.

Milcah [mĭl′-căh]. Daughter of Haran, wife of Nahor (*Gen.* 11, 29). She was Rebekah's grandmother (*Gen.* 24, 15). Another is daughter of Zelophehad (*Num.* 26, 33).

Mildew. Disease of grain produced by damp (*Deut.* 28, 22; etc.). ' Blasting ' in the ref. is the opposite —produced by drought.

Mile. *See* WEIGHTS AND MEASURES.

Miletus(m) [mĭ-lē′-tŭs]. City of the coast of Ionia, about 40 m. from Ephesus, at the place where the R. Meander joins the sea. Its temple to Apollo was famous. Paul visited the city twice (*Acts* 20, 15; *2 Tim.* 4, 20).

Milk. A very important article of diet in Scripture times. The milk was taken from sheep, goats, cows and camels (*Gen.* 32, 15; *Deut.* 32, 14; *Prov.* 27, 27). From milk they made curds and cheese, and a refreshing sour milk drink. Butter as we know it was not common, as it takes a lot of milk for little butter, and the butter quickly grows rancid. They boiled it, producing a clarified butter.

Mill, Millstone. The most primitive method of milling was to spread the grain on a large concave stone, and rub it with another rounded stone held in the hand: the ' rubbing stone.' Then there was the handmill or quern. The lower stone (*Job* 41, 24) was larger than the upper, and had a fixed spindle which passed through a hole in the upper stone. By this hole the grain was fed in (*Deut.* 24, 6). The upper stone was turned by hand, but not through the full circle. In NT times the stones were larger, and the upper one had a wooden pin by which it could be rotated. Sometimes 2 women worked it together (*Matt.* 24, 41). In humble homes milling was women's business; among the wealthy it was done by slaves (*Ex.* 11, 5; *Judg.* 16, 21). A moneylender was not allowed to take the handmill or part of it as a pledge (*Deut.* 24, 6).

Millet. It is not clear precisely what grain is meant, but it was used only as an ingredient of bread and not as a substitute for flour (*Ezek.* 4, 9).

Millo [mill'-ŏ]. A fortress at Shechem (*Judg.* 9, 6). Also a fortalice of Jerusalem rebuilt by Solomon, and strengthened by Hezekiah (*2 Sam.* 5, 9; *1 Kings* 9, 15; *2 Chron.* 32, 5).

Mine, Mining. The process is described in *Job* (28, 1-11). These were not pits, with hoists, etc. The shaft ran from the surface on a downward slope sometimes to considerable depth. The miners were criminals or prisoners of war (*Deut.* 8, 9). The principal metals mined were copper and gold, though there was little or none of it in Palestine; Ophir, Tarshish and Sheba being the main sources. Iron is found in the Lebanon area. They could not, of course, generate sufficient heat to make steel—the iron was forged (*Deut.* 4, 20; *Isa.* 44, 12). Lead was mined (*Jer.* 6, 29); and silver, though again there are no deposits in Palestine. When ' steel ' is used AV it is usually a mistrans. for brass Their brass was not an alloy of copper and zinc, but rather of copper and tin, which makes bronze. Flint was known, and was used for producing sparks to kindle fires, and in the early days for arrowheads and knives (*Ex.* 4, 25 RV, RSV; ' sharp stone ' in AV). Marble and limestone were quarried and used for fine building (*1 Chron.* 29, 2).

Minish. Diminish, as everywhere in RSV.

Minister. In a general sense, anyone who gives

service of any kind; but there are degrees. In one sense the minister is not at all a menial, but a personal assistant: like Joseph in Egypt (*Gen.* 39, 4). It was Joshua's relationship to Moses (*Ex.* 24, 13). It was John Mark's relationship to Paul (*Acts* 13, 5). In another sense the minister was not a personal attendant but one who served the state of God in an official capacity. Thus the priests and Levites were ministers (*Ex.* 28, 43). Other refs. are to the civil office (*2 Chron.* 22, 8; *Esth.* 1, 10). The third meaning is one specially delegated and appointed as official representative of another. That 'other' might be God (*Rom.* 13, 4; *1 Cor.* 3, 5).

Minstrel. Gen. means those skilled in playing on the harp or lyre, esp. those who sang to their own accompaniment. In the passage in Matthew (9, 23 AV) it is better as 'fluteplayers' as in RV and RSV. These were professional mourners.

Mint. Herb of the species *Mentha*. It could be peppermint or wild mint. There must have been a cultivated variety, for it was tithed (*Matt.* 23, 23).

Miphkad [mĭph′-kăd]. Gate on the E wall of Jerusalem called Hammiphkad in RV (*Neh.* 3, 31).

Miracles. Strictly these are 'deeds of power'; but generally they include wonders, signs and works of God. They have to be the witness of supernatural power, demonstrating the power of God. Undoubtedly some phenomena described as miracles have a natural explanation. Locusts are wind driven, and winds change (*Ex.* 10, 13 & 19). Quails migrate and need a rest (*Ex.* 16, 13). Much that appeared miraculous to the ancients has now been scientifically explained as being perfectly natural, but the miracle is nature itself. Before an event was accepted as a miracle, it had to tell something about God, and it had to be in character with God (*Deut.* 13, 1-3). If it did not do this it was a deception (*2 Thess.* 2, 9; *Rev.* 16, 14). The miracle must also have a sound reason behind it, and the miracle had to be vouched for, not by great numbers of people, but by people of proved trustworthiness. The miracles of the Bible fall into 4 periods of crisis: the Exodus, the wandering, and the conquest form the first group. Then comes the crisis of Judaism agst. paganism in the kingdoms at the time of Elijah and Elisha. The next period of miracles is the Exile, and finally the time of the beginning of the Christian era—the miracles performed by Jesus and the Apostles. The miracles of Jesus number 37, of which 18 are narrated in one Gospel only (7 in *Luke* and 8 in *John*). Six are narrated in 2 Gospels, 12 in 3 Gospels, and only 1, the feeding of the 5,000 in all 4. *See* LAZARUS.

Miriam. 1. Sister of Moses and Aaron (*Ex.* 15, 20). She was a prophetess and one of the accepted leaders of the people (*Ex.* 4, 15 & 29 & 30). Angry at Moses' marriage with a Cushite woman she led a grumbling faction who challenged his supreme authority, and became a leper, though she was later cured (*Num.* 12, 1-16; *Deut.* 24, 9). She eventually died at Kadesh (*Num.* 20, 1). **2.** A man of Judah (*1 Chron.* 4, 17).

Mirror. These were made not of glass but of copper or some alloy. RV is right to substitute ' mirror ' for ' glass,' in the famous passage in *1 Corinthians* (13, 12).

Mite. *See* MONEY.

Mithredath [mĭth'-rĕ-dăth]. Cyrus' treasurer who restored the sacred vessels after the Exile (*Ezra* 1, 8). Also another who objected to the rebuilding of Jerusalem's walls (*Ezra* 4, 7).

Mitre. The headdress of the High Priest, it was made of linen and had a golden plate with the words, ' Holiness unto the Lord ' (*Ex.* 28, 4 & 36-39). The word is once trans. ' turban,' (*see* DRESS), and once diadem (qv).

Mitylene [mĭt-y̆-lē'-ne]. City on Lesbos visited by Paul (*Acts* 20, 13-15).

Mizar [mĭ'-zar]. Hill E of Jordan (*Ps.* 42, 6).

Mizpah(peh) [mĭz'-păh]. Lit. ' a look-out point.' Thus it is better with the article before it. There was ' the ' Mizpah where Jacob and Laban made their compact (*Gen.* 31, 44-49). Another was a town in Gilead, prob. the same as Mizpeh of Gilead (*Judg.* 10, 17; *Josh.* 13, 26). This was also known as Ramoth Gilead and Ramah (*Deut.* 4, 43; *2 Kings* 8, 28). It was a key point in the many battles fought in the vicinity (*I Kings* 22, 3; *2 Kings* 8, 28). The ' land of Mizpeh ' (*Josh.* 11, 3) is the Valley of the Mizpeh. There is also a village of Judah (*Josh.* 15, 38); and a town in Benjamin (*Josh.* 18, 26). There was a Mizpah in Moab (*I Sam.* 22, 3).

Mnason [mnā'-son]. An early Christian of Cyprus who travelled with Paul on the last journey, and was to give him lodging (*Acts* 21, 16).

Moab, Moabites. Incestuous son of Lot (*Gen.* 19, 37). His descendants were akin to the Ammonites and worked in harmony with them to take the territory S of the Dead Sea from its orig. inhabitants (*Deut.* 2, 9). They refused permission to Israel to pass through their land (*Judg.* 11, 17). Alarmed by the nearness of the Israelites who had no intention of attacking him, the king of Moab sent for Balaam to curse Israel (*Num.* 22-24). This led to estrangement bet. Israel and Moab (*Deut.* 23, 3-6; *Neh.* 13, 1). Early in the time of the Judges, Eglon of Moab invaded Canaan, and sat in Jericho for

18 yrs. (*Judg.* 3, 12-30). David subdued Moab (*2 Sam.* 8, 2). But they threw off the yoke in the time of Ahaziah and Jehoram (*2 Kings* 1, 1; 3, 4-27). They made a federation with others agst. Judah but fell to quarrelling (*2 Chron.* 20, 1-30). They were conquered by Nebuchadnezzar and disappeared from hist. as a nation though they remained as a race (*Ezra* 9, 1).

Mole. In many refs. this is the chameleon (qv) (*Lev.* 11, 30 AV). In other refs. it translates the word for ' a burrower,' and might be any such rodent.

Molech (Moloch) [mō'-lĕch]. An Ammonite deity (*1 Kings* 11, 7). In Heb. it is written with the definite article, since it is not a proper name but a word meaning ' the one who reigns.' He was an offshoot of Baal and in his worship children were burned alive (*Lev.* 18, 21). Ahaz and Manasseh sacrificed their own children to Molech (*2 Kings* 21, 6; *2 Chron.* 28, 3). Josiah destroyed the altars and defiled them (*2 Kings* 23, 10).

Molten Sea. Also called the Brazen Sea. A great copper basin made by Solomon from David's store of plunder (*1 Chron.* 18, 8). It was intended for the priests washing their hands and feet before entering the sanctuary (*1 Kings* 7, 39). It was lily-shaped and stood on 12 brazen oxen, and was 15 ft. in diameter and 7 ft. 6 ins. high. It was destroyed by Nebuchadnezzar (*2 Kings* 25, 13).

Money. Coins are not old in terms of hist., barter being the means of exchange till c. the 8th cent. BC. Currency was gold or silver in bar form, and even when coins were introduced, their weight was more important than their stamped face value (*Josh.* 7, 21). Although talent, maneh, shekel, gerah and beka are referred to as money, they

were really weights. It was prob. the Persian
influence which gave the Jews a currency. The
daric (*Ezra* 2, 69) was a gold coin worth bet. 20
and 30 shillings (3 or 4 dollars). Later the Gk.
coinage was introduced, of talents and drachmas.
The silver drachma equalled the Rom. denarius
and was worth about a shilling. The silver stater
(*Matt.* 17, 27) was worth 4 times that. The mite
was a small copper coin called a lepton (*Luke* 12,
59). This was the smallest coin in the currency
equal to half a quadrans (*Mark* 12, 42). It was a
Jewish coin, for only Jewish coins could be offered
in the Temple. The talent (*Matt.* 18, 24) was the
Gk. talent made the lawful standard for the
empire of Alexander the Great. It was not itself
a coin, but a quantity of coins, 60 minas (*Luke*
19, 13) or 6,000 drachmas. The word rendered
' pound ' as money equalled 100 drachmas (*Luke*
19, 13 RSV). Rom. currency which became common under their rule was the silver denarius,
nearer to a shilling than a penny (*Matt.* 18, 28);
it was the tribute the Jews had to pay to the
imperial treasury (*Matt.* 22, 19). The as was a
small copper coin (*Matt.* 10, 29). The quadrans
was valued at a quarter of an as (*Matt.* 5, 26) and is
best rendered as farthing. The gold coin of NT
days was the denarius aureus, worth 25 silver
denarii.

Money changers. The importance of the money
changer, or exchanger, or banker, is seen from
examination of the various currencies in the
article above. It was his business to change one
currency for another, and from this he made his
profit. He changed large currency to small; he
changed Gk. or Rom. currency to Jewish, and
on each deal he charged a commission. His
importance in the environs of the Temple lay in

the fact that only Jewish money could be placed in the offering there (*Matt.* 21, 12).

Month. *See* TIME.

Monument. Lit. ' tomb ' (*Isa.* 65, 4). They thought they might receive supernatural information by sitting up all night in a cemetery.

Moon. The waxing and waning of the moon gave the natural division of the year into months. The feasts, such as the Passover, depended upon this timing (*Gen.* 1, 14; *Ps.* 104, 19). The moon, with the sun, was the general object of pagan worship, and from time to time moon worship was popular among the Israelites (*2 Kings* 21, 3; *Jer.* 7, 18; 8, 2; etc.). The word ' lunatic ' derives, of course, from the Latin name for the moon, and there was an idea that the moon might have a baleful influence upon humans (*Ps.* 121, 6). New moon was a holy day (*Num.* 28, 11-14). After the Exile the new moon of the 7th month became a kind of New Year's Day occasion. They reckoned that the shape and appearance of the new moon was very important, presaging good luck or bad, and when the new moon was obscured, the Sanhedrin would not officially sanction the start of another month.

Moph [mŏph]. *See* MEMPHIS.

Mordecai [mŏr′-dĕ-cā′-ĭ]. **1.** A Benjamite who in Babylonia thwarted the plot of Haman to have a putsch of the Jews. He was some kind of cousin to Esther and he used her influence with the king to discomfit his enemies. *See* ESTHER, HAMAN.

Moreh [mō′-reh]. A grove near Shechem where Abraham encamped (*Gen.* 12, 6). It developed sacred associations (*Josh.* 24, 26). There is also a hill of the name in the valley of Jezreel (*Judg.* 7, 1).

Moriah [mō-rī′-ăh]. Dist. prob. round Mt. Moriah, to which Abraham felt impelled to travel to sacrifice Isaac (*Gen.* 22, 2). Also the hill where David bought the threshing floor and built the altar (*2 Sam.* 24, 18).

Morning. *See* TIME.

Mortar. Mortar as understood nowadays was used in building; it was a wet mixture of sand and lime; but the word as used in the AV covers several other materials including mud and clay (*Nahum* 3, 14); bitumen (*Gen.* 11, 3). Straw was often mixed with the mortar to keep it from cracking.

Mortar and pestle. This is a very ancient way of crushing seeds, grains or solids of any kind (*Num.* 11, 8; *Ex.* 30, 36; *Lev.* 2, 14).

Mortify. Lit. ' make dead '; ' put to death.'

Moses. The Scriptural record of Moses is clear and precise, and he is the dominant character of the books from *Exodus* to *Deuteronomy*. He was the son of a Levite, Amram, by his wife, Jochebed, and was younger than his brother and sister, Aaron and Miriam. He was adopted as an infant by Pharaoh's daughter and received the education and upbringing of an Egyptian prince. In a fit of anger at seeing an Israelite abused by an Egyptian slavedriver, he killed the Egyptian and had to run for his life to Midian where he settled for a while and married Zipporah, daughter of a flockmaster named Jethro. While there, and at Mt. Horeb, he had the vision of the burning bush and heard God command him to return to Egypt and liberate Israel. This he did after dispute with Pharaoh. He led Israel out towards Canaan, and at Mt. Sinai received from God the Decalogue or Ten Commandments. For one reason or another he was fated not to set foot in the Promised Land. He died at Mt. Pisgah in old age, leaving 2 sons, Gershom and Eliezer. Jewish trad. credits him with the authorship of the first 5 books of the OT,

the Pentateuch. His name is often mentioned
with the utmost respect in the Koran, the ' Bible '
of Islam. The name ' Moses ' is Egyptian in its
form, and some have made much of this, claiming
that Moses was not Israelite but Egyptian. The
whole story of the period is so vague and uncertain that all sorts of theories can be held, for
reasons good or bad. But though scholars differ
about who Moses was, they agree that there certainly was a Moses, and that he certainly performed a work which still affects the life and
thought of the world. He stands right at the
beginning of monotheism—the Heb. worship of
Jehovah, the one God. He may have been the
interpreter of some other man's ideas; he may
have reached the conclusion himself, but he is
the one who persuaded the Hebs. that there is
but one God, and so made it possible for them
to produce, and then to reject the Son of God.
He is one of the shapers of world thought; he is
a religious pioneer. Whether he was Egyptian or
not it is a certainty that his idea of God did not
come to him in Egypt; such splendid sublime
thoughts are the product of loneliness. Hard
religions come out of the world's deserts. He
found his idea of God on Sinai when the light-
nings flashed and the thunders rolled and the
people trembled. His leadership, and the conquest, are historic. It is worth noting that when
the prophets railed agst. the twists and turns that
religion had taken, their accusation was that the
nation had fallen away from something old, simple
and pure—namely, the faith that had been taught
them by Moses. As a statesman and lawgiver
Moses is the creator of the Jewish people. He
found a loose conglomeration of Semitic people,
none of whom had ever been anything but a slave,

and whose ideas of religion were a complete confusion. He led them out and he hammered them into a nation, with a law and a national pride, and a compelling sense of being chosen by a particular God who was supreme. The only man of hist. who can be compared even remotely to him is Mahomet. The Scripture account tends to elaborate for the sake of impression, but behind all the elaborations stands a man of tremendous worth and achievement, whose mark upon the life of the world is as important as it is incalculable.

Mote. The word so translated means something that is dried up, and since Jesus was comparing something so small that it is almost invisible to a thing like a roof joist it can be assumed that he meant some little speck of flying dust that cannot even be seen till it is caught in a sunbeam (*Matt.* 7, 3; etc.).

Moth. The same creature that is still the housewife's bane, and agst. which she fights with mothballs (*Job* 13, 28; *Matt.* 6, 19).

Mount. A natural mountain, or the earthworks raised by a besieging force to enable them to overlook the walls of a city. In this meaning, 'mound' is better.

Mount of Congregation. A mountain far to the N. The idea of this as a dwelling place of the gods is found in many faiths, cf. Olympus.

Mourning. Although death had to be accepted by the individual in his relationship to God, quietly and with resignation, it was still necessary to let the world around know how grievous the loss was. Ornaments were taken off, the physical person was neglected (*Ex.* 33, 4; *Matt.* 6, 16; etc.). The clothes would be torn, the head shaved (*Lev.* 10, 6; *Joel* 2, 13; *Ezra* 9, 3). There was sackcloth, ashes, weeping and wailing (*Gen.*

37, 34; *2 Sam.* 3, 31; etc.). There were professional mourners (*Matt.* 9, 23; *Acts* 9, 39). There was a stated period of mourning (as there still is with royalty) which varied with the status of the person mourned (*Num.* 20, 29; *1 Sam.* 31, 13).

Mouse. Not simply the genus *mus*, but all the *muridae*, including field mice, hamsters, jerboa, dormice and the like. They were ceremonially unclean (*Lev.* 11, 29), but there were times when Israel ate them (*Isa.* 66, 17).

Mufflers. (*Isa.* 3, 19.) An article of attire not related at all to the muff, but to something which muffles or veils the face. In other words, the kind of veil still used in countries where purdah is observed for women.

Mulberry tree. Whatever these were they were not true mulberries which did not grow in Palestine. They may have been some kind of tree exuding balsam. The passage (*2 Sam.* 5, 23) seems to indicate the poplar.

Mule. The product of the mating of a mare with an ass stallion, very hardy, surefooted, and easily fed. The law forbade the crossing of species (*Lev.* 19, 19) and it was not till David's day that mules appear—imported (*1 Kings* 1, 33). One ref. is wrong; *Gen.* 36, 24 AV, should not be mules, but hot springs.

Munition. Stronghold or fortress (*Isa.* 29, 7; *Nahum* 2, 1).

Murder. See CRIME AND PUNISHMENT, CITY OF REFUGE.

Music (instruments). To begin with, music, even that assoc. with worship, was a ' noise made unto the Lord.' It may have been joyful and may not. It was harsh and cacophanous. There was some kind of choral system and convention but it is doubtful if it was based on anything remotely like mod. harmony or counterpoint (*1 Chron.* 15, 16; etc.). Music and dancing have always gone together and some of the orig. music may have been something like the 'mouth music' of the Gaels which is a rhythmic accompaniment to a dance. People have always had folk music of sorts, but the music of the sanctuary gradually assumed a set form which was brought to its perfection in the days of David and Solomon (*2 Chron.* 5, 12). This was retained during and after the Exile (*Neh.* 12, 27). Musical instruments were divided into: (1) Strings. Harp (sackbut) and the psaltery. These were different instruments and were used to accompany song, though there are indications that it was only song of the brighter sort (*Ps.* 137, 2). The strings were of gut, silk or metal. The string might be plucked by the fingers or struck by a plectrum. Both instruments could be carried and played simultaneously (*1 Sam.* 10, 5). (2) Wind instruments. The pipe was a kind of flute, or something like a 'penny whistle,' or it may have had a reed like a bagpipe or clarinet. But there would be no keys, as modern wind instruments have; there would just be the holes covered by the fingers. Although the word 'organ' is used in the AV, the instrument was nothing even remotely like the mod. organ. Poss. it was the Pan's pipes, a double tin whistle, with one mouthpiece but 2 pipes, or chanters, one for each set of fingers. (3) Percussion instruments. The tabret (qv) or timbrel was something like a tambourine. There were also cymbals—metal plates of sorts, clashed together. There was also another instrument which may have been the ancestor of the Spanish castanet—2 concave pieces of wood which, contained in the palm of the hand, could be 'clacked' together by the fingers in rhythm (*2 Sam.* 6, 5). In singing there was no harmony; not even in thirds or fourths. The lower voices would sing simply an octave lower than the higher. The congregation in the synagogue would not join in the singing but would unite at the close in the Amen (*1 Chron.* 16, 36).

Mustard. Among the Jews the seed of the annual plant referred to was proverbially connected with some ref. to the small becoming great. The plant, springing from a very small seed, did attain a height of 12 to 15 ft. It is not exactly a tree, though it grows to the height of a small tree (*Matt.* 13, 32; *Mark* 4, 32; *Luke* 13, 19; etc.).

Myra [mȳ'-ra]. A city of Lycia, now called Dembre, where Paul changed ships (*Acts* 27, 5 & 6).

Myrrh. There are 2 varieties. **1.** An extract from the tree *Balsamodendron myrrha*, which was used for perfumery (*Ps.* 45, 8; etc.), sacrament (*Esth.* 2, 12), and embalming (*John* 19, 39). **2.** A volatile oil derived from the *Cistus creticus*, related to laudanum (*Gen.* 37, 25; etc.).

Myrtle. The common evergreen myrtle, greatly used at the Feast of the Tabernacles (*Neh.* 8, 15).

Mysia [mȳs'-ĭ-ă]. Dist. in NW of Asia Minor. It came within the Rom. province of Asia. Paul passed through it on his 2nd missionary journey (*Acts* 16, 7 & 8).

Mystery. The word in Christian and in pagan religion means something which is revealed to some but not to all. The Mystery religions could not be appreciated or understood until the seeker had passed through certain formal initiation ceremonies with which mod. Freemasonry may be compared. The ' mystery ' is never something which can never be understood. It is always something which can be understood after one has passed through the approved drills or processes. In the NT there is the sense of an ordained and approved time when the mystery will be made plain (*Mark* 4, 11; *1 Tim.* 3, 16).

N

Naamah [nā'-ă-măh]. **1.** Daughter of Lamech (*Gen.* 4, 22). **2.** Wife of Solomon and mother of Rehoboam (*1 Kings* 14, 21). **3.** Town in Judah (*Josh.* 15, 41).

Naaman [nā'-ă-măn]. **1.** A son or grandson of Benjamin (*Gen.* 46, 21; *Num.* 26, 40). **2.** C.-in-C. of the armies of Benhadad of Damascus. He was a leper. His master, the king, wrote a letter to the king of Israel (or Samaria) who thought this was only an attempt to pick a quarrel. He consulted Elisha who advised him to have Naaman sent to himself; but when Naaman arrived, Elisha treated him in a rather off-hand fashion which offended the Syrian. Elisha's attitude was 'there is my advice, take it or leave it.' Naaman was inclined to leave it, but was persuaded to take a chance and he was cured. Elisha refused the rich rewards which Naaman was prepared to give, but his servant Gehazi reckoned that making something off the heathen was not a bad thing. He suffered for his temerity. Naaman knew that he had to appear in the temple of Rimmon with his master the king, and asked a dispensation to stand there with the king, but to worship Jehovah. Elisha had no objection. The whole story is in *2 Kings* (ch. 5).

Nabal [nā'-băl]. A sheepmaster of Maon who pastured his flocks about Carmel, and whose wife, Abigail, ultimately married David (*1 Sam.* 25, 1-42).

Nabataeans [nă-bă-tē′-ăns]. Also Nabathaeans;
Nabathites. An important Arabian people who
were at their height in the last 2 cent. BC, and in
the 1st cent. AD. Their capital was Petra.

Naboth [nā′-bŏth]. He was a man of Jezreel who
owned a vineyard near one of Ahab's summer
palaces. Ahab wanted it but Naboth would not
sell. Jezebel trumped up a charge agst. him and
had him executed and Ahab got his vineyard.
Elijah took the matter up, however, and told
Ahab he would have little luck. Elijah was right
(*2 Kings* 9).

Nac(h)on [nă′-kŏn]. Threshing floor where Uzzah
was struck dead for touching the Ark (*2 Sam.*
6, 6 & 7).

Nadab [nā′-dăb]. **1.** Oldest of the 4 sons of Aaron
(*Ex.* 6, 23). They were admitted to the priesthood
but were destroyed for making too much of it
(*Lev.* 10, 1-7). **2.** A man of Judah (*1 Chron.* 2, 28).
3. Son of Gibeon, a Benjamite (*1 Chron.* 8, 30).
4. Son and successor of Jeroboam who reigned
c. 913 BC. He led the people into idolatry and
was assassinated after less than 2 years' reign (*1
Kings* 14, 10; etc.).

Nahash [nā′-hăsh]. Former husband of David's
mother, father of his half sisters, Abigail and
Zeruiah (*2 Sam.* 17, 25; *1 Chron.* 2, 15-17). Also
an Ammonite king who determined to humiliate
the Israelites but was foiled by Saul (*1 Sam.* 11,
1-11).

Nahor [nā′-hŏr]. Abraham's grandfather (*Gen.* 11,
22).

Nahshon [nă′-shŏn]. Man of Judah whose sister
married Aaron (*Num.* 1, 7). He was an ancestor
of Boaz, and thus of David and of Jesus (*Ruth*
4, 20; *Matt.* 1, 4).

Nahum [nā′-hūm]. Of the man nothing is known

except that he had a consuming interest in Nineveh
and in its fate. Some of his ancestors may have
been deported thither in 722 BC. But that is con-
jecture. He seems, however, to have been an
inhabitant of Judaea (*Nahum* 1, 15). There is
another man of the name who was an ancestor
of Jesus (*Luke* 3, 25).

Nahum, Book of. The first 10 verses seem to be a
Psalm lauding the power of God and His ability
to do as He likes with Nineveh. The remainder
of the 1st ch. tells of God's intention to do what
He can do. The author then goes on in chs. 2
and 3, to describe in grim detail the fate that will
fall upon that mighty city. Nineveh was in fact
overthrown by the Persians and Babylonians in
612 BC, after a 3 year siege. The Book is prob.
a composite, but the passion agst. Nineveh is
plain and sustained. Oddly enough, as one of the
OT prophets, Nahum seems not at all concerned
with the sins of his own people. The prophets
usually cited the oppressions of the Assyrians as
just punishment for the faults and failings of
Israel and Judah. It may have been that Nahum
came just after the reforms of Josiah (qv) and
that he felt that the sin was purged and that all
was well—the Assyrians as the scourge in the hand
of God were no longer needed. The opening
Psalm (1, 1-10) is prob. in acrostic form (cf. *Ps.*
9; 10; 25; 34; 37; etc.).

Nail. 1. The fingernail. A sign of mourning was
to omit to trim the finger and toe nails (*Deut.* 21,
12; *2 Sam.* 19, 24). **2.** The tent peg, usually of
wood (*Judg.* 4, 21). **3.** Something thinner and
sharper, a kind of clothes peg, used to keep the
curtains hanging (*Ex.* 27, 19). **4.** The carpenter's
nail as understood to-day, and put to more or
less the same uses (*1 Chron.* 22, 3; *2 Chron.* 3, 9;

Isa. 41, 7). Nails were used in crucifixion (_John_ 20, 25).

Name. Among the ancients the name was very significant, and was often a combination of words expressing the parents' joy or otherwise, at the birth of the child. Some names were taken from the animal or vegetable kingdom. Terah is a wild goat; Leah a wild cow; Tabitha a gazelle; Tamat a palm tree (cf. Rosemary, Myrtle, Hazel, etc.). Some affirmed the faith of the parents: Nethaniah, ' God has given '; Elizur, ' God is a rock.' With Aramaic and Gk. both in use, a man might have 2 names: Thomas and Didymus simply mean ' twin ' in the 2 languages; just as Messiah and Christ both mean ' anointed.' The name, Joseph, under Gk. influence became Joses. Surnames were not used by the Hebs., the distinction bet. one and another of the same name being made by adding the place of habitation, or a word depicting some physical peculiarity. The Romans, however, had each 3 names. There was the prae-nomen, which was his personal name, the nomen, which was the name of his house or tribe, and the cognomen which was his family name. Mar-cus Antonius Felix was Marcus of the Antonia clan of the sept or family known as the Felixes.

Naomi [nā´-ō-mī]. Wife of Elimelech who emi-grated with her and his 2 sons to Moab. The sons married Moabite women, one of them being Ruth. When Elimelech and the sons died Naomi came home with Ruth (chs. 1-4).

Naphtali [năph´-tă-lī], **(Nephtalim). 1.** Sixth son of Jacob (_Gen._ 30, 8). **2.** The tribe or clan desc. from him. He had 4 sons and the clan had 4 septs (_Gen._ 46, 24). At the 1st census the warriors numbered 54,000; and at the 2nd census 45,400 (_Num._ 2, 30; 26, 50). They were given for their portion

N Palestine. a dist. bounded on the E by upper
Jordan and the Sea of Galilee. It bordered Issachar on the S, and Zebulun on the W (*Josh.* 19,
34). It formed a long narrow strip about 50 m.
long by 15 broad, and was hilly, though fertile
enough (*Josh.* 20, 7). Its main cities were Ramah,
Hazor, Kedesh, Hammoth-dor and Kartan. Kedesh was a city of refuge (*Josh.* 20, 7). They
played a heroic part in the fighting under Barak
(*Judg.* 4, 6 & 10; 5, 18). They rallied to David
in the fight agst. Ishbosheth (*1 Chron.* 12, 34).
Benhadad of Syria ravaged their country (*1 Kings*
15, 20), but Isaiah promised that all would be
restored (*Isa* 9, 1-7). Jesus spent much of His
ministry in the old land of Naphtali, of which
Chorazin, Capernaum and Tiberias were cities
in His day (*Matt.* 4, 12-16).

Napkin. A piece of cloth put more or less to the
same uses, including those of handkerchief, as it
is to-day.

Narcissus. A Rom. whose household was greeted
by Paul in the letter to the Romans (16, 11).

Nard. *See* SPIKENARD.

Nathan [nā'-thăn]. **1.** A man of Judah (*1 Chron.* 2,
36). **2.** A prophet working in the reigns of David
and Solomon. He told David that the building
of the Temple was to be his son's work (*1 Chron.*
17, 1-15). He also took David to task for the
affair with Bathsheba (*2 Sam.* 12, 1-15). When
there was doubt about the succession; Nathan
persuaded David to nominate Solomon and was
made one of the executors to see that Solomon
succeeded (*1 Kings* 1, 11-45). He wrote a hist. of
the events in which he had played a part (*1 Chron.*
29, 29; *2 Chron.* 9, 29). **3.** Relatives of two of
David's heroes (*2 Sam.* 23, 36). **4.** Third son of
David (*2 Sam.* 5, 14). He is a link bet. David

and Jesus (*Luke* 3, 31). **5.** Two returned exiles (*Ezra* 8, 16; 10, 39).

Nathanael [nă-thăn′-ă-ĕl]. Name of a disciple, occurring only in *John* and prob. identical with Bartholomew. He was a native of Cana and was called by Jesus ' an Israelite indeed ' prob. because he did not believe that anything good could come out of Nazareth (*John* 1, 45-51). He was in the boat when Jesus appeared after the resurrection (*John* 21, 2).

Nations. RV and RSV use this word often where AV has ' Gentiles ' and ' heathen.' It means what Kipling meant when he wrote of ' The Gentiles . . . . without the law.' Simply, people other than the Jews.

Naughtiness Wickedness (*Prov.* 11, 6).

Naughty. Worthless (*Jer.* 24, 2).

Nazarene. (*Matt.* 2, 23.) One born in, or a native of, Nazareth. It has no connection with Nazirite (qv). It may here be used as the fulfilment of the prophecy (*Isa.* 11, 1). Elsewhere it is used contemptuously (*Mark* 10, 47; *John* 19, 19; *Acts* 24, 5; etc.).

Nazareth. A town of Galilee, the home of Joseph and Mary, and the place where Jesus lived for the first 30 years of his life. He was held in high esteem until He started His ministry (*Luke* 2, 51-52; 4, 16 & 28-31). The town cannot have been of much size or importance, for it is not mentioned in the OT. It stood on an eminence in a valley of Lower Galilee, and is some 90 m. from Jerusalem.

Nazirite. A person, male or female who put himself or herself completely at the disposal of God, by vow, for a stated period. This did not mean that the Nazirite became either a hermit or an ascetic. The regulations governing Nazirites were laid down in law at Sinai, and by them he (they were usually men) must not touch strong drink, including wine, or eat any product of the vine. This was simply because cultivation of the vine was the symbol of a settled, instead of a nomadic life. Nor was he allowed to cut his hair. He had to avoid any kind of ceremonial uncleanness, like coming in contact with a corpse. At the end of the stated period of obligation he came to the priest, performed certain sacrifices, cut off his hair and burned it (*Num.* 6, 1-21). He then was at liberty to lead a normal life. The Nazirite might dedicate himself for life, or might be so dedicated from his birth, as Samson was (*Judg.* 13, 4) and Samuel (*1 Sam.* 1, 11). In the time of Amos there was a deliberate attempt to persuade Nazirites away from their vows (*Amos* 2, 11 & 12). John the Baptist was a Nazirite (*Luke* 1, 15); and Paul may have taken the vow (*Acts* 21, 20-26).

Neapolis [nē-ăp'-ō-lĭs]. The harbour of Philippi (*Acts* 16, 11).

Nebo [nē'-bō]. The Babylonian god of literature and science (*Isa.* 46, 1). It is also the name of a mt. in the Abarim range near Jericho (*Deut.* 32, 49; 34, 1). There are 2 towns called Nebo—one in Judah (*Ezra* 2, 29; etc.); and one in Moab (*Num.* 32, 3; etc.).

Nebuchadnezzar (Nebuchadrezzar) [nē'-bŭch-ăd-nĕz'-ăr]. His father, Nabopolassar, was a Chaldean who rebelled agst. Assyria and founded the Neo-Babylonian Empire c. 625 BC. Nebuchadnezzar, when prince, inflicted a heavy defeat upon Necho of Egypt who had already defeated and killed Josiah of Judah at the battle of Megiddo (608). This was the battle of Carchemish (605) which brought everything bet. Babylon and the Egyptian border under Chaldean sway. In the same year his father died and Nebuchadnezzar

became king. Judah paid him tribute for 3 yrs.,
then rebelled (*2 Kings* 24, 1) but were reconquered
(*2 Chron.* 36, 6). Later, under Zedekiah, they
revolted again, helped by the advance of an
Egyptian army (*Jer.* 37, 5). Jerusalem fell and
was burned and the exile began (586) (*2 Kings*
24-25). Nebuchadnezzar was at war with neighbouring peoples for the better part of his 43 yrs.
on the throne. He finally went out of his mind
and died in 562. With the forced labour of
deported populations he built several works of
note including the celebrated Hanging Gardens.
See BABYLONIA, JEREMIAH, JEHOIAKIM, JEHOIACHIN,
ZEDEKIAH, ISRAEL, ETC.

Nebuzaradan [nĕ′-bū-zăr-ă′-dăn]. Captain of the
Chaldean troops who finished off Jerusalem. He
showed kindness to Jeremiah (*2 Kings* 25, 8-11;
Jer. 39, 11-14).

Neck. The neck under the yoke was defeat and
subjection; to break the yoke was liberation
(*Deut.* 28, 48). Stiffnecked was ' hard to guide '
(*Deut.* 31, 27). To ' put the neck to work ' (*Neh.*
3, 5) was ' to get the sleeves rolled up '; ' put
the back into it.'

Necklace. *See* ORNAMENTS.

Necromancy. *See* MAGIC.

Needle's eye. (*Mark* 10, 25.) There is no need to
try to prove that there was a narrow street called
the Needle's Eye through which camels could
hardly go. The ordinary needle and the ordinary
camel are good enough for a sensible proverb.

Negeb [nĕg′-ĕb]. Fine grazing land S of Hebron
over which Abraham wandered (*Gen.* 12, 9; etc.).
The word is often used as an alternative for the
South, but it was a definite geographical area. Its
main towns were Kadesh Barnea, Beer-sheba,
Ziklag and Arad.

Neginah(oth) [nĕ-gīn'-äh]. A musical term appearing in Psalm titles. Gen. it means a stringed instrument (*Ps.* 61).

Nehemiah [nĕ-hē-mī'-äh]. There are 3 of the name, all of them returned exiles (*Ezra* 2, 2; *Neh.* 3, 16) but the important one is the prophet of the book. He was a Jew of the Exile, son of Hacaliah, and the king's butler, and wine taster. He begged permission to return to Jerusalem to see if there was anything he could do to repair its desolation, and he received permission to do so. The year was c. 445 BC. He was appointed governor of Judah, or of what was left of it; and various Persian governors were instructed to co-operate with him. Ezra the priest had preceded him to Jerusalem 13 yrs. before. He encouraged the people to tackle the job of rebuilding the walls, in the face of active opposition from Sanballat, Tobiah and Geshem, chiefs of neighbouring tribes. In 7 or 8 weeks the work was well advanced and was crowned by a religious revival and a new covenant. Nehemiah governed for 12 yrs., then returned to Susa c. 433. He then asked for further leave and returned to Jerusalem where he spent the rest of his life. He was a man of considerable character and accomplishment, and there is not quite another like him in Scripture.

Nehemiah, Book of. Part of the book is autobiographical, though there are obvious later additions. It is the last historical book of the OT. It was not Nehemiah who brought the Jews back from captivity, but Zerubbabel. Nehemiah followed him after about 90 yrs. By this time the Persian empire was at the start of its decline, and this may have been why Ezra was finding things so hard in Jerusalem. He had in fact 'lost the place' and the people had slid into heathen ways.

To them comes the man of action, Nehemiah. The first 7 chs. are a personal diary, and the whole book falls into 3 sections. There is the building of the wall, starting with Nehemiah's appeal to the king, and the granting of the king's permission, and the journey to Jerusalem (1—2, 20). This section proceeds with an account of the work and the difficulties encountered (ch. 3); and ends with the finished job (7, 1-3). The 2nd section (chs. 8-10) tells of the consecration of the people and the renewal of the covenant. The 3rd section (chs. 11-13) tells of the re-ordering of the life of the people, the cleansing of worship and conduct, and the dedication of the wall. As we have said, this is the last historical book of the OT. The period covered by the books bet. Joshua and Nehemiah is something over 1,000 yrs.

Nehiloth [nĕ'-hī-lŏth]. Psalm title (*Ps.* 5). Means prob. a wind instrument.

Nephew. (*Judg.* 12, 14; *Job* 18, 19; *Isa.* 14, 22; *1 Tim.* 5, 4.) The word should be ' grandson.'

Nephilim [nĕ'-phĭl-ĭm]. See GIANT.

Nephtoah [nĕph-tō'-äh]. Town on border of Judah and Benjamin, source of part of Jerusalem's water supply (*Josh.* 15, 9).

Nereus [nēr'-ēŭs]. Rom. Christian greeted by Paul (*Rom.* 16, 15).

Nergal [nēr'-găl]. Babylonian god of war and pestilence; ruler of the underworld (*2 Kings* 17, 30).

Net. Fishing nets were of two kinds—the casting net, thrown with a circular action to spread it out almost like a lasso (*Matt.* 4, 18); and the drag net with the bottom weighted and the top supported by floats (*Isa.* 19, 8). Nets were also used in fowling and hunting (*Prov.* 1, 17; *Isa.* 51, 20; etc.).

Nethanel [nĕ-thă'-nel]. **1.** Prince of Issachar (*Num.*

1, 8). **2.** Brother of David (*1 Chron.* 2, 14). There are 8 others of slight importance (*1 Chron.* 15, 24; 26, 4; *2 Chron.* 17, 7; 35, 9; *Ezra* 10, 22; *Neh.* 12, 21 & 36).

Nethinim [nĕth'-ĭ-nĭm]. A good deal of menial work was connected with temple sacrifices. Fires had to be lit and cleaned out, wood cut, blood and offal cleared away and the whole place, which from time to time looked and smelled like a slaughterhouse, kept from being offensive. Orig. this work was done by slaves and prisoners (*Num.* 31, 47; *Josh.* 9, 23). Later David gave servants to the Levites in the temple who seem to have made a kind of office of the job. These and their descendants were called Nethinim, but not till after the Exile. What they were called before that is not known. Those who came back after the Exile do not, by their names, seem to have been native Jews (*Ezra* 2, 43-54).

Nettle. Two words are so trans. There is the true nettle (*urtica pilulifera*) (*Prov.* 24, 31; *Isa.* 34, 13; *Hos.* 9, 6). Elsewhere it is simply quick-growing and wide-spreading weeds of some kind.

New Moon. *See* FEASTS.

New Testament. This is, of course, the name given to the 2nd section of the Bible, excluding the Apocrypha. The word 'Testament' is discussed under that name. In the NT there are 27 books, and all of them were written in the common Gk., now known as 'NT Greek.' This Gk. was, so to speak, the *lingua franca* of the world for some 300 yrs. before the birth of Jesus. None of the orig. MS is in existence, and the very earliest copies of any of the NT books are no more than 1,700 yrs. old. The paper on which they were written was papyrus which had a short life, and many of the earliest MS were sought out by the servants of Diocletian (AD 303) and were destroyed wherever found. It must be remembered, though it seems silly to point it out, that printing had not been invented. Every copy was made by hand, and any person who has tried to transcribe any ill-written document knows very well that it is possible to make mistakes. There are, in fact, some 4,500 copies of the NT in existence. As we have said, mistakes occur, and there are wide variations in the copies. Sometimes the man who copied thought that he knew better than his model what the sense of a passage should be. Sometimes they would write their observations in the margin, and then the man who copied them would get the marginal observations confused with the actual text. When all the extant MSS of the NT are compared, it is found that there is something like a quarter of a million variants—that is, differences: some large, some very small. Most of them do not matter a great deal one way or the other. Scholars, sifting through this great mass, have, however, come to an almost universally agreed text. The MSS are found in 2 main forms or patterns. In one all the letters are written as capitals with no space at all bet. the words. These are known as Uncials. In the other the words are written in running hand, like mod. writing, with spaces bet. the words. These are known as Cursives. But the Cursives date from about the year 1000. There are only half a dozen MSS of anything like completeness which are older than this. Here is a point which must always be borne in mind, for it is so easy to assume that the records of the events of the NT date almost from the time when they occurred. They do nothing of the kind. The very oldest of them dates from at least 500 yrs. later. There is no space to list the

various versions in any detail. The important
thing to remember is that the best we have is a
copy of a copy of a copy, almost ad infinitum, of
the originals; and that copyists are liable to error,
esp. in the Uncial convention, where the last
letter of one word might be read as the first letter
of another word. The difficulty with Uncials may
be seen from a sentence such as this: WHOMO-
THERSASCRIBE. That can be read as 'whom
others ascribe' or as 'who mothers a scribe.'
Scholars have been much criticised for what used
to be called the Higher Criticism, but their labours
have resulted in a text which can be accepted as
the nearest we are ever likely to get to the original.
When people talk of the verbal inspiration of the
English Bible they should not forget the devious
ways by which the words have come to us. But
those who scoff at the idea of verbal inspiration
after all these years must not forget that the Holy
Spirit has guided and still does guide the heart
and the head and the hand of man. *See* VERSIONS,
BIBLE, CANON.

Nicanor [nĭ-cā′-nŏr]. One of the 7 elected deacons
of the early Church (*Acts* 6, 5).

Nicodemus [nĭc′-ō-dē′-mus]. A Pharisee and member of the Sanhedrin to whom Jesus explained
the wonder of the new birth (*John* 3, 1-21). He
objected to the way in which the Sanhedrin condemned Jesus unheard (*John* 7, 50-52). He helped
in preparing the body of Jesus for the tomb (*John*
19, 39).

Nicolaitans [nĭc′-ō-lā′-ĭ-tăns]. A sect which arose
in the churches of Ephesus and Pergamos. They
argued that nothing was sin to the saved (*Rev.*
2, 6 & 14 & 15) in defiance of the Church position
(*Acts* 15, 29).

Nicolaus [nĭc′-ō-lā′-ŭs] (Nicolas, AV). One of the 7

elected deacons of the early Church (*Acts* 6, 5).

Nicopolis [nĭc-ŏ'-pŏl-ĭs]. Place on the R. Nestus which forms the border bet. Thrace and Macedonia. But it is doubtful if this was the place where Paul hoped to spend the winter (*Titus* 3, 12).

Niger [nī'-gēr]. The surname of Simeon of Antioch. It means ' black ' but he seems to have been of Jewish origin. ' Black ' is the surname of a good many white people (*Acts* 13, 1).

Night. *See* TIME.

Night hawk. A bird of unknown species, ceremonially unclean (*Lev.* 11, 16). It may be the nightjar, or even the owl.

Night monster. (*Isa.* 34, 14 RV marg.) In AV it is ' screech owl.' The Heb. means simply ' nocturnal,' and it might be any night flyer.

Nile. The river of Egypt, Nahum calls it a sea when flooding (*Nahum* 3, 8). Without the Nile, Egypt, of course, would be desert. The annual flooding of the river deposits silt along the banks which is the most fertile of soil, annually renewed. The total length of the river is over 3,500 m. The Blue and White Niles join at Khartoum, and the mainstream is joined 140 m. lower by the only other tributary, the Atbara.

Nimrod [nĭm'-rŏd]. A Cushite, warrior and hunter whose kingdom was in Shinar (*Gen.* 10, 8-10). He is prob. a completely legendary figure.

Nimshi [nĭm'-shī]. Grandfather of Jehu (*1 Kings* 9, 16).

Nineveh [nĭn'-ĕ-vĕh]. The great Assyrian city on the left bank of the Tigris. It was circled by a great wall with 15 gates and towers and partially surrounded by a moat. The enclosed area was 1,800 acres. The name derives from Nina, the fish god of a metal-using people from S Babylonia who followed a Stone Age people settled at the place (*Gen.* 10, 11). Nina developed into Ishtar, greatly worshipped in the reign of Hammurabi c. 2100 BC. Sennacherib was the main architect of Nineveh and of its greatness (*2 Kings* 19, 36).

Nisan [nī'-san]. Post-exilic name for Abib, the 1st month of the year. It corresponds roughly to the Eng. March (*Neh.* 2, 1). *See* TIME, YEAR.

Nisroch [nĭs'-rŏch]. Assyrian deity in whose temple Sennacherib was murdered (*2 Kings* 19, 37).

Nitre. This is not mod. nitre, which is saltpetre. It is an alkali like carbonate of soda. It was used in washing or bleaching (*Prov.* 25, 20; *Jer.* 2, 22).

No, Noamon (*Nahum* 3, 8). This is the ancient Egyptian city of Thebes. It became the capital of the 18th dynasty of Pharaohs, and was a place of great splendour and beauty, and was the heart and centre of Egyptian civilisation till the Assyrians conquered Egypt in 671 BC. The town was sacked in 663, but remained of some stature till it was razed to the ground by the Rom. Cornelius Gallus for participating in a revolt agst. taxation (29 BC).

Noah [nō'-äh], **Noe.** Simply the son of Lamech and father of Shem, Ham and Japheth, who being a good man in a bad world was bidden build an ark to rescue the best of man and beast from the waters of destruction. He seems also to have invented wine, and suffered for it (*Gen.* chs. 6-9). *See* FLOOD.

Noamon [nō-ā'-mŏn]. *See* NO.

Nob [nŏb]. A town of the priests in Benjamin. After the Ark of the Covenant had been captured, the Tabernacle was for a while at Nob. The High Priest of the time, Ahimelech, received David there when Saul was looking for him, allowed him and his men to refresh themselves with the shewbread, and gave David the sword of Goliath.

For this Saul killed him and massacred the inhabitants of Nob. Abiathar escaped and told
David (1 Sam. 21-22).

Nod [nŏd]. Country to the E of Eden where Cain
went (Gen. 4, 16).

Nogah [nō'-găh]. Son of David (1 Chron. 3, 7).

Noisesome. The word is used nowadays mostly for
something loathsome, esp. to the sense of smell.
The orig. meaning is ' annoys-some,' ie full of
annoyance of any kind. In AV it can mean hurtful.

Nose jewel. Indian women wear to-day a nose jewel
which is studded or riveted through the nostril
(Isa. 3, 21). It is very becoming.

Nose ring. A split ring inserted through a hole bored
in the nostril (cf. ear ring). It might be inserted
through the gristle bet. the nostrils (Ezek. 16, 12).
See ORNAMENTS.

Nought. The phrase to ' set at nought ' has a
meaning not always appreciated. ' Set ' does not
mean to place in a position, but to value. ' Set
at nought ' is ' value at nothing ' (Prov. 1, 25;
Mark 9, 12).

Novice. Lit. ' newly planted.' To-day it means one
who has not yet taken holy orders. In the early
Church it prob. meant no more than a ' new
member ' (1 Tim. 3, 6).

Number, Numeral. Most of the ancients reckoned
in a form of the decimal system. The natural way
to count is with the fingers, and normally there
are 10 of these. The highest number that can be
expressed in a single Heb. word is 20,000. AV
is wrong with ' millions ' (Gen. 24, 60). The word
should be ten-thousands. Big numbers are found
in the census of warriors (1 Chron. 21; 2 Chron.
17). In OT Heb. the numerals are represented
in the main by words, and the NT Gk. follows

suit. Arithmetic was not a science with the Hebs.
though it is obvious from the census that they could
count, prob. making a mark of some kind for
each hundred or so. They used round numbers a
great deal—' ten thousand times ten thousand '
which must simply be reckoned as a way of expressing a very large number indeed. Seven was
a sacred number with the Jews (*Gen.* 2, 2). But
this was due to religious considerations. *See*
SABBATH.

Numbers, Book of. The Book gets its name from
the two censuses, or numberings of the people
(chs. 1-4; 26). The period covers something
under 40 yrs. of nomadic life beginning at Sinai
and ending on the plains of Moab. Some of these
years are simply rushed over. 17 chs. out of the
27 that deal with the travelling, are given to the
last year of it (20-36). In the account no route
is described, so that ' wandering ' is a better word
than ' travelling ' to describe the progress. The 2
great heroes of the Book, who emerge as real and
clearly drawn characters are Joshua and Caleb
(qv). The great event is the 1st of the 3 Heb.
rebellions (chs. 13-14). The 2nd rebellion was
when they demanded of Samuel a king, and the
3rd was the split bet. Israel and Judah on the
death of Solomon. There is not a great deal of
spiritual teaching in the Book, though there is a
deal of poetry, or scraps of it (6, 24-26; 10, 35-36;
21, 14 & 15 & 17 & 18 & 27-30). The Book begins
with the ordering and preparation of the people
for the expedition (chs. 1-4). Certain laws of
health and conduct are then laid down (chs. 5-6).
The religious observances are defined and the
Passover taken (chs. 7 & 8 & 9, 1-4). There
follow general directions for the march—the cloud
and the trumpets (9, 15-23; 10, 1-10). From Sinai

they march with constant complaint and bickering culminating in the revolt at Kadesh Barnea when all the spies but Caleb and Joshua bring in unfavourable reports (10, 11-14, 45). They then move back from the borders of the Promised Land (15-19). They return and move on into the Plains of Moab where they encounter Balaam. They hold another census, promulgate some new laws, and decide on their military and civil policy for the invasion.

Nun [nŭn]. Non once (*1 Chron.* 7, 27). Father of Joshua (*Ex.* 33, 11). It is also the 14th letter of the Heb. alphabet approximating to the Eng. *N*.

Nurse. These are of 2 sorts—the wet nurse who suckled the child of another woman, obviously a woman who had given birth at about the same time. Children were suckled for as long as 3 yrs. (*Ex.* 2, 7-9; etc.; *Gen.* 24, 59). There was also the ' Nanny,' male or female, employed by the wealthy to look after their young children, or some infirm member of the household (*Num.* 11, 12; *Ruth* 4, 16; *2 Sam.* 4, 4).

Nuts. Two words are so trans. **1.** (*Gen.* 43, 11) is the pistachio nut. **2.** (*S. of S.* 6, 11). The walnut.

Nymphas [nўm'-phăs]. A Christian at Laodicaea or Colossae greeted by Paul (*Col.* 4, 15).

O

Oak. Heb. word *Elah* is sometimes used simply as a place name (*1 Sam.* 17, 2; 21, 9). Sometimes it is trans. terebinth, or elm. The Heb. word *elon* is trans. ' plain ' in the AV but correctly trans. ' oak ' in the RV (*Gen.* 12, 6; etc.).

Oath. A statement or promise made as in the presence of God and therefore absolutely binding (*Gen.* 21, 23; 31, 53; *Heb.* 6, 16; etc.). To retract it was an offence agst. God (*Ezek.* 17, 13). Sometimes the oath was made with the uplifted hand, sometimes by placing the hand under the thigh of the person to whom the contract was being given (*Gen.* 24, 2). The oath might be made before the altar and accompanied by gifts or sacrifices (*Gen.* 15, 8 & 18; 21, 27 & 31). A woman's oath might be disavowed by her father if she was a virgin, or by her husband (*Num.* 30). Jesus condemned the whole practice (*Matt.* 5, 33-37).

Obadiah [ā'-băd-ī'-ăh]. There are several of the name (*1 Chron.* 7, 3; 12, 9; 27, 19; 8, 38; *2 Chron.* 17, 7; *1 Kings* 18, 3), but the most important is the prophet.

Obadiah, Book of. Short book by the Prophet of Judah which bears his name. It foretells the destruction of Edom because of their hostility to Judah and warns them not to rejoice in the misfortunes of Judah for a day of reckoning was coming. Obadiah's vision dates from about the time of the fall of Jerusalem in 586 BC. The object of his attack is Edom. He foretold their destruction because they were the descendants of Esau, while Israel was descended from Jacob. Although the Edomites were then rejoicing at the discomfiture of Judah, their day would come, and Judah would be restored.

Obed [ō'-běd]. Several of the name (*1 Chron.* 2, 37; 11, 47; 26, 7; *2 Chron.* 23, 1). The most celebrated is the son of Boaz and Ruth, grandfather of David (*Ruth* 4, 17).

Obed-Edom [ō'-běd ē'-dŏm]. A Gittite who housed the Ark of the Covenant at Kiriath Jearim (*2 Sam.* 6, 10 & 12).

Oblation. An offering to God. *See* OFFERINGS.

Oded [ō'-běd]. **1.** Father of the prophet Azariah (*2 Chron.* 15, 1). **2.** Prophet in the reign of Pekah I of Israel who insisted that prisoners from Judah should be returned (*2 Chron.* 28, 9 & 15).

Offerings. Making offerings to God was a very ancient practice (*Gen.* 4, 3; 8, 20; *Ex.* 10, 25; etc.), and was known in Egypt and Babylonia long before patriarchal times. The form and order is laid down by law (*Lev.* chs. 1-7). The 3 types were: vegetable, animal and drink, and might be personal or national. The vegetable offering is called ' meat ' in the AV and ' meal ' in the RV, and the drink offering was always in connection with it. The offering was of white meal, unleavened bread, or roasted grain, always with salt and usually with olive oil. Animal offerings were usually cattle, sheep or goats and sometimes doves. They might be of either sex but must be free from blemish and not less than a week old. For the Burnt Offering the animal was male. The blood was sprinkled on and around the altar and the carcase was completely burned. For the Sin Offering there was a bullock, a goat, a she lamb or a dove. For the Guilt Offering, a ram. Only the fat was burned, the flesh going to the priests. Sin agst. another person could not be expiated by the offering—reparation had first to be made; and, of course, no offering could expiate an offence which deserved capital punishment (*Num.* 15, 30). Peace offerings were made in gratitude for favours received or simply as an expression of devotion, the flesh of the offering being shared by the person and the priest. It was eaten at the altar as a Communion meal. The Sacrificer brought the victim to the priest and laid his hands on its head. The priest then killed it, sprinkled the blood, and burned it.

Og [ŏg]. The king of Bashan (*Num.* 21, 33). He was
the last of the giant Rephaim. The celebrated
iron bedstead was more prob. a sarcophagus of
ironstone (*Deut.* 3, 11). He was killed at Edrai
(*Deut.* 3, 3).

Oholah [ō-hō′-läh], **(Aholah)**. Personification of
Israel as a loose woman (*Ezek.* 23, 4 & 44).

Oholibamah [ō-hō′-lĭ-bä′-mäh]. Wife of Esau (*Gen.*
36, 2).

Oil. Mainly olive oil. The olives shaken from the
tree were trampled in the press (*Isa.* 17, 6). The
oil was drained into vats and jars and allowed to
settle. It was a most important product in the
economy of the people (*Num.* 18, 12; etc.), and
was used for cooking and for lighting (*Ex.* 27, 20;
Ezek. 16, 13). It was also used medicinally (*Isa.*
1, 6; *Mark* 6, 13). After bathing, the body was
anointed (*2 Sam.* 12, 20). It was used as a hair
fixative (*Ps.* 23, 5).

Oil tree. Prob. not the olive tree but the pine (*1
Kings* 6, 23; *Isa.* 41, 19).

Ointment. Used in the toilet and for embalming.
The base was olive oil with various spices and
fragrant extracts added (*Esth.* 2, 12; *Matt.* 26,
6-13). There were also salves, used medicinally
(*Jer.* 8, 22; *Rev.* 3, 18).

Old Testament. See CANON, PENTATEUCH, VERSIONS.

Olive. A tree grown principally for the valuable oil
extracted from the ripe fruit, though the timber
was also used. It is the common *olea europaea*.
It was reckoned the symbol of peace, beauty,
strength and prosperity (*Ps.* 52, 8; *Jer* 11, 16;
Hosl 14, 6) *See* OIL.

Olives, Mt. of, (Olivet). A hill across the valley
of Kidron from Jerusalem on the E. Its distance
was a Sabbath's day journey (qv) (*Acts* 1, 12). It
had deep religious associations—Ezekiel had his

vision there (*Ezek.* 11, 23); and Zechariah saw
God standing on its summit (*Zech.* 14, 4) Jesus
was fond of the hill and travelled often to it (*Luke*
21, 37; 22, 39; *John* 8, 1). This is where the
crowds first welcomed Him with Hosannahs (*Luke*
19, 37) Gethsemane was to the W of the hill
(*Matt.* 26, 30); and Bethany and Bethphage were
on the E slope (*Matt.* 21, 1). It is really a short
range of hills with a maximum height of under
3,000 feet. One of the peaks is known as the Mt.
of the Ascension.

Olivet. *See above.*

Olympas [ō-lўm'-păs]. Rom. Christian (*Rom.* 16,
15).

Omer [ō'-měr]. *See* WEIGHTS AND MEASURES.

Omega [ŏ-mē'-gǎ]. Last letter of the Gk. alphabet,
used with Alpha of God as the first and the last
(*Rev.* 1, 8; etc.).

Omri [ŏm'-rī]. **1.** Descendant of Benjamin (*1
Chron.* 7, 8). **2.** Man of Judah (*1 Chron.* 9, 4).
3. Prince of Issachar (*1 Chron.* 27, 18). **4.** One of
the most important of Israel's kings. He was a
general in the army of Elah of Israel who was
murdered by Zimri. Civil war broke out. Omri
won the struggle and made Tirzah his capital (*1
Kings* 16, 17). Later he moved to Samaria.
During his reign, Israel for the first time came in
contact with Assyria, and the Assyrians called
Israel ' Omri's land.' He established alliances with
the Phoenicians which led to the disastrous
marriage bet. his son Ahab and Jezebel. He died
c. 874 BC. *See* ISRAEL.

On [ŏn]. **1.** Reubenite chief (*Num.* 16, 1). **2.** City
of Lower Egypt on the delta near Memphis,
where sun worship was practised (*Gen.* 41, 45).

Onesimus [ō-něs'-ĭ-mus]. Runaway slave whom Paul
induced to return to his master, Philemon. He

went back with Tychicus, bearing Paul's letter to Philemon (qv).

Onesiphorus [ŏn'-ĕs-īph'-ŏ-rŭs]. Christian orig. from Ephesus who showed much kindness to Paul in Rome (2 Tim. 1, 16-18; 4, 19).

Onion. *Allium cepa*, the bulbous root which was and is much cultivated in Egypt and Palestine (*Num.* 11, 5).

Ono [ō'-nō]. Benjamite city to which his enemies invited Nehemiah after the return from the Exile (1 Chron. 8, 12; Neh. 6, 2).

Onycha [ŏn'-ў̆-chă]. (*Ex.* 30, 34). An ingredient of incense prob. extracted from the lid of some mollusc.

Onyx. *See* JEWELS AND PRECIOUS STONES.

Ophel [ō'-phĕl]. Part of the wall of Jerusalem near the pool of Siloam (Neh. 3, 15-27). It was prob. a great tower.

Ophir [ō'-phĭr]. Tribe descended from Joktan (Gen. 10, 29). Also their country, which has been described variously as being in India, Arabia and Africa (1 Chron. 29, 4; 1 Kings 10, 11 & 22; 22, 48).

Ophni [ŏph'-nī]. (*Josh.* 18, 24.) Town of Benjamin.

Ophrah [ŏph'-răh]. 1. Man of Judah (1 Chron. 4, 14). 2. Town of Benjamin N of Michmash (Josh. 18, 23). 3. Home of Gideon, W of Jordan (Judg. 6-8).

Orator. (*Acts* 24, 1.) Term applied to Tertullus. It means a 'pleader' who attends law-courts hoping to get a case. In one OT ref. (*Isa.* 3, 3) it might be better rendered 'enchanter.'

Orchard. In AV it means any kind of garden. or even copse or forest.

Oreb [ō'-rēb]. With Zeeb, princes of Midian (Judg. 7, 25). They were killed on the advice of Gideon, by the men of Ephraim (*Judg.* 8, 2). Also the place of their death (*Isa.* 10, 26).

Organ. *See* MUSIC.

Orion [ō-rī′-ŏn]. A constellation in the heavens. Orion was a giant in mythology. He was slain by Diana and transferred to the heavens (*Job* 38, 31).

Ornaments. Sometimes worn as amulets for protection agst. evil influences; and sometimes merely as adornments. They were of precious metals or of sea-shells. Two Heb. words are so trans. The 1st is more lit. ' jewels ' (*Gen.* 24, 53; *Ex.* 3, 22; etc.); and the 2nd is trans. ' ornaments ' (*Ex.* 33, 4; *Ezek.* 16, 11; etc.). Women wore earrings, necklaces, pendants, brooches, finger rings, chains, bracelets and anklets. Men wore seal rings (*Dan.* 6, 17). In time of mourning, all ornaments were put off (*Ex.* 33, 4-6).

Orpah [ŏr′-păh]. Daughter-in-law of Naomi and sister-in-law of Ruth (*Ruth* 1, 4-14).

Osnappar [ŏs-năp′-per], Asnappar. An important Assyrian official who placed foreign tribes in Samaria after the captivity (*Ezra* 4, 10). He is prob. the heir-apparent to the Assyrian throne. He succeeded his father, Esarhaddon, in 669 BC and reigned for 43 yrs.

Ospray. Prob. the osprey, *pandion haliaetus*. It may mean any of the smaller eagles, fish-eating or not (*Lev.* 11, 13).

Ossifrage. (*Lev.* 11, 13). Trans. ' gier eagle ' RV. This is one of the great vultures—not an eagle (*Gypaetus barbatus*).

Ostrich. Various Heb. words are so rendered in AV. There are no true ostriches in Palestine to-day, and it is highly doubtful if the refs. are to this bird or to the owl. But the word really means ' a feather ' (*Ezek.* 17, 3 & 7).

Othniel [ŏth′-nĭ-ĕl]. Nephew of Caleb (*Judg.* 1, 13). He is the 1st of the Judges (*Judg.* 3, 8-11).

Owl. Half a dozen Heb. words are so trans. The screech owl is sometimes known as the ' night monster' (*Isa.* 34, 14 RV). All the owls were ceremonially unclean (*Lev.* 11, 16).

Ox, oxen. Sometimes there is no ref. to sex (*Ex.* 20, 17), but gen. the ref. is to the male of the species, *bos taurus*. It was used for ploughing (*1 Kings* 19, 19), and as a draught animal (*Num.* 7, 3; etc.). They trod out the grain (*Deut.* 25, 4); they were sacrificed (*Num.* 7, 87); they were eaten as food (*1 Kings* 1, 25). For ' wild ox,' *see* UNICORN.

Ox goad. *See* GOAD.

Ozem [ō′-zĕm]. **1.** Son of Jesse (*1 Chron.* 2, 15). **2.** Son of Jerahmeel (*1 Chron.* 2, 25).

Ozni [ŏz′-nĭ]. Son of Gad and founder of a clan (*Num.* 26, 16).

P

Padan, Paddan [pă′-dăn]. Also Padan Aram. The plain of Aram (qv), Syria.

Paddle. (*Deut.* 23, 13.) Not the paddle for a canoe, but a kind of spade.

Painfulness. (*Ps.* 73, 16; *2 Cor.* 11, 27.) Means laboriousness.

Paint. Paint and powder were used by Egyptian women much as they are to-day; the Hebs. frowned on the practice, at least the authorities did (*2 Kings* 9, 30; *Jer.* 4, 30). Antimony, lead, kohl and henna were employed. There was little painting in the artistic sense.

Palace. The word means simply ' a great house,' and since the king normally had the greatest, it became the title for a royal residence (*1 Kings* 7,

1). There is a detailed description of Solomon's palace in the passage quoted and the following verses. It took nearly twice as long to build (13 yrs.) as the Temple did and the main feature of it was the House of the Forest of Lebanon—a hall 150 ft. long, by 75 broad and 45 high, the ceiling supported by 4 rows of pillars.

Palestine. The coast of Palestine forms the E end of the Mediterranean sea, an almost straight, harbourless line where shore meets sea. The E frontier of the land is by and large the gorge of the Jordan and the few cultivated miles beyond till the desert is reached. The S border is the desert again, a line from Gaza to the Gulf of Akaba. The N border with Syria has always been a debatable land. The area bet. Jordan and the Mediterranean is roughly 9,000 sq. m. and the span from sea to desert is seldom more than 100 m. Moving E from the Mediterranean coast there is the shore, then the coastal plain, the hills of Judaea and Samaria, the Plain of Esdraelon, Galilee, and Lebanon. Last is the gorge of the Jordan towards which the watershed of the hills flows. The Dead Sea, at the S extremity of the Jordan is 1,300 ft. below sea level. It is part of the Great Rift Valley which can be traced from the Caspian sea to Lake Tanganyika in Africa, and is deeper than the celebrated Grand Canyon of Colorado. The climate, though it varies with distance from the sea, is gen. sub-tropical with a rainy season from October to May, and a very hot dry season from May till October. There is evidence a-plenty that the land was settled in the Stone Age, but it was sometime about 3000 BC that the Semites began to advance over the land, and with them, or in opposition to them, the Anakim and Rephaim from the S. By 2500 BC

Palestine was part of the Egyptian empire, though the Hittites contested their supremacy. Around 1200 BC various waves of immigrant nomadic peoples found their way to Palestine—the Arameans from Arabia, the Philistines from the coastal areas and the Hebs. from Egypt and the S desert. These achieved a pretty secure foot-hold and made common cause with the Canaanites agst. the Philistines. It was not till the age of the kings, Saul and then David and Solomon, that the Philistines were driven back and the land made reasonably secure. After the death of Solomon the kingdom split into Judah, roughly mod. Palestine, and Israel, or Ephraim, roughly mod. Syria. These 2 kingdoms led a very chequered career (see ISRAEL) till 1st the N kingdom, and then Judah were transported by the Assyrians. Later Judah was resettled by the released captives under the Persians. Then the Persian Empire fell to Alexander the Great (333 BC). After his death Palestine again came under the overlordship of Egypt. But as the surrounding great peoples wilted under the advance of the Romans, the Judaeans revolted under the Maccabees and were free again by 143 BC. Nevertheless in these years of conflict Palestine and its people had been acquiring a character and producing a literature which was to make a far greater impact upon the world than have any of the great empires who oppressed them. Palestine is the birthplace of the 2 great monotheistic religions of the older world, Judaism and Islam; and of course, of the Christian religion itself. Very important was the conquest of the E by the W under Alexander, which brought this small Middle Eastern land into the orbit of Gk. culture and language. Then came the orderliness of the Rom. sway and the Pax Romana. The soil is fertile, given rain, and crops are abundant. Palestine is a land of flowers. There is abundance of wild life, but nowadays the lion and the cheetah, the hippopotamus and the bear are pretty well extinct.

Palm tree. Of the first importance for sustaining life was the date palm (*Ex.* 15, 27). Every part of the tree, fruit, leaves, seed, is put to use. Palm trees appeared copied in the metal work of the Temple (*1 Kings* 6, 29-35). In the Feast of Tabernacles, palm branches featured (*Neh.* 8, 15).

Palmer worm. 17th cent. name for caterpillar. *See* LOCUST.

Palsy. Paralysis. *See* MEDICINE.

Pamphylia [păm-phўl′-liä]. Dist. on the S coast of Asia Minor bet. Lycia and Cilicia. The name was later used for a Rom. province which embraced neighbouring areas. The main town was Perga which was visited by Paul and Barnabas, and it was there that John Mark left them (*Acts* 13, 13; 14, 25). *See* PERGA.

Pannag [păn′-năg]. (*Ezek.* 27, 17.) It seems to have been some kind of cake or confection.

Paper. *See* PAPYRUS.

Paper reed. This is papyrus (qv).

Paphos [pā′-phŏs]. Town on the coast of Cyprus and capital of that Rom. province. It was visited by Paul (*Acts* 13, 6-13).

Papyrus [păp-ŷ′-rus]. Although called a reed, papyrus is not grass. It is a kind of sedge growing to 10 ft. tall. It grew in water at the edge of rivers and lakes and was used for all kinds of woven containers, including boats. For paper making, the pith of the plant was drawn out, and thin sections were laid down criss-cross with glue bet., and under pressure. This gave sheets some ten inches square, although there are some rolls of over 100 ft. long. But for the exceedingly dry climate

of Egypt it is doubtful if any papyri would have
lasted very long, as they tended to split and to
rot in damp. Writing was done with ink, and
many of the rolls and codices (writings more in
book form) are still remarkably readable.

Parable. A parable is really an extended simile or
metaphor with a teaching intention. There may
be the use of the word 'like,' eg, 'the kingdom
of God is like . . .' Or the parable may be a
straightforward story of events, real, or imaginary,
which quite clearly contain a deeper meaning, as
the Prodigal Son, or the Sower. Being easily
remembered, if the parable is well told, the meaning sticks, when a straightforward homily might
be forgotten. Thus neighbourliness is almost
synonymous with the parable of the Good Samaritan. It was possible, too, for a moralist to administer a very sharp rebuke to an important personage, by using parable. David was completely
'taken in' by Nathan's parable of the one ewe
lamb, and the gravity of his sin struck all the
harder when he realised that he was the man in
question. There are a number of parables in the
OT (*Judg.* 9, 8-20; *2 Sam.* 12, 1-14; 14, 4-20; *1
Kings* 20, 35-42; *2 Kings* 14, 9-11; *Isa.* 5, 1-7;
Ezek. 17, 1-10; 19, 1-9; 23, 1-49; 24, 1-14). It
was Jesus who brought the parable to perfection.
From the beginning of His ministry Jesus used
parable (*Mark* 3, 23; etc.) but later He used the
method more and more, explaining His reason
in the rather difficult passage in *Matthew* (13,
10-16). There has been much disagreement about
the precise meaning of this passage, but it seems
clear that Jesus had made up His mind that there
were some people who would never get beyond
the story, and others who would at once leap to
the meaning and grasp it. There is surely signi-

ficance in the fact that His explanation of His purpose came immediately after His parable of the good and bad ground. This is not a parable of sowing or of seed. There is nothing wrong with either the sower or the seed. It is a parable of the soil that the seed fell into. Parables as Jesus used them had no subtle or obscure meaning. They were produced at an appropriate moment for an immediate purpose, and they must always be read and interpreted as such. Nor must familiarity with the parables diminish appreciation of the genius behind their composition. In the great parables not a word can be added nor a word deleted which would effect an improvement.

PARABLES OF JESUS

Found in 1 Gospel

	Matthew	Mark	Luke
Tares	13, 24		
Treasure	13, 44		
Pearl	13, 45		
Dragnet	13, 47		
Unmerciful servant	18, 23		
Vineyard labourers	20, 1		
Two sons	21, 28		
Prince's marriage	22, 2		
Ten virgins	25, 1		
Talents	25, 14		
Secret seed		4, 26	
Absent householder		13, 33	
Two debtors			7, 41
Good Samaritan			10, 30
Importunate friend			11, 5
Rich fool			12, 16
Waiting servants			12, 35
Faithful steward			12, 42
Barren fig tree			13, 6

PARABLES OF JESUS

Found in 1 Gospel

	Matthew	Mark	Luke
Great supper			14, 16
Tower and war cost			14, 28
Lost coin			15, 8
Prodigal son			15, 11
Unjust steward			16, 1
Rich man: Lazarus			16, 19
Unprofitable servants			17, 7
Unrighteous judge			18, 1
Pharisee: publican			18, 9
Pounds			19, 11

Found in 2 Gospels

	Matthew	Mark	Luke
Rock and sand	7, 24		6, 47
Leaven and Lump	13, 33		13, 20
Lost sheep	18, 12		15, 3

Found in 3 Gospels

	Matthew	Mark	Luke
Candle and bushel	5, 14	4, 21	8, 16
New patch	9, 16	2, 21	5, 36
New wine	9, 17	2, 22	5, 37
Sower	13, 3	4, 2	8, 4
Mustard seed	13, 31	4, 30	13, 18
Wicked husbandmen	21, 33	12, 1	20, 9

Paraclete [pă′-ră-clēte]. Lit. 'the Counsel for the defence'; he was an advocate. The term is applied to Jesus, on earth and in heaven (*Luke* 22, 31; *1 John* 2, 1). It is also applied to the Holy Spirit (*John* 15, 26). This is the proper meaning of 'comforter.' The Holy Spirit 'advocates' Christ, 'pleads His cause' to the believer.

Paradise. Orig. simply an enclosed pleasure ground —a pleasant fenced-off spot (*S. of S.* 4, 13). Since

this was the place that man had lost through his
sin, it became the ultimate and desirable end. In
the NT (*2 Cor.* 12, 4; *Rev.* 2, 7) it means ' heaven '
as now understood. The place of bliss and reward, the opposite of Gehennah.

Paran [pā'-răn]. Desert bet. Sinai and Canaan
(*Num.* 10, 12). Here Israel wandered for something under 40 yrs.

Parbar [păr'-băr]. Lit. ' suburbs ' or ' precincts.'
Additional buildings round the Temple with
dormitories and cattle stalls (*2 Kings* 23, 11).

Parched corn. Roasted grain, as in certain mod.
breakfast cereals (*Lev.* 23, 14).

Parchment. Properly this is the skin of sheep or
goat with the wool and hair removed, and treated
till it is clean and soft and smooth. The name is
thought to derive from Pergamum where it was
once greatly used. This is pretty well only a
tradition as it was used extensively everywhere,
being more lasting than papyrus.

Parents. *See* FAMILY.

Parlour. An upper chamber of the house with
lattices admitting the evening breeze. *See* HOUSE
(*Judg.* 3, 20).

Parmenas [păr'-mĕ-năs]. One of the 7 elected deacons of the early Church (*Acts* 6, 5).

Parousia [păr-ōū'-sĭă]. Gk. word important in the
Christian faith. It means the ' appearance ', the
' advent ', the ' Second Coming ' of the Lord. The
early Christian writers expected this to take place
within their lifetime (*1 Thes.* 4, 15; etc.). It was to
be preceded by much trouble and by the appearance of the Antichrist (*2 Thes.* 2, 8) and also by
the conversion of the Jews (*Rom.* 11, 25). This
belief led to many abuses in the early days of the
church. Even today there is constant search for far-
fetched evidence and Scriptural warrant for the

parousia in this day and generation. That has always been the way; it is always NOW. In God's good time it will come.

Parthians. An ancient people who orig. inhabited a country SE of the Caspian Sea. They came under the Persian Empire, revolted, were suppressed, revolted again c. 255 BC when the Persian Empire had been taken over by Alexander and his successors the Seleucidae. They later increased in power and established a considerable empire under Mithridates c. 174-138 BC. They invaded Judea, took Jerusalem and placed Antigonus on the throne. They fell under Persian power once more in AD 226.

Partridge. A game bird which the Jews seemed to confuse with the cuckoo (*Jer.* 17, 11 RV, RSV). ' Like the partridge which gathers a brood which she did not hatch.'

Passion. There are 2 meanings as used in the AV. One is simply ' feelings ' or ' emotions ' (*Acts* 14, 15). The other is ' suffering ' (*Acts* 1, 3).

Passover. The first certain ref. to the Passover is in *Exodus* (12, 21-27) and it is fair to assume that the feast, or something of its nature was already in existence and known at that time (*Ex.* 3, 18). The directions were that a lamb was to be killed and its blood sprinkled on the lintel and doorposts. This is connected with the death of the Egyptian firstborn. Later the feast became regularised as a commemoration of the Exodus and was to be held in the month Abib (*Deut.* 16, 1-8). It was then not a private and domestic celebration. At this time the Passover, and the *Mazzoth*, or Feast of Unleavened Bread, seem to have been part and parcel of one another. The sacrifice was in the Temple. This merging of the 2 Feasts is apparent in the time of *Ezekiel* (45, 21-24), although earlier a clear distinction had been made (*Num.* 28, 16-25). The fact is that the various OT reasons given for the inception of the Feast and for its conventions, are not at all consistent. By the time of *Ezra* (6, 19-22) the Passover and the Feast of Unleavened Bread were being observed as 2 distinct celebrations. It is prob. that the start of the feast was a shepherd's sacrifice of a lamb, symbolising the 1st fruits of the flock, and that it was in existence long before the Exodus. It may, however, derive from ancient human sacrifice, the lamb being the substitute for the child. In a Sin offering, blood was sprinkled. In a Burnt offering the animal was roasted whole. In a Peace offering the animal was eaten entirely. The Passover regulations insist upon all 3 practices. It was a spring festival, and such have always been connected with the firstborn. Its connection with the Feast of Unleavened Bread is not one of character, but simply a question of the overlap of seasons. After the Exile the mode changed. Formerly there had been a killing of the lamb at home, the sprinkling of the doorposts and the meal eaten standing, with staff in hand and ready for the road. By the time of Jesus, the lambs were killed in the temple, and the blood sprinkled before the altar by the priests. Then the carcases were dressed, and the fat offered on the altar while the priests chanted the Hallel (*Ps.* 113-118). The lambs were then roasted at home and were served with bitter herbs; each guest (it was not necessarily a family affair) bringing 4 cups of red wine. By this time they had copied the Greek and Roman manner of reclining at table, though the Pharisees gave as their reason, that reclining symbolised the rest which God had given to His people. Before the 1st cup of wine

a blessing was asked (*Luke* 22, 17). This was
followed by ceremonial hand washing, and a
prayer. When the 2nd cup was poured, the son
of the house, or the youngest present, would ask
why this was being done. Whereupon the father,
or the oldest member present, explained the
significance of the feast and of the Exodus.
Psalms 113 and 114 were then sung, and the 3rd
cup poured. Prayer was offered, followed by the
4th cup and the singing of Psalms 115, 116, 117
and 118. There were always very big crowds at
Jerusalem for the Passover in Rom. times, and
the authorities were always nervous until it was
over. The custom of releasing a prisoner may
have been due to this.

Pathros [păth′-rŏs]. Upper Egypt (*Isa.* 11, 11).

Patmos [păt′-mŏs . Small island of the Gk. archepelago (mod. Patino). Here John had the visions
which inspired the *Book of the Revelation* (1, 9).
He had been banished thither by Domitian.

Patriarch. Lit. ' the father of a chief of a clan or
race.' The word is usually applied to the great
men of *Genesis* before Moses, and esp. to Abraham, Isaac and Jacob.

Paul. Saul of Tarsus, later Paul the Apostle, appears
on the scene at the critical point. The apostles
who had been the disciples were not men of much
imagination. They had no vision of a great new
faith transcending the greatness of Judaism and
the splendour of Greek philosophy (of which they
knew little or nothing). After the excitement of
Pentecost (*Acts* 2) they were excited about the
religion. Converts were flocking in. But they
could not see beyond this. When Philip baptised
the Gentile Ethiopian, who was also a eunuch
(*Acts* 8, 26) they were a bit doubtful, but they
accepted him. Then Cornelius the Rom. officer

came to Peter, and the Apostle was faced with the
perplexity—should a Gentile embrace the Jewish
faith before being admitted to the new religion
by profession of faith and baptism? In short, was
Christianity (though it was not yet so called)
something entirely new and divorced from Judaism, or was it an extension of Judaism? (*Acts*
10-11.) At Antioch, and without Apostolic sanction Gentiles were being baptised, and it was
there, in fact, that they were first called Christians
(*Acts* 11, 26). While they had been able to make
exceptions of the Ethiopian and of Cornelius, the
Apostles felt that the wholesale admission of
Gentiles was either the natural, logical and ordained way of doing things, or that it was going
too far (*Acts* 15, 1 & 5 & 24). To that time and
situation came Saul of Tarsus. Saul was a Jew,
born and brought up at Tarsus, the chief town
of Cilicia in Asia Minor. He was, like all orthodox
Jews, steeped in the traditions and convinced of
the exclusiveness of his nation. Nevertheless he
was living in a wider world, speaking and reading
Greek, and in daily contact with the advanced
ways of Greek thinking. Furthermore his father,
and so himself, was a Roman citizen. This was a
privilege of immense worth and importance,
granted to non-Romans as a reward for services
of importance. In Saul, therefore, the 3 great
forces of the ancient world met—the monotheism
of Judaism, the liberal exciting speculation of
Greece (with its language which was universally
spoken) and the authority, the order and the
discipline of Imperial Rome. His ancestry was
Heb. to the core, and of the tribe of Benjamin,
one of the more ' select ' clans (*Phil.* 3, 5). He
was a Pharisee (qv). Good Pharisees were good
men. They were patriotic, and they were zealous,

but they were exclusive to, and beyond, a fault. Among the Jews it was customary for the sons even of the easeful wealthy to be taught a trade. Weaving goat-hair for tentage was a thriving industry of Tarsus and that was the trade Saul learned. At about the age of 13 he was sent to Jerusalem to the College, to be trained in the Law of his fathers. His chief tutor was Gamaliel, who was a man of liberal ideas for his time and place (*Acts* 22, 3). He was afire, young Saul, with zeal for God. His training for the office and dignity of rabbi took 10 yrs.; he then returned to Tarsus and carried on normal activities for another 10 yrs. It was during that 10 yrs. that Jesus appeared in Galilee, and the 3-year ministry took place. Pentecost came, and this new faith began to reach out from the tiny corner of Palestine to the world around. Where Paul first met the new faith is unknown. He may not have been aware of what was happening until he went back to Jerusalem after his 10 yrs. at home in Tarsus. His anger agst. it knew no bounds, for he saw what this new teaching was likely to do to his precious Judaism. The Jew would no longer be exclusive if this teaching were to be believed. If it were true that the Messiah had already come, what was there to wait for and pray for? Jewry was finished if Zion hill was not to be the lamp of the nations. There could be no dignity or worth in the sacred Law if sins were to be forgiven by faith in a man. Where was the kingdom where the Jew would be free of Rome, if the kingdom had already come? For the sake of Jewry, and for the sake of the world whose saviour Jewry would yet be, this new thing had to be crushed. Not for him the temporising of Gamaliel, logical though it might be (*Acts* 5, 38). The execution of Stephen had to

be, and it could be, only a beginning. Much
blood must flow, but it was worth it. In Jerusalem
and dist., and wherever this new thing had
taken root, it must be pulled up. The Sanhedrin
approved the passion of Saul, and gave him
authority to hunt the heretics. He accepted the
office with an enthusiasm that was utterly sincere.
He was no sadist. What conflict there was in
Paul's own soul and conscience at this time there
is no way of knowing. But conflict there must
have been. Although the change in a man's life
and thinking may appear to be instantaneous,
there is usually a history of thinking, even almost
unconscious thinking behind it. Every increase
in emotional disturbance led, naturally, to another
excess, because something was disturbing him.
For one thing he could not shake Stephen out of
his mind (*Acts* 22, 20). In this confusion and
turmoil of thought and emotion, Paul set out for
Damascus with authority to arrest any Jews guilty
of the new heresy and to bring them back for trial
to Jerusalem. Something happened as they were
approaching Damascus. It may have come from
outside, it may have come from inside, but it
came. That is the fact, and the only one that
matters. He found himself blind. The instrument
who finally brought Saul to the Lord was a simple
soul called Ananias who showed Saul a mercy that
Saul would not have shown him under similar
circumstances. That was the end and the beginning, and it is a mistake to attribute all of his
conversion to the blinding light and the voice. Without this fine fellow, Ananias, it might not have
worked at all. Paul had no second thoughts:
not a single moment of vacillation. He was in the
new thing with all the enthusiasm that he had
shown in the old. Paul was never in any doubt

about his own special position and he would not
let the others have any doubts either. He had
never been a very easy man to get on with. When
the call came on the Damascus road Paul would
be, about 31 yrs. old. He was executed at
Rome when he was about 64. These 33 yrs. were
of vital importance to the purposes of God. The
story of what he did in them is by no means complete, but enough is known to draw a pretty complete picture of the man and his work. Possibly
Paul had once had an idea that Judaism might
become a universal religion (*Rom.* 9-11). Now he
knew that there was something better and that
God's purpose was to make this indeed a universal
religion. There was not much of Paul physically
(*paulis* means ' little ' in Latin). But he must have
possessed stores of physical strength, as well as the
dynamism which is of the mind and of the spirit.
He endured what could well have broken much
stronger men (*2 Cor.* 10, 10). He himself spoke
about a ' thorn in the flesh ' (*2 Cor.* 12, 7) but
what it was nobody knows, though there has been
a deal of speculation about it. It must have been
something fairly serious and painful (*2 Cor.* 5, 2;
12, 8-10). There was, however, real toughness in
him (*2 Cor.* 11, 23-27). Some of the experiences
which he touches upon to justify his claim to
apostleship can be traced in the *Acts;* more than
half of them cannot (*2 Cor.* 11, 23-27). The *Acts*
does not record that 5 times he received the maximum flogging that a Jewish court could award;
and only once records that he was flogged by the
Romans. Paul claims 3 such floggings. *Acts*
records 1 shipwreck; Paul claims 3. Of his
physical courage there can be no doubt. There
is nothing wrong with a man's courage when he
recovers consciousness outside the walls of Lystra,

having been thrown there on the assumption that he was dead after a stoning, and immediately goes back into the town (*Acts* 14, 19). It was the same during the Ephesus riots (*Acts* 19, 23-30). What he had to put up with and overcome on his travels can only be imagined, but to follow his route in these present times is bad enough; what it was in Paul's day must have been infinitely worse. His 1st missionary journey took 2 yrs., and he did not grow fat on it (*Acts* 14, 27; *2 Cor.* 12, 10). In good times and in bad it was his clear conviction that Jesus had called him and that Jesus would not let him down, which carried him through (*Phil.* 4, 11-13; *2 Tim.* 4, 17). He had his bad times and his low times (*2 Cor.* 7, 5 & 6). But God comforted him, and sometimes the unlooked for affections of men and women sustained him (*Acts* 28, 15). His constant worry and anxiety was about the Church, or rather, the churches (*2 Cor.* 11, 28). He felt that he was responsible for their existence, and therefore was responsible if anything went wrong, eg if the new faith took a wrong twist and went the wrong way. News of the faithfulness of the churches could bring him back almost from the gates of death while news of their failure could nearly drive him out of his mind (*2 Cor.* 7, 5). He did not, however, immediately and without thought and preparation, dash into the Christian work. After the excitement of Damascus he went down into Arabia to think things out, just as Jesus had gone into the wilderness after He was convinced of the genuineness of His call (*Gal.* 1, 16). Paul was there for at least a year, then he came back to Damascus, having eventually to run for his life (*2 Cor.* 11, 32-33). He travelled the 150 m. to Jerusalem, and found himself not at all popular

with the Apostles. Only when Barnabas spoke
up for him would they have anything at all to do
with him. He had talks with Peter and James
(*Gal.* 1, 18-20). He found himself odd man out,
his preaching only caused riots, so he went home
to Tarsus. For the better part of 10 yrs. he stayed
there, but what he was doing is not even hinted
at (*Gal.* 1, 21). Then Barnabas gets in touch with
him from Antioch, where the new faith was making
a great advance (*Acts* 11, 21). Barnabas did
not know what to do, for the issue was demanding
a ruling—must Gentile converts come to Christianity by way of Judaism? Paul accepted the
invitation to grapple with this question which was
of paramount importance. He travelled to Antioch, and established the Church of the new way,
not the old. It was that new Church at Antioch
which decided that since Paul and Barnabas had
done so much for them, they must send the 2 out
into the world to do as much for others (*Acts*
13, 3). The 2 set out on the 1st missionary tour
prob. c. AD 46-48), with John Mark, who was
Barnabas' relative. They sailed to Cyprus, landing at Salamis, and preached in the Jewish synagogues. They toured the island and at Paphos,
after an altercation with the magician, Bar-Jesus,
they succeeded in convincing the Rom. governor,
Sergius Paulus, to become a Christian (*Acts* 13,
6-12). They then sailed to Perga in Pamphylia,
where John Mark left them. They moved on N
into Phrygia to Pisidian Antioch, capital of
Galatia, where Paul preached a powerful sermon
in the synagogue (*Acts* 13, 16). They fell out with
the Jews and concentrated on the Gentiles, but
influential Jews turned the civic leaders agst. them
and they were expelled from the city. They went
on to Iconium but again met with hostile Jews, and

they moved to Lystra and Derbe, where they were taken for Mercury and Jupiter (*Acts* 14, 12-18). Timothy was prob. converted at Lystra (*Acts* 16, 1). And at Lystra Paul was stoned. They came back by the same route, establishing the Churches they had inaugurated in the various towns. They then sailed back from Perga to Syrian Antioch. This established the convention which Paul was to follow, preaching first to Jews, then to Gentiles, and founding Churches. Because of the fine Rom. roads, protected by patrols, and because of their knowledge of the common language, Greek, they found their task much eased. But one result of the success was to bring to a head the whole business of the relationship bet. Christianity and Judaism. Many Jewish Christians reckoned that entry into Judaism was a necessary step bet. the Gentile state and the Christian. They insisted that converts should be circumcised. Peter had taught otherwise (*Acts* 10, 1—18) but his view was not accepted by the most orthodox. Paul and Barnabas were sent to Jerusalem to thresh the thing out (*Acts* 15; *Gal.* 2, 1-10). A Council was held and the verdict, supported by James, was that there need be no circumcision, but Gentile converts were to be recommended not to indulge in any practices which were offensive to their fellow Christians who were Jews. It was also decided that while the other apostles would concentrate on the conversion of Jews, Paul and Barnabas would concentrate on the Gentiles. Nevertheless, although the unity of the Church seemed to have been preserved, this thorny question kept raising its head (*Gal.* 2, 11-21). After the Council (AD 50) Paul invited Barnabas to another tour, but indicated that he did not want the company of John Mark. Barnabas

insisted that if John Mark did not go, he himself
would not go. The result was that Paul went
without Barnabas, taking Silas instead. They
passed through Syria to Cilicia, then N through
the Taurus mts. to revisit the Churches established on the 1st journey. He decided to take
Timothy with him from Lystra, and circumcised
him so that there need be no offence anywhere
they went. Timothy's mother was a Jewess. There
is some doubt about their subsequent route, but
at Troas Paul had the vision of the man from
Macedonia. Paul was ill at this time and prob.
in high fever, but the vision was clear enough.
His decision to obey it was momentous, for
Macedonia was in Europe (*Acts* 16, 9). Luke was
with him now as medical adviser, and they sailed
for Neapolis and went inland to Philippi, and then
to Thessalonica, Berea and Athens, where he was
heard politely enough but achieved nothing of
importance. At Corinth, however, he had marked
success and stayed there for a year and a half,
lodging with Aquila and Priscilla (*Acts* 18, 1-3). He
returned to Syrian Antioch by way of Jerusalem.
The Church was now established in Europe. About
AD 54 he set off again taking in Galatia and Phrygia, and spending a good deal of time in Ephesus
(*Acts* 19, 8). Here he began his letter writing with
an epistle (now lost) to the Corinthians, followed
by the existing 1st epistle, sending Titus with it.
From Macedonia he wrote the 2nd epistle. From
Corinth he sent the epistle to the Romans. He
then set out for Jerusalem again carrying generous
gifts from Gentile Christians to the poor Jewish
Christians of Judea. This was an attempt to break
down the Jewish prejudice which still existed.
After a very roundabout tour which enabled him
to greet many old friends (*Acts* 20, 18-35), he

arrived at Jerusalem where he was at first made
very welcome. Later, however, he was asked to
show his allegiance to the old ways of his people
by taking a Nazirite vow (qv). He agreed, but
was later accused of defiling the Temple by
bringing Gentiles further in than the Court of
the Gentiles (*Acts* 21, 27-29). There was a riot,
and the Roman commander, Claudius Lysias
rescued him from a lynching. Learning that he
was a Roman citizen, he released Paul but
ordered the Sanhedrin to be convened to ascer-
tain the rights and wrongs of the matter. This
led to another riot (*Acts* 23, 1-10). Paul was
placed in protective custody, and Lysias sent
him to Caesarea, having heard rumour of an
attempt on Paul's life, and turned the whole case
over to the governor Felix. Paul was charged
before Felix with profanation of the Temple and
incitement to riot. Felix temporised, being
strangely impressed by Paul, but unwilling to
offend the Jews (*Acts* 24). Paul was remanded,
and remained under open arrest for 2 yrs. till
Porcius Festus succeeded Felix as procurator. Paul
would have been in danger if he had been sent for
trial to Jerusalem, but Festus refused to allow this.
He was tried again, after having claimed his right
as a Roman citizen, to appeal to Caesar. So well
did he plead his cause before Festus and Agrippa
that he was told that but for his appeal to Caesar
he would have been found not guilty and liber-
ated. However, Paul had made up his mind that
the thing for him to do was to take the challenge
of Christianity to the emperor himself. He had
no wish to be set at liberty till he had done this.
In the autumn of AD 60, with other prisoners
he sailed for Rome, but the ship was wrecked on
the coast of Malta. They joined another ship 3

months later (*Acts* chs. 27-28). Eventually he was handed over to the authorities in Rome. For 2 yrs. he was in very open confinement, being able to continue with his preaching and administration, and the book of the *Acts* concludes on that note, the story of his life. The rest must be gathered from his letters. With him in Rome were many enthusiastic Christians who put themselves at Paul's disposal, writing for him, and carrying messages near and far. There were Timothy, Philemon, Tychycus, Aristarchus, John Mark and Luke. He even influenced members of Caesar's household to accept the faith (*Philip.* 4, 22). Eventually he appeared in court in Rome and was acquitted. At this time the Romans had nothing in particular agst. the Christians, whom they regarded as a sect of the Jews. There is a warranted early tradition that he then travelled to Spain, but there is no proof of this. He seems to have returned to Greece and Macedonia, visiting churches, settling disputes, confirming orders. Then he was rearrested; why or where is not known, though it seems very likely that this took place in Rome during a later visit, and when the persecution of the Christians was beginning c. AD 64. He was imprisoned again, and it was in prison that he wrote *2 Timothy*, which gives a moving portrait of the old man in jail, thinking of the past and of the future. Tradition states that he was executed (as a Roman citizen he had the right to be beheaded) on the Ostian way. Some have said of Paul that he released Christianity from the restrictions of its Jewish ancestry, but that he forced it into the confinement of his own theology, which for centuries was accepted as being final and indisputable. He made a conservative thing liberal, then made it conservative again in that new form. This is true enough. But at the same time he gave Christianity a direction and an order and an organisation which it did not have and which it certainly needed. His emphasis on the social gospel, the inter-responsibility of all classes, the fact that each man is directly answerable to God for what he does or does not do to his fellow man, the concept of wealth as a stewardship, not a right, have had a tremendous impact upon life ever since. His training in Greek philosophy with its Platonic conception of man as a being of 2 natures, matter and spirit, was largely responsible for bringing into Christianity the idea of the constant warfare bet. the flesh and the spirit, and the fact of the re-birth into the purely spiritual state. Insistence on this ' warfare ' has had good results and bad, one of the bad results being the withdrawal of the believer from the rush and hurry of life, into monasticism. But the social urge of the teaching of Paul has at times overcome this and sent the Christian raging out to reform the world. The secret may well lie in a proper balance, which Paul himself never quite found.

Paulus Sergius [paŭ'-lŭs sĕr'-gĭ-ŭs]. Proconsul of Cyprus when Paul and Barnabas landed there on the 1st missionary journey (*Acts* 13, 7).

Pavement. *See* GABBATHAH.

Pavilion. Simply a tent.

Pe [pē]. Seventeenth letter in the Heb. alphabet. Usually the Eng. *P*, but when a single *Pe* appears before a vowel it is *Ph*.

Peace offering. *See* OFFERINGS.

Peacock. The word appears in connection with imports from India (*1 Kings* 10, 22; *2 Chron.* 9, 21). The peacock is indigenous to India and would be imported as a bird ornamental to royal gardens. As used in *Job* (39, 13 AV), 'ostrich' is a better translation.

Pearl. This includes both the pearl as known to-day, and mother of pearl, which is the lining of the shell.

Peep. (*Isa.* 8, 19; 10, 14.) This is not 'looking,' but 'chirping,' or 'cheeping,' like a nestling.

Pekah [pē'-käh]. One of the last kings of Israel. He headed unrest agst. Israel's subservience to Assyria by murdering the King Pekahiah (*2 Kings* 15, 25), and usurping the throne. He tried to form a federation agst. Assyria and when Judah refused to come in, he and Rezin of Syria invaded Judah. The Assyrians swiftly dealt with the situation. Israel and Syria were devastated and the people transported. Hoshea, a friend of the Assyrians, murdered Pekah, and succeeded him, but he was only delaying the inevitable subjugation of Samaria and enslavement of the people.

Pekahiah [pē'-kā-hī'-äh]. Son and successor of Menahem, King of Israel. Assassinated by Pekah after reigning 2 yrs. c. 733 BC.

Pelethites [pē'-lĕ-thī'-tes]. Members of David's bodyguard, of Philistine ancestry (*2 Sam.* 15, 18; 20, 7).

Pelican. Twice trans. 'cormorant' AV (*Isa.* 34, 11; *Zeph.* 2, 14). Prob. the true pelican *Pelicanus onocrotalus* still common around the waters and in the wildernesses of Palestine.

Pen. There were 2 kinds. **1.** The stylus, a sharp, pointed graving tool used for cutting letters on stone (*Job* 19, 24). **2.** A pen cut from a reed with a pen knife (*Jer.* 36, 23) and used for writing with ink on papyrus (*3 John* 13). It was sharpened with a pen knife.

Pen knife. See PEN.

Penny. See MONEY.

Pentateuch [pĕn'-tă-tēūch]. The first 5 books of the
OT: *Genesis, Exodus, Leviticus, Numbers* and
Deuteronomy are so called, the word meaning
' consisting of 5 books.' They were not called
this by the Jews, of course; the word does not
occur in Scripture. They called them the Law,
the Book of the Law, the Law of Moses, the Book
of the Law of God, and other names. Orig. they
were prob. not divided into 5. The Books were
not in the main written at the time of the events
recorded, or even near that time. Everything in
Genesis was handed down orally in the hist. of the
people. That is not to say that writing was not
practised in the very early days, but the traditions
are older than the written Heb. language. By
AD 80 they had been separated into the 5 Books.
The names of the Books are all Gk. and not Heb.
Moses' title to the authorship has been challenged by scholars, causing a great deal of
controversy. Undoubtedly, however, there are
passages which must be attributed directly or
indirectly to him (*Ex.* 17, 14; *Num.* 33, 2; *Deut.*
31, 19; *Ex.* 15, 1-18; etc.). There is no space here
to go into the discussion and debate which has
raged around the authorship of these 5 books,
but in fairness we must state that the subsſance
of the proof is certainly with those who believe
that Moses' hand was not one of the many which
wrote the words of the Pentateuch. Scholars
prefer to name the authors by initials. Without
a very good knowledge of Heb. it is impossible to
detect the great differences in language and style
which occur in these books. The reader of the
Eng. Bible will prob. have noticed that in some
passages God is referred to as ' Lord ' and in
others as ' Jehovah,' but that is only one difference which occurs, and the others are almost as

clear in the Heb. as the use of 2 names for God is in Eng. These distinctions are plain to those who know the original language well. Moses was the original lawgiver and nothing could be more natural than for tradition to give Moses credit for all the legislation which stemmed from original Law. We suggest that the student who has not recognised that there are many contradictions in the accounts of happenings in these books, should read *Genesis* 37, the story of Joseph and his brothers. Was he sold to Ishmaelites or to Midianites? Was it Reuben who suggested the pit, or was it Judah who tried to rescue him by selling him? It is possible, and it has been done, simply by observing differences in the story and differences in style in the Eng. of the AV to produce 2 distinct accounts of this incident. When the scholar turns to the whole Pentateuch, with the account before him in Heb., it is infinitely easier for him to reach conclusions about authorship. There are, for example, 2 stories of Creation (*Gen.* 1, 1—2, 3 and *Gen.* 2, 4-25). There are 2 accounts of the Flood (*Gen.* 6 & 7 & 8). Not only are some of the details different, but it is clear that 2 hands have been at work—one a pithy, forceful, precise writer; and one far more copious, discursive and wordy. Criticism moved along these lines in the work of separating one author from another and reached the conclusion that at least 4 were involved. One (or more than than one but all with very similar styles) used the word ' Jehovah ' and wrote concisely; they called him J. Another used the title ' Lord ' and was called E (Heb. *Elohim*). He was more voluble, but there was another, using 'Lord,' who had a style quite different from E's, and quite a different way of thinking. They called him P. In *Deuter-*

onomy it was plain that a new hand was at work, quite different from the others. They called him D. There have been those who wanted a further breakdown into J.1, etc., but for our purposes it is enough to recognise the 4 main ones. P passages, roughly, are: *Genesis* 1, 1—2, 4; 5, 1-28 & 30-32; 6, 9-22; 7, 6 & 11 & 13-16 & 18-21 & 24; 8, 1-5 & 13-19; 9, 1-17 & 28-29; 10, 1-7 & 20 & 22 & 23 & 31 & 32; 11, 10-26 & 27 & 31 & 32; 12, 4-5; 13, 6 & 11-12; 16, 1 & 3 & 15 & 16; ch. 17; 21, 1-5; ch. 23; 25, 7-17 & 19 & 20 & 26; 26, 34 & 35; 27, 46 to 28, 9; 29, 24 & 28 & 29; 34, 1 & 2 & 4 & 6 & 8-10 & 13-18 & 20-24 & 27-29; 35, 9-13 & 15 & 22-29; ch. 36; 37, 1-2; 41, 46; 46, 6-27; 47, 5 & 6 & 7-11 & 27 & 28; 48, 3-7; 49, 1 & 28-33; 50, 12 & 13. *Exodus* 1, 1-5 & 7 & 13 & 14; 2, 23-25; 6, 2 to 7, 13 & 19 & 20 & 21 & 22; 8, 5-7 & 15-19; 9, 8-12; 11, 9-10; 12, 1-20 & 28 & 37 & 40 & 41 & 43-51; 13, 1 & 2 & 20; 14, 1-4 & 8 & 9 & 15-18 & 21-23 & 26-29; 16, 1-3 & 6-24 & 31-36; 17, 1; 19, 1-2; 24, 15-18; chs. 25-31, 18; 34, 29-35; chs. 35-40. *Leviticus*—the whole book. *Numbers* 1, 1 to 10, 28; 13, 1-17 & 21 & 25 & 26 & 32; 14, 1 & 2 & 5 & 7 & 10 & 26-30 & 34-38; ch. 15; 16, 1-7 & 16-24 & 27 & 32 & 35 & 41-50; chs. 17 to 20, 1-4 & 6-13 & 22-29; 21, 4 & 10 & 11; 22, 1; 25, 6-18; chs. 26-31; 32, 18 & 19 & 28-32; chs. 33-36. (In some of these refs. there are half verses). These passages seem in ref. very disjointed but to read them through in order gives a clear and ready account of things, complete in itself. A consistent style will be observed, and the use of certain words rarely come upon elsewhere in the OT. P's idea of God is of one all powerful and not condescending to walk with men. Creation is by decree, not by action on the part

of God. He begins by calling God Elohim (Lord),
but he moves on (*Gen.* 17, 1) to call Him El
Shaddai (God Almighty). Finally he arrives at
Jehovah (I am). The RV by the constant, and
wrongful, use of 'Lord' conceals this change of
name. J's contributions are: *Genesis* 2, 4-25;
chs. 3 & 4 & 18 & 19 & 24 & 26, 1-33; 27, 1-45;
chs. 38 & 39 & 43 & 44. For purposes of comparison with P, no passage is better than the
creation story. Where P is longish and discursive
and somewhat cold, J's is human and alive. It is
a story which compares with the Nativity story
for sheer skill of simplicity. Theologically, in the
conception of the greatness of God, P is far above
J, but one feels that God was nearer to J than
He was to P. In the Deluge story (*Gen.* 6-9, 17)
J and P are mixed, but the 2 accounts can be extracted and compared. The character of the 2
remains. The E passages make up the remainder
of the 1st 4 books, and D is confined to *Deuteronomy*. Many passages are a mixture of J and E
and are best called simply JE. *See* further under
the names of the 5 books.

Pentecost [pĕn'-tĕ-cŏst]. During the Feast of Unleavened Bread a barleysheaf was offered, the 1st
cut. After 49 days (a week of weeks) came the
Feast of Pentecost when harvest officially ended.
This seems a long time but there was a great
difference of time bet. the ripening of grain in the
valleys and on the hills. The Feast was also called
the Feast of Weeks (*Ex.* 34, 22), Feast of Harvest
(*Ex.* 23, 16), and the Day of Firstfruits (*Num.* 28,
26). It fell on the 6th day of Sivan. It lasted only
for one day. Two leavened loaves of wheat flour
were 'waved' before the Lord, as well as 2 year-
ling lambs. Seven lambs, one bullock and 2 rams
were the Burnt offering, and one kid the Sin offer-

ing (*Lev.* 23, 17-21). Later there was a special offering (*Deut.* 16, 10-11). It was at Pentecost that the Holy Spirit came upon the apostles.

Peor [pē'-ŏr]. Mt. in Moab (*Num.* 23, 28). Also a Moabite god worshipped there (*Num.* 25, 18).

Perfumes. Gums, resins, roots, bark, spices such as aloes, cassia, cinnamon, myrrh, frankincense and spikenard formed the substance of the preparations designed to delight the nose. Sometimes they were hung in a bag like a mod. lavender bag (*S. of S.* 1, 13); sometimes crushed, dried, and burned as incense; sometimes distilled and mixed with oil.

Perga [pĕr'-gă]. Town and Rom. capital of Pamphylia. Paul and Barnabas visited it (*Acts* 13, 13).

Pergamum [pĕr'-gă-mŭm], **Pergamos.** Chief city of Mysia. In 241 BC its people defeated the Gauls and settled them in Galatia. In ancient days it was celebrated for its library. Parchment takes its name from Pergamum, where it was early used. Although there was a branch of the Church at Pergamum it seems to have been a city hostile to Christianity (*Rev.* 1, 11; 2, 12-17).

Perizzites [pĕr'-ĭz-zītes]. Section of the Canaanite people (*Gen.* 15, 20). They were settled there earlier than the time of Abraham (*Gen.* 13, 7). Their territory was given to Ephraim and Manasseh.

Persia. The land of the Persians, lying bet. Great Media and the Persian Gulf, and bounded E and W by Carmania and Susiana. Its area was less than 50,000 sq. m. At the height of its greatness the Persian Empire stretched from India to the Greek islands, and from the Caspian sea to the Nubian desert. They first came to the front when they conquered the Elamites who had been their friends and neighbours. Cyrus II c. 558 BC came to the throne and started to build the empire, taking Media, Lydia and Babylonia. He allowed the Hebs. of the Exile to return home. He was succeeded by Cambyses who invaded Egypt. Darius came to the throne c. 521 facing revolt all through the empire. He suppressed it and strengthened and extended the empire. During his reign the Temple at Jerusalem was rebuilt. His son was Xerxes, called Ahasuerus in Scripture (*Esther* and *Ezra* 4, 6). He attempted the invasion of Europe through Greece but was defeated. He was assassinated in 465 and his son Artaxerxes Longimanus succeeded. Under him Ezra and Nehemiah returned to Jerusalem. From the end of his reign the Persian empire began to decline. The last king, Codomannus, was defeated by Alexander in 331 and that was the end of the empire. The main cities were Persepolis, Susa or Shushan, Ecbatana or Achmetha and Babylon (*Ezra* 6, 1 & 2). The Persian religion was Zoroastrianism, which was a faith of some spirituality and not idolatrous.

Pestilence. Any infectious or contagious disease. Three scourges are usually mentioned together: sword, famine and pestilence (*Ezek.* 6, 11). That is still the normal order.

Peter. Simon the disciple was surnamed Peter. He was the son of Jonas, or John (*Matt.* 16, 17; etc.). He lived in Bethsaida with his wife, brother Andrew, and his mother-in-law (*Mark* 1, 29-31) and earned his living as a fisherman, very prob. in partnership with Zebedee, James and John (*Matt.* 4, 21). He was caught up in the revival of John the Baptist and first came in contact with Jesus at Bethany, being introduced by Andrew. Jesus named him *Cephas* which is the Aram. equivalent of *Petros*, a rock. He was with James,

John and Andrew, one of the first 4 called into discipleship. Peter was with Jesus, sometimes to his credit, sometimes to his shame, in all the big moments. He was intensely loyal at some of the times of testing (*John* 6, 66-69) but in the moment of crisis he denied Him (*John* 18, 12-17). He had in fact the qualities and the failings of the impulsive (*Matt.* 14, 28). After Pentecost Peter was recognised as the leader of the Apostles, and there was never again any shrinking from duty through timidity. He figured prominently in the great controversy which broke out when, after the martyrdom of Stephen, believers were scattered, and the Church spread far beyond the environs of Jerusalem and Palestine. The question was whether or not Gentiles must become Jews before they could be called true Christians. Peter at first was inclined to say that they should, but experience of Philip's work in Samaria persuaded him otherwise (*Acts* 8, 1-25; 10—11, 19). Controversy increased, however, after the start of the work of Paul and Barnabas at Antioch. Peter, with James, at the Council of Jerusalem affirmed religious liberty (*Acts* 15, 1-29). However, on a visit to Antioch, Peter did give some sanction to the narrow opinions of the Jews and was rebuked by Paul (*Gal.* 2, 11-21). The trad. is that he went to Rome and ended his days there as one of Nero's victims. It is justifiably believed that the Gospel according to Mark (qv) is largely the reminiscences of Peter.

Peter, Epistles General of. The 1st letter claims to be from Peter's hand, though there is more than one opinion about this. Some attribute it to Silvanus, others to Barnabas. If Peter did write the letter it must have been done in the early sixties, and before the Nero persecution in which

Peter prob. met his death. The source would be
Rome; the destination was the Christians throughout the existing Church. Although there are refs.
to the Jews of the Dispersion, Peter was thinking
bigger than that. Peter by this time felt that the
true Israel was not the Jews, but the Christians,
Jewish or not. In fact, some of the refs. seem to
apply to non-Jewish Christians, far more than
they do to converted Jews (2, 10; 4, 2 & 3). In
another ref. (3, 6) it seems quite clear that Peter
reckoned that they had inherited the Covenant
only when they became Christians. Undoubtedly
the influence of the thinking of Paul is very clear
through the Epistle, but this is not necessarily a
proof that Peter did not write it. Peter was prob.
far more under the influence of Paul than either
of them imagined. Even a casual reading of the
Gospels will make it clear that Peter did not
become the man he was until after the Crucifixion
and the Resurrection. It was only then that Peter
seemed to grasp the meaning of a good deal of
Jesus' teaching; and it is perfectly understandable
that Peter should have attached far more importance to the saving work of Christ, than he would
give to the actual teaching of Jesus. For it was
the saving work, not the teaching, that had made
all the difference to himself. When Jesus had
decided to set His face towards Jerusalem, Peter
was the one who objected most violently, because
he could see no earthly reason for it. After the
death and the rising he realised that there was no
earthly reason; it was a heavenly reason. Peter
knew what had happened, but Peter did not have
the mental capacity to explain it. Paul had, and
it is perfectly natural and understandable that
Peter should have accepted the explanations of a
more clever man than himself. They had both

reached the point of knowing that Christ died
for the sins of the world. Paul was prepared to
explain how and why; Peter knew only the result.
He was prepared to subscribe to Paul's ideas. The
conclusion of the matter is that it is perfectly poss.
that the 1st Epistle was not written by Peter, but
that there is very little evidence in the Epistle
that it was not. The 2nd Epistle is completely
bound in with the Epistle of *Jude* (qv). But the
internal evidence points pretty shrewdly to the
conclusion that Jude came first, and that *2 Peter*
is an attempt, and a very good one, to take some
of the conclusions of *Jude* a bit further. As we
have said, in the part on the 1st Epistle, there is
no reason at all why Peter should not have
borrowed from Paul. Peter was not an intellectual,
but rather reached his conclusions, right or wrong,
by instinct and emotion. But it is one thing to
borrow from Paul and it is another thing entirely
to borrow from one so obscure as *Jude*. And the
fact of the matter is that *2 Peter* contains pretty
well everything that is in *Jude*. Is this in character
with the leader of the Apostles, who, after all,
had his pride and his distinctiveness? As one
scholar has said: to accept Peter as author of the
2nd Epistle is to accuse him ' of plagiarising in a
remarkable way.' This does not seem characteristic of Peter. Another scholar, comparing 1st
and 2nd *Peter*, has concluded that for one ' agreement ' bet. the 2, there are 6 disagreements. The
1st intimation that there was such an Epistle at
all comes from Origen in the 3rd cent. and he is
not at all sure who wrote it. In the 2nd Epistle
the hope of the immediate second coming of the
Lord has grown very faint. The change is too
great to have occurred within a lifetime. When
the writer refers to the Epistles of Paul he seems

to imply that they have been gathered together and that they are already Scripture—something which certainly did not happen within the lifetime of Peter. The evidence, in fact, points with fair certainty, to some hand other than Peter's and to a date at least 100 yrs. after his death.

Pharaoh [phăr'-rōah]. Title of the Egyptian rulers, meaning ' royal house.' There were many of them but the only ones of immediate interest are those mentioned in scripture. **1.** The Pharaoh of Abraham's time (*Gen.* 12, 10-20) is indefinite. **2.** Pharaoh of Joseph's day (*Gen.* 39 ff.). Prob. one of the Hyksos dynasty c. 950 BC. **3.** One of the Rameses was Pharaoh of the oppression and the Exodus (*Ex.* 1, 11). It might be Rameses II or Merenptah, c. 1350 BC. **4.** (*1 Chron.* 4, 18). There is no evidence who she was, and Bithiah is Heb. not Egyptian. **5.** (*1 Kings* 3, 1; 9, 16.) Some Pharaoh living towards the end of the 21st dynasty when Egypt was on the way out. **6.** (*1 Kings* 11, 18). Another unidentified Pharaoh who befriended Hadad. **7.** (*2 Kings* 18, 21; *Isa.* 36, 6). Some one of the Ethiopian dynasty, but prob. not an individual at all, and just a gen. title. *See* EGYPT.

Pharisees [phăr'-ĭ-sēes]. There were 3 main parties among the Jews: the Pharisees, the Sadducees and the Essenes. The Pharisees have suffered a great deal from Jesus' general condemnation of them. Their origin was prob. as a protest agst. the encroaching Gk. influence in Judea, before the time of the Maccabees, and led to them adhering even more strictly than was necessary to the old Mosaic ways. Bet. 175-163 Antiochus Epiphanes launched a punitive persecution of Jewry and tried to destroy everything that was dear and traditional. This led to the war bet. him and the

Hasidim. The Pharisees sprang out of the defeated Hasidim c. 135-105 BC. Where the rebellious were now concerned with political issues, the Pharisees still recognised that the differences bet. themselves and others were not political but religious. Their beliefs included predestination which did not make freewill meaningless; the immortality of the soul; the resurrection of the body; and judgment in the world to come (*Acts* 23, 8). But the standard of judgment was the Law; the good were those who conformed absolutely and strictly to the Law; the bad were those who did not. This led them to pay far more attention to the external adherence to detail, and not enough attention to obedience to the spirit of the Law. The business of the expositor, or lawyer, became completely concerned with the application of the Law to the most minor and unimportant activities of people (*Matt.* 15, 2 & 3 & 6). At the beginning they were the pick of the people, when they were identified with revolt. But they degenerated into a party of talk and no action (*Matt.* 5, 20; 16, 6 & 11 & 12; 23, 1-39). Some there were who still remembered what Pharasaism had orig. been, but they were much in the minority. Paul was not ashamed of having been one (*Acts* 23, 6; 26, 5-7). Gamaliel was a good example of the better sort (*Acts* 5, 34).

Pharpar [phăr'-păr]. A river of Damascus (2 *Kings* 5, 12). It may be the Awaj.

Philadelphia [phĭl-ă-dĕl'-phĭ-ă]. This was a name given late to the town of Rabbah; but the noted Philadelphia was in Lydia, built by Attalus Philadelphus. It was destroyed by an earthquake and rebuilt in AD 17. In it was about the only one of the 7 churches to be complimented (*Rev.* 1, 11; 3, 7-13).

Philemon, Epistle of Paul to [phī-lē'-mŏn]. From the earliest days this has been recognised as a genuine letter written by Paul. The style and the purpose are unmistakably Pauline. It and *Colossians* were written at the same time and sent to their destination by the same messenger. It was almost certainly written from Rome. A slave by the name of Onesimus, belonging to Philemon, had escaped and landed in Rome. Philemon was a Christian living in Colossae, but prob. converted under Paul's ministry at Ephesus. In Rome, Onesimus, escaped slave and thief (vv. 18, 19) became converted (v. 10). Paul felt that the true test of the sincerity of the conversion of both Philemon and Onesimus would be their reaction to this situation. He asked Onesimus if he was prepared to go back and face the music, and he asked Philemon to make the music pleasant, offering to pay back what Onesimus had stolen. Off Onesimus went in company with Tychicus who had a letter for the Colossians (*Col.* 4, 7-9), and one for the Ephesians (*Eph.* 6, 21). What happened is not known but it is pretty certain, from the way the situation was dealt with, that all was well.

Philetus [phī-lē'-tŭs]. A teacher of false doctrine of the resurrection (*2 Tim.* 2, 17 & 18).

Philip. There was a Philip, king of Macedonia and father of Alexander. There was another of Macedonia who fought with Hannibal agst. the Romans. A 3rd was foster brother of Antiochus Epiphanes. They are mentioned in the Apocrypha but not in the Bible. The 1st of the 'Bible' Philips is the son of Herod the Great and original husband of Herodias (*Matt.* 14, 3). He prob. is not Philip the Tetrarch (*Luke* 3, 1). It is almost impossible to sift out the children of Herod the Great.

Philip the tetrarch was also a son of Herod the Great, but out of Cleopatra of Jerusalem. He was brought up in Rome, ultimately he was appointed over Batanea, Trachonitis and Auranitis. Then he married Salome about the time when John the Baptist was starting his ministry. He built the town of Caesarea Philippi. He was not at all a bad ruler bet. AD 4 and 34. Philip the Apostle is another of the name (*Matt.* 10, 3). He was a citizen of Bethsaida as were Andrew and Peter. Jesus called him as a disciple at Bethany where he brought Nathanael to the Lord (*John* 1, 43-48); and called him ' apostle ' about a year later. He did not take a prominent part in affairs during Jesus' ministry or, according to the information, in apostolic times (*John* 6, 5 & 6; 12, 20 & 23; 14, 8-12; *Acts* 1, 13). Finally there is Philip the Evangelist, one of the 7 good men and true appointed as the Church's first deacons (*Acts* 6, 5). He did good work in Samaria, including the conversion of Simon Magus (8, 9-25), and the Ethiopian eunuch (8, 26-39). This latter conversion brought many issues to a head in the early Church. He had 4 daughters who seem to have inherited some of his eloquence (21, 8 & 9).

Philippi [phĭl'-lĭp-pī]. City on the E border of Macedonia about 10 m. inland. Paul visited the town on his 2nd missionary journey and founded a church.

Philippians, Epistle to the. This is included among the letters written during Paul's imprisonment in Rome, and there is no genuine doubt about Paul's authorship, the date being c. AD 63. The Church at Philippi had sent him a gift in his need, and the prime purpose of the letter is to acknowledge this (4, 15). He takes the chance, however, to speak to them in a kindly 'elder brother' way of the dangers of wrong thinking, not because there is any immediate exhibition of this, but because the danger is always there. Epaphroditus had come with the gifts from Philippi, but there had taken ill. Now he was better and ready to return. Paul got him to carry the letter (2, 25-30). He thanks them for their goodness and speaks of what he has been able to do even as a prisoner (ch. 1). He pleads with them to stand firm and to stand together, and to remember that the power that binds them is the Lord Himself (2, 1-18). He hopes to come to them soon himself, but in the meantime will send them Timothy, when possible, and Epaphroditus right away (2, 19-30). He professes to be happy for them and for himself, but warns them not to let too much satisfaction go to their heads (ch. 3). Then he thanks them again and gives them his blessing.

Philistines. The people settled in the coastal plain of Palestine looking W across the Mediterranean. Samson is the first who seems to have been seriously at war with them (*Judg.* 13-16). In the time of Eli the Philistines were trying to move E, pushing the Israelites back (*1 Sam.* 4-6). Saul and Jonathan inflicted heavy defeats on them (*1 Sam.* 13-14). But they pushed back and by the end of Saul's reign had a substantial foothold (*1 Sam.* 31, 10). David, however, brought them to heel (*2 Sam.* 5, 22; 8, 1). Their main cities were Gaza, Ashkelon, Ashdod, Ekron and Gath, the chiefs of these cities being known as the Lords of the Philistines. They broke away again when the kingdoms split after Solomon's death (*1 Kings* 15, 27). They had a pretty chequered career at the hands of Assyrians, Egyptians and Israelites for many years (*2 Kings* 18-19). After the time of

Assyrian supremacy they disappear from the records.

Phinehas [phĭn'-ē-ăs]. **1** Son of Eleazar, grandson of Aaron (*Ex.* 6, 25). He became Chief Priest (*Judg.* 20, 28). **2.** Younger of Eli's evil sons, killed in fight agst. the Philistines when the Ark was captured (*1 Sam.* 1, 3; etc.). **3.** A returned exile (*Ezra* 8, 33).

Phoebe [phoē'-bĕ]. Deaconess of the church at Cenchreae, commended by Paul to the Church at Rome (*Rom.* 16, 1 & 2).

Phoenicia(ns) [phō-ĕn-ĭ'-cĭ-ă]. The narrow coastal strip of Palestine towards the Mediterranean. Its length was upwards of 120m. The Hebs. knew it as Canaan (*Gen.* 17, 8), its inhabitants being the Canaanites (*Gen.* 10, 15). Orig. they came from Arabia, and were thus Semites as the Hebs. were. They were a maritime people, building their boats from wood from the slopes of Lebanon, and having excellent natural harbours. Carthage was their colony on the N African coast near mod. Tunis, and long wars (the Punic wars) were carried out bet. them and the Romans. Hannibal and Hasdrubal (the ' bal ' being ' BAAL ') were the great Carthaginian generals. Eventually the Carthaginians were defeated after the Romans had copied their ships, built a navy, and invented new tactics. Tyre and Sidon were their great towns (*Matt.* 15, 21). After the murder of Stephen, several Jewish families emigrated to Phoenicia (*Acts* 11, 19). Paul and Barnabas visited the country (*Acts* 15, 3). Paul sailed on one of their vessels on his last missionary journey (*Acts* 21, 2 & 3).

Phrygia [phrў'-gĭ-ă]. Important Asia Minor pro-. vince surrounded by Bithynia, Galatia, Lydia and Mysia. It is a plateau bounded by the Mts.

Olympus, Taurus and Temnus. There was a considerable Jewish colony there and Paul visited it twice (*Acts* 2, 10; 16, 6; 18, 23). Four towns are mentioned in the NT: Laodicea, Colossae, Hierapolis and Antioch of Pisidia.

Phylactery [phўl-ăc′-tĕrў]. (*Matt.* 23, 5 & 6.) The word means a safeguard or amulet in Gk., but the Jews used another name for them meaning 'prayers.' They consisted of 2 small leather cases about 1½ in. square, one worn on the forehead and the other on the upper left arm. The one for the forehead contained 4 sections or compartments; the one for the arm, only one. In the forehead phylactery were placed small pieces of parchment with, for each compartment, one of the following passages written on them: *Ex.* 13, 1-10; 13, 11-16; *Deut.* 6, 4-9; 11, 13-21. The arm case contained them all written on one parchment. The strap binding the case to the forehead was tied behind the head in a knot shaped like the Heb. letter *Daleth*. The letter *Shin* was on each side of the forehead case. The arm thong formed the letter *Yod*, and the whole made up *Shaddai*, the Almighty. These had to be worn by all males over the age of 13 when reciting morning prayer on all days but Sabbaths and Festivals. In later times many, esp. the Pharisees, made great parade of phylacteries and earned the scornful rebuke of Jesus.

Physician. *See* MEDICINE.

Piece. The orig. translators were not sure of the exact values of precious metals and coins and used this word instead (*Gen.* 33, 19; *1 Sam.* 2, 36).

Piety. Respect for parents (*1 Tim.* 5, 4).

Pigeon. *See* DOVE.

Pilate. Nothing is known of his antecedents, but he was 5th procurator of Judea and was appointed by Tiberius as successor to Valerius Gratus c. AD 26. He brought his wife to Judea with him (*Matt.* 27, 19). He first offended the Jews by allowing the troops to retain the emblems on their standards, which were reckoned by the Jews to be idols. This was agst. Rom. practice which was pretty tolerant of foreign religions. Jewish pressure forced his hand, however. Later he seized the Temple offerings (*see* CORBAN) and used the money to build an aqueduct. This caused a riot in which some Jews were killed and many injured. He gave offence again by hanging decorative shields in honour of Tiberius in Herod's palace. Prominent Jews appealed to the Emperor who ordered Pilate to remove the shields. Giving offence and tyrannising seemed to be his great delight, and his regime was notable for oppression and corruption. His troops were responsible for the murder of many of the Galileans who were among the wilder elements who came up to the Jerusalem feasts (*Luke* 13, 1 & 2). Herod objected and he and Pilate came to an understanding about division of authority (*Luke* 23, 6-12). The character of the man comes out clearly in his treatment of Jesus. He allowed expediency and self-interest to take the place of courage and justice. His brutality is shown by his allowing the Roman soldiers to abuse and torture Jesus. There was no need for this and it was not part of the sentence. Vitellus, the legate of Syria removed him from his post, and sent him to Rome to account for his deeds. Trad. has it that he was banished to Vienne in the S of France and that he committed suicide.

Pill AV. (*Gen.* 30, 38.) Peel.

Pillar. Two Heb. words are so trans. One means the column which supports the roof or the lintels of a house (*Judg.* 16, 25; *1 Kings* 7, 2). This word is used figuratively in the pillar of fire and smoke (*Ex.* 13, 21; etc.). The 2nd Heb. word meant simply 'something set up' (Mod. 'standing stones'). These might be erected over a grave (*Gen.* 35, 20); or to commemorate some incident of importance (*Josh.* 24, 27). The 3rd type were the columns set up beside Canaanite altars and frequently mistranslated in the AV as 'images' (*Hos.* 3, 4; 10, 1). *See* ASHERAH, HIGH PLACES.

Pillow. *See* BOLSTER. The pillow in the boat (*Mark* 4, 38) would be an oarsman's cushion.

Pinnacle. The word means 'a little wing' and the pinnacle of the temple was not the top of a spire, but a projection at some considerable height from the ground (*Matt.* 4, 5).

Pipe. *See* MUSIC.

Pisgah [pĭs'-găh]. Mt. in N of Moab overlooking W Palestine (*Num.* 21, 20). Balaam built his 7 altars there (*Num.* 23, 14). On its top Moses died after having his first sight of the Promised Land (*Deut.* 3, 27; 34, 1). It was also called Nebo (*Deut.* 32, 49).

Pisidia [pĭ-sĭd'-ĭ-ă]. Part of the Rom. province of Galatia whose chief town was Antioch. Paul visited it (*Acts* 13, 14).

Pitch. *See* BITUMEN.

Pitcher. Earthenware water jar usually with 2 handles at the neck.

Plague. *See* MEDICINE.

Plagues of Egypt. There is a good deal of confusion in the accounts of these and the various literary sources are sometimes at odds. *See* PENTATEUCH. The oldest source, J, does not mention blood in connection with the 1st plague, but simply the death of the fish in the river, prob. due to a poisonous silting up, or the accumulation of algae.

On this frogs would thrive, breed and die (*Ex.* 8, 14). This in turn would produce flies of every sort, including malarial mosquitoes (*Ps.* 105, 31), producing the murrain and the cattle pest. Hailstorms are, of course, a dreadful menace to crops in eastern countries. The author himself has experienced one storm which left not a leaf on a tea garden, and which was followed by an outbreak of infectious diseases thought to have been not unconnected with the fact that all the small birds in the vicinity were killed by the hail. The coming and going of locusts depends upon the wind—a change of wind will bring them or remove them. Most, if not all of the plagues, can be ' explained ' without stretching the imagination. It is the hammer blow incidence of them that compels respect for the hand of God.

Plain. The word is the translation of 7 Heb. and one Gk. word in the AV. One word means simply a broad valley bet. hills (*Gen.* 11, 2; *Neh.* 6, 2; *Isa.* 40, 4; *Ezek.* 3, 22 & 23; 8, 4; *Dan.* 3, 1). Another is ' level land ' mostly in the sense of a high plateau (*Deut.* 3, 10; *Josh.* 13, 9; *1 Kings* 20, 23; etc.). The word *arabah* means ' plain ' but is sometimes transliterated as ' the Arabah ' (qv). Still another word ' *kikkar* ' is used of the region where the Jordan flows into the Dead Sea and is a word of shape, better rendered as ' circle ' (*Gen.* 13, 10). Another word, ' *shephelah* ' means rather lowland, low hills, than plain (*Deut.* 1, 7; *Josh.* 10, 40; etc.). Matthew makes the great sermon ' on the mountain ' (*Matt.* 5, 1). Luke makes it ' on a level place ' (*Luke* 6, 17 RV, RSV.).

Plain, Cities of the. Sodom, Gomorrah, Admah, Zeboiim and Bela or Zoar. They were in the ' circle ' of Jordan (*see* PLAIN). They were burned out by some natural cataclysm.

Plaster (Plaister). *See* MORTAR. The plaister (*Isa.* 38, 21) was a poultice made of figs (*2 Kings* 20, 7).

Plane tree. (*Gen.* 30, 37; *Ezek.* 31, 8.) *Acer pseudo platanus.*

Plead. Always in the sense of pleading a cause in a law court.

Pledge. By law a lender was entitled to accept collateral for a loan, even household articles or clothing. But if the pledge were the *simlah*, or warm cloak, it had to be returned to the borrower before nightfall, as it might well be his only blanket (*Ex.* 22, 26; *Deut.* 24, 12). This adds point to Jesus' words about the coat and the cloak (*Matt.* 5, 40; *Luke* 6, 29). The mill or millstone could not be pledged (*Deut.* 24, 6). The word is used also of a lost wager (*Isa.* 36, 8). *See* DEBT, USURY.

Pleiades [pleï'-ā-dēs]. (*Job* 9, 9; *Amos* 5, 8. ' Seven stars ' in AV). Group of stars in the constellation Taurus.

Plough. *See* AGRICULTURE.

Plumbline, Plummet. A cord with a weight attached, held agst. a wall while it is being built to check its perpendicular. Among the Hebrews it would prob. be of stone, not lead (*2 Kings* 21, 13; *Isa.* 34, 11; *Amos* 7, 7).

Poetry. In Scripture this is the rhythmic ordering of words, and care must be taken not to confuse the rhythms of AV Eng. with the cadences of Heb. poetry. Some very rhythmic Eng. passages are in fact prose in the original. There was no rhyme, and it would be hard to discover iambuses, spondees and other conventional metres in the Heb. There were 4 main conventions which can be called ' parallelism.' In one, the 2 parallel lines say the same thing in a slightly different way: ' How shall I curse whom God hath not cursed?

And how shall I defy whom Jahweh hath not defied?' (*Num.* 23, 8). In another parallelism, the 2nd line repeats the truth of the 1st line, but does it the other way round. 'A wise son maketh a glad father, But a foolish son is the heaviness of his mother' (*Prov.* 10, 1). Another common form of words, again in 2 lines, consists in the 2nd line repeating most of the 1st line, and then carrying the thought a stage further: 'Till Thy people pass over, Jahweh, Till Thy people pass over, which Thou hast purchased (*Ex.* 15, 16). Finally there is a form, still in 2 lines, where the 2nd line does not repeat anything of the 1st, but carries on the sense and completes it: 'Answer not a fool according to his folly, Lest thou also be like unto him' (*Prov.* 26, 4). Most Heb. poetry, then, is in couplets, but there are examples of grouping in 3, 4 and 5 lines (*Ps.* 1, 3; 27, 4 & 9; etc.). *Psalms* 42 and 43 are really one poem divided into 3 stanzas (42, 5 & 11; 43, 5) by the recurrent 'Why are thou cast down my soul?' *Ps.* 46 is divided into stanzas by 'Selah' (qv). There are also the alphabetical *Psalms*, the verses starting in order with the letters of the Heb. alphabet (*Ps.* 25 & 34 & 37). *Psalm* 119 has 22 groups of 8 vv, the 1st in each group beginning with the appropriate letter of the alphabet. The Book of *Lamentations* has a similar arrangement. The whole of the Book of Job can qualify as poetry, and so can the Sóng of Solomon. New versions of scripture usually follow the practice of printing poetic passages as such.

Poll. The head (*Num.* 3, 47).

Pollux [pŏll'-ŭx]. *See* CASTOR AND POLLUX.

Pomegranate. The *punica granatum.* It grows on a tree some 12 to 15 ft. high, and is about the size of an orange, with a hard red skin containing a red pulpy fruit full of seeds. The pulp is juicy and refreshing. Replicas were used in decoration and carvings (*Ex.* 28, 33; *1 Kings* 7, 20).

Pommel. Not the pommel of a saddle but a rather similar shape in the capital of a column; called 'bowl' in RV (*2 Chron.* 4, 12; *1 Kings* 7, 41).

Pontus [pŏn'-tŭs]. A province of Asia Minor on the shores of the Black Sea. The common name of its kings was Mithridates, the dynasty beginning in 337 BC. It lasted till 63 BC. There was a colony of Jews in Pontus (*Acts* 2, 9; *1 Pet.* 1, 1). Aquila was born in Pontus (*Acts* 18, 2).

Pool. An artificial reservoir to collect water from springs or rainfall, but not one into which stream water flowed. The water might be led to houses or gardens by channels (*Eccl.* 2, 6). Bethesda, Siloam and Gihon were pools at Jerusalem. There is a mistrans. in one passage AV (*Isa.* 19, 10). The words should be ' and all who work for hire will be grieved.'

Poor. *See* POVERTY.

Porch. Not simply a small structure erected outside the front door, but rather a portico or covered walk, like cloisters.

Porpoise. *See* SEAL.

Port. (*Neh.* 2, 13.) Simply 'gate.'

Porter. Doorman or gatekeeper (*1 Chron.* 9, 22; 26, 1-19).

Possession. *See* DEMONIAC.

Post. A messenger or courier; runner or bearer of dispatches (*2 Chron.* 30, 6; *Job* 9, 25; *Jer.* 51, 31).

Post (door). *See* HOUSE.

Pot. *See* HOUSE.

Potiphar [pŏt'-ĭ-phär]. Captain of Pharaoh's guard who bought Joseph as a slave. He imprisoned Joseph when his wife falsely charged the Heb.

after he had resisted her blandishments (*Gen.* 39, 1).

Potter. Member of an ancient craft (*2 Sam.* 17, 28). Nomadic people have little use for pottery since it is so breakable. Its use requires a settled life. The potter trod the clay and water into a mixture of the right consistency (*Isa.* 41, 25). He then placed the lump on a flat wheel which he turned with his hand, moulding the clay as it spun. The vessel was then baked and sometimes glazed (*Jer.* 18, 3).

Potter's Field. See AKELDAMA.

Pound. See MONEY, WEIGHTS AND MEASURES.

Poverty. The main causes of poverty in OT times were bad seasons, with failure of crops and diseases of cattle (*2 Kings* 8, 1-6); war; land grabbing (*Isa.* 5, 8); taxation and forced labour (*Jer.* 22, 13); debt and high interest charges (*Neh.* 5, 1-6). The old freehold land system of the early days usually managed to provide some kind of living and food, but the growth of landed gentry, royal luxury, commerce and city life, with oppression and corruption, changed for the worse the tempo of living (*Isa.* 1, 23; *Amos* 4, 1; 6, 3-6; *Micah* 2, 1). Those who suffered most were widows and orphans, and foreigners who possessed no land. Levites outside Jerusalem seem to have been badly off (*Deut.* 12, 12). After the return from the Exile there was gen. poverty for years; and the constant marching and counter-marching of armies left misery behind them. The Law devoted a lot of attention to the plight of the poor (*Deut.* 14, 28; 24, 15 & 21). See ALMS. The early Christians followed this excellent Jewish practice (*Rom.* 12, 13; 15, 26; *Gal.* 2, 10). In the *Psalms* and in the Beatitudes the word 'poor' has rather the sense of 'the pious.'

Praetor [prāe'-tŏr]. An important civil magistrate of a Rom. colony. There were usually 2, elected by the colonials (*Acts* 16, 20 & 35).

Praetorium [prāe-tō'-rĭ-ŭm]. The seat of a provincial governor. In the NT the word is used of: (1) Pilate's residence at Jerusalem (*Mark* 15, 16; etc.). (2) Herod's palace at Caesarea (*Acts* 23, 35). (3) The Emperor's personal bodyguard (*Philip.* 1, 13).

Prayer. Personal communion with God who is a Person. It implies a right relationship bet. God and man (*Prov.* 15, 29; 28, 9). The classic contents of prayer are adoration, thanksgiving, confession and petition (*Neh.* 1, 4; *Dan.* 9, 3; *Philip.* 4, 6). If properly presented by the proper person, prayer will be answered (*John* 14, 13; *James* 5, 16). But the answer, the timing and the nature of it, must be left entirely to God (*1 John* 5, 14). In the NT prayer is to be in the name of Jesus, for man's sin has made the direct approach impossible. There was early recognition of the three Persons of the Godhead of God, to whom prayer could be made (*2 Cor.* 13, 14). Many early prayers were addressed directly to the risen Jesus (*Acts* 7, 59; *2 Cor.* 12, 8 & 9; *1 Thes.* 3, 11; *1 Tim.* 1, 2; *Rev.* 1, 5 & 6).

Preparation. The day before the Sabbath or any religious festival.

Presbyter [prĕs'-bў-tĕr]. The elder, as interpreted by Presbyterians; the bishop as interpreted by Episcopalians. They were one and the same person. The Presbytery was the presbyters meeting as a body (*1 Tim.* 4, 14). *See* LAYING ON OF HANDS.

Press. Winepress, or wine vat.

Prevent. Lit. ' to go before,' to forestall, to anticipate (*Ps.* 18, 5; 59, 10; 119, 147).

Priest. The full account of the status and functions

of the priesthood dates from about the time of
Nehemiah, and constitutes an important part of
the P documents. *See* PENTATEUCH. There were
3 grades of priest: the High Priest, the ordinary
priest and the Levite. We will take them in order:
(1) The High Priest. This was a hereditary office
falling to the oldest son of the last High Priest.
He was installed with considerable ceremony (*Ex.*
29; *Lev.* 8). For his functions, vestments, etc
see HIGH PRIEST. (2) The ordinary priests were
set apart with some ceremony (*see passages ref.
to above*). They wore breeches, coats parti-
coloured, girdles and head bands. They offered
the sacrifices. They diagnosed the presence of
disease and performed the offices for getting rid
of it (*Lev.* chs. 13 & 14). They blew the trumpets
for mobilisation of the people either to war or to
religious observance (*Num.* 10, 10; *Lev.* 23, 24;
25, 9). They had a tenth of the Levitical tithe
(*Num.* 18, 28); and they had the profit of the
first fruits, which could be in money (*Num.* 18,
12-18; *Lev.* 7, 30-34). (3) Orig. the Levites were
selected as the functionaries of the priests (*Num.*
3, 5 ff.). They were supported by the tithe (*Num.*
18, 21). Cities were allocated to the Levites after
the conquest, since the Levites owned no land
(*Num.* 35, 1 ff.). David divided the priests and
Levites into courses or shifts, 24 of them. They
performed the sacred offices in turn, for a week,
the shift beginning on the Sabbath before evening
service (*1 Chron.* 24, 1-19). Immediately after the
Exile there were enough priests only for 4 courses
(*Ezra* 2, 36-38) but eventually the original number
was restored (*Luke* 1, 5 & 9). By Gospel times
the office of High Priest had ceased to be strictly
hereditary.

Prince. Various Heb. words with different shades

of meaning are so trans.—governor, ruler, deputy, chieftain, noble, etc. It means generally a person of authority and influence acting in some official capacity, and can be anything from a king (*1 Kings* 14, 7) to a councillor (*Ezra* 7, 14).

Prisca, Priscilla [prĭs′-că prĭs-cĭll′-ă]. *See* AQUILA.

Prison. In times when human life was cheap and capital punishment common for crimes which would to-day be regarded as trivial, there was little use for prisons as they are known to-day. Generally confinement was temporary until something worse happened to the prisoner. Joseph in Egypt was confined in some kind of ' round-house ' (*Gen.* 39, 20). Samson was in a prison of sorts where he was put to work, though the main instrument of detention was his blindness (*Judg.* 16, 21). Jeremiah was thrown into a dungeon or oubliette (*Jer.* 37, 15-16). The Romans had prisons usually attached to the procurator's palace or castle (*Acts* 23, 10). Peter was confined in the Mamertine prison at Rome. Paul experienced prisons of different sorts, varying from a kind of ' open arrest ' (*Acts* 28, 30) to something much grimmer (*Acts* 16, 24).

Prize. *See* GAMES.

Prochorus [prŏ-chō′-rŭs]. One of the 7 original deacons (*Acts* 6, 5).

Proconsul. Rom. provincial governor appointed for 1 yr. by the Senate. He acted as consul in the province (*Acts* 13, 7; 18, 12).

Procurator [prŏ′-cŭ-rā′-tŏr]. Orig. the manager, factor and chief steward of private property. Naturally the status of a procurator was enhanced by the position of the man he served. The greatest man was the Emperor, and his stewards could be appointed to administer parts of the empire as if they were private estates. Gen. they were subordinate to the Rom. governor of the province, but in Judea the procurator was supreme. Judea, Samaria and Idumaea together constituted the Rom. province of Judea of which the procurators were Coponius, Ambivius, Rufus (Augustus died during his term), Valerius Gratus, Pontius Pilate (qv), Marullus, Cuspius Faddus, Tiberius Alexander, Cumanus (after the death of Herod), Felix (qv), Porcius Festus (qv), Albinus, and Gessius Florus (in the 12th year of Nero's reign). They usually lived at Caesarea on the Mediterranean coast, coming up to Jerusalem on important occasions.

Profane. The word is used to-day mostly of speech, but in the AV it means any kind of ceremonial uncleanness (*Heb.* 12, 16).

Prophet. Although the whole OT is of immense value, it is certain that the greatest glory of it is the books of the prophets, as these men and others were the glory of the Jewish people. They made the Jewish contribution to religion and philosophy quite unique. They worked and preached over a fairly lengthy space of time and their progress towards the supreme heights where Jeremiah stands was slow, but it was progressive. The first occurrence of the name is in connection with Saul (*1 Sam.* 10, 12), an expression which seems to have been proverbial. These first prophets seem to have been little different from frenzied mullahs or dervishes (*1 Sam.* 19, 23 & 24). But the frenzy was a passion of patriotism (*1 Sam.* 11, 4 ff.). Samuel is not called a prophet, but a seer, that is, one possessing (or thought to possess) second sight. Later the meanings of the 2 words merge and the distinction disappears; patriotic fervour, and the ability to trace tendencies to their logical and inevitable end become allied qualities of the prophet. Orig. the prophets were not literary; they did not write books. There were people like Deborah, and Nathan, who is the first example of an abiding characteristic of later prophets— criticism of established religious practice which has lost its meanings and spirit (*2 Sam.* 7, 6 & 7). The greatest of the older prophets were, of course, Elijah and Elisha. Elijah's passion was to drive out foreign worship, and Elisha's business was to keep it out. The fierce patriotism amounting almost to fanaticism is apparent in Elijah (*1 Kings* 18, 46; 19, 8). Moving to the literary prophets we find that most of the books are collections of prophecy not all from the head, heart and hand of the man whose name is in the title. *Jeremiah* and *Ezekiel* are by and large the product of these 2 men; *Isaiah* is not from one hand alone, but likewise not from many. The 12 books of the Minor Prophets, however, contain the gist of the prophecy of over 300 yrs., brought together, edited, and titled, at some time before 200 BC. The gap in time bet. the editor and the oldest of the Minor Prophets (*Amos*) is equal to the gap bet. the present time and the age of Shakespeare. For more detailed examination of the particular books, see under their titles. What were the qualities of a prophet? In the first place he had to possess the combination already referred to of vision and understanding of man and God. He had to be a patriot for the sake of the Covenant; one who wanted the nation to be in the right relationship to God, and who could foresee the inevitable consequences of rebellion agst. God's will. He believed that his vision was the gift of God. They were disturbing people to live with, therefore they were gen. solitary. They believed also that their vision was not a sudden and fleeting glimpse into the mind of God, but that it was continuous; God would keep them informed (*Amos* 3, 7). With Isaiah there comes the idea that God at His discretion will act without informing the prophets, and will in fact make them incapable of prophecy (*Isa.* 29, 10). Prophetic silence could therefore be as terrible as prophetic speech. Ezekiel was able to prophesy nothing for 5 yrs. (*Ezek.* 3, 25 ff.; 24, 27). Jeremiah on one occasion took 10 days to make up his mind about a course of action on which his advice had been sought (*Jer.* 42, 7). Again it must be remembered that the prophets were not always right; things did not always turn out as they had foretold. Sometimes, in fact, they changed their minds (*2 Kings* 20, 5). Sometimes, they deliberately concealed the truth (*Jer.* 38, 14-28). Sometimes they gave instructions about the treatment of enemies which, by Christian standards, show that they had an idea of God's will which to-day would be condemned as devilish. But at their best the prophets were men of the highest moral character, obedient to the inspiration of the Holy Spirit, which it must be remembered, was not created at Pentecost. In their own time they were regarded with veneration amounting to fear. The people looked on them as men not only with superhuman knowledge, but with superhuman power. Prophecy in the strictest sense of the word, continues in the NT with such people as Simeon (*Luke* 2, 25 ff.), Anna (*Luke* 2, 36) and John the Baptist (*Matt.* 14, 5; etc.). The Messiah was to come in the line of the prophets (*Deut.* 18, 15 & 18; *John* 6, 14). The people knew Jesus as a prophet (*Matt.* 21, 11; etc.). His disciples called Him a prophet and He even referred to Himself as such (*Luke* 24, 19; *Matt.* 13, 57). The coming of the Holy

Spirit at Pentecost was the ordination of the
Church as a prophet in fulfilment of Joel's prophecy (*Acts* 2, 16 ff.; *Joel* 2, 28). The accent on
preaching in the early Church is indication enough
of their prophetic sense—prophecy was among the
' diversity of gifts.' The 3 types of prophecy found
in the NT are: (1) Ordinary preaching for edi-
fication and comfort (*1 Cor.* 14, 3). (2) Action
under inspiration in particular situations within
the Church (*Acts* 13, 1). (3) Very occasionally,
prediction of the future (*Acts* 11, 28; 21, 10).
Judas and Silas are named as prophets (*Acts* 15,
32) as are Agabus (*Acts* 11, 27) and the daughters
of Philip (*Acts* 21, 9). There is only one example
of literary prophecy in the NT—the book of the
Revelation. By Gospel times, however, there were
so many false prophets, claiming to have special
powers and visions, that people were a bit suspicious even of the name, though the main reason
for the virtual disappearance of the office as such,
was the power and influence of a preaching and
teaching church. All through Christian hist., of
course, men have appeared in the classic mantle
of the prophet to recall the Church to its origins
and to its duty.

Prophetess. The word is once used as a title for the
wife of a prophet (*Isa.* 8, 3). Elsewhere it means
a woman called by God to the work of prophecy.
These were Miriam (*Ex.* 15, 20); Deborah (*Judg.*
4, 4); Huldah (*2 Kings* 22, 14); Noadiah (*Neh.*
6, 14); Anna (*Luke* 2, 36); and Jezebel (*Rev.* 2,
20). This last may mean something rather
opposite, however.

Prophetic Schools. There was a band of fanatical
prophets in Saul's day (*1 Sam.* 10, 5). Samuel was
head of a band or company of prophets who lived
together, and no doubt instructed one another and

exchanged ideas (*1 Sam.* 19, 18-20). 'School' is not the most appropriate name for this assoc. It was a time of religious stagnation and there was nothing more natural than that men of spiritual awareness should gather round Samuel, the only possible mouthpiece of God. In Samaria after the time of Elijah, similar associations appeared, prob. inspired by him and by his memory. They were called the 'sons of the prophets.' This was a guild of people with the same outlook and function (*1 Kings* 20, 35-38; *2 Kings* 2, 3 & 5; 9, 1). They lived together at Bethel, Gilgal and Jericho, which were notorious strongholds of heathen worship. They held Elisha in high esteem and affection (*2 Kings* 4, 38 & 40; 6, 1-7; etc.). After the time of Elisha, these guilds seem to have disappeared.

Proselyte [prŏ'-sĕ-lȳte]. A convert from the state of being a Gentile to Judaism. The Jews were keen missionaries and thought it a splendid thing to pluck such brands from the burning (*Matt.* 23, 15). Two classes were recognised: (1) The 'proselytes of righteousness' who accepted the whole law and were circumcised. (2) 'Proselytes at the gate' who accepted the 'seven precepts of Noah.'

Provender. 1. Cattle food (*Gen.* 24, 25; etc.). 2. Savoury food (*Job* 6, 5; etc.).

Proverbs, Book of. With *Job* and *Ecclesiastes*, one of the Wisdom Books. In the book itself, authorship is attributed to various sources: Solomon (1, 1 to 25, 1); The Wise (22, 17); Men of Hezekiah (25, 1); Agur (30, 1); King Lemuel and his mother (31, 1). Solomon is, of course, the king; 'Men of Hezekiah' could have been Isaiah and Micah (*2 Chron.* 31, 13). Nobody knows who the others may have been. They are collections of the lore of a nation, the proverbs, wise sayings and earthy philosophy of a people, brought together, arranged and edited by men of wisdom and ability who wanted all this treasure of the spoken word put into permanent form. Proverbs exist in all languages, and such collections are very common. Some of this collecting and editing was done in the time of Hezekiah (25, 1); some of it as late as the time of Ezra. The whole function of the proverb, like that of the epigram, is to compress as much as possible into the smallest possible form, and to produce something pithy and full of meat, which can express a great deal in few words, every one of which has its punch and pungency. This is done in various ways in the book. (For the rhythmic form *see* article on POETRY). Along with collections of single proverbs on a common theme (24, 3-12; etc.) there is enlargement of a single proverb (23, 4 & 5; etc.); and monologue with personification of, say, wisdom (1, 20-33). There is also a form which might be called a sonnet (3, 1-10). The general break down of the book is as follows: (1) Introduction (1, 1-6). (2) Proverbs of Solomon on the value of wisdom and the means to acquire it (1, 7 to 9, 18); (3) Proverbs of Solomon on practical morality and good behaviour (10, 1 to 22, 16); (4) Proverbs of the Wise, being advice on the getting of wisdom (22, 17 to 24, 34); (5) Proverbs of Solomon arranged by the men of Hezekiah, on the subjects of ethics and business (chs. 25-29); (6) Words of Agur and Lemuel, mostly on domestic matters (chs. 30-31).

Providence. (*Acts* 24, 2.) Simply ' foresight.'

Province. Lit. ' a sphere of magisterial duty.' With the extension of the Roman Empire these spheres increased in number so that they became actually

of more importance than the administration of
the city itself. Gradually the word came to mean
every place that was not the city (cf. ' London
and the provinces.'). The administrator of a
province was the praetor. During the Republic,
senators were appointed by the senate as provincial governors, usually after having served as
praetor within the city. The job was expensive
and unpaid, and this system of appointment led
to a good deal of corruption. Under Augustus
an arrangement was made, in 27 BC, that peaceful
provinces were to remain under the Senate, while
disturbed provinces were to be under the Emperor.
The senatorial provinces were governed by a
proconsul (qv) while the larger Imperial provinces
were placed under a legate, and the smaller ones
under a procurator. Judea was one of these. The
proconsul held office for a year, the procurator
at the discretion of the Emperor. The terms of
rule and administration were laid down, and
provincial government under the Empire was
vastly better than under the Republic. *See*
PROCURATOR.

Provoke. To persuade a person to any action good
or bad. ' Provocation,' however, is always used in
a bad sense (*2 Cor.* 9, 2; *Ps.* 95, 8).

Psalms, Book of. This is the hymnal of the Jews
and has as much diversity as any Church Hymnal.
(For the poetical form *see* article on POETRY).
There are 150 *Psalms* and of them 73 are assigned
to David, 10 to the School of Korah, 12 to the
School of Asaph, 2 to Solomon, and 1 each to
Ethan, Heman and Moses. Fifty are anonymous.
In the LXX Jeremiah is named as author of one
(137), and Haggai (146) and Zechariah (147).
Possibly one was written by Ezra (119) and several
by Hezekiah (120-134, cf. *Isa.* 38, 9-20). If we can

accept David and Hezekiah as authors, then it appears that the golden age of Heb. poetry was in the 300 yrs. bet. them (c. 1050-750 BC). All but 34 of the *Psalms* have titles. There are many ways in which the *Psalms* can be classified, and of course some *Psalms* would fall into several departments, but a fairly general and useful division might be: Psalms of Prophecy (2, 16, 22, 40, 45, 68, 69, 72, 97, 110, 118); Psalms of the Messiah (16, 22, 24, 40, 68, 69, 118); Penitential (6, 32, 38, 51, 102, 130, 143); Praise (106, 111, 112, 113, 117, 135, 146-150); Teaching (1, 5, 7, 15, 17, 50, 73, 94, 101); Psalms of travelling (120-134); Prayers (17, 86, 90, 102, 142); King's psalms (92-100); Devotional (3, 16, 54, 61, 86, 28, 41, 59, 70, 67, 122, 144); Morning praise (3-5, 19, 57, 63, 108); Evening praise (4, 8, 143); Psalms of anguish (4, 5, 11, 28, 41, 55, 59, 64, 109, 120, 140, 143); Psalms of the story of Israel and Judah (78, 105, 106); Contemplation (16, 56, 60). Out of some 280 OT quotations in the NT, 116 are from the Psalms which were part and parcel of the lives of the Jews, as they are to-day of the life of the Christian Church. There are still in Scotland denominations who sing nothing but Psalms and Paraphrases. The late J. P. Struthers, a most distinguished minister of the Reformed Presbyterian Church, once said, ' Show me anything expressed in a hymn and I will show you it expressed better in a Psalm.' It is still the great devotional Book, for in it all the time man is seeking God at every phase and chance and turn of life from the supremely happy to the completely miserable. Jesus was very familiar with the *Psalms* and it is quite clear that they had an enormous influence in shaping His thought and in feeding His soul. Some of the *Psalms* include musical and other directions. These are: *Neginah* (*Neginoth*), stringed instrument(s), and *Nehiloth*, wind instruments (4 & 5 & 61); *Alamoth*, female or treble voices (46); *Gittith*, either a vintage song or a march (8 & 81 & 84); *Selah* (qv) (3, 2; etc.); *Maschil*, a didactic or reflective Psalm (32; etc.); *Michtam*, epigrammatical (16 & 56-60); *Mizmor*, a lyric ('psalm,' AV); *Shiggaion*, a dissonant choric hymn (7); *Aijeleth hash-shahar*, a well-known melody, 'hind of the dawn' (22); *Jonath elem rehokim* 'the quiet dove of the faraway' (56); *Mahalath*, sickness (53 & 88); the songs of ascent, (or degrees) were sung by pilgrims on their way up to Jerusalem.

Psaltery. *See* MUSIC.

Ptolemy [tŏl'-ĕ-my]. Dynastic title of Egyptian Pharaohs descended from Ptolemy Soter who died in 283 BC. He had been one of Alexander's generals and the last of his line was Cleopatra, who died at the Roman conquest of Egypt. Ptolemy II reigned from 285-246, and Ptolemy III till 221. They were efficient kings, patrons of arts and science, and it was under them that the greatness of Alexandria (qv) developed. The later Ptolemies were of a different stamp altogether.

Publican. The word has nothing to do with public houses, but was the title of a tax-farmer. The Herods auctioned to the highest bidder the right to exact and collect taxes in specific areas. The buyer would subdivide the area and auction portions of it to smaller men. Agents employed in the actual collecting of the taxes were called publicans. Naturally the tax farmers wanted to get in as soon as possible the money they had 'staked,' with the result that the publicans were in the main extortioners (*Luke* 3, 12 & 13; 19, 8). The fact that Jews would serve the Romans and the Herods in this way made them hated and despised (*Matt.* 9, 10-13). Jesus chose one of them to be a disciple (*Matt.* 9, 9; 10, 3). Jesus was not blind to their faults but he never forgot that they were human beings and children of God (*Matt.* 21, 31 & 32).

Publius [pŭb'-lĭ-ŭs]. First citizen of Malta. He befriended Paul after the shipwreck. Paul healed his father of dysentery (*Acts* 28, 7 & 8).

Pulse. Prob. any kind of vegetable grown for food and not simply peas, beans, etc. Ref. (*2 Sam.* 17, 28) is an insertion, it is parched grain. *See* FOOD.

Punishment. *See* CRIME AND PUNISHMENT.

Purification. 1. From uncleanness encountered by touching a corpse (*Num.* 19). The ashes of a red heifer, killed outside the camp, and burned with cedar, hyssop and scarlet (qv) were kept in readiness and were sprinkled by a clean person upon the unclean with a sprig of hyssop on the 3rd and 7th days after contamination. The defiled person then washed himself and his clothes. The ceremony was more elaborate for a Nazirite so defiled (*Num.* 6, 9-12). **2.** From uncleanness due to an issue (*Lev.* 15). The defiled washed in running water on the 7th day, and washed his clothes. On the 8th day he offered 2 doves in the Temple. **3.** Of a mother after childbirth. The woman remained unclean for a week after the birth of a boy, and for a fortnight after the birth of a girl. Her purification lasted 33 or 66 days thereafter, when she could not enter the sanctuary. She then brought for sacrifice a first year lamb, though the poor were allowed to substitute 2 pigeons or doves (*Lev.* 12, 8; *Luke* 2, 12-24). **4.** For a leper (*Lev.* 14). The applicant came to the gate, where the priest killed a ' clean ' bird, bleeding it into a bowl of water. With a sprinkler made of hyssop bound to a cedar stick by a scarlet thread he sprinkled the leper, at the same time dipping a living bird into the bowl and then releasing it. The applicant then washed his clothes, shaved his head, and bathed. Seven days later he did the same, and might then mix with his fellows, after bringing for sacrifice 2 male lambs and 1 ewe lamb, or, if he were poor, 1 lamb and 2 pigeons with a meal and oil offering. The priest sprinkled blood on the man's right ear, right thumb, and right big toe. He repeated this with the oil and poured the remainder of the oil on the man's head.

Purim [pū'-rĭm]. **1.** In the OT, the feast of Purim, or Lots, was celebrated on the 14th and 15th of Adar (March). It was later called Mordecai's Day, as it celebrated the deliverance of the Jews from the pogrom planned by Haman (*Esth.* 3, 7; 9, 15-32). There was at first no religious ceremonial, but later the people gathered at the Temple where the *Book of Esther* was read. Its true origin is obscure. **2.** In the NT some believe that there is one ref. to Purim (*John* 5, 1) but this is unlikely. It was not a very important festival.

Purple. Colour varying bet. violet and near crimson and in ancient times including red. The dye was derived from the shellfish, *murex trunculus*, and was hard to get and expensive. The colour for this reason was always assoc. with wealth, position and royalty.

Purse. A money bag.

Puteoli [pū-tē'-ō-lī]. Italian port near Naples. Paul landed there and found Christians (*Acts* 28, 13).

Pygarg [pўg'-ärg]. (*Deut.* 14, 5.) Prob. the addax, a white rumped antelope.

Python [pŷ'-thŏn]. (*Acts* 16, 16 AV marg.). This is

not the snake, but a person of Pytho near Delphi.
In fable Apollo slew the snake here, hence the
snake name, python. Soothsayers were known as
pythons, and were prob. ventriloquists.

Q

Quail. (*Ex.* 16, 13; *Num.* 11, 31; *Ps.* 105, 40). The
smallest of the partridge family, it migrates from
Africa to Europe.

Quarrel. (*Col.* 3, 13 AV). This is the old meaning
of a complaint, not an argument (*Mark* 6, 19).

Quartus [quăr'-tŭs]. Corinthian Christian (*Rom.*
16, 23).

Quaternion [quă-tĕr'-nĭ-ŏn]. Squad of 4 soldiers
(*Acts* 12, 4).

Queen. Used as now both of the consort of a king
and of a woman who reigns in her own right.
The consort was of very little importance in olden
days but the queen mother did have very considerable influence, like Bathsheba, Jezebel and
Athaliah.

Queen of Heaven. Prob. the Phoenician goddess
Astarte or Ashtaroth (qv) (*Jer.* 7, 18; 44, 15-30).

Quick, quicken. In AV means life, and to enliven
or bring to life, cf. ' the quick and the dead '
(*Acts* 10, 42; *2 Tim.* 4, 1; *1 Pet.* 4, 5).

Quicksands. This is not quicksand in the mod.
sense of a bed of loose wet sand in which solid
objects can be immersed. ' Quick ' has the sense
of ' lively ' or moving. ' Shifting sands ' is better
(*Acts* 27, 17).

Quirinius [quĭ-rĭn'-ĭ-ŭs]. Also **Cyrenius**. The Rom.
governor of Syria in AD 6. During his time in
office the census was ordered which brought
Joseph and Mary to Bethlehem (*Luke* 2, 1-5).

Quiver. A case for carrying arrows worn either on the back (the arrows being extracted over the shoulder) or at the side (*Isa.* 49, 2; *Lam.* 3, 13).

R

Raamah [rā′-ă-măh], **Raama.** A Cushite people of traders (*Gen.* 10, 7; *1 Chron.* 1, 9; *Ezek.* 27, 22).

Rabbah [răb′-băh]. There are 2 cities of the name; one, unidentified, in Judah (*Josh.* 15, 60). The other was the capital of the Ammonites, situated on a hill 20 m. from the Jordan. It was on the E boundary of Gad (*Josh.* 13, 25).

Rabbi [răb′-bī]. Straight Heb. word meaning ' my master,' and used by the pupil in respect to his spiritual teacher (*Matt.* 23, 7; etc.). Some think that there is a distinction of degree bet. Rabbi and Rabboni, but this is more likely to be an Aram. version of the same word (*John* 1, 38; 20, 16).

Rabsaris [răb′-să-rĭs]. 1. An Assyrian official in the time of Hezekiah (*2 Kings* 18, 17). 2. Two officials of the time of Nebuchadnezzar. It is not a proper name but an official title (*Jer.* 39, 3).

Rabshakeh [răb′-shă-kĕh]. Another official title in the Assyrian court (*Isa.* 36).

Raca [rā′-că]. Occurs only once (*Matt.* 5, 22). It was an expression of contempt and unbelief, perhaps better trans. colloquially as ' You silly ass.'

Race. *See* GAMES.

Races. All races were supposed to be desc. from the sons of Noah. Those mentioned in Scripture include: 1. Sons of Japheth (Aryans): Greeks, Parthians, Persians, Medes, Romans. 2. Sons of Ham: Egyptians, Cushites, Lybians. 3. Sons of

Shem (Semites): Babylonians, Assyrians, Aramaeans, Ammonites, Amorites, Canaanites, Edomites, Hivites, Israelites, Jebusites, Moabites, Phoenicians. **4.** Unclassified: Cimmerians, Elamites, Hittites, Horites, Philistines. With class 3, can be counted Amalekites, Ishmaelites and Midianites.

Rachel [rā′-chĕl] **(Rahel).** Younger daughter of Laban and the love of Jacob's life (*Gen.* 29, 28-30). Her older sister married Jacob first by a piece of deception. Both made good wives to him (*Gen.* 31, 14-16 & 19). Rachel bore him 2 sons, Joseph and Benjamin, and died giving the latter birth. Jacob buried her near Bethlehem (Ephrath) and erected a pillar over the grave (*Gen.* 35, 20; *1 Sam.* 10, 2).

Raddai [răʹ-dă-ī]. Fifth son of Jesse, brother of David (*1 Chron.* 2, 14).

Rahab [rāʹ-hăb]. **1.** A woman of easy virtue in Jericho to whose house the 2 Israelite spies found their way. They were discovered and Rahab saved them (*Josh.* 2). In return her house and kin were spared at the sack of Jericho (*Josh.* 6, 22-25). She is mentioned in the genealogy of Jesus (*Matt.* 1, 5). **2.** A poetic title for Egypt as the dragon, or mythological monster subdued by Jehovah, which dwelt in the depths (*Ps.* 87, 4; 89, 10; *Isa.* 51, 9).

Raiment. *See* DRESS.

Rain. The Israelites spoke of the former and the latter rains. The former rains fell in Oct.-Nov., and without them the hard-baked earth could not be made soft enough for the plough. The latter rains fell intermittently till about March, and without them the seed would not germinate and the crops grow. The average rainfall is only about 30 inches and it all falls in the six months.

Rainbow. All natural phenomena had to have a religious significance; so the rainbow became to the Hebrews the witness that God would not destroy the world again by flood (*Gen.* 9, 12-17).

Raisins. Grapes, dipped in a solution of potash and dried in the sun (*1 Sam.* 25, 18; 30, 12; *Hos.* 3, 1 RV; etc.).

Ram. For the animal, *see* SHEEP.

Ram. For the battering ram, *see* FORTIFICATION AND SIEGE.

Ramah [rā´-măh], **Rama. 1.** Town of Benjamin near Bethel (*Josh.* 18, 25; *Judg.* 4, 5; *Jer.* 40, 1; *Neh.* 11, 33). **2.** Samuel's birthplace and burial place (*1 Sam.* 1, 19; 2, 11; 7, 17; 25, 1; 28, 3; etc.). **3.** Town in Asher (*Josh.* 19, 29). **4.** Town in Naphtali (*Josh.* 19, 36). **5.** Town of Ramoth Gilead (*2 Kings* 8, 29). **6.** Town in Simeon (*Josh.* 19, 8).

Ramath [rā´-măth]. *See* 6 above.

Rameses [rā´-mē-sĕs]. Town of Egypt in the land of Goshen where Pharaoh allowed Jacob and his sons to settle (*Gen.* 47, 11).

Ramoth Gilead [rā´-mŏth gĭ´-lĕ-ăd]. Levitical city in Gilead, and City of Refuge (qv) (*Josh.* 21, 38; 20, 8; *Deut.* 4, 43). Ahab was killed here in battle agst. the Syrians (*1 Kings* 22). Agst. the enemy here Jehoram was wounded (*2 Kings* 8, 28 & 29). Some think it identical with Mizpeh or Mizpah (qv).

Rapha(h) [rā´-phă]. **1.** Son of Benjamin, prob. born in Egypt (*1 Chron.* 8, 2). **2.** Desc. of Jonathan (*1 Chron.* 8, 37).

Raven. Ceremonially unclean bird (*Lev.* 11, 15). It is the common raven, *corvus corax*, which feeds on carrion. Hebrew was written in consonants only till the Massoretes supplied vowel points. The consonants of the Heb. word trans. ' ravens '

are the same as those of the word 'Arabs,'
suggesting an alternative to the 'ravens' which
fed Elijah by the brook Cherith (*1 Kings* 17, 2-7).

Raven (ravin). As a verb, this means to prey upon.

Razor. Sharp knife for shaving with (*Isa.* 7, 20;
Ezek. 5, 1).

Reba [rē'-bă]. One of 5 Midianite kinglets slain in
battle with Israel under Moses (*Num.* 31, 8; *Josh.*
13, 21).

Rebekah [rĕ-bĕ'-kăh]. (Rebecca *Rom.* 9, 10).
Daughter of Bethuel, who was son of Abraham's
brother Nahor (*Gen.* 22, 23). Her brother was
Laban and she married Isaac (*Gen.* 24). Rebekah
late in life produced twins, Jacob and Esau (*Gen.*
25, 24-26). She favoured Jacob before Esau, and
secured the birthright from Isaac, who was senile
by this time, for Jacob (*Gen.* 27). She had the
qualities of a great wife and mother in fair measure, but she had also the faults possessed by all
possessive people.

Receipt of Custom. *See* CUSTOM.

Rechab [rē'-chăb] (**Rechabite**). There was a Rechab
who, with his brother Baanah murdered Ishbosheth (qv) (*2 Sam.* 4). The more important
one was Rechab the father of Jehonadab (*2 Kings*
10, 15-28). Jehonadab was known as the Rechabite, as were his descendants. He threw in his lot
with Jehu in the attempt to overthrow Ahab and
to get rid of idolatry. On the success of the venture
Jehu treated him with considerable respect. The
Rechabites, inspired by his example, would not
drink wine, live in roofed houses, sow seeds, or
plant vineyards. They reckoned, and Jehonadab
had believed, that Israel was better off in the old
nomadic days than under the settlement (*Jer.* 35).
They were not, however, Nazirites (qv).

Red heifer. Prop. a red cow. The ashes of a red

cow, burned, added to running water removed defilement from contact with a dead body. This was the ' water of separation;' the whole ceremony is described (*Num.* 19).

Red Sea. The thousand-mile long stretch of water bet. Africa and Arabia. It is part of the Great Rift Valley running from Lake Tanganyika to the Caspian Sea. Main scriptural interest centres round the northern end with the Gulf of Suez, the Bay of Akabah, and the Sinaitic peninsula. In olden times the Gulf of Suez extended further N, maybe as far as the Bitter Lakes and along the line of the present canal. Its Arabic name is the Sea of Weeds (*Ex.* 10, 19; 15, 4). This, called also the Sea of Reeds, is what the Israelites crossed dry shod. From time to time a favourable combination of wind and tide will shallow what is left of the Sea of Reeds so much that it can be walked over almost dry shod. The Israelites, being on foot, managed this. The Egyptian chariots were bogged down, however, and a shift of wind and change of tide was their end.

Reed. Several Heb. words are so trans. **1.** Any tall broad-leaved grass growing in wet ground or in water (*1 Kings* 14, 15; *Isa.* 19, 6; etc.). Some reeds are short and fragile, others grow to a considerable height and are strong (*Matt.* 27, 29 & 30 & 48). This is prob. *arundo donax.* **2.** A unit of measurement deriving from the use of reeds as measuring wands. It was 6 cubits, or approx. 9 feet. **3.** (*Jer.* 51, 32). Marshes.

Refiner, Refining. Tradesman and his trade of purifying metals, esp. precious metals by heat. Silver and lead are placed in a crucible in a very hot furnace, oxide of lead forms and is blown off (*Jer.* 6, 29). Figuratively it is the purifying influence of suffering (*Mal.* 3, 2 & 3).

Refuge, Cities of. See CITY OF REFUGE.

Refuse. In the AV has a meaning stronger than the mod. meaning. It is more ' to reject ' (*Ps.* 118, 22).

Rehob [rē'-hŏb]. **1.** Place near Hamath (*Num.* 13, 21). **2.** Two towns in Asher. one on the border (*Josh.* 19, 28; 21, 31; *1 Chron.* 6, 75). **3.** Father of Hadadezer of Zobah (*2 Sam.* 8, 3 & 12). **4**: Levite, returned exile (*Neh.* 10, 11).

Rehoboam [rē'-hō-bō'-ăm]. Son of Solomon and Naamah (*1 Kings* 14, 21). Under him Israel, the N kingdom, and Judah, the S kingdom, parted company (*1 Kings* 12). Relations had been strained bet. the 2 for some time, but the rivalry was most bitter bet. Ephraim, the most powerful of the 10 tribes, and Judah. Rehoboam went to Shechem in Ephraim to be crowned. He was asked to release the people from the forced labour imposed on them by Solomon. Discourteously and provocatively he refused. Israel thereupon decided to split away from Judah with their own king Jeroboam. During his reign Judah was invaded by the Egyptians (*1 Kings* 14, 26; *2 Chron.* 12). He maintained a large and fruitful harem (*2 Chron.* 11, 21) and after a reign of about 17 yrs. died c. 915 BC, and was succeeded by Abijah. See ISRAEL.

Rehoboth [rĕ-hō'-bŏth]. **1.** A well, dug by Isaac's servants, subject of a dispute with Abimelech of Gerar (*Gen.* 26, 22). **2.** King of Edom (*Gen.* 36, 37). There was a town called after him.

Reins. See KIDNEYS.

Rekem [rē'-kĕm]. One of 5 kings of Midian slain in war by Moses (*Num.* 31, 8; *Josh.* 13, 21). Also a Benjamite city (*Josh.* 18, 27).

Religion. The AV use of the word applies not to the inner spiritual faith, but rather to the outward and visible form. James uses the word in contrast bet. the two (*James* 1, 26 & 27).

Remnant. *See* ISRAEL. The hist. of this people was one of selection and rejection. The remnant was the portion left selected after the majority had been rejected. This remnant was always to be the nucleus of the new Israel (*Ezra* 9, 8; *Zech.* 14, 2; etc.).

Repent. Lit. ' to change the mind,' though with the mind is included the affections.

Rephaim [rĕ'-phă-ĭm]. People of considerable physique who were in Palestine before Abraham (*Gen.* 14, 5; 15, 20; *Josh.* 17, 15). Also a valley near Jerusalem where David twice defeated the Philistines (*2 Sam.* 5, 18-22; 23, 13). Prob. the valley of Baca.

Rephan [rĕ'-phăn] (**Remphan**). The *Acts* (7, 43) quoting *Amos* (5, 26) substitutes this word for Chiun, by a slight confusion of letters. This was a heathen godling, worshipped by Israel in the wilderness.

Rephidim [rĕ'-phĭ-dĭm]. Camping ground of Israel where the people grumbled at the lack of water and Moses smote the rock and obtained it (*Ex.* 17). They fought agst. Amalek there.

Reprobate. (*Jer.* 6, 30 AV.) Descriptive of false metal that cannot stand the test or the refiner's fire. RV trans. ' refuse,' the noun. This idea of counterfeit remains in the NT (*Rom.* 1, 28; etc.).

Resh [rĕsh]. 20th letter of the Heb. alphabet: Eng. R. Copyists often confused *resh* with *daleth* (qv).

Rest. Not the physical sense of the word, but rather freedom from care and anxiety; complete peace of mind and soul.

Resurrection. *See* IMMORTALITY.

Reuben [reu'-bĕn]. First child of Jacob and Leah (*Gen.* 29, 31 & 32). After an involvement with a

concubine of his father's he lost the birthright
which was his due, and played a very minor role
indeed in the story of the beginnings of Israel
(*Gen.* 35, 22; 49, 3 & 4). He had 4 sons, Hanoch,
Phallu, Hezron and Carmi (*Gen.* 46, 8 & 9). His
descendants formed the tribe of Reuben, divided
into the clans desc. from his sons (*Num.* 26, 5-11).
In the first 2 censuses they numbered about 45,000
men of military age (*Num.* 1, 20 & 21; 26, 7).
They asked Moses to be allowed to settle E of
Jordan, reckoning the country to be well suited
to their flocks. This was granted on condition
that they still supplied troops for the crossing of
Jordan and the invasion (*Num.* 32, 1-42). Relations were strained, however, bet. them and those
living W of Jordan (*Josh.* 22, 1-34). Their Levitical
cities were Bezer, Jahaz, Kedemoth and Mephaath
(*Josh.* 21, 7 & 36 & 37). Bezer was a city of refuge
(*Josh.* 20, 8). *See* TRIBES OF ISRAEL.

Revelation. Lit. ' an unveiling of something concealed.' ' Apocalypse ' means an uncovering (*Rev.*
1, 1). Man by his best nature is a seeker after
God, but there is a limit to what man can discover.
The searching by man must coincide at some point
with a revealing of Himself by God. Without this
it is impossible for man to come to anything like
an appreciation and understanding of the nature
of God. Man seeks knowledge and God leads him
into knowledge by making things known that
cannot possibly be discovered. Man can communicate with God by means of prayer, but God
can communicate with man in various ways. This
may be through the works of nature. ' The heavens declare the glory of God.' There is also the
sense of the purposefulness of Creation (*Rom.* 1, 20).
There is also the sense that the best of men know
because they feel that something in them derives

from something great outside themselves. The thoughtful, looking back on their own and on their country's experiences feel driven to the conclusion that here and there a hand has guided. Men like the OT prophets felt this so completely that they had to preface their exhortations and warnings with the words, ' Thus saith the Lord.' We have used of men the words, ' the best,' ' thoughtful.' And this must be borne in mind, that unless there is a particular quality in the human being, God cannot make himself ' en rapport ': He cannot ' get through.' The whole OT is the story of persons, and even of a people, trying to get a portrait of God. The portrait is almost always imperfect, though it is progressive. But it was not until God, by a physical act, projected Himself into the realm of human experience in the person of Jesus, that the portrait became complete. Most people are perfectly satisfied with this revelation. Jesus at the Ascension disappeared from human view, leaving the conviction that the revelation continues in the work of the Holy Spirit in the hearts and souls of men.

Revelation, Book of. *See* JOHN THE DIVINE, REVELATION OF ST.

Revenge. *See* AVENGER OF BLOOD.

Revive. Mod. meaning is to bring to life again. AV meaning is to come to life again (*1 Kings* 17, 22; *Neh.* 4, 2; *Rom.* 7, 9; etc.).

Rezin [rē′-zin]. King of Damascus, subject to Assyria, who joined a federation with Israel agst. Judah. He was killed by the Assyrians (*Isa.* 7, 1 —9, 11; *2 Kings* 16, 5-9).

Rezon [rē′-zŏn]. Founder of the Syrian kingdom after David destroyed Zobah (*1 Kings* 11, 23).

Rhoda [rhō′-dă]. Maidservant in the house of John Mark's mother (*Acts*, 2, 13).

Rhodes [rhŏd′-es]. City of Greece on the island of the same name. It was founded in 408 BC. It became a great commercial centre of the ancient world. Paul's ship called at Rhodes on the voyage from Troas to Caesarea. The Colossus, 105 ft. tall, straddled the harbour bet. 280 and 224 BC.

Riblah [rĭb′-lăh]. Town on the Orontes, headquarters of Nebuchadnezzar in the control of Syria and Palestine (*2 Kings* 25, 6; etc.).

Riddle. Any remark or question that has to be thought about before an answer can be found (*Num.* 12, 8). Where it is called ' dark speeches ' the riddle can also be a parable or ' dark saying ' (*Ps.* 49, 4; 78, 2). Well-known riddles were those of Samson (*Judg.* 14, 12-19) and several of Solomon and Hiram ref. to by Josephus.

Rie. Old spelling of rye (*Ex.* 9, 32; *Isa.* 28, 25 AV). RV trans. ' spelt ' a poor quality grain. Elsewhere AV has ' fitches ' (*Ezek.* 4, 9).

Rimmon [rĭm′-mŏn]. **1.** A Benjamite whose sons murdered Ishbosheth (*2 Sam.* 4, 2). **2.** Town in the S of Judah (*Neh.* 11, 29). **3.** Border town of Zebulun assigned to the Levites (*Josh.* 19, 13 AV Remmon). **4.** Rock to which the remnants of the Benjamites fled after defeat (*Judg.* 20, 45-47).

Rimmon. A Syrian god worshipped at Damascus (*2 Kings* 5, 18). He was god of rain, thunder and tempest.

Ring. *See* ORNAMENTS.

River. Three Heb. words are so trans. **1.** *Nahar*, a stream of some considerable size: the Nile, Pharpar, Euphrates, etc. **2.** *Nahal*, usually a seasonal stream, carrying water only during the rains but dry otherwise, a wadi. **3.** *Yeor*, almost entirely confined to the Nile, and esp. the delta, but once used of the Tigris (*Dan.* 12, 5-7).

River of Egypt. The Nile, esp. the E channel

(*Gen.* 15, 18). In this passage the 2 rivers, Nile and Euphrates, are named as the boundaries of the land promised to Abraham and his people. This is not the 'brook of Egypt' or the great wadi, which is a *nahal*, while the Nile is a *nahar*. *See* RIVER. The names are sometimes confused (*Num.* 34, 5; etc.), but the distinction is plain in the Heb.

Rizpah [rĭz′-păh]. Concubine of Saul, and cause of the quarrel which took Abner away from Ishbosheth and back to David (2 *Sam.* 3, 6-8).

Road. Old form of 'inroad' or 'infiltration' (*1 Sam.* 27, 10). RV has 'raid.' When the highway is meant, the word 'road' is seldom used, 'way' or 'path' being preferred. 'Byways' (*Judg.* 5, 6) are 'round-about roads' (cf. by-pass): 'by-paths' (*Jer.* 18, 15) are new ways as opposed to old.

Robber. *See* THIEF, CRIME AND PUNISHMENT.

Rock badger. (*Lev.* 11, 5.) Trans. 'coney' except RV mar. It is *hyrax syriacus*, which is more like the tapir than either the rabbit or the badger.

Roe. Also called roebuck (2 *Sam.* 2, 18; etc.). *See* GAZELLE. It is one of the deer family, *capreolus capraea* or *cervus capreolis*. Some think the word so trans. however, is of the antelope family. The beast was ceremonially clean (*Deut.* 14, 5).

Roll. *See* PAPYRUS, PARCHMENT, WRITING.

Romans. 1. Inhabitants of Rome (*Acts* 2, 10). **2.** Officials representing the Rom. authority (*John* 11, 48; *Acts* 25, 16; etc.). **3.** Citizens of the Rom. Empire of any nationality (*Acts* 16, 21; 22, 25; etc.). Citizenship could be conferred in return for a service, though it could on occasion be bought (*Acts* 22, 28). In early Christian times it was a great privilege. Paul was a Rom. citizen, and that is why he had to be given special treat-

ment A Rom. citizen could not be bound,
scourged, or killed without ref. to the emperor.
A citizen on trial had only to call out 'I am a
Roman citizen' and the trial ended *pro tem*. That
is why Lysias suddenly stopped the scourging of
Paul (*Acts* 22, 25) and why the scourging of
Paul caused fear and alarm at Philippi (*Acts* 16,
36-38). Yet Paul claimed several scourgings to his
credit. *See* PAUL.

Romans, Epistle of Paul the Apostle to the. There is
abundant evidence that the letter was written by
Paul, and, apparently at Corinth just after he had
written another letter (*2 Cor*. 1-9). It is hard to
decide if the Church at Rome was predominantly
Jewish or predominantly Gentile. The weight of
evidence, however, is that, as in many of the cities
at that time, the number of Gentile Christians
surpassed the Jewish element. The date is towards
the close of the 3rd missionary journey, bet.
AD 55-56. Paul always had a reason for writing a
letter. What was his reason here? The first great
controversy of the Church had been bet. those who
believed that Christianity was a development from
Judaism, and those who believed that it was something quite new and distinct: that the Christian
Church had, in fact, taken over the trad. Jewish
role of ultimately bringing all humanity into the
knowledge of Jehovah and to obedience to the
Mosaic law. The case was hammered out at the
Council of Jerusalem and Paul's point of view,
accepted by Peter and James, won the day:
Christianity (though it did not then have the name)
was new, and a faith in its own right. But in Asia
Minor, where Jewish influence was strong, pressure was still being brought to bear on converts
to submit to circumcision and to old Jewish
regulations and taboos. Paul wrote a letter to the

Galatians beseeching them to resist this pressure.
It was a passionate document, which has been
called the Magna Carta of Christianity. Later he
felt that he would have to set down the arguments
more dispassionately, soberly and logically. To
this end he wrote the Epistle to the Romans. This
is the Constitution of Christianity as Paul saw it.
His main theme is that Christianity is the one and
only means of salvation. In ch. 1 he introduces
himself and makes his main statement about the
faith as the only means of salvation, and the need
for righteousness. The Gentile world is a world of
sin. In ch. 2 he points out that the Jewish world
is no different, but with hypocrisy added. In ch.
3 he shows how ' acquittal ' for sin can be granted
by God if He is approached in faith. He will do
this because of the atoning death of Jesus. Ch. 4
is an argument about Abraham: was he justified
by faith or by works? Paul reckons it was by
faith. In ch. 5 he speaks of the peace which
springs from certainty of redemption, and goes
on in the next 2 chs. to speak of the complete
break with the old life that comes with baptism,
which is a mystical death and resurrection (6, 1-11);
at the same time it is the point of leaving the
service of King Sin for the service of King God
(6, 12-14). In the third place baptism is the act of
liberating the slave from the bondage of sin into
the free service of God (6, 15-23). Finally, baptism
is the end of the marriage with Sin, who is now
dead, and the beginning of the marriage with God
(7, 1-7). Ch. 8 is a call to courage in those who
have the spirit within them, of the assurance of
regeneration, and of the confidence that comes
from knowing that all this was ordained by God.
He turns to the Jews again in ch. 9, asking how and
why they have got themselves out of the right

relationship with God, and how they can win back again. Chs. 12, 13, 14 and 15 are general exhortations about belief and conduct, with a plea for toleration and harmony. He ends with greetings to personal friends in Rome.

Rome. City on the left bank of the Tiber, under 20 m. from the sea. By the middle of the 6th cent. BC its walls enclosed a considerable town built on seven hills. In early days the Romans were one of several members of a Latin League, but fairly soon became the dominant power in it. At first they were ruled by kings but when these tended to treat the people like slaves they were expelled, and in their place 2 rulers called consuls were appointed to serve each for 1 yr. The whole system of government consisted of devolution of authority, with one office acting as a brake on the others. Under the republic the Rom. conquest stretched out over the entire known world. But the seeds of its own destruction were within it. The struggle bet. the aristocracy and the plebeians had resulted in all offices of state being open to all citizens, but soon a ' governing class ' evolved, and the republic came to an end after bitter struggles for power bet. representatives of that governing class, Julius Caesar, Crassus, Pompey, Mark Antony, Brutus and others. Octavius, nephew of Julius Caesar, became emperor, with the title Augustus, and before very long the emperors had usurped all the democratic offices which had still remained in name. Enormous wealth poured into Rome and into the luxurious Rom. cities of the world. Society was uneasily perched on the shoulders of millions of slaves. Rome itself degenerated into an incredible and almost insane licentiousness, while in the provinces alone did some semblance of the old rugged grandeur persist. On the whole the provinces were fairly well governed. *See* PUBLICAN. The emperor appointed the governors who were directly responsible to him. *See* GOVERNOR. Rome gradually decayed, but its work had been done; and along the straight roads, protected by the legions, the Gospel had gone out to the ends of the earth. Christianity became the official religion of the Rom. empire in the 4th cent. under Constantine.

Roof. *See* HOUSE.

Room. *See* HOUSE. There is also in the AV an obsolete use of the word, meaning a place at table. These 'rooms' were the couches on which guests reclined when eating, following the Gk. and Rom. practice (*Matt.* 23, 6; *Luke* 14, 7 & 8; 20, 46). *See* MEALS.

Rose (*S. of S.* 2, 1; *Isa.* 35, 1). Unlikely to be the true rose as we know it. Various suggestions have been made as to its identity. **1.** *Narcissus tazetta.* **2.** The crocus. **3.** Meadow saffron: *colchicum autumnale.* **4.** A water plant, *cyperus syriacus.* **5.** Poss. the true rose.

Ruby. *See* JEWELS AND PRECIOUS STONES.

Rue. *Ruta graveolens;* a shrubby plant used medicinally and even as a culinary flavouring. So valueless that Jesus used it to ridicule the Pharisees (*Luke* 11, 42).

Rufus [rū′-fŭs]. Son of Simon of Cyrene, who may poss. have been the Christian at Rome to whom Paul sent greetings (*Mark* 15, 21; *Rom.* 16, 13).

Ruhamah [rū-ha′-măh]. Part of a word-play in Hosea (1, 6 & 8; 2, 1 & 23). The prophet gave strange meaningful names to his children by Gomer. Lo-ruhamah means 'unpitied,' the 'lo' meaning 'not.' Hosea says, to console the people, that God will have pity on her who had obtained no pity: ' ruhamah ' on ' Lo-ruhamah.'

Ruler. Anyone who exercises authority; but particularly: **1.** Ruler of the synagogue (*Luke* 8, 41). *See* SYNAGOGUE. **2.** Ruler of the city, or civil magistrate (*Acts* 16, 19). **3.** A member of the Sanhedrin (*John* 3, 1; 7, 26; etc.). **4.** The ruler of a feast, or master of ceremonies. *See* MAGISTRATE, SANHEDRIN, MEALS.

Runners. A king's bodyguard (*1 Sam.* 22, 17). Called ' footmen ' AV; and ' guard ' RV. It is poss. that they ran before the king's chariot. *See* FORERUNNER. But their main duties were escort (*1 Kings* 14, 28).

Rush. More or less any kind of reed (qv), but particularly the papyrus.

Rust. Any corrosion or tarnish on metals (*Matt.* 6, 19 & 20; *Jas.* 5, 3).

Ruth. Moabite wife and widow of Mahlon, a Bethlehemite. He, with his father, mother and brother had been driven into Moab by famine. There he and the brother married, and, with the father, died. Ruth left Moab with her mother-in-law Naomi and came to Bethlehem. It was customary for a near kinsman to marry the widow of his kin. One relative turned Ruth down, but another, Boaz, married her. They were ancestors of David, and so of Jesus.

Ruth, Book of. The book must be fairly historical for it is hardly likely that post exilic writers with the record of Ezra having persuaded so many returned exiles to put away their foreign wives, would have felt encouraged to tell the story of one who married a foreigner and so helped to produce David. Israel and Moab were for a time fairly friendly (*1 Sam.* 22, 3 & 4). The touching words of Ruth to Naomi are well known (1, 16 &

17) and seem to indicate a belief or at least an idea, that foreigners could come within the Promise and the Covenant. Among the Jews the book was placed immediately after the Judges and is one of the Megilloth, or Festal Rolls publicly read. This book was read at Pentecost, a harvest feast.

Rye. *See* RIE.

S

Sabachthani [să-băch-thă′-nĭ]. *See* ELI.

Sabaoth [să′-bā-ŏth]. Lord of Hosts. *See* HOSTS.

Sabbath. According to one account of the origin of the Sabbath, God, after completing the work of creation, rested on the 7th day and hallowed it (*Gen.* 2, 1-3). *See* CREATION. But the word simply means, 'to stop working,' and was used of the Day of Atonement, which fell not on a 7th but on a 10th day (of the 7th month) (*Lev.* 16, 31). The name has become assoc. with the 7th day of creation when it was hallowed for human rest, though the Decalogue does not indicate how it should be spent (*Ex.* 20, 8; *Deut.* 5, 12). It became a day of rest, sacred to God. Even in the OT there was the idea that it was made for man (*Ex.* 23, 12; *Deut.* 5, 14). It is not till post exilic times, however, that the obligation to worship is emphasised. Nehemiah insisted that the observance of the Sabbath was the symbol of the difference bet. the Jew and all others (*Neh.* 10, 31; 13, 15 ff.,). By the time of Jesus, the Sabbath was no longer a simple Covenant day, to be observed as a witness. It was hedged about with conventions, regulations, artificialities, and restrictions. Jesus' claim to be the Messiah was unforgivably blasphemous in the ears of the Scribes, but their wrath at His cavalier treatment of Sabbath observance was hardly less bitter than their indignation at His claim (*Matt.* 12, 1 ff.; *Luke* 13, 14 ff.; *John* 5, 5 ff.). But Jesus saw the point and the reason for the Sabbath (*Luke* 4, 16). Observance of the Sabbath in Apostolic times was not obligatory (*Col.* 2, 16 ff.). *See* LORD'S DAY.

Sabbath day's journey. This was the distance which the Scribes reckoned to be the maximum which a person could walk and still observe the Sabbath obligation to rest (*Acts* 1, 12). It seems to have been something just over half a mile (*Num.* 35, 5). This was for journeys outside the city; there was no limit to walking inside the city.

Sabbatical Year. There are various interpretations according to the source of the legislation. In one, all field work had to stop every 7th year (*Ex.* 23, 10 & 11). This was for the sake of the poor, to rest animals and the like, but it seems more likely that it was designed to rest the overworked ground in sections. Or it may have meant that in every 7th year the produce of sections of the land was to be given to the poor. The poor (*see* POVERTY) were by and large the landless. It was also the law that a Heb. slave was released in the Sabbatical, or 7th year (*Ex.* 21, 2-6). But in *Deuteronomy* there is another picture entirely. In the 7th year all liabilities of Jews to Jews were to be cancelled (*Deut.* 15, 1-3). There is no word of redemption of mortgaged land. *Leviticus*, on the other hand, mentions the 7th year fallow period (*Lev.* 25, 1-55) but says nothing about the poor. It is here that the Jubilee Year (qv) is mentioned, when all slaves were to be freed. But the Jubilee year is not the Sabbatical year: the Jubilee year is the 7th Sabbatical year, the period bet. Jubilee years

being 49 years. Behind all this legislation, however, and the various readings and interpretations,
is the awareness that land, like people, gets tired
and needs rested. There is also the awareness that
human dignity is entitled to land, liberty, and the
pursuit of happiness. It must be remembered that
this kind of law may have seemed a fine thing
when nobody had any land, but a different thing
entirely when they had (*Luke* 4, 18 & 19).

Sabeans [să-bē´-ăns]. People of Sheba, or Seba
(*Isa.* 45, 14; *Joel* 3, 8).

Sackbut. *See* MUSIC.

Sackcloth. Not mod. sackcloth, which is made of
jute, but a coarse cloth woven usually of goats'
hair (*Rev.* 6, 12). It had nothing to do with
sacks. The Eng. word derives from the Heb. *sak*,
a garment worn often by prophets as a kind of
uniform, and by mourners, penitents and prisoners
(*2 Sam.* 3, 31; *Isa.* 20, 2; *Isa.* 3, 24).

Sacrifice. *See* OFFERING.

Sadducees [săd´-dū-cēes]. A Jewish politico-
religious party, opposed to the Pharisees (qv).
They were named after Zadok the High Priest
(qv). Where the Pharisees were traditionalists,
the Sadducees took their guidance from Scripture
alone and not from the rulings of the elders. They
denied the Pharasaic doctrine of the resurrection
of the body, and of existence in Sheol (qv). They
denied the doctrine of the reality of angels (*Mark*
12, 18; *Acts* 23, 8). One clear sign of their fear
of the effects of Jesus' teaching was the assoc.
of Sadducees and Pharisees to discomfit him
(*Matt.* 16, 1-4; 22, 23-33). They were bitter
enemies of the early Church (*Acts* 4, 1-22; 23,
6-10).

Saffron. A variety of crocus (*c. sativus*), source of
a yellow dye, and of a fragrant flavouring for food.

Sails. *See* SHIPS AND BOATS.

Salamis [să′-lă-mĭs]. City of Cyprus, visited by Paul, the mod. Famagusta. It is not to be confused with the scene of the naval battle bet. Gks. and Persians in 480 BC (*Acts* 4, 36; 11, 19; 21, 16).

Salecah [să′-lē-căh]. Also appears as Salcah and Salchah. The most N city of Gad, and so of all Israel (*Deut.* 3, 10; *Josh.* 12, 5; *1 Chron.* 5, 11).

Salem [să′-lĕm]. Abbreviation of Jerusalem. *See* SHALEM (*Ps.* 76, 2).

Salmon [săl′-mŏn]. Father of Boaz (*Ruth* 4, 20). So, an ancestor of Jesus (*Matt.* 1, 4).

Salmone [săl-mō′-nĕ]. Cape Sidero, promontory on NE Crete (*Acts* 27, 7).

Salome [să-lō′-mĕ]. **1.** Wife of Zebedee; mother of James and John (*Mark* 15, 40; 16, 1). **2.** Daughter of Herodias (qv) who asked for the head of John the Baptist (*Mark* 6, 17-28).

Salt. There was no shortage of salt in Palestine, for 100 lbs. of Dead Sea water yields nearly 25 lbs. of salt. It was used in food and accompanied sacrifices (*Lev.* 2, 13). Newly born children were rubbed with it (*Ezek.* 16, 4). Fish, meat, and fruit were pickled in it. The Covenant of Salt (*Num.* 18, 19; *2 Chron.* 13, 5) has in it some thought of the permanence which salt could give to something which otherwise would rot (*Matt.* 5, 13). But it has also the sense of the irreplaceable; the thing for which there is no substitute. They ploughed salt into enemy land (*Judg.* 9, 45).

Salt, City of. A town near the Dead Sea (*Josh.* 15, 62).

Salt Sea. Dead Sea.

Salt, Pillar of. *See* LOT.

Salt, Valley of. Plain S of the Dead Sea where David had victories over Edom (*2 Sam.* 8, 13; *1 Chron.* 18, 12).

Saltwort. RV rendering of ' mallows ' (*Job* 30, 4
AV). Prob. it is sea purslane; *atriplex halinus*.

Salutation. Most mod. greetings derive from the
more elaborate and punctilious salutations of long
ago: ' Peace be upon you '; ' And on you ';
' May your day be happy '; ' May yours be happy
and blessed.' Eastern greetings were usually prolonged and elaborate. The greeting, ' blessed be
he that cometh ' (*Judg.* 18, 15; *Matt.* 10, 12) was
a very common salutation from one approaching
another. The court greeting was ' Let the king
live forever ' (cf. Long live the king). A bow went
down to the ground (*Gen.* 18, 2; 19, 1). The
parting salutation was, ' Go in peace,' which is
just the same as ' Fare thee well ' (*1 Sam.* 1, 17).

Salvation. Redemption from sin by act or grace of
God; and deliverance from the fate foretold by
the OT prophets. This work is effected by the
Saviour. **1.** In the OT the word lit. means ' enlargement ' the broadening of horizons (*Ex.* 14,
13; 15, 2; *Ps.* 34, 6). It is clear that in any circumstances there must be a right spiritual state
before God can save (*Ps.* 18, 1-3). If this state is
absent it must be found again by penitence and
prayer. This is the point emphasised by the
prophets: the enemy from which the individual
and the nation had to be saved was sin itself (*Jer.*
31, 32-34; *Ezek.* 36, 26-28; *Hos.* 14). **2.** In the
NT salvation means the work of the Saviour,
who is, of course, Jesus (*Matt.* 1, 21; *Luke* 2, 11;
19, 10; *Rom.* 5, 9 & 10). According to *Acts* (4,
12) He is the only source of salvation, and His
instrument is the Gospel (*Acts* 13, 26; *Ephes.* 1,
13).

Samaria [să-mā′-rĭ-ă]. **1.** City, the capital of the
N kingdom of the 10 tribes. Building was started
by Omri (*1 Kings* 16, 24). It became the seat, and

the burying place, of the kings of Israel (*1 Kings* 16, 28 & 29; 20, 43; etc.). Omri had a disagreement with Ben Hadad of Syria, and as a sign of his subservience, was forced to allow Syrian merchants to trade in the city (*1 Kings* 20, 34). Ben Hadad II besieged the town in the reign of Joram (*2 Kings* 6, 8—17, 20). The Jews of Judea loathed the Samaritans for their idolatry (*1 Kings* 16, 32; 18, 19), their immorality was a byword (*Hos.* 7, 1-8; *Amos* 4, 1; 8, 14). Elijah thundered agst. them (*1 Kings* 18), as did Elisha, who lived there (*2 Kings* 5, 3-9; 6, 32). Other prophets denounced them (*Isa.* 7, 9; *Jer.* 31, 5; *Ezek.* 16, 46). The Assyrians besieged the city from 724 till 722 BC, when it fell (*2 Kings* 17, 3-6). The people were taken captive and foreigners were settled in it. Alexander gave it the same treatment in 332 BC. John Hyrcanus besieged it in 108 BC and ultimately demolished it (*Micah* 1. 6). Herod rebuilt it and called it Sebaste. Philip the Apostle worked there (*Acts* 8, 5-13) as did Peter and John (*Acts* 8, 14-25). **2.** The whole territory of the 10 tribes: the kingdom of Israel (*1 Kings* 21, 1; *Isa.* 7, 9; etc.). **3.** The district of Samaria bet. Galilee on the N and Judea on the S.

Samaritan [să-mă'-rĭ-tăn]. The name occurs only once in the OT (*2 Kings* 17, 29) and means simply an inhabitant of the N kingdom. In the NT it is not an inhabitant of the kingdom of Samaria, for by that time there was none. It was an inhabitant of the district. By this time the Samaritans were reckoned to be foreigners. The orig. inhabitants had been taken away by Sargon in 722 BC and the remnant de-nationalised by the import of colonists from Babylonia (*2 Kings* 17, 24). Idolatry had persisted and triumphed (*2 Kings* 17, 25; *Ezra* 4, 2 & 9 & 10). Josiah of

Judah destroyed the High Places there (qv) (*2 Chron.* 34, 6 & 7), and numbers of Samaritans began to come, for their worship, to Jerusalem. After the exile (of Judah) some of them even asked to have a share in rebuilding the Temple (*Ezra* 4, 2). The Jews would have nothing or little to do with them (*Ezra* 4, 3; *Luke* 9, 52 & 53; *John* 4, 9). Even in NT times the Jews remembered that when Nehemiah had been rebuilding the walls of Jerusalem he had been opposed by Samaritans under Sanballat (*Neh.* 4, 1-23). Jesus' choice of a Samaritan as the hero of His parable was very deliberate.

Samech [sä'-měch]. 15th letter of the Heb. alphabet, approximating to Eng. S.

Samos [sā'-mŏs]. Aegean island SW of Ephesus. With Pergamos it passed to the Romans in 133 BC, and received virtual independence under Rome in 17 BC. Paul visited it (*Acts* 20, 15).

Samothrace [să'-mō-thrāce]. Island off the coast of Thrace (*Acts* 16, 11).

Samson [săm'-sŏn]. The rather 'dumb' heavyweight champion of the OT, and also its practical joker. His is a J story. *See* PENTATEUCH. It tells the kind of story that mod. films delight in, of the simple man who becomes champion, falls to a woman's wiles, keeps falling; then goes out in a blaze of glory. He was one of the Judges (qv). Born in the tribe of Dan he was vowed by his parents as a Nazirite (qv) (*Judg.* 13, 1-24). Judah and Dan had become isolated territorially from the other tribes, and the Philistines were taking full advantage of the fact. With them Samson carried on a one-man guerrilla war (*Judg.* chs. 14 & 15). There is no space or need to recount the familiar story, but undoubtedly this was a historic figure round whom a great deal of legend has gathered, as it has gathered round Robin Hood, Wyatt Earp, and all such.

Samuel [săm'-ū-ĕl]. Also appears as Shemuel (*1 Chron.* 6, 33 AV). He stands as the last of the Judges (qv) and the first of the Prophets (qv). He was a man of Ephraim, born into a Levitical family; his father being Elkanah, whose wives were Penninah and Hannah (*1 Chron.* 6, 26; *1 Sam.* 1, 1-2). Hannah made a vow that if she had a son, she would make him a Nazirite (qv). She did bear a son, Samuel, and took him early to the Tabernacle at Shiloh, to the High Priest Eli (*1 Sam.* 1; 2, 1-11). There he stayed, and there, while still a young lad, he had a vision which Eli interpreted for him (*1 Sam.* 3, 1-18). As Samuel grew, so did his fame, and all Israel knew that there was a prophet in the land (*1 Sam.* 3, 20 & 21). Eli's 2 sons were killed in the battle when the Ark was lost to the Philistines, and Eli had a stroke and died (*1 Sam.* 4, 1-22). Samuel accepted the challenge to reform the nation: the task which was thenceforward to be the traditional task of the prophet. He had to lift religion from the static, conventionalised, priestly form in which it stagnated, to a new and higher level. He called the nation to Mizpah for an act of penitence and dedication. The Philistines, always looking for a chance, thought that here it was, and attacked. A timely thunderstorm interfered with their plans. The people reckoned that this was the hand of God. They defeated the Philistines who thereafter stayed away while Samuel was in charge of Israel (*1 Sam.* 7, 3-14). Of course this greatly enhanced Samuel's reputation, and his status with the Israelites. He decided to train a group who might be called his disciples, and at Ramah, where he lived, he established a School of Prophets (*1 Sam.*

7, 15-17; 19, 18-20). In his old age he nominated his 2 sons as his successors in the office of Judge, but he was better at judging other folks' children than he was at judging his own. The people, who knew Samuel's sons a lot better than Samuel did, were scared of what might happen when Samuel died and left the nation to the tender mercies of this pair. They asked Samuel to give them a king. He was unwilling, being afraid that Israel, a theocracy (acknowledging God as king) might become an autocracy under an earthly king. He prayed over the matter, then chose Saul and anointed him king. He made clear to Saul, however, the division of responsibility bet. Saul the new king, and Samuel, the old Judge and Prophet. Saul crossed this borderline once or twice, and Samuel told Saul that for this he must consider himself to be rejected by God. Samuel then chose David. There was not, of course, any arrangement that the monarchy was to be hereditary. Samuel died and was buried at Ramah, with all Israel mourning his passing (*1 Sam.* 25, 1). He made an 'appearance' when Saul asked the Witch of Endor (qv) to conjure up the old man and to ask his advice before the fatal battle of Gilboa (*1 Sam.* 28, 3-25). *See* SAMUEL, BOOKS OF.

Samuel, Books of. The division of the Book into 2 was made in AD 1516-17. Orig. it was one, but scholars decided that since part of it was the story of Samuel himself, and part the story, in the main, of Saul and David, it should be divided at the point where the kings took over political authority from the Judges. The LXX calls *Samuel* (*1* and *2*) and *Kings* (*1* and *2*) the 1st, 2nd, 3rd and 4th books of the Kingdom. The natural divisions are: **1.** Samuel himself; his birth, call and rise to power (chs. 1-7). **2.** The reign of Saul, beginning

with his selection and going on to his success,
and then to success going to his head. Saul's
defiance of Samuel: the various campaigns and
battles in which Saul and Jonathan distinguished
themselves (chs. 8-15). Then comes Samuel's
judgment on Saul, leading to the choice of David,
and the strains and stresses bet. Saul and David
(chs. 16-31). **3.** David becomes king and rules
(*2 Sam.* 1-24). Some of the work may have come
from Samuel's own hand, but not much of it.
After all, he was dead before the accession of
David (*1 Sam.* 10, 25; 25, 1). Other contemporary
works are ref. to: The History of Samuel the
Seer; the History of Nathan the Prophet; the
History of Gad the Seer (*1 Chron.* 29, 29). It
seems as if there are 2 main streams in the work,
one early and one quite late. Both are prob.
earlier than *Deuteronomy* and are poss. not later
than 700 BC.

Sanballat [săn-băl′-lăt]. *See* SAMARIA, SAMARITANS.
He was the sworn enemy of Nehemiah, as the
Jew tried to rebuild the walls of Jerusalem. Sanballat was of Babylonian origin. With his con-
federates, Tobiah the Ammonite, and Geshem the
Arabian, he made things as hard as poss. for
Nehemiah, and even planned to attack him and
his workers. When he came to Jerusalem the second
time, Nehemiah found one of Sanballat's agents
at work in the city, Manasseh, his son-in-law.
Nehemiah banished him (*Neh.* 2, 10 & 19; 4, 1
ff.; 13, 28).

Sandal. *See* DRESS.

Sanhedrin [săn-hē-drĭn]. It derives from a Gk.
word meaning council. Rabbinical trad. affirmed
that the Sanhedrin was created by Moses (*Num.*
11, 16). But the fact is that it was instituted by
Jehoshaphat (*2 Chron.* 19, 8). It was a court of

justice and had no other function, which does not
identify it with the Sanhedrin as it was later constituted. Something very like the beginning of
something very like the Sanhedrin as later known
is seen in *Ezra* (5, 5 & 9; 6, 7 & 14; 10, 8) and
in *Nehemiah* (2, 16; 4, 14; 5, 7; 7, 5). The
Sanhedrin which dealt with Jesus and Stephen,
however, is something very much different from
that, and was constituted at a much later date,
certainly not before the time of Antiochus Epiphanes (qv). That is when it is first mentioned
by that name (223-187 BC). It was abolished after
the destruction of Jerusalem in AD 70. Its chairman was the High Priest, and it was made up of
the nobility, who were mainly Sadducees (qv).
Herod did not care for them, however, and tried
to pack the Sanhedrin with Pharisees (qv). There
were 71 members, vacancies being filled by co-
option followed by the ceremony of laying on of
hands (qv). By the time of Jesus, the authority
of the Sanhedrin, though trad. over all Jews everywhere, was in fact restricted to Judea. That is why
Jesus was safe in Galilee. Later, however, the
scope of the Sanhedrin's authority broadened to
cover the whole world where orthodox Jews lived.
It issued warrants for the arrest of Jews in Damascus (*Acts* 9, 2), etc. Although it was a court of
justiciary, dealing with cases which the provincial
courts were not competent to deal with, and as a
court of appeal in all matters which were not the
business of the procurator (qv), its principal work
was to make pronouncements on the Mosaic law
and the interpretation thereof; much as the
Supreme Court of the U.S.A. safeguards the
Constitution. It was the Sanhedrin that charged
Jesus with blasphemy (*John* 19, 7; etc.). It
charged Paul with transgression of the Law (*Acts*

22, 30). Peter and John were charged by it for
posing as prophets (*Acts* 4, 5 ff.). By the Sanhedrin Stephen was charged and condemned for
blasphemy (*Acts* 7). The Sanhedrin had its own
officers empowered to arrest the accused (*Matt.*
26, 47). Without consulting the Rom. authority
they could prosecute and impose any sentence
other than death (*Acts* 4, 5). Stephen's death may
seem to contradict this, but it was more in the
nature of an inspired lynching. They sat in a
semi-circle with the clerks in front, and immediately behind the clerks, the ' disciples ' of the
members. The accused was dressed in mourning
garb. One who spoke in favour of the accused
could not thereafter speak agst. him. A straight
majority could acquit, and usually announced
their verdict that day. A two-thirds majority was
needed for a condemnation, and the verdict was
always announced the next day, or even later.

Sapphira [să-phī′-ră]. *See* ANANIAS.

Sapphire. *See* JEWELS AND PRECIOUS STONES.

Sarah [sā′-răh], **Sarai** or **Sara. 1.** Wife of Abraham, married before they left Ur (*Gen.* 11,
29-31). She was his half sister (*Gen.* 20, 12). Even
in middle age she was a woman of considerable
beauty for Abraham passed her off as his full
sister in case some amorous Egyptian should
decide to acquire his wife by getting rid of him
(*Gen.* 12, 10-20). He did the same thing in Gerar
(*Gen.* 20, 1-18). Hopeless of bearing a son who
would continue the Covenant, she persuaded
Abraham to mate with her bondslave Hagar, who
produced Ishmael (*Gen.* 16, 1-16). Sarah regarded
Ishmael as her own son until at last she became
pregnant herself and produced Isaac. It was then
that she changed her name from Sarai to Sarah—
a princess (*Gen.* 17, 15-22; 18, 9-15; 21, 1-5·)

Naturally this prejudiced her agst. Ishmael, and her regret at having compacted with Hagar became jealousy which was fanned by Hagar's superior airs. Sarah demanded that Hagar and Ishmael should be turned out (*Gen.* 21, 9-21). Sarah died at Kiriath-Arba (Hebron) and was buried in the cave of Machpela, the family sepulchre (*Gen.* 23, 19.) **2.** (*Num.* 26, 46 AV). *See* SERAH.

Sardis [săr'-dĭs]. Capital of ancient Lydia in Asia Minor. In AD 17 it was largely destroyed by an earthquake, but was rebuilt by the Romans. The Church made little progress in Sardis in the early days.

Sardius. *See* JEWELS AND PRECIOUS STONES.

Sardonyx. *See* JEWELS AND PRECIOUS STONES.

Sarepta [să-rĕp'-ta]. *See* ZAREPHATH.

Sargon [săr'-gŏn]. (*Isa.* 20, 1.) Successor to Shalmaneser IV of Assyria, c. 722-705 BC. Father of Sennacherib. He took Samaria (qv) and carried off 30,000 Samaritans. He had to face insurrection led by Merodach-baladan (qv). Finally he recaptured Babylon where Merodach-baladan was entrenched. He was killed in 705 BC. *See* ASSYRIA.

Sarid [să'-rĭd]. Frontier town of Zebulun (*Josh.* 19, 10-12).

Satan. Lit. ' the Adversary ' (*Num.* 22, 22; *2 Sam.* 19, 22). This is not a specific single being. The first real appearance of a person who is by nature the adversary of all, including God, is in *Job* (chs. 1 & 2). He is one of the ' Sons of God,' called ' The Satan.' Orig. he is not the tempter, but the ' snooper ' who finds out about human sins and reports them to God. Obviously the step is short bet. the informer and the agent provocateur, who tempts the innocent into sin. Later the name becomes a proper name for this malevolent being, acting on his own initiative, and not under instruction from God (*1 Chron.* 21, 1), cf. this account with the parallel passage (*2 Sam.* 24, 1). The act of God has become the act of God's enemy. In the NT the Heb. name Satan is often changed to the Gk. *Diabolos*, which is trans. devil, but which is more accurately the Accuser, or the Slanderer. There is also identification with Beelzebub (qv) sometimes called the Evil One (*Matt.* 12, 26 & 27; 13, 19). It may be that the petition in the Lord's prayer is ' Deliver us from the Evil One.' In the NT are also the ideas expressed in the Apocryphal Book of Enoch; a revolt in heaven and the expulsion of the rebel angels led by Satan (*Jude* 6; *2 Pet.* 2, 4, cf. Milton's *Paradise Lost*). They are kept imprisoned in eternal darkness, and the demons are their offspring (*Matt.* 12, 43-45; *Luke* 11, 24-26). These demons are the subjects of Satan in the Kingdom of Evil (*Matt.* 12, 26; *Luke* 11, 18). Through them, Satan tempts humans to evil (*Matt.* 4, 1-11; *Luke* 22, 31) and accuses them (*Rev.* 12, 10). In John's writings the lesser demons have disappeared, and the fight is on bet. Christ and the Devil, who is the ruler of the world. Jesus' work is to destroy him and his power (*1 John* 3, 8). Paul frequently calls Satan ' The Serpent ' (*Rom.* 16, 20; *2 Cor.* 11, 2 & 3). Paul believed that the angels lived in the upper atmosphere and that Satan and his demons lived in the lower atmosphere (*Eph.* 2, 2; 6, 12). Jesus believed in the reality of a kingdom of evil whose king was Satan or Beelzebub. He also believed that the Messiah's work was to destroy it and them (*Mark* 1, 13; 3, 11; etc.). *See* DEVIL, POSSESSION.

Satchel. *See* BAG.

Satrap [săt′-răp]. Persian viceroy of a number of

minor colonies (*Ezra* 8, 36; *Esth.* 3, 12, 'lieutenant' in AV).

Satyr [sā´-tẏr]. Woodland god of the Greeks and Romans. He is depicted as being half goat, half man. The word so trans. in AV (*Isa.* 13, 21; 34, 14) is commonly a he-goat, but is used elsewhere as an object of idolatrous worship (*Lev.* 17, 7; *2 Chron.* 11, 15 RV).

Saul. 1. King of Edom (*Gen.* 36, 37) called Shaul in RV. **2.** Son of Kish, a Benjamite who became 1st king of Israel. The people demanded that Samuel should choose a king for them, since it was obvious that the day of the judges would end with Samuel (*1 Sam.* 8, 1 & 3 & 20; 12, 12). It was a sign of lack of faith in God, though there was nothing in the Law to prevent the election of a king (*Gen.* 17, 6; *Deut.* 17, 14-20). Samuel warned them that they might be worse off under a king, but they insisted and he gave them their wish. He selected Saul, who would be in his middle thirties at the time. He was a striking man, being head and shoulders taller than his fellows. Samuel explained his kingly responsibilities to him, then anointed him. He called the people to Mizpah to acclaim their king. Benjamin was the border clan bet. Ephraim and Judah, and the choice of a Benjamite was wise. Some were not happy about the choice and Saul did not try to take over until mutterings had died down. He got a chance to show his prowess when the Ammonites besieged Jabesh in Gilead (*1 Sam.* 10, 27; ch. 11). The people took this as a sign that there need be no more disputing the choice of king. They carried him to Gilgal, where Samuel resigned his judgeship and Saul was installed as king (*1 Sam.* chs. 11-12, 35). Saul was older than 30 when this happened, and the text which says

that he was just 30 is corrupt (*1 Sam.* 13, 1).
Jonathan, his son, was old enough for a command.
Saul raised a small standing army, keeping 2,000
men under his own command at Michmash and
Bethel, and 1,000 under Jonathan at Gibeah (*1
Sam.* 13, 2 ff.). In his first real tussle with the
Philistines Saul and Samuel fell out. Saul pre-
sumed to make the sacrifice which was the prerogative of Samuel (*1 Sam.* 13, 8 ff.). For this
sin, Samuel told Saul that he had been rejected;
he would not be the 1st of a dynasty (*1 Sam.* 13,
13). Samuel still had confidence in Saul's soldierly
abilities, however, and ordered him to attack and
exterminate the Amalekites and all that was their's.
Saul spared their king, and their best cattle as a
sacrifice. Samuel told him that for this disobedience he could no longer be regarded as fit
to rule (*1 Sam.* 15, 1-35). In his place, Samuel
anointed David at Bethlehem (*1 Sam.* 16, 1-13).
All this greatly troubled Saul, and no wonder.
He became melancholic and violent by turns.
David was selected as a minstrel to cheer him up
—a singularly unwise choice, for no man likes
to be confronted constantly with his successor.
The more Saul saw of David the less he liked
him; after David's victory over Goliath Saul
could not abide him at all, and David had to take
to the hills (*1 Sam.* 17-30). Encouraged by this
internal trouble in Israel, the Philistines made
another raid. Saul had no one to rely on. He
consulted the Witch of Endor (qv) who produced,
or pretended to produce the shade of Samuel.
Samuel from the grave prophesied Saul's death
and the extinction of his house. In spite of this,
however, or maybe because of it, Saul went into
battle with his usual courage. Jonathan and his
brothers were killed, and Saul severely wounded.

He asked his armour bearer to run him through, but the man would not, and Saul died by his own hand rather than fall into the hands of his enemies. The Philistines beheaded him and his sons, and nailed the heads and bodies to the walls of Bethshan, sending Saul's armour to the Temple of Ashtaroth. The men of Jabesh Gilead, by night, took the bodies down and gave them honourable burial. David lamented them sincerely (*1 Sam.* 31; *2 Sam.* 1). Saul must have reigned for about 40 yrs. **3.** Original name of the apostle Paul (*Acts* 7, 58). *See* SAMUEL, ISRAEL.

Saviour. *See* SALVATION.

Savour. Lit. ' to taste or to smell ': transitive or intransitive. It is used also of a person's reputation (*Ex.* 5, 21), cf. mod. ' His name stinks.'

Saw. The Egyptians used a bronze one-handed saw. The Assyrians had a two-handed iron saw (*I Kings* 7, 9; *Isa.* 10, 15). A horrible form of capital punishment was to be sawn asunder. Though the Heb. words in this passage, with very slight alteration, could mean ' exacted forced labour ' (*Heb.* 11, 37).

Scapegoat. *See* AZAZEL; ATONEMENT, DAY OF.

Scarlet. Crimson obtained from the insect *coccus ilicis* (*Lev.* 14, 4; *Num.* 19, 6; *Heb.* 9, 19).

Sceptre. The word means both a short royal rod or staff, or wand of office (cf. ' Black Rod '). It was a symbol of authority, not always royal (*Ps.* 45, 6; *Amos* 1, 5; *Judg.* 5, 14; *Gen.* 49, 10; *Esth.* 4, 11). The reed put into Jesus' hand was an imitation sceptre (*Matt.* 27, 29).

Sceva [scē'-vă]. A Jewish exorcist at Ephesus (*Acts* 19, 14).

School(master). (*Acts* 19, 9; *Gal.* 3, 24 & 25.) The Eng. word pedagogue derives from the Gk. *paidagogos*, who was not a teacher in the sense of being an instructor, but a personal slave who attended the sons of the wealthy. The word has come to mean teacher. In the early days of the Jews, education was given at home and was concerned in the main with religion (*Gen.* 18, 19; *Deut.* 6, 7; *2 Tim.* 3, 15). Just before the Christian era, however, teaching was being given in the synagogue (qv) (*Luke* 2, 46). In the time of Gamaliel this teaching was compulsory at the age of 6, but it was still mainly religious. *See* EDUCATION.

Science. (*Dan.* 1, 4; *1 Tim.* 6, 20.) Simply knowledge.

Scorpion. Member of the spider family armed with a sting in the tail which could produce severe illness and even death (*Deut.* 8, 15). The scorpions compared with whips (*1 Kings* 12, 11) were prob. a kind of cat o' nine tails.

Scourge. Whipping a delinquent was a recognised punishment; the victim lying on the ground (*Deut.* 25, 2 & 4). Canes or rods were used for the beating, and, for scourging, whips (*2 Cor.* 11, 25). The maximum number of strokes was 39.

Screech owl. (*Isa.* 34, 14.) Prob. the tawny owl: *syrnium aluco*.

Scribe. Usually named in assoc. with Pharisees (qv). The Scribes occupied more or less the same position and had the same authority as the Supreme Court of the U.S.A. The Constitution of Israel was the Mosaic law, and the scribal responsibility was to apply that law to the changing conditions of changing times. He was lawyer, scholar, preacher and magistrate in one (*Matt.* 23, 1 ff; *Acts* 5; etc.). Hillel, Shammai and Gamaliel were Scribes of the best sort (*Acts* 22, 3). The Scribes had no official financial reward for their work. The office, however, tended to produce pride, vanity and the closed mind. By their very nature they were opposed to change, and blind to the need for reform. Jesus was very sore on them (*Matt.* 23).

Scrip. A pouch or wallet, usually carried slung over the shoulder. It was big enough to carry provisions for several days. A leather haversack (*Matt.* 10, 10).

Scripture(s). Lit. ' something written,' but by use and assoc., ' The Bible: the Holy Scriptures.' Prob. the first writing so called was *Deuteronomy* (*2 Kings* 22, 8). The early Church was quick to call the writings of Paul, ' Scriptures.' In the use of the word there is always the implication of inspiration.

Scythian(s) [scȳth'-ĭ-ăn]. Nomadic race living bet. Danube and Don in the Caucusus mts., and round the Caspian Sea. To civilised people of the day the word Scythian meant more or less what barbarian means to-day.

Sea. The ocean as distinct from the dry land (*Gen.* 1, 10; etc.), but more particularly the Mediterranean, or Sea of the Philistines (*Ex.* 23, 31). Also known as the Great Sea (*Num.* 34, 6; etc.). The other seas familiar to the Jews were the Sea of Galilee, also called Sea of Chinnereth, Sea of Tiberias, and Lake of Gennesaret: the Dead Sea was known also as the Salt Sea, the Sea of the Akabah, and the Eastern Sea. Large rivers with their drainage area might be called seas (*Jer.* 51, 36; *Nahum* 3, 8). The name was given to the enormous laver in Solomon's Temple (*1 Kings* 7, 39). *See* MOLTEN SEA.

Seamew. (*Lev.* 11, 16 RV.) A bird ceremonially unclean and trans. ' cuckoo ' in AV. Prob. the tern.

Sea Monster. Any great fish (*Gen.* 1, 21; *Job* 7, 12).

One ref. (*Lam.* 4, 3 AV) is prob. an error for jackal.

Seal (signet). These were known and common from the earliest days (*Gen.* 38, 18 RV). Usually they were cut from semi-precious stones, and with the Hebrews were normally oval in shape. Smaller ones were set in rings, while larger ones were worn on a chain round the neck (*Jer.* 22, 24). These seals did not depict figures of persons and always carried 2 carved lines close together dividing the seal longitudinally into 2. The person's name was carved on the seal which was used to authenticate documents (*1 Kings* 21, 8; *Jer.* 32, 10). The seal was impressed on the wax which had to be broken to open the document. They were also used on wine jars (*Job* 38, 14). Doors might be sealed (*Dan.* 6, 17; *Matt.* 27, 66). Paul used the word figuratively (*1 Cor.* 9, 2; etc.).

Seal (mammal). The common seal, but the word is wrongly trans. ' porpoise ' RV and ' badger ' AV (*Ex.* 26, 14; *Ezek.* 16, 10).

Seba [sē'-bă]. Eldest son of Cush and his descendants (*Gen.* 10, 7; *Ps.* 72, 10). The name is interchangeable with Sheba. The people lived bet. the Nile and its tributary the Atbara, or on the Red Sea coast.

Secundus [sē-cŭn'-dŭs]. Thessalonian companion of Paul (*Acts* 20, 4).

Secure. In AV does not mean ' safe ' but rather ' feeling safe ' (*Judg.* 8, 11; *Matt.* 28, 14).

Seed. The animal or vegetable germ of life (*Gen.* 1, 11; *Lev.* 15, 16-18). It is used of one's descendants (*Gen.* 3, 15; *John* 7, 42). ' Seed of Abraham' was a favourite Pauline phrase for Israel (*Rom.* 11, 1). John uses it in the sense of the life of God within man: divine vitality (*1 John* 3, 9).

Seer. See PROPHET.

Seethe. In AV means to boil. The past tense is sod, sodden. The latter word does not have the mod. meaning of saturated (*Ex.* 23, 19; *Lam.* 4, 10; etc.).

Seir [sē'-ĭr]. Mt. range in Edom orig. populated by Hororites or cave dwellers (*Gen.* 36, 21; 14, 6). The name Mt. Seir is synonymous with Edom (*Josh.* 15, 10).

Seirah [sē-ĭ'-răh]. Place near Mt. Ephraim to which Ehud fled after the murder of Eglon (*Judg.* 3, 26).

Sela [sē'-lă]. Lit. ' a cliff or crag,' but appears also as a proper name (*Judg.* 1, 36; *2 Kings* 14, 7; etc.).

Selah [sē'-lăh]. The word appears 71 times in the *Psalms* and should not be pronounced when the Psalm is being read aloud. It appears also in *Habakkuk* (3, 3 & 9 & 13). It has some ref. to music, though the meaning is obscure. It may have been the sign of an instrumental interlude in a vocal piece; or a kind of Amen; or a point at which some well-known doxology was sung during the Psalm.

Seleucia [sĕl-ēu'-cĭ-ă]. Port of Syrian Antioch at the mouth of R. Orontes. Paul and Barnabas sailed from it (*Acts* 13, 4).

Seleucus [sĕl-ēu'-cŭs]. **1.** Officer in the army of Alexander the Great, who became satrap (qv) of Babylon c. 312 BC. Later he became ruler of Syria and built Antioch and Seleucia (*Dan.* 11, 5). **2.** Son of Antiochus Soter c. 246-226 BC (*Dan.* 11, 7-9). **3.** Son of above (*Dan.* 11, 10-16). **4.** Son of Antiochus the Great, c. 187-176 BC (*Dan.* 11, 20).

Semite, Semitic [sĕ'-mĭte] [sĕ-mĭt'-ĭc]. Lit. 'a desc. from Shem ' (qv). It describes a people of common origin, but is used particularly of their languages, of which there are 4 main groups. **1.** East Akkadian, Babylonian, Assyrian. **2.** Northern Amorite and Aramaic. **3.** Western Ugaritic, Canaanite, Moabite, Phoenician, Punic, and Heb. **4.** Southern Arabic and Ethiopic. *See* RACES.

Senate. (*Acts* 5, 21.) Not the Rom. senate, but the Sanhedrin.

Seneh [sĕ´-nĕh]. Scene of a daring exploit of Jonathan in Michmash (*1 Sam.* 14, 4).

Senir [sĕ´-nīr]. Also **Shenir.** Amorite name for Mt. Hermon (*Deut.* 3, 9).

Sennacherib [sĕn-nă´-chĕr-ĭb]. Son of Sargon, he succeeded to the Assyrian throne c. 705 BC. He drove Merodoch-baladan (qv) out of Babylon, warred agst. the Kassites and the Elamites, then set out to bring the W to heel (701 BC). He took Tyre and Sidon and the whole of Phoenicia. Ashdod, Moab and Edom became his tributaries. Under the threat of invasion, Hezekiah of Judah enlisted the help of Egypt, but Sennacherib inflicted a heavy defeat on the Egyptians, then moved in to devastate Judah. Hezekiah tried to buy him off, but the surrender of Jerusalem was demanded (*2 Kings* 19, 8 ff.). Plague struck the Assyrian army, however, and Jerusalem was saved. All through his reign Sennacherib was plagued by insurrection in Babylon, and he destroyed it completely in 689 BC. He created Nineveh as his capital, and was murdered in 681 (*2 Kings* 19, 37). *See* ASSYRIA, ISRAEL.

Septuagint [sĕp-tū´-ă-gĭnt]. *See* VERSIONS.

Sepulchre. *See* TOMB.

Serah [sĕ´-răh]. Daughter of Asher (*Gen.* 46, 17).

Seraiah [sĕr-āī´-ăh]. **1.** Official of David, also called Shausha. **2.** High Priest in reign of Zedekiah (*2 Kings* 25, 18 & 21). **3.** Soldier who joined Gedaliah at Mizpah (*2 Kings* 25, 23). **4.** Father of Joab (*1 Chron.* 4, 13). **5.** Prince of Simeon (*1 Chron.*

4, 35). **6.** Name of several returned exiles (*Ezra* 2, 2; *Neh.* 10, 2; 11, 11 etc.; *Jer.* 36, 26; 51, 59).

Seraphim(s) [sĕr′-ă-phīm]. They are described in *Isaiah* (6, 2 & 3) but this is, of course, a vision. This is the only mention of these real or imaginary celestial creatures.

Sered [sĕr′-ĕd]. Son of Zebulun (*Gen.* 46, 14).

Sergius Paulus. *See* PAULUS.

Sergeants. (*Acts* 16, 35 & 38 AV.) The lictors who were the officials in attendance on Rom. magistrates, and who carried out sentences involving physical punishment.

Serpent. A dozen Heb. words are so trans., and differentiation does not matter a great deal. Some are adders, some are vipers, some are called dragons (*Ex.* 7, 9 & 10 & 12; *Ps.* 91, 13). These are prob. lizards of one kind or another. Many of the snakes found in the Holy Land are harmless. The venomous ones are the Egyptian cobra, often trans. ' asp ' in OT, and the horned viper. When ' fiery serpent ' is used, the adjective prob. refs. to the result of the bite rather than to the cause. ' Cockatrice ' AV, and ' basilisk ' RV, appear along with serpents (*Isa.* 11, 8; 59, 5; *Jer.* 8, 17). These were entirely imaginary monsters.

Serpent, Brazen. (*Num.* 21, 4-9.) ' Brazen ' should be ' bronze.' Serpent worship always has been common, and there was a belief that the image of a harmful thing could repair the damage (cf. ' hair of the dog that bit you '). The Lord Jesus saw himself in the same saving role (*John* 3, 14). The verb in the text means a voluntary, concentrated looking at.

Servant. General term for anyone acting in the service of another, and including captive slaves and trusted officials. It is used also of man's relationship to God (*Ex.* 32, 13; *Acts* 16, 17). *See* BONDAGE, MINISTER.

Servant of Jehovah. Or ' the suffering servant' (*Isa.* 40-66). Some commentators reckon that this is the whole nation of Israel, but there is more in it than that. On occasion the prophet may mean the whole nation; elsewhere he may mean a select part of the nation; but the implication also is that there is the one person, the blameless Messiah, whose fate will be to atone for the sin of the whole nation. The Messiah must be of Israel, and must personify all that is best in Israel so that He can say to God that in Him all Israel has atoned. At the same time He must be quite free from the taint of the sins of Israel, and must have no personal axe to grind as he offers himself to suffering and sacrifice.

Seth. Son of Adam born after the murder of Abel (*Gen.* 4, 25; etc.).

Seven. The only interest is in the sacred use of the numeral, a sanctity which is very ancient in the ME. Wisdom's House has 7 pillars (*Prov.* 9, 1); Samson's hair was braided in 7 locks (*Judg.* 16, 13); to atone for a broken vow 7 sacrifices were needed (*2 Sam.* 21, 6). How 7 came to be so regarded is a moot point, but there were the 7 lights of heaven—sun, moon and 5 planets; and 7 is a quarter of the 28 days of the moon, which has four phases. Its sanctity with the Jews, however, was due to their conviction that God at creation had hallowed the 7th day. *See* SABBATH.

Seven words. Jesus' words from the Cross. They are in order: **1.** (*Luke* 23, 34). **2.** (*Luke* 23, 43). **3.** (*John* 19, 26 & 27). **4.** (*Matt.* 27, 46; *Mark* 15, 34). **5.** (*John* 19, 28). **6.** (*John* 19, 30). **7.** (*Luke* 23, 46).

Shaaph [shā-ă-ph]. A kinsman of Caleb, and a son of Caleb (*1 Chron.* 2, 47 & 49).

Shadrach [shăd'-rach]. One of the 3 men of the fiery furnace. Hananiah was his other name (*Dan.* 1, 7; 3, 12-30).

Shalem [shā'-lem]. Town near Shechem. Not Salem (*Gen.* 33, 18).

Shallecheth [shăl'-lĕch-ĕth]. W gate of Solomon's Temple (*1 Chron.* 26, 16).

Shallum [shăl'-lŭm]. There are 15 of the name. Son of Naphtali (*1 Chron.* 7, 13); desc. of Simeon (*1 Chron.* 4, 25); desc. of Judah (*1 Chron.* 2, 40); chief porter of the Temple (*1 Chron.* 9, 17); murderer of King Zechariah (*2 Kings* 15, 10); father of Jehizkiah (*2 Chron.* 28, 12); ancestor of Ezra (*Ezra* 7, 2); husband of Huldah (*2 Kings* 22, 14); uncle of Jeremiah (*Jer.* 32, 7); another name of Jehoahaz (*2 Kings* 23, 30); returned exiles (*Ezra* 10, 24 & 42; *Neh.* 3, 12).

Shalman [shăl'-man]. Prince of Moab who may be referred to under a slightly different name (*Hos.* 10, 14).

Shalmaneser [shăl'-măn-ē'-sĕr]. **1.** King of Assyria 1280-1260 BC. **2.** King of Assyria 860-825 BC. A territorially ambitious king, he made constant threats agst. Syria and Israel, being resisted by a confederation called the Syrian league, in which Ahab's army was occasionally involved. In 842 he crushed the League and Jehu of Israel became his tributary. **3.** King of Assyria and successor to Tiglath Pileser 728-722 BC. Hoshea was his tributary. Later Hoshea refused to pay, relying on help from Egypt. The Assyrians crushed them, Hoshea was taken and imprisoned. Shalmaneser besieged Samaria for 3 yrs., then took it (*2 Kings* 17, 1-6; 18, 9 & 10). *See* SARGON, ASSYRIA, ISRAEL.

Shamgar [shăm′-gar]. Son of Anath (*Judg*. 3, 31). He carried on a one man fight agst. the Philistines before the time of Deborah, but is not classed as one of the judges.

Shamir [shăm′-ĭr]. **1.** Town in Judah (*Josh*. 15, 48). **2.** Town in Mt. Ephraim (*Judg*. 10, 1). **3.** A Levite (*1 Chron*. 24, 24).

Shammah [shăm′-măh]. **1.** Chief of Edom (*Gen*. 36, 13 & 17). **2.** David's brother (*1 Sam*. 16, 9). **3.** One of David's heroes (*2 Sam*. 23, 11). **4.** Another of the same (*2 Sam*. 23, 35).

Shammua [shăm′-mū-ă]. **1.** The Reubenite spy (*Num*. 13, 4). **2.** Son of David and Bathsheba (*2 Sam*. 5, 14). **3.** Several returned exiles (*Neh*. 11, 17; 12, 18).

Shaphan [shă′-phăn]. Scribe of Josiah's time who read the book of *Deuteronomy* to the king. He was one of the deputation which interviewed Huldah (*2 Kings* 22, 8-14). His sons were Ahikam (*Jer*. 26, 24); Elasah (*Jer*. 29, 3); Gemariah (*Jer*. 36, 10); and the idolater Jaazaniah (*Ezek*. 8, 11).

Shaphat [shă′-phăt]. **1.** Spy from Simeon (*Num*. 13, 5). **2.** Gadite (*1 Chron*. 5, 12). **3.** David's chief herdsman (*1 Chron*. 27, 29). **4.** Elisha's father (*1 Kings* 19, 16). **5.** Desc. of David (*1 Chron*. 3, 22).

Sharezer [shă′-rĕ-zĕr]. Son of and murderer of Sennacherib (qv) (*2 Kings* 19, 37; *Isa*. 37, 38). Name also of one of a religious deputation after the Exile (*Zech*. 7, 2).

Sharon [shă′-rŏn]. Region on the coast bet. Joppa and Carmel (*Isa*. 35, 2). For Rose of Sharon, *see* ROSE. Lydda was one of its main towns (*Acts* 9, 35). There was another region of the name E of Jordan (*1 Chron*. 5, 16).

Shaul [shă′-ūl]. **1.** Prince of Edom (*Gen*. 36, 37) also called Saul. **2.** Son of Simeon (*Gen*. 46, 10). **3.** Levite (*1 Chron*. 6, 24).

Shaveh [shā'-věh]. Valley near Jerusalem (*Gen.* 14, 17; *2 Sam.* 18, 18).

Shavsha [shăv'-shă]. Also **Shisha**. Scribe of David and Solomon prob. identical to Seraiah and Sheva (*2 Sam.* 8, 17; 20, 25; *1 Kings* 4, 3).

Shealtiel [shē'-ăl-tī'-ĕl]. In NT Salathiel. Son of King Jeconiah (*1 Chron.* 3, 17; *Matt.* 1, 12). Father of Zerubbabel (*Ezra* 3, 2). There is, however, confusion of relationships (*1 Chron.* 3, 17-19).

Shearing house. This may be a place name, Bethe-ked; or it may simply be a place where sheep were shorn or shepherds gathered. Jehu slew the kinsmen of Ahaziah there (*2 Kings* 10, 12-14).

Sheba [shē'-bă]. People of Cushite stock and their land (*Gen.* 10, 7). They are also named as being of Semitic stock by way of Joktan (*Gen.* 25, 3). They moved into Arabia (*Matt.* 12, 42) and carried on a prosperous trade with their neighbours (*1 Kings* 10, 1; etc.). The capital of their territory was Mareb. There may or may not have been a queen of Sheba in the time of Solomon. Many think it is a story worked in by priestly writers to demonstrate Solomon's greatness (*1 Kings* 10, 1-13). But the country of Sheba was pretty prosperous and it is hardly likely that its queen would have been dumbfounded by the magni-ficence of Solomon's court.

Shebuel [shĕb'-ū-ĕl], **Shubael. 1.** Priest and his family in David's day (*1 Chron.* 24, 20). **2.** Levite in Hezekiah's reign (*2 Chron.*31, 15). **3.** Priest of importance, a returned exile (*Neh.* 12, 3 & 7). **4.** Desc. of David, kin to Zerubbabel (*1 Chron.* 3, 21 & 22). **5.** Various returned exiles, priests and Levites (*Ezra* 8, 5; 10, 2 & 3; *Neh.* 3, 29; 6, 18).

Shechem [shĕ′-chĕm]. Once Sichem (*Gen.* 12, 6).
Twice Sychem (*Acts* 7, 16). **1.** Town in the hill
country of Ephraim nr. Mt. Gerizim. Abraham
camped here (*Gen.* 12, 6; 33, 18; *Judg.* 9, 7;
Josh. 20, 7). It was then Hivite territory (*Gen.*
34, 2). Joseph was buried here (*Josh.* 24, 32).
Luke is confused in his ref. (*Acts* 7, 16). After
the conquest the tribes met at Shechem to hear
and to subscribe to the Law (*Josh.* 8, 30). It
became a Levitical city and a City of Refuge
(*Josh.* 20, 7; 21, 21). Here Joshua made his
valedictory speech (*Josh.* 24, 1). Gideon destroyed
the town (*Judg.* 9). After the death of Solomon
the 10 tribes of the N (Israel) at Shechem rejected
Rehoboam, Solomon's son, and elected Jeroboam
as their own king (*1 Kings* 12, 1-19). Shechem
then became his capital (*1 Kings* 12, 25). It lies
about 30 m. N of Jerusalem. **2.** A prince of
Shechem (*Gen.* 34). **3.** Son of Gilead, and his clan
(*Num.* 26, 31).

Sheep. The animal as known to-day, though a less
carefully bred one. Palestine was very suitable
for sheep herding. In the W sheep normally do
not drink, receiving enough liquid from herbage;
in the ME they had to be watered. The person
least likely to understand v. 2 of the 23rd Psalm
is the western shepherd (*Gen.* 29, 7-10). Ceremonially
sheep were clean and could be eaten (*1 Sam.* 14,
32). Ewe milk was valued (*Deut.* 32, 14). The
wool (qv) was very important for domestic use
and for trade. Shearing time was a rural fiesta
(*Gen.* 38, 12; *1 Sam.* 25, 4). Rams horns were
made into trumpets and flasks (*Josh.* 6, 4; *1 Sam.*
16, 1). Sheep were used in sacrifice (*Lev.* 1, 10;
4, 32; 5, 15; 6, 6; 22, 21). Normally Palestinian
sheep were white, though there were browns,
blacks, and variegated (*Isa.* 1, 18; *Gen.* 30, 32).

The commonest breed is the broad-tailed sheep *ovis laticaudata. See* LAMB, RAM.

Sheepfold (cote). Gen. sheep were not left out grazing all night for fear of wild animals but were brought back in the evening to the safety of an enclosure. The shepherd remained with them overnight (*Num.* 32, 16; *Jer.* 23, 3; *Ezek.* 34, 14; *John* 10, 1). Sometimes there were watchtowers used as look-out posts agst. raiders (*2 Chron.* 26, 10). *See* SHEPHERD.

Sheepgate. Gate in walls of Jerusalem (qv).

Sheepmarket. Same as above.

Shekel. *See* WEIGHTS AND MEASURES, MONEY.

Shelah [shē′-läh]. **1.** Pool at Jerusalem. Also, wrongly, Siloah and Siloam (qv) (*Neh.* 3, 15). **2.** Son of Arphaxad (*Gen.* 10, 24). **3.** Son of Judah (*Gen.* 38, 2 & 5 & 11).

Shelemiah [shĕ′-lĕ-mī′-äh]. **1.** Doorkeeper in David's day (*1 Chron.* 26, 13). **2.** Son of Cushi (*Jer.* 36, 14). **3.** Son of Abdeel (*Jer.* 36, 26). **4.** Son of Hananiah (*Jer.* 37, 13). **5.** Father of Jucal (*Jer.* 38, 1). **6.** Various returned exiles (*Ezra* 10, 39 & 41; *Neh.* 3, 30; 13, 13).

Sheleph [shĕ′-lĕph]. Son of Joktan, and his clan (*Gen.* 10, 26).

Shem [shĕm]. One of the sons of Noah, and ancestor of all the Semitic peoples. It may simply be a geographic locality, or a people (*Gen.* 5, 32; 10, 21 & 31; 9, 20 & 27). *See* RACES.

Shema [shē′-mä]. **1.** Town in S Judah (*Josh.* 15, 26). **2.** Man of Judah (*1 Chron.* 2, 43). **3.** Reubenite (*1 Chron.* 5, 8). **4.** Benjamite, called also Shimel and Shimhi (*1 Chron.* 8, 13). **5.** Returned exile (*Neh.* 8, 4).

Shemaiah [shĕm-āī′-äh]. **1.** Simeonite (*1 Chron.* 4, 37). **2.** Reubenite (*1 Chron.* 5, 4). **3.** Levite connected with the Ark (*1 Chron.* 15, 8-11). **4.** Levite and Scribe (*1 Chron.* 24, 6). **5.** Son of Obed-edom (*1 Chron.* 26, 4). **6.** Prophet and historian in the time of Rehoboam (*1 Kings* 12, 22-24). **7.** Levitical teacher (*2 Chron.* 17, 8). **8.** Levite reformer in Hezekiah's reign (*2 Chron.* 29, 14 & 15). **9.** Another of the same (*2 Chron.* 31, 15). **10.** Levite in Josiah's reign (*2 Chron.* 35, 9). **11.** Father of Urijah (qv) (*Jer.* 26, 20-33). **12.** Father of Delaiah (*Jer.* 36, 12). **13.** False prophet during the Exile (*Jer.* 29, 24 ff.). **14.** A large number of returned exiles, high and low, good, bad and indifferent (*Ezra* 8, 13 & 16; 10, 21 & 31; *Neh.* 3, 29; 6, 10-13; 10, 8; 11, 15; 12, 6 & 34 & 35 & 36 & 42).

Shemer [shĕm'-ēr]. **1.** Owner of the hill on which Samaria was built (*1 Kings* 16, 24). **2.** A Levite (*1 Chron.* 6, 46). **3.** An Asherite. Also Shomer (*1 Chron.* 7, 34).

Sheminith [shĕm'-ĭ-nĭth]. Musical term poss. meaning ' in a low key ' (*1 Chron.* 15, 21; *Ps.* 6 & 12, titles). *See* PSALMS.

Shen [shĕn]. Place where Samuel set up the stone called Ebenezer. The text is prob. corrupt for Jeshanah (qv) (*1 Sam.* 7, 12).

Sheol [shē'-ōl]. *See* HELL.

Shepher [shē'-phēr]. Mt. where Israel camped (*Num.* 33, 23 & 24).

Shepherd. *See* ARTS AND CRAFTS, SHEEP, AGRICULTURE, SHEEPFOLD. He was responsible to the owner for loss or hurt, but was protected by law (*Gen.* 31, 39; *Ex.* 22, 10-13). Sheep were herded into the sheepfold at night, and there might be several flocks together. In the morning each shepherd called his own sheep and they recognised his voice (*John* 10, 2-5). The shepherd walked ahead of his flock to pasture. He did very much the work of the mod. shepherd (called in Kent, the ' looker '). He carried a plaid in case he had to sleep out, a haversack of food, and some kind of weapon agst. wild animals (*1 Sam.* 17, 40; *Jer.* 43, 12). This may have been a crook (*Ps.* 33, 4; *Micah* 7, 14; *Zech.* 11, 7). The dog of the E shepherd was a poor thing compared with the mod. sheepdog (*Job* 30, 1). God (*Gen.* 49, 24) and Jesus (*John* 10, 1-18) are Good Shepherds. Certain humans could be pastors, or under shepherds (*Isa.* 56, 11).

Sheshach [shĕ′-shăch]. (*Jer.* 25, 26; 51, 41). The word does not appear in LXX and is prob. an interpolation by editors. It is a cryptic form of the word Babel, the substitution being for each letter, another letter counted from the end of the alphabet to the same number. Thus in Eng. ' Babel ' counted from the beginning of the alphabet is, 2, 1, 2, 5, 12. The code word, counting similarly from the end of the alphabet, would be yzyvo.

Shesh Bazzar [shĕsh băz′-zăr]. Prince of Judah into whose custody Cyrus gave the Temple vessels pillaged by Nebuchadnezzar. He brought them back to Jerusalem after the Exile and laid the foundations of the temple. It may simply be a Babylonian form of the Heb. name Zerubbabel (qv), as Belteshazzar was the Babylonian form of Daniel (*Ezra* 3, 8 & 11; 5, 14 & 16).

Sheth [shĕth]. **1.** Same as Seth (qv). **2.** Descriptive name for Moabites as troublemakers (*Num.* 24, 17 AV).

Shetharboz(e)nai [shĕ′-thăr-bŏz′-(ĕ)-nă-ī]. Persian official who tried to interfere with the building of the Temple (*Ezra* 5, 3 & 6; 6, 6)

Shewbread. The first mention (in point of date of writing) is in the account of David's flight from the wrath of Saul (*1 Sam.* 21, 1-6). It is also called the ' bread of the presence.' The word used in *1 Chron.* (9, 32; 23, 29) might be better rendered, ' piled up bread.' Bread was baked, not into loaves (though they are so called) but rather into flat scones. The ' altar of cedar ' in Solomon's temple is better as the table of the shewbread (cf. *1 Kings* 7, 48). The shewbread offering consisted of 12 unleavened scones, each containing one-fifth of an ephah (*see* WEIGHTS AND MEASURES) of flour. These were renewed each Sabbath, and those removed were eaten by the priests within the sanctuary (*Lev.* 24, 5-9). The origin of the practice undoubtedly dates back to times when it was believed that the deity had to be fed (cf. *Ex.* 25, 29 RV; *Num.* 4, 7). The latter ref. gives another name for the shewbread in the AV. It had to be there always in 2 piles. The 12 loaves were reckoned to refer to the 12 tribes, but in Babylonia the same practice was observed and the same number of loaves. The 12 may well have been connected with the waxing and waning of the moon.

Shibah [shī'-bäh], **Shebah.** Well at Beer-sheba so named by Jacob to memorialise his covenant with Abimelech (*Gen.* 16, 33).

Shibboleth [shĭb'-bō-lĕth]. Word used as a test by the men of Gilead to discover the Ephraimites escaping over the Jordan fords after the battle bet. the 2 clans. The Ephraimites could not get their tongue round the word, and said Sibboleth. Just as Englishmen cannot easily say, ' It's a braw bricht moonlicht nicht, the nicht.' The inability cost the men of Ephraim their lives (*Judg.* 12, 5 & 6).

Shield. *See* ARMOUR.

Shiggaion [shĭg'-gāī'-ŏn]. The pl. is *shiggonath* It is a musical term prob. meaning ' with passion ' (*Ps.* 7 title; *Hab.* 3, 1).

Shihor [shī'-hŏr], **Sihor** AV. A river. Some think it is the E branch of the Nile; some that it is the ' River of Egypt ' (qv). *See* NILE. It may have been a canal, but it formed the boundary bet. Egypt and Canaan (*Josh.* 13, 3; *1 Chron.* 13, 5; *Isa.* 23, 3; *Jer.* 2, 18). In these refs. consult RV marg. and RSV.

Shilling. *See* MONEY.

Shiloah [shĭ-lō'-ăh]. *See* SILOAM.

Shiloh [shī'-lōh]. Town bet. Shechem and Bethel (*Judg.* 21, 19). Here Joshua set up the Tabernacle (*Josh.* 18, 1), and divided by lot the remainder of Canaan (*Josh.* 18, 8-20; etc.). An annual feast was held here during the time of the Judges (*Judg.* 21, 16-23). The Tabernacle and the Ark remained there till they were lost during the time of Eli (*Judg.* 18, 31; *1 Sam.* chs. 1 & 2 & 3 & 4). The prophet Ahijah lived there (*1 Kings* 14, 2 & 4). In the *Genesis* ref. (49, 10) there are difficulties which the RV recognises. Shiloh being a sacred place it is quite poss. that the name may have been transferred to a person deemed to be sacred; as The Messiah. Or the word may not be a proper name at all, but a composite, meaning ' that which is his,' or ' his very own.' The ref. may simply be to the covenant which was witnessed by the first placing of the Tabernacle and Ark at that place, and then the name of the place may have been used instead of the Covenant.

Shimea(h) [shĭm'-ē-ă]. **1.** Two Levites (*1 Chron.* 6, 30 & 39 & 43). **2.** Brother of David, also called Shimma and Shaminah (*2 Sam.* 13, 3; 16, 9; 7, 13; *1 Chron.* 2, 13). **3.** Son of David also called Shammua (qv). **4.** (*1 Chron.* 8, 32) is Shimeam, a Benjamite of Jerusalem.

Shimron [shĭm'-rŏn]. **1.** Son of Issachar and his

clan (*Gen.* 46, 13; *Num.* 26, 24). **2.** Town on Zebulun border (*Josh.* 11, 1).

Shimshai [shǐm´-shāī]. Opponent of the returned Jews after the exile (*Ezra* 4, 8).

Shin (sin). 21st letter of Heb. alphabet. In Eng. sometimes ' S ' and sometimes ' SH.'

Shinar [shǐn´-är]. The plain of Babylon by the rivers. In it were the cities of Babel, Erech, Accad and Calneh (*Gen.* 10, 10; 11, 2; *Dan.* 1, 2).

Ships and boats. The Israelites were not a sea-going people. They disliked the sea. In the blessed place there would be ' no more sea ' (*Rev.* 21, 1). They were not even greatly interested in their own coastland and left it in the main to the Phoenicians. In the older Akkadian story of the Flood the Ark was a ship which could be navigated. In the Heb. Flood story it was an elaborate piece of driftwood. They knew little of ships and nothing of navigation. Asher and Dan had some maritime experience, but prob. not much (*Judg.* 5, 17). Zebulun and Issachar are mentioned as having some maritime commerce (*Gen.* 49, 13; *Deut.* 33, 19). Sea trade reached its peak in the reign of Solomon, and mainly in connection with the transporting of materials by sea (mostly on rafts) for the building of the Temple (*I Kings* 5, 9; *2 Chron.* 2, 3-18). Eventually Solomon had a merchant navy of sorts sailing from Ezion Geber on the gulf of Akabah, and manned by Phoenicians. Even on longer voyages, ships tended to hug the coast (*I Kings* 9, 26; 10, 22 & 28 & 29). There must have been some kind of sea-borne trade in the time of Isaiah to inspire the ships of Tarshish to be included in his general denunciation. Ships of Tarshish are not ships belonging to Tarshish, but ships capable of sailing to Tarshish (qv). There was not much difference bet. a merchantman and a warship (*Isa.* 33, 21). The primitive type of boats were simply inflated goatskins, or coracles supported by inflated skins. The vessels of papyrus (*Isa.* 18, 2 *Job* 9, 26) were prob. bundles of reeds tied together into rafts rather than coracles woven out of papyrus. It is very hard to tell just how large or how small were the ships of these times, but it is safe to say that in design and size the mod. dhow is not much different from its older counterparts. Sails would prob. be of the lateen type (*Ezek.* 27, 7; *Isa.* 33, 23). Oars were the common mode of propulsion, and from single banks of oars they developed the trireme, with 3 banks of oars. Ezekiel gives a pretty good description of a ship of his day (*Ezek.* 27). The writer of *Ps.* 107, certainly knew what he was writing about (vv. 23-27). There is much about ships and boats in the NT of course, for much of Jesus' ministry was spent around Galilee, and Paul was a great voyager. The Galilee fishing boats were able to accommodate quite a number of people, but they were not so big that a full catch of fish might not threaten their free-board. Paul had been shipwrecked 3 times before the wreck on Malta (*2 Cor.* 11, 25; *Acts* 27). The description of the voyage in the 2nd ref. shows that Luke knew more than a little about ships and the sea. The ship on that voyage from Caesarea to Puteoli was of fair size, with nearly 300 people on board. It was not a galley (ie with oars). The oars mentioned were used for steering over the stern. The ' foresail ' mentioned would be another lateen, or a square sail used for steadying the ship in high winds. This ship carried one small boat. The ' helps,' and ' undergirdings ' tell of ancient practice of seamanship which is still used by small

vessels in emergency. The word is ' frapping,'
which consists of dropping a bight of rope over
the bows and letting it run to midships, then
drawing it tight to hold together the sprung seams.
In winter they were not so much afraid of actual
stormy seas, as they were of heavy cloud which
obscured the sky, and thus their only navigational
aids. Paul voyaged twice in wheat ships out
of Alexandria, and the Latin writer Lucian
has left a description of one such. It was 180 ft.
long, with a beam of 45 ft. and a displacement of
over 1,000 tons. The mainmast was amidships and
carried usually 1 great sail, though there might
be a topsail. The foremast was more in the nature
of a bowsprit. Bow and stern the bulwarks curved
upwards, and were often ornamented. The rudder
paddles or sweeps went out through holes in the
deck and in the sides of the ship. They were withdrawn when anchoring, and the holes became the
hawsepipes for the anchor cables, when the ship
was anchored by the stern. James made an analogy of the rudder (*Jas.* 3, 4). And the Boys'
Brigade have taken their symbol and motto from
the ref. to the anchor in Hebrews (6, 19).

Shittah tree. Called the acacia in RV. Much of
the Temple furniture was made of its timber
(*Ex.* 25, 5 & 10 & 13 & 23; 26, 15 & 26 & 32;
27, 1 & 6; 30, 1 & 5). It is a close-grained hard-
wood.

Shittim [shĭt'-tĭm]. **1.** Place where Israel encamped
E of Jordan on the plains of Moab, ready for the
assault on Jericho (*Num.* chs. 21 & 22). This was
where Balaam (qv) was persuaded to curse Israel's
arms (*Num.* chs. 22-24). At Shittim Joshua was
publicly proclaimed to be Moses' successor (*Num.*
27, 12-23). Some order was brought into religious
ceremonies at this momentous hour (*Num.* chs.

28-30). Five Midianite tribes who had been
seducing Israel to idolatry were dealt with (*Num.*
ch. 31) and Reuben and Gad, who had asked for
the doubtful privilege, were granted land E of
Jordan. At Shittim the plans for the invasion
were drawn up, and the general allocation of the
country still to be conquered, was made (*Num.*
chs. 33-35). Moses was clearing up the odds and
ends of legislation, knowing that his end was near.
He then gave his valedictory speech (*see* DEUTER-
ONOMY) and disappeared in the heights of Mt.
Nebo, after committing Israel to the care and
charge of Joshua. Joshua sent out spies to in-
vestigate Jericho, and, satisfied with their report,
abandoned the Shittim camp and crossed the
Jordan (*Josh.* chs. 2 & 3). **2.** A notorious valley
in which nothing grew but the acacia tree (Shittim
wood) (*Joel* 3, 18). It may have been the Kidron
valley, or at least the course of the Kidron wadi,
a watercourse during the rains, dry otherwise.
Joel uses it as an illustration of the state of the
kingdoms of the world after Jehovah has judged
them (*Joel* 3, 9-21). The water from the hills of
Judah will make the wadis flow brimming full,
and the barren valley of the acacias will blossom
like the rose (cf. *Rev.* 22, 1 & 2).

Shittim wood. *See* SHITTAH TREE.

Shobab [shō′-băb]. Man of the house of Caleb.
Also a son of David (*2 Sam.* 5, 14; *1 Chron.* 2,
18).

Shock, stack. RV has shocks. But the building
of shocks, that is sheaves of corn leaning agst.
each other to dry, is a convention of western, not
of Palestinian farming. There is no need for
drying out the sheaves in Palestine. They piled
the sheaves into something like a stack, but only
for convenience in carting them to the threshing

floor. This kind of heap or pile, is what is meant (*Ex.* 22, 6; *Judg.* 15, 5; *Job* 5, 26).

Shoe. Almost always the sandal, fastened to the foot by straps called latchets. They were removed indoors. It seems as if the priests performed their office barefoot. Sandals were exchanged as sign of a compact or contract (*Ruth* 4, 7). In taking possession of a new piece of land the shoe could be thrown on to it (*Ps.* 60, 8). The shoe also had part in a rather unpleasant ceremony when a man refused to be responsible for his brother's widow (*Deut.* 25, 9).

Shoshannim [shō'-shăn-nim]. Word found in titles of *Psalms* 45 and 69. There is no certainty about the meaning. But it is prob. a popular tune to which it was to be sung. It appears as *Shoshannim Eduth* (*Ps.* 80) and *Shushan Eduth* (*Ps.* 60). These mean respectively, Lily (lilies) for a testimony; a phrase like ' roses for love.'

Showbread. *See* SHEWBREAD.

Shovel. A utensil for removing ashes from the altar. Another word so trans. is the broad wooden shovel used for throwing up the grain and chaff for winnowing (qv) (*Ex.* 27, 3; *Num.* 4, 14; *Isa.* 30, 24).

Shroud. (*Ezek.* 31, 3.) Not the garment of the dead, but shelter, or covering.

Shulammite [shū'-lăm-mīte]. A woman of Shunem, known also as the Shunammite. It may be a kind of titular name, feminine of Solomon (*S. of S.* 6, 13).

Shunem [shū'-nĕm]. Town in Issachar nr. Mt. Gilboa, where the Philistines camped before the battle in which Saul was killed (*Josh.* 19, 18; *1 Sam.* 28, 4; *2 Kings* 4, 25).

Shur [shūr]. Place on the Egyptian border which gave its name to a desert over which escaping

Israel travelled for 3 days (*Gen.* 16, 7; *Ex.* 15, 22). Also called the wilderness of Etham (*Num.* 33, 8).

Shushan [shū'-shăn]. Royal city of Persia (*Esth.* 1, 2; *Neh.* 1, 1). This is the ancient city of Susa. Cyrus made it a capital city equal in status to Ecbatana and Babylon after he overthrew the Babylonian empire. Alexander the Great pillaged it in 331 BC. It gradually declined in importance.

Shushanchites [shū-shăn'-chītes]. Natives of Shushan above. When the Samaritans were transported, these were brought to fill their place (*Ezra* 4, 9).

Shuttle. (*Job* 7, 6 only.) May be the shuttle rod or the loom itself (*Judg.* 16, 14. The same Heb. word). *See* SPINNING AND WEAVING.

Sibbecai [sĭb'-bē-cāi]. One of David's heroes. Also called Mebunnai (*2 Sam.* 21, 18; *1 Chron.* 27, 11).

Sibboleth. *See* SHIBBOLETH.

Sibmah [sĭb'-măh] **Shibmah.** Town of Reuben near Heshbon, which reverted to the Moabites. It was famed for its vines (*Josh.* 13, 19; *Isa.* 16, 8; etc.).

Siccuth [sĭc'-cūth]. (*Amos* 5, 26.) Its assoc. in this verse with Chiun makes it seem likely that this is a Massorete error. It is the Assyrian god Sakkut, who is really Kaiwanu (Chiun) (qv).

Sick (sickness). *See* MEDICINE.

Sickle. These were successively of flint, bronze and iron, the curved blade being set in a handle of wood or bone. In 1 or 2 refs. the true sickle is not the correct trans. (*Joel* 3, 13; *Rev.* 14, 19 & 20 AV) should be the grape knife, a somewhat smaller but similarly shaped instrument. AV marg. is wrong in several instances to give scythe as an alternative. Scythes were unknown.

Siddim, Vale of [sĭd'-dĭm]. Place where Amraphel and his allies defeated the 5 Canaanite kings (*Gen.*

14, 8 ff.). It is near the Dead Sea. The slime pits are, of course, deposits of bitumen.

Sidon (Zidon) [sī'-dŏn]. *See* ZIDON.

Siege. *See* FORTIFICATION.

Signet. *See* SEAL.

Sign. Something visible and remarkable which serves as witness (qv) to God or the Will of God. The rainbow (*Gen.* 9, 12); the rite of circumcision (*Gen.* 17, 11); the plagues of Egypt (*Ex.* 10, 2) were signs. Gideon and Saul were granted signs (*Judg.* 6, 17; *1 Sam.* 10, 7). The Jews demanded miracles of Jesus, as signs (*Matt.* 12, 38; 16, 1). The end of the age was to be preceded by signs (*Matt.* 24, 30; *Luke* 21, 25; *2 Thess.* 2, 9). *See* WONDERS.

Sihon [sī'-hŏn]. King of the Amorites who refused to allow marching Israel to pass through his territory. They overcame him at Jahaz (*Num.* 21, 21-24; *Deut.* 2, 26-36; *Judg.* 11, 19-22). His capital, Heshbon, fell, and the whole land was given to Reuben, Gad and half Manasseh. Ref. (*Jer.* 48. 45) is to Heshbon.

Silas [sī'-lăs]. This is his name in the *Acts*; in the epistles he is called Silvanus (*2 Cor.* 1, 19; *1 Thes.* 1, 1; *2 Thes.* 1, 1). He was an early convert and took a prominent place in the early church. With Judas, called Barsabbas, he was sent out with Paul and Barnabas to announce the findings of the Council of Jerusalem (*Acts* 15). He was prob. a Jew, and possibly a Rom. citizen (*Acts* 16, 37). When Barnabas and Paul parted company, Paul chose Silas to accompany him on the 2nd missionary journey. He was imprisoned at Philippi. Paul left Silas and Timothy in Thessalonica while he himself went on to Athens. They followed him to Athens, then were sent back into Macedonia (*1 Thes.* 3, 1). They were with Paul in Corinth and are mentioned in the various letters written there. Paul thought a great deal of him (*2 Cor.* 1, 19), as did Peter (*1 Pet.* 5, 12).

Silk. The fine cloth woven from the threads produced by the silkworm and other caterpillars. It was imported, and was lit. worth its weight in gold (*Ezek.* 16, 10 & 13; *Rev.* 18, 12).

Siloah [sĭ-lō'-ăh]. (*Neh.* 3, 15 AV). Should be Siloam (qv).

Siloam [sĭ-lō'-ăm]. A pool at Jerusalem (*John* 9, 7) whose waters 'went softly' (*Isa.* 8, 6). It is the same as Siloah, and Shelah (*Neh.* 3, 15 RV). It is really the catchment of the water passing from the Fountain of the Virgin, by way of the aqueduct called the Siloam tunnel. There is still a masonry cistern 58 ft. long, by 18 broad, and 19 deep. It was near the city wall, and the Tower of Siloam (*Luke* 13, 4) was prob. part of the fortifications.

Silvanus. *See* SILAS.

Silver. Weighed silver was used as money (*Gen.* 23, 16; *Job* 28, 15). Ornaments, musical instruments, and even crowns were made from it (*Gen.* 24, 53; *Num.* 10, 2; *Zech.* 6, 11). Many of the temple furnishings and utensils were of silver (*Ex.* chs. 26 & 27; etc.).

Silverling. (*Isa.* 7, 23 only AV). 1,000 shekels of silver.

Simeon [sĭm'-ē-ŏn]. Twice Symeon (*Luke* 3, 30; *Acts* 15, 14 RV). **1.** Second son of Jacob and Leah (*Gen.* 29, 33). His full brother Levi and he massacred the inhabitants of Shechem for the assault on their full sister Dinah (*Gen.* 34, 24-31). Jacob does not seem to have been as fond of his children by Leah as he was of his children by Rachel. He certainly was not very fond of Simeon and Levi (*Gen.* 49, 5-7). **2.** The tribe which sprung

from him. His six sons were Nemuel (or Jemuel)
Jamin, Ohad, Jachin (Jarib), Zohar (Zerah) and
Shaul (*Gen.* 46, 10; *Num.* 26, 12-14; *1 Chron.* 4,
24). At the 1st census they numbered just under
60,000 adult males (*Num.* 1, 23; 2, 13), but by
the 2nd census they had diminished to 22,000
(*Num.* 26, 12-14). Their spy was Shaphat (*Num.*
13, 5). Their portion at the partition of Canaan
was a strip of land in the S of the country surrounded by land given to Judah (*Josh.* 19, 1-9).
Their cities were Beer-sheba, Ziklag and Hormah.
They carried on some minor forays agst. neighbouring peoples (*1 Chron.* 4, 24-43). 3. An
ancestor of Jesus (*Luke* 3, 30). 4. A man who
believed that he would not die until he had seen
the Messiah. He was present when Joseph and
Mary brought the infant Jesus to the Temple, and
knew that this was He for whom he waited (*Luke*
2, 25-35). 6. Simon Peter (qv) (*Acts* 15, 14). 7.
Christian teacher at Antioch called Niger, or
Black. He may have been a negro (*Acts* 13, 1).
Simon. 1. Father of Judas Iscariot (*John* 6, 71). **2.**
Simon Peter (qv) (*Matt.* 10, 2). **3.** Simon Zelotes,
the Zealot (qv), one of the apostles (qv). *See*
CANAANITE. **4.** One of Jesus' brothers (*Matt.* 13,
55). *See* BRETHREN OF THE LORD. **5.** A Pharisee,
host to Jesus (*Luke* 7, 36-50). **6.** Man of Bethany
who had been a leper. In his house Mary of
Bethany anointed Jesus' feet (*Matt.* 26, 6-13;
Mark 14, 3-9). He was prob. related to Mary,
Martha and Lazarus, but there is no evidence that
he was their father, or that he was husband of
Martha. **7.** Man of Cyrene forced by the Romans
to carry Jesus' cross. He was father of Alexander
and Rufus (*Matt.* 27, 32). **8.** Simon Magus, Simon
the magician, who made a very good thing out of
impressing the Samaritans with his magical powers.

He was baptised by Philip, but obviously had not got rid of his showground ways, for he offered to buy the right to confer the Holy Spirit by the laying on of hands. Peter would have none of this, and Simon asked forgiveness and Peter's intercession for him (*Acts* 8, 9-24). Trad. has it that he went back to his old ways and was one of the inspirers of the heresy of Gnosticism. **9.** A tanner at Joppa with whom Peter lodged (*Acts* 9, 43; 10, 6).

Simple (simplicity). In the OT is trans. of the Heb. *pethi*, which means ' openness.' This is a virtue when it is candour, but is not so virtuous when it means lack of thoughtfulness, or ingenuousness. Sometimes the simple would be the better of being more prudent (*Prov.* 1, 4; 8, 5 RV marg. and RSV). Simplicity (*2 Sam.* 15, 11) is integrity. NT (*Matt.* 10, 16 AV and RV marg.) means ' all of one good substance,' RV gives trans. ' innocent.' Same meaning is in (*Rom.* 16, 19 AV ' harmless ' in in marg.). Moffat once trans. same Gk. word as ' single ' (*2 Cor.* 11, 3).

Sin. The sin of omission is to neglect to do what the Law of God commands. The sin of commission is to do what the Law of God forbids (*Rom.* 3, 23; *1 John* 3, 4; *Gal.* 3, 10-12). Since the revelation of God, His nature, and His will, is progressive throughout Scripture, it is perfectly natural that ideas of what constitutes sin should change. In the Iron Age of Israel actions were supposed to be inspired by God, which the Christian would condemn as being essentially wicked and sinful. The domestic and matrimonial habits of the patriarchs could find no place in a Christian civilisation. Sin, therefore, depends very largely upon the individual's understanding of the revealed will of God. Jesus was very conscious of this when he said,

' If I had not come and spoken unto them, they had not had sin: but now they have no cloak for their sin ' (*John* 15, 22). In other words they were not sinners by the standards which they knew, but now they were sinners because He had shown them other standards. There has been much argument about the exact meaning of the unforgiveable sin; the eternal sin of blasphemy agst. the Holy Spirit (*Mark* 3, 29; *Luke* 12, 10; *Matt.* 12, 31 ff.). Jesus may well have meant the constant resisting of the promptings of the Holy Spirit until a man reaches a state when he is impervious to these promptings, and incapable of either feeling them or responding to them. He is now immune from God. It is not that God has stopped wanting to forgive, and to give the blessed sense of forgiveness. God cannot get in at all. The doors have been shut so long that they are rusted solid and cannot open. The key has been thrown away.

Sin. 1. Desert through which Israel marched from the Red Sea to Sinai (*Ex.* 16, 1; 17, 1; *Num.* 33, 11 & 12). **2.** An Egyptian city (*Ezek.* 30, 15). It was prob. the mod. Syene.

Sinai [sī′-nä-ī]. Twice **Sina** (*Acts* 7, 30 & 38 AV). Also called Horeb. The Israelites reached it when 3 months out from Egypt (*Ex.* 19, 1). Moses climbed the mt. and returned with the Law, which he then announced to the people. The Covenant was then ratified, setting up Israel as a theocratic (God-governed) nation (*Ex.* chs. 20-24). The only ref. apart from those connected with the giving of the Law, and occurring bet. *Ex.* 20 and *Num.* 10, is when Elijah fled to Sinai to escape from Jezebel (*I Kings* 19, 8). The exact location of Sinai is a matter of guesswork. There is an ancient trad. that it is Mt. Serbal; another, almost as ancient, is that it is Jebel Musa.

Sincere. Lit. ' unmixed, pure,' free from adulteration (*1 Pet.* 2, 2).

Sinew. (*Gen.* 32, 32.) The Hebrews did not eat the sciatic muscle. This passage is the explanation for it, but it is prob. a much older taboo (RV trans. 'the sinew of the hip'). It is not mentioned in the listed food taboos of the Pentateuch.

Sinim, Land of [sĭn'-ĭm]. This land has not been identified (*Isa.* 49, 12). The wilderness of Sin was not far enough away to make this a dramatic statement, nor was the town of Syene. There was a race of Shinas who lived among the Hindu Kush mts. of India, and some think Sinim was farther off still; China in fact. But Isaiah is not trying to be precise; he is trying to be dramatic. What he means is ' from the ends of the earth '; or even ' from the back of beyond.'

Sin offering. *See* OFFERING.

Sion. Another name for Mt. Hermon. But Mt. Sion is Zion (qv).

Sirah, Well of [sĭr'-äh]. Place where Joab's men overtook Abner (*2 Sam.* 3, 26).

Sirion [sĭr'-ĭ-ŏn]. Sidonian name for Mt. Hermon (*Deut.* 3, 9; *Ps.* 29, 6).

Sisera [sĭs'-ĕ-rä]. Captain of the army of Jabin (*Judg.* 4, 2 ff.). Also given as a ruler in his own right (*Judg.* 5). He was defeated by Barak at the R. Kishon and sought sanctuary with Heber the Kenite. Heber's wife, Jael, killed him by hammering a tent peg into his head while he slept.

Sister. The word is wider than it is to-day. Matrimonial complications rather dulled the edges of relationships. It can be a full sister or a half sister, or simply a female relative (*Gen.* 20, 12; *Deut.* 27, 22). It can even be a wife (*S. of S.* 4, 9); or a fellow tribeswoman (*Num.* 25, 18); or a member of the same church (*Rom.* 16, 1).

Sistrum [sĭs'-trŭm]. Musical instrument consisting of metal rods which were shaken together (*2 Sam.* 6, 5 RV marg.).

Sith. Since (*Jer.* 15, 7; etc.).

Sivan [sī'-văn]. Third month of the Jewish year; May-June. *See* TIME, YEAR (*Esth.* 8, 9).

Slave, Slavery. *See* BONDAGE.

Sleight. (*Eph.* 4, 14.) Dice playing.

Slime. *See* BITUMEN.

Sling. The common form of the weapon was a piece of leather with 2 strings attached. A stone was laid on the leather which became a pouch. The sling was whirled round the head by both thongs. When one thong was released the stone was flung with considerable force and accuracy (*1 Sam.* 17, 40). *See* ARMOUR.

Smith. Worker in metals, using charcoal furnace, bellows, anvil, and the other tools of the trade. *See* ARTS AND CRAFTS.

Smyrna. City on W coast of Asia Minor, inhabited by Aeolian and Ionian Greeks. It was destroyed by the Lydians about 580 BC, and remained in ruins till it was rebuilt just after the time of Alexander the Great, ie, 200 years later. It became a wealthy centre of trade and was part of the Rom. province of Asia by 133 BC. Its church was one of the 7 churches of Asia named in the *Revelation* (1, 11; 2, 8-11).

Snail. Two words are so trans. One is not the snail, but a sand lizard as in RV (*Lev.* 11, 30 AV). The other is the true snail (*Ps.* 58, 8).

Snow. Snow is common in the hill country of Palestine, falling usually in January and February. Normally it does not lie long, though in mts. like Hermon it never melts. Such snow, packed in deep holes in the ground, was used for cooling beverages (*Prov.* 26, 1). It is used as a figure for purity (*Ps.* 51, 7; *Isa.* 1, 18; etc.).

Snuffers. Not candle snuffers, used for trimming the wick. They had no candles. *See* CANDLESTICK. The snuffers are tongs, and the snuff dishes are the plates for the burned wick of the lamps.

So [sō]. King of Egypt with whom Hoshea tried to effect an alliance when he was threatened by Assyria, about 724 BC (*2 Kings* 17, 4).

Soap. Also **sope**. The word means lit. ' that which cleanses,' but it is certain that nothing like mod. soap existed then. In one ref. (*Isa.* 1, 25) RV marg. and RSV have ' lye.' The substance seems to have been alkaline and was used for washing the body and clothes, and in smelting (*Job* 9, 30; *Mal.* 3, 2; *Isa.* 1, 25). Two refs. allude to it as grass (*Jer.* 2, 22; *Mal.* 3, 2 LXX). Glasswort and saltwort when burned produce a soda bearing ash.

Soco(h) [sō'-cō]. **1.** Fortified town of Judah, under the charge of Ben Hesed in Solomon's day (*1 Sam.* 17, 1; *1 Kings* 4, 10; *2 Chron.* 11, 7). **2.** What seems to be another town of the name occurs (*Josh.* 15, 48). It must have been near Hebron.

Sod (sodden). *See* SEETHE.

Sodom [sŏ'-dŏm]. *See* PLAIN, CITIES OF: LOT.

Sodomite. Native of Sodom, but particularly one addicted to sodomy (ie, homosexuality). It was a practice notorious in that town, where it was related to the worship and rites of Ashtoreth (Asherah). At various times it broke out in Israel and was suppressed (*Gen.* 38, 21 & 22; *1 Kings* 14, 24; 15, 12; 22, 46; *Hos.* 4, 14).

Sojourner. *See* STRANGER.

Soldier. *See* ARMY, WAR, LEGION, ETC.

Solemn(ity). Has nothing to do with seriousness. It means 'stated,' 'regular.' 'Solemn assembly' is a regular meeting. 'Solemn feast' is a recognised and official feast.

Solomon [sŏl'-ō-mŏn]. Youngest of the sons of David and Bathsheba (*2 Sam.* 12, 24). Nathan the prophet called him Jedidiah, 'beloved of the Lord' (*2 Sam.* 12, 25). Towards the end of David's life, Adonijah, his oldest surviving son, tried to set himself up as king, or at least as regent. Nathan rallied the forces that mattered; Zadok, the High Priest and Benaiah, commander of the standing army, and they proclaimed Solomon king (*1 Kings* 1, 5-40). David did not live long after this and Solomon began to reign in his own right about 970 BC. He had Adonijah, and Joab, who was implicated, killed (*1 Kings* 2, 1-46). He married a princess of Egypt (*1 Kings* 3, 1). The Tabernacle was still at Gibeon, and it was while worshipping there that Solomon had a vision, in which God offered him any gift of his choice. He asked for an understanding heart. He appears to have received it, for his judgments became famous (*1 Kings* 3, 2-28). This promise was renewed to him 20 years later, with the promise that his line would continue (*1 Kings* 9, 1-10). His only military campaign seems to have been agst. Hamath, but he fortified the borders, mainly agst. Rezin and Hadad of Damascus and Edom. He fulfilled his father's dream to build the Temple, using much of the material which David had gathered for the purpose. It took 7 years to build (*1 Kings* chs. 5 & 6). He played a prominent part in the dedication and renewed his promises (*1 Kings* 7, 13; 8, 66). He then built a palace for himself which took almost twice as long (*1 Kings* 7, 1-12). He was an astute rather than an eminently wise king,

and he chose his advisers and subordinates with
discretion (*1 Kings* 4, 2-6). He reorganised local
government and maintained a strong and well
deployed standing army. He organised a considerable commerce with neighbouring countries
and even with others far distant (*1 Kings* 10, 22
& 23). Although much is said of the splendour
of his court and of his many virtues, it is possible
that writers made a little more of him than he was
worth because it was he who had built the Temple.
Sheba (qv) was a wealthier land than Israel, and
it is hardly likely that its queen would have been
struck dumb by what she saw at Solomon's court
(*1 Kings* 10, 1-13). His harem was very considerable, though many of the women would be presents from foreign rulers, and the size of a harem
was the ancient royal way of keeping up with the
Joneses. Many of the women were foreigners and
Solomon was enticed away from the austerities
of Jehovah worship into easier and more congenial
practices. He was punished for this (*1 Kings* 11,
1-13). His luxurious way of living made heavy
taxation necessary and this was resented bitterly
by the 10 tribes of the N, who complained that
all the revenues were being poured into Judah
and Jerusalem. This was one of the causes of the
split in the country on Solomon's death, when the
10 tribes refused to accept his son Rehoboam, and
elected their own king Jeroboam. Solomon
reigned for about 40 years and several records of
his reign are referred to. These records are,
however lost (*1 Kings* 11, 41-43; *2 Chron.* 9
29-31). *See* ISRAEL.

Solomon, Song of. *See* SONG OF SOLOMON.

Solomon, Wisdom of. *See* APOCRYPHA.

Solomon's Porch. *See* TEMPLE.

Solomon's servants. *See* NETHINIM.

Sometime. Simply ' sometimes,' and occasionally
' once upon a time.'

Son. *See* FAMILY, BIRTHRIGHT, CHILD, etc. The word
is used in a wider sense than it is to-day. It can
mean the male child (*Gen.* 27, 1). But it can also
mean: **1.** A grandson, or an even more remote
descendant (*2 Kings* 9, 20). **2.** An adopted
male (*Ex.* 2, 10). **3.** ' My son ' as an aged man
might refer to a dear young friend (*Josh.* 7, 19).
4. Member of a society or guild (*2 Kings* 2, 3;
Neh. 3, 8). **5.** Citizen or national (*Gen.* 10, 4;
Lam. 4, 2). **6.** One possessing a quality or characteristic (*1 Sam.* 25, 17 AV; 14, 52; *Luke* 10,
6).

Son of God. There is one ref. in OT AV (*Dan.* 3,
25). RV correctly alters this to ' son of the gods.'
The words were spoken by a heathen. In the NT
it is a title of the Messiah (qv) except once when
it is used of Adam (*Luke* 3, 38). The phrase is
more common in the RV than in the AV, occurring 44 times in ref. to Jesus. It signifies a very
special relationship bet. God and Jesus. He is of
the Father, sent by the Father, and the instrument
of the Father's will. Jesus is of exactly the same
nature as God. It was Jesus' insistence upon this
relationship which incensed the Sanhedrin (*Matt.*
26, 63-66) for this was blasphemy. The claim was
made for Jesus by the Baptist (*Matt.* 3, 16 & 17;
Mark 1, 10 & 11); it was substantiated at the
Transfiguration (*Matt.* 17, 5; *Mark* 9, 7; *Luke*
9, 35). Paul and the Apostles accepted this sonship without question, and placed it centrally in
their preaching (*Rom.* 1, 4). *See* SON OF MAN.

Son of Man. This denotes an essentially human
being (*Num.* 23, 19; *Job* 25, 6; etc.). Both Daniel
and Ezekiel were so addressed by divine voice
(*Dan.* 8, 17; *Ezek.* 2, 1). In *Daniel* the ultimate

triumph was to be of 'one like unto a son of man' over the beasts. This is the victory of humanity itself, surely (*Dan.* 7, 13 & 14 & 27 RV). The title was therefore quite traditional and Jesus adopted it for Himself, quite poss. with a mind to the *Daniel* passage indicated (*Matt.* 24, 30; *Mark* 14, 62; etc.). Jesus used the title of Himself almost 80 times in the Gospels, and it was used of him by Stephen and the apostles (*Acts* 7, 56; *Heb.* 2, 6; *Rev.* 1, 13; 14, 14). So long as Jesus used the title of Himself, and encouraged others to do so, He might offend authority, but He was not transgressing. He could not be charged with blasphemy. They might question His claim to be the Son of Man of *Daniel*, but it was not an indictable offence to make the claim. The real trouble began when He claimed Messiahship and used the title Son of God. It is significant that He asked the disciples for their idea of who the Son of Man was. They might have answered that He was the triumphant human of *Daniel* in the battle with the beasts, but Peter replied, 'Thou art the Christ, the Son of the living God.' Jesus congratulated Peter on his insight, but told him to say nothing about it (*Matt.* 16, 13 & 16 & 17). Nevertheless Jesus seems to have identified the 2 designations; for when the High Priest asked Him if He claimed to be the Son of God, Jesus referred to Himself as the Son of Man, but claimed that the Son of Man would be seen in the position in which they would expect the Son of God to be (*Matt.* 26, 63 & 64). *See* SON OF GOD, MESSIAH, JESUS CHRIST.

Song. The word means more or less what it means today, and refs. not merely to the sacred. The song might, however, merely be a rhythmic arrangement of words without a set tune which might be spoken to some kind of instrumental accompaniment.

Song of Solomon. Solomon is credited with over 1,000 ' songs ' (*1 Kings* 4, 32) though many of these may have been very short indeed. This book (which we will call ' Canticles ') has only 117 vv., and many of these are repetitions. It is not at all surprising that the rest have been lost when one remembers what happened to the country in the years up to the Exile. Refs. to Canticles in other books which can be dated, indicate that it is not later than 200 BC, and internal evidence seems to show that it is not older than 400 BC. There are Greek influences on the language which lead to the conclusion that the work was written after the conquests of Alexander about 350. Some regard the work as being a dramatic poem, parts of which certainly are in dialogue. But if the intention is dramatic there does not seem to be any plot or story. Is this a king falling in love with a country girl, trying to persuade her to yield to his blandishments and then finding that she is faithful to her humble rustic lover? Or is this the king, tired of the sophisticated ways of the court and of his harem, finding his true love in a humble and simple walk of life? It seems more likely that Canticles is a collection or anthology of bits and pieces of remembered verses and songs, and even possibly of some simple dramatic mimes, where the actors went through the motions while the words were spoken by a chorus. The title of these mimes might be ' Scenes from the life of Solomon the Great Lover.' It is possible to argue for a continuity, but the evidence must be considerably distorted to ' prove ' the point. To regard Canticles as an essentially religious book, and as an allegory of the relationship bet. God and Israel, and later bet. Christ and His Church, is to strain the evidence too far. This interpretation is written into the chapter headings of the AV. If there is any worship in Canticles it is the worship of Love itself; the love of a man for a maid, which Solomon regarded as one of the world's wonders. Canticles is not mentioned in the OT, NT or Apocrypha; nor do Josephus or Philo refer to it. The name of God does not appear in it. In the Hebrew canon it is one of the Hagiographa or Writings, and the first of the 5 'Rolls' or Megilloth, which include *Ruth, Lamentations, Ecclesiastes* and *Esther*. These were read at the annual festivals of Pentecost, Booths and Purim.

Song of the Three Holy Children. *See* APOCRYPHA.

Sons of God. The 1st ref. is in *Genesis* (6, 1-4), where the sons of God discovered that the daughters of men were fair and married some of them. This kind of relationship bet. superhuman 'men' and human women is found in all mythology, and is given as reason for the appearance of demi-gods, Titans and 'heroes.' The *Genesis* passage has been variously interpreted as meaning that the best men were tempted to mate with unworthy women, whose only claim to distinction was their beauty; or that angels deliberately chose the physical delights of earth in preference to the more austere state of heaven; or that men of deep religious sense, who abstained from all physical contacts and delights, were lured away by the blandishments of women and became as other men. Although the demi-god idea cannot be rejected out of hand (as we have said it appears in every mythology), it seems more likely that this *Genesis* passage is an attempt to explain religious deterioration before the Flood. Something must have made the Flood necessary. How did it come

about that the desc. of Adam through Seth, good
men that they were, should ultimately land up in
a state so evil that it was necessary for God to
revise His plan, obliterate all but a chosen group
of his created creatures, and start all over again?
Some influence must have brought His sons (and
there are many refs. all through Scripture to men,
and esp. to Israelites, as being the children of
God) to this sorry state. There is nothing new in
attributing the fall of men to women, as the old
Genesis story attributes the fall of man to a woman.
This seems to be the correct interpretation.

Sons of the Prophets. *See* PROPHET, SAMUEL. These
were associations or guilds, or schools of prophecy which may have been instituted by Samuel,
but which may have been older (*1 Sam.* 10, 5).
They were in existence from Samuel's time to
beyond Elisha's time, and functioned at Ramah,
Naioth, Bethel, Jericho, Gilgal and other centres.
Exactly what they studied, and how they went
about it, is not known. Music played a part in
their activity Saul came under their influence
(*1 Sam.* 10, 10-13). Maybe one great service
which they rendered was by their devotion to
preserve the old traditions of the race which were
later written down and became Scripture. To
refer to them as a 'school' does not, however,
imply a place of instruction. The word means
rather, the same as 'a school of thought.' It is
significant that later prophetic associations made
their headquarters in or near centres of pagan
worship (*2 Kings* 2, 3 & 5; 4, 38). They had great
respect and affection for Elisha (*2 Kings* 6, 5). The
ref. (*2 Kings* 22, 14 AV) to Huldah living in a
'college' is wrong. The word refers to a district
of the city as in RV. It is very unlikely that these
associations persisted after the time of Elisha.

Soothsayer. Fortune teller and interpreter of dreams. *See* MAGIC, DIVINATION.

Sopater [sō´-pā-tĕr]. Son of Pyrrhus (*Acts* 20, 4 RV). He was a Christian of Berea who accompanied Paul on the last stages of the 3rd missionary journey. He is ref. to as a kinsman (fellow countryman) of Paul (*Rom.* 16, 21). This may poss. be a different man.

Sope. *See* SOAP.

Sorcery. *See* MAGIC.

Sosipater. Prob. same as Sopater above.

Sosthenes [sŏs´-thĕ-nēs]. **1.** Ruler of the Corinth synagogue, beaten up by the crowd after their accusation of Paul had failed (*Acts* 18, 17). **2.** Christian mentioned in greetings to Corinth (*1 Cor.* 1, 1). This may be the same man converted.

Soul. Its use in the OT is quite different from its use in the NT. In the OT its sense is the same as the mod. ' I didn't see a living soul.' It is in fact simply an animated being. In the NT the word is the Gk. *psyche*, which is the non-material substance which is the source of the body's life. It also has the meaning of ' personality '; the factor which ' makes you, you ' (*Matt.* 6, 26 RV marg. and RSV). In the assessment of the make-up of man there is a school of thought (bipartite)which argues that he is body and soul. There is another school of thought which maintains that he is body, soul and spirit (tripartite). Certainly the NT uses an entirely different word for spirit: *pneuma*. Sometimes the 2 words, *psyche* and *pneuma*, appear to mean exactly the same (*Luke* 1, 46 & 47; *Philip.* 1, 27 RV). In other refs. there appears to be a clear distinction. *Psyche* is the quality of life in the individual, while *pneuma* is the principle of life in all created things. Man possesses *psyche*, which gives him a life apart from and distinct from God; he has a personality which is his own. But the origin of that life is God, who has breathed the spirit into man, as he has breathed it into all living creatures. By exercising the rights of his personality man can live apart from God if he so chooses, but whether he does or not, he cannot alter the fact that his life derives from God. There is no space here to go fully into a matter which the reader will recognise as being very intricate indeed, but it is obvious that it is the person who recognises and realises that his personality has its origin in God, and that therefore he has an obligation to God, who finds that the elements in himself are not in a state of discord, but in a state of harmony.

South, the. *See* NEGEB.

Sower (sowing). *See* AGRICULTURE.

Spain. More or less mod. Spain, the Iberian peninsula, or at least the coastal portions of it. Paul wanted to visit it, and poss. did (*Rom.* 15, 24 & 28).

Span. *See* WEIGHTS AND MEASURES.

Sparrow. The word prob. includes all ' twittering' birds, as distinct from songsters, as used in the OT. In the NT it is more prob. the true sparrow, *passer domesticus*, or *p. italiae*, or *p. hispaniolensis*.

Spear. *See* ARMOUR.

Spearmen. Lightly armed infantry, as distinct from the cavalry and the legionaries (*Acts* 23, 23).

Speckled bird. (*Jer.* 12, 9 only) The text is very corrupt here. The ref. seems to mean that Israel as a speckled bird attracts and falls easy victim to birds of prey. But the fact of the matter is that the speckles on a bird are protective colouring.

Spelt. A poor kind of wheat, called rie in AV (*Ex.* 9, 32; *Isa.* 28, 25), and called fitches (*Ezek.* 4, 9 AV). *See* RYE, FITCHES.

Spice(s). Trans. of 4 words. **1.** Heb. *bosem:* a vegetable substance which is fragrant and aromatic, as myrrh, cinnamon, calamus and cassia (*Ex.* 25, 6; *1 Kings* 10, 10; *S. of S.* 4, 10 & 14) Certain refs. are specifically to balsam (balm of Gilead) (*S. of S.* 5, 13; 6, 2). **2.** Nekoth Tragacanth (qv) (*Gen.* 37, 25; 43, 11). **3.** Sammim. Substances with a sweet smell used in the preparation of incense (qv). Opobalsamum, onycha and galbanum are mentioned (*Ex.* 30, 7 & 34). **4.** Gk. *aroma:* term which covers all such substances including myrrh and aloes (*Mark* 16, 1; *John* 19, 40).

Spice merchant. (*1 Kings* 10, 15.) The word means a merchant of any sort.

Spider. One of the many of the *genus arachnidae.* One ref. (*Prov.* 30, 28 AV) should be lizard as in RV.

Spikenard. The fragrant extract of an Indian plant, *nardostachys jatamansi.* It was both rare and precious in Palestine (*S. of S.* 1, 12; 4, 13; *Mark* 14, 3; *John* 12, 3).

Spindle. *See* SPINNING AND WEAVING.

Spinning and weaving. The materials were flax, wool and goats' hair. The wool was scoured and carded. The flax was prepared by steeping and beating the flax leaves which had been sun dried. The thin threads were then heckled, or combed. The threads of all 3 materials were spun by distaff and spindle. The distaff was simply a piece of wood or cane split at the top to hold the wool. The spindle was a cylinder of wood about a foot long. The bottom rested in a hole in another block of wood or stone, and there was a hook at the top for catching the wool or flax. The spindle was rotated in the hole in the ' whorl ' (*Ex.* 35, 25; *2 Kings* 23, 7; *Prov.* 31, 19). Ref. (*2 Sam.* 3,

29) should have for ' one that leaneth on a staff,'
' one that holdeth a spindle '; the meaning being
that Joab's descendants would be fit only for
women's work. The word loom does not occur
in the AV, and is used wrongly in RV and RSV.
It should be trans. thrum, which is the pile of a
cloth, and to thrum is to tease out threads to make
a pile or a rough surface. In this case the thrum
is the cut ends of the threads of the warp
left attached to the beam when the complete web
has been removed from the loom. The ' beam'
(*Judg.* 16, 14) is prob. the loom of which there
were 3 varieties, one horizontal and 2 upright. On
the upright loom the threads of the warp hang
down from a horizontal beam supported by 2
posts, each thread having a small weight attached
to keep it taut. In NT times the loom was an
improvement upon this, and consisted of 3 horizontal beams on uprights, thus allowing a longer
bolt of cloth to be woven. Loom weaving is simply
a development of plaiting with the fingers; the
threads of the weft or woof, being drawn alternately over and under the threads of the warp.
On the loom the threads of the warp were attached
to the beam or beams (*Lev.* 13, 48 ff.; *Isa.* 19, 9;
Job 10, 11). The threads of the warp had then to
be divided into odds and evens, one being brought
forward and the other taken back to admit the
passage of the shuttle which carried the weft.
After each complete passage of the shuttle the
thread of the weft had to be pushed or beaten
upwards to keep the fabric close. The threads of
the warp were then reversed so that the weft thread
was gripped bet. them. The shuttle was then passed
back, and the threads of the warp reversed once
more. The process sounds slow, but it was not
with a skilled weaver at work. (*Job* 7, 6) may refer

to the shuttle itself or to the shuttle rod which carried it; or it may be the loom itself. After each passage of the shuttle rod, the batten came into play to beat the thread of the weft up tight. On the upright loom the web was woven from the top down, as Jesus' seamless garment (*John* 19, 23). The loom on which Delilah wove Samson's hair into a web was a horizontal loom (*Judg.* 16, 13 f.). ' If thou weavest the seven plaits of my head with the warp and beatest them up with the batten, then shall I become weak and as other men.' And she made him sleep and wove the 7 plaits of his head with the warp and beat them up with the batten (AV, ' fastened them with the pin '). When the weaving was complete, the weaver cut the ends of the threads of the warp, leaving the ends hanging. This is the thrum. The ref. (*Isa.* 38, 12) where the RV marg. alone is correct, is a figure for premature death; the threads are cut and the web rolled up. New cloth (*Matt.* 9, 16; *Mark* 2, 21 AV) is cloth fresh from the loom, before it has been taken to the fuller. *See* ARTS AND CRAFTS. The weavers had their guild (*1 Chron.* 4, 21) but their trade was reckoned not an honourable one. Paul, being a tentmaker, or weaver of tent curtains, would work with goats' hair (*2 Cor.* 11, 9). Wool and flax could not be mixed in the warp and woof.

Spirit. *See* SOUL, HOLY SPIRIT.

Spitting. Spitting into another's face was the ultimate in insult (*Num.* 12, 14; *Isa.* 50, 6; *Matt.* 26, 67).

Sponge. These are common in the waters of the Mediterranean and have been used from early times (*Matt.* 27, 48; etc.).

Spring. *See* FOUNTAIN.

Stacte [stăc′-tĕ]. (*Ex.* 30, 34.) A fragrant gum,

storax or myrrh. The Heb. means lit. ' a drop.'

Stall. *See* MANGER.

Standard. *See* BANNER.

Stars. The ancients were keen observers of the stars, and it was they who saw them grouped as constellations whose names have remained (*Gen.* 22, 17; *Job* 9, 9; 38, 31 & 32). The Hebrews believed that the stars were made and controlled by God (*Gen.* 1, 16; *Ps.* 8, 3; *Isa.* 13, 10; *Jer.* 31, 35). Among heathen peoples there was star worship (*Deut.* 4, 19; *2 Kings* 17, 16; 21, 5; 23, 5). They believed that their fault could be in their stars and not in themselves (*Judg.* 5, 20). There was a science of astrology (qv) which claimed to be able to read the future in the stars. Almost every popular newspaper has such a section to-day. The day star (*2 Pet.* 1, 19) may be the sign of the Second Coming, or the light of the Holy Spirit in the human heart. The morning star (*Rev.* 2, 28) refs. prob. to older apocalyptic literature (*Dan.* 12, 3; etc.). The other ref. (*Rev.* 22, 16) is to Christ as the herald of the destruction of darkness.

Star of the Magi. Various attempts have been made to relate the appearance of the star of the nativity to natural phenomena, arguing that it could have been a comet, or that it was a conjunction of Jupiter and Saturn which is known to have occurred in 7 BC; or of Venus and Jupiter which occurred in 6 BC. It is known that all over the Mediterranean world at the time of the birth of Jesus there was an expectancy of the arrival of a great one. The appearance of any starry phenomenon might very readily have been connected to this, and set the Magi (qv) travelling. It is just possible that Babylonian scholars remembered the old prophecy of Balaam, and that this expectancy was traditional (*Num.* 24, 17).

Stater. A shekel (*Matt.* 17, 27 RV marg.). *See*
MONEY.

Steel. The metal as it is known to-day was not
widely known in scriptural times, though the
Chalybes of Pontus had the secret of hardening
and tempering iron. Where the word is used in the
AV it should be brass as in RV. In one ref (*Nahum*
2, 3) RV correctly has steel, while AV wrongly
has ' torches.' *See* MINES AND MINING.

Stephanas [stĕ'-phă-năs]. A Corinthian of some
status whose family were the first converts of Paul
in Achaia. Paul baptised them. Stephanas later
came to Paul's help in Ephesus (*1 Cor.* 1, 16;
16, 15 & 17).

Stephen. The first Christian martyr. He was one
of 7 ' deacons' appointed to relieve the apostles of
administrative work (*Acts* 6). He did not confine
himself to the distribution of charity, however,
but became a forceful and successful evangelist.
He was prob. a Hellenist (qv). This roused the
hostility of other Hellenists in Jerusalem, and the
synagogues of the Libertines (qv) and of the
Cyrenians and Alexandrines charged him with
blaspheming agst. Moses and God, and with
preaching that Jesus would destroy the Temple
and the Mosaic law. He was charged with this
before the Sanhedrin, and made a long defence
which is really a summary of Heb. history from
Abraham to the building of the Temple of Solomon. the argument being that the Jews had read
their own Law wrong; God was not confined to
Tabernacle and Temple. He had been there and
in communication with men long before either
was thought of. The people who had persecuted
the prophets for saying this, had now killed Jesus
for saying it. They would hear no more, but
dragged him out and stoned him. The Sanhedrin

(qv) had no authority to sentence to death, and this was really a lynching. It was followed by general persecution during which the apostles had to escape from Jerusalem, thus bringing the new faith out and beginning its world wide mission. It is quite prob. that the young man at whose feet the executioners laid their outer garments was Saul of Tarsus, and that his ultimate conversion was partly made possible by the haunting memories of that dreadful day, and of Stephen whose face like was an angel's, who died saying, ' Lord, lay not this sin to their charge.'

Stocks. A wooden frame in which the feet were clamped so that a condemned person had to sit in an uncomfortably upright position, exposed, of course, to the public view and insult. There was another form involving shackles, where the body was twisted into a position of extreme discomfort and pain (*Job* 13, 27; 33, 11; *Acts* 16, 24; *Jer.* 20, 2; 29, 26). *See* CRIME AND PUNISHMENT.

Stoics. The name derives from Gk. *stoa*, a porch or portico, in which the philosopher Zeno of Cyprus taught c. BC 340-265. Their maxim was ' live naturally.' The highest essence of nature is reason, which is the animating spirit of all things, and the very soul of man. It is wrong to assume that they had a god whom they called the world spirit (*Acts* 17, 28). They were pantheistic; they believed that God and the universe were identical. God was not a being; He was everything but had no separate existence. They insisted so much on the rule of reason that they resisted every impulse which might be called emotional. They were moralists, but in a cold, austere way. It was, however, of all the philosophies, the only one whose moral standards approached those of

Christianity. Paul may have had the idea of bringing the two together, but neither he nor anyone else succeeded in doing that (*Acts* 17, 18).

Stomacher. A kind of feminine waistcoat covering the breast and the pit of the stomach and often richly embroidered or ornamented. It is not certain if this is the exact meaning of the Heb. RSV trans. simply 'robe' (*Isa*, 3, 24).

Stone(s). The word has the same wide use as the Eng. word. Palestine is a very rocky and stony country, and stones were put to all kinds of uses, from a pillow (*Gen.* 28, 18) to a well-cover (*Gen.* 29, 2). There were stone (flint RV) knives and implements (*Ex.* 4, 25; etc.). In building there were foundation stones and corner stones. *See* HOUSE. The headstone is really the finial, or ornamental stone on the top of roof or gable (*Zech.* 4, 7). Masonry was a recognised trade, as was stone-dressing and quarrying (*2 Sam.* 5, 11; *2 Kings* 12, 12). Stones were used in fighting. *See* SLING. And, of course, stoning to death was a common means of execution. For precious stones *see* JEWELS AND PRECIOUS STONES. Stones were also used as memorials (*Gen.* 31, 45; *Josh.* 8, 29; 24, 26); and as boundary and landmarks (*Josh.* 15, 6; *Deut.* 19, 14). In worship, stone pillars and altars were common (*Gen.* 28, 18 & 22; 31, 45; etc.). Important writings were inscribed on stones (*Ex.* 24, 12; *Deut.* 27, 2; *Josh.* 8, 30; etc.). The 'white stone' (*Rev.* 2, 17) is some kind of amulet used figuratively. A 'living stone' is the natural unworked stone (*Eph.* 2, 20-22; *1 Pet.* 2, 4-8). The word is used also of the hard heart (*1 Sam.* 25, 37; *Ezek.* 36, 26), and of firmness (*Job* 6, 12; 41, 24). The word is also used for the testicles (*Lev.* 21, 20; *Deut.* 23, 1; *Job* 40, 17) as RSV.

Stonesquarers. (*1 Kings* 5, 18 AV.) This is more prob. Gebalites or men of Gebal (*Ezek.* 27, 9).

Stoning. Always took place outside the city. The executioners placed their hands on the victim's head in token that the guilt was all his. The actual witnesses threw the first stones. Thereafter all took part. The body might be hung up after death (*Lev.* 24, 14; *Deut.* 13, 9; 21, 23; *Josh.* 7, 25; *John* 8, 7; *Acts* 7, 58). *See* CRIME AND PUNISHMENT.

Stool. More or less any kind of seat. The ref. (*Ex.* 1, 16) is to a birthstool (qv) but is really 2 stones upon which a Heb. woman sat or crouched during childbirth.

Stork. Migrant storks arrive in Palestine in the spring, and are great favourites (*Jer.* 8, 7). They clear the growing crops of pests. Although it is named as being ceremonially unclean (*Lev.* 11, 19; *Deut.* 14, 18) it is quite prob. that this was to protect the stork. Its name in Heb. means ' devotedly affectionate,' a tribute to the bird's care for its young. In Palestine it is mainly the white stork that is known, *ciconia alba*.

Strait. Narrow and, by allusion, strict.

Stranger. Sometimes the word means foreigner as distinct from Israelite, and may even have the sense of one estranged (*Hos.* 7, 9; 8, 7; etc.). There is also a meaning of a layman as distinct from a Levite or priest (*Num.* 1, 51; etc.). RSV here has ' if anyone else come near.' Otherwise the word means more or less the same as in mod. Eng.: a person not known, an incomer, a visitor. RV often uses sojourner in preference to stranger. Orig. the Heb. *ger*, was a man who exchanged one tribe or clan for another, seeking the rights and privileges of a native. The Gibeonites (*Josh.* 9) and the Beerothites, were *gerim*, or stranger clans,

as all Israel were sojourners in Egypt (*Ex.* 22, 21).
The sojourner was to be helped and protected,
and allowed to take part in the 3 great feasts, but
he did not have to adopt his 'host's' religion
(*Deut.* 10, 18; 14, 29; 24, 14 & 17; 16, 11; *I
Kings* 11, 7). The sojourner is not allowed to
marry into the clan (*Deut.* 10, 18; 23, 4). Later
the word proselyte becomes almost interchangeable with sojourner. He is the non-Jew, living in
the Jewish way, and expected to perform religious
offices (*Lev.* 16, 29). He eats unleavened bread
during Passover week (*Ex.* 12, 19). He cannot
belong to the congregation until he is circumcised.
There is no compulsion that he must be circumcised, however (*Ex.* 12, 47; etc.). After the Exile
the sojourner seems to have been completely drawn
into Jewry as the proselyte who had been circumcised (*Matt.* 23, 15; *Acts* 2, 10).

Strangling. Death by suffocation, not necessarily
by hanging (*2 Sam.* 17, 23) where AV has ' hanged
himself' (*Job* 7, 15). Christians were urged to
refrain from eating ' things strangled' (*Acts* 15,
29). This was a food (qv) taboo. All things killed
had to be bled.

Straw, Stubble. Neither word means quite what the
mod. Eng. word means. In Scripture straw is
chopped stalks of wheat or barley, mixed prob.
with pulses and used as animal fodder. In other
words, the threshings. Stubble is the stalk as it
was left in the ground after reaping. They did not
cut down to the ground but left a fair amount of
stalk standing. This was later burned to fertilise
the ground before the next ploughing (*Jer.* 23,
28). In this ref. RV uses straw and AV chaff.
Neither word conveys quite the meaning. RSV
also has straw. The 2 Heb. words are *teben* and
qash. In Egypt the Hebrews gathered ' stubble

for straw.' In other words they were not given *teben* to mix with the clay, so they gathered *qash*. *Teben* is the word also in other refs. where the trans. is ' driven stubble ' (*Isa.* 5, 24; 41, 2; 47, 14).

Stripes. *See* CRIME AND PUNISHMENT.

Strong drink. *See* WINE AND STRONG DRINK.

Stubble. *See* STRAW.

Stuff. (*Luke* 17, 31; etc. AV.) Furniture in the mod. sense.

Stumbling block. Lit. ' the spring of a trap ': that which trips up or ensnares. Also trans. ' offence '; occasion to fall ': ' cause to stumble.'

Suburb. **1.** Within the precincts (*1 Kings* 23, 11; *1 Chron.* 26, 18 AV). **2.** Pasture ground immediately outside the walls of Levitical cities, set apart for the Levites (*Num.* 35, 2 ff.).

Succoth [sŭc'-cŏth]. **1.** Place E of Jordan where Jacob built a house with byres for his cattle, after which he called the place (*Gen.* 33, 17; *Judg.* 8, 4 & 5). It was near Zarethan in the Jordan and by the time of Gideon was of some importance (*Judg.* 8, 5-16). **2.** Camping ground of Israel after leaving Rameses (*Ex.* 12, 37; *Num.* 33, 5 & 6).

Succoth Benoth [sŭc'-cŏth bĕn'-ŏth]. Babylonian idol in Samaria (*2 Kings* 17, 30).

Sumer(ians). *See* BABYLONIA.

Sun. Regarded as the greatest and most important of the heavenly bodies (*Gen.* 1, 16). One case of death by sunstroke is mentioned (*2 Kings* 4, 18 & 19). There is a description of a sundial of sorts (*2 Kings* 20, 9 & 11; *Isa.* 38, 8). *See* TIME. They knew of and described eclipses, attributing them to the power of God (*Joel* 2, 31; *Rev.* 6, 12). Sun worship is, of course, common among primitive peoples (*Gen.* 37, 9; *Deut.* 4, 19). The punishment for sun worship among the Hebrews was death

(*Deut.* 17, 3). Sun images were popular in the reign of Asa (*2 Chron.* 14, 5), but Josiah stamped out all practices connected with sun worship (*2 Kings* 23, 5 & 11; *2 Chron.* 34, 4 & 7). Sun worship was actually practised in the Temple, with the worshippers facing away from the Temple and to the E (*Ezek.* 8, 16).

Suph [sūph]. (*Deut.* 1, 1 RV and RSV.) If this is a place its locality is unknown. The AV could well be right in calling it the Red Sea, or Sea of Weeds. *Suph* means ' weeds ' and it could be that the word for ' sea ' has been lost in the Heb. text. This would make sense. It would then be the Gulf of Akabah.

Supper. *See* MEALS.

Supper, Last. *See* LORD'S SUPPER.

Surety. A person who stands as guarantor of another's obligations (*Prov.* 22, 26 & 27). The writer of *Proverbs* had evidently suffered from going surety for a stranger (*Prov.* 11, 15; 17, 18; 20, 16).

Susa [sū'-sa]. *See* SHUSHAN.

Susanna. Woman who served Jesus (*Luke* 8, 3).

Susanna, Book of. *See* APOCRYPHA.

Swaddling band. A cross bet. diapers and what the Scots call a barry coat. It was a wrapping for new born children (*Job* 38, 9; *Ezek.* 16, 4; *Luke* 2, 7 & 12).

Swallow. Not all refs. are to the true swallow, which nests under the eaves of buildings, quite regardless of whether they are the houses of men or the House of God, but some are (*Ps.* 84, 3; *Prov.* 26, 2). There is some uncertainty about the bird ref. to (*Isa.* 38, 14; *Jer.* 8, 7). Some think it is the crane, others that it is the swift.

Swan. The true swan is not at all common in Palestine and there is more chance that the bird ref. to is the horned owl, or even a lizard of sorts. (*Lev.* 11, 18 RV marg.; *Deut.* 14, 16).

Swearing. *See* OATH.

Sweat, bloody. In medicine this is not uncommon. It is known as diapedesis. It is the oozing of blood through the capillaries (*Luke* 22, 44).

Swine. There is a theory that in very ancient times pigs were regarded as sacrosanct, and that this is the reason why Jews (and Mohammedans) are not allowed to eat their flesh (*Lev.* 11, 7; *Deut.* 14, 8; *Isa.* 65, 4; 66, 3 & 17). The word 'pig' was a byword then as it is to-day (*Prov.* 11, 22; *Matt.* 7, 6; *2 Pet.* 2, 22).

Sword. *See* ARMS AND ARMOUR.

Sycamine. The black mulberry, *morus nigra* (*Luke* 17, 6).

Sychar [sȳ'-chär]. A town of Samaria. It is not Shechem (*Gen.* 48, 22; *John* 4, 5).

Sycomore. *Ficus sycomorus.* It is not the sycamore tree, but is in fact a fig tree. The figs are not of much worth, but the timber is valuable (*1 Kings* 10, 27; *Isa.* 9, 10; *Amos* 7, 14).

Symeon. **1.** Ancestor of Jesus (*Luke* 3, 30). **2.** Teacher at Antioch (*Acts* 13, 1). **3.** Simon Peter (qv) (*Acts* 15, 14 AV).

Synagogue. It is a Gk. word meaning simply a place of meeting. For the Jews it was at once the local place of worship, a court of law and the day school for the children of the town or village. Although before the Exile the real place of worship was the Jerusalem Temple, there was a great deal that could be done at the local level in the synagogue (*Jer.* 36, 6 & 10 & 12-15). During the Exile there was, of course, no access to the Temple, and it was during this period that the synagogue became really important. It could never take the place of the Temple as the centre of sacrifice, but it became the place of instruction which kept the old religion alive. The word is used only once in the OT (*Ps.* 74, 8 AV where RV has ' place of assembly '). But by NT times there was a synagogue wherever there was a colony of Jews (*Acts* 13, 5; 14, 1; 17, 10). In Jerusalem there were many synagogues (*Acts* 6, 9). Each synagogue was controlled and administered by its own board of elders (*Luke* 7, 3-5). There was one or more ' ruler of the synagogue ' (*Acts* 18, 8). He or they were responsible for the proper conduct of the services (*Luke* 13, 14). There was no fixed ministry, but any person, qualified in the opinion of the ruler, might take part (*Matt.* 4, 23; *Luke* 4, 16). In this regard it was not unlike a Quaker meeting. When Paul and Barnabas came to the synagogue at Pisidian Antioch, they were asked to speak (*Acts* 13, 15). With the rulers there were subordinates who carried on the work more or less of church officer, except that when necessary they carried out the sentences of the synagogue on people who had transgressed. There were other officials who attended to matters charitable (*Matt.* 6, 2). They assembled every Sabbath (*Acts* 15, 21) and on the 2nd and 5th days of the week for scripture reading. The readings were in the main out of *Deuteronomy* (6, 4-9; 11, 13-21) and *Numbers* (15, 37-41). The people stood during the prayers (*Matt.* 6, 5; *Mark* 11, 25). Prayers were offered ' from the floor of the house ' and anyone might come forward to read Scripture. There could be an exposition of the passage read (*Luke* 4, 16-22). There was a reading desk, seats for some of the more important worshippers, and a chest, or press, for holding the scrolls of the Scriptures (*Matt.* 23, 6; *Jas.* 2, 2 & 3). Men sat on one side, and women on the other. There was a kind of punishment chamber where the sentences of the synagogue were carried out (*Matt.* 10, 17; *Acts* 22, 19). The Great Synagogue was organised by Nehemiah c. 410 BC to be a kind of House of Commons. Ezra was its president, but later its functions were taken over by the Sanhedrin (qv).

Synoptics. *See* GOSPELS.

Syntiche [sўn'-tĭch-ē]. Christian woman of Philippi (*Philip.* 4, 2).

Syracuse [sȳr'-ă-cūse]. Sicilian city founded c. 735 BC. It was at its height c. 400, but was taken by the Romans c. 212. Paul was there on his voyage to Rome (*Acts* 28, 12).

Syria. An ancient country which embraced old Canaan and Aram. It became a Rom. province with the governor living at the main city, Antioch. The name came to mean the territory lying to the W of the Euphrates and the Taurus mts. to the Egyptian border.

Syrian. Native of Syria. But in the OT when the word is used it means an Aramean (*Gen.* 28, 5.)

Syrtis [sўr'-tis]. Quicksands (qv).

T

Taanach [tā'-ă-năch]. Canaanite city taken by Joshua (12, 21). The battle bet. Sisera and Barak was fought in the vicinity (*Judg.* 5, 19).

Tabeal [tă'-bē-ăl] **Tabeel.** Puppet claimant for the throne (*Isa.* 7, 6). Also a Persian magistrate (*Ezra* 4, 7).

Taber, Tabering. (*Nahum* 2, 7 AV). Tabor is a drum or tambourine. Tabering is drumming—'beating the breast.'

Tabernacle. The tent set up to shelter the Ark of

Tab 578 **Tab**

the Covenant when Israel was travelling to the
Promised Land. The oldest documents describe
it as a simple thing which stood outside the camp
(*Ex.* 33, 7-11). Later writers, prob. under priestly
influence, make it much more elaborate, and site
it in the centre of the camp (*Ex.* 25-27). The
materials for its building were all available at the
place and time (*Ex.* 35, 21-29). It contained the
Ark, the table for the shewbread and the candela-
brum (*Ex.* 25, 10-40). The whole service and
approach to it is laid down (*Ex.* chs. 28 & 29).
Dimensions were 45 ft. by 15 ft., and the entrance
was on the E. On 3 sides of the walls were boards
which could be dismantled, and the other side
was curtained. The walls were 15 ft. high. Pillars
held the curtains and there were more pillars
inside, supporting curtains to screen off the Holy
of Holies, which was 15 ft. square. The ceiling
was a tent of linen or muslin, and cloth draped
the walls too. Drapes of goats' hair hung down
outside, and the whole stood in a fenced enclosure
150 ft. by 75 ft. The laver and the altar stood in
the enclosure but outside the Tabernacle, while
the Ark was in the Holy of Holies and just outside
it the altar of incense with the table of shewbread
on its right and the Golden Candlestick on the
left. The Levites were responsible for dismantling
and re-erecting it (*Ex.* 40, 34-38). After the conquest Joshua brought it out from its temporary
site at Gilgal to Shiloh (*Josh.* 18, 1). The erection
was prob. made more permanent. When the
Philistines captured the Ark (*Ps.* 78, 60) in Saul's
day, the Tabernacle was at Nob (*1 Sam.* 21, 1;
Mark 2, 26). In David's and Solomon's day it
was at Gibeon (*1 Chron.* 16, 39). When the new
Temple was built to double the scale of the Tabernacle, the old Tabernacle was dismantled and

Tab 579 **Tac**

stored in the Temple (*1 Kings* 8, 4). *See* TENT OF MEETING.

Tabernacles, Feast of. One of the 3 Feasts of obligation, it was a harvest festival (*Deut.* 16, 16; etc.). Booths, or rough brush shelters were built (*Lev.* 23, 40; *Neh.* 8, 16) to remind them of the march to Canaan; but also prob. because such shelters were useful in the fields at harvest time so that the ripe crops might be watched and guarded (*Ex.* 23, 16). It was held in the 7th month on the 15th day and lasted a week. Sacrifices were made (*Num.* 29, 12-34). It followed the Day of Atonement. Later the celebrations achieved an elaborate pattern and ritual (*Isa.* 12, 3) which included libations and illuminations, and these were prob. used by Jesus to point a moral (*John* 7, 37; 8, 12).

Tabitha [tă'-bĭth-ă]. *See* DORCAS.

Table. *See* HOUSE.

Table, tablet. A writing tablet usually of stone (*Ex.* 24, 12), but also of wax (*Luke* 1, 63). In some refs. the trans. is prob. wrong and the words should be necklaces, or bracelets as RSV (*Ex.* 35, 22; *Num.* 31, 50 AV).

Tabor [tā'-bŏr]. Mt. in Issachar (*Jer.* 46, 18) where the armies gathered to fight Sisera (*Judg.* 4, 6). It is almost 2,000 ft. high. There is a trad. that the mt. was the scene of the Transfiguration (*Mark* 9, 2-8).

Tabret. A timbrel (qv) (*1 Sam.* 10, 5). One AV passage is wrong (*Job* 17, 6). ' Aforetime I was as a tabret ' should be ' I have become someone to be spat on in the face.'

Taches [tă'-ches]. Hooks, cleats or clasps (*Ex.* 26, 6).

Tackling. The running and standing gear of a ship (*Isa.* 33, 23; *Acts* 27, 19).

Tahpanhes [tăhp'-ă-nĕs]. Egyptian city where Jews settled (*Jer.* 44, 1; *Ezek.* 30, 18).

Tahpenes [tăh'-pĕn-ĕs]. Queen of Egypt in time of Solomon (*1 Kings* 11, 19).

Talent. See MONEY, WEIGHTS AND MEASURES.

Talitha Cumi [tă-lĭth-ă cū'-mĭ]. Aram. ' Get up, lassie ' (*Mark* 5, 41) addressed by Jesus to Jairus' daughter.

Talmai [tăl'-mă-ĭ]. Son of Anak (*Josh.* 15, 14). Also king of Geshur whose daughter was Absalom's mother (*2 Sam.* 3, 3).

Talmud [tăl'-mŭd]. A compilation of Jewish writings over several centuries. Jewish scholars spent much time debating points of law—the Torah. These discussions of the years bet. AD 70 and AD 200, were gathered together in the Mishna, and were committed to writing. During the next 300 years these Mishna were debated, discussed, amended and expanded, and the combined work became the Talmud.

Tamar [tă-măr], **Thamar. 1.** Wife of Er the son of Judah; mother of Perez and Zerah (*Gen.* 38, 24-30). **2.** Absalom's sister, seduced by Amnon (*2 Sam.* 13). **3.** Daughter of Absalom (*2 Sam.* 14, 27). **4.** Desert town; also spelled Tadmor (*1 Kings* 9, 18). **5.** Frontier town of Palestine (*Ezek.* 47, 19).

Tamarisk. A small tree, *tamarix articulata*, thought to yield the food known as manna (qv).

Tammuz [tăm'-mŭz]. Babylonian god, who gave his name to the 4th month of the Jews. He was king of the underworld (*Ezek.* 8, 14).

Tanner. A dresser of hides. *See* ARTS AND CRAFTS.

Taphath [tăph'-ăth]. Daughter of Solomon (*1 Kings* 4, 11).

Tares. (*Matt.* 13, 24-30). Prob. the bearded darnel, a poisonous grass not unlike wheat when green.

The true tare is a vetch which looks nothing like wheat.

Target. A targe or shield. *See* ARMOUR.

Targum [tăr'-gŭm]. A trans. of Scripture from Heb. into Aram. (*Ezra* 4, 7). This was for use in synagogues where the people did not understand classical Heb.

Tarshish [tär'-shĭsh], **Tharshish**. The town to which Jonah was sent (*Jonah* 1, 3). Its site has not been positively identified but it was far to the W, poss. in Spain. Ships of Tarshish were orig. ships in the Tarshish trade, but the name came to be applied to any ship capable of making the voyage.

Tarsus [tär'-sŭs]. Asia Minor city of Cilicia on the R. Cydnus. It is very ancient, having been established about 1000 BC, or even earlier. It became the seat of government under the Romans and its universities were world famous. Here Paul was born, and he revisited it at least once (*Acts* 21, 39; 22, 3; etc.).

Tartan [tär'-tăn]. The official title of the commander-in-chief of the Assyrian army (*2 Kings* 18, 17; *Isa.* 20, 1).

Tassel. *See* BORDER OF GARMENT.

Tattenai [tăt'-těn-āī]. Persian Governor who opposed Ezra (*5*, 3; 6, 6).

Tau [tau]. Last letter of the Heb. alphabet, T, or Th when followed by a vowel.

Taverns, Three. Village on the Appian way about 33 m. S of Rome (*Acts* 28, 15).

Taxes. At the time of the Judges there were ecclesiastical but not civil taxes. When the monarchy was introduced civil taxes appeared. These were in kind rather than in cash (*1 Kings* 4, 7-28). Tribute was exacted from conquered peoples (*2 Sam.* 8, 6). The people objected to Solomon's taxes (*1 Kings* 12, 4). In the Persian Empire each territory had its quota of taxes to meet (*Neh.* 5, 15). Under the Romans the system varied, but latterly the taxes (or the right to levy them) was farmed out by auction. The right to gather the taxes of a district was sold to the highest bidder. The tax on the soil remained, plus a poll tax (*Matt.* 22, 17) and a property tax. In addition there were Customs duties. After the exile, each Israelite over 20 years of age had to pay half a shekel each year for the Temple (*Matt.* 17, 24-27). *See* PUB-LICAN, TRIBUTE.

Taxing. (*Matt.* 2, 5 & 6; *Luke* 2, 1-7.) This was really a census. A later one caused riots. *See* QUIRINIUS, THEUDAS.

Teaching, Teacher. *See* EDUCATION.

Teil tree. Mistrans. for terebinth (qv) or oak (qv) (*Isa.* 6, 13).

Tekel [tĕ-kĕl]. *See* MENE.

Tekoa(h) [tĕ-kō'-ä]. Town of Judah near Engedi, fortified by Rehoboam. Here Amos lived (*2 Chron.* 11, 6; 20, 20; *Neh.* 3, 5 & 27; *Amos* 1, 1).

Telaim [tē-lā'-ĭm]. Prob. the same as Telem below (*Josh.* 15, 24). Saul concentrated his army here agst. Amalek (*1 Sam.* 15, 4). It was in the S of Judah.

Telem [tēl'-ĕm]. *See* TELAIM.

Tema [tĕ'-mă]. Son of Ishmael, and his clan (*Gen.* 25, 15; etc.).

Teman [tĕ'-măn]. Tribe desc. from Esau and their country in the N of Edom (*Gen.* 36, 11).

Temanite. Name applied to a friend of Job (2, 11).

Temperance. Trans. of Gk. word meaning ' self control ' (*Acts* 24, 25; *Gal.* 5, 23). Its opposite is also found (*Matt.* 23, 25; *1 Cor.* 7, 5; *2 Tim.* 3, 3). Self indulgence is not confined to drink (*1 Thes.* 5, 6; *2 Tim.* 4, 5; *1 Pet.* 1, 13; 4, 7; 5, 8). This grace is a gift of the Holy Spirit (*Eph.* 3, 16).

It is the control over every appetite and the
avoidance of any excess, eg, lust (*1 Cor.* 7, 5);
drink (*1 Tim.* 3, 3); quarrelling, lying, boasting and
greed (v. 8); conceit (v. 6). All through the NT
it is hailed as a cardinal virtue.

Temple. Generally, any building erected for the
worship of a god, but the main ref. is to the Temple
at Jerusalem. There was more than one. **1.** Solomon's Temple. David started to collect the
materials for the building of the first permanent
abode of Jehovah, but it was left to his son to
start and complete the work (*2 Sam.* 7; *1 Chron.*
22; 28, 11—29, 9). The total cost was 108,000
talents of gold, 10,000 darics of gold, and 1,017,000
talents of silver. *See* MONEY. At least that is what
Chronicles says about it, though there may well
be exaggeration. The money was not all spent
(*1 Kings* 7, 51). It took 7½ years to build and the
site was Mt. Moriah (*1 Kings* 6, 1 & 38; *2 Chron.*
3, 1). The plan was simply the Tabernacle (qv)
on a larger scale. Inside it was 90 ft. long, 30
broad and 30 high—twice the scale of the Tabernacle. It was, however, built of stone (*1 Kings* 6),
with a roof of cedar and a floor of fir. The inside
walls were overlaid with gold. The Holy of Holies
followed the same convention as the Tabernacle,
and was 30 ft. square and high, with latticed windows, or ventilators, in the roof or near it. The
altar of incense stood outside the Holy of Holies.
There were 10 candelabra, really lampstands, and
10 tables for the shewbread. On the outer walls
there was lodging for the priests, and in front was
the portico with the 2 brazen pillars, Boaz and
Jachin. The main court was the Court of the
People, and within it, at a different level, was the
Court of the Priests. These were separated by a
low wall. The altar of sacrifice was in the Priests'

Court ((*1 Kings* 8, 64) with water for the priests to wash themselves, and lavers to wash the vessels (*1 Kings* 7, 23-39). Solomon's Temple was plundered and burned by the Babylonians in 586 BC (*2 Kings* 25, 8-17). **2.** Jerubbabel's Temple was authorised by Cyrus after the return from the exile, and was to be 90 ft. square and high. Work was started in the 2nd year after the return, and then was stopped because of the opposition of the Samaritans (qv). It was begun again in 520 BC, and was finished 5 years later. In the end it turned out to be more or less a copy of Solomon's Temple but more modest and less elaborate. Some of the captured Temple vessels were returned (*Ezra* 1, 7-11). There was the altar of incense, one candlestick, and one table for the shewbread. There was also the priests' lodging and the usual courts (*Neh.* 10, 37-39). **3.** Herod's Temple. The old building was demolished and the new begun in 20 BC. Work went on intermittently till AD 64. The plan followed the shape of Solomon's Temple, but the new one was 60 ft. high and built of blocks of white stone. The Holy of Holies was of course still empty—there was no Ark of the Covenant, and was separated from the Court by a veil (*Matt.* 27, 51). The gate to the Holy of Holies was on the E, and had doors 75 ft. high and 24 ft. broad. The whole structure stepped up towards the Holy of Holies, which was of 2 storeys. Surrounding the Temple was a great pillared Court—the Court of the Gentiles. On the E Solomon's Porch looked down to the valley of the Kidron; and on the W was the Tyropoeon Valley. The Royal porch was on the S side. The Temple itself had the Beautiful Gate, or Gate of Nicanor, on the E, opening on to the Court of the Women, surrounded by the Women's Gallery. Moving W straight through an opening was the Court of Israel, with a vast altar of Burnt Offering. Contained within the Court of Israel was the Court of the Priests, and within it, the Holy Place, reached by a porch and with the Holy of Holies beyond. The Jews used this Temple as a citadel when Titus besieged Jerusalem, and with the Rom. victory, the Temple was completely destroyed in AD 70.

Temptation. Gen. in the OT, to tempt means to test or to prove, except, poss. (*Deut.* 4, 34; *Mal.* 3, 15). The Heb. word is *Nissah* which has been misread in one ref. (*Ps.* 95, 8) where it should be the place name Massah (*Deut.* 33, 8). The same idea of temptation as a test or proof persists in the NT, though it can have the sense of enticement to sin (*Matt.* 4, 1; *1 Cor.* 7, 5; *Rev.* 2, 10). The use of the word in the Lord's Prayer is different, however, for it is unthinkable that God would ever try to persuade His children to sin (cf. *Jas.* 1, 13). Prob. the best way to think of this is to remember the nature of Jesus' own Temptation (*Matt.* 4). This must have been in His mind when he formed the prayer that we now know as the Lord's Prayer. In it He asks God not to require Him to go through again what He went through before in the wilderness. The same idea appears again in His Gethsemane prayer (*Matt.* 26, 42).

Ten. *See* NUMBERS.

Ten Commandments. Trad. is that these laws or ' words ' were given orally by God to Moses on Sinai. Moses engraved them on 2 stones which were accidentally broken. They were re-inscribed. Later these stones were placed in the Ark of the Covenant and were lost when the Ark was lost (*Ex.* 20; 24, 12; 31, 18; 32, 19; *Deut.* 10, 1-5; *1 Kings* 8, 9). Two versions of the Command-

ments appear (*Ex.* 20; *Deut.* 5) and these are
prob. expanded versions of something much
earlier and much shorter (even single) clauses
which revisionists reckoned should be more detailed. Whether they originated in Moses or not,
they form the earliest and the fundamental law
of the Heb. people. As Church and State evolved,
the laws became more precise and definite, and
even complicated; but the foundation is still the
first statement from which the 2 Decalogues sprang.
See LAW, DEUTERONOMY, SABBATH, etc. Jesus went
back to the simple, pithy form without elaborations (*Mark* 10, 19).

Tent. This was exactly what is meant to-day by a
tent. There were and are many shapes and sizes,
but in Bible times they were made mainly of a
dark cloth woven from goats' hair. They were
supported by guys (*Job* 4, 21 RSV) and by tent
pegs (*Judg.* 4, 21). In the army, when on the
march, they built bivouacs (*2 Sam.* 11, 11). A
newly married couple had a new tent pitched for
them (*Ps.* 19, 5). Priscilla, Aquila and Paul were
tent makers.

Tent of Meeting. The Tabernacle of the Congregation. After the incident of the Golden Calf,
Moses told the people that God was estranged,
and pitched his tent away from the rest of the
camp (*Ex* 33, 7). From it he dispensed justice,
and there the people could consult God (*Ex.* 18,
13-26).

Terah [tě'-răh]. Father of Abraham, Noagor and
Haran (*Gen.* 11, 24-32).

Teraphim [tě'-ră-phĭm]. Household gods (cf. Rom.
Lares et Penates). They were gen. small images
(*Gen.* 31, 19) but could be any size (*1 Sam.* 19,
13). Samuel condemned them (*1 Sam.* 15, 23).

Terebinth [tě'-rě-bĭnth]. The word does not occur

in the AV. It is the turpentine tree, and may be
the tree of refs. in addition to those in RV (*Isa.*
6, 13).

Teresh [tē'-rĕsh]. Chamberlain of Ahasuerus (*Esth.*
2, 21).

Tertius [tĕr'-tĭ-ŭs]. Clerk who wrote the Epistle
to the Romans at Paul's dictation (*Rom.* 16,
22).

Tertullus [tĕr-tŭl'-lŭs]. Counsel for the Prosecution
at the trial of Paul before Felix (*Acts* 24, 1-8).

Testament. The word does not occur in the OT. In
the NT it is sometimes trans. Testament and sometimes Covenant. LXX sometimes trans. the Heb.
as *diatheke*—a testamentary disposition; where it
should have been *syntheke*—a covenant. Lat.
versions trans. always as *testamentum* which
changed the Books of the Old and New Covenants
into the Books of the Old and New Testaments.
Covenant is better. *See* NEW TESTAMENT.

Testimony. *See* ARK, TABERNACLE, WITNESS,
ORNAMENTS (*2 Kings* 11, 12).

Teth. 9th letter of Heb. alphabet; pronounced *T*.

Tetrarch. Lit. ' ruler of a quarter of a territory,'
the word came to mean a minor prince. Herod
was T. of Galilee, Philip T. of Ituraea; and
Lysanius T. of Abilene (*Luke* 3, 1).

Thaddaeus [thăd-dae'-ŭs]. Name of one of the 12
disciples (*Matt.* 10, 3; *Mark* 3, 18); elsewhere
called Judas, not Iscariot (*Luke* 6, 16).

Thank Offering. *See* OFFERINGS.

Theatre. Has more or less the same meaning as
to-day, but it was usually in the open air—a semi-
circular excavation in a hillside, cut into steps for
seats. These theatres held very large crowds of
people (*Acts* 19, 29).

Thebes [thēbes]. *See* NO.

Theophilus [thē-ŏ'-phĭl-ŭs]. Person addressed in

Luke's prefaces to the Gospel and the Acts (*Luke* 1, 3; *Acts* 1, 1).

Thessalonians, Epistles of Paul the Apostle to the. The book is accepted as genuinely Pauline, and has been from the time of Irenaeus. It was written shortly after Paul had left Thessalonica and had arrived at Athens (*1 Thess.* 3, 1). From there he went to Corinth and was rejoined by Timothy. Allowing time for these journeys and for residence and work at Athens and Corinth where he wrote the letter, the date of the 1st epistle must be about AD 52. The authenticity of the 2nd epistle is not quite so clear, mainly because one passage (*2 Thess.* 2, 1-12) seems out of character with Paul's convictions on the Second Coming, as they are expressed in the 1st letter. The chances are, however, that some members of the church at Thessalonica had taken too lit. Paul's view that the Second Coming was imminent. The 2nd epistle, in this regard, could be a corrective to the 1st. Neither letter can be classed as one of Paul's great statements of faith. He deals in the main with practical matters. They had been neglecting their work and their duty under the impression that the end of the world was at hand; and they were at the same time worried in case Christian friends of theirs who had died would miss the glories of the Kingdom. Paul gives them sound practical advice about their responsibilities. In date, the 2nd letter follows the 1st closely. *See* ANTICHRIST.

Thessalonica [thĕs'-să-lŏn'-ĭ-kă]. City on the Gulf of Salonika called orig. Therme and later renamed in honour of Thessalonike, daughter of Alexander the Great and wife of Cassander. It was the Rom. capital of a quarter of Macedonia. The Jews had a synagogue there, and Paul visited it (*Acts* 17, 1-13).

Theudas [theū'-däs]. Could be Judas the Gaulonite of Gamala, who raised a revolt during the governorship of Quirinius (qv). What sparked off the rebellion was this man's objection to the enrolment, the same one that brought Mary and Joseph to Bethlehem (*Acts* 5, 36 & 37). There is a ref. to another Theudas, a magician, and there always has been some doubt about identification.

Thief. A general term for a sneak-thief (*John* 12, 6), a highwayman or foot-pad (*Luke* 10, 30), a burglar or housebreaker (*Matt.* 6, 20). Barrabas (*Mark* 15, 7), would be more of a political outlaw living by banditry. In Mosaic law a convicted thief had to repay twice what he stole. If he were killed in the dark while housebreaking it was not homicide. During daylight, it was (*Ex.* 22, 1-4). The thieves at Calvary had been responsible, on their own admission, for something fairly serious (*Luke* 23, 41).

Thigh. Hip and thigh, or leg and thigh (*Judg.* 15, 8) is subject to several explanations, but in hand-to-hand fighting it was a tactic to slash at the genitals. Caesar used to order his veterans to do this. The same meaning is latent in the description of children coming out of the thigh (*Gen.* 46, 26) and in the practice of putting the hand under the thigh when making an oath (*Gen.* 24, 2).

Thistle. *See* THORNS.

Thomas. One of the Twelve, though only John tells us of anything which he said or did. Thomas is not a name at all but, like Didymus, means simply a twin. He is notorious for his doubts and depressions (*John* 14, 5; 20, 24). But when Jesus decided to go to Bethany when Lazarus was ill, and the rest tried to dissuade Him, it was Thomas who said, 'Let us go and die with Him' (*John* 11, 16). He later became a missionary to the E, Parthia and Persia, and is said to have died in India near Madras.

Thorns. Over 20 Heb. and Gk. words are so trans. or called thistles in the AV. Some are genuine thorns and thistles, but others are different plants. All are prickly. The Crown of Thorns may have been made from a species of lotus tree, the *zizyphus spinci Christi. See* BRAMBLE, BRIER, NETTLE.

Thought. In certain passages (notably *Mark* 13, 11 AV) the word has a 17th cent. sense of worry, grief, anxiety.

Thousand. Division of the Tribe or of the Army (qv).

Three Taverns. *See* TAVERNS.

Threshing. *See* AGRICULTURE.

Thresholds of the Gates. Storehouses (where the threshings were held) as in RV (*Neh.* 12, 25 AV).

Throne. Chair of state, royal, ecclesiastical or legal. It was often portable (*1 Kings* 22, 10). Solomon's was of cedar inlaid with ivory and overlaid with gold. The arms had lion carvings and there was a footstool, the seat of the chair being higher than usual from the ground. It was approached by 6 steps (*1 Kings* 10, 18-20).

Throughly. Thoroughly.

Thumb. A common punishment of an enemy taken in war was to cut off the thumbs thus making an archer or swordsman useless (*Judg.* 1, 6 & 7). Blood was sprinkled on the thumbs in certain ceremonies, eg, the consecration of Aaron (*Ex.* 29, 20) and the cleansing of a leper (*Mark* 1, 40).

Thummim [thŭm'-mĭm]. *See* URIM AND THUMMIM.

Thunder. Was understood to be the voice of God (*Job* 37, 4; *Ps.* 104, 7; etc.). The ' voice ' could be interpreted (*John* 12, 29). There is a fine description of a thunderstorm (*Ps.* 29).

Thyatira [thў'-ă-tĭ'-ră]. City in Lydia, Asia Minor,

famous for dyeing. The woman Lydia, of Philippi, came from the town (*Acts* 16, 14). It had one of the 7 churches of Asia (*Rev.* 2, 18-29).

Thyine [thȳ'-īne]. Fine wood of the cypress family, used for making furniture (*Rev.* 18, 12).

Tiberias [tī-bē'-rī-ăs]. Town built by Herod on the W shore of the Sea of Galilee, sometimes called the Sea of Tiberias. It was named in honour of the Emperor Tiberius. Since it was built on the site of an old graveyard the Jews would live in it only under compulsion. There is only one ref. to it (*John* 6, 23); and no indication that Jesus ever visited it.

Tiberius. *See* CAESAR.

Tiglath Pileser [tĭg'-lăth pĭl-ē'-sĕr]. King of Assyria (qv), c. 746-727 BC. He revived the military fortunes of the nation. Menahem of Syria paid him tribute (*2 Kings* 15, 19). When Pekah and Rezin combined agst. Ahaz of Judah he called in the Assyrians to his aid (*2 Kings* 16, 7). Pileser destroyed the Philistines, and took Reuben, Gad and half Manasseh into captivity (*2 Kings* 15, 29; *1 Chron.* 5, 26). He took Damascus in 732. Also called Pul by Israel.

Tile, Tiling. Clay used for impressed writing then baked hard (*Ezek.* 4, 1). The Greeks used similar baked tiles for roofing, but it was not common in Israel. When the men were trying to get their friend to Jesus (*Luke* 5, 19) they would not remove tiles but would come through the roof, chipping away the solid baked clay and then parting the laths which held it up.

Timaeus [tĭm-āe'-ŭs]. Father of Bartimaeus (*Mark* 10, 46).

Timbrel. A tambourine played for dancing and used also in worship. *See* MUSIC.

Time. According to Scripture there was nothing

but God before time began; and after time is
done, selected humans and the angels will share
eternity with God. Time is only a fragment (*Ps.*
90, 4; *2 Pet.* 3, 8). It has a definite beginning and
a definite end (*Rev.* 10, 6). The day began and
ended with the sun, and was divided into morning,
noon and evening. The word trans. ' hour ' in
the OT is a fairly vague space of time. In the NT
it is more precise, owing to Gk. and Rom. influence (*John* 11, 9). In NT times the day was
divided into watches following the military pattern, 4 of 3 hours each (*Matt.* 14, 25). The Jews
spoke more of 3 watches of 4 hours each (*Luke*
12, 38). Months, of course, derived from the
waxing and waning of the moon. New moon and
full moon were feast days (*Ps.* 81, 3). The time of
visibility of the moon is 28 days, dividing naturally
into 4 weeks of 7 days (*Gen.* 29, 27). Two Heb.
words are used for week—one means ' seven ' and
the other means ' Sabbath ' (qv). The Sabbath
was the last day of the Jewish week. In Christianity the 1st day of the week is the day of the Resurrection, when the faithful gathered for the breaking
of bread (*Acts* 20, 7), and to make offerings for
the needy (*1 Cor.* 16, 2). It is also called ' The
Lord's Day ' (qv) (*Rev.* 1, 10). The 7th year is a
week of years and was called a Sabbatical year.
Seven Sabbatical years makes a Year of Jubilee.
The days of the week had no names—only numbers. The seasons were Seedtime (Spring);
Summer; Harvest; and Winter (*Gen.* 8, 22).
' Autumn ' is never mentioned in the AV, although there are 4 refs. in the RSV (*Job* 29, 4;
Prov. 20, 4; *Jer.* 5, 24; *Jude* 1, 12). There is one
mention of a sundial (*2 Kings* 20, 9-11; *Isa.* 38, 8).

Timna(h) [tĭm´-nă]. Mother of Amalek (*Gen.* 36,
12).

Timon [tī'-mŏn]. Man chosen to relieve the apostles of some secular duties (*Acts* 6, 5).

Timotheus [tĭm-ō'-thē-ŭs]. Fellow worker with Paul. *See* TIMOTHY.

Timothy. A young man of Lystra chosen by Paul as his companion on the 2nd missionary journey. His father was Greek, his mother a Jewess (*Acts* 16, 1). He had been raised as a good Jew by his mother Eunice and his grandmother Lois (*2 Tim.* 1, 5; 3, 15). He was ordained by Paul and the Lystra presbyters (*1 Tim.* 4, 14; *2 Tim.* 1, 6). But he had to be circumcised, as he was not a true Jew. Gentile converts did not have to be circumcised in Paul's view at least (*Acts* 16, 3). Timothy went with Paul to Troas and Macedonia, and remained there till summoned by Paul from Athens (*Acts* 17, 14). He was then sent back to Macedonia to report on the state of the Church at Lystra. They met again at Corinth, and in the light of Timothy's report Paul wrote the Epistles to the Thessalonians (qv). He was with Paul at Ephesus on the 3rd journey and was sent ahead into Macedonia again (*Acts* 19, 22). Paul was with him in Macedonia when *2 Corinthians* was written (*2 Cor.* 1, 1). They came together to Corinth where Paul wrote the letter to the Romans (*Acts* 20, 2; *Rom* 16, 21). They then came back to Troas (*Acts* 20, 4). Timothy was with Paul during his imprisonment (*Col.* 1, 1; *Philem.* 1). On Paul's release, Timothy was left as his delegate in Ephesus (*1 Tim.* 1, 3; 3, 14). During his 2nd imprisonment, Paul sent for Timothy (*2 Tim.* 4, 9 & 21). He may himself have been imprisoned (*Heb.* 13, 23). Nothing more is known of him.

Timothy, Epistles of Paul the Apostle to. With the letter to Titus, these form the Pastoral Epistles. Many scholars do not accept Paul as the author,

and place the letters in the 2nd cent. But even
if this is true there must be fragments in them that
are Pauline. They purport to be written to Timothy
of the last article. The 1st letter is very practical
—advice on the responsibilities of the ministry
and the dangers of heresy. Paul then moves on to
suggest how to achieve good Church organisation
and management, with some very worldly-wise
observations on widows, especially young ones,
and the tactful handling of aged office-bearers by
a young minister. The 2nd letter continues the
good advice and repeats some of it. This letter
is very personal, and particularly touching is the
obvious aching of the old man facing death, for
the young man facing life.

Tin. *See* MINES AND MINING.

Tire. *See* DRESS.

Tirhakah [tĭr′-hă-kăh]. King of Cush. One of the
Ethiopian Pharaohs (*2 Kings* 19, 9; *Isa.* 37, 9).

Tirshatha [tĭr′-shä-thă]. Persian title of the governor
of Judah (*Ezra* 2, 63; *Neh.* 8, 9).

Tirzah [tĭr′-zäh]. City captured by Joshua (*Josh.*
12, 24). It was the royal seat till the time of Omri
(*1 Kings* 15, 21). It is also found as a woman's
name (*Num.* 26, 33).

Tishbite. Prob. the inhabitant of a town of similar
sound. Elijah is often ref. to as the Tishbite (*1
Kings* 17, 1; etc.).

Tishri [tĭsh′-rī]. The 7th month.

Tithes. The tenth part of personal income dedicated
to God (*Gen.* 28, 22). It was an obligation under
Mosaic law (*Lev.* 27, 30). Grain was threshed,
and grapes and olives pressed and processed before
tithing them (*Num.* 18, 26 & 27). The law of tithing
was fairly complicated (*Deut.* 12). There was no
tithing in a Sabbatical Year (qv). The tithe was

taken to the Sanctuary and part of it was eaten by the giver and by the Levites; the remainder was at the disposal of the Levites. Tithing came and went as enthusiasm for religion fluctuated (*2 Chron.* 31, 4 & 11). By NT times the tithes went to the priests who collected them personally (*Luke* 11, 42; 18, 22).

Title. (*John* 19, 19.) The account of a crime, written on a board and fastened round the neck of the criminal or carried before him (*Mark* 15, 26). This public warning could be nailed to the cross on capital punishment (*Matt.* 27, 37).

Tittle. A point, or slight penstroke, used to distinguish similar letters of the Heb. alphabet. Hence a minute point of law (*Matt.* 5, 18).

Titus. A convert of Paul's (*Gal.* 2, 3; *Titus* 1, 4). He is not mentioned in the *Acts of the Apostles.* Titus went with Paul from Antioch to Jerusalem for the circumcision conference (*Gal.* 2, 1; *Acts* ch. 15). Titus was the test case in the dispute. In *2 Corinthians* he is mentioned 9 times, indicating that he was well known there. He had been sent there, prob. 3 times to set their house in order, and on the last occasion he carried the 2nd epistle. Paul sent him to Crete on the same kind of mission (*Titus* 1, 5; 2, 1 & 15; 3, 9). He was with Paul during the 2nd imprisonment in Rome (*2 Tim.* 4, 10). There was another Titus at Corinth, surnamed Justus qv, (*Acts* 18, 7).

Titus, Epistle of Paul to. The 3rd of the Pastoral Epistles, the others being the letters to Timothy, written near the end of Paul's life c. AD 66. It was written from Rome to Titus in Crete where he was establishing a church. Paul tells him what his aim should be and how he should go about the job. He deals with the character of the good minister, the danger of imitation Christians, the duty of freemen and slaves alike, and the attitude of the Christian to the civil authority.

Toi, [tŏĭ] **(Tou).** King of Hamoth, friendly to David (*2 Sam.* 8, 9).

Tola [tōl´-ä]. **1.** Son of Issachar and his clan (*Gen.* 46, 13). **2.** One of the first of the Judges (*Judg.* 10, 1).

Tomb. Also grave, and sepulchre. The Jewish dead were always buried, but embalming was not prescribed. The spices and unguents were prob. for overcoming the smell of corruption in a hot country. With a shortage of cultivable land, the cemetery would normally be where the ground was poor and rocky. A hole would be excavated, and, after the interment, covered with stones to prevent jackals digging up the body; or the tomb would be cut in the rock itself if there was insufficient depth of earth. More important people had a quarried or built mausoleum of fair size. The stone door of this would be cemented in place. Under Gk. influence before NT days a more elaborate mausoleum would be carved out for the wealthy, with several recesses to hold sarcophagi. The sepulchre of Joseph of Arimathea was prob. one such (*John* 20, 12).

Tongs. *See* ARTS AND CRAFTS.

Tongue. The word can mean the part of the body or the actual speech or language (*Gen.* 10, 5; *Acts* 2, 8; etc.). Differences of speech, according to Genesis, were the judgment of God upon the ambitions of Babel (*Gen.* 11, 1-9).

Tongues, Gift of. The gift was made to the disciples on the day of Pentecost which followed Jesus' death (*Acts* 2, 1-4). There is little doubt that the implication of the passage is that these were intelligible languages and not the babbling of physical tongues gone mad. Paul accepted this

(*1 Cor.* 12, 10 & 30; 14, 13-16 & 27 & 28). There are other parallel refs. (*Mark* 16, 17; *Acts* 10, 44-46).

Tools. *See* ARTS AND CRAFTS.

Topaz. *See* JEWELS AND PRECIOUS STONES.

Tophet(h) [tŏ′-phĕt]. Name given to High Places (qv) in the Valley of Hinnom, where those who had gone over to Baalism made burnt offerings of their children to Moloch (*2 Kings* 23, 10; *Jer.* 7, 31). Josiah defiled the place.

Torch. *See* LAMP, LANTERN.

Tormentors. Torturers (*Matt.* 18, 34; *Acts* 22, 24).

Tortoise. *See* LIZARD.

Tower. *See* FORTIFICATIONS.

Tower of Babel. *See* BABEL, TONGUE.

Town Clerk. Mayor or provost appointed by the Romans over a town. Not elected (*Acts* 19, 35).

Trachonitis [tră′-chŏ-nī′-tĭs]. Region S of Damascus, part of Philip's tetrarchy (*Luke*, 3 1).

Trade and Commerce. Canaan was in the main an agricultural country, with little in the way of raw materials for manufacture. There was olive oil which could be exported (*Hos.* 12, 1); there was wine (*2 Chron.* 2, 10). Some wheat, barley, timber and balsam might be exported but beyond these there was little surplus of anything. It was not an industrial community, most of the manufactures being for the use of local people. Skilled artificers, esp. in the metal crafts had to be brought in during the early years of the settlement (*1 Sam.* 13, 19; *2 Sam.* 1, 24). Most of the armour and weapons were taken in raids on their enemies. There was a fiscal system of sorts in the days of David and Solomon (*1 Kings* 10, 14). There was no native gold—even then the universal currency; any they had was pillaged. Silver was the more

popular currency (*1 Kings* 10, 29). Almost all the
luxuries enjoyed by the wealthy were imported,
prob. in exchange for precious metals stolen or
extorted. There was a certain amount of trade in
selling prisoners of war (*Joel.* 3, 48) The word used
for 'merchant' really means 'traveller' which
indicates a profession of pedlars or chapmen.
Not till after the Exile did there appear to be
shopkeepers in anything like the mod. sense, and
settled together in districts of the towns. Nehemiah
mentions goldsmiths (3, 32), grocers and fish-
mongers (13, 16). But the market appears to have
been more on the lines of the eastern Bazaar
(*Neh.* 10, 32; 13, 30), with the usual bargaining
of the E (*Prov.* 20, 14; *Ezek.* 7, 12). In other
words, trading and shopkeeping were not Jewish
occupations before the Exile. There was, however,
some 'fiddling' in the corn exchange (*Prov.* 11,
26; *Amos* 8, 4-7; *Micah* 6, 10). The Mosaic Law
has almost nothing to say on the subject of honest
trading, which surely means that trading was not
important enough to need regulation. Palestine
was, however, the cross roads of the Eastern
caravan routes. Sea trade was slight (*1 Kings* 10,
11; *Isa.* 60, 4). There were financiers and money
lenders (*Matt.* 25, 27).

Trades. See ARTS AND CRAFTS.

Tragacanth [trǎ'-gǎ-cǎnth]. A vegetable gum (*Gen.*
37, 25).

Trance. A state of suspended animation as practised by yogi. Peter fell into them, as did Paul
(*Acts* 11, 5; 22, 17). See VISIONS.

Transfiguration. An occurrence in the life of Jesus
at Mt. Hermon. It was a mystical and visionary
occurrence in which the spirit which possessed
Jesus became visible to others. It was Jesus'
warrant and sanction publicised to His disciples,

though it seems to have had little permanent effect upon them (*Matt.* 17, 1-9; etc.).

Travail. A French word taken into Eng. and meaning both labour and trouble. It is mainly used of childbirth 'labour' nowadays. It appears sometimes as 'travel' which was a travail in those days. But one ref. (*Num.* 20, 14 AV) is not travel but travail as in RV.

Treasure, Treasury, Treasurer. A treasure is a store of wealth and a treasury is where it is stored. The words are sometimes interchanged in the AV (*Job* 38, 22). Treasures should be treasuries as in RV. While treasury would be better as treasure in others (*Josh.* 6, 19 & 24; *Ezra* 2, 69 RV). The 'treasure cities' (*Ex.* 1, 11) were cities where provisions were stored. The same slight confusion occurs in the NT. The ref. (*Matt.* 12, 35) should be 'treasury.' In another the Gk. word is *korbanas*, which means the place where a man keeps the Corban (qv). The Temple treasuries were the offering boxes which stood in the colonnade. This would be where Jesus was standing when he spoke of the widow's mite (*John* 8, 20). Treasurer is the guardian of the treasury, and in the royal connection is the Chamberlain or Chancellor of the Exchequer (*Neh.* 12, 25; *Ezra* 1, 8; *Isa.* 22, 15; etc.).

Tree. Poetical word for the Cross (*Acts* 5, 30; 10, 39; etc.).

Trespass Offering. See OFFERINGS.

Tribes of Israel. Careful study shows that the number of the Tribes was not 12 or not always 12 (*Gen.* 17, 20; 25, 13-16; 36, 15-19; 40; 43; 49, 7). The Genealogies (*Gen.* 29-30) make 13 tribes—Reuben, Simeon, Levi, Judah, Dan, Naphtali, Gad, Asher, Issachar, Zebulun, Joseph (which was really 2 tribes, Manasseh and Ephraim) and Benjamin (*Gen.* 35, 22-26). Maybe the number 12 was chosen because of the months, or Solomon's division of the land into 12 parts.

Tribute. In the OT the word very often means forced labour rather than payment in kind or coin (*2 Sam.* 20, 24; *1 Kings* 9, 21). Solomon enjoyed both varieties (*1 Kings* 4, 7-19; 5, 13 ff.). He also taxed caravans passing through (*1 Kings* 10, 15). See PUBLICAN, CUSTOMS, TAXES.

Troas [trō-ăs]. Seaport town of Mysia (*Acts* 16, 8). In this town Paul had the vision of the man from Macedonia, which brought him into Europe (*Acts* 16, 8-10). He was back at Troas bet. his 2nd and 3rd missionary journeys and there he left some of his gear which he asked Timothy to bring to him at Rome (*2 Tim.* 4, 13).

Trogyllium [trŏ-gўl'-lĭ-ŭm]. Promontory and town on the coast of Asia Minor opposite the island of Samos. The ship in which Paul was returning from his 3rd missionary journey anchored there (*Acts* 20, 15).

Trophimus [trŏ'-phĭ-mŭs]. Gentile Christian of Ephesus who travelled with Paul. Jews in Jerusalem accused Paul of having taken Trophimus beyond the barrier of the court of the Gentiles and there was a riot which led to Paul's arrest (*Acts* 20, 4; 21, 29).

Trumpet. See MUSIC.

Trumpets, Feast of. The 1st of the lunar festivals in the Jewish calendar, it fell on the 1st day of the 7th month. Trumpets were blown to remind the Jews that they were men, and God that He was God. Special offerings were made and no servile work was done (*Lev.* 23, 24 & 25).

Tsadhe (Tzaddi) [tsä′-dhĕ]. 18th letter of the Heb. alphabet. It was a stronger sound than the Eng. S; more like *TS*, or *TZ*.

Tubal [tū'-băl]. Country and tribe desc. from Japheth (*Gen.* 10, 2). They traded with Tyre (*Isa.* 66, 19).

Tubal Cain. The Tubal people, above, were skilled metal workers; 'Cain' means a smith. Tubal Cain, son of Lamech and Zillah, is credited with being the first of the metal workers (*Gen.* 4, 22).

Turban. See DRESS, DIADEM.

Twin brothers. See CASTOR AND POLLUX.

Tychicus [tych'-ĭ-cŭs]. Was Paul's companion on the journey to Jerusalem. He was a native of the Rom. Province of Asia. He was the bearer of the Epistle to the Ephesians and the Epistle to the Colossians. Paul called him ' the beloved brother.' Paul made great use of him and he must have been a very trustworthy fellow. He was for a while in Crete either with Timothy or as his immediate successor (*Acts* 20, 4; *Ephes.* 6, 21; *Col.* 4, 7; *2 Tim.* 4, 12; *Titus* 3, 12).

Tyrannus [tўr-ăn'-nŭs]. A philosopher or teacher of sorts in Ephesus. These teachers had their own schools, where they spoke, argued and taught. When Paul was in Ephesus, very anxious to have a platform for Christian teaching, he seems to have been made welcome in this man's ' school,' prob. after the Jews there had denied him the use of the synagogue for his teaching. It is impossible to say if Tyrannus was alive at the time or whether this was some kind of lecture hall or open air forum named after him (*Acts* 19, 9).

Tyre. The name means The Rock (*Josh.* 19, 29). Tyre was on the coast of Palestine midway bet. Beirut and Carmel. Immediately behind the town the mountains rise sharp and high, and the place is practically impregnable from the landward side. It was a very ancient city indeed, even by OT reckoning (*Isa.* 23, 7). Yet it was younger

than Sidon (*Isa.* 23, 2 & 12). The district was
assigned to Asher at the conquest (*Josh.* 19, 29).
Hiram, who was contemporaneous with David
and Solomon, restored the fortunes of Tyre, and
carried out a magnificent piece of civil engineering
which made Tyre a splendid port. The main industry had been the collection of the shellfish
murex and the extraction and preparation of the
celebrated purple dye—Tyrian purple. But under
Hiram the inhabitants, Phoenicians, became more
ambitious and started a sea trade which embraced
the known world and made new parts known.
They sailed round Africa and reached India; they
traded with Cornwall in Britain for tin. Some
time after the days of Hiram their connection
with Israel became more close by the marriage
of Jezebel, daughter of Eth-baal of Tyre, to
Ahab, King of Israel (*1 Kings* 16, 31). This led to
trouble. *See under their names,* ISRAEL, ELIJAH.
A sister of Jezebel may have been the Dido of
the Aeneid, who founded Carthage. They carried
on a long war with the Assyrians, who, being a
military nation, found the naval genius of the
Tyrians too much for them till in c. 644 BC the
two agreed to live in peace, with Tyre acknowledging Assyria's suzerainty. The fluid state of
ME politics brought Tyre to the top again when
Nineveh collapsed and she had her greatest days
c. 630-600. (*Ezek.* 27-28) Assyria faded from the
scene and Nebuchadnezzar of Babylonia became
the menace. He besieged Tyre for 13 years (*Ezek.*
26, 7-12). Though they destroyed Old Tyre, they
could not subdue the New Tyre, which had open
access to the sea (*Ezek.* 29, 18). But though the
city was never taken, her trade was ruined, and
they were never the same again. The Heb. prophets were no admirers of Tyre (*Amos* 1, 9 & 10;

Joel 3, 4-6; *Jer.* 44, 30; *Ezek.* 28, 2). In the end, after a gallant defence the city fell to Alexander the Great, who reached the island port by building a mole out from the shore. Thereafter Tyre was a vassal of Antioch and of Egypt, and then of Rome. The Romans made her a free city. Jesus was well received in the neighbourhood of Tyre (*Mark* 7, 24-31; *Luke* 10, 13). Paul visited the town and a church was established (*Acts* 12, 20; 21, 3-7). There is little left of the place now.

Tzaddi [tzăd'-dĭ]. *See* TSADHE.

U

Ulai [ū'-lāī]. River flowing through Elam into the Persian Gulf (*Dan.* 8, 2).

Uncle. Not merely the brother of a parent, but any fairly near kinsman on the father's side,

Unclean. *See* PURIFICATION. Unholy and unclean are not to be confused. One is a breach of the moral law, the other merely of the ceremonial law. The only connection is that the truly holy person would never wilfully transgress the ceremonial laws. There is also a distinction bet. purely physical cleanliness, due to careful attention to personal and social hygiene, and ceremonial uncleanness (*Ex.* 19, 12 & 14; 30, 18-21; *Josh.* 3, 5). *See below.*

Unclean animals. Abhorrence from the eating of certain living creatures is natural and ingrained in certain peoples. The Anglo-Saxons in general loathe the French idea of eating frogs and snails. When they try them they find them very palatable. The Hebrews felt the same about certain creatures, and at the same time they knew, poss. from experience, that certain others, like carnivores, did not make good eating. They therefore drew up a list of the permitted and the forbidden. The general rule was that the following were unclean: (1) Animals that do not both part the hoof and chew the cud (*Lev.* 11, 2-8); this includes all animals with 4 paws. Paws do not completely separate the hoof (v. 27). Thus the only clean animals were cattle, sheep, goats and the deer family (*Deut.* 14, 4 & 5). (2) All birds of prey and carrion, including bats, which are, of course, not birds (*Lev.* 11, 13-19; *Deut.* 14, 12-18). (3) All insects except the locust, sometimes called grasshopper (*Lev.* 11, 20-23). (4) Any water creature which had not both fins and scales (*Lev.* 11, 9 & 10). Eels and crabs were unclean. (5) All creeping creatures (*Lev.* 11; 29, 30). In addition, meat was unclean that had been offered to idols, or which had not been bled. Blood was sacred to the Lord and for Him alone (*Lev.* 17, 10-14).

Unicorn. This is, of course, a legendary animal. The animal referred to in scripture is the two-horned wild ox (*Deut.* 33, 17). One ref. may be to the oryx, a kind of antelope (*Num.* 23, 22).

Unknown god. (*Acts* 17, 23.) This may well have been an altar erected by some person in thankfulness for a favour received in some foreign country whose god and the method of whose worship was unknown.

Unleavened bread. *See* BREAD, LEAVEN, PASSOVER.

Untoward. Not the mod. meaning of ' unfortunate' or ' unexpected,' but rather ' not well disposed to' (*Acts* 2, 40 AV).

Upharsin [ū-phär-sĭn]. *See* MENE.

Uphaz [ū'-phäz]. Place whose site is unknown. A source of gold, it may be Ophir (*Jer.* 10, 9; *Dan.* 10, 5).

Ur [ûr]. **1.** Father of one of David's heroes (*1*

Chron. 11, 35). **2.** City of ancient Sumer, then of Babylonia, then of Chaldea after various conquests. It was a city c. 4000 BC and was the birthplace of Abraham (*Gen.* 11, 28 & 31; etc.).

Urbanus [ŭr-bā′-nŭs], **Urbane.** A Rom. Christian (*Rom.* 16, 9).

Uriah [ū-rī′-ăh] **Urijah. 1.** One of David's heroes whose wife David coveted. He ordered Uriah to be exposed to the greatest danger, and being a brave man he was killed (*2 Sam.* 11, 1-27; *Matt.* 1, 6). Others of the name are priests.

Urijah [ū-rī′-jăh]. High Priest in the reign of Ahaz (*2 Kings* 16, 10).

Urim and Thummim [ū′-rĭm thŭm′-mĭm]. These were the oracle by which the Hebrews sought guidance on the will of God. The names start with the 1st and last letters of the Heb. alphabet. They mean light and darkness, yes and no, life and death. But there are differences of opinion about this. Exactly what they were is not known but whichever one was ' pulled out of the hat ' first, determined the answer to a single question (*1 Sam* 14, 41 ff.; 23, 2 & 4; 30, 7 & 8). The tribe of Levi had charge of them and they were connected with the ephod (qv) (*Deut.* 33, 8; *Ezra* 2, 63). They were kept in a pouch of the High Priest's breastplate. But by the time the account was written it is highly prob. that Urim and Thummim had long ago disappeared and that even the priests did not know really what they had been. They would claim the High Priestly oversight of them to scotch any idea that divination had been practised in the old days.

Usury. The word has a bad sense nowadays, but it used to mean simply the normal, not the exorbitant, interest on a loan. In the old days a Heb. was not supposed to charge interest of another

Heb. (*Ex.* 22, 25). To-day the Jew is so much identified with business and with moneylending that there may be some idea that this started in Bible times. But it did not. The kind of loan referred to was not the provision of capital for business expansion, but rather the ' hand-out ' to the needy (*Lev.* 25, 47). By NT times investment in another man's business was common enough, and the advancing of money on banking lines (*Matt.* 25, 27; *Luke* 19, 23). ' Bankers ' is a better trans. than ' usurers.' The rate of interest was usually high.

Uzziah [ŭz-zī́-ăh]. **1.** A Levite (*1 Chron.* 6, 24). **2.** Father of one of David's officers (*1 Chron.* 27, 25). **3 & 4.** Returned exiles (*Ezra* 10, 21; *Neh.* 11, 4). **5.** King of Judah, also called Azariah. He came to the throne c. 785 BC a few years before the death of his father Amaziah, but after the great defeat of Judah by Israel (*2 Kings* 14, 22). He was 16 years old when he began to reign (*2 Kings* 14, 21). One ref. (*2 Kings* 15, 1) is misleading; it seems to mean no more than that at this point Uzziah began to rule over a free Judah. He was a good and careful soldier and had victories over several of Judah's traditional enemies (*2 Chron.* 26, 6-8). He worshipped Jehovah but did not remove the High Places. Finally he dared to offer incense in the Temple and became a leper. He made his son Jotham regent. A notable earthquake took place during his reign (*Amos* 1, 1; *Zech.* 14, 5). He died c. 734 BC (*2 Kings* 15, 1-7). This was the beginning of a great age of Prophets (*Isa.* 1, 1; *Hos.* 1, 1; *Amos* 1, 1). There are 2 returned exiles of the same name (*Ezra* 10, 21; *Neh.* 11, 4).

V

Vagabond. (*Gen.* 4, 12; *Acts* 19, 13 AV). This does not have any sense of misdemeanour, but is simply a wanderer.

Vail. Veil. *See* DRESS, TABERNACLE, TEMPLE.

Vale, Valley. Five Heb. words are so trans. It can be a glen or ravine, or it can be, and frequently is in the AV, the lowlands of a country as a highlander regards them—the easier, more fertile country.

Vanity. In the AV of the OT vanity may be that which is unsubstantial and temporary (*Ps.* 144, 4; *Isa.* 57, 13). In many refs., esp. in *Ecclesiastes*, it means that which is fleeting and profitless—utter futility (*Eccl.* 1, 2; 12, 8; *Jer.* 10, 15). Again the word may have the more evil sense of lack of moral worth (*Isa.* 41, 29; *Job* 15, 35; *Ps.* 10, 7; 41, 6). Another meaning is ' futureless,' doomed to failure (*Ps.* 4, 2; *Hab.* 2, 13). In the AV of the NT, ' vain ' is used for 2 Gk. words, one meaning ' empty ' and the other ' worthless.' ' Vanity ' appears 3 times, meaning ' worthlessness' (*Rom.* 8, 20; *Eph.* 4, 17; *2 Pet.* 2, 18). In the Epistle of James (2, 20) the meaning of ' vain ' is clearly ' swollen-headed.'

Vashni [văsh'-nī]. Second son of Samuel, not the first. The text is corrupt (*1 Sam.* 8, 2; *1 Chron.* 6, 28).

Vashti [văsh'-tī]. *See* ESTHER.

Vav [văv]. 6th letter of the [Heb. alphabet, pronounced as Eng. *W*.

Veil. *See* DRESS, TABERNACLE, TEMPLE.

Vermilion. Ground cinnabar, used for painting and decoration (*Jer.* 22, 14; *Ezek.* 23, 14). Really any red pigment.

Versions. These are simply translations of the oldest manuscripts into any language of people who want to read them and hear them and understand them. The original writing is the ' Text,' and the translation is the ' Version.' (1) The 1st real version of the OT was the Septuagint (LXX), which was the Heb. scripture done into Gk. The name means ' the seventy ' for that was the number of translators who worked on it. The work was done in Alexandria for the great library there. The date of starting the work is not known, but it was certainly finished by 150 BC. The work is uneven in quality, the translation of the 1st 5 Books being the best of it. Origen in AD 245 and Lucian in AD 311 revised the LXX, but the work as a whole is unreliable, though it achieved the very important object of making the Judaism of the ME known throughout the Greek speaking world. There are several versions of the OT in Syriac. (2) By the end of the 2nd cent. work had begun on Latin versions of the OT, but the outstanding one is the Vulgate upon which the OT of the Roman Catholic Church is based. It was undertaken by Jerome who in AD 384 published the Gospels in Latin and revised old Latin versions of the Psalms. Beginning in 387 he made new Latin translations of the OT direct from the Heb., finishing it in 405. This was the Bible of the Mediaeval Church and remains the Bible of the Roman Catholic Church. It was the 1st book ever to be printed, the date being c. 1455. There have been several mod. versions of the Vulgate, the most recent being an excellent piece of work by Father Ronald Knox. Other versions are the Coptic, the Ethiopic, the Gothic, the Arabic, the Armenian and the Slavonic.

But our main concern is Eng. versions. Portions had been translated into Anglo-Saxon before 1066, and more were done into the Anglo-Norman tongue after the Conquest. (1) But Wycliffe and Purvey were the 1st to try to produce a complete Eng. version of the Bible. They worked bet. 1382 and 1388, the original from which they worked being the Vulgate—itself a version, of course, and not an original text. (2) Then came Tyndale. He had fled from England to avoid persecution c. 1526, and worked in Germany. He went back to the original Gk. of the NT and his Eng. version of the NT was printed in Germany and imported to England. As correctives he used a Gk. version by Erasmus, Luther's German version, and the Vulgate. His English version was condemned and publicly burned by the Roman Catholic Church. By 1534 Tyndale had translated into Eng. from the original Heb. text, the Pentateuch (first 5 Books of the present Bible) and the Book of *Jonah*. In style and language this set the pattern for the Authorised Version. (3) Coverdale produced the 1st complete Eng. Bible to be printed. That was in 1535, but only the OT from *Job* to *Malachi* is really Coverdale's; the rest is Tyndale. Other versions which there is no space to describe in detail were Matthew's Bible of 1537; Taverner's Bible, 1539; the Great Bible (Cranmer's), 1540. This was the 1st to be appointed to be read in churches, during the reign of Henry VIII. The Geneva Bible is sometimes called the Breeches Bible for that is the word used in *Gen.* (3, 7). This was published in 1560 and was the 1st to be divided into verses. It contained the best of all that had gone before. Then came the Bishops' Bible of 1568 which was based mainly on the Great Bible, but which was not uniform in quality. It was revised in 1572 and

again in 1602. The last formed the basis for the
Authorised version of 1611. Before that, however,
there had come a Roman Catholic version in Eng.,
the OT appearing in 1582, and the NT in 1610.
This was a translation of the Vulgate, and contained some ' coined ' words, created out of the
Latin to express ideas for which there seemed to
be no then-existing Eng. equivalent, words like
' propitiation,' ' remission,' ' impenitent.' Unfortunately these words found their way into the
Authorised version to the confusion of thought.
This English translation of the Vulgate is known
as the Rheims and Douay Bible. The inspiration
for the AV came, under God, out of a conference
bet. Anglicans and Presbyterians in 1604—the
Hampton Court Conference. King James I being,
like many Scots, something of a theologian,
accepted a proposal by Dr. Reynolds of Oxford
that a new version should be prepared, and 54
scholars were appointed to the work. Only 47
of them actually worked on the translation, and
they operated in groups. In 1611 they produced
the miracle of the Authorised Version (the King
James Bible), which not only shaped the thinking
of Britain but moulded the Eng. language. With
the passing of time older and better Gk. texts
have been discovered, and knowledge of NT Gk.
has greatly increased. It was felt that a Revised
version was needed, and scholars under the aegis
of the Convocation of Canterbury, got down to
work, with American scholars co-operating. That
was in 1870 and more than 10 years later the NT
Revised Version was published, followed by the
OT in 1885. It had immediate success, but somehow, partly because of affection for the AV, and
partly because the RV tried to run with the hare
of the old and hunt with the hounds of the new,

its influence was not what it might have been. Scholarship was spoiled by conservatism. American scholars brought out their own Standard Version in 1900 and 1901. Since then single scholars like Weymouth, Moffat, Rieu, Phillips and others have produced translations of the whole and parts of the Bible, which are commonly seen as paperbacks on stationers' counters, and which are very widely read indeed. In Scotland in 1958 the Presbytery of Stirling and Dunblane overtured the General Assembly of the Church of Scotland to consult with other churches about the possibility of an entirely new translation. On the 350th anniversary of the publication of the AV, a completely new translation of the whole New Testament was published. It immediately became a best seller, and many ministers now use it during public worship, esp. when the reading is from one of the more obscure portions of the Epistles. It is absolutely sound, though it lacks a rhythm and a cadence which seemed to call for a poet on the panel. But it has certainly caught the imagination and will no doubt catch the affection of the Anglo-Saxon world. Work is proceeding on the OT and Apocrypha. The Bible, or parts of it, have been translated of course, into every written language in the world, and even into languages for which a script had to be invented. The various Bible Societies pour out an almost endless stream of scripture; but these are not properly versions, in that the authors do not normally go back to the original text. They are more commonly translations of translations.

Vessels. The word is usually self-explanatory, though sometimes the meaning is more 'furniture' than 'containers.' One ref. is quite wrong (*Gen.* 43, 11 AV). The word is ' saddlebags.'

Vestry. (*2 Kings* 10, 22.) The meaning is really ' wardrobe '; not the room which contains one.

Vesture. Usually simply means what people wear, but once or twice the word is used of a specific garment (*Deut*. 22, 12; *Rev*. 19, 13). See DRESS.

Vial. In OT this is the container of oil. In the NT it is prob. more often a flat, saucer-shaped dish for pouring libations (*Rev*. 5, 8; etc.).

Village. In OT days it was very dangerous to be alone, or even to be a dweller in any small community. There had to be a city into which the villager could escape when enemies came raiding. The word ' village ' does not mean what it means now. Nobody would have lived long in what moderns call a village. The distinction bet. village and city is more one of status than of size, like ' city ' and ' burgh.' Some Scottish burghs are bigger than some Scottish cities.

Vine. The word means not simply the grape bearing plant, but any plant with a long climbing stem (*2 Kings* 4, 39). Usually, however, it is the vine as it is now gen. understood. It played a very large part in the economy of the Holy Land. There is one passage which gives a pretty good idea of the processes of vine cultivation (*Isa*. 5, 1-7). Failure of the vintage was a serious business and was regarded as a visitation from God in punishment for some offence (*Ps*. 78, 47; *Jer*. 8, 13). Jesus used the analogy of Himself as the parent stem when talking of the relationship bet. Himself and His disciples (*John* 15). In the OT Israel was compared to a vine (*Ps*. 80, 8-16). Connected with vine are vineyard (which normally was nothing like a yard, but more often a hillside), winepress, watchtower, and vats (*Isa*. 1, 8; *Matt*. 21, 33-41). Palestine grapes were red and they ripened in August (*Rev*. 14, 19).

Vine of Sodom. A plant which looks like a vine, and which bears fruit that look like grapes but which are unpalatable. It could be *citrullus colocynthus*.

Vinegar. This is wine gone sour through over fermentation (*Num.* 6, 3; *Prov.* 10, 26). Mixed with oil it was the poor man's thirst quencher (*Ruth* 2, 14). Rom. soldiers drank a thin sour wine which might be classed as vinegar (*Mark* 15, 36).

Viol. *See* MUSIC.

Viper. More or less any poisonous snake. Vipers were, of course, common.

Virgin. This does not always mean *virgo intacta*, although the importance of virginity in the mod. sense at marriage was stressed (*Deut.* 22). The word can mean an unmarried maiden, but it can also mean 'fit for marriage, mature, nubile.' It is used also of men, and then means 'chaste' rather than 'celibate' (*Rev.* 14, 14). *See* MARY.

Virtue. In the AV has the old sense of power or of possessing power (*Mark* 5, 30; *Luke* 6, 19; 8, 46).

Visions. It could be said that the dream is what is seen, and that the vision is the addition of significance to what is seen. They believed that this was a means of communication bet. God and man; and this is particularly true of the visions of the prophets. But clearly their visions were exceptional simply because the prophets were exceptional men.

Vows. The vow was a covenant bet. God and a man and was usually inspired by the fact that the man was in some kind of jam and wanted God to get him out of it. The man was aware that there was a power which could help, if that power so cared. The job was to persuade or bribe the power to take an interest and intervene. Vows are found in all religions (*Jonah* 1, 16). Very often the undertaking is conditional, the operative word being 'if' (*Gen.* 28, 18-22). A person could be vowed to the special service of God, and so could animals or material things (*Lev.* 27, 1-27; *1 Sam.* 1, 11 & 24 & 28). The person or article so vowed could be redeemed, but the sacrificial animal could not. There was also the vow which involved the renunciation of some activity or delight (cf. Nazirite). There was no obligation to make vows, but once one had been made it had to be kept (*Deut.* 23, 23). For that reason vows should not be made rashly or impulsively (*Prov.* 20, 25). *See* JEPHTHAH.

Vulgate. *See* VERSIONS.

Vulture. Word used to trans. a number of words like 'kite', 'eagle', 'gier eagle' (qv). The common vulture of the E is not a bird of prey but a bird of carrion—a scavenger. Some of them are prob. the griffon, *gyps fulvus.*

W

Wafer. A thin cake of unleavened wheat flour anointed with oil and used in offerings (qv) (*Ex.* 16, 31; etc.).

Wages. In an agricultural community there was not a great deal of room for the 'hired servant.' The family did most of the work, though there might be a few slaves. Even for the hired man, wages were not high (*Deut.* 15, 18), and were usually in kind. Micah hired and paid a domestic chaplain (*Judg.* 17, 10). The wages paid in Jesus' parable were about a denarius (one shilling) a day (*Matt.* 20, 1 ff.). By Mosaic law, wages had to be paid daily (*Deut.* 24, 15). The prophets had much to say about withholding wages (*Jer.* 22, 13; *Mal.* 3, 5; *Jas.* 5, 4).

Wailing. *See* MOURNING.

Walk. A person's behaviour and manner of life (*Ezek.* 9, 20; *Rom.* 8, 1).

War. Early wars were not at all on a large scale, but were rather border raids and their repulse. Saul and David mobilised the fit men of the whole nation, and created at the same time, the germ of a standing army. *See* SAUL, DAVID, ARMY. Certain classes were exempt from military service (*Deut.* 20, 5-8). All wars were religious wars, fought at the call of and on behalf of Jehovah (*Num.* 21, 14). Before battle there were religious ceremonies (*Josh.* 3; *1 Sam.* 7, 9; etc.). Later, the prophets were consulted (*1 Kings* 22, 5). In a campaign, when they had exhausted the food they were able to carry, they lived off the country (*Judg.* 20, 10). Scouts or spies were sent out ahead of the main force (*Judg.* 1, 24; *1 Sam.* 26, 4). They slept in the open or in bivouacs (*2 Sam.* 11, 11). They might camp within a ring of wagons, as in the old American West (*1 Sam.* 17, 20; 26, 5-7). The average battle was a straightforward test of strength and courage rather than of skill, strategy and tactics. The 2 armies faced one another in line, and at a sign from the commanders, raised the battle cry and advanced (*Judg.* 7, 18-21; *Amos* 1, 14; *Jer.* 4, 19). No quarter was asked or given (*2 Kings* 15, 16). Prisoners were enslaved. Defeated nations had to pay indemnities (*2 Kings* 3, 4). The wages of the victor was the plunder (*Judg.* 8, 24; *1 Sam.* 30, 26).

Wars, Book of the. A lost book, quoted (*Num.* 21, 14).

Washing. *See* HOSPITALITY.

Watch. *See* TIME.

Watchman. Night guard of a city (*Isa.* 62, 6; etc.).

Water of Bitterness. *See* JEALOUSY.

Water of Separation. *See* PURIFICATION, RED HEIFER.

Waterpot. *See* HOUSE.

Waterspouts. Poss. waterfalls or cataracts (*Ps.* 42, 7).

Wave Offering. A ceremony of offering and sacrifice in which the right thigh and shoulder of the animal were heaved aloft, and the breast waved from side to side before the Lord. This was the consecration of the Peace offering. The first-fruit sheaf was waved, as were the loaves made from the 1st of the grain. The guilt offering of the leper and the jealousy offering were also waved. In these offerings most of the meat went to the priests; the remainder being eaten by the offerer. The priest laid the offering on the extended hands of the offerer, placed his own hands underneath, and then raised the whole up to arms' length (*Ex.* 29, 24; *Num.* 6, 19 & 20). *See* OFFERINGS.

Waymark. (*Jer.* 31, 21.) Something like a milestone.

Wax. Always beeswax.

Wealth. The wealth of Palestine reached its height under the earlier monarchy (*Isa.* 2, 7 & 8). Wealth did the wealthy little good (*Isa.* 5, 8 & 11 & 18; *Micah* 2, 2 & 11). Various individuals are named as being very wealthy: Abraham (*Gen.* 13, 2); Nabal (*1 Sam.* 25, 2); Barzillai (*2 Sam.* 19, 32); Zaccheus (*Luke* 19, 2); Joseph of Arimathea (*Matt.* 27, 57). This was regarded as a sign of God's favour (*Ps.* 1, 2-4). Even Paul reckoned that virtue was worth rather more than its own reward (*2 Tim.* 4, 8). Jesus did not believe in poverty for poverty's sake, but His own observation of people and life had taught Him that wealth was more of an obstacle to spiritual peace than poverty was (*Mark* 10, 21; *Luke* 12, 20; 16, 19). When Jesus described as a fool a man of property, it was not because the man was wealthy, but because the man thought that being wealthy was enough (*Luke* 12, 21). Jesus saw money not as a possession, but as a trust, a stewardship (*Matt.* 25, 14-29; *Luke* 19, 12-26). What He condemned was not so much money as materialism. In the early Church they held all things in common (*Acts* 2, 44 ff.; 4, 34 ff.), but they did not question the right to own private property (*Acts* 5, 4). The sin of Ananias was not that he withheld something, but that he pretended that he had given everything. Both Paul and James found it necessary to condemn the rich (*1 Tim.* 6, 9 & 10; *Jas.* 2, 1-8; 5, 1-6).

Weapons. *See* ARMOUR.

Weaving. *See* SPINNING AND WEAVING.

Wedding. *See* MARRIAGE.

Wedge of gold. *See* MONEY.

Week. *See* TIME.

Weeks, Feast of. *See* PENTECOST.

Weights and Measures: Measures of length. The cubit. The length of the cubit varied from time to time and in various localities, though it bore the same relationship to other lineal units. It consisted of 2 spans, or 6 palms, or 24 finger breadths, and was itself one-sixth of a reed. The cubit of *Deuteronomy* (3, 11) seems to have been the same as the cubit of *2 Chronicles* (3, 3); but the cubit of *Ezekiel* (40, 5; 43, 13) was longer, consisting of an old cubit and a hand's breadth. Since these 'big' cubits were connected with the building of the Temple and its rebuilding, the 'big' cubit can be called the Royal cubit, as agst. the common cubit. Estimates vary of the exact length of these, and they can be anything bet. 16 and 25 inches. Rabbinical trad. had it that a cubit was 144 grains of barley side by side. This makes very nearly 18 inches, and that can be taken as a fair average standard. The following table gives as good an estimate as any:

Royal system.

Finger's breadth = 0.022 metres = 0.86 inches
Palm = 4 fingers = 0.88 metres = 3.44 inches.
Span = 3 palms = 0.262 metres = 10.33 inches
Cubit = 2 spans = 0.525 metres = 20.66 inches
Reed = 6 cubits = 3.15 metres = 124.02 inches

In the *Common system* the lengths in metres and inches would be:

Finger's breadth = 0.019 m. = 0.74 in.
Palm = 0.075 m. = 2.95 in.
Span = 0.225 m. = 8.86 in.
Cubit = 0.45 m. = 17.72 in.
Reed = 2.7 m. = 106.32 in.

Measures of area. One method of calculation was the area which a yoke of oxen could plough in a day (*Isa.* 5, 10). It is hard to say exactly how many sq. yds. this would be, poss. about 100 Royal cubits square. Another measure was the amount of land which could be sown from a given measure of seed (*Lev.* 27, 16). One ref. (*1 Kings* 18, 32) is wrong. The trench was not ' as great as would contain 2 measures of seed.' The trench was as big as a house which would occupy the ground which 2 seahs of seed could sow. This would be about 1,650 sq. yds.

Measures of capacity. Liquid measure was:

12 logs = 1 hin
6 hins = 1 bath
10 baths = 1 homer or cor

The log was about a pint, which makes the hin about 1½ gallons, the bath 9 gallons, and the homer 90 gallons (English).

Dry measure was:

4 logs = 1 cab
6 cabs = 1 seah
3 seahs = 1 ephah
10 ephahs = 1 homer

The seah is often called a measure. The log was about a pint dry measure, which makes the dry homer about 11 bushels. The omer is not to be confused with the homer. It was the 100th part of a homer. Bushel (*Matt.* 5, 15) is trans. of the Latin *modius*, and was roughly the same as the seah. Firkin (*John* 2, 6) is the trans. of Gk. *metretes*, and is roughly the bath. 'Measure' (*Rev.* 6, 6) is the trans. of the Gk. *choinix*, roughly 2 pints.

Measures of weight. Scales and weights were used (*Lev.* 19, 36), and money was also counted by weight (*Jer.* 32, 10). Orig. weights were stones, replaced later by metal. There were, however, wide variations in weight in various places. The Heb. table of weights was:

20 gerahs = 1 shekel
50 shekels = 1 maneh
60 manehs = 1 talent

This seems to disagree with *Ezekiel* (45, 12) by 10 shekels to the maneh, but his may have been an attempt to bring the commercial weight up to the Temple weight. There is, however, another reading of this passage: 'five shekels are five, and ten shekels are ten, and fifty shekels shall be your maneh.' The same sentiment as 'pay twenty shillings to the pound.' Of every weight there was a heavy and a light variety, the heavy being twice the weight of the light. The shekel as far as can be ascertained (which is not very far) weighed about two-fifths of an ounce. The shekel as weight is not to be confused with the shekel as money: nor must the talent. *See* MONEY, TALENT. The word 'pound' is usually the trans. of the Lat. *libra* (lb.). 2¼ libra of gold = about 1 maneh.

Well. A narrow excavation dug down into water-bearing strata and filled by seepage to the water table level. Sometimes there was a constant flow of water under the dry bed of a wadi which could be reached by the knowledgeable (*Gen.* 21, 30 & 31; 24, 19). The mouth of the well would be covered by planks or by a circular stone (*Gen.* 29, 2; *Ex.* 21, 33). There was a shallower well, more like a broad cistern, the water being reached by a series of steps. Water was hauled up from the deeper well by a pitcher on a rope.

Wench. In the 17th cent. the word was perfectly respectable (*2 Sam.* 17, 17 AV). A young woman.

Whale. The Hebrews did not know the true whale. The words so trans. mean no more than a fish of very considerable size; or a monster of the sea. One ref. should be dragon (*Ezek.* 32, 2). Another (*Matt.* 12, 40), is any large sea creature.

Wheat. The wheat harvest fell bet. April and June, depending on the locality and elevation of the fields. It made one of the seasonal divisions of the year (*Ex.* 34, 22; *Judg.* 15, 1; *1 Sam.* 12, 17). The fat of wheat is flour of the first quality (*Deut.* 32, 14; *Ps.* 81, 16; 147, 14). Bread was made from the flour, but the ears were also roasted whole. This is 'parched corn' (*Lev.* 2, 14 & 16). Egyptian wheat was famous in Rom. times. Peasants made a kind of porridge from unground wheat. A delicacy was pounded wheat mixed with scraps of meat, and called kibbeh (*Prov.* 27, 22).

Wheel. Chariot wheels are described (*1 Kings* 7, 30 & 32 ff.). Wells were equipped with a wheel over which the rope passed for hauling up the pitcher (*Eccl.* 12, 6). The wagon wheel was solid, creaking round a fixed axle.

Whirlwind. A furious storm of any sort, though the true whirlwind, with moving vortex, is described (*2 Kings* 2, 1-11; *Job* 38, 1).

White of an egg. (*Job* 6, 6 AV.) RV marg. has 'juice of purslain,' and it could be a plant juice. But the AV rendering is so expressive that it deserves to be right.

Widow. The widow was particularly helpless, and was reckoned to be the special care of God, because few others troubled (*Ps.* 68, 5; 146, 9). To show them kindness was to qualify for God's approval and blessing (*Job* 29, 13; *Isa.* 1, 17; *Jer.* 7, 6). The early Church accepted this responsibility but found it a considerable burden (*Acts* 6, 1). Paul found them something more than a mere burden on finance, and warned young Timothy about their manners and blandishments (*1 Tim.* 5, 3-16). An Order of Widows developed in the Church in the 2nd cent. and lasted into the 4th. It was abolished by the Council of Laodicaea in 364. *See* RUTH.

Wife. *See* MARRIAGE.

Wilderness (desert). Several Heb. words are so trans. **1.** *Midbar*—this is uninhabited scrub land, for not all deserts are of sand. Sometimes even the scrub is absent. The haunt of wild animals. Nomads might wander over it (*Josh.* 15, 61; *Isa.* 42, 11). The Arabian desert is called 'Wilderness of the wandering.' **2.** *Arabah* (qv). This is the great plain from the Jordan valley to the gulf of Akabah. The word is applied gen. to 'steppe' country and is sometimes trans. 'plain.' **3.** *Chorbah*—a place once inhabited but now abandoned and desolate. **4.** *Tsiyyah*—dry ground. **5.** *Tohu*—the howling wilderness; the great empty waste where caravans perish (*Job* 6, 18).

6. The NT Gk. word is *eremos, eremia*, trans. desert place. The wilderness of the wanderings of Israel was the triangle of land with its base on the Mediterranean and its 2 sides formed by the Gulf of Suez and the Gulf of Akabah. Its area is about 22,000 sq. miles. It is both desert of sand and desert of rock seamed with wadis which are raging torrents during the rains, but are otherwise dry. The central tableland was the wilderness of Paran (*Num.* 10, 11; etc.). This place could not have sustained 2 million people for 40 years. Water was always insufficient (*Ex.* 17, 1; *Num.* 20, 2). They were often hungry (*Deut.* 1, 19; 8, 15-16).

Willow. Several varieties of the genus *salex* are found in Palestine (*Ezek.* 17, 5). Another Heb. word so trans. might be the weeping willow, or might be the poplar (*Lev.* 23, 40; *Isa.* 44, 4; *Job* 40, 22; *Ps.* 137, 2).

Willows, Brook of. A brook in Moab (*Isa.* 15, 7).

Wimple. A long kerchief which framed the face, covering the sides of the face, the neck and the chin (*Isa.* 3, 22 AV). RV has ' shawl.'

Wind. The Hebrews were content with 4 winds —N, S, E, W. The winds were under the control of God (*Job* 28, 25; *Ps.* 78, 26; 107, 25; etc.). The W winds were rain-bearing, but the E winds were dry and destructive (*Gen.* 41, 6). S and SE winds were hot and dry (*Job* 37, 17; *Luke* 12, 55). The Levanter (Euroclydon) is described (*Acts* 27, 14).

Window. Windows were unglazed and are better described as lattices (*Judg.* 5, 28; etc.).

Wine and strong drink. These are 2 words. *Yayin* is wine, and *shekar* is strong drink, covering every other kind of intoxicating liquor. Another word is *tirosh*, sometimes trans. ' new wine ' in the AV, and always so trans. in RV. This is really the fresh grape juice before it becomes wine. From the earliest times Palestine has been a land of vines and wines (*2 Kings* 18, 32). The wine-press was in 3 parts—2 stone troughs, the press vat and the wine vat (*Isa*. 63, 2) connected by a pipe or channel. The grapes were put into the press vat, where they were trampled, the juice running down the conduit into the wine vat. When all the juice had been extracted by this method, the mush was pressed again by a heavy beam weighted with stones. The extracted juice—the must—was left in the wine vat for the beginning of fermentation. It was then ladled out or run out into jars or wineskins (*Hag*. 2, 16; *Matt*. 9, 17). After 40 days it was decanted to other jars or skins, through a strainer. Periodically it was re-decanted to prevent it from settling on the lees (*Zeph*. 1, 12 RV). Finally the wine was poured into jars lined with pitch, sealed, and stored in wine cellars (*I Chron*. 27, 27). There was no such thing as unfermented wine. There was a kind of date wine, and a kind of cider, though the European apple was unknown, the fruit being prob. the apricot or quince. There was a sweet wine made from pomegranates (*S. of S*. 8, 2 RV). The fruits were crushed and allowed to ferment. In NT times wines were usually tempered with water, though Palestine wines were usually light. Isaiah denounced ' mixing drinks ' (5, 22). What he really condemns is the adding of spices and flavourings (*S. of S*. 8, 2). Cf. the wine mingled with myrrh (*Mark* 15, 23). Wine was drunk by all except Nazirites and Rechabites. Priests on duty in the sanctuary had to abstain (*Lev*. 10, 9). A libation was poured out before the burnt offering. Over-indulgence was denounced (*Isa.* 5, 11 ff.; *1 Cor.* 5, 11; 6, 10; etc.).

Winepress. *See* WINE.

Wink at. Elizabethan slang, meaning to overlook (*Acts* 17, 30).

Winnowing. Tossing the threshed grain into the air so that the wind would separate the grain from the chaff. *See* AGRICULTURE.

Wisdom. Among the Hebrews, knowledge was divided into law, prophecy and wisdom. The law states the obligation, prophecy passes judgment upon those who have not accepted it; while wisdom seeks to find reasons. Where law and prophecy are divine, wisdom is human in its origin. Its beginning is the fear of the Lord (*Ps.* 111, 10; *Prov.* 9, 10). The Books of Wisdom are *Job*, *Proverbs* and *Ecclesiastes*.

Wisdom of Solomon. *See* APOCRYPHA.

Wise Men. *See* MAGI.

Wist. *See* WIT.

Wit. To wit means 'to know.' The present tense is I wot, the past tense is I wist. 'Do to wit' means 'make to know' (*2 Cor.* 8, 1 AV). The noun 'wit' means 'knowledge' (*Ps.* 107, 27). Witty is knowledgeable, 'knowing' as Dickens used the word (*Prov.* 8, 12). Wittingly is knowingly (*Gen.* 48, 14).

Witch(craft). *See* MAGIC, WIZARD.

Withered hand. *See* MEDICINE.

Withs. Supple willow wands. But this ref. (*Judg.* 16, 7) is prob. bowstrings.

Witness. 1. Evidence, testimony or sign, eg, a cairn or heap of stones, or a monument (*Josh.* 24, 27). Moses' song was in this sense a witness (*Deut.* 31, 26) as were poor Job's boils (*Job* 16, 8). As a witness the disciples were to shake off the dust of towns that did not receive them (*Mark* 6, 11).

It was thus a significant gesture, a meaningful act. **2.** A person who testifies or vouches for a happening or on behalf of another person in some debatable cause (*Gen.* 31, 50; *Job* 16, 19; *2 Cor.* 1, 23). The person vouched for may, of course, be God. **3.** Witness in the strictly legal sense (*Ruth* 4, 9; *Jer.* 32, 10). There were also false, or lying witnesses—perjurers (*Prov.* 12, 17; 19, 5-9; etc.). The apostles witness, or testify about Jesus (*Luke* 24, 48; *Acts* 1, 8; 2, 32; etc.). The faithful are the cloud of witnesses (*Heb.* 12, 1). Jesus is the faithful witness (*Rev.* 1, 5; 3, 14). The Gk. word is *martys, martyreo;* and the martyr is simply the one who witnesses by his willingness to die for the ' other person.'

Witty. *See* WIT.

Wizard. One who professed to be able to converse with the spirits of the dead (*Isa.* 8, 19). It was agst. the law for a Heb. to consult a wizard (*Lev.* 19, 31; 20, 27; *2 Kings* 23, 24). Manasseh made a practice of it (*2 Kings* 21, 6). The wizards were prob. ventriloquists. *See* MAGIC.

Wolf. *Canis lupus.* Its habits are nocturnal, but the wolf of the ME does not run in packs like the wolves of the N (*Jer.* 5, 6). Another Heb. word is trans. ' howling creature ' (*Isa.* 13, 22; *Jer.* 50, 39). This may be the wolf, but it may well be the jackal.

Woman. In the OT woman is always in a position inferior to that of the man (*Gen.* 3, 16). She still had a place and dignity of sorts (*Gen.* 2, 18-24). Some of the great men had great wives and may well have owed something of their greatness to them—Sarah, Rebekah, Rachel. Miriam stood equal to Moses and Aaron. Deborah was both prophetess and Judge (*Judg.* 4, 4). Jezebel was a great evil woman, but still great—the OT'S Lady

Macbeth. The Law of *Deuteronomy* had many safeguards for women's rights, and Malachi declared agst. divorce (*Mal.* 2, 14-16). The writer of the *Proverbs* gives a fine description of the virtuous woman, though he indicates that this type was by no means common (ch. 31). In many ways the position and status of women had not changed a great deal by Jesus' day. In fact it had somewhat deteriorated, cf. the 2 incidents at wells (*Gen.* 24, 10 ff.; *John* 4, 27). No one did more to change this than Jesus did (*Matt.* 5, 27 ff.; 19, 3 ff.). Women early found a place in their own right in the Apostolic Church (*Acts* 1, 14; 2, 1 ff.; *Rom.* 16, 1 ff.; *Philip.* 4, 2 ff.). An office of deaconess (qv) evolved (*I Tim.* 3, 11), and there was an Order of Widows (qv) (*I Tim.* 5, 3). Paul seemed a bit uncertain about women, though it is hard to say whether they disturbed him or merely annoyed him (*I Cor.* 7). In this passage the expectation of the early return of Jesus must be borne in mind. Paul certainly disliked talkative types (*I Cor.* 14, 34 ff.). He distrusted young widows (*I Tim.* 5, 11-15). But he does affirm that a woman is a person and a personality in her own right (*Gal.* 3, 28).

Wonders. These are always mentioned in assoc. with ' signs.' The word is used of the plagues of Egypt (qv) (*Ex.* 7, 3; etc.). It also describes the miracles of Jesus (*Acts* 2, 22; etc.). It conveys the impact of the miracle upon the beholder, but the addition of ' sign ' indicates the kind of reaction which should follow. The ' wonder ' is a sign of the power of God.

Wool. Garments were made mainly of wool (*Lev.* 13, 47; *Prov.* 31, 13) though linen was preferred for undergarments. In the ME they keep the heat out by wearing fairly heavy protective clothing. Wool and flax were not to be mixed in weaving (*Lev.* 19, 19; *Deut.* 22, 11). The Hebrews traded in wool (*Ezek.* 27, 18).

World. In the OT this was 'the heavens and the earth' (*Gen.* 1, 1; *Ps.* 89, 11). The NT idea of the world as naturally sinful is not found in the OT, although even then they believed that it would be judged, and, if necessary, punished (*Ps.* 96, 13; *Isa.* 13, 11). The wickedness of materialism, the folly of setting too much store on the world, is pointed out (*Ps.* 49). Two Gk. words are trans. 'world' in the NT: (1) *Aeon.* Here there is the element of time in the meaning of the word, the alternative word being 'age' (*Luke* 1, 70; *John* 9, 32; *Acts* 15, 18; *Heb.* 9, 26). There is always the contrast bet. the world of time, and the world to come (*Matt.* 12, 32; *Eph.* 1, 21; *Titus:* 2, 12; *Heb.* 6, 5). (2) *Cosmos.* This is gen. the earth as the abode of mankind. It typifies material things in contrast to the things of the spirit (*Matt.* 16, 26; *Luke* 9, 25). The reason for the contrast is that sin was introduced into the world (*Rom.* 5, 12). But the world can be and will be redeemed because of the incarnation (*2 Cor.* 5, 19; *Heb.* 10, 5; etc.). Paul maintained that the bad bit of the world was the very bit that most greatly attracted humans, and that the good bit of the world was the bit they despised (*1 Cor.* 1, 20 & 21 & 27; *2 Cor.* 7, 10). Only those who have received the gift of the Spirit see the distinction; only the saints can judge (estimate or assess) the world (*1 Cor.* 2, 12; 6, 2). John uses the word *cosmos* very often. The 4th Gospel is largely the account of the Light of the World (*John* 1, 9; etc.), which the world refused to see (*John* 1, 10). Paul thought of the 'world spirit' as evil, but John means rather 'blind humanity.' The disciples were chosen out of the world and will therefore be hated by the world as Jesus was (*John* 13, 1; 15, 18 & 19). In his 1st Epistle John pleads with the Christian to have nothing to do with a world which is essentially evil, although God's purpose is to redeem it through the work of Jesus (*1 John* 2, 18 & 22; 4, 3). There is a power in control of the world—the Antichrist (*1 John* 4, 4; 5, 19) and this power cannot be persuaded, it is unredeemable. It must be resisted and opposed.

Worm. Any small, creeping, limbless creature. Its characteristics and conduct are self explanatory (*Deut.* 28, 39; *Jonah* 4, 7; *Isa.* 14, 11; *Acts* 12, 23). Applied to a human it was an expression of contempt, though not in the mod. sense of one who ' never turns ' (*Job* 25, 6; *Isa.* 41, 14). Classifications are: (1) Maggots (*Ex.* 16, 24; *Job* 21, 26). The larva of the bluebottle or blow fly. (2) Larva of the moth (*Isa.* 51, 8). (3) The coccus worm, which is really an insect (*Micah* 7, 17). *See* SCARLET.

Wormwood. *Artemisia absinthium;* a plant with a bitter juice (*Deut.* 29, 18; *Prov.* 5, 4). It could be poisonous if taken regularly over a period (*Rev.* 8, 11). Figuratively it is used of the effects of injustice (*Amos* 5, 7) or of punishment (*Jer.* 9, 15), or of suffering (*Lam.* 3, 19).

Worship. Honour, respect and reverence shown to a person (*Luke* 14, 10 AV). From this broad meaning the word has narrowed and concentrated upon the showing of respect, honour and reverence to the divine Person (*Matt.* 14, 33; *Rev.* 14, 7). Though the old meaning still remains in the ' your worship ' in a court of law. The outward act of worship of God, the courtly bow, reaching to the ground, was the same as the courteous greeting of one person to another. In the original the word for this greeting is the same as the word for an obeisance to God (*Gen.* 33, 3; 42, 6). The gesture must not be made to idols (*Ex.* 20, 5).

Worshipper. (*Acts* 19, 35 AV.) Should be ' temple keeper ' as RV.

Writing. The first writing was pictorial or pictographic, and from these pictures, cunieform writing evolved, the wedge-shaped characters being made with a stylus with a triangular point, the different ' letters ' being formed by the angle at which the stylus was held to impress the clay. Thus Abraham might have written. The Hebrews, or at least some of them, could write before the Exodus (*Ex.* 17, 4; 24, 4; 39, 14 & 30; *Num.* 33, 2). From the use of clay tablets which required fairly heavy indentation, the next step was writing with pen and ink on papyrus and parchment. *See* BOOK, PARCHMENT, PEN, INKHORN, VERSIONS, etc.

Writings. *See* CANON.

X

Xerxes [xĕr′-xēs]. *See* AHASUERUS.

Y

Yarn. *See* SPINNING AND WEAVING.

Year. The divisions of the year accorded with the agricultural seasons. They divided the year into 12 lunar months of 28 days each, which, of course is not quite accurate. They would lose something like 10 days a year, which would soon throw their seasons badly out. They brought in an extra month every leap year, though the practice is not recorded in scripture. Leap years were calculated on a lunar cycle of 19 years, the leap years being the 3rd, 6th, 8th, 11th, 14th, 17th and 19th. Abib or Nisan was the 1st month (*Ex.* 12, 17), that being the new moon immediately before or after the vernal equinox. After the Exile, for some reason or other, the day of the new moon of the 7th month came to be regarded as New Year's Day. The refs. (*Ezra* 3, 6; *Neh.* 8, 2) may have had something to do with this, but certainly not everything. *See* TIME.

Yodh [yōdh]. The 10th letter of the Heb. alphabet. Its sound falls bet. Eng. *I* and *J*, and is prob. best rendered as *Y*. In transcribing the Heb. scriptures it was easy to confuse this letter with *Waw*.

Yoke. Bullocks worked gen. in pairs. A bar of wood, curved to fit the necks of the beasts was láid across the 2 necks and held in position by pins which passed through on either side of the necks of the 2 animals. The traces were then attached to the yoke, which, when the animals were working, rested in front of the ' hump ' which E cattle possess (the ' withers '). Obviously if a yoke was not well made it would not be ' easy ' (*Matt.* 11, 30) but would gall the animals badly. Jesus, as a carpenter, would make many yokes, and He knew the difference bet. a well-made one and a badly made one. To ' pass under the yoke ' was a sign of enslavement (*1 Kings* 12, 4).

Z

Zabad [zā'-băd]. A common personal name, but the most imp. are: **1.** A desc. of Ephraim (*1 Chron.* 7, 21). **2.** A man of Judah (*1 Chron.* 2, 36-37). **3.** A form of the name Jozacar. **4.** Three returned exiles (*Ezra* 10, 27 & 33 & 43).

Zabdi [zăb'-dĭ]. There are several of the name (*Josh.* 7, 1; ' Zimri ' in *1 Chron.* 2, 6). Others are: (*1 Chron.* 8, 19; 27, 27; *Neh.* 11, 17).

Zabud [zā'-bŭd]. Solomon's Prime Minister (*1 Kings* 4, 5).

Zabulon [zăb'-ū-lŏn]. *See* ZEBULUN.

Zacchaeus [zăc-chāe'-ŭs]. A publican (qv) who became a follower of Jesus. Jesus saw him up in a tree as he passed by, for Zacchaeus was a very small man (*Luke* 19, 1-10).

Zachariah [ză'-chăr-ī'-ăh] (**Zacharias**). Common name, but principally the father of John the Baptist (*Luke* 1). There is another mentioned in the NT (*Matt.* 23, 35; *Luke* 11, 51).

Zadok [zā'-dŏk]. Most important was the founder of a branch of the priesthood, and desc. from Aaron (*1 Chron.* 24, 3). He is prob. the same as David's hero (*2 Sam.* 8, 17; *1 Chron.* 12, 27). He remained loyal to David in the Absalom rebellion (*2 Sam.* 15, 24-29). He was also instrumental in securing the succession for Solomon (*2 Sam.* 19, 11; *1 Kings* 1, 7 & 8 & 32-45; 2, 35.

Zaham [zā'-hăm]. Son of Rehoboam (*2 Chron.* 11, 19).

Zain (Zayin) [ză'-ĭn]. 7th letter of the Heb. alphabet. Eng. Z.

Zalmon (Salmon) [zăl'-mŏn]. One of David's heroes (*2 Sam.* 23, 28). Also a mt. in Shechem (*Judg.* 9, 48).

Zalmunnah [zăl-mŭn'-năh]. King of Midian killed by Gideon (*Judg.* 8, 4-28).

Zaphenath Paneah [ză'-phĕ-năth păn-ē'-ăh]. Name given by Pharaoh to Joseph, meaning prob. ' this is the one responsible for life ' (*Gen.* 41, 45).

Zarephath [zăr'-rēph-ăth], **Sarepta**. A town belonging to Sidon. There Elijah healed the widow's son (*1 Kings* 17, 8-24).

Zarethan [zăr'-ĕ-thăn] **Zaretan, Zartanah, Zarthan.** Village near Jezreel. Bronze work for the Temple was cast there (*1 Kings* 7, 46).

Zayin. *See* ZAIN.

Zealot. Member of a patriotic party of the Jews inspired by Judas the Galilean agst. the Romans when Cyrenius was governor. Later it degenerated and became a band of assassins. Simon was a Zealot (*Luke* 6, 15; *Acts* 1, 13).

Zebadiah [zĕ-băd-ī′-ăh]. Common name possessed by no one of very great importance (*1 Chron.* 8, 15; 12, 7; 26, 2; 27, 7; *2 Chron.* 17, 8; 19, 11; *Ezra* 8, 8; 10, 20).

Zebah [zē′-băh]. King of Midian slain by Gideon (*Judg.* 8, 4 f.).

Zebedee [zĕ′-bĕd-ēē]. A prosperous Galilee fisherman, father of James and John (*Matt.* 4, 21; *Mark* 1, 19).

Zebidah [zĕ′-bid-ăh], **Zebdah** AV. Mother of Jehoiakim (*2 Kings* 23, 36).

Zeboim [zĕ-bō′-ĭm]. One of the Cities of the Plain (*Gen.* 10, 19). It was destroyed with the others by fire from heaven. There was another town of the name repopulated after the Exile (*Neh.* 11, 34).

Zebul [zē′-bŭl]. Faithful governor of Shechem in Abimelech's time (*Judg.* 9, 28 & 36-39, 41).

Zebulun [zĕ′-bū-lŏn], **Zabulon.** 1. The 10th son of Jacob, 6th son of Leah (*Gen.* 30, 19 & 20). His descendants formed the tribe of that name (*Gen.* 49, 13). 2. The tribe itself. It sprung from his 3 sons—Serod, Elon and Jahleel. In the wilderness after the Exodus the chief was Eliab; he was later succeeded by Elizaphan (*Num.* 1, 9; 10, 16; 34, 25). At the 1st numbering they mustered 57,400 men of military age (*Num.* 1, 30); and at the 2nd numbering 60,500 (*Num.* 26, 27). Jacob had foretold that Zebulun would settle near the sea, and they did, but not on the coast (*Deut.* 33, 18). Men of Zebulun played an important part in the army of Barak (*Judg.* 4, 6-10); and in the army of Gideon (*Judg.* 6, 35). They acclaimed David as king (*1 Chron.* 12, 33 & 40). They suffered sorely at the hands of the Assyrians, but a good future was prophesied for them (*Isa.* 9, 1 & 2; *Ezek.* 48, 33; *Matt.* 4, 12-16).

Zechariah [zěch'-ă-rī'-äh]. There are several of the name. **1.** A Benjamite of the family of Jeiel (*1 Chron.* 9, 35-37). **2.** A Levite of David's time (*1 Chron.* 9, 21). **3.** Other Levites of the same period (*1 Chron.* 15, 18 & 24; 24, 25; 26, 11; 27, 21) **4.** Later Levites kept the name (*2 Chron.* 17, 7; 20, 14). **5.** Son of King Jehoshaphat (*2 Chron.* 21, 2). **6.** Son of Jehoiada the High Priest who inherited his father's high principles in the reign of Joash of Judah. He was stoned to death for his bold preaching agst. king and people (*2 Chron.* 24, 20-22). Jesus remembered him with respect (*Luke* 11, 51). Abel was the first righteous man whose death for righteousness is recorded. Zechariah is the last, for 2 Chronicles is the last book in the Heb. scriptures. **7.** There are a score of other Zechariah's of little importance. The most important of the name was the prophet—son of Berechiah (*Zech.* 1, 1). He began his work c. 520 BC, and was contemporary with Jerubbabel and Haggai (*Zech.* 3, 1; 4, 6; 6, 11; *Ezra* 5, 1 & 2). With Haggai he pleaded with leaders and people to go on with the work of rebuilding the Temple.

Zechariah, Book of. The Book is the account of 8 visions which Zechariah had. They are: (1) The angels on horseback (1, 7-17). (2) The horns and the smiths (1, 18-21). (3) The man with the measuring line (ch. 2). (4) Joshua and the High Priest (ch. 3). (5) The candlestick and the olives (ch. 4). (6) The flying roll (5, 1-4). (7) The ephah (qv) and the woman (5, 5-11). (8) The chariots (6, 1-8). The prophecy is of the millenium when Messiah will come (6, 1-8). Zechariah then gives his views on religious ceremonial, pointing out that fasting is meaningless unless its meaning and purpose are known (7, 4-7). The inward, not the outward state is what matters (7, 8-14). He goes on to promise the coming of the day of compensation (8, 1-23). The restoration of Israel is assured, but first there will come a bad time because of the rejection of the Messiah (chs. 9-14). The 3 'heads' of the sermon are that God has an unswerving purpose; that this purpose includes the coming of the Messiah; and that, therefore, God is king. It is pretty plain that the Book is not all from the one hand, or, if it is, that hand had been writing over a fair number of years, and the mind had changed with their passing. If it is one author then these are the observations of a long lifetime. He begins by encouraging the returned exiles to get on with the job of rebuilding the Temple, which is, to him, the symbol and warrant of their faith. Then he seems almost to change his mind and to ask what is the point of ceremonial religious convention. He looks deeper into this and finds that there is much in it after all if people think. In the end he reaches, by way of faith in the coming of the Messiah, to a point of confidence in the sovereignty of God.

Zedekiah [zĕ′-dĕ-kī′-ăh]. **1.** A false prophet who gave bad advice to Ahab and suffered for it (*1 Kings* 22, 11-25). **2.** Another of the same in Jeremiah's time (*Jer.* 29, 21-23). **3.** Prince of Judah in the reign of Jehoiakim (*Jer.* 36, 12). **4.** King of Judah, vassal to Nebuchadnezzar (*2 Kings* 24, 17). He reigned c. 597-586 BC, and not very successfully as far as religion is concerned (*2 Chron.* 36, 11-14; *Jer.* 21, 11-12). Jeremiah warned him agst. coming revolt; he ignored the warning and the revolt came (*Jer.* 27, 2-22). During his reign the Babylonians besieged Jerusalem but had to retire under threat from Egypt (*Jer.* 37, 5). They returned to the siege but Zedekiah and others escaped through their lines. He was later captured, blinded, and his sons killed (*2 Kings* 24, 17-20; 25, 1-7; *Jer.* 39, 1-14). He died in prison in Babylon (*Jer.* 52, 11). **5.** A returned exile (*Neh.* 10, 1).

Zela [zē'-lă]. Town in Benjamin where Saul was buried (*Josh.* 18, 28; *2 Sam.* 21, 14).

Zelophehad [zĕ-lō'-phĕ-hăd]. A Manassite with no sons, whose daughters established their right to the estate, and so established a law of succession to female issue, failing male (*Num.* 26, 33; 27, 1-8; 36, 1-12).

Zelotes [zĕ-lō'-tĕs]. *See* ZEALOT.

Zemaraim [zĕm'-ă-rā'-ĭm]. Town and mt. The town was in Benjamin and the mt. in Ephraim, from which Abijah of Judah addressed the 10 tribes before fighting them (*Josh.* 18, 22; *2 Chron.* 13, 4).

Zenas [zē'-năs]. A lawyer friend of Paul, Apollos and Titus (*Titus* 3, 13).

Zephaniah [zĕph'-ă-nī'-ăh]. There are several of the name : **1.** A priest (*1 Chron.* 6, 36). **2.** A priest who shewed Jeremiah a letter whose contents were dangerous to him, and who was later killed (*Jer.* 29, 24-29). **3.** A man of Zechariah's time (*Zech.* 6, 10).

Zephaniah, Book of. The prophet. It is prob. that he was descended from King Hezekiah (1, 1) and the date of his work is c. 630-610 BC. His prophecies fall into Josiah's reign and are concerned with the reforms the king was busy about. In

time he is bet. Nahum and Jeremiah. He spoke
of the day of the Lord, Judgment Day, not only
for Judah, but for all the world. The most revealing verses are (1, 14-18 and 3, 14-17). There are
only 3 chapters in the book, but in this short space
he treats of Judgment—what judgment is; what
makes it necessary; who must undergo it. He
then tells of the doom which threatens all, including Judah, and shows how it may be avoided.

Zerah [zēr′-ăh]. **1.** Desc. of Esau (*Gen.* 36, 13). **2.**
Twin son of Judah and Tamar (*Num.* 26, 20).
3. Son of Simeon (*Num.* 26, 13). **4.** A Levite
(*1 Chron.* 6, 21). **5.** An Ethiopian general (*2
Chron.* 14, 8-15).

Zerahiah [zěr′-ă-hī′-ăh]. **1.** A priest desc. of Phineas
(*1 Chron.* 6, 6). **2.** Son of Pahath-moab (*Ezra* 8, 4).

Zered [zē′-rĕd]. Valley and stream; the limit of
Israel's wilderness wanderings (*Num.* 21, 12).

Zereda(h) [zě′-rĕd-ă], **Atha.** A village poss. in
Ephraim which was the orig. home of Jeroboam
(*1 Kings* 11, 26).

Zeresh [zēr′-ĕsh]. Wife of Haman (*Esth.* 5, 10 &
14).

Zeruah [zĕr-ū′-ăh]. Mother of Jeroboam I (*1 Kings*
11, 26).

Zerubbabel [zĕr-ŭb′-băb-ĕl]. He was desc. of David
and heir to the throne of Judah, though he had
spent most of his life in captivity during the Exile
(*Ezra* 2, 2; *Neh.* 7, 7). After the release he became
governor of Judah (*Hag.* 1, 1). He is pointed out
as one worthy of reward in the Day of the Lord
(*Hag.* 2, 23). His mission is to rebuild the Temple
(*Zech.* 4, 1-14; *Ezra* 5, 2). Some regarded him as
the Messiah (*Zech.* 3, 1-10). He is an ancestor of
Jesus (*Matt.* 1, 12 & 13). His governorship under
the Persians lasted till at least 515 BC.

Zeruia [zěr′-ū-ĭ-ă]. Sister, though prob. half-sister

of David (2 Sam. 17, 25; 1 Chron. 2, 16). She was the mother of Abishai, Joab and Asahel (2 Sam. 2, 18).

Zethar [zēth'-är]. Chamberlain of Ahasuerus (Esth. 1, 10).

Ziba [zī'-bä]. Servant of Saul (2 Sam. 9, 9). David attached him to Saul's grandson, Mephibosheth (2 Sam. 9, 9-12). During the Absalom rebellion he remained faithful to David though his master did not and David transferred Mephibosheth's estates to Ziba (2 Sam. 16, 1-4).

Zibiah [zĭb'-ĭ-äh]. Wife of Ahaziah and mother of Jehoahash (2 Kings 12, 1).

Zidon [zī'-dŏn]. Sidon. Town on the Mediterranean coast bet. Beyrout and Tyre, with first class harbourage and anchorage. It was the chief city of Phoenicia (Gen. 10, 15). The Phoenicians were the merchant adventurers of the ancient world who traded as far W and N as Britain, and as far E as India. They were highly skilled metal workers and weavers. Their dye, Tyrian purple from the shellfish murex, was famous and greatly sought after. They planted colonies all round the Mediterranean, but by Solomon's time they were under the Assyrians. Tyre (qv) their other great city was destroyed after a revolt (Ezek. 26, 7 ff.). Under the Romans Zidon was a free city and is mentioned in the Gospels (Matt. 11, 21 ff.). Paul's ship touched the port on its way to Rome (Acts 27, 3). The gods of Zidon were Baal and Ashtoreth (1 Kings 16, 31).

Ziklag [zĭk'-lăg]. City of Judah, lost to Amalek, but recovered by David (Josh. 15, 31; 1 Sam. 30, 1-31).

Zillah [zĭl'-läh]. Wife of Lamech; mother of Tubal Cain (Gen. 4, 19-23).

Zilpah [zĭl'-päh]. Maid to Leah, and mother of

Jacob's sons, Gad and Asher (*Gen.* 29, 24; 30, 9-13).

Zimri [zĭm′-rĭ]. **1.** Grandson of Judah (*1 Chron.* 2, 6). **2.** Prince of Simeon (*Num.* 25, 14). **3.** Desc. of Jonathan (*1 Chron.* 8, 36). **4.** Soldier who assassinated Elah, King of Israel, and usurped the throne. The army preferred Omri, who marched agst. Zimri. Seeing the inevitable fate, Zimri set fire to Tirzah, which he had selected as his capital, and died in the blaze (*1 Kings* 16, 8-20).

Zin [zĭn]. Desert land crossed by Israel on the march. It was on the borders of Edom and Judah (*Josh.* 15, 1-3). This is not the same as the wilderness of Sin (qv).

Zion [zī′-ŏn]. One of the hills on which Jerusalem was built. David captured it when Jerusalem was a Jebusite fortress (*2 Sam.* 5, 7). It was made sacred when David brought the Ark of the Covenant to it (6, 10-12). In Solomon's time the Ark was moved to Mt. Moriah which then claimed the title (*1 Kings* 8, 1; *2 Chron.* 3, 1; 5, 2). On Moriah the Temple was built and the title ' Zion ' was reserved for the Temple (*Isa.* 8, 18; 18, 7; etc.). Usually when the word ' Zion ' is used, the Temple is meant, though sometimes the ref. is to the whole of Jerusalem. The word also came to mean the Church and the faith of the Jews (*Ps.* 126, 1; 129, 5; etc.). In the NT it can mean ' heaven ' (*Heb.* 12, 22).

Ziph [zĭph]. **1.** Town in the S of Judah (*Josh.* 15, 24). **2.** A town in the hills of Judah (*Josh.* 15, 55). **3.** A man of Judah (*1 Chron.* 4, 16).

Zippor [zĭp′-pŏr]. Father of Barak of Moab (*Num.* 22, 4).

Zipporah [zĭp′-pŏr-äh]. Daughter of Jethro, priest of Midian. She married Moses (*Ex.* 2, 21 & 22).

There was trouble bet. him and her over the question of the circumcision of their son (*Ex.* 4, 18-26).

Ziv [zĭv], **Zif.** The 2nd month of the Jewish year, roundabout mod. May (*1 Kings* 6, 1 & 37). *See* YEAR.

Zoan [zō'-ăn]. Ancient Egyptian city, at one time capital of the country, fortified by the Hyksos dynasty and renamed Avaris. Here Moses and Pharaoh met (*Ps.* 78, 12 & 43). *See* EGYPT.

Zoar [zō'-är]. One of the Cities of the Plain (*Gen.* 19, 20 & 22). It was the smallest of the 5.

Zohar [zō'-här]. **1.** A Hittite (*Gen.* 23, 8). **2.** Son of Simeon (*Num.* 26, 13). **3.** Man of Judah (*1 Chron.* 4,7). Also called Zerah (qv).

Zophar [zō'-phär]. A friend of Job (*Job* 2, 11).

Zorah [zō'-räh]. Town of Judah, where Samson was buried (*Josh.* 15, 33; *Judg.* 16, 31).

Zuph [zūph]. A Levite ancestor of Samuel (*1 Chron.* 6, 35). Also a district over the Benjamin border (*1 Sam.* 9, 4 & 6).

Zur [zūr]. **1.** King of Midian in Moses' day (*Num.* 25, 15). **2.** A Benjamite (*1 Chron.* 8, 30).

COLLINS GEM

Other Gem titles that may interest you include:

Gem Bible Guide
A compact guide to the content and meaning of all 66 books in the Bible **£2.99**

Gem Daily Light
A selection of readings composed entirely of Biblical verses chosen from the Good News Bible **£3.50**

New Testament and Psalms
The Good News New Testament and Psalms in compact form (GNB93) **£5.50**

Gem Quotations
A fascinating selection of quotations drawn from over 900 authors **£3.50**

Gem Flags
Up-to-date, full-colour guide to over 200 flags of the world, explaining their history and significance **£3.50**

Gem Ready Reference
A unique compilation of information on the world of measures, with quick-reference conversion tables and helpful illustrations **£2.99**